OTH[
THE S

MW01532631

1. *The A to Z of Buddhism* by Charles S. Prebish, 2001. *Out of Print. See No. 124.*
2. *The A to Z of Catholicism* by William J. Collinge, 2001.
3. *The A to Z of Hinduism* by Bruce M. Sullivan, 2001.
4. *The A to Z of Islam* by Ludwig W. Adamec, 2002. *Out of Print. See No. 123.*
5. *The A to Z of Slavery and Abolition* by Martin A. Klein, 2002.
6. *Terrorism: Assassins to Zealots* by Sean Kendall Anderson and Stephen Sloan, 2003.
7. *The A to Z of the Korean War* by Paul M. Edwards, 2005.
8. *The A to Z of the Cold War* by Joseph Smith and Simon Davis, 2005.
9. *The A to Z of the Vietnam War* by Edwin E. Moise, 2005.
10. *The A to Z of Science Fiction Literature* by Brian Stableford, 2005.
11. *The A to Z of the Holocaust* by Jack R. Fischel, 2005.
12. *The A to Z of Washington, D.C.* by Robert Benedetto, Jane Donovan, and Kathleen DuVall, 2005.
13. *The A to Z of Taoism* by Julian F. Pas, 2006.
14. *The A to Z of the Renaissance* by Charles G. Nauert, 2006.
15. *The A to Z of Shinto* by Stuart D. B. Picken, 2006.
16. *The A to Z of Byzantium* by John H. Rosser, 2006.
17. *The A to Z of the Civil War* by Terry L. Jones, 2006.
18. *The A to Z of the Friends (Quakers)* by Margery Post Abbott, Mary Ellen Chijioke, Pink Dandelion, and John William Oliver Jr., 2006.
19. *The A to Z of Feminism* by Janet K. Boles and Diane Long Hoeveler, 2006.
20. *The A to Z of New Religious Movements* by George D. Chryssides, 2006.
21. *The A to Z of Multinational Peacekeeping* by Terry M. Mays, 2006.
22. *The A to Z of Lutheranism* by Günther Gassmann with Duane H. Larson and Mark W. Oldenburg, 2007.
23. *The A to Z of the French Revolution* by Paul R. Hanson, 2007.
24. *The A to Z of the Persian Gulf War 1990–1991* by Clayton R. Newell, 2007.
25. *The A to Z of Revolutionary America* by Terry M. Mays, 2007.
26. *The A to Z of the Olympic Movement* by Bill Mallon with Ian Buchanan, 2007.
27. *The A to Z of the Discovery and Exploration of Australia* by Alan Day, 2009.
28. *The A to Z of the United Nations* by Jacques Fomerand, 2009.
29. *The A to Z of the "Dirty Wars"* by David Kohut, Olga Vilella, and Beatrice Julian, 2009.
30. *The A to Z of the Vikings* by Katherine Holman, 2009.
31. *The A to Z from the Great War to the Great Depression* by Neil A. Wynn, 2009.
32. *The A to Z of the Crusades* by Corliss K. Slack, 2009.
33. *The A to Z of New Age Movements* by Michael York, 2009.
34. *The A to Z of Unitarian Universalism* by Mark W. Harris, 2009.
35. *The A to Z of the Kurds* by Michael M. Gunter, 2009.
36. *The A to Z of Utopianism* by James M. Morris and Andrea L. Kross, 2009.
37. *The A to Z of the Civil War and Reconstruction* by William L. Richter, 2009.

38. *The A to Z of Jainism* by Kristi L. Wiley, 2009.
39. *The A to Z of the Inuit* by Pamela K. Stern, 2009.
40. *The A to Z of Early North America* by Cameron B. Wesson, 2009.
41. *The A to Z of the Enlightenment* by Harvey Chisick, 2009.
42. *The A to Z Methodism* by Charles Yrigoyen Jr. and Susan E. Warrick, 2009.
43. *The A to Z of the Seventh-day Adventists* by Gary Land, 2009.
44. *The A to Z of Sufism* by John Renard, 2009.
45. *The A to Z of Sikhism* by William Hewat McLeod, 2009.
46. *The A to Z Fantasy Literature* by Brian Stableford, 2009.
47. *The A to Z of the Discovery and Exploration of the Pacific Islands* by Max Quanchi and John Robson, 2009.
48. *The A to Z of Australian and New Zealand Cinema* by Albert Moran and Errol Vieth, 2009.
49. *The A to Z of African-American Television* by Kathleen Fearn-Banks, 2009.
50. *The A to Z of American Radio Soap Operas* by Jim Cox, 2009.
51. *The A to Z of the Old South* by William L. Richter, 2009.
52. *The A to Z of the Discovery and Exploration of the Northwest Passage* by Alan Day, 2009.
53. *The A to Z of the Druzes* by Samy S. Swayd, 2009.
54. *The A to Z of the Welfare State* by Bent Greve, 2009.
55. *The A to Z of the War of 1812* by Robert Malcomson, 2009.
56. *The A to Z of Feminist Philosophy* by Catherine Villanueva Gardner, 2009.
57. *The A to Z of the Early American Republic* by Richard Buel Jr., 2009.
58. *The A to Z of the Russo-Japanese War* by Rotem Kowner, 2009.
59. *The A to Z of Anglicanism* by Colin Buchanan, 2009.
60. *The A to Z of Scandinavian Literature and Theater* by Jan Sjåvik, 2009.
61. *The A to Z of the Peoples of the Southeast Asian Massif* by Jean Michaud, 2009.
62. *The A to Z of Judaism* by Norman Solomon, 2009.
63. *The A to Z of the Berbers (Imazighen)* by Hsain Ilahiane, 2009.
64. *The A to Z of British Radio* by Seán Street, 2009.
65. *The A to Z of The Salvation Army* by Major John G. Merritt, 2009.
66. *The A to Z of the Arab-Israeli Conflict* by P. R. Kumaraswamy, 2009.
67. *The A to Z of the Jacksonian Era and Manifest Destiny* by Terry Corps, 2009.
68. *The A to Z of Socialism* by Peter Lamb and James C. Docherty, 2009.
69. *The A to Z of Marxism* by David Walker and Daniel Gray, 2009.
70. *The A to Z of the Bahá'í Faith* by Hugh C. Adamson, 2009.
71. *The A to Z of Postmodernist Literature and Theater* by Fran Mason, 2009.
72. *The A to Z of Australian Radio and Television* by Albert Moran and Chris Keating, 2009.
73. *The A to Z of the Lesbian Liberation Movement: Still the Rage* by JoAnne Myers, 2009.
74. *The A to Z of the United States–Mexican War* by Edward R. Moseley and Paul C. Clark, 2009.
75. *The A to Z of World War I* by Ian V. Hogg, 2009.
76. *The A to Z of World War II: The War Against Japan* by Ann Sharp Wells, 2009.
77. *The A to Z of Witchcraft* by Michael D. Bailey, 2009.

78. *The A to Z of British Intelligence* by Nigel West, 2009.
79. *The A to Z of United States Intelligence* by Michael A. Turner, 2009.
80. *The A to Z of the League of Nations* by Anique H. M. van Ginneken, 2009.
81. *The A to Z of Israeli Intelligence* by Ephraim Kahana, 2009.
82. *The A to Z of the European Union* by Joaquín Roy and Aimee Kanner, 2009.
83. *The A to Z of the Chinese Cultural Revolution* by Guo Jian, Yongyi Song, and Yuan Zhou, 2009.
84. *The A to Z of African American Cinema* by S. Torriano Berry and Venise T. Berry, 2009.
85. *The A to Z of Japanese Business* by Stuart D. B. Picken, 2009.
86. *The A to Z of the Reagan–Bush Era* by Richard S. Conley, 2009.
87. *The A to Z of Human Rights and Humanitarian Organizations* by Robert F. Gorman and Edward S. Mihalkanin, 2009.
88. *The A to Z of French Cinema* by Dayna Oscherwitz and MaryEllen Higgins, 2009.
89. *The A to Z of the Puritans* by Charles Pastoor and Galen K. Johnson, 2009.
90. *The A to Z of Nuclear, Biological and Chemical Warfare* by Benjamin C. Garrett and John Hart, 2009.
91. *The A to Z of the Green Movement* by Miranda Schreurs and Elim Papadakis, 2009.
92. *The A to Z of the Kennedy–Johnson Era* by Richard Dean Burns and Joseph M. Siracusa, 2009.
93. *The A to Z of Renaissance Art* by Lilian H. Zirpolo, 2009.
94. *The A to Z of the Broadway Musical* by William A. Everett and Paul R. Laird, 2009.
95. *The A to Z of the Northern Ireland Conflict* by Gordon Gillespie, 2009.
96. *The A to Z of the Fashion Industry* by Francesca Sterlacci and Joanne Arbuckle, 2009.
97. *The A to Z of American Theater: Modernism* by James Fisher and Felicia Hardison Londré, 2009.
98. *The A to Z of Civil Wars in Africa* by Guy Arnold, 2009.
99. *The A to Z of the Nixon–Ford Era* by Mitchell K. Hall, 2009.
100. *The A to Z of Horror Cinema* by Peter Hutchings, 2009.
101. *The A to Z of Westerns in Cinema* by Paul Varner, 2009.
102. *The A to Z of Zionism* by Rafael Medoff and Chaim I. Waxman, 2009.
103. *The A to Z of the Roosevelt–Truman Era* by Neil A. Wynn, 2009.
104. *The A to Z of Jehovah's Witnesses* by George D. Chryssides, 2009.
105. *The A to Z of Native American Movements* by Todd Leahy and Raymond Wilson, 2009.
106. *The A to Z of the Shakers* by Stephen J. Paterwic, 2009.
107. *The A to Z of the Coptic Church* by Gawdat Gabra, 2009.
108. *The A to Z of Architecture* by Allison Lee Palmer, 2009.
109. *The A to Z of Italian Cinema* by Gino Moliterno, 2009.
110. *The A to Z of Mormonism* by Davis Bitton and Thomas G. Alexander, 2009.
111. *The A to Z of African American Theater* by Anthony D. Hill with Douglas Q. Barnett, 2009.

112. *The A to Z of NATO and Other International Security Organizations* by Marco Rimanelli, 2009.
113. *The A to Z of the Eisenhower Era* by Burton I. Kaufman and Diane Kaufman, 2009.
114. *The A to Z of Sexspionage* by Nigel West, 2009.
115. *The A to Z of Environmentalism* by Peter Dauvergne, 2009.
116. *The A to Z of the Petroleum Industry* by M. S. Vassiliou, 2009.
117. *The A to Z of Journalism* by Ross Eaman, 2009.
118. *The A to Z of the Gilded Age* by T. Adams Upchurch, 2009.
119. *The A to Z of the Progressive Era* by Catherine Cocks, Peter C. Holloran, and Alan Lessoff, 2009.
120. *The A to Z of Middle Eastern Intelligence* by Ephraim Kahana and Muhammad Suwaed, 2009.
121. *The A to Z of the Baptists* William H. Brackney, 2009.
122. *The A to Z of Homosexuality* by Brent L. Pickett, 2009.
123. *The A to Z of Islam, Second Edition* by Ludwig W. Adamec, 2009.
124. *The A to Z of Buddhism* by Carl Olson, 2009.
125. *The A to Z of United States–Russian/Soviet Relations* by Norman E. Saul, 2010.
126. *The A to Z of United States–Africa Relations* by Robert Anthony Waters Jr., 2010.
127. *The A to Z of United States–China Relations* by Robert Sutter, 2010.
128. *The A to Z of U.S. Diplomacy since the Cold War* by Tom Lansford, 2010.
129. *The A to Z of United States–Japan Relations* by John Van Sant, Peter Mauch, and Yoneyuki Sugita, 2010.
130. *The A to Z of United States–Latin American Relations* by Joseph Smith, 2010.
131. *The A to Z of United States–Middle East Relations* by Peter L. Hahn, 2010.
132. *The A to Z of United States–Southeast Asia Relations* by Donald E. Weatherbee, 2010.
133. *The A to Z of U.S. Diplomacy from the Civil War to World War I* by Kenneth J. Blume, 2010.
134. *The A to Z of International Law* by Boleslaw A. Boczek, 2010.
135. *The A to Z of the Gypsies (Romanies)* by Donald Kenrick, 2010.
136. *The A to Z of the Tamils* by Vijaya Ramaswamy, 2010.
137. *The A to Z of Women in Sub-Saharan Africa* by Kathleen Sheldon, 2010.
138. *The A to Z of Ancient and Medieval Nubia* by Richard A. Lobban Jr., 2010.
139. *The A to Z of Ancient Israel* by Niels Peter Lemche, 2010.
140. *The A to Z of Ancient Mesoamerica* by Joel W. Palka, 2010.
141. *The A to Z of Ancient Southeast Asia* by John N. Miksic, 2010.
142. *The A to Z of the Hittites* by Charles Burney, 2010.
143. *The A to Z of Medieval Russia* by Lawrence N. Langer, 2010.
144. *The A to Z of the Napoleonic Era* by George F. Nafziger, 2010.

145. *The A to Z of Ancient Egypt* by Morris L. Bierbrier, 2010.
146. *The A to Z of Ancient India* by Kumkum Roy, 2010.
147. *The A to Z of Ancient South America* by Martin Giesso, 2010.
148. *The A to Z of Medieval China* by Victor Cunrui Xiong, 2010.
149. *The A to Z of Medieval India* by Iqtidar Alam Khan, 2010.
150. *The A to Z of Mesopotamia* by Gwendolyn Leick, 2010.
151. *The A to Z of the Mongol World Empire* by Paul D. Buell, 2010.
152. *The A to Z of the Ottoman Empire* by Selcuk Aksin Somel, 2010.
153. *The A to Z of Pre-Colonial Africa* by Robert O. Collins, 2010.
154. *The A to Z of Aesthetics* by Dabney Townsend, 2010.
155. *The A to Z of Descartes and Cartesian Philosophy* by Roger Ariew, Dennis Des Chene, Douglas M. Jesseph, Tad M. Schmaltz, and Theo Verbeek, 2010.
156. *The A to Z of Heidegger's Philosophy* by Alfred Denker, 2010.
157. *The A to Z of Kierkegaard's Philosophy* by Julia Watkin, 2010.
158. *The A to Z of Ancient Greek Philosophy* by Anthony Preus, 2010.
159. *The A to Z of Bertrand Russell's Philosophy* by Rosalind Carey and John Ongley, 2010.
160. *The A to Z of Epistemology* by Ralph Baergen, 2010.
161. *The A to Z of Ethics* by Harry J. Gensler and Earl W. Spurgin, 2010.
162. *The A to Z of Existentialism* by Stephen Michelman, 2010.
163. *The A to Z of Hegelian Philosophy* by John W. Burbidge, 2010.
164. *The A to Z of the Holiness Movement* by William Kostlevy, 2010.
165. *The A to Z of Hume's Philosophy* by Kenneth R. Merrill, 2010.
166. *The A to Z of Husserl's Philosophy* by John J. Drummond, 2010.
167. *The A to Z of Kant and Kantianism* by Helmut Holzhey and Vilem Mudroch, 2010.
168. *The A to Z of Leibniz's Philosophy* by Stuart Brown and N. J. Fox, 2010.
169. *The A to Z of Logic* by Harry J. Gensler, 2010.
170. *The A to Z of Medieval Philosophy and Theology* by Stephen F. Brown and Juan Carlos Flores, 2010.
171. *The A to Z of Nietzscheanism* by Carol Diethe, 2010.
172. *The A to Z of the Non-Aligned Movement and Third World* by Guy Arnold, 2010.
173. *The A to Z of Shamanism* by Graham Harvey and Robert J. Wallis, 2010.
174. *The A to Z of Organized Labor* by James C. Docherty, 2010.
175. *The A to Z of the Orthodox Church* by Michael Prokurat, Michael D. Peterson, and Alexander Golitzin, 2010.
176. *The A to Z of Prophets in Islam and Judaism* by Scott B. Noegel and Brannon M. Wheeler, 2010.
177. *The A to Z of Schopenhauer's Philosophy* by David E. Cartwright, 2010.
178. *The A to Z of Wittgenstein's Philosophy* by Duncan Richter, 2010.
179. *The A to Z of Hong Kong Cinema* by Lisa Odham Stokes, 2010.

180. *The A to Z of Japanese Traditional Theatre* by Samuel L. Leiter, 2010.
181. *The A to Z of Lesbian Literature* by Meredith Miller, 2010.
182. *The A to Z of Chinese Theater* by Tan Ye, 2010.
183. *The A to Z of German Cinema* by Robert C. Reimer and Carol J. Reimer, 2010.
184. *The A to Z of German Theater* by William Grange, 2010.
185. *The A to Z of Irish Cinema* by Roderick Flynn and Patrick Brereton, 2010.
186. *The A to Z of Modern Chinese Literature* by Li-hua Ying, 2010.
187. *The A to Z of Modern Japanese Literature and Theater* by J. Scott Miller, 2010.
188. *The A to Z of Old-Time Radio* by Robert C. Reinehr and Jon D. Swartz, 2010.
189. *The A to Z of Polish Cinema* by Marek Haltof, 2010.
190. *The A to Z of Postwar German Literature* by William Grange, 2010.
191. *The A to Z of Russian and Soviet Cinema* by Peter Rollberg, 2010.
192. *The A to Z of Russian Theater* by Laurence Senelick, 2010.
193. *The A to Z of Sacred Music* by Joseph P. Swain, 2010.
194. *The A to Z of Animation and Cartoons* by Nichola Dobson, 2010.
195. *The A to Z of Afghan Wars, Revolutions, and Insurgencies* by Ludwig W. Adamec, 2010.
196. *The A to Z of Ancient Egyptian Warfare* by Robert G. Morkot, 2010.
197. *The A to Z of the British and Irish Civil Wars 1637–1660* by Martyn Bennett, 2010.
198. *The A to Z of the Chinese Civil War* by Edwin Pak-wah Leung, 2010.
199. *The A to Z of Ancient Greek Warfare* by Iain Spence, 2010.
200. *The A to Z of the Anglo–Boer War* by Fransjohan Pretorius, 2010.
201. *The A to Z of the Crimean War* by Guy Arnold, 2010.
202. *The A to Z of the Zulu Wars* by John Laband, 2010.
203. *The A to Z of the Wars of the French Revolution* by Steven T. Ross, 2010.
204. *The A to Z of the Hong Kong SAR and the Macao SAR* by Ming K. Chan and Shiu-hing Lo, 2010.
205. *The A to Z of Australia* by James C. Docherty, 2010.
206. *The A to Z of Burma (Myanmar)* by Donald M. Seekins, 2010.
207. *The A to Z of the Gulf Arab States* by Malcolm C. Peck, 2010.
208. *The A to Z of India* by Surjit Mansingh, 2010.
209. *The A to Z of Iran* by John H. Lorentz, 2010.
210. *The A to Z of Israel* by Bernard Reich and David H. Goldberg, 2010.
211. *The A to Z of Laos* by Martin Stuart-Fox, 2010.
212. *The A to Z of Malaysia* by Ooi Keat Gin, 2010.
213. *The A to Z of Modern China (1800–1949)* by James Z. Gao, 2010.
214. *The A to Z of the Philippines* by Artemio R. Guillermo and May Kyi Win, 2010.
215. *The A to Z of Taiwan (Republic of China)* by John F. Copper, 2010.

216. *The A to Z of the People's Republic of China* by Lawrence R. Sullivan, 2010.
217. *The A to Z of Vietnam* by Bruce M. Lockhart and William J. Duiker, 2010.
218. *The A to Z of Bosnia and Herzegovina* by Ante Cuvalo, 2010.
219. *The A to Z of Modern Greece* by Dimitris Keridis, 2010.
220. *The A to Z of Austria* by Paula Sutter Fichtner, 2010.
221. *The A to Z of Belarus* by Vitali Silitski and Jan Zaprudnik, 2010.
222. *The A to Z of Belgium* by Robert Stallaerts, 2010.
223. *The A to Z of Bulgaria* by Raymond Detrez, 2010.
224. *The A to Z of Contemporary Germany* by Derek Lewis with Ulrike Zitzlsperger, 2010.
225. *The A to Z of the Contemporary United Kingdom* by Kenneth J. Panton and Keith A. Cowlard, 2010.
226. *The A to Z of Denmark* by Alastair H. Thomas, 2010.
227. *The A to Z of France* by Gino Raymond, 2010.
228. *The A to Z of Georgia* by Alexander Mikaberidze, 2010.
229. *The A to Z of Iceland* by Gudmundur Halfdanarson, 2010.
230. *The A to Z of Latvia* by Andrejs Plakans, 2010.
231. *The A to Z of Modern Italy* by Mark F. Gilbert and K. Robert Nilsson, 2010.
232. *The A to Z of Moldova* by Andrei Brezianu and Vlad Spânu, 2010.
233. *The A to Z of the Netherlands* by Joop W. Koopmans and Arend H. Huussen Jr., 2010.
234. *The A to Z of Norway* by Jan Sjåvik, 2010.
235. *The A to Z of the Republic of Macedonia* by Dimitar Bechev, 2010.
236. *The A to Z of Slovakia* by Stanislav J. Kirschbaum, 2010.
237. *The A to Z of Slovenia* by Leopoldina Plut-Pregelj and Carole Rogel, 2010.
238. *The A to Z of Spain* by Angel Smith, 2010.
239. *The A to Z of Sweden* by Irene Scobbie, 2010.
240. *The A to Z of Turkey* by Metin Heper and Nur Bilge Criss, 2010.
241. *The A to Z of Ukraine* by Zenon E. Kohut, Bohdan Y. Nebesio, and Myroslav Yurkevich, 2010.
242. *The A to Z of Mexico* by Marvin Alisky, 2010.
243. *The A to Z of U.S. Diplomacy from World War I through World War II* by Martin Folly and Niall Palmer, 2010.
244. *The A to Z of Spanish Cinema* by Alberto Mira, 2010.
245. *The A to Z of the Reformation and Counter-Reformation* by Michael Mullett, 2010.

The A to Z of United States–Russian/ Soviet Relations

Norman E. Saul

The A to Z Guide Series, No. 125

The Scarecrow Press, Inc.
Lanham • Toronto • Plymouth, UK
2010

Published by Scarecrow Press, Inc.
A wholly owned subsidary of
The Rowman & Littlefield Publishing Group, Inc.
4501 Forbes Boulevard, Suite 200, Lanham, Maryland 20706
http://www.scarecrowpress.com

Estover Road, Plymouth PL6 7PY, United Kingdom

British Library Cataloguing in Publication Information Available

Library of Congress Cataloging-in-Publication Data

The hardback version of this book was cataloged by the Library of Congress as
follows:

Saul, Norman E.
  Historical dictionary of United States–Russian/Soviet relations / Norman E.
Saul
    p. cm. (Historical dictionaries of U.S. diplomacy ; 8)
    Includes bibliographical references.
    1. United States—Foreign relations—Soviet Union—Dictionaries. 2. Soviet
Union—Foreign relations—United States—Dictionaries. 3. United States—
Foreign relations—Russia—Dictionaries. 4. Russia—Foreign relations—United
States—Dictionaries. 5. United States—Foreign relations—United States—
Dictionaries. I. Title.
  E183.8.R9S3835 2008
  327.73047—dc22   2008022955

ISBN 978-0-8108-7550-0 (pbk. : alk. paper)

Contents

Editor's Foreword   *Jon Woronoff*   xiii

Acknowledgments   xv

Readers' Notes   xvii

Acronyms and Abbreviations   xix

Chronology   xxiii

Introduction   xlv

THE DICTIONARY   1

Appendix 1: Ministers/Ambassadors from the United States
    to Russia/Soviet Union   375

Appendix 2: Ministers/Ambassadors from Russia/
    Soviet Union to the United States   381

Selected Bibliography   385

About the Author   435

Editor's Foreword

Anyone familiar with relations between the United States and Imperial Russia, the Soviet Union, or present-day Russia will most likely find them a rather odd couple. Interests sometimes coincided and sometimes collided, with tsars and ordinary people being attracted to revolutionary America and dictators in the Kremlin becoming foes of U.S. presidents. Mutual anxiety began with the Bolshevik Revolution, was muted in the struggle against fascism during World War II, and became almost catastrophic during the cold war. One would think—or at least hope—that with the collapse of the "evil empire," relations would warm. For a brief while, that seemed to be the case. But now "capitalist" Russia is again worried about American aggressive actions in certain areas (Middle East, Ukraine, and other independent states of the former Soviet Union), while Americans find the actions of Vladimir Putin of major concern. It might take more time than expected to overcome history and establish good relations, but doing so would be of great benefit not only for the parties involved but also for the rest of the world.

The A to Z of United States–Russian/Soviet Relations contains a chronology, which traces the evolution from the first contact to the present, and the introduction also examines the different phases of interaction. People and events; basic institutions; and political, economic, social, and especially diplomatic facets are examined in more depth in the dictionary section. This is truly a vast field, one on which no end of articles and books have been written; thus, a substantial bibliography directs readers to other sources.

Norman Saul is professor of history and of Russian and East European studies at the University of Kansas, and one of his main interests is U.S.–Russian relations, on which he has written no less than four books and coedited a fifth: *Distant Friends: The United States and Russia, 1763–1867*; *Concord and Conflict: The United States and Russia,*

1867–1914; *War and Revolution: The United States and Russia, 1914–1921*; *Friends or Foes? The United States and Soviet Russia, 1921–1941*; and *Russian–American Dialogue on Cultural Relations, 1776–1914*. From these dates, it's obvious that his focus is earlier, which is somewhat unusual among Russian/Soviet specialists but certainly advantageous for this book, since the earlier period is often overlooked.

Jon Woronoff
Series Editor

Acknowledgments

My research on Russian and Soviet–American relations has been nurtured and encouraged by a number of scholars, both American and Russian. Of special importance on the American side are Walter La Feber, John Lewis Gaddis, and Basil Dmytryshyn, whose work has been an inspiration to my own. Without the support and assistance of my Russian colleagues, none of what follows would have been possible; chief among them are Grigory Sevostianov, Nikolai Bolkhovitinov, Eduard Ivanian, Gennady Kuropiatnik, and Robert Ivanov. I also appreciate the friendship and fresh insights of younger Russian scholars such as Vladimir Pozniakov, Viktoria Zhuravleva, Ivan Kurilla, and Alexander Petrov. My American colleagues David Foglesong, David Engerman, Bertrand Patenaude, and many others have kept me abreast of their and others' research. It is nice to know that Russian–American studies are alive and well on both sides.

I also owe much to the support of the University Press of Kansas, its director, Fred Woodward, and his staff in guiding me through the publication of more than 2,000 pages on Russian/Soviet–American relations. In those pages, and especially in those that follow in this volume, I am in debt to Pam Lerow, senior associate administrator of the Word Processing Center of the University of Kansas, for her expertise in electronic communications and manuscript massaging. I also owe a special thanks to Luba Ginsburg, a graduate student in American studies from St. Petersburg, who was researching the American colony in St. Petersburg as this work unfolded.

Finally, but not certainly not last in the production of this volume, is Jon Woronoff, who stalwartly guided a sometimes temperamental author toward a better balance between the prerevolutionary and the Soviet and post-Soviet periods. He definitely helped shape the book.

Readers' Notes

The existence of a different alphabet in the Russian language presents a challenge. In general, the Library of Congress transliteration system from the Cyrilic alphabet to the Latin English, especially in the bibliography, has been followed in the dictionary. This will ease cross-references to library catalogs, since that form is universally followed in American libraries with the significant exception of the old catalog of the New York Public Library. Adaptations of current usage, however, are exceptions. For example, instead of the "skii" common ending, "sky" is used for well-known names, for example, Leon Trotsky instead of Leon Trotskii and not his real name, Lev Bronstein. Thus, the changing of names from actual to revolutionary is another problem: Lenin for Ulyanov, Stalin for Dzugashvili, and so on.

More important for alphabetical entries, however, are the common spellings of such names as Tchaikovsky, the composer, rather than Chaikovsky in transliteration, while the same name (no relation) of the revolutionary Nikolai Chaikovsky is to be found under *C* rather than *T*. English has been used for important rulers such as Peter the Great and Catherine the Great, in place of the true Russian of "Petr velikii" or "Ekaterina velikii." Similarly, journalistic practice has been followed with such names as Yeltsin rather than the formal transliteration, Eltsyn. Such discrepancies also occur as a result of the author's choice, resulting in Boris Bakhmeteff, the ambassador of the Provisional Government to the United States, and his predecessor, Georgi Bakhmetev (same name, no relation), simply because the former preferred and used that spelling throughout his life in the United States. The Russian "soft sign" has also generally been omitted in the dictionary entries: Svinin, rather than Svin'in, the Russian artist/diplomat who painted America.

Common usage also prevails in regard to revolutionary pseudonyms: for example, Vladimir Lenin rather than Ulyanov, Leon Trotsky instead of Lev Bronstein, Joseph Stalin for Iosif Djugashvili (the real names are usually indicated in parentheses). This helps simplify the entries, although we are stuck with Mstislav Rostropovich and many other pure Russian names. First names are somewhat an arbitrary choice: "Alexander" Solzhenitsyn instead of Aleksandr and Nicholas or Michael in many cases instead of Nikolai or Mikhail, depending usually on familiarity. Thankfully, Igor is Igor and Ivan is Ivan, not John. Persons with multiply rendered names are arbitrarily entered, usually with subentries. Thus, Vladimir Geins, also known as Wilhelm Frei and William Frey, is listed under Frey.

Another problem is the changing place names, since many cities of Russia were converted to honor heroes of the Soviet regime: Petrograd = Leningrad; Tsaritsyn = Stalingrad; Nizhni Novgorod = Gorky; Ekaterinburg = Sverdlovsk; Tver = Kalinin. Fortunately, many retained their original names (Moscow, Smolensk, Vologda, Rostov, Kiev, Kharkov) and others reverted back to the original Russian name, for example, St. Petersburg, Tver, and Nizhni Novgorod. Moscow has always been Moscow, although Tsaritsyn/Stalingrad has been stuck with the de-Stalinized Volgograd. Standard English rendering for many names prevails, for example, Moscow, not the transliterated Moskva.

Variances in dates can also be confusing. Before February 1918, Russia officially employed the Julian calendar, 13 days behind the Western (or Gregorian) calendar in the 20th century, 12 days behind in the 19th. The "October Revolution" is the common usage through the Soviet period for the Bolshevik seizure of power, though it occurred in November by the Western calendar. I have used Bolshevik Revolution rather than November Revolution to avoid confusion. With few exceptions, however, the Western calendar prevails in regard to years of birth and death, events, and so on. Fortunately, the new Soviet regime in early 1918 adopted the Western calendar, eliminating the problem.

Acronyms and Abbreviations

AAASS	American Association for the Advancement of Slavic Studies
ABM	Anti-ballistic missiles
ACTR	American Council of Teachers of Russian
AEF	American Expeditionary Force (Siberia, North Russia, 1918)
Amtorg	American [Soviet] Trading Corporation
ARA	American Relief Administration
ARC	American Red Cross
ARCC	American Russian Chamber of Commerce
CER	Chinese Eastern Railway
CIA	Central Intelligence Agency
CIS	Commonwealth of Independent States
COMINTERN	Communist (Third) International
CPSU	Communist Party of the Soviet Union
CPUSA	Communist Party of the United States of America
FBI	Federal Bureau of Investigation (U.S.)
FER	Far Eastern Republic
FSB	Federal Security Service (Russian Federation, 1991–)
GARF	State Archives of the Russian Federation
GAZ	State Automobile Works
GAZPROM	Gas Industry, large natural gas and oil company
ICBM	Intercontinental ballistic missiles
IH	International Harvester (U.S.)
INF	Intermediate-range Nuclear Forces
INTOURIST	Foreign Tourist Agency (Soviet)
IREX	International Research and Exchanges Board

ISKAN	Institute of the USA and Canada (Russian Academy of Sciences)
IWW	International Workers of the World ("Wobblies")
JJDC	Jewish Joint Distribution Committee
KGB	Committee on State Security (Soviet)
LC	Library of Congress
MAD	Mutual assured destruction
MAT	Moscow Art Theater
MGU	Moscow (Lomonosov) State University
MIRV	Multiple independently targetable reentry vehicle
NARA	National Archives and Records Administration
NARKOMINDEL	Peoples' Commissariat for Foreign Affairs (Foreign Ministry)
NASA	National Aeronautical and Space Administration (U.S.)
NATO	North Atlantic Treaty Organization
NEP	New Economic Policy
NKVD	People's Commissariat of Internal Affairs (Soviet political police, 1927–46)
NYLIC	New York Life Insurance Company
NYPL	New York Public Library
OSS	Office of Strategic Services (U.S.)
Politburo	Political bureau of the Central Committee of the Communist Party of the Soviet Union (CPSU)
RAC	Russian America Company
RF	Russian Federation
RFE	Radio Free Europe
RGASPI	Russian State Archives of Social and Political History (Party Archive)
RL	Radio Liberty
RSDLP	Russian Social Democratic Labor Party
RSFSR	Russian Socialist Federal Soviet Republic
SALT	Strategic Arms Limitation Talks I and II
SDI	Strategic Defense Initiative ("star wars")
SORT	Strategic Offensive Reductions Treaty
SOVNARKOV	Council of People's Commissars (Soviet executive cabinet)
START	Strategic Arms Reduction Talks

UN	United Nations
USSR	Union of Soviet Socialist Republics
VOA	Voice of America
VOKS	All-Russian Society for Cultural Relations with Foreign Countries
YMCA	Young Men's Christian Association
YWCA	Young Women's Christian Association

Chronology

1698 Peter the Great meets with William Penn during a visit to England.

1725 Danish explorer Vitus Bering carries out the first official Russian expedition to the Pacific, inaugurated by Peter the Great.

1732 Ivan Gvozdev and Ivan Fedorov "discover America," sighting the mainland of Alaska.

1733–41 Bering's second expedition proves that America was separated from Asia by a strait, later named after the explorer.

1763 An American merchant ship, the *Wolfe*, makes the first direct voyage from Boston to St. Petersburg. This is followed by more each year until interrupted by the Revolutionary War.

1766 Direct scholarly communication is initiated between Benjamin Franklin and Russian-German mathematician Franz Epinus.

1775 The Russian expedition of Grigory Shelikhov establishes a hunting camp in the Aleutian Islands.

1777–83 Russian Fedor Karzhavin supports the cause of American independence. Russian subjects Tadeus Kosciusko, Casimir Pulaski, and Gustavus Rosenthal (John Rose) provide distinguished services for the colonial army in the American Revolutionary War (although the first two were Polish, the third Baltic German).

1780 Catherine the Great initiates the Russian declaration of armed neutrality during the Revolutionary War to protect the ships of neutral countries trading with America.

1781 Francis Dana is sent to Russia to secure recognition of U.S. independence.

1783 End of American War for Independence. Direct and legal commercial voyages resume between the United States and Russia after the Revolutionary War. This usually involves a triangular pattern: New England–Spanish West Indies (mainly Cuba)–Baltic ports (mainly St. Petersburg); Alexander Radishchev praises American independence and its leader George Washington.

1784 Grigory Shelikhov establishes Russian hunting camp on Kodiak.

1787 American adventurer John Ledyard arrives in St. Petersburg on an expedition to Siberia.

1788 John Paul Jones enters Russian naval service during the Second Turkish War.

1789 Ekaterina Dashkova is elected a member of the American Philosophical Society. Benjamin Franklin becomes an honorary member of the Russian Academy of Sciences.

1790 Alexander Baranov becomes a director of Russian America Company.

1792 Dmitri Golitsyn arrives in Baltimore as the first permanent Russian immigrant to the United States; as Father Augustine he becomes a renowned Roman Catholic priest and missionary in Pennsylvania.

1794 A Russian Orthodox mission is sent to Kodiak, resulting in the first permanent Russian settlement in Alaska.

1799 Ukaz (decree) of Emperor Paul establishes the Russian America Company (RAC) as the first Russian joint stock company with a monopoly over the natives and resources of Northwest America. Alexander Baranov, the first chief administrator of the Russian America Company, establishes a Russian fort at Sitka; it soon becomes the "capital" of the territory.

1803 Ivan Kruzenshtern and Yuri Lisiansky begin around-the-world voyage under overall command of Nikolai Rezanov.

1803 Levett Harris establishes first U.S. consulate in St. Petersburg.

1804–05 Tsar Alexander I and President Thomas Jefferson correspond.

1805   John D'Wolfe sails to Alaska on the *Juno*; he has sold the ship to the Russian America Company and travels by sea and across Siberia to collect on the sale.

1806   Nikolai Rezanov visits San Francisco Bay and Monterey to negotiate with Spanish authorities on supplies for Russian America Company.

1807   Negotiations in London between M. M. Alopeus and James Monroe and William Pinckney about diplomatic recognition between the two countries.

1808   Andrei Dashkov arrives in Philadelphia as the first Russian minister to the United States.

1809   John Quincy Adams settles in St. Petersburg as the first U.S. minister to Russia.

1810   John D. Lewis of Philadelphia establishes mercantile trading firm in St. Petersburg. It serves more than 200 "American" ships calling at Russian Baltic ports annually in 1810–12.

1812   Ivan Kuskov establishes an RAC outpost at Fort Ross on the northern California coast; beginning of U.S. war with Great Britain.

1813–14   American peace commission headed by James Bayard and Albert Gallatin in St. Petersburg to settle War of 1812 with Russian mediation.

1815   Napoleonic Wars and War of 1812 end; Congress of Vienna; Kozlov affair in Philadelphia.

1820   Henry Middleton and family from Charleston establish residence as minister in St. Petersburg for 10 years.

1821   Ukaz (decree) of Alexander I establishes a 100-English-mile zone of Russian control over water from the coast of its Northwest American territories to protect its shores from smuggling by mainly American ships to natives, but it has little effect before being reversed by the Convention of 1824.

1823   **December:** The Monroe Doctrine is outlined in the president's State of the Union address; essentially drafted by John Quincy Adams, it restricts European expansion in North America, including Russia in Alaska.

1824   Convention of 1824 on Russian–American boundaries and sea limits in North America, essentially annulling the Ukaz of 1821.

1825   The Decembrist Revolt occurs in St. Petersburg with a prominent American constitutional influence on the program of the Northern Society.

1832   The Russian American Commercial Treaty is negotiated and signed in St. Petersburg; William H. Ropes of Boston/Salem founds a substantial American trading firm in St. Petersburg; his family will remain in business in Russia for three generations.

1837   Visit of USS *Independence* to St. Petersburg.

1839–40   Melnikov–Kraft mission to United States; William Darby's columns in *National Intelligencer* on Russia.

1840   **November:** The steam warship *Kamchatka* is launched for the Russian navy in New York with much publicity, followed by its equally celebrated delivery to Kronstadt.

1841   Fort Ross (*Krepost Rossia*) in northern California is sold by the RAC to an American rancher, Captain John Sutter.

1842   George Washington Whistler arrives with his family to be the chief surveyor of the Moscow–St. Petersburg rail line, the first Russian long-distance railroad.

1843   Harrison, Eastwick and Winans Company of Baltimore obtains a long-term contract for the manufacture of locomotives and rolling stock for the Russian railroads.

1848   Gold is discovered on former Russian territory in northern California, triggering the California gold rush of 1849, in which the Russian America Company participated.

1852   The American Russian Commercial Company (ARCC) is established in San Francisco specifically for trade (mainly purchase of ice) with the Russian colonies in Alaska. Peter Kostromitinov establishes Russian consulate in San Francisco.

1854–56   During the Crimean War, American support for Russia is demonstrated with more than 30 American surgeons volunteering for service in Russia; American military observers also operate on Russian combat side.

1854   Commercial treaty between RAC and ARCC to avoid possible occupation of Alaska by British forces; Beverley Sanders mission to Russia. Arrival of American volunteer physicians to assist the Russian army in Crimean War. Publication in the United States of Adam Gurowski's *Russia As It Is*.

1855   **June:** Arrival of U.S. military commission of Mordecai, McClellan, and Delafield to observe Crimean War.

1856   Crimean War ends with a treaty in Paris. Extensive tour of Alexander Lakier in the United States. First exchange of books between Smithsonian Institution and Russian Academy of Sciences.

1857   Siberian journeys of Bernard Peyton and Perry McDonough Collins.

1858   **September:** Launch in New York of *General Admiral* for Russian navy; purchase of *Tsaritsa* for Russian America Company.

1859   **February:** African American Ira Aldridge first performs Shakespeare on the Russian stage.

1860   Beginning of "Perkins affair."

1861   The emancipation of serfs edict by Alexander II wins favorable American opinion and launches a parallel with the abolition of slavery during the American Civil War.

1863   Emancipation Proclamation is pronounced by President Abraham Lincoln. Russian naval squadrons under command of Stepan Lesovsky and Alexander Popov visit New York and San Francisco, respectively, to demonstrate Russian support for the Union forces.

1865   American Civil War ends. U.S. government endorses the Western Union Collins Overland Telegraph line, initiated simultaneously in Siberia and Alaska, to connect North America with Europe (abandoned in 1867 upon successful laying of Atlantic cable).

1866 July: Gustavus Fox mission to Russia aboard Union monitor *Miantonomoh* to extend thanks for Russian support during Civil War and to celebrate the escape of Alexander II from assassination. Astronomer Cleveland Abbe begins studies at Pulkovo Observatory, near St. Petersburg.

1867 March: Sale of Alaska to the United States by treaty for $7,200,000. **August:** Visit of an American squadron under Admiral Farragut to St. Petersburg. **August:** Arrival of Mark Twain at Yalta on *Quaker City*. **October:** Official transfer of Alaska from Russia to United States in Sitka.

1868–71 Perkins claim disrupts Russian–American relations.

1869 Hiram Berdan arrives in St. Petersburg to supervise production of his rifle, the "Berdanka," as the principal infantry weapon of the Russian army.

1871 November: Arrival in New York of a Russian squadron with Grand Duke Alexis for a celebrated tour of the United States. Establishment of Russian utopian commune in Kansas by William Frey (Vladimir Geins). First major immigration of Russian Jews to the United States.

1872 January: Buffalo hunts in Nebraska and Colorado for Grand Duke Alexis that feature Buffalo Bill (William Cody), George Armstrong Custer, and Pawnee Indian chiefs. Katakazi affair. **April:** Alexis sails from Pensacola after being crowned king of Mardi Gras in New Orleans.

1874 "To-the-people" movement galvanizes Russian revolutionary movement. Mennonite emigration from Russian Ukraine to Great Plains region of United States.

1875 Volga German exodus from Russia begins.

1876 U.S. centennial of independence in Philadelphia with Russian exhibition. Chemistry professor Dmitri Mendeleev visits Pennsylvania oil fields.

1877–78 Russo-Turkish War; covered by military attaché Francis Greene, war correspondent Januarius MacGahan, and historian Eugene Schuyler.

1878   Visit of former U.S. president Ulysses Grant to Russia.

1887   November: Beginning of George Kennan's series of articles in *Century Magazine*, "Siberia and the Exile System."

1880s   Tolstoy craze in United States. Rise of American reaction to Russian anti-Semitism (pogroms).

1891   March: Russian artist Vasily Vereshchagin visits United States. **April/May:** Peter Tchaikovsky visits United States to open Carnegie Hall in New York. **June/July:** Severe famine in Russia.

1892   Launching of construction of Trans-Siberian Railroad. Major American relief effort to Russian famine, involving American Red Cross and state agencies. Andrew Dickson White becomes ambassador to Russia.

1893   Chicago World's Fair with major Russian presence in large Russian pavilion. International arbitration of Bering Sea Fur Seal controversy in Paris.

1890s   Establishment of major American companies in Russia: Singer, International Harvester, Westinghouse, Baldwin locomotives, New York Life Insurance, Equitable Assurance, and New York City Bank. Jewish "passport question" raised.

1894   Archibald Cary Coolidge introduces at Harvard the first course at an American university on Russian history.

1896   June: Coronation of Nicholas II in Moscow.

1897   Publication in New York by Putnam of Zenaida Ragozin's translation of Anatole Leroy-Beaulieu's *Empire of the Tsars and the Russians* (three volumes).

1898   Hague Peace Conference receives Nicholas II's proposal for arms limitations and arbitration of international disputes, perhaps in response to Spanish–American War.

1900   Meeting of Charles Crane, William Rainey Harper (University of Chicago), Charles Hutchinson (Chicago Art Institute), and Martin Ryerson with Leo Tolstoy.

1902 Alexis Babin founds Slavic Division of Library of Congress. Zenith of Enoch Emery's Siberian commercial empire.

1903 Paul Miliukov's lecture series in United States in Boston and Chicago. Second Congress of the Russian Social Democratic Labor Party in Brussels and London, where the split between Bolsheviks and Mensheviks occurs.

1904 **February:** Russo–Japanese War begins with Japanese attacks on Port Arthur and Vladivostok.

1905 **January:** Bloody Sunday, beginning of Revolution of 1905. **May:** George von Lengerke Meyer appointed ambassador to Russia. Battle of Tsushima is a Russian naval disaster. **August:** Sergei Witte arrives in United States to negotiate peace with Japan. **September:** Treaty of Portsmouth negotiated in Kittery, Maine, arbitrated by Theodore Roosevelt, ends Russo–Japanese War. **October:** General strike and issue of October Manifesto establishing a quasi-constitutional regime. Jewish emigration increases.

1906 Library of Congress acquires Yudin Collection from Siberian merchant. Maxim Gorky visits the United States.

1908 William Howard Taft tours Russia on Trans-Siberian Railroad.

1911 Vote by U.S. Senate to abrogate the Commerce Treaty of 1832. American Atlantic fleet visits St. Petersburg.

1912 Herbert Hoover involved in an international copper enterprise in Urals.

1914–18 World War I.

1915 Second Division of American embassy formed to oversee German and Austrian prisoner of war camps in Russia and enlarge U.S. presence in Russia.

1916 **May:** David Francis appointed ambassador to Russia.

1917 **February/March:** Abdication of Nicholas I. U.S. recognition of Provisional Government. **April:** United States enters World War I. **May:** Root Commission arrives in Russia. Imperial ambassador Georgy Bakhmetev replaced by Provisional Government ambassador Boris

Bakhmeteff. **August:** Substantial loans issued by United States to Alexander Kerensky's Provisional Government. **September:** YMCA and American Red Cross expand activities. **October/November:** Bolshevik seizure of power in Russia; United States refuses to recognize new Soviet government.

1918   January: Russian Railway Service Corps from United States enters Siberia and Manchuria. President Woodrow Wilson presents Fourteen Points program for peace negotiations, which provides for an independent Poland and the integrity of Russia. **March:** Treaty of Brest–Litovsk signed and ratified by Fourth All-Russian Congress of Soviets, allowing Soviet Russia to withdraw from war. Capital moves from Petrograd to Moscow. American embassy transfers from Petrograd to Vologda in North Russia. **July–August:** Beginning of Allied Intervention in Russia. **September:** The American Expeditionary Force (AEF) arrives in Murmansk and Archangel in the north and Vladivostok in the east. **October:** Anti-Bolshevik forces form in North Russia, Ukraine, and Siberia. **November:** World War I ends with armistice on western front. Civil war in Russia begins.

1919   January: Paris Peace Conference opens with Russia absent. **March:** Prinkipo conference proposed. Bullitt–Steffens mission to Russia. Civil war continues in Russia. AEF in Siberia in contact with Alexander Kolchak's Omsk government. Beginning of Allied forces withdrawal. **October:** Labor unrest in Seattle reaches crisis in a general strike. Beginning of Red Scare.

1920   Russian civil war ends with Red Army victories in Ukraine and Siberia. **August:** Secretary of State Bainbridge Colby issues note declaring nonrecognition policy. **October:** Petrograd Children's Colony returns home assisted by the American Red Cross. **November:** Massive Russian refugee exodus through the Black Sea to Constantinople assisted by American Red Cross. **December:** Ludwig Martens designated official Soviet representative in United States. Red Scare continues with prosecution and deportation from United States of suspected radicals, including Martens.

1921   March: End of the period of war Communism and beginning of the more moderate New Economic Policy (NEP), approved by Tenth

Party Congress. **July:** Appeal by Maxim Gorky for famine relief. **August:** Riga agreement for the American Relief Administration to enter Russia for distribution of massive relief assistance. **September:** First trainloads of aid and relief workers enter Soviet Russia. **November:** Armand Hammer signs agreement for development of asbestos mines in Urals, the first of a number of business concessions.

1921–22 Washington Naval Conference meets with participation of Far Eastern Republic but not Russia.

1922 April: Soviet delegation arrives in Italy for Genoa Conference. Signing of Treaty of Rapallo between Germany and Soviet Russia. **June:** Washington Conference concludes by setting limits on warships of major powers. **September:** Russian émigré impresario Nikita Beliaev takes Broadway by storm.

1923 Russian Information Bureau established by Boris Skvirsky in Washington. Inauguration of the All-Russian Society for Cultural Relations with Western Countries, directed by Olga Kameneva.

1924 Establishment of Amtorg in New York. Stanislavsky and the Moscow Art Theatre perform in New York. Deaths of Vladimir Lenin and Woodrow Wilson.

1925 Soviet poet Vladimir Mayakovsky visits New York and other American cities.

1926 American engineer Hugh Cooper commissioned to design largest dam in the world on the Dnieper River below Kiev.

1927 Expulsion of Leon Trotsky from USSR. **October/November:** Visits of American writers Theodore Dreiser and Sinclair Lewis to Moscow on occasion of the 10th anniversary of the Bolshevik Revolution. **December:** Approval of First Five-Year Plan by Fifteenth Party Congress.

1928 Signing of Kellogg–Briand Pact in Paris; the USSR is the first country to ratify (6 September). Several Russian–American institutes founded in major American cities.

1929/1930 Major contracts signed by Soviet agencies with American companies for large construction projects, such as Magnitogorsk, that are an important part of the First Five-Year Plan.

1930 Maxim Litvinov replaces Chicherin as commissar of foreign affairs.

1931 Japanese aggressive actions in the Far East, especially in Manchuria, concern both the United States and the Soviet Union. Height of U.S. Great Depression.

1932 The number of American engineers and workers in Russia surpasses 3,000.

1933 **10 October:** President Franklin D. Roosevelt invites Soviet "president" Mikhail Kalinin to begin negotiations for diplomatic recognition. **15 November:** Soviet Commissar of Foreign Affairs Litvinov arrives in Washington for negotiations. **16 November:** General agreement on exchange of diplomatic representatives. **17 November:** William C. Bullitt designated first ambassador to the USSR. **20 November:** Alexander Troyanovsky appointed first Soviet ambassador to the United States.

1934/1935 Zenith of Litvinov's initiatives of "collective security" to contain the aggressive actions of Germany, Italy, and Japan with membership in the League of Nations and defensive alliances with France and Czechoslovakia.

1938 **October:** Munich Agreement among Germany, France, and Great Britain, signaling Allied appeasement of Adolph Hitler and the defeat of Litvinov's collective security policy.

1939 **May:** Litvinov replaced by Vyacheslav Molotov as commissar of foreign affairs. **August:** Signing of Nazi–Soviet Pact (Molotov–Ribbentrop Agreement), providing for a division of a major part of Eastern Europe. **September:** Soviet and German invasions of Poland, beginning World War II, when Great Britain and France support Poland. **November:** Beginning Soviet–Finnish Winter War that demonstrated Red Army weaknesses.

1940 Fall of France, German supremacy in Western Europe. Air battle over Great Britain. President Roosevelt begins more active preparations for involvement with the initiation of the Committee to Defend America by Aiding the Allies.

1941 **May:** U.S. Congress passes lend-lease bill aimed at aiding Great Britain. **22 June:** Operation Barbarossa—German invasion of USSR.

July: Beginning of American lend-lease shipments to USSR. **30–31 July:** Harry Hopkins mission to Moscow as special assistant to the president. **29 September–1 October:** Moscow conference of foreign ministers to solidify opposition to Germany. **15 October:** American embassy evacuated from Moscow to Kuibyshev on the Volga. **28 October:** Roosevelt extends lend-lease to USSR. Battle of Moscow begins. **November:** Litvinov appointed ambassador to United States. **6 December:** Soviet counterattack at Moscow. **7 December:** Japanese attack on Pearl Harbor. **8 December:** United States enters World War II in Europe as well as Pacific. Litvinov arrives in Washington via Hawaii and San Francisco.

1942   1 January: Declaration of United Nations signed by the four Allied powers, United States, USSR, Great Britain, and China, and 22 other countries. **August:** Soviet leaders informed of delay in the opening of a second front in Western Europe owing to concentration on North African campaign. **November:** German offensive south of Moscow culminates in siege of Stalingrad; large German forces are enveloped and defeated by the following January.

1943   14–24 January: Casablanca conference of leaders of United States, Great Britain, and France (Roosevelt, Winston Churchill, and Charles de Gaulle). Plans made for invasion of Italy, delay of cross-channel invasion, and pronouncement of policy of unconditional surrender with the huge Soviet war effort in mind. **April:** Germany announces the discovery of mass graves of Polish officers in Katyn Forest, near Smolensk, blaming the Soviet Union. **July:** Impressive Soviet victory at the battle of Kursk. **August:** Soviet capture of Kharkov and sweep through Ukraine. **28 November–1 December:** Tehran conference, first meeting of Joseph Stalin with Churchill and Roosevelt, pledging cooperation and coordination in the defeat of German forces.

1944   6 June: D day, opening of second front in Western Europe with landing of Allied forces in Normandy. Soviet forces advance westward, halted briefly by the battle of Warsaw and the Warsaw uprising.

1945   4–11 February: Yalta (Crimean) conference of the "Big Three" reaches major decisions regarding the future position of Poland (in Soviet sphere), Soviet agreement to support United Nations, occupation zones for Germany, and that the USSR would enter the war against

Japan. **April:** Death of Roosevelt. Harry S. Truman becomes president. Meeting of American and Soviet armies on the Elbe. San Francisco Conference on postwar problems and United Nations. **26 May–6 June:** Second visit of Harry Hopkins to Moscow. **June:** San Francisco Conference of representatives of 50 nations, culminating in the signing of the Charter of the United Nations; the Soviet Union was represented by Vyacheslav Molotov and Andrei Gromyko. **25 June:** President Truman addresses the final session of the San Francisco Conference. **17 July–2 August:** Potsdam (Berlin) conference on settling remaining issues, such as the administration of occupation zones and Soviet entry into the war against Japan. U.S. atomic bomb tested successfully. **6 August:** Atomic bomb dropped on Hiroshima. **8 August:** Soviet declaration of war on Japan and invasion of Manchuria. **14 August:** Japan announces surrender. **2 September:** Surrender formalized on the USS *Missouri* in Tokyo Bay without Soviet participation. **24 October:** United Nations officially comes into existence with the ratification of the charter by the United States, USSR, Great Britain, France, China (the "Big Five"), and a majority of other signees.

1946   January: First meetings of the General Assembly and Security Council of the United Nations in London with decision to establish permanent headquarters in the United States. **February:** George F. Kennan, first councilor of embassy in Moscow, sends "long telegram" to Secretary of State George C. Marshall warning of Soviet aggressive actions. **5 March:** Churchill's speech at Fulton, Missouri, defining an "iron curtain" that had descended across Europe. **May:** After United States voices strong concern, the Soviet army withdraws from Iran.

1947   17 February: First broadcast of Voice of America to USSR. **12 March:** Truman Doctrine, a proclamation by President Harry S. Truman of a military aid program to Greece and Turkey to prevent them from falling under Communism. **July:** Marshall Plan inaugurated as a reconstruction program for Europe (European Recovery Program). USSR refuses to participate in Marshall Plan. Publication of George F. Kennan's "X" article in *Foreign Affairs Quarterly*.

1948   February: Communist takeover of Czechoslovakia. **March:** Foreign Minister Jan Masaryk found dead in Prague; whether by murder or suicide remains in dispute. Considerable American reaction to this "brutal

Soviet aggression." Expulsion of Yugoslavia from Cominform. **15 June:** Soviet declaration closing access to Berlin after the consolidation of the American, British, and French occupation zones in West Germany. **25 June:** Allied airlift of supplies to Berlin begins. Founding of Russian Institute at Columbia University and Harvard Russian Research Center.

1949 Victory of Communist People's Army in China. McCarthy era in United States. **30 September:** Berlin blockade lifted. East Berlin proclaimed capital of the German Democratic Republic.

1950 **June:** Invasion by North Korean forces of South Korea, beginning Korean War. United Nations on American initiative joins the resistance.

1951 **Summer:** Successful Allied offensive occupies most of North Korea, resulting in Chinese intervention and retreat of UN forces. Stalemate results approximately along original border.

1953 **March:** Death of Stalin and beginning of succession struggle. Truce in Korean War.

1954 American Kremlinologists observe power struggle in USSR.

1955 **21 July:** First U.S.–Soviet summit meeting in Geneva between Nikita Khrushchev and Dwight D. Eisenhower. Austrian State Treaty allowing for withdrawal of occupation forces and a free, neutralized Austria.

1956 **February:** "Secret speech" by Khrushchev attacking Stalin's crimes and his cult of personality. Announcement of "peaceful coexistence." Exchange of *USSR* and *Amerika* publications. **September:** Hungarian Revolution and its suppression by Soviet troops.

1957 **June:** Khrushchev overcomes reaction against his new policies in suppression of the "Anti-Party" coup. **4 October:** Soviet launch of Sputnik I, first orbital object around the earth, creating a sensation in United States but followed early the next year by the first American satellite, setting off a space race.

1958 **27 January:** Signing of the Lacy–Zarubin (Eisenhower–Khrushchev) agreement on student and cultural exchanges. **April:** Van Cliburn wins Tchaikovsky Piano Competition in Moscow. **31 October:** Negotiations begin in Geneva on cessation of nuclear weapons testing among United States, USSR, and Great Britain.

1959 **June–July:** Cultural exchange expositions: a Soviet one on science and technology in New York and an American one in Sokolniki

Park on domestic economy. The latter results in the "kitchen debate" between Khrushchev and Vice President Richard Nixon. **15–17 September:** Visit of Nikita Khrushchev to United States, where he addresses United Nations, tours the United States, and meets with President Eisenhower at Camp David.

1960 1 May: A U.S. high-altitude U-2 surveillance plane is shot down by a Soviet missile over the Urals. Pilot Gary Powers is captured on the ground as proof of the overflight of Soviet airspace violation. **16–17 May:** Summit between Eisenhower and Khrushchev in Paris disrupted by Soviet demands in connection with U-2 incident. **29 October–4 November:** Dartmouth conference of American and Soviet political and cultural leaders.

1961 3–4 June: Vienna summit between Khrushchev and President John F. Kennedy with a general discussion of issues. **August:** Erection of the Berlin Wall separating East and West Berlin to stop increasing defection of East Germans to the West.

1962 Publication of *One Day in the Life of Ivan Denisovich*, a fictional autobiographical account of life in a labor camp, by Alexander Solzhenitzen. **October:** Cuban (Caribbean) Missile Crisis over a Soviet plan to install intermediate-range missiles in Cuba. A major threat of nuclear war peacefully resolved.

1963 June: Signing of hotline agreement for direct telephone connection between U.S. and Soviet leaders. **July:** W. Averell Harriman visits with Khrushchev in Moscow. **August:** First large-scale Soviet importation of grain from the United States.

1964 1 June: Consular convention signed in Moscow, enlarging diplomatic presence in both United States and USSR. **October:** Khrushchev removed as Soviet leader; Leonid Brezhnev replaces him as Soviet leader. **December:** Fishing convention signed for waters of Northeastern Pacific.

1967 June: Glassboro, New Jersey, summit between Soviet Chairman of Council of Ministers Andrei Kosygin and American President Lyndon Johnson with the new Brezhnev policy of *detente*. **December:** Foundation of the Institute of the USA and Canada of the Russian Academy of Sciences ("think tank" on American affairs). Growing reform movement in Eastern European satellite countries, especially in Poland and Czechoslovakia.

1968 **September:** Soviet invasion of Czechoslovakia to suppress its movement away from Warsaw Pact. Crisis averted by American decision not to intervene.

1969 **17 November:** Beginning of strategic arms limitation talks (SALT I) in Helsinki.

1971 **30 September:** Agreement on measures to reduce the threat of nuclear war between United States and USSR.

1972 **22–30 May:** First visit of a president of the United States, Richard Nixon, to the Soviet Union. **26 May:** Signing of Anti-Ballistic Missile (ABM) Treaty by Nixon and Leonid Brezhnev. A series of minor agreements leading to the inauguration of SALT I negotiations.

1973 **18–25 June:** Official visit of Leonid Brezhnev to United States, reciprocating Nixon's visit to the USSR the previous year. A number of minor agreements signed. **June/July:** Soviet consulate established in San Francisco and U.S. consulate in Leningrad. **November:** Establishment of Fulbright lectureship in American history at Moscow State University.

1974 **27 June–3 July:** Visit of President Richard Nixon to USSR. **23–24 November:** Vladivostok summit between Brezhnev and President Gerald Ford. **20 December:** U.S. Congress approves trade agreement with USSR with the Jackson–Vanik amendment, restricting most-favorite trade policy because of lack of freedom of emigration from USSR.

1975 **17 July:** "Apollo–Soiuz" space cooperation agreement. **30 July–2 August:** Brezhnev–Ford summit meeting in Helsinki. **September:** Agreement on five-year term of grain purchases by USSR from United States.

1976 **28 May:** Signing of treaty on banning of underground nuclear tests.

1979 **15–18 June:** Summit meeting between Brezhnev and President Jimmy Carter in Vienna, ending with signing of SALT II agreement; beginning of negotiations for Strategic Arms Reduction Treaty (START I). **25 December:** Soviet invasion of Afghanistan.

1980 **4 January:** President Carter suspends exports of grain to the USSR as part of an economic embargo in reaction to the Soviet invasion of Afghanistan. **12 April:** U.S. Olympic Committee announces that the United States will not participate in the Moscow Olympic games that summer. Kennan Institute for Advanced Russian Studies is founded in Washington to be associated with the Woodrow Wilson Center of the Smithsonian Institution.

1981   28 December: Declaration of President Ronald Reagan of temporary suspension of Aeroflot flights to the United States in protest of Soviet suppression of events in Poland.

1982   29 June: Beginning of Soviet–American negotiations in Geneva on limitation and reduction of strategic weapons (START I). **21 October:** Russian Institute at Columbia University endowed by W. Averell Harriman family and renamed as the Harriman Institute.

1983   8 March: President Reagan uses term *evil empire* as applied to the USSR for the first time in a speech to the National Association of Evangelicals in Orlando, Florida. **23 March:** President Reagan announces beginning of work on Strategic Defense Initiative, "star wars." **8 September:** Reagan suspends all Aeroflot flights from United States in reaction to the shooting down of South Korean Air flight 007 over Sakhalin Island.

1984   8 May: USSR national Olympic committee decides not to participate in Los Angeles Olympic games, in apparent retaliation for U.S. boycott of Moscow games in 1980.

1985   12 March: Negotiations begin in Geneva on control of nuclear weapons in outer space. **15 March:** Death of Viktor Chernenko and ascendancy of Mikhail Gorbachev to Soviet leadership. **8 April:** Declaration by Gorbachev of moratorium on use of nuclear weapons; response by President Reagan as a propaganda ploy. **1 July:** Announcement of the "retirement" of Andrei Gromyko as foreign minister. **4 July:** Very large Soviet attendance at a gala Fourth of July reception at Spaso House in Moscow. **19–21 November:** Summit meeting between President Reagan and Gorbachev in Geneva.

1986   1 January: Telecasts of Reagan and Gorbachev to audiences in respective countries. **15 January:** Gorbachev proposes a plan for the dismantling of atomic weapons by the year 2000. **26 April:** Nuclear power station accident at Chernobyl in Ukraine causes widespread dissemination of radioactive fallout. Soviet admission of the incident as an example of the new policy of *Glasnost*. **11–12 October:** Summit meeting of Gorbachev and Reagan in Rekyavik, Iceland.

1987   14 January: First round of talks in Geneva on the reduction of nuclear threat. **15 April:** Agreement signed on cooperation in space explorations. **15 September:** Two protocols signed on the reduction of nuclear threat. **7–10 December:** Meeting in Washington between Gorbachev and Reagan; treaty signed on gradual elimination of intermediate- and short-range missile deployments. **27 December:** Gorbachev selected by *Time Magazine* as "man of the year."

1988   29 May–2 June: Meeting in Washington between Gorbachev and Reagan; series of agreements on limitations on intermediate-range missiles signed. **7 December:** Meeting on Governor's Island between Gorbachev and Reagan, joined by President-Elect George H. W. Bush.

1989   30 March: General trade agreement signed between United States and USSR. **9–17 September:** Unofficial visit of Boris Yeltsyn to the United States, including a meeting with President Bush and a visit to the Harriman Institute at Columbia University. **23 September:** Memorandum of understanding between United States and USSR regarding the cessation of production of chemical weapons. **2–3 December:** Summit conference between Gorbachev and Bush at Malta, concluding with the first joint press conference. **24 December:** *Time Magazine* selects Gorbachev as "man of the decade."

1990   30 May–5 June: Visit of Gorbachev to United States, meeting with President Bush; joint press conference and signing of a series of agreements, extending previous ones and initiating new proposals. **June:** "Meeting for Peace" brings more than 200 representative Soviet citizens to Lawrence, Kansas, to stay with American families and discuss world affairs. **8 July:** Agreement on joint training of Russian and American cosmonauts. **9 September:** Conference of Gorbachev and Bush in Helsinki. **15–19 September:** Visit to Russia by invitation of Gorbachev of former president Ronald Reagan and his wife. **4 October:** Meeting of Foreign Minister Edouard Shevardnadze with Secretary of State James Baker. **30 December:** President Bush grants long-term credits to USSR, which has met the restrictions of the Jackson–Vanik amendment of 1974 regarding freedom of emigration.

1991   28 April: Direct flights begin between Moscow and Miami. **29 July–1 August:** Gorbachev and Bush summit meeting in Moscow;

signing (31 July) of Strategic Arms Reduction Treaty (START I). **19 August:** August coup; declaration of President Bush of extraordinary situation in USSR. **6 September:** ABC press conference with Gorbachev and Yeltsin. **30 October:** Meeting of Bush and Gorbachev in Madrid. **25 December:** Resignation of Gorbachev; disintegration of USSR into 15 independent states.

1992 Beginning of First Chechen War. **1 February:** Meeting of President George H. W. Bush and Russian Federation president Boris Yeltsin at Camp David (his first trip to United States) and signing of a new declaration on Russian–American cooperation. **17 June:** Visit of Russian President Yeltsin to Washington and signing of a number of agreements on mutual cooperation. **29 June:** First delegation (around 100) of Peace Corps volunteers to Russia. **22 September:** Opening of American consulate in Vladivostok. **5 October:** NASA agreement on space research cooperation leading to future joint missions.

1993 **2–3 January:** At summit in Moscow Bush and Yeltsin sign SALT II treaty (not ratified by Russian Duma). **21 January:** Bill Clinton inaugurated as president. **25 February:** Meeting of Secretary of State Warren Christopher and Russian Foreign Minister Andrei Kozyrev in Geneva. **23 March:** Kosyrev in Washington proposes creation of special Gore–Chernomyrdin commission. **3–4 April:** Clinton and Yeltsin meet for their first summit in Vancouver, Canada. **9–10 July:** Clinton and Yeltsin meet again in Tokyo; Group of Seven announces $28 billion assistance for former Soviet states. **1–2 September:** Vice President Al Gore and Russian Chairman of Council of Ministers Viktor Chernomyrdin meet in Washington. **17 September:** Patriarch Aleksei II of the Russian Orthodox Church visits United States to celebrate 200th anniversary of the Orthodox Church in America. **September–October:** Yeltsin crisis with Russian parliament.

1994 **12–15 January:** Visit of Clinton to Moscow for meeting with Yeltsin; a number of agreements are signed, including one on human rights. **3 February:** *Discovery* launched from Cape Canaveral with a joint Russian–American crew. **February:** Conference of Russian and American historians in Moscow to honor the 20th anniversary of the Fulbright American history professorship at Moscow State University. **15–16 March:** Russian–American conference at Harvard University on the conversion of nuclear weapons to peaceful purposes. **27–28 September:** Meeting of Clinton and Yeltsin in Washington with a number of declarations, for example, on strategic stabilization of nuclear threat, for a "partnership for economic progress," and that the enlargement of the North Atlantic Treaty Organization membership will be gradual and will not exclude Russia.

1995   **6 February:** American spaceship *Discovery* docks with Russian space station *Mir*. **8 April:** Fiftieth anniversary of the meeting of American and Soviet forces on the Elbe. **10 May:** President Clinton and Yeltsin meet in Moscow on the occasion of the 50th anniversary of the end of World War II. **16–17 June:** Clinton–Yeltsin meeting in Halifax, Nova Scotia. **23 October:** Clinton and Yeltsin meet at the Roosevelt Library in Hyde Park, New York. Agreement on Russian participation in Bosnian peace settlement. **26 October:** Yeltsin suffers heart attack upon return to Moscow. **November:** Agreement on Bosnian peace in negotiations in Dayton, Ohio. **17 December:** Communist Party gains in Russian parliamentary election.

1996   **9 January:** Yevgeny Primakov replaces Kosyrev as Russian foreign minister. **19–21 April:** Clinton visits St. Petersburg and Moscow. **June:** After achieving a narrow plurality in first round of the presidential election, Yeltsin forms an alliance with Alexander Lebed and wins reelection though suffering from heart problems. **31 August:** Lebed signs peace ending First Chechen War. **17 October:** Yeltsin dismisses Lebed as minister of defense.

1997   **20–21 March:** Clinton–Yeltsin meeting in Helsinki; unsuccessful Russian appeal that NATO will not include states of former Soviet Union. Outline of START III agreement. **27 May:** Yeltsin attends NATO summit in Paris. **20–22 June:** Meeting in Denver of eight leading industrial nations, attended by Clinton and Yeltsin. **28–29 July:** Russian–American conference in Los Angeles on trade and development.

1998   **23 March:** Chernomyrdin replaced as chairman of council of ministers by Sergei Krylenko. **16–17 May:** Yeltsin and Clinton meet in Birmingham, Alabama. Russian Federation officially becomes a member of G8 (Group of Eight economic council). **14–17 August:** Russian financial crisis. **September:** Aleksei Primakov becomes Russian prime minister, Igor Ivanov foreign minister.

1999   **23–24 April:** Fiftieth anniversary of NATO summit in Washington welcomes Poland, Hungary, and the Czech Republic into alliance; the main concern is the crisis in Kosovo, an Albanian-speaking province of the former Yugoslavia. **19–20 June:** Clinton and Yeltsin attend G8 summit in Cologne. **9 August:** Vladimir Putin becomes chairman of council of ministers (prime minister). **12 September:** Putin and Clinton meet in Auckland, New Zealand. **31 December:** Yeltsin resigns as president; Putin becomes acting president.

2000 **26 March:** Putin elected president. **3–5 June:** Clinton–Putin summit in Moscow. **21 July:** Putin and Clinton meet at G8 summit in Okinawa. **6 September:** UN summit in New York attended by Putin and Clinton. **30 October:** Successful joint Russian–American mission to international space station.

2001 **20 January:** George W. Bush inaugurated as president. **April:** United Russia Party founded in Moscow as a pro-Kremlin, pro-Putin political party. **16 June:** Bush and Putin meet for first time in Lubljana, Slovenia. **13–15 November:** President Bush hosts Putin at his ranch in Crawford, Texas. **15 December:** United States withdraws from ABM Treaty, signed in 1972.

2002 **11 March:** Mikhail Gorbachev delivers lecture at Harriman Institute at Columbia University. **28 April:** Death of Alexander Lebed in helicopter accident. **23–26 May:** Bush visit to Moscow and signing of Strategic Offensive Reductions Treaty (SORT). **14 June:** Russia announces withdrawal from START II negotiations in protest of American actions in Iraq and Kosovo.

2003 **26–27 September:** Putin visits New York, speaks at UN and at Columbia University on Russian–American relations, and is hosted by President Bush at Camp David; Putin opposes U.S. invasion of Iraq. **25 October:** Arrest of Mikhail Khodorkovsky, director of Yukos petroleum company and Menatap banking concern, charged with fraud and tax evasion.

2004 **14 March:** Putin reelected to presidency for a second term with 71 percent of the vote. **20 November:** Meeting of Putin and Bush in Santiago, Chile.

2005 **24 February:** Meeting of Putin and Bush in Bratislava, Slovakia. **8 May:** The leaders meet again in Moscow. **16 September:** Putin–Bush conversations in Washington on a number of current issues; financial and economic cooperation advanced.

2006 Mikhail Khodorkovsky, director of Yukos oil company, tried for tax evasion. **September:** French President Jacques Chirac awards Putin

Knight of the Legion of Honor. Putin chairs G8 meeting. **November:** Alexander Litvinenko, former FSB officer and critic of Putin, falls ill and dies under suspicious circumstances in London, leading to charges of a Putin-directed assassination.

2007 February: Conference on 200th anniversary of Russian–American relations at Russian State Humanities University in Moscow. **7 June:** Vladimir Putin publicly opposes the deployment of U.S. missile shield in Eastern Europe at G8 summit with George Bush. **1–2 July:** Bush hosts Putin at his summer home in Kennebunkport, Maine. **16 October:** Putin visits Tehran for Second Caspian Summit, first visit of a Russian leader to Iran since 1943. **30 September:** Garry Kasparov formally enters presidential election contest for 2008. **8–9 November:** Conference at the Russian Academy of Sciences on the bicentennial of Russian–American relations, featuring Henry Kissinger as keynote speaker. **10 December:** Putin officially backs First Deputy Prime Minister Dmitri Medvedev as his successor as president in March 2008 election. **December:** Putin named "person of the year" by *Time Magazine.*

2008 January: Human Rights Watch issues critical report on Putin's crackdown on civic freedoms and freedom of assembly. **March:** Dmitri Medvedev elected president of the Russian Federation by a large majority. **April:** Medvedev announces that he will appoint Putin as prime minister upon assuming the presidency in May. The two Russian and American outgoing presidents, Putin and Bush, meet at Sochi, a Russian Black Sea resort; major differences remain over the proposed missile shield deployment in Poland and Ukraine, the continuing war in Iraq, and the independence of Kosovo, all opposed by Putin and the Russian Federation. Putin is elected chairman of United Russia Party at its congress. **May:** Medvedev is inaugurated as president and Putin is ratified as prime minister (chairman of the council of ministers) by the Russian Duma. **August:** An attack by the Georgian Army on the enclave of South Ossetia results in a strong Russian military response and occupation of Georgian territory near the capital of Tbilisi. The U.S. and Western powers attempt to mediate, but also support Georgia and condemn the Russian overreaction. Though Russia responds with a withdrawal from most of the territory, media commentary suggests a renewed U.S. confrontation with Russia and a revival of the cold war. Ethnic tensions both in Russia and on its periphery remain a major problem.

Introduction

Russian–American relations dominated much of the world history of the 20th century, as the two great powers after World War II contested for supremacy during the cold war in a generally hostile and dangerous competition. Prior to 1945, they had relatively friendly contacts in culture, commerce, and diplomacy. With the apparent end of the cold war with the collapse of the Soviet Union and of Communism in 1991, the relationship modified, but renewed tensions, when Vladimir Putin, the president and then prime minister of the Russian Federation in the 21st century, revived some of the cold war rhetoric and atmosphere.

Though early connections between Russia and America were somewhat episodic and inconsequential in terms of the historical development of the two countries, they matured into an enduring and mutually advantageous relationship economically and in international relations. Obviously of diametrically opposed political orientations, the two countries were nonetheless friendly and cordial throughout the late 18th century and most of the 19th century, especially during the mid-century conflicts of the Crimean War and the American Civil War. It was only late in that century that rifts began to appear that concerned revolutionary movements, Russian anti-Semitism, and aggressive Russian actions in the Far East.

Outside of the immediate European context, however (France, Great Britain, Germany, and Russia), perhaps the most important relationship of two countries in modern history has been that between the United States and Russia in its various constructions: tsarist empire, revolutionary state, Stalinist state, Soviet Union world power, and the current Russian Federation under Vladimir Putin. While the United States has remained fairly consistent in its policies despite major advances in its geopolitical position, Russia has passed through a number of dramatic changes, providing major challenges to both, as well as to other nations.

EARLY RUSSIAN–AMERICAN RELATIONS

Relations between the two foremost American and Eurasian nations were shaped by world currents that often originated in Europe, chief among them being the creation of colonial empires and the Enlightenment and the commercial revolution of the last half of the 18th century. Both the British colonial provinces of North America and the Russian Empire were emerging as significant economic and political presences in that period. The Seven Years War, known as the French and Indian War in America, was a significant catalyst in establishing the first contacts. The war created a significant increase in the demand for naval and commercial fleets. The average number and size of vessels in both categories more than doubled during the course of the war. Russia was the major source of vital materials for shipbuilding: coarse linen sailcloth, iron for anchors, chains, and nails, and rope made from Russian hemp. These "naval stores" became important Russian exports that produced a very favorable balance of trade and provided the capital for impressive construction projects of summer palaces around St. Petersburg, Moscow, and elsewhere.

The American colonies in the 1760s were especially influenced by this development and the need for shipbuilding materials. Thus began the first commercial voyages directly between Atlantic ports, especially from Boston to St. Petersburg, in violation of the British Navigation Acts that required colonial ships destined for the European continent to stop at British ports and pay duties. The Boston ship *Wolfe*, owned by Nicholas Boyleston, was probably the first to make a round trip to Russia in 1763. Many more would follow, asserting the fact of the growing independence of American commerce from that of Britain. This would expand considerably after the interruption of the Revolutionary War to include a regular triangular route: New England–West Indies–Russia, importing colonial goods such as sugar and coffee in exchange for the "naval stores" that were brought back to America or sold to British merchants. This trade would reach a high point during the Napoleonic Wars, when as many as 200 American flagships per year would enter Russian Baltic ports, benefitting from their neutral status.

Meanwhile, during the war for American independence, Russia provided important support by promoting commercial contacts (smuggling) with the rebellious colonies from France and the West Indies.

Several prominent Russian subjects provided important auxiliary military support as volunteers; they included Thadeus Kosciuscko, Kasimir Pulaski, and John Rose (Rosenthal). Fedor Karzhavin acted as an important agent in delivering supplies and in establishing relations with the Continental Congress. Catherine the Great, in opposition to British naval practices, if not in direct support of the American Revolution, issued the Declaration of Armed Neutrality that clearly favored the American cause. The first official American mission, that of Francis Dana, followed in order to seek additional Russian support for the cause of independence. Though that effort proved abortive, the idea was planted, especially in the minds of John Adams and his son John Quincy Adams, who accompanied Dana on his trip to Russia.

Although direct diplomatic relations did not result from this initial contact, nor did they follow upon the success of American independence, commercial relations continued to grow as well as new political/philosophical communications. Leaders of the Russian Enlightenment, such as Alexander Radishchev and Nikolai Novikov, praised the American accomplishments in the 1780s, though the praise was muted by the Russian reaction to the French Revolution after 1789. Direct contacts, however, remained minimal but not nonexistent. John Ledyard traveled into Russia as far as Siberia, and a few early Russian immigrants, such as Dmitri Golitsyn, reached the American shores.

Two other developments in the last half of the 18th century would have major impacts upon the relationship between the two countries. The first was the Russian presence and explorations of the North Pacific as a result of the Russian conquest of Asian Siberia and the quest for fur resources. The voyages of Vitus Bering, promoted by Peter the Great, and a number of subsequent ventures into that area, resulted in the "Russian discovery of Alaska" and settlement in Northwest America by the 1790s, instigated especially by the Nootka Sound incident between British and Spanish squadrons under George Vancouver and Juan Francisco de la Bodega, respectively. Soon after the establishment of Russian presence in North America, an intersection occurred between Russian needs and the developing Russian–Chinese trade. American ships, "Bostonians," served as intermediaries in the Russian sale of Alaskan furs to China in exchange for tea that was shipped to Russia. A number of prominent American merchant families, for example, D'Wolfe and Heard, were involved in these transactions that extended well into the

19th century: Americans providing supplies to Russian Alaska and hauling furs to China. The Russian establishment in North America was formalized by the charter of the Russian America Company of 1799, granted by Emperor Paul.

Another, rather different and extended aspect of the 18th-century Enlightenment was the effort by Catherine the Great to encourage settlement in Russia by Germans, especially from areas devastated by the Seven Years War, and by Dutch-speaking Mennonites in vacant areas on the Volga and in southern Russia near the Black Sea. This practice would continue through the reign of Alexander I. Many seeking better opportunities and new homes would prefer the land route to Russia over the sea voyage to America. These Russian semiautonomous colonies would prosper under the privileges granted by the Russian government, and about 100 years later many of their descendants would emigrate to the Great Plains of the United States and Canada. The inspiration behind both of these migrations was in the physiocratic theories on the development of the land by state initiative: free land, tax abatement, freedom from conscription on the Russian side, and later in the United States, the Homestead Act and railroad land grants, both stimulating new and permanent settlement by foreign colonists. The Volga German, Black Sea German, and Mennonite contributions to the agricultural development of both the Russian steppe and the American plains would be enormous.

THE ESTABLISHMENT OF DIPLOMATIC RELATIONS

A community of interests, especially involving increased commerce, but also mutual antagonism toward Great Britain, fostered a closer relationship in the early 19th century. An American consulate in St. Petersburg, headed by John Levett Harris, existed by 1804, to be followed by a friendly exchange of communications between President Thomas Jefferson and Tsar Alexander I and more serious negotiations between Russian and American representatives in London and Paris resulted in an agreement in 1807 to establish regular diplomatic relations. John Quincy Adams left his temporary professorship at Harvard College to accept the appointment as minister to Russia. He and his extended family reached St. Petersburg after a difficult voyage in October 1809.

Meanwhile, a Russian presence in the United States had begun under Andrei Dashkov as consul-general and representative to the U.S. Congress in 1808, settling in Philadelphia. Though briefly "displaced" by Fedor Pahlen, the first official Russian minister, Dashkov continued to solidify the Russian base in the United States along with the erudite Aleksei Evstafev as consul in Boston. Evstafev would remain there until the 1850s.

Both Dashkov and Adams succeeded in establishing firm foundations for future official relationships. While Adams met Alexander I on the streets of St. Petersburg for informal talks, Dashkov called on President Jefferson at Monticello. Both were assisted—and perhaps constricted—by the presence of compatriots. In some ways, Dashkov was overshadowed by an ambitious writer-artist, Pavel Svinin, as secretary, and Adams by a host of American traders and adventurers. While Svinin traveled widely and depicted in art and words the American scene for a Russian audience, Adams was beset by a number of ambitious and opportunist Americans, such as Edward Wyer, Levett Harris, and John Delaware Lewis. The latter would bring his brother from Philadelphia, William David Lewis, who was sort of an "American Svinin," traveling through the country, becoming fluent in Russian, writing the Russian scene, and translating Russian poetry into American English.

Relations between the two countries were not always so cordial or successful in this period. Episodes disturbed the general harmony, such as the Kozlov affair in Philadelphia (alleged rape of a young woman) and the Harris-Lewis commercial feud in St. Petersburg. Svinin's effort to recruit Robert Fulton to develop Russian steamboat navigation failed, as did the projected sale of the *Savannah* to Russia in 1818. A series of mediocre ministerial appointments on both sides, with the exceptions of Henry Middleton (1820–30) from South Carolina and Alexander Bodisko, was a handicap in developing a firm foundation during the first half of the 19th century. At least James Buchanan finally put an official stamp on commerce by signing the Russian–American Treaty of Commerce in St. Petersburg in 1833.

On another front, American contacts with Russian settlements in Northwest America increased, as an extension of the booming "China trade." Among the first of a considerable number of "Bostonians" to visit that area was John D'Wolfe, of Bristol, Rhode Island, who reached the new Russian–American "capital" at Sitka in 1807 to sell his ship to the Russian company and have a wild adventure back to America. Others followed to provide a valuable shipping service for Alaskan fur to China. At the same time, the Russian America Company moved farther down the Pacific coast to establish an outpost at "Fort Ross [Rossia]" in northern California in 1815 and also to face a Russian outreach into the Hawaiian Islands. These ventures were bringing Russian–American relations into a new focus.

OUR MANIFEST DESTINIES

With both Atlantic and Pacific connections established, Russians and Americans began to think of the wider dimensions of the relationship. The result was a number of articles in the press of both countries on the other and the broader sense of common interest. Comparisons were naturally in order. In the United States, the leading newspaper, *National Intelligencer*, and a leading New England literary journal, *The North American Review*, focused much attention in Russia; similarly, Russian periodicals such as *Dvukh Zhurnalov* [Soul of Journals] and *Syn Otechestvennaia* [Son the Fatherland] carried a surprising amount of information about the United States. Authors such as Pavel Svinin and William Darby stressed what they saw as a community of interests based upon geography, settlement patterns, and cultural progress in the 1820s and 1830s. Soon the growing number of Americans and Russians in residence in the other country would be speaking of "our manifest destinies"—Russia going eastward to found a Eurasian empire and the United States moving westward to expand the original colonies into a continental domain. A common thread—or threat—that both sides perceived was Great Britain and its imperial aspirations. A mutual Anglophobia thus united the United States and Russia, perhaps somewhat superficially, through most of the 19th century.

A simultaneous mutual interest developed in literature. While Alexander Pushkin, Mikhail Lermontov, and Nikolai Gogol became popular in the United States, Russia witnessed a "craze" for the works of James Fenimore Cooper that would persist through the 20th century, as well as for Washington Irving and Edgar Allan Poe. Cooper especially seemed to strike a chord for both Russian and American frontier developments that would include the "white man's burden" of "civilizing" native peoples. Along with this interrelationship, both in literature and political-social discussion, was a common pursuit of abolition, the freeing from inhumane treatment of African Americans and of Russian serf peasants. Harriet Beecher Stowe's *Uncle Tom's Cabin* would be one of most popular books in Russia.

Aiding this mutuality of development and progress was the Russian tendency to look to the United States for its first major railroad advance, the route from St. Petersburg to Moscow launched in the 1840s with George Washington Whistler from Connecticut as chief surveyor and supervisor and the Winans company of Baltimore as the manufacturer of locomotives and cars for the railroad. Meanwhile, commerce shifted from mainly Russian exports of "naval stores" to the predominant import of colonial products and especially cotton from American southern ports. Firms, such as that of William H. Ropes in St. Petersburg, flourished in the superintending of this trade. By this time, the 1840s, a substantial American colony had been established in St. Petersburg with a church, the legation, and mercantile houses as its nucleus. Another advance in the relationship occurred on the Pacific coast, where Americans and Russians were also developing mutually favorable connections, especially after the 1849 discovery of gold in California, by now part of the United States. The need for supplies such as ice promoted new and closer contacts with the Russian America Company.

Not surprisingly, the United States would be a defender and advocate of Russia in the Crimean War (1853–55). A number of American surgeons would volunteer for service with the Russian army, Colt revolvers would be smuggled into Russia, and an American military observer team would sympathetically cover the war scene. American enterprise would generally benefit from the increased Russian hostility toward Britain and France. This political and economic cooperation would carry over into the American Civil War. Long-term Russian minister Alexander Bodisko was instrumental in enhancing the relationship as dean of the diplomat colony and as a major social presence in Washington at his Georgetown estate.

LINCOLN AND THE RUSSIANS

The American Civil War, fought both to preserve the Union and to abolish slavery, attracted much Russian attention, at least partly because of the move of the reform-minded Alexander II to emancipate the serfs in Russia, but perhaps mainly because it served Russian interests vis-à-vis Britain and France to have the United States preserved as a significant power, neither divided nor reduced to a weak status. American support for Russia during the Crimean War contributed to Russian support. Russian diplomacy and military presence in the form of supportive naval squadrons in New York and San Francisco supported this effort and that of restraining a more active British and French support of the Confederacy. Lincoln himself had reservations about an alignment with the Russian empire and its continued oppression of the peasantry and ethnic peoples. Two Russian naval squadrons to New York and San Francisco demonstrated the empire's support for the Union, an important boost in the wake of the Battle of Gettysburg. A few Russians, such as Ivan Turchininov (John Turchin), served with distinction in command positions in the Union army.

In recognition of Russian support, the United States sent a mission, headed by Gustavus Fox, assistant secretary of the navy, to Russia in 1866. This event received much publicity owing to the lavish reception in St. Petersburg as well as the voyage to St. Petersburg on a Union monitor warship, the *Miantonomoh*. The Western Union launch of the construction of a telegraph line from North America through Siberia also attracted much attention, especially with George Kennan's publication of his experiences. Siberia had definitely become a new frontier for many Americans, especially demonstrated by the journey of Perry McDonough Collins through the region and down the Amur River to the Pacific. And a Union army ordinance officer, Hiram Berdan, sold his breech-loading rifle design to the Russian army; it would be the army's main infantry weapon through World War I. Finally, a son of Alexander II, Grand Duke Alexis, would tour the United States with much fanfare in 1871–72.

Perhaps the greatest impact of the Civil War on Russian–American relations was the purchase/sale of Alaska, the transfer of a large area of Northwest America from Russia to the United States in 1867. Although the idea of the sale arose before the Civil War, especially because of Russian America's vulnerability during the Crimean War, the possibility of an exchange was delayed by the war and was really not feasible until after the Union victory and at a point that Russia was ready to sell. Largely engineered by Secretary of State William H. Seward at the cost of $7,200,000, the purchase was widely opposed and caricatured as "Seward's folly" or "Seward's icebox." Nevertheless, the income to the U.S. Treasury from only the harvesting of fur seals on the Pribyloff Islands more than reimbursed the purchase price during the first 20 years, while administrative costs were practically nonexistent. Moreover, the United States gained a sizeable population of Native Americans, most of whom had been converted to Russian Orthodox Christianity. Most of the relatively small number of Russians in Alaska returned home, though some chose to settle in San Francisco.

Another related aspect of a closer Russian–American involvement after the American Civil War was the considerable emigration from the Russian Empire to the United States. Among the first immigrants were Jews escaping poverty, Russian anti-Semitism, and violent pogroms, who found new residences initially in eastern cities, especially on the Lower East Side of New York; Volga Germans, Mennonites, and Black Sea Germans, who settled as agriculturalists in the Great Plains region; and Poles, Ukrainians, Lithuanians, Armenians, and others from the Russian Empire, who became an important part of the labor force in the new American industrial cities. Though often considered as "Rooshians," none were of Russian ethnicity nor Russian Orthodox in religion. This large East European immigration to America (including Canada) would constitute an immense contribution to its social, economic, and cultural advance and diversity well into the 20th century. The United States also provided exile for Russian radical socialists, such as William Frey, Nikolai Chaikovsky, Grigory Machtet, and many others, in the 1870s, while George Kennan described the horrible conditions of those less fortunate who were condemned to Siberian prisons in *Siberia and the Exile System* (1887).

On the cultural level, there was a fascination in America for considerable Russian literary, musical, and artistic productions. Beginning with Pushkin and Gogol, the interest increased with a fascination with the works of Ivan Turgenev and Fedor Dostoyevsky, but above all with Leo Tolstoy, whose classic works created a virtual "Tolstoy craze" in the 1870s and 1880s. On the music front, Modest Mussorgsky and Peter Tchaikovsky were celebrated, especially with the latter's personal appearance to direct his works at the opening of Carnegie Hall in 1891. Major expositions of Russian arts and crafts at the Chicago World's Fair (Columbia Exposition) in 1893 and personal engagements contributed to an increased American appreciation of Russian culture. A highlight of the fair was a Russian choral ensemble performing Slavic folk songs. By that time the artistic works of Russian artists such as Vasily Vereshchagin had received American interest and patronage.

THE UNITED STATES AND THE RUSSIAN INDUSTRIAL REVOLUTION

Among the reasons for the surprisingly large Russian presence in Chicago in 1893 were the new policies of Minister of Finance Sergei Witte to promote industry in Russia. The policies were designed to bring Russia out of its relative backwardness into the modern era largely through increased loans from abroad, borrowing of technological expertise, and government promotion. About 40 special delegates were sent to investigate the exhibits and especially to survey American developments in rail and river transportation, agriculture, grain storage and handling, fuel extraction, and industrial enterprises in general. They also studied foreign exhibits at the fair. The result was a government and social trait of *amerikanism*, looking to the United States for new technology and models of development, a continuation of the developments of the 1840s in regard to the construction of the St. Petersburg–Moscow railroad.

Railroads would again be a keystone of Russian development, but this time to serve industrial and agricultural expansion, as well as to develop new markets, especially in the Far East. The major pump primer for economic growth was the launch of the Trans-Siberian Railroad, and a number of American industries would become involved in this enterprise. Among the first was a partnership of Westinghouse and Crane Plumbing that secured a contract to construct a plant near St. Petersburg to manufacture air brakes for the new railroad. Charles Crane, who had already traveled widely through the Russian Empire, was a catalyst for this project and supervised the construction of the factory. Even more significant was the penetration of the Russian economy by major American companies such as Singer Sewing Machines and International Harvester (agricultural implements), which built substantial factories in suburbs of Moscow. By 1914 each had labor, sales, and repair employees that numbered more than 30,000, the largest private companies in the Russian Empire. The Singer office building on Nevsky Prospect in St. Petersburg became—and still is—a landmark of the city.

Unfortunately, much of this expansion came at considerable cost to Russia. While major—and smaller—American and other foreign companies made handsome profits, the Russian peasantry continued to sink deeper into poverty. Russian fiscal practice reduced the price of grain in order that Russian exports could compete with American agricultural products in the world market. Russian transport and storage facilities added to the circumstances of a major famine in 1892. Relief shipments from Midwestern states and the American Red Cross rescued much of the rural population from certain death. Meanwhile, American financial and insurance institutions, such as New York Life Insurance, Equitable Assurance Society, and New York City Bank, controlled a considerable portion of Russia's private capital market. At the same time, the Russian government borrowed immense amounts from foreign banks, chiefly in France, some of which was earmarked for military modernization, a continuing drain on capital for economic development and social improvements.

By the turn of the century, American opinion was turning more critical toward Russia, especially because of Russian anti-Semitic policies, in addition to its treatment of political liberals as well as radicals. The term *pogrom* became familiar in the American press, owing to the increased frequency and violence of these murderous incursions into Jewish sections of cities, culminating in wide publicity given to one in Kishinev (1903). The "passport question," Russian consular officials denying visas to those who admitted to being Jewish in religion, also aggravated American disposition toward separation of religion and state. At the same time, there was a movement in the United States to understand Russia better through the inauguration of Russian language, history, and literature courses at universities. Archibald Cary Coolidge started the first course in Russian history at Harvard University. Charles R. Crane, who had supervised the early operations of the Westinghouse air brake factory in Russia, commissioned the first scholarly history of Russia in English, as well as the works of several other Americans interested in Russian studies. In 1900 he brought to Russia William Rainey Harper and other prominent citizens of his native Chicago to visit with Tolstoy, Witte, Nicholas II, and Paul Miliukov. The latter, along with other Russian academics—Sergei Volkonsky and sociologist

Maxim Kovalevsky—would soon be lecturing at the University of Chicago and other American universities.

THE UNITED STATES AND THE RUSSIAN REVOLUTION

It should be emphasized at this point that climaxes of the Russian revolutionary movements in the events of 1905 and 1917 coincided with the emergence of the United States as a significant world power. Thanks to Miliukov, Volkonsky, Coolidge, Crane, Kennan, and others, Americans began to perceive Russia as inevitably headed toward major political and social changes in the early 20th century. The American physical presence in Russia committed to practical, capitalistic, and liberal beliefs played a part, symbolized by the influential social positions of Walter Dixon (Singer), Frederick Corse (New York Life), Henry Hiller (Tiffany), William S. Smith (Westinghouse), and a number of first-rate ambassadors: Andrew Dickson White, George von Lengerke Meyer, and Curtis Guild. The Trans-Siberian Railroad provided additional access to the "new Russia" and was used by William Howard Taft on the campaign trail in 1908.

At the outset of the Russo-Japanese War (February 1904), American opinion was strongly in favor of Japan. This is explained not only by the general antipathy toward Russian practices in regard to political prisoners and Jews, but also by American concern about Russian aggression in the Far East in contradiction to the "open door" doctrine of Secretary of State John Hay, and by Japan's being considered the "underdog." American banks, especially that of Jacob Schiff, provided low-interest loans to Japan. As the war progressed, however, and especially after the Bloody Sunday incident of January 1905 that signaled the beginning of a truly revolutionary crisis, American opinion shifted dramatically in favor of Russia. Both the sense of Russia finally headed toward an American model of development and also the fear of a changing balance of force in the Far East that would be exacerbated by the Japanese naval victory at Tsushima (May 1905) were catalysts. Another American concern was that the Russian Revolution was headed left toward a more radical conclusion, especially from the mutiny in June on the Battleship *Potemkin*.

The result was an American effort, orchestrated by President Theodore Roosevelt, to arbitrate and end the conflict with minimal loss to Russia. Thanks to his intervention, Russian and Japanese delegations, the former headed by Witte, met on the neutral ground of the Portsmouth Naval Shipyards in Kittery, Maine, to negotiate the end of the war in the Treaty of Portsmouth (September 1905). Russia gave up the lease on Port Arthur and half of Sakhalin Island but was saved from an embarrassing and costly indemnity by American arbitration. What was clear from the course of the revolution, however, was that Russia had both liberal and radical alternatives for a new political direction. For the time being, the liberal ideal held the edge in the new concession of Nicolas II for an elected Duma. Though the restrictions confirmed a conservative majority, the Duma included a "Progressive bloc" of liberals and radicals, who heralded a new nonautocratic Russia.

In the process of shifting revolutionary aspirations, the radical movements in Russia were divided between two parties. The Socialist Revolutionaries supported a peasant socialist basis for Russia and sometimes used violent terrorist tactics; most notable among their leaders were Alexander Kerensky, Victor Chernov, Ekaterina Breshko-Breshkovskaya, and Nikolai Chaikovsky. The other major radical party, the Social Democrats, was inspired by Marxist ideology but had split into two factions, Menshevik and Bolshevik, at their second congress (1903). A leader of the latter wing, Vladimir Lenin, argued that the inevitable proletarian revolution had been delayed by imperialism (exploitation of colonial populations) but would have unique opportunities during war (as in the Russo-Japanese War), and that Russia would have a unique opportunity to lead the way to revolution because of the weakness of its imperial/capitalist existence, though it would be dependent on peasant support to supplement the small proletarian base.

Russia was swept into World War I because of Witte's dependence on French loans for industry that were tied to a political and military alliance and a German offensive strategy that would concentrate initially on France (Schlieffen Plan). The result was stagnation on both Eastern and Western fronts that left Russia vulnerable to a war of attrition. The resulting conditions, including breakdown of transportation and resulting shortages and dissatisfaction with leadership, would precipitate a political crisis in February 1917 that led to the abdication of Nicholas II and the ascendancy of the liberal democratic Provisional Government. It was challenged at the beginning, however, by the more radical Soviet of Workers' and Soldiers' Deputies and a slogan of a returned revolutionary exile, Lenin, "All Power to the Soviets." Aided especially by Leon Trotsky, who returned from New York exile in May, Lenin's Bolshevik party rose to predominance in staging the October Revolution.

Meanwhile, the United States entered the war in April, partly inspired by the removal of the autocratic Russian regime, "to make the world safe for democracy," including especially Russia. America provided considerable support to the new Russia through loans, shipments of supplies, the American Red Cross, the Young Men's Christian Association, and other agencies, but was handicapped by the Allied concentration on winning the war on the western front. As conditions continued to worsen in Russia, the Bolsheviks took advantage of the situation to urge an end to a disastrous war for Russia, achieved in the Treaty of Brest-Litovsk in March 1918. This left the decision to the Allies of what to do about a disappearance of the vital eastern front and the threat of more radical revolutionary activity elsewhere. Finally, intervention forces were sent with significant American involvement in North Russia and Siberia to protect supplies and restore a commitment to a non-Bolshevik Russia. This cause was frustrated by the absence of creditable leadership by Alexander Kerensky, Alexander Kolchak, or Anton Denikin during the resulting civil war, the end of the war in the West, and the peace conference, which left Russia totally out of the picture.

SOVIET RUSSIA BECKONS AMERICA

Even before the dust had settled on war, revolution, and civil war, the American attitude toward a really new Russia coalesced into opposing views. Some, such as John Reed, Raymond Robins, Albert Rhys Williams, and many others connected with the socialist Industrial Workers of the World, envisaged the advent of the Bolshevik Communist-socialist state as the herald of a new socialist world that promised a much kinder, fairer future for mankind. Many others, however, considered their appearance as leaders of a major world power as a threat to civilization and institutions. This line would be followed by the American government, under Bainbridge Colby and Charles Evans Hughes, to forge a policy of nonrecognition and to pursue deportations of a large number of Americans as suspected threats (Palmer raids) in 1919–20, one of the blackest marks in American history. The Bolshevik suppression and persecution of religious freedom was an important factor in American hostility toward the new regime, reinforced by the Soviet nationalization of American and other foreign enterprises and the refusal to pay debts (the wartime loans).

Another factor was the Soviet resentment of American presence and military intervention in Russian territory during the civil war. Supporting the resulting formal nonrecognition by the United States was the East European division of the State Department under the leadership of Robert F. Kelley and his assistants at the Riga (Latvia) "listening post," who included George F. Kennan. In the interim, the Russian Information Bureau in Washington, under the direction of Boris Skvirsky, provided the services of an embassy in terms of visas and other contacts, while the American Trading Corporation (Amtorg) in New York handled Soviet business affairs in the United States.

During the 1920s there was genuine interest in "the new experiment" in Russia and about an American opportunity to participate and even influence that development, especially since Soviet Russia, initially weak, provided no specific or immediate threat to American imperial interests. What was still surprising, however, was the compatibility of cultural developments. In the 1920s era of the new economic policy, Soviet developments in arts, literature, music, and so on were relatively free. American influence was especially pronounced owing to its leadership of the Jazz Age. And Russia was quite receptive to this current, as manifested by the popularity of American performers in Russia such as Benny Peyton and his orchestra and many other African American performers during the 1920s and by the adaptation of it by the new Soviet cultural elite: Valentin Parnakh, Vseslod Meyerhold, and Dmitri Shostakovich. This mutual cultural appreciation was also advanced by the Soviet Society for Relations with Foreign Countries, under Olga Kameñev. It sponsored the visits of Theodore Dreiser, Sinclair Lewis, John Dewey, and many other prominent Americans.

On the other side, the United States hosted a large number of émigré and Soviet artists, professors, and talents. Some were already here and forced to stay by the revolution; foremost among them were Igor Stravinsky, Sergei Diaghelev, and a host of Russians who chose to emigrate: historians Michael Florinsky, George Vernadsky, Michael Karpovich, and Boris Bakhmeteff, who established an archive at Columbia University dedicated to preserving the record of the old Russia. Others, such as Paul Miliukov and Alexander Kerensky, would locate mainly in Western Europe (hoping for a return) but would visit the United States on speaking tours. Nikita Baliev would take Broadway by storm with his "Russian vaudeville" in 1922, while a number who remained committed to the Soviet cause would come for celebrated visits: Konstantin Stanislavsky, Vladimir Mayakovsky, and satirists Ilya Ilf and Yevgeny Petrov. There seemed to be a revival of a Russian–American cultural community of interests in the 1920s, despite nonrecognition and official American condemnation of the Soviet regime.

STALIN'S AMERICAN ENGINEERS

Even before the dramatic initiation of the First Five-Year Plan by Joseph Stalin in 1928, Soviet Russia looked to the United States for technical leadership. First among these large industrial projects was the building of the Dnepropetrovsk dam in Ukraine to provide electrical power to the Donetsk industrial basin. American hydroelectric engineer Hugh Cooper was contracted to design and supervise the dam's construction in 1926 and remained on the scene until its completion in 1931.

During the First Five-Year Plan, American assistance was essential in construction as part of the long-standing *amerikanizm* tendency of the Russian government, that is, looking to American business organization and superior technology as the model for Russian economic advances, in this case negotiated by Amtorg. Almost all major projects of the plan were advanced by American contributions: a large steel complex in the Urals (Magnitogorsk) designed and supervised by McKee and Company of Cleveland, tractor factories in Kharkov and Stalingrad (International Harvester), the State Automobile Works (GAZ) near Nizhny Novgorod (Austin Company and Ford), a heavy tractor plant in Cheliabinsk (Caterpillar), an auto factory in Leningrad (Ford), and electrical plants in Moscow and elsewhere (General Electric). Several of these involved training Soviet workers in American plants and putting American experts on the scene in Russia. In addition, many individuals, seeking lucrative—or any—employment during the Depression, signed on to work on various projects in the USSR in the 1930s.

One result of this greatly increased pace and economic significance of the Soviet–American relationship was a move to end nonrecognition through negotiations in Washington between Commissar of Foreign Relations Maxim Litvinov and President Franklin D. Roosevelt in October–November 1933. The United States wanted more guarantees of freedom, especially for religion, in Russia and increased trade and cooperation in the Far East vis-à-vis Japanese expansion, while the Soviet Union negotiated for debt forgiveness (from World War I) and favorable loans for future development. The urge toward accommodation prevailed, with details on the major issues to be worked out later, though little progress would be made. The first American envoy, William Bullitt, settled into quarters at Spaso House in 1934 (still the official ambassadorial residence in Moscow), while the first Soviet ambassador repossessed the old Russian embassy on 16th Street in Washington. Though the respective missions encountered obstacles in pursuit of their goals, especially in trust, in access to information, and in solving unsettled issues of debts and loans, a stable foundation was established, especially in the Soviet Union during the tenure of Ambassador Joseph Davies and military attaché Philip Faymonville and in the growing expertise in regard to the country, especially from the American perspective.

THE SOVIET–AMERICAN GRAND ALLIANCE

An important aspect that surmounted many problems between the two countries in the 1930s was mutual concern about the threatening policies and actions of Japan and Germany. Litvinov's policy of collective security had created a partial alliance against fascism but ultimately failed because of Western appeasement of Germany (the Munich Agreement of 1938). This led to a Soviet turn toward accommodation with that country in the Nazi–Soviet Pact (1939) and the subsequent beginning of World War II with their joint invasion and division of Poland, opposed militarily by France and Great Britain. The following surprising quick defeat of France left Stalin's Russia isolated and vulnerable, while Britain—with American support—held out through the Battle of Britain during the winter of 1939–40. Meanwhile, American policy under Roosevelt veered toward intervention and the supply of vital assistance under the program of lend-lease, initially to support British defense against German attacks.

Though most Americans were dismayed by Soviet military actions during the "peaceful" interval (1939–41) in Poland, the Baltic states, and especially Finland, the United States was quick to offer assistance after the "surprise" German invasion of the Soviet Union in June 1941 by an immediate extension of lend-lease to the Union of Soviet Socialist Republics. Most immediate and crucial were the shipments of aircraft and aviation fuel into Russian northern ports in the late summer of 1941 that would be of importance in the Battle of Moscow (November–December). This would be followed by much more after American entry into the war after the Japanese attack on Pearl Harbor. The main routes of supply, besides the Arctic one, were through the Persian Gulf and Iran into the Volga region, especially for the supply of American Studebaker trucks, over the North Pacific to Vladivostok by safe and unhindered "liberty" ships under the Soviet flag, and by air from Alaska. The latter two routes were possible and vital because the USSR remained neutral in the war with Japan, and the ships delivering supplies could fly the Soviet flag, thus allowing a considerable amount of war material to enter freely for use against Germany at Stalingrad, Kursk, and on the eastern front in general in 1942–45.

During the World War II Grand Alliance, the Allies met in conferences at Tehran (1943), Yalta (1945), and Potsdam (1945) to coordinate policies and goals. These meetings of the "big three" (Roosevelt, Churchill, and Stalin—the first replaced by Truman at Potsdam) were undermined and overshadowed by major Soviet military successes in the drive on Berlin, the delayed Allied "second front," and subsequent Soviet efforts to control the future of most of Eastern Europe, as well as by concessions of the Western Allies in order to achieve cooperation in the creation of a United Nations and Soviet participation in the ongoing war against Japan. The dropping of atomic bombs on Hiroshima and Nagasaki brought a quick end to the latter but left a residue of resentment and quandary about the future dimensions of power on the Soviet side, especially in regard to jurisdiction over the pacification and stabilization of a ruined Europe and on the Asian mainland, both left unsolved by the informal peace arrangements in both arenas. The triumph over the tyranny of Germany and Japan and their makeshift empires produced a bipolar world of the United States and its weak allies and the Soviet Union and its subservient client (satellite) states in Eastern Europe.

THE COLD WAR

With so much unsettled in regard to postwar arrangements after V-E day and the American dedication to the Pacific area and to the creation of a United Nations, new conflicts were inevitably to arise, especially on the war-torn European continent, where Communist influence was paramount in taking advantage of the disillusionment with the prewar political hegemony, especially in France, Italy, and Greece. Though the beginnings of the cold war that dominated most of the last half of the 20th century can be traced to long-term ideological differences and the results of World War II, perhaps the gun that signaled the actual start of the cold war was fired from Moscow by senior foreign service officer George F. Kennan in his "long telegram" of 22 February 1946 that sent a shot over the bow of the Soviet cruiser perceived to be sailing unchecked through Europe. It was echoed by Winston Churchill's speech later that year at Fulton, Missouri, in which he described "an iron curtain" descending upon Europe.

The results were a militant Western response, led by the United States in the form of the Truman Doctrine (major and immediate assistance to Greece and Turkey) in 1947 and the Marshall Plan (1948) to rehabilitate Western Europe with massive American economic aid, including the Western occupation zones of Germany, to withstand Communist propaganda and the threat of Soviet military threats. The first face-off was the Soviet embargo of West Berlin in June 1948, countered by a dramatic and successful airlift that continued until the lifting of the blockade the following May. This was an important power and psychological victory for the West that had additional repercussions in forging a unity of the West in the creation of the North Atlantic Treaty Organization. Little understood at the time was that the appearance of Soviet aggression was a cover for significant weakness at home. Nevertheless, Soviet atomic weapons testing and apparent massive ground forces added to the fear of a conquest of Europe. This sense of vulnerability to Communist perfidy created a regrettable hysteria in the United States that culminated in the McCarthy era witch hunt, seeking Communist infiltration in government agencies, in Hollywood, in universities, and elsewhere.

The threat was real, especially in Asia, where Communist parties rose to power in the wake of the decline of corrupt nationalist and colonial political forces and added to the vulnerability of traditional Western interests, especially in China, North Korea, and French Indochina. An arbitrary dividing line of the 38th parallel between Soviet and American zones and apparent American withdrawal of interest in the area produced the Korean War, the one real hot spot of the cold war, in which many Americans but very few Russians would die, though their North Korean and Chinese clients definitely would. The war significantly ended with the Stalin era and would be followed by an easing of tensions during the "peaceful coexistence" initiative of Nikita Khrushchev. Though certainly not without its cold war reversions, including the U-2 incident (1960) and the Cuban missile crisis (1962), the new approach brought better understanding and more dialogue, such as the Camp David meeting (1958) and the "kitchen debate" (1959), and formal agreements on scholarly student and cultural exchanges. Though tensions remained, the "curtain" was fading.

The accession of Leonid Brezhnev brought a more sophisticated form of the Khrushchev policy in the form of "détente" and expanded relations, including more frequent summit meetings of leaders, increased exchanges, and the beginning of negotiations on the limiting and even reduction of missile-delivered offensive nuclear weapons. These advances, however, were dampened by concerns over Soviet violations of the civil rights of its citizens, including permission to leave, and enforcement of its controls over Eastern Europe through the suppression of the Polish "spring" and the invasion of Czechoslovakia in 1968. Still, the Soviet Union became more susceptible to world opinion, less effective in controlling pliant Eastern Europe, and more dependent on the United States for essential food imports. It also succumbed to a widely unsanctioned and unpopular invasion of Afghanistan in late 1979 that resulted in military disaster and repercussions such as the Western boycott of the 1980 Moscow Olympic games. The geriatric leadership was ill equipped to deal with the new world situation, especially in the Middle East—as would also be the case eventually of the United States.

The reform movement in Russia gathered steam in the 1980s under the successors of Brezhnev, especially during the tenure of Mikhail Gorbachev as "Communist leader," during which détente morphed into a "common cause" of East and West in reducing the dangers of a nuclear catastrophe and in a mutual support for democratic processes, illustrated by the creation of free elections, representative assemblies, and the liberation of eloquent (now free) spokesmen such as Andrei Sakharov. An important advisor to this "new course" for Russia was Alexander Yakovlev, a veteran of the student exchange in the United States of the 1960s who pioneered the Russian democratic direction, but he was far from being alone. By 1991 the cold war was over, and so was the Soviet Union and Communism in a dramatic, virtually bloodless revolution, signaled especially by the failure of the August coup of that year to reverse the direction toward dissolution.

RUSSIAN–AMERICAN RELATIONS IN THE POST-SOVIET ERA

The collapse of the Soviet Union hardly had time to be celebrated before the consequences emerged as new problems. Instead of one central government, the United States now had 15 newly independent entities to deal with, many weak, divided, and uncertain. All needed outside support and guidance, including the major residual nation in the form of the Russian Federation under the new and rather unpredictable leadership of Boris Yeltsin. Under Bill Clinton and his Russian advisor, Strobe Talbot, the United States provided substantial, but often confused and misguided, economic and psychological support during the economic and political chaos that resulted from uncertain efforts at the transition from a socialist to a market economy in Russia. The other new nations often presented even greater challenges in their efforts to define their identity and fully separate from their Soviet past. To aggravate the situation, new international problems such as drug traffic, AIDS, and subjection to world economic and civil rights influences entered the scene. The former Soviet Union was not yet safe for democracy.

The instability of the Yeltsin era of the 1990s gave way to his self-appointed and more self-confident successor, Vladimir Putin, who would continue to cultivate a more sophisticated, distant, and critical relationship with the United States. Major issues remain: the Russian valid criticism of American policy and armed intervention in the Middle East, and American concerns about disregard of civil rights in Russia and pressures of former constituent parts of the Soviet empire such as Ukraine. Putin, however is supported by successes in stabilizing the economy and in moving the country forward, selectively but rather dramatically with major construction projects, primarily based on state income and control of oil and natural gas resources—and on dependence on the "new rich." Cordial meetings between Putin and President George W. Bush and many other "conversations" and political and academic conferences inspire the possibility of a new and more equal and stable relationship in the 21st century under Putin and his appointed successor, obviously to remain active on the Russian political scene for some time to come. Questions still remain regarding how the presidency of Dmitri Medvedev, beginning in May, will differ from the Putin administration that preceded it. The future of Russian–American relations relies, as in the past, on leadership, study, contacts, and understanding.

As in the past, the relationship between America and Russia is also shaped by events and geopolitical circumstances and can be disrupted by such matters as interruptions in energy supplies, ethnic disputes, periphery concerns, and political posturing. One important sign of progress in recent years has been an informal "council" of ambassadors, consisting of five former Russian heads of mission to the U.S. and an equal number of previous American ambassadors to Russia, who meet and communicate with each other and provide a moderation to possible rash reactions of either power toward the other.

The Dictionary

– A –

ABBE, CLEVELAND (1838–1916). As an American astronomer and meteorologist, Abbe received important training as one of the first American "exchange students" to Russia in the 1860s. He studied at the Pulkovo Observatory near St. Petersburg under the supervision of August Wagner and **Otto Struve**, both renowned Russian and world astronomers. Returning to the United States, Abbe was director of the Cincinnati Observatory and the first daily weather forecaster in the country. He maintained contact with his Russian colleagues and provided hospitality during their visits to the United States. Abbe concluded his career in the early 20th century as the director of the U.S. Weather Bureau in Washington, D.C.

ABEL, RUDOLPH (NE WILLIAM FISHER) (1903–1971). Born in Newcastle, England, of a Russian-Jewish immigrant family, Abel returned to Russia in 1920 with his parents and became a Soviet citizen. After service in the Red Army, Abel entered the foreign department of OGPU (Soviet Secret Police) in 1927. Fluent in English, he worked for its successor, the **People's Commissariat of Internal Affairs (NKVD)**, in Canada and the United States during **World War II**. Reassigned to the United States in 1948, Abel was a major secret agent in the transfer of documents regarding atomic research until his arrest by the Federal Bureau of Investigation (FBI) in 1956. Although tried and convicted of espionage and receiving a sentence of 32 years, he was formally released to the Soviet Union in February 1962 in exchange for **U-2** pilot Gary Powers. Celebrated as a Soviet hero of the **cold war**, Abel concluded his Soviet service as a consultant to the **Committee on State Security (KGB)**.

ACADEMY OF SCIENCES. Founded in 1724 by Peter the Great on French and British models as the supreme citadel of learning in the country, the academy, at first composed mainly of foreign scholars, continued to carry on major research in ethnography, history, philosophy, and natural and physical sciences through nearly three centuries. It developed the first cultural and scientific contacts with American scholars, mainly through the American Philosophical Society in Philadelphia during the last half of the 18th century, and continuing with regular exchanges of publications with the **Smithsonian Institution** in the 19th century. It expanded considerably during the 20th century, as Soviet leaders placed high priority on research. The academy members were typically devoted to research, while "professors" at universities were focused on teaching. During the cultural exchanges between the United States and the Union of Soviet Socialist Republics (USSR) beginning in the 1950s, the academy hosted many American and other scholars and many seminars and colloquia devoted to common concerns that contributed considerably to lessening the tensions caused by the **cold war**. An example is one hosted by its **Institute of General History** held in November 2007 on the 200th anniversary of the beginnings of diplomatic relations between the two countries.

ACHESON, DEAN GOODERHAM (1893–1971). A graduate of Yale University (1915) from the "Eastern liberal establishment," Acheson served as private secretary to Justice Louis Brandeis before entering private law practice in the 1920s. A long career in public service began with his appointment as undersecretary of the treasury in the first administration of **Franklin D. Roosevelt**, though he soon resigned over disagreement with the president's economic policies. He returned to Washington at the beginning of **World War II** as assistant secretary of state and then undersecretary before assuming the highest post in the State Department from President **Harry S. Truman**. Acheson was instrumental in the foundation of the **North Atlantic Treaty Organization (NATO)** and in the diplomacy that resulted in the inauguration of the **Marshall Plan** and the successful military defense of South Korea (**Korean War**), although he was strongly attacked by Senator Joe McCarthy and accused of lukewarm support of Nationalist China (Taiwan). After the election of **Dwight D. Eisen-**

hower as president and Acheson's replacement by **John Foster Dulles**, Acheson played the role of elder statesman and author of reminiscences, especially *Present at the Creation* (1969), reemerging as a key advisor to President **John F. Kennedy**. *See also* COLD WAR.

ACKERMAN, CARL (1890–1970). A journalist for the *New York Times*, covering Russia during **World War I**, the **Bolshevik Revolution**, and the **American intervention**, Ackerman is best known for his reporting on the Siberian adventures of the **American Expeditionary Force (AEF)** in 1918–19, subsequently compiled in his book *Trailing the Bolsheviki: Twelve Thousand Miles with the Allies in Siberia* (1919). *See also* AMERICAN EXPEDITIONARY FORCE.

ADAMS, JOHN (1735–1826). An American "founding father" and second president of the United States (1797–1801), Adams was a member of a prominent Boston family that was among the first to support American independence from Great Britain. He served as the diplomatic representative of the American republic in The Netherlands during the Revolutionary War, where he initiated the mission of **Francis Dana** to Russia to win the support of **Catherine the Great**. This was against the advice of **Benjamin Franklin**, who was the American emissary to Paris. He also assigned his teenage son, **John Quincy Adams**, to accompany Dana to St. Petersburg to groom him for later diplomatic and political careers.

ADAMS, JOHN QUINCY (1767–1848). Sixth president of the United States, 1825–29, and first American minister to Russia, 1809–15, John Quincy Adams was the son of "founding father" **John Adams** of Boston. He first became acquainted with Russia as a youthful companion-secretary of **Francis Dana** during his mission to St. Petersburg in 1781. He subsequently studied at Harvard (1786–88), was appointed to diplomatic posts (Holland in 1794 and Portugal in 1796), served as interim senator from Massachusetts in Congress (1803–08), and then briefly was the Boyleston Professor of Rhetoric at Harvard University before his appointment to head the first American legation in Russia by President **Thomas Jefferson** in 1809. Portraying the parsimonious New England puritan at Tsar Alexander's court to the hilt, Adams developed good relations with officials and society in St. Petersburg during the Napoleonic Wars, vital to the expanding American commerce with Europe. The plain dressing and acting of Adams and his expanded family (to include three related secretaries) were a new experience for formal St. Petersburg society. Though never venturing outside the capital, Adams walked the streets of the city systematically, meeting **Alexander I** for brief informal conversations, all recorded in his detailed memoirs. He resigned his post in Russia to participate in the negotiations to end the **War of 1812** at Ghent and resume a political role in the United States.

Subsequently, Adams served as secretary of state (1817–25) during the administration of James Monroe and was instrumental in drafting what became known as the **Monroe Doctrine** (1823) that aimed at limiting and eliminating the presence of Britain and other European powers from Central and South America, but the policy was also directed toward the new, aggressive Russian designs in the North Pacific. Especially annoying to Americans was the Russian Ukaz of 1821 that claimed an extraordinary 100-mile territorial jurisdiction off the coast of Russian possessions. Adams would later serve one term as president (1825–29), but he then became a long-tenured congressman, seated for several subsequent terms (1831–48) from Massachusetts as a firm opponent of slavery; his career as a foremost public servant ended when he was literally carried from the floor of the House of Representatives to the Speaker's office, where he died.

ADDAMS, JANE (1860–1935). An American social worker born and educated in Illinois, Addams is best known as the founder and longtime director of Hull House in Chicago, one of the first and most enduring of the settlement houses for the poor in the United States. As a dedicated pacifist, in 1896 she visited Russia specifically for the purpose of conferring with **Leo Tolstoy** at his Yasnaya Polyana country estate. She was quite impressed with his conversation, demeanor, and her simple lunch of black bread and kasha (cooked barley); Tolstoy, however, lectured her on her fancy, frilly blouse as an insult to plain, simple living. All of this received wide publicity in the United States and helped nurture the "Tolstoy craze." As a subsequent supporter of the Russian liberal/radical cause, Addams welcomed and befriended visiting dissident Russians who ranged from anarchist **Pe-**

ter **Kropotkin** (1897 and 1901), socialist **Ekaterina Breshko-Breshkovskaya**, and Marxist writer **Maxim Gorky** (1906). She was also a friend and supporter of other sympathizers with Russia such as **Charles R. Crane** and **Raymond Robins**.

AFGHANISTAN, SOVIET INVASION OF (1979–1989). Afghanistan has long constituted an important part of the Middle East and Central Asia. At least since the middle of the 19th century Russia's long southern border with the country was of major military and political concern owing to the unsettled nature of the region that invited Great Power interference. An on-and-off conflict at a distance resulted, especially between Great Britain and the Russian Empire that became known as the "Great Game," which created few heroes and many victims. The region continued to be of interest to Soviet Russia after the 1917 revolution because of **Vladimir Lenin**'s concentration on fostering national independence and socialist movements in what became known as the "third world." Soviet diplomatic relations were established as early as 1920, but higher priorities absorbed most Soviet attention. Nevertheless, the **Comintern** and independent adherents to Communism stimulated nascent Marxist movements in these underdeveloped countries. These emerged in force after **World War II** owing to the serious weakening of imperialist powers, such as Great Britain and France, and the emerging global contest between the United States and the USSR for influence in the area.

The Middle East and Central Asia were of vital interest during the **cold war** because of oil resources, the existence of Israel, supported by the United States, and the instability of the region in general. It included a number of minority peoples related to ethnic groups in the Soviet Union—Azeris, Tadzhiks, and Turkmen. Afghanistan, especially, was sharply divided between city and country, mountainous regions and plains, and ethnic and tribal rivalries. Although overwhelmingly Moslem in religion, the population is divided between Pashtun (40 percent) and Persian-speaking Tadzhik (30 percent) and between Sunni (30 percent) and Shia (70 percent). Afghanistan's population (30 million) and area is about twice that of Iraq and about equal to that of Iran. Lacking the oil resources of those countries, the country also shares a long, mountainous frontier with Pakistan. Hostility between Afghanistan and Pakistan and the transition from monarchy to republic thus further complicated the situation in the 1970s.

The quasi-democratic and moderate Marxist government of Hafizullah Amin requested assistance from the Soviet Union to deal with a mixed array of insurgent forces of both militant Communist as well as radical Islamic positions, but Moscow refused to intervene until 24 December 1979. In a rash act of the **Leonid Brezhnev** regime, Soviet armed units landed at the Kabul airport. One of the first actions was to attack Amin's palace and kill him. Communist leader Babrak Karmal was then installed as a Soviet puppet ruler. This was the beginning of a protracted Soviet–Afghan War that resembled the American invasion of Vietnam several years earlier. The substantial Soviet force of more than 100,000 consisted mostly of armor, air, and support units. Tribal guerrillas from mountain strongholds were quite effective in resistance to it, thanks in part to supplies, especially handheld missiles, and encouragement from the United States.

President **Jimmy Carter** reacted to the Soviet invasion by issuing an embargo against the shipment of grain to the Soviet Union and by a boycott of American participation in the Moscow **Olympic Games** of 1980. The United States also facilitated the shipment of supplies, especially Stinger handheld missiles, through Pakistan to the resisting groups in Afghanistan. The conflict essentially meant the end of Brezhnev's **détente** and constituted a major deterioration in Soviet–American relations. Opposition to the Soviet operation grew internationally but also within the Soviet Union—a parallel to the U.S. experience in the Vietnam War. With the deaths in the invading Soviet army reaching 15,000 and no successful outcome in sight, in 1985 **Mikhail Gorbachev** initiated a gradual withdrawal from Afghanistan. With public pressure mounting in the Soviet Union, the Soviet leader speeded up the evacuation of military forces in 1988 into a complete withdrawal by 1989, leaving the terrain to a mix of local tribal control of the countryside and militant Taliban ascendancy in the major cities. By 2000 the Taliban jurisdiction extended over 95 percent of the country, and it had practically suppressed any Communist remnants as well as the lucrative poppy cultivation.

Afghanistan had become a haven for training bases of Islamic militants headed by Osama bin Laden and his inauguration of the radical Islamic movement of Al Qaeda. After Al Qaeda's initiation of the 11 September 2001 attacks, the United States launched Operation Enduring Freedom, the goal of which was the destruction of the Al Qaeda strongholds, in cooperation with the remaining opposition headed by the Afghan Northern Alliance. This time the states of the former Soviet Union supported the American effort out of concern, by the Russian Federation, for the war against the Islamic Chechens and the vulnerability of the large Central Asian region of Turkic and Iranian Islamic peoples, especially in Tadzhikistan and Uzbekistan. Even American support airbases were established in that area for the involvement in Afghanistan. American objectives were assisted by a capable Afghan leadership, headed by Hamid Karzai, who was elected president in 2004. Taliban forces, however, remained formidable, and Osama remained at large well into 2008 when conflict escalated and American military presence was increased.

AFRICAN AMERICANS IN RUSSIA. The first African Americans to reside in Russia were from American commercial ships in the late 18th century and servants of Americans who joined the staff of the Imperial Palace. Very few records of them exist, except that they were a popular adornment of court occasions. The wife of one of them, **Nancy Prince**, however, left a record of her Russian experiences in the first half of the 19th century. Shakespearean actor **Ira Aldridge** was also well known for his performances in Russia, where he died and was buried in Russian Poland. Russians were also fascinated by the plight of the black population of the United States, Harriet Beecher Stowe's depiction in *Uncle Tom's Cabin*, and the resulting **Civil War in America.**

By the early 20th century the appearance of African Americans was common as performers and as servants of American residents. Most prominent of these were Frederic Thomas, owner and impresario of the Aquarium, a prominent Moscow restaurant-nightclub and **Philip Jordan**, the assistant, valet, and counselor for Ambassador **David Francis** (1916–18). A number of others performed in minstrel-type entertainments across the Russian empire as individuals or in groups.

After the **Bolshevik Revolution** several African Americans were attracted by Soviet and **Comintern** propaganda of a nondiscriminatory society to visit or take up residence in Soviet Russia. Most prominent of them were **Claude McKay**, Emma Harris, and **Coretta Arle-Tietz**. While the first two would eventually return to the United States, Arle-Tietz, a noted operatic and jazz singer, would have a successful career that would merit her burial upon her death after **World War II** in the artist's section of the Novodeivichi Cemetery. One notable event in the early 1930s was an invitation to more than 20 African Americans to make a film in Moscow that would emphasize racial discrimination in the United States. Included in this group was **Langston Hughes**, who would write about their experiences. A few others would seek employment in Russia during the Depression years, such as **Robert Robinson**, who would also publish his experience. Perhaps the best-known sympathizer with the Soviet cause was singer **Paul Robeson**. Few African Americans would become scholars of the Soviet Union, but they would include Allison Blakely, who is the leading scholar on the subject, and Secretary of State **Condoleezza Rice**.

ALASKA. Defined as the present state of Alaska, it includes a north–south straight-line border with Canada, the Aleutian Islands, the **Pribylov Islands** in the **Bering Sea**, and other offshore islands. Many of the native inhabitants—Aleuts, Tlinglits, and Inuit—were converted to the Russian Orthodox religion during the Russian control of the region, leaving a permanent Russian impact on the region. While it was administered by the **Russian America Company (RAC)**, Alaska was not only a source of fur skins, but also an area of exploration, of exploitation of native labor, and of cultural integration. Though a strategic Russian possession—to deny Great Britain of occupying it—RAC from the beginning encountered difficulties in administration of this large territory. The main problem was supply because of the distance from ready sources of food and other essentials. This led the company into an abortive attempt to gain a foothold in Hawaii and to establish a base in California at **Fort Ross** in 1815. Trading Alaskan furs for tea in China and shipping ice to San Francisco, the RAC became profitable until political and economic factors forced the Russian government to decide in late 1866 to sell the region to the United States at the first opportune moment, which occurred in March 1867. *See also* ALASKA PURCHASE.

ALASKA PURCHASE (1867). The sale of Northwest America by Russia to the United States. The Russian Empire for a number of years, beginning at least as early as 1854, was interested in selling its North American territory because of the expense of supplying and administering the colony, the strained relations with the native population, and the vulnerability of the area to other powers, specifically the United States and Great Britain. The possibility of American purchase, seriously considered in 1860, was delayed by the **American Civil War**. In the meantime, the idea of a Russian sale was advanced in government circles, especially by Minister of Navy **Grand Duke Constantine**. The decision was essentially made by a private meeting with **Alexander II** in December 1866 to await an opportune time. The United States, recovering from the war and with **William H. Seward** in charge of an aggressive foreign policy, readily but secretly agreed to the purchase price, and the "treaty" was signed by him with Russian minister **Eduard Stoekl** at the end of March 1867 for an amount of $7,000,000. A subsequent amount ($200,000) was added to facilitate the sale's passage through Congress. *See also* ALASKA; RUSSIAN AMERICA COMPANY.

ALDANOV, MARK (NE LANDAU) (1889–1957). Russian American scientist, philosopher, and novelist born in Kiev, Aldanov studied science and law at the University of Kiev and published his first articles there and in Paris. He immigrated to France in 1919 to become an active novelist specializing in historical fiction and to become one of the most popular writers in **Russia Abroad**. His subjects ranged from the French Revolution and Napoleon to the recent Russian political and social past. In 1941 he left war-threatened France for the United States, where he was associated with Ivan Bunin and Russian émigré publications *Novyi Zhurnal* (*New Journal*) and *Novoe Russkoe Slovo* (*New Russian Word*).

ALDRIDGE, IRA (1807–1867). An African American actor born and educated in New York City, Aldridge began his theater career in the early 1820s, but, discouraged by discrimination against black performers, he immigrated to England, where he soon established a reputation as a leading Shakespearian tragedian in the title roles of Romeo, Hamlet, and Othello, earning top billing at London's Coberg Theatre by 1825. Subsequently, he toured Dublin, Edinburgh, and Bath and appeared on the continent for the first time in 1852. On another visit in 1858, he performed in Russia, where he was very popular. Most of his remaining years were spent there, though he planned to return to the United States after the **American Civil War**. He died and was buried in the Polish-Russian city of Lodz.

ALEKSANDROVSK. The location and name of the largest industrial factory in Russia during much of the 19th century, it originated during the Napoleonic Wars for armaments manufacture in an eastern suburb of St. Petersburg on the Neva River and was leased to the American firm of **Harrison, Eastwick and Winans** in the 1840s for the production of locomotives and railroad cars, patterned after those constructed by Thomas Winans in Baltimore for the Baltimore & Ohio Railroad. They were specifically made for use on the St. Petersburg–Moscow Railroad and for subsequent railroad expansions through the 1860s for about 25 years. The Winans family made a fortune on the Russian business, witnessed by two lavish estates in Baltimore, "Crimea" and "Aleksandrovsk," the latter demolished in the 1920s, the former serving as a city park headquarters. The Russian factory continued to be one of the major industrial enterprises in Russia through the end of the 19th century and stood as a symbol of the introduction of American technology into Russia.

ALEXANDER I (1777–1825). Tsar of Russia (1801–25), Alexander was the ruler of the Russian Empire during the very difficult, stressful, and destructive times of the Napoleonic Wars that featured a major Russian defeat at Austerlitz and the extraordinary invasion of Russia in 1812 that resulted in a French occupation and the destruction of Moscow. But the cost in lives and materiel contributed to Napoleon's ultimate defeat. Alexander I began his reign with draft programs of democratic reform with American models in mind. He corresponded indirectly with President **Thomas Jefferson**, whose term was beset with uncertainties of quasi-neutrality and embargo reaction. Alexander I approved the preparations for diplomatic recognition of the United States that began in 1807, and he went out of his way to welcome the first American minister, **John Quincy Adams**, in 1809.

In reaction to the upheavals of the period and the defeat of Napoleon, which his armies were instrumental in accomplishing, Alexander I turned much more conservative after 1815 and was a bulwark of the Holy Alliance, created at the Congress of Vienna, that aimed to stabilize and protect legitimate regimes against liberal and radical reforms. This led to secret efforts to reverse the government's course that led to the **Decembrist revolt** immediately after Alexander's death in 1825. Throughout his rule, Alexander I supported advances of Russia in the Pacific region by the operations of the **Russian America Company (RAC)** in Northwest America, its ventures into Hawaii, the launch of several costly naval expeditions, and the establishment of **Fort Ross** (1814) in California that helped instigate the **Monroe Doctrine** (1823). But Russian policy was often contradictory, as in the tsar's issue of the Ukaz of 1821 and its subsequent retraction in the Russian–American **Convention of 1824**. Accurately termed "the enigmatic tsar," Alexander I admired the United States, yet withdrew from any commitment to emulating its institutions, much of this owing to the perceived need to maintain a large military force to safeguard Europe, and especially Russia, from any future invasion.

ALEXANDER II (1818–1881). The reign of Alexander II (1855–81) is best known as an era of liberal reforms. He was also well aware of American friendship to Russia during the **Crimean War** (1854–56) and the nearly coincident emancipation of the Russian serfs in 1861 and **Abraham Lincoln**'s Emancipation Proclamation of 1863, releasing the black population in the United States from slavery. The tsar, with the important support of his brother, Minister of Navy **Grand Duke Constantine**, lent important support to the Union cause, sending two naval squadrons to New York and San Francisco, respectively, in 1863, at a crucial time (Battle of Gettysburg) for the fate of the Union's military campaigns. Russian policies also discouraged more direct action by Britain and France in favor of the Confederacy. In thanks for this demonstration of support, the United States sent a naval mission to St. Petersburg in 1866, headed by Assistant Secretary of Navy **Gustavus Fox**. Alexander II went out of his way to welcome and visit the squadron at the Kronstadt naval base and host its officers onshore. Much credit for the success of this Russian–American rapprochement is owed to his chancellor, **Alexander Gorchakov**. Subsequently, Alexander II sent his son, **Grand Duke Alexis,** on a tour of the United States in 1871–72, a high point of Russian–American relations in the

19th century. The tsar's liberal reforms, however, were cut short by his assassination in 1881, often compared with the fate of American contemporary **Abraham Lincoln**. A conservative reaction under his successor, **Alexander III**, resulted in the persecution of liberals and revolutionaries and anti-Jewish measures, contributing to a deterioration in Russian–American relations. *See also* ALEXIS, GRAND DUKE; FOX MISSION.

ALEXANDER III (1845–1894). Tsar of Russia (1881–94), his reign is known as a period of reaction and for the consolidation of a repressive police state that naturally caused problems with previously close Russian–American relations. The particular American objections concerned the severe treatment of political prisoners in Siberian exile that was exposed by **George Kennan** and several others and the increased discrimination against the Jewish population of the empire that resulted in bloody pogroms and stimulated considerable immigration to the United States; this policy was instigated by the main power behind the throne, **Konstantin Pobedonostsev**, the reactionary procurator of the Holy Synod (director of religious affairs). Despite political and social problems, however, American business continued penetration into Russia, illustrated by expansion of the **Singer**, **Westinghouse**, **New York Life**, and **International Harvester** enterprises during his reign. Russian foreign affairs were distinguished in the early 1890s by an alliance with France that would herald Russia's participation on the Allied side during **World War I**.

ALEXANDERWOHL MENNONITE COLONY. Established in 1819 in the **Molochna** region in Southeastern Ukraine, about 50 miles north of the Sea of Azov port of Berdiansk, the village derived its name from the settlers who encountered **Alexander I**, who gave them his "best wishes," on their trek into Russia from the Danzig area of West Prussia. These Mennonites settled in Russia, attracted by free land and the promise of exemption from conscription into military service. When these conditions were threatened by the reforms of **Alexander II** that aimed to eliminate special privileges, most of the colony's members, joined by many others, immigrated in 1874 to the United States. Those from Alexanderwohl reestablished their church-community about 50 miles north of Wichita, Kansas, where it remains as one of the largest Mennonite congregations in the United States. The Russian/Ukrainian/Dutch Mennonites had a major impact in the economy of the area, mainly involving the cultivation of turkey red wheat, brought from Crimea, and the introduction of new milling technology by **Bernhard Warkentin** that made the Great Plains region the greatest flour exporter in the world by the 1920s.

ALEXIS, GRAND DUKE (1850–1908). The third son of **Alexander II** and younger brother of **Alexander III**, Alexis was sent as a naval officer—at age 21—on an around-the-world cruise in 1871–72, the highlight of which was an extensive tour of the United States, where he was given a royal welcome. Landing in New York City in early December 1871, Alexis visited Boston, Philadelphia, and finally Washington, D.C., where he received a cold, cursory reception at the White House (because of the **Katakazi** affair) but was entertained by gala receptions, fancy balls, and elaborate dinners before venturing on a cross-country journey that included sightseeing in fire-ravaged Chicago and a buffalo hunt in western Nebraska at the end of January 1872, the latter staged by Buffalo Bill (William Cody), General George Armstrong Custer, Civil War hero General Philip Sheridan, and an assemblage of temporarily peaceful Sioux chiefs. Expertly guided by Admiral **Konstantin Pos'et** and legation secretary Vladmir **Bodisko**, Alexis's return trip included a reception by the state legislature in Topeka, Kansas, a visit to Mammoth Cave, a conversation with ex-president of the Confederacy Jefferson Davis in Memphis, and a steamboat trip down the Mississippi to New Orleans, where he was crowned "King of the Mardi Gras." It concluded in Pensacola, where he embarked on the Russian squadron to resume his around-the-world voyage.

This sensational and widely publicized three-month journey through the United States by a Russian grand duke marked a high point in Russian–American relations, especially since it came shortly after the expressions of Russian support for the Union during the **American Civil War**. Later, when minister of navy, Alexis would recall fondly his experiences in the United States to visiting Americans and relish his buffalo-head souvenir mounted in the Naval Ministry in St. Petersburg. His administrative tenure would be marred, however, by the Russian naval debacle (Tsushima) during the **Russo–Japanese**

War (1904–05). He died prematurely soon afterward, thus saved from witnessing the end of the Romanov dynasty and the **Bolshevik Revolution**.

ALLIED AMERICA CORPORATION. *See* HAMMER, ARMAND.

ALLILUYEVA, SVETLANA (1926–). As the only daughter of **Joseph Stalin**, Svetlana, by all accounts, had a close relationship with her father but later adopted the maiden name of her mother. She was married first to a fellow student at **Moscow State University** and, after their divorce in 1947, to Yury Zhdanov, the son of a prominent Soviet leader. This marriage was dissolved after the birth of a daughter in 1950. After a later infatuation with an Indian Communist who soon died, she left the Union of Soviet Socialist Republics (USSR) to accompany his ashes to his native India in 1967. She remained abroad, first in Switzerland and then in the United States, becoming a celebrated defector from the USSR, supported by the proceeds of her memoirs, *Twenty Letters to a Friend* (1967) and *Only One Year* (1969) and befriended by Harrison Salisbury and **Louis Fischer**. Briefly married to American architect William Peters, who was associated with Frank Lloyd Wright, she left the United States with her daughter (by Peters) and moved to Cambridge, United Kingdom, but they subsequently became itinerant, returning to the Soviet Union in the 1980s and then to the Georgian republic. Eventually, they came back to New York with minimum income, the daughter working in a flower shop in the 1990s, and then went back to England. Rather reclusive, Svetlana reemerged briefly in March 2008 for an interview on Russian television.

ALL-RUSSIAN SOCIETY FOR CULTURAL RELATIONS WITH FOREIGN COUNTRIES (VOKS). Soviet cultural agency (1922 to c. 1940) under the initial direction of **Olga Kameneva**, the wife of **Lev Kamenev** and sister of **Leon Trotsky**. VOKS coordinated and advanced the cultural relations of Soviet Russia with the West—and especially the United States—in the 1920s and 1930s. It sponsored a number of exchanges of performing artists and groups of Russians in the United States and Americans in Russia. These included poets, musicians, jazz combos, and literary figures. It assisted with the establishment of **American Russian Institutes** in major American cities and arranged exhibits, both cultural and propagandistic, for display. While Kameneva was in charge of VOKS, American visitors could count on assistance, whether simply visiting or working in archives. Among those it hosted were writers **Theodore Dreiser** and **Sinclair Lewis** and scholars such as **Geroid Robinson, George Counts**, and **John Hazard**. After Kameneva's departure (owing to the purges), the agency declined with much of its role taken over by new organizations such as **Intourist**.

AMERICAN AID TO FAMINE IN RUSSIA (1892–1893). During a severe Russian famine concentrated in the Volga region, the United States formed a major food and relief effort, one of the first of its kind. It was supported by the **American Red Cross**, the milling industry, eastern cities, and various state committees in the Midwest. Leading organizers were William Edgar of Minneapolis, **Clara Barton** of the Red Cross, Charles Tillinghast of Iowa, and Rudolf Blankenburg of Philadelphia. Several shiploads of grain, mainly corn, were shipped to Russia, where a relief organization, headed by Andrei Bobrinskoi, managed the shipping into the interior. Though opposed by **George Kennan** and other critics of Russian policies toward Jews and radicals, the relief effort constituted a high point in Russian–American relations and became a model for many future American relief operations. One difficulty was that much of the food shipment was Midwestern corn, which was unfamiliar to Russians, though instructions on its use were provided.

AMERICAN ASSOCIATION FOR THE ADVANCEMENT OF SLAVIC STUDIES (AAASS). Professional scholarly organization founded in 1948 and devoted to the Slavic-speaking world. Several loosely affiliated academic groups promoted the importance of the study of Russia in the 1930s. The **cold war** and the accompanying creation of a number of academic study centers on Russia and Eastern Europe, initially at Columbia University and Harvard University, inspired the organization of a national association to promote scholarship in annual meetings and through its quarterly journal, *Slavic Review*. The association and the journal includes all disciplines pertaining to the geographic area of the Slavic and Eurasian world and thus is much more broadly conceived than, for example, the *Russian Review*, which is published independently of an organization. The AAASS headquarters, editorial offices, and meeting places have varied over the years but are currently at Harvard University, Indiana University, and Washington, D.C., respectively. The association also has a number of regional affiliates, which have regular meetings, and it publishes a newsletter, *Newsnet*, that provides current information about the profession and the activities of the organization and its affiliates.

AMERICAN COUNCIL OF TEACHERS OF RUSSIAN (ACTR). An organization devoted to facilitating opportunities for scholars and students of the Russian language, ACTR was founded in 1974 and would serve as a supplement to the **International Research and Exchanges Board (IREX)** to meet the special needs and explore exchange arrangements for American students and teachers of the Russian language. In the mid-1880s, as the possibilities for exchanges increased, an affiliated group was created, the American Council for Collaboration in Education and Language Study (ACCELS). Both ACTR and ACCELS in 1998 became branches of a new organization, the American Councils for International Education (ACIE). ACTR is the professional unit, focusing on programs for U.S. citizens, while ACCELS administers exchange and research programs with not only Russia but other countries of Eurasia and Eastern Europe.

AMERICAN EXPEDITIONARY FORCE IN SIBERIA (AEF) (1918–1920). After much delay and hesitation, the American government under **Woodrow Wilson** sent military units into Russia, in the north at **Murmansk** and Archangel under British command, and larger contingents from the Philippines and California under General **William S. Graves** to **Siberia** in August and September 1918. A major reason for the American military presence in Siberia was to safeguard the exit of the **Czechoslovak Legion** from a Bolshevik Russia in order that it could be deployed on the western front and to support the cause of Czechoslovak independence. Another, perhaps equally important, purpose was to prevent Japan, which was sending a much larger military force into the area of southwest Siberia and Manchuria, from dominating the region—and perhaps annexing it. The American contingent of about 11,000, compared with more than 70,000 Japanese, was concentrated in the area in and around **Vladivostok** under vague direction from Washington. By General Graves's own preference, it remained aloof from civil war action in Siberia as much as possible. One incident, however, an ambush by unidentified insurgents near the Suchan coal mines on an American infantry company being sent to guard the mines, resulted in several American casualties.

After the successful evacuation of the Czechoslovak units and continued upheaval in the area, the mission of the American forces became obscure, causing considerable opposition among the troops and at home for their continued deployment well after the world war was over. The last contingents were finally withdrawn in the spring of 1920, leaving control of a large part of eastern Siberia very loosely in the hands of the Japanese military forces and a **Far Eastern Republic (FER)** government, centered in Chita and leaning toward adherence to the Soviet government in Moscow. American presence remained in Manchuria for another year in the form of the Russian **Railway Service Corps** that controlled the **Chinese Eastern Railway (CER)**.

AMERICAN FRIENDS SERVICE COMMITTEE. Society of Friends (Quaker) relief organization. Already active in Russia before and during **World War I**, it was among the first to "go back" to provide essential relief to Russia during the great famine of 1920–23. In cooperation with the **American Relief Administration**, whose director, **Herbert Hoover**, was sympathetic to the committee's dedication but desiring an overseeing role, the Service Committee concentrated its relief work on one of the areas that was especially in dire need, the Tatar and Bashkir regions around Kazan and Ufa. Because of the independent and nongovernmental nature of their work, the Soviet leadership appreciated their contributions and grudgingly tolerated their religious mission for the duration of the famine.

AMERICAN FUR COMPANY. *See* ASTOR, JOHN JACOB.

AMERICAN JEWISH JOINT DISTRIBUTION COMMITTEE ("JOINT"). Stemming from American assistance to the immigration of Russian Jews to the United States, this New York–based organization, founded in 1914, was devoted to providing assistance to Jewish-Russians during their severe distress during **World War I** and the **Russian Civil War**. It solicited funds and sent relief directly to Jewish communities in Russia, attempted to provide assistance to many refugees, and cooperated with the **American Relief Administration** in its program of 1921–23, sending many relief parcels through its organization, while receiving some criticism from both American and Soviet authorities for its "targeting" efforts. It continued in operation to assist Jewish victims of Soviet persecution through the Stalin era, suspending its activities in 1952.

AMERICAN RAILWAY SERVICE CORPS. During **World War I** the Russian railroads deteriorated rapidly owing to the strain on their service and lack of adequate replacement and repair capability. Shortage of coal was another factor. After the United States entered the war in April 1917, a technical commission was sent to Russia to investigate, especially because of a large amount of supplies being delivered to Russian ports, such as **Murmansk** and **Vladivostok**, and piling up because of the decrease of rail traffic. The commission, headed by **John F. Stevens**, recommended that a special group be assembled and sent to supervise and assist the Russian management and also to place high priority on shipments of new cars and locomotives from the United States.

An American service corps of approximately 300 technical experts was assembled and sent to Siberia in early 1918 to improve the shipment of supplies from Vladivostok and to safeguard telegraphic communications. It arrived in early March 1918 and established headquarters in Harbin, a major center along the **Chinese Eastern Railway (CER)** that was a crucial link on the **Trans-Siberian Railroad** to Chita. This was just in time to greet a large Japanese army that arrived in April at Port Arthur and proceeded north into Manchuria. The corps then received a secondary mission of preventing the Japanese from seizing control of rail and telegraph lines. Because of the continuing deterioration of Russian civic and military forces in 1918, the small corps could achieve little except to aid the extraction of the **Czechoslovak Legion** from Russia and to resist Japanese efforts to gain control of the region through 1921, when the mission was finally withdrawn

The actual administration and the payment of expenses of this "expedition" were complicated. It was formally under the jurisdiction of the State Department and funded by withdrawals from loans granted in 1917 to the Russian **Provisional Government** and countersigned by Ambassador **Boris Bakhmeteff**. The members, however, wore uniforms and carried arms for self-protection. They later claimed military service pension rights, which were granted after several years by the U.S. Supreme Court. This small corps thus became the first Allied **Intervention** force on Russian soil—except that its activity was mainly confined to Manchuria.

AMERICAN RED CROSS (ARC). Founded in 1881, by the 1890s the ARC had grown rapidly under the inspired leadership of **Clara Barton** to become an important humanitarian relief organization with a focus on natural and human disasters both at home and abroad. Barton led the organization's first international relief effort for the Russian famine of 1892–93. The ARC was especially active in Russia during the period of revolution and civil war. A mission headed by **Raymond Robins** and William Boyce Thompson arrived there in the summer of 1917 to bolster the **Provisional Government**'s effort to continue participation in the war, despite rapidly deteriorating economic conditions. It represented a visible and welcome American presence in revolutionary Russia. Later, however, under the influence of Robins, the ARC turned toward sympathizing with the new Bolshevik-led government in hopes of making an arrangement that would continue the relief mission and keep Russia in the war. Red Cross supplies and assistance would be a major presence and saver of many lives during the **Russian Civil War** in Siberia and North Russia and in assistance to thousands of refugees in Constantinople and elsewhere. During the subsequent major relief effort by the **American Relief Administration (ARA)** in 1921, Red Cross supplies were among the first to cross the Soviet border, and a number of the personnel of ARC would become involved in the administration of that relief. The ARC also played a major role in Siberia in organizing the "typhus train" and filling a major relief need where the ARA was not present.

AMERICAN RELIEF ADMINISTRATION (ARA). The American agency for providing relief to Eastern Europe and Soviet Russia was technically a private organization with headquarters in New York City but directed by Secretary of Commerce **Herbert Hoover** from his government offices in Washington. Hoover was chosen to head the ARA because of his successful relief efforts in Belgium during **World War I**. Initially the agency responded in 1919 to the economic devastation and politically unstable situation in Eastern Europe. The plight of refugees and prisoners of war required assistance, but the American aid was partly motivated by a desire to support the new government of Poland, created as an independent entity by Wilson's Fourteen Points and the Versailles Treaty arrangements. Its operation was aided by the presence of leftover food and medical supplies from the world war that were largely in the hands of the **American Red Cross (ARC)**.

The conditions in Soviet Russia were also of considerable concern, owing to the destruction of much of the infrastructure of transportation and political authority by the war, the revolution, and a brutal civil war. Adding to the misery was the Bolshevik War Communism policy of seizing food in the countryside for the Red Army. It also attempted to install a utopian Communist program among the Russian peasantry that allowed them to keep only what they needed for their own support, while turning what remained to the Soviet state. Peasants responded by producing only what they needed, which was still seized. On top of this, there was a genuine drought along the Volga River and in Ukraine, which left the population with virtually nothing to eat. The desperation was known to the outside from refugees, a few visitors, and agents of the **American Friends Service Committee**, who were among the first to reach some of the worst afflicted areas early in 1921.

The Soviet appeal for Western aid came from **Maxim Gorky**, with the approval of **Vladimir Lenin**, in the summer of 1921. Hoover responded to Gorky on 23 July with a willingness to assist provided certain conditions were met. The arrangement was negotiated in the **Riga Agreement** in August by Walter Lyman Brown for the ARA and **Maxim Litvinov** for the Soviet government. The American conditions granted by the Soviet government involved release of all American prisoners, only about 10, but including an American spy, **Xenophon Kalamatiano**, and, more important, the right of the ARA to supervise distribution of relief directly in the provinces, not through Soviet channels. Also, the ARA would have complete control on the selection of personnel who would be given diplomatic status, freedom to come and go with unhampered mail privileges.

William N. Haskell, an army officer with relief experience in the Near East, was selected by Hoover to direct the operation from a headquarters in Moscow. His military command operation tended to conflict regularly with many other personnel recruited from the ARC, the **American Society of Friends**, and others with Russian expertise in academic positions. The relief came to Russia almost immediately, owing to the existing ARA organization in Eastern Europe and the rapid assembly of a special organization for Russian relief. Supply trains were headed into Russia within days of the signing of the agreement and ARA personnel, to total about 300 at the height of the effort, were quickly investigating the worst famine areas and documenting the seriousness of the situation in grizzly detail, especially in the Volga German colony near Saratov and in the Bashkir lands near Ufa. Problems were naturally encountered with Soviet authorities, especially those designated with direct liaison, but a surprising degree of mutual interest evolved with **Lev Kamenev** (Soviet director of relief), Felix Dzerzhinsky (commissar of transportation), and Lenin, who clearly and more than once voiced his appreciation of the American assistance.

The ARA was financed by a $20 million appropriation from Congress in December 1921, by $10 million in Soviet gold, and by a variety of other contributions, totaling more than $60 million. One of the major problems, naturally, was coordination with Soviet authorities, especially in regard to transportation and in the hiring of more than 6,000 Russians, many from the old intellectual class who knew some English and who were also in desperate circumstances. Among notable Americans involved in the relief were Harvard historian **Archibald Cary Coolidge**, Stanford historian **Frank Golder**, whose responsibility was the supervision and safeguarding of the records of the operation (more than 600 boxes in the **Hoover Institution**), and Governor **James P. Goodrich**, who was sent as a special investigator and troubleshooter by Hoover. Though about 7,000,000 perished, about the same number were saved from death by the American relief effort, which closed down its operations in July 1923 with banquets and much Soviet appreciation. Remembered by many recipients, the role of the ARA was "forgotten" during the **cold war** but revived afterward with studies by both American and Russian scholars, including Bertrand Patenaude's *The Big Show in Bololand: The American Relief Expedition to Soviet Russia in the Famine of 1921* (2002).

AMERICAN RUSSIAN CHAMBER OF COMMERCE (ARCC). American organization dedicated to fostering trade with Russia. Though founded in 1916 under the direction of a New York–based organization that was strongly anti-Bolshevik, it quickly shifted in the early 1920s to promote business association with Soviet trade agencies under the presidency of **Reeve Schley**, vice president of Chase Manhattan Bank, which handled much of the Soviet monetary needs in the United States. **Samuel Bertron**, another prominent New York banker, served for many years as its active chairman. The chamber received the support of a wide range of major American companies, such as **Ford**, **Westinghouse**, General Electric, and **International Harvester**. It was a major proponent of increased American contact with the Soviet Union and of recognition. The ARCC provided essential services and encouragement to a number of individuals and companies who would participate in the gigantic construction projects of the **First Five-Year Plan**.

AMERICAN RUSSIAN COMMERCIAL COMPANY (ARCC). With the encouragement of Russian consul **Peter Kostromitinov**, a group of San Francisco businessmen, headed by **Beverley C. Sanders**, formed a company in 1853 to trade with the **Russian America Company (RAC)** in **Alaska.** The increased population and business in the area, owing to the gold rush, was the major catalyst. This fostered a need for a special commodity—ice—that was previously furnished from New England around South America and sold for a dollar a pound. With capital generated from sale of stock, ARCC invested in equipment and construction in Sitka and on Kodiak Island for the production of ice from inland lakes to be shipped to California. The yearly average production during this period was 4,000 tons hauled by the ships of RAC. The ARCC also expanded into importing lumber and fish from Alaska. Sanders journeyed to St. Petersburg in 1854 to negotiate a far-reaching contract and to discuss a fictitious sale of Alaska to the United States to avoid possible British seizure during the **Crimean War**. The company continued operations until the sale of the Russian possessions in America (1867).

AMERICAN RUSSIAN INSTITUTES. As part of a growing campaign for closer relations with the Soviet Union during the **First Five-Year Plan**, "institutes" were established in leading American cities to foster greater understanding and appreciation of culture. The leading one was, of course, in New York, headed by Lucy Branham, along with the one in Chicago, also very active, under the leadership of Agnes Jacques. Others in Philadelphia (led by orchestra director Leopold Stokowsky) and San Francisco had spurts of activity. Most of these activities originated around 1930 and were supported by the Soviet **All-Russian Society for Cultural Relations with Foreign Countries (VOKS)**, which provided publications, exhibits, and hospitality services for those members who joined tours of the Soviet Union. Their significance was in maintaining an active American interest in Soviet cultural relations and in promoting the cause of diplomatic recognition in the early 1930s. Some of them continued into the **cold war** but came under increased political pressures for their sympathetic leanings toward Communism.

AMERICAN SOCIETY OF FRIENDS OF RUSSIAN FREEDOM. A philanthropical and political activist organization, founded by **George Kennan** and others in 1891 as an American affiliate of a similar British "Friends of Russian Freedom," it was devoted to supporting those who advocated a liberal political agenda for Russia, which left them vulnerable to Russian arrest and incarceration and forced to seek exile abroad. It published an influential journal, *Free Russia*, that succeeded in raising modest amounts of money for its cause. The leaders, such as **Ekaterina Breshko-Breshkovskaya**, Sergei Kravchinsky (Stepniak), and **Paul Miliukov** pursued a moderate agenda of a liberal, though somewhat socialist, political agenda that soon went out of favor under the Allied commitment to continuing Russian participation in **World War I** and because of the much more radical rise of the Bolshevik alternative, leaving most of the surviving members after the Russian Revolution as frustrated Russian émigrés.

AMERICAN TRADING CORPORATION (AMTORG). Although the American government in the administrations of **Woodrow Wilson**, Warren Harding, **Calvin Coolidge**, and **Herbert Hoover** refused to recognize formally the Soviet government, it removed restrictions on regular trade in July 1920, while warning Americans that any business with Soviet Russia would be at their own risk. To take advantage of Western business desires to resume normal commerce, especially in regard to Russia's vast natural resources but backward technology, the Soviet government sent special trade missions abroad to negotiate and facilitate arrangements. The first "permanent" agency was the Anglo-Russian Company (Arkos), established in London in 1920, which soon had an American subsidiary. Meanwhile, other Soviet agencies and commissariats were negotiating separately, in regard, for example, to the purchase of cotton and locomotives from the United States. It became apparent that these ventures needed to be under central control. Thus Amtorg was chartered with headquarters in New York in 1923. Technically, it was a private company, but everyone was aware of its Soviet affiliation. Under the direction of Saul Bron and **Peter Bogdanov**, especially, Amtorg expanded into a major commercial enterprise by 1930 with more than 100 employees, mostly American Jews with a knowledge of Russian. In its formative period, Amtorg was very careful to clear any legal hurdles through a leading New York law firm headed by Thomas Thacher.

Amtorg was especially useful for the USSR in negotiating contracts with major companies such as **Ford Motor Company**, General Electric, **International Harvester**, and many others, during the **First Five-Year Plan**, taking advantage of the desperation of American individuals and companies during the Great Depression. Though frequently charged by American opponents as a Communist tool of world revolution in the middle of American financial institutions, Amtorg maintained its virtual monopoly on economic contacts between the two countries and especially during the **Nazi–Soviet Pact**, when it became clear that the organization had been harboring agents of the **People's Commissariat of Internal Affairs (NKVD)**. It revived, however, in **World War II** as supervisor of American support for the Soviet war effort through **lend-lease**. Amtorg ceased to exist in 1946 after the end of lend-lease and the advent of the **cold war.**

AMERIKA **(1945–1988).** A periodical published monthly in the Soviet Union to promote the best side of American life during the **cold war**, *Amerika* had limited circulation due to Soviet restrictions, even after it became part of the cultural exchanges in the 1950s, when, in exchange, *Soviet Life* became available in the United States. Typically, the American journal "borrowed" copyrighted articles from popular media such as *Life Magazine*. It later became a private venture under Russian commercial auspices in the 1990s, similar to *Russian Life*.

AMERIKANIZM. Beginning in the 19th century and continuing well into the 20th, Russia looked to the United States for economic and political solutions to its problems of development. The term is also related to the Soviet construction program of *gigantomania*. The phenomenon was especially explored and described in articles by American scholar Hans Rogger. More specifically, the term refers to technological borrowing by Russia that stemmed from seeing parallel situations, especially in regard to settlement, expansion, consolidation, and progress over a whole continent. In the 19th century Russia preferred to negotiate contracts with American companies such as **Winans** (railroad equipment), **International Harvester (IH)** (agricultural machinery), and **Singer** (sewing machines). Similarly, during the **First Five-Year Plan**, a number of American companies and individuals were contracted to assist in the great industrialization drive. A corollary to *amerikanizm* was *Fordism*, an emphasis on mass assembly-line production. This theme was also emphasized in the scholarly works of **Nikolai Bolkhovitinov**, Alan Ball, Norman Saul, and Antony Sutton. The Russian leaders who ascribed to this policy direction ranged from **Nicholas I** to **Sergei Witte** and **Peter Stolypin** before the revolution to Communist leaders **Vladimir Lenin**, **Joseph Stalin**, and **Nikita Khrushchev**.

AMERIKANSKII EZHEGODNIK (AMERICAN YEARBOOK). Founded in 1970, especially by **Grigory Sevostianov** of the **Institute of General History**, the yearbook published scholarly and only mildly biased articles on American history and society. Under the guidance of leading Russian scholar **Nikolai Bolkhovitinov**, *Amerikanskii Ezhegodnik* represents the best scholarship on American history in the Soviet Union and Russia. Sponsored by the **Center**

for North American Studies, it played a leading role in maintaining and advancing American studies in the Soviet Union and the **Russian Federation**. Many of its authors were Russian or American participants in the academic exchanges during the **cold war** and beyond. It continues this mission in the 21st century under the expert leadership of Bolkhovitinov, **Gennady Kuropiatnik,** Valery Malkov, Larissa Troitskaya, Boris Shpotov, Irina Beliavskaia, and others. Americans, such as Martin Zuckerman, Walter LaFeber, and Norman Saul, serve on its advisory board.

AMTORG. See AMERICAN TRADING CORPORATION.

ANDERSON, PAUL (1898–1975). After several years of service with the **Young Men's Christian Association (YMCA)** during **World War I** and the **Bolshevik Revolution**, Anderson became the major administrator and catalyst of initiatives toward assistance to the many Russian refugees in Western Europe after the **Russian Civil War**. He developed an educational program for Russian refugees directed toward adjustment to their new non-Russian environment. Most significantly, he and the YMCA promoted a series of correspondence courses for these new Russian settlers in Europe, while also supporting exiled Russian intelligentsia who wrote the textbooks in the 1920s, mainly for the Soviet market. This study program helped sustain the values of old Russian culture from its center in Berlin. This led to the establishment of a major émigré press in Paris that would foster the new literature of the émigré community, while sustaining its cultural life in the 1920s and 1930s and again during the **cold war**, such as in the publication of Boris Pasternak's *Doctor Zhivago* in a Russian edition by YMCA Press in Paris.

ANDROPOV, YURY (1914–1984). As general secretary of the Communist Party of the Soviet Union (CPSU) from 1982 to 1984 and director of the **Committee on State Security (KGB)** from 1967 to 1980, Andropov was perhaps the last **cold war** leader of the Soviet Union but was better educated and advised than most of his predecessors. Unfortunately, he soon developed a kidney disease that left him incapacitated and shortened his tenure. In the meantime, Andropov faced an offensive policy of the administration of President

Ronald Reagan in the form of a Strategic Defense Initiative and the epithet of **"the evil empire"** (1983). These hostile initiatives seemed justified by one of the last serious events of the cold war, known as the **Korean airliner incident**, the shooting down of a South Korean passenger plane (flight 007) that had strayed over Soviet territory due to erred navigation on a flight from Anchorage to Seoul. Andropov, however, had prepared the way for future reforms—and the end of the Soviet Union—by establishing and protecting a liberal coterie (brain trust) in the 1960s in Prague, dubbed the "men of the sixties" (*shestidesiatniki*), who would emerge as trusted consultants under **Mikhail Gorbachev**. The latter was also advanced from provincial leadership to a position of succession in the top leadership by Andropov.

ANGLO-AMERICAN CHURCH. From the early 19th century, when it was founded, until the revolution of 1917, the Anglo-American Church served the British Protestant and, especially, the growing **American colony in St. Petersburg**. Leaning toward nonconformist or Congregational services, the church on Vasilevsky Island served as a center of religious, missionary, and social life for many of the American residents who were involved in business pursuits, such as the family of **William H. Ropes** of Boston, who were of New England (Puritan) background. African American **Nancy Prince** and **George Washington Whistler** and his wife Anna and their children were also involved in the congregation's relief work, such as during the St. Petersburg flood of 1824, and in missionary activities in **Siberia**, especially in the region of Buryatia. The congregation's long-term ministers, such as John Hall, were usually British, but the church welcomed and received most of its support from Americans, especially "tracts" and funds from the New England Bible Society. It paralleled—and is sometimes confused with—the more pretentious "English Church" on the Nevsky embankment, which was Church of England (or Episcopalian) in orientation.

ANTI-BALLISTIC MISSILE (ABM) TREATY. The arms race that predominated in the **cold war** between the United States and the USSR by the 1960s had reached a point of a multitude of missile systems and antimissile countermeasures that were bewildering even to experts in the field, especially with the development of the multiple independently targetable reentry vehicle (MIRV) system, leading to mutual assured destruction (MAD). The United States first proposed a suspension of the race in 1967 during the period of **Leonid Brezhnev**'s **détente**. Negotiations during the **Strategic Arms Limitation Talks (SALT I)** resulted in an interim agreement on limiting missile defense systems that was signed in Moscow on 26 May 1972 and became effective when ratified by the U.S. Senate on 3 August. A subsequent protocol in 1974 limited the antimissile sites to one each.

The arrangement continued for a number of years until it was challenged by the Strategic Defense Initiative (SDI) in 1983 accompanied by a narrow American definition of the treaty. The collapse of the USSR left the treaty in a vacuum, and eventually President **George W. Bush** announced the American withdrawal from the treaty on 13 December 2001, though under much criticism, to clear the way for a new U.S. **missile shield** technology. The ABM treaty was partially replaced by the signing of the **Strategic Offensive Reductions Treaty (SORT)** in May 2002 by Bush and Russian president **Vladimir Putin**.

ANTI-SEMITISM, RUSSIAN. Based on a common European Christian and Middle Eastern Islamic rivalry and opposition to Judaism, the Russian government developed legal restrictions against its Jewish subjects, who were acquired mainly by the partitioning of Poland in the last half of the 18th century. The "Pale of Settlement" regulations restricted these peoples to that area. This confinement was periodically loosened, especially during the liberal reform era of **Alexander II** in the 1860s and especially for relatively open admission to major Russian universities outside the "Pale." The appearance of Jews in considerable numbers outside the "Pale" and their participation in major occupations and in the growing revolutionary movement of the 1870s and 1880s caused resentment and reaction by "official Russia" and ordinary Russians (especially owing to a simultaneous Russification policy); **Konstantin Pobedonostsev** was among the high-ranking officials who voiced and carried out punitive measures against the Jewish population, encouraging them to emigrate, to pay extra dues and fines, or to convert to Orthodoxy. Not officially condoned—but also not discouraged—were violent incursions into Jewish settlements, called **pogroms**.

One result by the 1880s was the departure of large numbers of East European Jews to the United States, where they received initial assistance from immigrant aid societies but were left to settle in crowded ghettos, such as in the Lower East Side of New York, where they preserved their Russian-Jewish customs and language. In Russia, however, pogroms continued, usually during a few days after Easter, especially around 1881 and in 1905, when Jews were also associated with radical movements. Russian anti-Semitism also was spurred by the circulation of such devices as the fictitious "Protocols of the Elders of Zion" and a widespread belief in Jewish ritual sacrifice of Christians, as well as exaggerated reports of their economic and political dominance. The conservative government, pursuing policies of Russification, encouraged popular movements against the Jewish population. All of this caused an outcry by American Jews and new immigrants, resulting in the **passport question**, an additional strain on the relations between Russia and the United States in the early 20th century.

Some of the worst anti-Semitic violence took place after the assassination of **Alexander II** in 1881 and during the **Revolution of 1905**, **World War I**, and the **Russian Civil War**. This was followed, however, by a period of relative freedom and opportunity for Jews in the 1920s, owing to a high percentage of them within the Bolshevik leadership, many returning from exile or from re-immigration. A reaction to Jewish success as leaders in politics, science, and the arts led to a large number of Jewish victims of the purges and a lingering anti-Semitism throughout the 20th century. By the 1970s large numbers of Jews were pressing for the right to emigrate. After a restricted number were allowed to leave, the dam began to burst into a large migration, especially to Israel and the United States by the 1980s. *See also* BRIGHTON BEACH.

ARBATOV, GEORGY (1923–). Specialist on the United States; director of the **Institute of the U.S.A. and Canada (ISKAN)** of the Russian Academy of Sciences (1967–95). Along with **Yury Andropov**, **Alexander Yakovlev**, and the "men of the sixties," Arbatov strove for a more open, liberal approach to relations with the United States and served as a principal advisor to **Leonid Brezhnev**, Yury Andropov, **Mikhail Gorbachev**, and Boris Yeltsin on American affairs—but with limited success. In ISKAN, which concentrated on recent American history and politics, he nurtured a number of excellent Russian scholars with new perspectives, many of whom studied in the United States under the **Lacy-Zarubin** scholarly exchange agreement of 1958.

ARCHANGEL (ARKHANGELSK). The Russian port on the White Sea about 600 miles north of Moscow first became important in the mid-17th century when the London Muscovy Company opened direct navigation to Russia through the White Sea; it was Russia's early half-opened "window on the west." After the founding of St. Petersburg at the beginning of the 18th century, it naturally declined in importance because of its much greater distance from Western ports. Archangel reemerged, however, as an important access to Russia during **World War I**, when the Baltic and Black Seas were closed by German and Turkish control. In 1917, Russia acquired a new ally, the United States, which sent major shipments of military supplies into Archangel, and it regained its status as an alternate entry to Russia from the West, along with the new port of **Murmansk** that was free from ice all year. After the **Bolshevik Revolution**, the large accumulation of supplies in these ports over the summer of 1917—caused by breakdowns in Russian rail transportation—became an issue that resulted in the sending of an Allied expeditionary force in September 1918 to safeguard these materials. The Archangel Soviet, chaired by **Nikolai Chaikovsky**, a supporter of the anti-Bolshevik units, appealed for Allied support against the Bolshevik efforts to take over the region. The American embassy fled from **Vologda** in August 1918 to Archangel, but a few months later, in early 1919, it abandoned the city. For similar reasons the port would once again regain strategic significance during **World War II** as the summer terminus of the **northern convoy route**.

ARLE-TIETZ, CORETTA (1894–1951). African American Coretta Alfred went to Russia in 1910 from Philadelphia as part of a "Kristy Creole" duo and "Coretta and the Creole Girl" ensemble. She subsequently studied at the St. Petersburg Conservatory and the Moscow Conservatory during **World War I** and married her pianist, Boris Tiz (Tietz). Under the name of Arle-Tietz, or Alfred-Tietz, she attracted considerable Soviet attention in 1921 in her performance in the title role of Verdi's *Aida*. She was also instrumental in the introduction of American **jazz** into Russia in the 1920s via her syncopated jazz renditions with Louis Mitchell's Jazz Kings and with leading Soviet jazz ensembles. Remaining in Russia, she was better known in the 1930s and 1940s for her recordings and performances of Negro spirituals that included "Sometimes I Feel Like a Motherless Child" and "Roll, Jordan, Roll," especially for Soviet troops behind the lines during **World War II**. She is a leading example of a Soviet–American cross-cultural success story. Her grave is in the artists' section of the Novodevichy Monastery cemetery in Moscow.

ARMED NEUTRALITY, DECLARATIONS OF (1780, 1800). Annoyed by British practices at sea, especially directed at neutral shipping and opposition to Russian imperial advances, **Catherine the Great**, with the support of Vice Chancellor Nikita Panin, issued a surprisingly progressive and clearly formulated defense of the freedom of the seas, much of which would become the foundation of international maritime law. This move placed Russia at the head of a "league" of smaller northern European countries that included Sweden, Denmark, Prussia, and the Netherlands in defending the right of neutral countries to trade with countries at war, except with goods, narrowly, not broadly, defined as contraband. It also restricted the use of embargoes to being real (that is, enforced by naval presence) as opposed to being only on paper (a simple pronouncement). The declaration had the effect of encouraging neutral trade with the American colonies through the loose British blockade of North America, much to their benefit, and was widely interpreted as a Russian measure that favored the American cause of independence, though its actual intent was more self-serving. Twenty years later, Emperor Paul renewed a declaration of these principles, again aimed at similar British naval practices during the Napoleonic Wars that would be a major cause of the **War of 1812**.

ARMSTRONG, HAMILTON FISH (1893–1973). A founding editor of *Foreign Affairs Quarterly*, Armstrong devoted most of his life as managing editor of *Foreign Affairs Quarterly* and as secretary of its parent organization, the New York **Council on Foreign Relations**.

He followed the proclivity of his co–founding editor, **Archibald Cary Coolidge**, emphasizing the new Soviet Russia in his effort to secure and publish articles on that country's international outlook. He was born—and lived his whole life—in Greenwich Village of New York City, except for his university education at Princeton. Armstrong set something of a record in editing the leading American journal on current international relations for more than 50 years. His papers, as well as those of the Council, are in the Seeley Mudd Library at Princeton University. Armstrong also wrote a perceptive memoir, *Peace and Counter-Peace: From Wilson to Hitler* (1971).

ARMSTRONG, LOUIS "SATCHMO" (1900–1971). Although details are vague, Louis Armstrong acknowledged several times his debt to a Russian-Jewish family in his native New Orleans for the acquisition of his first trumpet and for two principal pieces of his large repertoire of jazz renditions: "Russian Lullaby" and "Ochi Chyorni" ("Dark Eyes"). Armstrong also corresponded with Adolph (Eddie) Rosner, a major European (Polish-Jewish and later Soviet) jazz musician, referring to him as the "white Louis Armstrong." They reportedly entered a trumpet contest in Italy in the 1930s that Armstrong won—narrowly. Influenced by Armstrong, Rosner would become the leading "big band" conductor in the USSR during **World War II**, basically the "Soviet Glenn Miller." Though invited, Armstrong did not visit the Soviet Union; a fellow jazz musician and orchestra leader, Duke Ellington, did tour the Soviet Union in 1972 with great success. *See also* JAZZ IN RUSSIA.

ASTOR, JOHN JACOB (1763–1848). As a classic story of "rags to riches," Astor arrived in the United States as an impoverished immigrant from Germany in the late 18th century and quickly became one of the leading American merchant-bankers and entrepreneurs. One of his several early enterprises involved the fur trade on the West Coast of North America, where his Pacific Fur Company was established at Astoria, Oregon. Though initially in rivalry with the **Russian America Company (RAC)** in their territories to the north, Astor shrewdly developed a cooperative arrangement, essentially creating a Russian–American monopoly over the Pacific fur resources, that furthered both companies' interests. He, especially through experienced captains such as John Ebbets, performed essential supply and marketing services for the Russian company in **Alaska**. A mission to St. Petersburg in 1810 by his son-in-law Adrian Bentzon consolidated this arrangement, which also expanded Astor's lucrative operations in Northwest America in return for assistance to the Russian company in regard to shipping and other matters. The RAC was able to survive the international turmoil of the time, as well as its own lack of resources, while Astor expanded what at the time was the largest American commercial empire.

ATOMIC DIPLOMACY. An interpretation by some "New Left" revisionist historians that the United States was mainly responsible for the **cold war** because of its use of "atomic blackmail." The theory originated from a particular reading of the evidence that the decision to drop atomic bombs on Hiroshima and Nagasaki was made not so much to shorten the war against Japan as to demonstrate American strength to the **Soviet Union** and to keep that ally out of a shared occupation of the Japanese islands; and this policy was followed up by an emphasis on building an atomic arsenal with detailed plans for the use of these weapons against the Union of Soviet Socialist Republics (USSR) with the aim to force that country to withdraw from Eastern Europe. The leading proponent of this interpretation was Gar Alperovitz in his *Atomic Diplomacy: Hiroshima and Potsdam, the Use of the Atomic Bomb and the American Confrontation with Soviet Power* (1965), re-argued in *The Decision to Use the Atomic Bomb and the Architecture of an American Myth* (1995). The theory is largely dismissed by other American cold war historians, such as Robert Ferrell and **John Gaddis**.

AUGUST COUP (1991). The time when USSR government officials attempted to force President **Mikhail Gorbachev** to resign—or to renounce his reform agenda. The immediate issue was the signing of a "union treaty," which would have granted more autonomy to the 15 constituent republics; some of them, especially the Baltic republics and Ukraine, were already moving rapidly in the direction of independence. Despite clear signs of the threat of action by conservatives, who had been installed by Gorbachev himself, and a direct warning from American ambassador **Jack Matlock**, the Soviet leader was unprepared for the event and suffered the humiliation of house arrest in Crimea. In Moscow popular support against this reactionary move rallied behind **Boris Yeltsin**, the dynamic president of the Russian republic and the site of his power, "the White House." The defeat of the "coup" was thus the result of Yeltsin's opposition and the failure of the Soviet military commanders to obey orders from the Kremlin. The resignation and arrest of coup leaders and the sudden rise of Yeltsin's authority and prestige, as well as in the other independent-minded republics, led to the isolation of Gorbachev and his resignation in December—and the end both of the Soviet Union and the Soviet Communist Party. This, along with a series of events in Eastern Europe signaled the end of the **cold war**, though tensions would revive between a strong **Russian Federation** under **Vladimir Putin** and **Dmitri Medvedev** and adjacent states, such as Georgia and Ukraine, and the West.

AUGUSTINE, FATHER (DMITRI GOLITSYN) (1770–1840). From one of the most distinguished and oldest Russian noble families, Dmitri Golitsyn was the son of the Russian ambassador to The Netherlands during the American Revolutionary War and thus a contemporary of **John Adams** at The Hague. His mother converted to Catholicism, along with her son. Golitsyn, partly because of the connection with Adams, immigrated to Baltimore in 1792 to study at St. Mary's Seminary under the name of Schmidt. Ordained as a priest in 1795 by Bishop John Carroll, as Father Augustine, he established a mission at Loretto in western Pennsylvania that quickly became known for its conservatism and missionary zeal—and for its founder's skill in horsemanship. Known also as Augustine Schmett (after his mother's maiden name) or as "Demetrius A. Galitzen," he was one of the first permanent Russian residents in America.

AUGUSTINE HEARD COMPANY. This large American enterprise involved in the Far Eastern trade was established by "Gus" Heard Sr. and pioneered in American–Chinese trade from the 1830s to the 1890s. The company he founded flourished through successive generations, holding a dominant position in Shanghai, Canton, and other Chinese ports. Besides being leaders in the American trade in the Pacific, the Heards developed a business relationship with the **Russian America Company (RAC)** that involved the exchange of furs from **Alaska** for Chinese tea to be shipped overland or later, more often, by ship to St. Petersburg. This also entailed family members and agents visiting Russia and serving as Russian consuls in Chinese ports in the 19th century. The Heard Company is an excellent example of Americans serving as middlemen between Russia and other countries and of an emerging American global economic role. The extensive records of the company are maintained in the archives of the Baker Library of the Harvard University Business School.

AUSTIN COMPANY. This Cleveland engineering firm was well known by the 1920s for its innovative "Austin method" of designing everything, down to the last nut and bolt, on the drawing boards before beginning any construction; the company built several large American factories, including the Pontiac plant in Michigan, according to that plan. Looking for American expertise and ingenuity for the **First Five-Year Plan,** Soviet agents were especially attracted to the Austin "planning" concept. The Soviet **American Trading Company (Amtorg),** based in New York, first approached **Ford** about an automobile plant, but that company reported that they made cars but did not build factories. This led to the contract with the Cleveland concern for the construction of what would be the largest automobile factory (machinery provided by Ford) in the world, about 15 miles north of **Nizhny Novgorod** on the Oka River.

The first half of the three-year contract was spent on designs in Cleveland. Then approximately 25 Austin engineers, including recent Yale graduate Allan Austin, grandson of the founder, came to the plant site to supervise the project, which included a novel model city for workers. The plant itself was the size of 10 football fields and began producing the GAZ 1 automobile and associated trucks, essentially the Ford Model A car and AA truck, in 1932 and helped usher the Soviet Union into the auto age. Though badly damaged by German bombing in the summer of 1941, the plant still performed essential service in assembling Studebaker military trucks on the surviving Ford assembly line in the open air. Later, the plant, still the largest in the **Russian Federation,** produced the basic family and taxi car, the "Volga." Austin Company, though no longer associated with the Austin family, is still in existence, building factories, office complexes, and airports and proud of its contribution to Soviet industrialization. It reestablished contact with the GAZ plant in Russia in the 1990s.

AUSTRIAN STATE TREATY (1955). In return for a neutralization (no offensive military capability), Austria became united and essentially part of the Western bloc during the **cold war**. The treaty was a result of relaxed tensions (the **Geneva Conference**) and the "**peaceful coexistence**" initiative of Soviet leader **Nikita Khrushchev**. Like Germany, Austria had been divided into occupation zones with the capital, as Berlin, also jointly administered by the victorious Allies. The result of the treaty was a resolution of the "Austrian problem" in contrast to the unresolved German problem by unification of zones, Soviet armed withdrawal, and the creation of a viable Austria, neutralized but democratic and oriented toward the West. The treaty, signed on 15 May, and the atmosphere of agreement instead of hostility led to the **Lacy-Zarubin** cultural exchange agreement in 1958 and the visit of Khrushchev to the United States the following year.

– B –

BABINE, ALEXIS (NE ALEKSEI BABIN) (1866–1930). A **Library of Congress** official, Babine was educated in Saratov and St. Petersburg. He left Russia as an employee on a German steamer in 1890 and entered Cornell University, where he earned a degree in American history while working as a cataloguer in the library (1891–96). He then accepted a position as librarian at Indiana University before moving on to Stanford in 1898. In 1902 Babine transferred to the Library of Congress, where he was instrumental in the acquisition of the **Yudin collection**, 80,000 volumes of rare books discovered in Siberia that remains a mainstay of the library's special collections on Russian studies. He soon, however, returned to Russia as an agent of the Associated Press in St. Petersburg, while writing one of the best histories of the United States in Russian. Back in Saratov to care for aging parents during **World War I** and the **Russian Civil War**, he taught English at the local university. Managing to escape Soviet Russia in 1923, Babine resumed his career as a librarian at Cornell, and then again returned to the Library of Congress in 1927, not long before his premature death from cancer in 1930. He left a remarkable memoir of his Russian experiences during war and revolution, edited by Donald Raleigh, *A Russian Civil War Diary: Alexis Babine in Saratov, 1917–1922* (1988).

BAIDUKOV, GEORGY (1907–1994). A Soviet pilot, sometimes referred to as "the Charles Lindbergh of Russia," Baidukov was the chief of a three-man crew of a Soviet plane that made the first nonstop flight from the Soviet Union to the United States via the Arctic Circle route in 1937. The flight received much attention at the time in the press, especially the reception of the crew by President **Franklin D. Roosevelt** and General **George Marshall**, and through Baidukov's own description of the flight published the same year. He returned to the United States in 1941 as a member of a Soviet air force delegation to supervise the shipments of military planes and aviation fuel through the **lend-lease** program.

BAKER, JAMES ADDISON III (1930–). As a Republican Party activist, Baker advised the administrations of **Ronald Reagan** and **George H. W. Bush** on foreign and defense policies. He served as secretary of state for the latter at a critical time, when the Soviet Union was in transition out of Communism and state-controlled economy (1989–90) and consulted with **Mikhail Gorbachev** and Foreign Minister **Eduard Shevardnadze** on easing the resulting international tensions. He accompanied the president to a summit conference in Malta (December 1989) and in negotiations on the first Iraq war, on the unification of Germany, and in controlling nuclear weapon proliferation. Baker recounted his experiences in *Politics and Diplomacy* (1996).

BAKER, NEWTON DEIHL (1871–1937). As an influential member (secretary of war) of the administration of **Woodrow Wilson,** Baker was a firm opponent in 1917 of American military aid to Russia, which he considered a waste of important resources; he believed Russia would leave the war one way or another during **World War I** and that the United States needed all possible funding and materiel for its own war effort on the western front in 1917. This turned out to be the case, but his opposition to assistance for Russia may have prevented, or at least slowed, crucial aid for the government of **Alexander Kerensky** during a critical period, May–June 1917, as well as for a major publicity effort to forestall Bolshevism urged by Ambassador **David Francis**. Ironically, Baker was a strong advocate of American military intervention in Russia, formed the **American Expeditionary Force (AEF)** to Siberia, and presented its commander, General **William S. Graves**, with his secret orders personally in July 1918 at Union Station in Kansas City.

BAKHMETEFF ARCHIVE. This major collection of papers housed in the Rare Book and Manuscript Collection in the Butler Library of Columbia University was founded by former Russian **Provisional Government** ambassador to the United States, **Boris Bakhmeteff**, and others, such as Professors Phillip Mosely and **Geroid T. Robinson**. Organized and maintained for many years by Lev Magerovsky, the archive is one of the most valuable collections of papers of Russian émigrés, such as **Paul Miliukov**, and Americans who were involved with Russian affairs, especially during the period of the **Bolshevik Revolution** and **Russian Civil War**. Bakhmeteff's own extensive papers are supplemented by many others, such as those of Alan Wardwell, **Charles R. Crane**, and Professors **Michael Florinsky** and Robinson of Columbia. Supplementary materials continue to be added. Along with the collections of the **Hoover Institution** at Stanford, the archive contains resources for many future research projects.

BAKHMETEFF, BORIS (NE BAKHMETEV) (1880–1951). Ambassador of the Russian **Provisional Government** to the United States (1917–23) and professor of engineering at Columbia University, Bakhmeteff was born in Tiflis (Tbilisi) in the Georgian province of the Russian Empire. Bakhmeteff studied engineering in St. Petersburg, which included a year of study in the United States (1904). He returned to Russia to teach theoretical mechanics and hydraulic engineering at the University of St. Petersburg. In 1915, Bakhmeteff was selected to head a technical purchasing commission to the United States to place orders and supervise previous ones on behalf of the Russian war effort. His knowledge of English and technical and communicative skills impressed his hosts.

After the **February Revolution** and the elevation of **Paul Miliukov** to the post of minister of foreign affairs, Bakhmeteff was designated ambassador to the United States by the new Russian government. Assuming control of the large embassy building on 16th Street in Washington, as well as all of the Russian business and political affairs in the United States, Bakhmeteff skillfully cultivated the support of the U.S. government, which was now a military and political ally. One result was the award of several substantial U.S. loans to the Provisional Government that were used largely for the purchase of badly needed military supplies that would arrive at Russian ports later in 1917 and cause concern about their eventual destination—Germany or Bolshevik. After the **Bolshevik Revolution** in November 1917, the United States, avoiding recognition of the new government, maintained official relations with Bakhmeteff, who continued to supervise expenditures from the loans to maintain the embassy and in order to deal with the extensive legal disputes regarding cancelled military orders in the United States after Russia left the war. An uncertain amount of these funds was also used to aid anti-Bolshevik forces and provide American "support" for the former government, such as the expenses of the **American Railway Service Corps** in 1918–21. Under pressure by a number of individuals and organizations that were either disenchanted with the government of **Alexander Kerensky**, in favor of recognition of the legitimacy of the Soviet government, or both, Bakhmeteff resigned his official post in April 1922, leaving the remaining legal problems and maintenance of the embassy in charge of his financial attaché, **Sergei Ughet**. After brief and largely unsuccessful careers as a freelance consultant on Russian trade and as a lecturer, Bakhmeteff resumed his earlier career as a professor of civil engineering at Columbia University and continued to be a modest and moderate spokesman for a liberal Russia at public forums. He left a legacy in the rich **Bakhmeteff Archive** of papers of Russian political émigrés and Americans involved in the complicated affairs of revolutionary Russia.

BAKHMETEV, GEORGY (1848–1928). The last ambassador of the Russian Imperial Government to the United States (1911–17), this experienced Russian diplomat (having the same surname as his successor but of no relation), owed his appointment to his 1877 marriage to American socialite Mary Beale, whose family was influential in Washington as publishers of the *Washington Post* and a special request made to President **William Howard Taft**. As a cautious and unimaginative diplomat, Bakhmetev failed to solve sensitive problems in Russian–American relations, such as the **passport question** that involved Russian refusals of visas to Jews for travel to Russia. He and his wife, however, maintained a lavish and active social life at the imposing Russian embassy on 16th Street that attracted both praise and criticism. After the **February Revolution**, he resigned in protest and spent the remainder of his life as one of many unhappy Russian political émigrés in Paris.

BAKUNIN, MIKHAIL (1814–1876). A Russian revolutionary and international anarchist from an aristocratic Russian background, Bakunin rose quickly to fame during the Revolution of 1848 in Europe and as a rival of Karl Marx in establishing revolutionary goals for the future. Arrested in the 1850s in Russia and exiled to Siberia, Bakunin escaped in 1861 and crossed the Pacific and the United States to reach London, where he associated with a contemporary Russian revolutionary, Alexander Herzen. Active in the First International, Bakunin's conflict with Marx led to his expulsion from that organization and the initiation of a "Russian path to world revolution." Bakunin's ideas inspired later American anarchist and radical movements, a leading exponent being **Alexander Berkman** in the 1890s, and helped inspire the formation of the **Industrial Workers of the World (IWW)** in the early 20th century.

BALABANOVA, ANGELICA (1878–1965). Russian revolutionary born in Chernigov of Jewish parentage, Balabanova was soon recognized for her intellectual and social skills, receiving a doctoral degree from the University of Brussels. She quickly moved into the international socialist world at the turn of the century by serving as secretary to Benito Mussolini and through an attachment to **Maxim Gorky** during his stay at Capri. She met **Vladimir Lenin** there and again in Switzerland during **World War I**. She returned to Russia in April 1917 to support the Bolshevik cause and to be an active worker for the **Comintern**, associated with American Communists **John Reed** and **Louise Bryant** at its first congress. Balabanova soon became disillusioned with Soviet Communism and left Russia in 1921 to settle in the United States in 1924, living in relative poverty while writing for socialist publications and penning a remarkable memoir, *My Life as a Rebel* (1938).

BALANCHINE, GEORGE (NE GEORGY BALANCHIVADZE) (1904–1983). Ballet master and choreographer, son of a Georgian-Russian composer, Balanchine was born in St. Petersburg and studied at the Imperial School of Ballet, the St. Petersburg Conservatory, and the Marinsky Ballet School during the period of **World War I** and the **Russian Revolution**. He performed in Europe with a Russian ballet troupe in the 1920s before devoting the rest of his career to choreography, first in Great Britain and, by 1933, in the United States, where he directed the ballet at the Metropolitan Opera House (1934–37) and founded the School of American Ballet; in 1948, he became the long-term artistic director and choreographer of the New York City Ballet. In this role he was noted for his demanding direction, reinterpretations of classical ballet, and innovations in new music and styles, as well as for his frequent and exhausting world tours.

BALIEFF, NIKITA (1877–1936). Russian American actor and entertainer. Along with Will Rogers, Balieff was one of the most popular comedians and vaudevillians in the United States during the 1920s and 1930s. Of Armenian origin, born in Rostov-on-Don, Balieff joined the company of the illustrious **Moscow Art Theater (MAT)** in the early 20th century. He soon found, however, that his talents were more suitable for light entertainment. In 1908 he established in Moscow the "Letushaya Mysh" ("Fledermaus" or "The Bat") nightclub in a below–ground level (cave) cabaret, mainly for the benefit of late-night, after-theater patrons and casts. Excelling in satire and even winning the support of government authorities, Balieff soared to success. His venue, however, did not fit well with Bolshevik taste after 1917, so he emigrated and reassembled his company in Paris in 1919 under the name *Chauve Souris*, retaining the "bat" name. Discovered by American talent searchers, he and his troupe were imported to New York in 1922, where they took Broadway by storm, establishing new records for successive full houses and easily outstripping their main rival, the Ziegfeld Follies. In their performances, a variety of Russian vaudeville acts were superintended by Balieff, a large, rotund (Zero Mostel–like) individual, who scampered around in the background delivering insincere, inappropriate, but penetrating comments on all and sundry in broken English, a prototype of the master of ceremonies in the musical version of "Cabaret."

Balieff was featured on the cover of *Time Magazine* in 1927. The "Who's Who" of American theater—such as John Barrymore, Lillian Gish, and Al Jolson—were often found in attendance at *Chauve Souris*. The widely acclaimed performances in Russian also convinced New York impresarios of the probability of success of MAT, which was subsequently well received during its 1923 and 1924 tours of the United States. Balieff and *Chauve Souris* toured worldwide in subsequent years, returning to Paris and New York for regular seasons, until its founder's sudden death in New York in 1936, just after starring in a film, *Once in a Blue Moon*. Balieff was one of many great entertainers of that particular era in both Russian and American performance history, but perhaps the most neglected. More than a thousand people, however, attended his funeral in New York.

BARANOV, ALEXANDER (1747–1819). A Russian merchant and first chief administrator (governor) of the **Russian America Company (RAC)** territories in the North Pacific and North America from 1797 to 1818, Baranov was born in Olonets province and established his credentials as a successful entrepreneur in Moscow before heading east to Irkutsk in 1780. There he joined the fur company of **Grigory Shelikhov**. As a leading *promyshlenik* (fur hunting and trading entrepreneur) in the lucrative Siberian fur business, he earned respect from the central government and from **Nikolai Rezanov**, who promoted the expansion of the "harvesting" of sea otters to the coasts of North America. On behalf of this enterprise, Shelikhov ventured as far as Unalaska and **Kodiak** in the Aleutian Islands by 1790 and in 1795 visited the future site of **Sitka**. Upon the establishment of the government chartering of the Russian America Company in 1797, the experienced Baranov was designated the chief administrator (or governor) of the territory that it claimed under its jurisdiction in the North Pacific and in Northwest America. After first establishing his "command post" at Kodiak, the first Russian settlement in America, Baranov moved the administrative center to "New Archangel," later known as Sitka, on an island off the coast of southern **Alaska**, that was more central to territorial supervision. Though Baranov faced difficult relations with the natives (Tlingits) of the area, he nevertheless ruled and conquered effectively by conversion of most of them to the Russian Orthodox religion with the help of active church missionaries.

In consideration of the endurance of the company's fur profits, Baranov welcomed the assistance of the **Bostonians**, American ship captains who provided the vital shipments of furs to China in the early 19th century. His enterprises were also advanced by Russian naval explorations, such as those of Ivan Kruzenstern and **Ivan Kuskov** to California (1803–06), and the mission of Rezanov (1805) that resulted in the expansion of the Russian presence in America into California at **Fort Ross**. From these initiatives and the thriving fur trade, Baranov built a new Russian empire on behalf of the RAC and established its "capital" in North America with a striking Russian Orthodox church and a substantial company administrative building, the "Baranov Castle," which are still featured on contemporary Alaskan cruises. He probably deserved the title of "Lord of Alaska."

BARLOW, JOEL (1754–1812). A well-known American writer and diplomat, Barlow achieved European recognition with his satirical poetry and essays about the results of the French Revolution, for example, *Hasty-Pudding* (1793). A friend of Semen Vorontsov, Russian ambassador to Great Britain, Barlow facilitated a direct exchange of letters between **Thomas Jefferson** and **Alexander I** that would lead to diplomatic recognition between Russia and the United States. Because of his knowledge of European affairs and proven diplomatic ability (as consul in Algiers), Barlow was appointed U.S. minister to France in 1811 expressly to sort out the confusion of the impact of the Continental System on American–European commerce. Pressing his mission, Napoleon I agreed to meet him at Vilna, in French-occupied Russia in 1812. He arrived in time to witness the horrible results of the French retreat, which he immortalized in a condemnation of war and tyranny (Napoleon's) in "Advice to a Raven in Russia." He died shortly afterward in Zarnowiec (near Krakow). *See also* ADAMS, JOHN QUINCY.

BARNES, RALPH W. (1899–1940). As a distinguished reporter on Europe for the *New York Herald Tribune*, Ralph Barnes won the respect of colleagues, such as **Walter Duranty** of the *New York Times*, from his debut in Paris in 1926 until his premature death aboard a British bomber that crashed in Yugoslavia in 1940. He was thus one of the first American casualties of **World War II**. Barnes was especially known for his perceptive and critical reports from Moscow for the *Herald Tribune* during the period from spring 1931 to September 1935 that included the great industrial campaign of the **First Five-Year Plan**. His career, especially in Moscow, is recaptured by Barbara Mahoney in *Dispatches and Dictators: Ralph Barnes for the Herald Tribune* (2002).

BARROWS, DAVID PRESCOTT (1873–1954). After receiving his Ph.D. from the University of Chicago (1897), Barrows taught at the University of California and served with distinction in **World War I**, mainly in the Far East. He was then appointed chief intelligence officer for the **American Expeditionary Force (AEF)** in **Siberia** under General **William S. Graves** (March 1918–March 1919). As director of a sizable intelligence staff, he was instrumental in advising against direct engagement in the complex **Russian Civil War** in Siberia. Resuming his scholarly career in 1919, he was elected president of the University of California, Berkeley, was a visiting faculty member at a number of universities, received several fellowships, wrote a number of scholarly books, and participated in the Institute of Politics in Williamstown, Massachusetts, as a prominent opponent of Japanese expansionist policies in the Pacific arena.

BARTON, CLARA (1821–1912). For many years a school teacher in Massachusetts, Barton volunteered for dangerous service in the Union army as a nurse on the battlefields and devoted the rest of her long life to humanitarian causes. As a founder of the **American Red Cross (ARC)**, she was a strong supporter and leader of the U.S. effort to send food shipments and medical supplies to Russia during the 1892–93 famine, though she was initially hesitant about the inclusion of corn products that were unfamiliar to Russians and about the ARC not being given prominence in relief distribution. Barton also inspired the formation of Red Cross organizations in other countries, including Russia; she finally visited Russia herself in 1903 for an International Congress of the Red Cross in St. Petersburg. Her spirit of inspiring the ARC mission of relief abroad would become a symbol of American charity through the 20th century and into the next.

BARYSHNIKOV, MIKHAIL (1948–). Born in Riga, the son of a Soviet army officer, Baryshnikov joined the Leningrad Kirov Ballet Company in 1967 and quickly became a highly regarded star with a wide repertoire. While touring Canada with the company in 1974, he defected and joined the American Ballet Theatre in New York, becoming its artistic director in 1979; with that company, he staged many classical and modern ballets and toured widely. He also starred in film productions and on television. After retirement from dance performance, he became a noted elder statesman of American ballet and a gifted actor on the Broadway stage.

BAY OF PIGS (1961). A misconceived and unsuccessful invasion of Cuba staged by about 1,500 Cuban exiles supported by the **Central Intelligence Agency (CIA)** and by the administration of **John F. Kennedy**. Aimed at the overthrow of the Communist-leaning and anti-American Cuban government of Fidel Castro, the project was doomed from the beginning by poor planning and lack of adequate training and military support and was widely condemned by the Soviet leaders, who had adopted Cuba as a client nation. The resulting defeat led to plans for a larger engagement with American participation, but it also inspired a similar but more dangerous Soviet adventure to place intermediate-range missiles in Cuba the following year that precipitated the **Cuban missile crisis**.

BEATTY, BESSIE (1886–1947). From California, Beatty began her journalistic career as a reporter for the *Los Angeles Herald* (1904–07) and the *San Francisco Bulletin* (1907–18). The latter newspaper assigned her to Russia to cover the revolutionary activities in 1917. There she associated with other American journalists, who included **John Reed**, **Louise Bryant**, and Albert Rhys Williams, and developed contacts with Soviet leaders **Vladimir Lenin** and **Leon Trotsky**. Beatty captured the Russian turmoil eloquently in *The Red Heart of Russia* (1918), a compilation of her articles. Subsequently, she was an editor of women's magazines *McCall's* and *Good Housekeeping* and had her own daily radio program in the 1930s.

BELIAVSKAYA, IRINA (1915–). A distinguished Russian historian of American history, Beliavskaya made her mark for objective scholarship during the **cold war** with a number of studies concentrating on early U.S. history involving the impact of **World War I** on American economic institutions, biographies of Robert La Follette and **Theodore Roosevelt**, and studies of American reforms at the beginning of the 20th century. She is also a model of modest demeanor and an inspiration to younger scholars of the **Center for North American Studies** of the Russian **Academy of Sciences**, where her striving for objective history was protected by **Grigory Sevostianov** and **Nikolai Bolkhovitinov**.

BERDAN, HIRAM (1823–1893). From service as a Union army ordnance officer during the **American Civil War**, Berdan's improvements in breech-loading rifle mechanisms and accompanying metallic cartridges attracted the attention of a visiting Russian officer to the United States, Alexander Gorlov. Though Berdan lost a postwar contract bid for the employment of his improved rifle by the U.S. army to Remington and Springfield, his model was produced by the Colt works in Hartford, Connecticut, for a few years and then acquired by the Russian army with modifications by Gorlov and others. Berdan and his family resided in Russia for several months in 1869 to supervise the initial manufacture of his modified "Berdanka," which—with subsequent improvements—served as the basic Russian infantry weapon through **World War I**, manufactured at the Izhevsk arms works and financed by the Russian Nobel brothers. Besides being durable and simple in design, one distinguishing feature of the Russian Berdanka was that the bayonets were permanently attached and not removable, naturally something of a problem for new recruits and in parades and mass formations. Berdan's Russian adventures are adeptly recorded by Joseph Bradley in *Guns for the Tsar* (1990).

BERING SEA. This large body of water in the North Pacific bordered by **Alaska**, the Aleutian Islands, Kamchatka, and the coast of **Siberia** is known for its cold climate and fog but also as a rich fishing ground and as the main habitat of the **fur seals** of the **Pribylov Islands**. During the Bering Sea Fur Seal Controversy, adjudged by an international court of arbitration in Paris in 1893, the United States claimed that the sea was U.S. territory, purchased along with Alaska in 1867. The U.S. delegation produced a map from the purchase negotiation that showed a line drawn from the **Bering Strait** through the western extension of the Aleutian Islands as proof that the purchase included most of the sea. The general law of freedom of the seas, however, prevailed, and the Bering Sea remained international waters, much to the detriment of the large numbers of seals that were being harvested without restriction by pelagic hunting.

BERING STRAIT. Between northeast Asia and northwest North America connecting the Arctic Ocean with the **Bering Sea**, the strait, probably initially discovered by Cossack explorer Simon Dezhnev in the 17th century, became a border between Russia and the United States after the purchase of **Alaska**. It was the scene of geographic and exploring interest in the last half of the 19th century in the search for a northeast passage between the American continent and Europe via the Siberian coast. The unfortunate American *Jeannette* **Expedition** of 1879–81 was an example. Though the strait is more than 50 miles wide, the Diomede Islands in the middle are divided between the two countries and separate political jurisdictions by only a few miles, causing some tension during the **cold war**. With the emergence of formal Russian claims to a large portion of the land under the Arctic in 2007, the Bering Strait again attracts attention for the potential establishment of the Arctic zones of the two countries.

BERING, VITUS (1681–1741). Of Danish origin, Bering was contracted by Peter the Great to explore the Pacific coast of the Russian Empire with the goal of determining whether Asia and North America were separated by water. His first voyage left the Baltic in 1725, just before the death of the emperor, and would be inconclusive by 1730, although it would define the coasts of the Kamchatka peninsula. A second "Kamchatka expedition," authorized by Catherine I, was better organized from Okhotsk bases, beginning in 1733. The main voyage, begun only in 1740, proved the separation of the continents and sighted the **Alaska** mainland, though many of the crews of the two ships and Bering himself perished in this successful attempt, which concluded in 1741. One result was the prominent appearance of the name of Bering on the map for the straits and sea that the expedition charted, although the main "discoverer" was probably A. I. Chirikov, who commanded one of the ships.

BERKMAN, ALEXANDER (1870–1936). Born in Vilnius, educated in St. Petersburg, and related to the Russian Peoples' Will leader Maxim Natanson, Berkman immigrated to the United States in 1888 and joined the anarchist movement, influenced by **Bakunin**. He was a leader of the volatile Homestead Strike (1892). After sensationally attempting the assassination of one of the leaders of the steel industry, Henry Frick, Berkman was arrested and sentenced to prison for 22 years. For this he also became a celebrated martyr of the radical movement. Released, however, in 1906, Berkman edited the anarchist journal *Mother Earth*, was an organizer of the **Industrial Workers of the World (IWW)**, and became a close associate of **Emma Goldman**. He was arrested again in 1917 along with her, and they were both deported to Soviet Russia in 1919. Berkman remained, however, an advocate of revolutionary terror, supported the radical opponents to Bolshevism, and, as in the case of Goldman, soon became disillusioned with the Soviet style of Communism. They left Russia in 1921 to spend most of their remaining years in unhappy exile—radicals with a cause but without a home—in Western Europe. Depressed by the international decline of idealistic anarchism and by his poor health, Berkman committed suicide in 1936.

BERLIN BLOCKADE AND AIRLIFT (1948–1949). A major crisis of the **cold war**. The Western occupation zones of Germany were becoming united and rehabilitated through the **Marshall Plan** in 1948, while the Soviet Union, recovering from its own devastation, was still consolidating Communist rule in Poland, Czechoslovakia, and Hungary. Meanwhile, a negotiated peace with Germany remained elusive. The Western occupation zones of Berlin, the former German capital, were a sore point, since the infusion of American aid brought about a stark contrast between the zones and Soviet East Berlin. A Soviet effort to force Western withdrawal was initiated in June 1948 by the cutting off of land and water routes through the Soviet Eastern zone of Germany into the city. The earlier-stipulated air corridors, however, were left open. The Western allies, chiefly the United States and Great Britain, responded with a massive airlift of supplies into the city, consisting mainly of fuel and food, which proved to be a surprising success owing to pilot experience and expertise, aircraft availability, and the use of radar for coordinated navigation and landing. A total of 277,000 flights landed, often arriving at three-minute intervals and delivering an average of 8,000 tons per day.

As a result, West Berlin was better supplied than East Berlin during the winter of 1948–49. Having lost both the physical and moral battle, the Soviet leaders called the whole thing off and lifted the blockade in May 1949. The Berlin blockade and airlift were proof that the West could resist Soviet aggressive moves without causing a major conflict and that Berlin would remain an embarrassing and significant Western democratic outpost behind the **iron curtain**. The problem of the ease of exit through East Berlin for subjects of the "captive nations" of Eastern Europe culminated in the erection of the **Berlin Wall** in 1961, which would become a symbol of the **iron curtain**.

BERLIN CONFERENCE. *See* POTSDAM CONFERENCE.

BERLIN, IRVING (NE IZZY BALIN) (1888–1988). Born in Odessa (a few accounts claiming **Siberia**), Berlin immigrated with his parents to America in 1893, where he grew up on the Lower East Side of New York and soon became one of the most popular songwriters of the 20th century, writing the music and lyrics to such hits as "Alexander's Ragtime Band," "God Bless America," "Easter Parade," and "White Christmas." Along with George Gershwin, whose family was also from Russia, he represented the East European Jewish imprint upon African American **jazz** themes (ragtime, swing, and blues), the American compositions that defined a century of popular music.

BERLIN WALL (1961–1989). After the unsuccessful effort to force the Western powers out of their occupied zones of Berlin by means of a **Berlin blockade** in 1948–49, Soviet leader **Nikita Khrushchev** resorted to the erection of a substantial barrier between Eastern and Western zones in 1961, especially in dividing Berlin physically by concrete barriers. This became a symbol of the division of Europe and of Western solidarity in opposition (President **John F. Kennedy's**

visit: "Ich bin ein Berliner"). More perhaps than anything else, the Berlin Wall symbolized the **cold war**, the **iron curtain**, and the failure of the Soviet system to keep its subjects confined to their region. Similarly, the destruction of the wall in 1989 heralded the end of the cold war, the collapse of the Soviet Union and the Communist threat, and the subsequent reunification of Germany.

BERTRON, SAMUEL READING (1865–1938). As a leading New York international financier, Bertron was included as a member of the special mission to Russia in 1917 led by **Elihu Root**. He became an advocate of substantial loans to Russia in 1917, pleading this cause repeatedly to President **Woodrow Wilson**, who was advised against it by Secretary of War **Newton Baker**. The advocates in favor of loans included **Cyrus McCormick** and **Raymond Robins**, and they finally achieved the first major commitment in August 1917, too late to make a difference for **Alexander Kerensky** and the **Provisional Government**. Bertron continued to be a promoter of Soviet–American business after the revolution as a director of the **American Russian Chamber of Commerce** and a strong proponent of recognition of the Soviet government in the 1920s.

BESSMERTNYKH, ALEXANDER (1933–). A career Soviet diplomat, Bessmertnykh worked in the Ministry of Foreign Affairs (1957–60 and 1966–70), in the **United Nations** Secretariat (1960–66), and as counselor in the Soviet embassy in Washington (1970–83). After a stint during the tenure of **Mikhail Gorbachev** as assistant minister of foreign affairs, where he helped chart Gorbachev's foreign policy of "**new thinking**," he was appointed ambassador to the United States in 1990, earning the distinction of being the last to represent formally the Soviet Union. Bessmertnykh later in retirement served in honorary and consultative roles at universities and in foreign policy groups and by 2007 was a leading organizer of the "conference" of former American and Russian ambassadors that was devoted to heading off a new "**cold war**."

BILLINGTON, JAMES H. (1929–). Before becoming Librarian of Congress (1987–), Billington was a historian of Russia. He graduated from Princeton University and received his doctorate from Oxford

University while a Rhodes Scholar. Billington then taught Russian history at Harvard University (1957–62) and Princeton (1963–74). From 1974 to 1987 he was director of the Woodrow Wilson International Center for Scholars and founded a branch, the **Kennan Institute for Advanced Russian Studies**. His many scholarly publications include *The Icon and the Axe* (1966), *Fire in the Minds of Men* (1980), and *The Face of Russia* (1998). At the **Library of Congress** he initiated several programs pertaining to Russian–American relations, such as the microfilming of the records of the **Communist Party of the United States (CPUSA)** from Russian archives and the "Meeting of Frontiers" online web site.

BLACKWELL, ALICE STONE (1857–1950). As a leading women's rights advocate, Blackwell continued the ardent campaign charted by her parents, Henry Blackwell and Lucy Stone, through the early 20th century as a leading suffragette; she adopted a Russian revolutionary, **Ekaterina Breshko-Breshkovskaya**, and actively supported her cause of a liberal, democratic Russia—one that appeared a real possibility after the **February Revolution** in 1917. Blackwell sponsored the lecture engagements of the Russian populist before and after the **Bolshevik Revolution**, campaigning for and contributing to her relief causes. Blackwell also promoted the idea of a Russian democracy through her social campaigns and publication of her biography of Breshkovskaya in 1928.

BOCHKAREVA, COLONEL MARIA (1889–1920). A Russian female soldier and officer (1915–18), Bochkareva achieved renown in 1917 as commander of the first women's battalion in the Russian army, sponsored by the government of **Alexander Kerensky**. In an innovative move, women were recruited for direct combat service on the front lines. The idea was to try to bolster the male ranks by proving that women had the will and capability of fighting. This novel experiment attracted wide attention in the United States, since it showed that Russia had gone well beyond what American women's rights groups advocated—equal military responsibility and service. Though demonstrating true courage and ability in direct combat in June, the limited number of women combatants had little possibility of reversing the collapse of the eastern front in the summer of 1917.

Bochkareva was celebrated as a heroine, especially during a visit to the United States in 1918, when she brought President **Woodrow Wilson** to tears in an audience at the White House. She also won a symbolic medal for bravery for returning to "her people" to face certain execution by the Bolsheviks.

BODISKO, ALEXANDER (1786–1854). As minister to the United States (1837–54), Bodisko was a collegial, socially active representative who meshed well with the Southern aristocratic dominance of Congress and American foreign policy during his tenure in Washington. He leaned toward the Whig Party and cultivated friendships with Henry Clay and Daniel Webster. Bodisko was instrumental in consolidating close relations between the two countries that involved expanded trade and reinforcing a mutual Anglophobia that set the stage for American friendship to Russia during the **Crimean War** and Russian support of the Union during the **American Civil War**. In this he was ably assisted by a son of his first marriage, Vladimir, who served as a secretary and courier. Arriving in the United States a widower, Bodisko surprised Washington society in 1840 by his marriage in his fifties to a teenage Georgetown debutante, Harriet Brooke Williams. His stately (and surviving) Georgetown mansion (3322 O Street) quickly became a hub of the capital's social life, the marriage endearing him to many by the birth of several children and by his regular lavish entertainments that were continued and expanded at summer resorts in Saratoga and Newport. For many years the dean of the diplomatic colony in Washington, Bodisko suffered an accidental death by a fall from a horse in Rock Creek Park in January 1854, leaving his secretary and successor, **Eduard Stoekl**, to pursue American friendship through the Crimean War and the American Civil War as minister. His length of tenure as head of the Russian mission in the United States would remain unsurpassed until that of **Anatoly Dobrynin** in the 1960s–80s.

BOGDANOV, PETER (1882–1939). A leading Soviet economic expert and director of the **American Trading Corporation (Amtorg)** (1930–34), Bogdanov joined the **Bolshevik** faction of the **Russian Social Democratic Labor Party (RSDLP)** in 1905, becoming a reliable and flexible party worker. In 1921 he supported **Vladimir**

Lenin's retreat from the extreme measures of War Communism to the **New Economic Policy (NEP)** and served as chairman of the Soviet Supreme Economic Council (1921–25). After a few years directing an economic delegation in London, Bogdanov was appointed head of the rapidly expanding Amtorg in New York. He supervised its operation during a very busy and responsible period that saw many major contracts with leading American companies negotiated. Bogdanov thus deserves considerable credit for the implementation of the **First Five-Year Plan**. He was transferred back to London and then to economic posts in Moscow until his arrest and execution during the Great Purge.

BOHLEN, CHARLES E. "CHIP" (1904–1974). Entering the U.S. foreign service in 1929, Bohlen was one of a small group of experts on Russia nurtured by **Robert F. Kelley** that included **George F. Kennan** and **Loy Henderson**, with whom he served as the first contingent of the American embassy staff in Moscow in 1934. In an apparent attempt to break up the "Kelley control" of the Soviet diplomatic scene, Bohlen was transferred in 1940 to Tokyo, where he would be at the beginning of **World War II** (as Kennan in Berlin). He reemerged, however, in 1942 as a leading interpreter and advisor to President **Franklin D. Roosevelt** at wartime conferences in **Tehran** (1944), **Yalta** (1945), and **Potsdam** (1945). Valued highly for this service, Bohlen would remain a leading advisor and high-ranking official in the Moscow embassy and in the State Department until his appointment as ambassador. In that position he managed the American presence in Moscow through the volatile times of the ascendancy of **Nikita Khrushchev**, the **"Secret Speech"** (1956), the **Hungarian Revolution** (1956), and the transition to **peaceful coexistence**.

BOKER, GEORGE HENRY (1823–1890). As U.S. minister to Russia (1875–78) Boker was one of the few American diplomats to Russia with previous international experience, having been transferred to the Russian post from the Ottoman Empire in 1875; this was especially useful for his service on the eve of, and during, the Russo–Turkish War, 1877–78. His main contributions were in facilitating access to the battle fronts for American observers and journalists, such as **Januarius**

MacGahan and **Francis Greene**, and furthering the diplomatic and historian careers of **Eugene Schuyler**. His support for Russia promoted American sympathy for the Russian "crusader" cause, as depicted in a Thomas Nast cartoon on the cover of *Harper Weekly Magazine* (26 May 1877).

BOLKHOVITINOV, NIKOLAI (1930–2008). As a scholar of early Russian–American relations from the 1760s, Bolkhovitinov quickly established a reputation in the Soviet Union and in the United States as an honest and direct interpreter of documentary evidence, often in contradiction with Soviet **cold war** preferences. His initial work on the **Monroe Doctrine** and many subsequent books on Russian–American relations are acknowledged as fundamental studies in the profession by American scholars. His works on Russians in America in the 18th and 19th centuries, based on both American and Russian archival materials, provide the foundation for many future studies, especially in regard to the history of **Russian America**. Bolkhovitinov worked closely with, and actively supported, a remarkable generation of scholars of American history that included academician **Grigory Sevostianov** and historians **Gennady Kuropiatnik**, **Irina Beliavskaya**, Mikhail Al'perovich, **Alexander Nikoliukin**, **Robert Ivanov**, and Eduard Ivanian. He also helped nurture a new generation of Russian Americanists that included Vladimir Pozniakov, Boris Shpotov, Larisa Troitskaya, Alexander Petrov, Vladimir Sogrin, Sergei Zhuk, Viktoria Zhuravleva, Ivan Kurilla, Ilya Gaiduk, and others.

Bolkhovitinov serves as editor of ***Amerikanskii Ezhegodnik*** (*American Yearbook*) and multivolume works, such as a monumental *Istoriia Russkoi Amerika* (*History of Russian America*) (1997–2000). As the director of the **Center for North American Studies** of the Institute of General History of the Academy of Sciences, Bolkhovitinov has been instrumental in stimulating (and inspiring) the study of American history in the Soviet Union and the Russia Federation. His considerable contributions to historical scholarship in this field were recognized by a *festschrift*, *Russkoe otkryti Ameriki* (*The Russian Discovery of America*) (2002) and the award of honorary membership in the American Historical Association at its annual meeting in Philadelphia in January 2006. Unfortunately, he succumbed to an illness that year and was unable to be present to accept the award. He was, however, present and honored at a conference commemorating the 200th anniversary of the beginning of diplomatic relations between the United States and Russia in Moscow in November 2007.

BOLSHEVIK REVOLUTION (OCTOBER REVOLUTION) (NOVEMBER 1917). The achievement of power during the Russian revolution of 1917 by the **Bolshevik** faction of the **Russian Social Democratic Labor Party (RSDLP)** and its Left Socialist Revolutionary and anarchist supporters. Though the essential "seizure of power" occurred in a relatively short period of time, as depicted in **John Reed**'s *Ten Days That Shook the World*, the history of the radical Russian revolutionary movement was long and tumultuous. The basic division was between Populists (agrarian socialists) and Marxists (social democrats), who advocated the Marxist doctrine of a proletarian (workers') revolution. The latter, however, were divided between traditionalists (Mensheviks) who were prepared to wait for a proletarian majority in backward Russia, and the extremist Bolsheviks, led by **Vladimir Lenin**, who followed the model of "revolution now" through terrorist and dictatorial means. Given the weakness of the Russian government under both Tsarist and **Provisional Government** administrations in 1917 and the deteriorating conditions in the country due to **World War I**, the Bolsheviks had a definite advantage with the superior leadership of Lenin and **Leon Trotsky**. Many Americans contributed to the Bolshevik victory by providing exile to Russian revolutionaries, such as Trotsky and Nikolai Bukharin, by expressing sympathy with radical causes in general, as well as through a distrust and lack of support to **Alexander Kerensky**, the Russian leader from May to November 1917.

BOLSHEVIKS. At the Second Congress of the **Russian Social Democratic Labor Party (RSDLP)** meeting in London in 1903, the Russian Marxist party split into two major sections over a number of issues and control of the newspaper. A major factor was the definition of membership—those obtaining a majority, led by **Vladimir Lenin**, argued that only those who worked full time for the revolution could be members. They were henceforth known as Bolsheviks, while the minority were labeled Mensheviks. A fictional unity was maintained into 1917, when the formal identity was RSDLP (b). A number of Russian social democrats, such as **Leon Trotsky**, refused to join either side—until 1917. The name, meaning "majority," gave Lenin and his followers a psychological advantage over their opponents. After the seizure of power and the formation of a "Soviet" government, the party became officially known as the Communist Party of the Soviet Union (CPSU). The party continued to function in the **Russian Federation** as a diminishing challenge to the administrations of Boris Yeltsin and **Vladimir Putin**.

BORAH, WILLIAM E. (1865–1940). A long-term Republican senator from Idaho (1907–40), Borah is best known for his opposition to the Treaty of Versailles (1919) and American membership in the **League of Nations** and as an advocate of conservative causes. His position as chairman of the Senate Committee on Foreign Relations was instrumental in defeating the Wilsonian internationalist agenda and in steering the United States into isolationism in the 1920s. Nevertheless, Borah, along with his friend **Raymond Robins**, was a strong advocate of American recognition of the Soviet Union in the 1920s, simply on the commonsense grounds that the country existed and the best way to solve problems was to deal with it directly. In the meantime, he worked with the unofficial Soviet "ambassador," **Boris Skvirsky**, to solve many personal problems of Americans in Russia who desired to leave or, conversely, Americans outside Russia who wanted to enter. He was probably the most widely respected American politician by Soviet authorities during the interwar period, excepting **Franklin D. Roosevelt**. Borah thus cancelled out much of the Republican Party's resistance to recognition when Roosevelt began negotiations that would accomplish it in 1933.

BOSTONIANS. American captains and ships (c.1790–1825) in the Pacific and Far Eastern trade were not only from Boston, but from a number of New England ports. These American commercial adventurers sought lucrative trade along the shores of the North Pacific, which included the coasts of Northwest America under the control of the **Russian America Company (RAC)**, with China the special target. Many of these independent, freelance captains established reciprocal, mutually profitable arrangements with the Russian authorities in Northwest America in regard to the harvesting and shipping of furs of the region to China. Among those who brought back profits to their New England bases and shipping families were Joseph O'Cain (Boston), **John D'Wolfe** (Bristol, Rhode Island), Jonathan Winship (Boston), and John Ebbets (New York). The New England–Russian America–China trade was a boon to both the success of the RAC and to the Atlantic American commercial seacoast towns. The commerce also led to the New England whaling industry, which was based primarily on hunting in the Sea of Okhotsk.

BOURKE-WHITE, MARGARET (1904–1971). Already in her twenties, Margaret Bourke-White became renowned for seeking out the unusual, as well as the commonplace, to capture on film around the world, especially for *Life Magazine*. Her lens focused especially on construction (such as skyscrapers) and industrialization (machines and workers, clearly sympathetic to the latter over the former). In the early 1930s she visited Soviet Russia three times to record the progress of industrialization and especially the American contributions to them for *Fortune*. She returned with her husband, Erskine Caldwell, in 1941 to take some memorable pictures of Russia at the beginning of **World War II**, including a revealing portrait of **Joseph Stalin**. Pressed by the American embassy, she and Caldwell reluctantly left Russia in the early winter of 1941 by way of **Archangel** and the **northern convoy route**. She died in 1971 after a 14-year battle with Parkinson's disease. Her photographs of a Russia in transition and at war, published in various magazines and books, are a valuable legacy for an understanding of the times, as is her poignant memoir, *Portrait of Myself* (1963).

BOYER, PAUL (NE JEAN MARIE BOYER) (1864–1949). Professor of Russian language at the University of Paris (Sorbonne School of Oriental Languages), Boyer was the first Western, largely self-taught, professional expert on the Russian language and the teaching of it to Western students. His Russian grammar (in French) was also the first widely used in the American universities for courses in elementary Russian (later revised and adapted into English by **Samuel Harper** for American students). He traveled extensively in Russia, interviewing philologists and literary figures, such as **Leo Tolstoy**.

Among his early American students in Paris were Harper, **Elizabeth Reynolds (Hapgood)**, and **Robert F. Kelley**. When the United States suddenly needed expert guidance in the 1920s and 1930s for teaching Russian to its foreign service officers, such as **Charles Bohlen**, Boyer was again called upon. He was praised for his methods of learning grammatical rules simply and easily and for recommending that students then live with a Russian family, preferably in Russia, to master accents and fluency, a practice far ahead of its time.

BRESHKO-BRESHKOVSKAYA, EKATERINA (CATHERINE BRESHKOVSKY) (1844–1934). Russian populist revolutionary. She won attention in the 1870s as one of the most active women in the *narodnichestvo* or "to the people" movement that climaxed in the summer of 1874, the anniversary of the Pugachev revolt of 1774, when a number of university students descended on peasant villages with the expectation of stirring the masses to revolt. Though a major failure, several of the instigators became martyrs to the cause of revolution in Russia by suffering difficult years of Siberian exile. This experience, especially that of Breshko-Breshkovskaya, was dramatically revealed by **George Kennan** in his *Siberia and the Exile System* in the 1880s. World reaction helped gain her release and ability to travel abroad to advocate her cause of a liberal, democratic Russia. She lectured widely in the United States with the help and support of Kennan and **Alice Stone Blackwell**, a leading advocate of women's rights in America, in the 1890s and subsequently. Though a poor speaker with a heavily accented English, with their help she nonetheless galvanized audiences and raised considerable American contributions for Russian radical and liberal causes, which mainly paid for publicity materials.

Though for a time an advocate of terror and assassination, she became more moderate by 1917 and actively supported **Alexander Kerensky** and the Socialist Revolutionary Party, earning the epithet of "the little grandmother of the Russian revolution." After the overthrow of the Kerensky government in the **Bolshevik Revolution**, she again went into exile, devoting her considerable energy to the maintaining of orphanages for homeless children in Czechoslovakia with funding from sympathetic Americans. A touching memoir/biography of Breshkovskaya was published in the 1920s by Blackwell.

BREST-LITOVSK, TREATY OF (MARCH 1918). During 1917, the opponents of the **Provisional Government** gained much support by their public campaign to end Russian participation in **World War I**. This was made official by the peace decree of the Second All-Russian Congress of Soviets that met during the **Bolshevik Revolution** in November. An armistice soon followed. The German motive in agreeing was in order to shift sizable forces to the hard-pressed western front. Negotiations were soon underway for a definitive peace at the border town of Brest-Litovsk, the chief Soviet representative being **Leon Trotsky**, the first Soviet commissar for foreign affairs, assisted by **Karl Radek**, who was an authority on Germany. Under their leadership, the Bolshevik tactics were to stall, reject reasonable settlements, and follow Trotsky's formula of "no war, no peace." This was based on the expectation that world revolution would soon occur in any event. The Germans broke off talks and resumed military advances. This brought the Bolsheviks back to the table—without Trotsky. The final result was the acceptance of the German terms and the ceding of most of the territory under German occupation, namely Poland and the Baltic states. Also, the Soviet government was forced to recognize an earlier (January 1918) treaty of the Central Powers with a separatist Ukrainian government, thus recognizing Ukrainian independence. This draft treaty was then presented to the Fourth Congress of Soviets, meeting in Moscow in early March, for ratification.

In the meantime, **Raymond Robins** and a few other Americans were working behind the scenes to secure a promise of substantial American aid in return for refusing ratification—and continuing the war—the object being to keep as many German troops as possible in the East. Communications with Washington were somehow delayed, and when **Vladimir Lenin** advanced to the podium of the congress to present the treaty, he stopped at Robins in a front-row seat to ask whether he had heard from America. Hearing the negative, Lenin then asked the congress to ratify the treaty. Though the treaty would be nullified by the demise of the German and Austro-Hungarian empires later that year, it brought about mutual diplomatic recognition, arrangements for the exchange of prisoners, and reestablishment of normal trade. Little really resulted that would affect the outcome of the war in the West, since Germany undertook occupation authority for a very large territory, including Ukraine. Besides, the peace was tenuous, since the treaty had considerable internal opposition in Soviet Russia, especially from left-wing Socialist revolutionaries and anarchists. This produced terrorist activity and civil war in the streets of Moscow, during which the new German ambassador would be assassinated. Another important effect of Brest-Litovsk was the **Allied Intervention** to safeguard supplies in ports and attempt to maintain a semblance of an eastern front.

BREZHNEV DOCTRINE (1968). Soviet limitation on the independence of members of the **Warsaw Pact**. The doctrine was issued in response to the 1960s initiatives of separate, more detached policies free from Soviet control and especially in foreign relations, first initiated by Poland but more directly by Czechoslovakia in the late summer of 1968, "socialism with a human face," the latter requiring suppression by Soviet armed forces. The doctrine justified that invasion and was best defined in a speech by **Leonid Brezhnev** at the Fifth Congress of the Polish United Workers' Party on 13 November 1968: "When forces that are hostile to socialism try to turn the development of some socialist country towards capitalism, it becomes not only a problem of the country concerned, but a common problem and concern of all socialist countries." The explicit meaning was that one country could not withdraw from the Warsaw Pact without the permission of all of its members, which, of course, included the Soviet Union.

BREZHNEV, LEONID (1906–1982). Soviet apparatchik; general secretary of the Communist Party of the Soviet Union (CPSU) and head of the Soviet government from 1964 to 1982. Born of Russian parentage in the Donbas industrial region of Ukraine, Brezhnev worked his way through party ranks in Ukraine and Moldava and in 1954 became director of the Virgin Lands program in Kazakhstan. An early supporter of **Nikita Khrushchev**, Brezhnev followed others, such as Mikhail Suslov and Nikolai Podgorny, in denouncing him in 1964 and ascended to his place as first secretary of the party. His era as Soviet leader was at first well regarded for major improvements in the lives of citizens, due largely to affluence gained from the sales of oil, gas, gold, and other resources—and the recovery from the disastrous economic effects of **World War II**. The growing confidence of the

Soviet leadership reflected the rise in military capabilities (missiles) and gains abroad through a new, more aggressive peace offensive and summitry, defined as **détente**.

Détente led to more summit meetings and more serious arms limitations negotiations and discussions, including **Strategic Arms Limitation Talks (SALT I and SALT II)**. This progress was marred, however, by the Soviet stemming of liberal movements in Poland and Czechoslovakia (1968) that led to the **Brezhnev Doctrine**. Much of the gain internationally and domestically was also reduced by stagnation of the economy (roughly after 1976) and the aging of the leadership, which was often referred to as a "gerontocracy." The Union of Soviet Socialist Republics (USSR) seemed to be no longer able to respond to the escalation in the technical/scientific advances of the West (computer revolution). In addition, the Brezhnev regime charted a new and more dangerous course in the military invasion of **Afghanistan** (1979) that not only led to worldwide condemnation with resulting boycotts and embarrassments, but also proved very costly—and a complete failure.

BRIGHTON BEACH. A community on the southern edge (seaside) of Brooklyn, New York. Many of the 1970s and 1980s immigrants from the Soviet Union, mainly Jews who were allowed to leave, settled in an area in Brooklyn neighboring on Coney Island; it is also referred to as "Little Odessa." In years since, its population of "Russians" has swelled and represents an enclave of Russian culture in New York City. As a polyglot of Jews, Russians, Ukrainians, and Caucasians, Brighton Beach is perhaps more "Soviet" than "Russian" in consciousness. It is noted for its lively cosmopolitan atmosphere of nightclubs, shops, and restaurants that feature "Russian-style" cuisine and drinks. In the fall of 2006 the state electoral district encompassing Brighton Beach elected the first Soviet-born legislator to the New York State General Assembly.

"BRINKMANSHIP." This American foreign policy characteristic is generally associated with Secretary of State **John Foster Dulles** during the administration of **Dwight D. Eisenhower** in the 1950s. It meant in the parlance of that time "standing up to the Soviets," or reacting aggressively to apparent Soviet offensive moves, some of which (China, Korea, Hungary) may have been beyond Soviet control. In one sense, it was what **George F. Kennan** would condemn as not what he meant by **containment** in 1946. The policy led the USSR to deprive its already hard-pressed economy (because of **World War II** destruction) in order to devote major resources to catching up militarily. The policy would also minimize the possibility of realizing more opportunities from the launching of **peaceful coexistence** by **Nikita Khrushchev**. Even President Eisenhower would criticize its American domestic manifestation in the "military industrial complex." As an American stance toward world affairs, "brinkmanship" would leave a legacy of favoring military priorities over social and environmental needs in later administrations, for example, that of **George W. Bush** in the early 21th century.

BRISTOL, ADMIRAL MARK (1868–1939). After active service as a naval officer in the Spanish–American War, Bristol served at various naval posts in the United States. Upon American entry into **World War I** in 1917, he was appointed commander of the American Eastern Mediterranean squadron that would be based at Constantinople upon conclusion of the war. At the time of the **Paris Peace Conference** in 1919, Bristol was designated Allied High Commissioner for the former Ottoman Empire (1919–27). In this post he was responsible for relief to a variety of destitute populations, including a large number of Russians fleeing the Bolshevik occupation of Ukraine, Crimea, and the Caucasus region and for maintaining communications and intelligence operations in the whole Black Sea area, and especially in regard to the Turkish Armenian genocide. These tasks he accomplished with considerable skill and with the assistance of Russian expert and friend Rear Admiral **Newton McCully**. In November 1920, upon final defeat of the anti-Bolshevik forces in South Russia, the relief capabilities in the region of the Straits, mainly operated by the **American Red Cross**, were literally swamped by the arrival of more than 100,000 Russian refugees, many of them remnants of the Russian White armies. Bristol and his wife Helen, along with **Charles R. Crane** and **Thomas Whittemore**, devoted much time and many resources to the problem and would remain committed to Russian relief efforts through the 1920s. Bristol served as an American delegate to the Lausanne Conference in 1923. After his retirement in 1932, he returned to the United States from the Far East via the Soviet Union without approval from the Department of the Navy, a breach of protocol soon quieted by the 1933 **Recognition Agreement**.

BRODSKY, JOSEPH (1940–1996). A Russian poet and dissident; recipient of the Nobel Prize in Literature in 1987. Of Russian Jewish heritage from St. Petersburg, Brodsky was one of the earliest dissidents, composing "unofficial" verse in the 1960s and protesting police interference with other dissident writers. Arrested and tried for "parasitism" (no legal occupation), Brodsky was sentenced to five years in prison in 1964. In 1972 he was formally expelled from the Soviet Union and sought asylum in the United States; a visiting scholar at several universities, he was mainly resident at the University of Michigan in Ann Arbor. Brodsky became an American citizen in 1980 and was later "rehabilitated" in Russia; his collected works in four volumes were published in Moscow in 1992. After his death, his remains were transported to his favorite European city, Venice, for burial in 1997.

***BROOKLYN,* USS.** American cruiser and flagship of Admiral **Austin Knight**, commander of the American Pacific Squadron during **World War I** and the **Russian Civil War**. After the Russian Revolution and during the period of American military intervention in Russia (1918–19), the ship was stationed in the harbor of Vladivostok, serving as a symbol of American presence and as a "safe" Allied command post. Knight also served as a primary supporter of the mission of the **American Expeditionary Force (AEF)** under General **William Graves**. The presence of a major American warship in a strategic Russian port helped achieve the evacuation of the **Czechoslovak Legion** and whatever cooperation was possible among the Allied, and especially Japanese, commanders in the area. During its return voyage to Pearl Harbor in 1919, an explosion occurred in the boiler room, described in its surviving logbook. Though towed into port without loss of life, the ship was soon afterward scuttled for scrap.

BROWDER, EARL (1891–1973). An American socialist, arrested for his opposition to the draft during **World War I**, Browder joined the

Communist Party of the United States (CPUSA) in 1919 and rose rapidly in its ranks to replace **William Foster** as its leader in 1930. Browder was subsequently the party's dull and uninspiring candidate for president in 1936 and 1940, drawing relatively few votes despite the Depression's devastating impact on the working population of America. During **World War II**, he urged close Soviet–American cooperation, which suited the times, but his continued advocacy of this cause after the war did not, and he was subsequently removed from all offices and from the party.

BRYANT, LOUISE (1885–1936). Bryant was born in San Francisco, the daughter of Hugh and Anna Mohan (Moen). Her parents soon divorced, and she adopted the name of her stepfather, Sheridan Bryant. Graduating from the University of Oregon in 1909, when she married a local dentist, Bryant began her journalistic career as illustrator and society editor of the *Portland Spectator* and was active in the women's suffrage movement. She met **John Reed** in 1915, and they had a tumultuous romantic affair, leading to her divorce. Bryant followed Reed to New York, where they were married in 1916, each pursuing separate careers as foreign correspondents during **World War I**, Reed covering the eastern front with Boardman Robinson. She rejoined Reed on his second trip to Russia in 1917 and fully supported his infatuation with the **Bolshevik Revolution**, which they covered in syndicated columns in the American press. Her book, *Six Months in Red Russia* (1918), was initially more successful than Reed's much better-known classic, *Ten Days That Shook the World* (1919), as was her lecture tour of the West Coast. Separated by Reed's commitment to lend support to the Soviet cause in 1919–20, she was able to rejoin him in Soviet Russia in August 1920 shortly before he died of typhus, the whole story dramatically developed in Warren Beatty's 1981 film *Reds*.

Bryant returned to the Soviet Union in 1922, writing another series of articles and another book, *Moscow Mirrors* (1923), that contained vivid character sketches of Bolshevik leaders she had interviewed. Also in 1923, she met in Paris—and married—**William Bullitt**, who would later become the first American ambassador to the Soviet Union, and gave birth to a child, Anne Moen Bullitt. Unfortunately, in 1926 she succumbed to the painful and debilitating Dercom's disease while also developing a lesbian relationship and suffering from alcoholism. Bullitt divorced her in 1930, obtaining custody of their daughter. Bryant died suddenly of a cerebral hemorrhage in early 1936. Her papers were deposited in 2004 by her daughter in the Yale University Library.

BRZEZINSKI, ZBIGNIEW (1929–). A scholar and diplomat, Brzezinski is best known as national security advisor during the administration of **Jimmy Carter**. Born in Warsaw, Poland, he accompanied his family to the Soviet Union (1936–38) during the purges and then to Canada in 1938 due to his father's diplomatic appointments. The invasion of Poland the following year and its inclusion in the Soviet bloc after 1946 caused the family to secure political asylum in Canada, where Brzezinski received B.A. and M.A. degrees from McGill University in Toronto and was awarded a Ph.D. in political science at Harvard University in 1953. After a brief stint of teaching at the latter university, Brzezinski moved to Columbia University, where he adapted a definition of totalitarianism to fit the Soviet model and wrote his first major book, *The Permanent Purge: Politics in Soviet Totalitarianism* (1956).

Early in his professional career, Brzezinski became involved in national politics as a strong critic of the **"brinkmanship"** of Secretary of State **John Foster Dulles** as only increasing the Soviet domination of Eastern Europe. He became a vocal champion of dissidents in both the Soviet Union and Eastern Europe and was likewise a critic of the foreign policy of **Richard Nixon** and **Henry Kissinger** in their support of **détente** and accommodation, which he believed only encouraged Soviet aggressive moves in the world. The election of Carter gave Brzezinski an opportunity to implement his policy as the new president's national security advisor. With Carter's support, he pressed the Soviet Union on human rights issues in the **Helsinki Accords**, despite the opposition of Secretary of State **Cyrus Vance,** who placed higher priority on achieving progress in the **Strategic Arms Limitation Talks (SALT)**. Brzezinski also encouraged the opposition of the Roman Catholic Church to the Polish Communist government, a move that would lead to the formation of Solidarity and may have assisted in the election of a Polish cardinal as pope.

Brzezinski also orchestrated the strong American reaction to the Soviet invasion of **Afghanistan** (1979–80), which was later criticized for aiding the rise of the Taliban and Al Qaeda. He also helped plan the attempt to liberate American embassy hostages in Iran. This and his continuing rift with Vance may have discouraged Carter from seeking reelection and led to Brzezinski being criticized within the Democratic Party, which in turn led to his break with the party and transfer of support to the camp of **Ronald Reagan** and **George H. W. Bush** and to his former student and disciple, Madeleine Albright, who was foreign policy advisor to Michael Dukakis and later secretary of state in the administration of **Bill Clinton**. Brzezinski continued to play an advisory role but remained outside of government as a critic of such "foolish" adventures as the Gulf War, the invasion of Iraq, and the "war on terror" of the Clinton and Bush eras from his professorship at the Johns Hopkins University's School for Advanced International Studies.

BUCHANAN, JAMES (1791–1868). A country lawyer in Pennsylvania, Buchanan served several terms in Congress before receiving his first diplomatic appointment as minister to Russia (1832–33). In that post he negotiated the **Commercial Treaty of 1832** that defined commercial and political relations between the two countries until its abrogation in 1912. Subsequently, Buchanan was a conservative stalwart of the Democratic Party, serving as secretary of state (1845–49) under President James Polk and as minister to Great Britain (1853–56) under Franklin Pierce, during the **Crimean War**, before succeeding him as president (1856–60). His mission to Russia, excepting the treaty, was undistinguished, as was the rest of his political career; as president he received much criticism for his failure to prevent the advent of a bloody civil war.

BULLARD, ARTHUR (1879–1929). Born in St. Joseph, Missouri, Bullard attended Hamilton College in New York, and, beginning in 1905, he became a foreign correspondent for *Harper's Weekly*, *Collier's Weekly*, *The Outlook*, and *Atlantic Monthly*. He traveled extensively through North Africa, the Middle East, the Balkans, and Russia, while filing penetrating, revealing reports. During **World War I**, he joined the **Committee on Public Information** and was appointed director of its Russian operations in 1917, a position he continued to hold in **Vladivostok** after the **Bolshevik Revolution**, while publishing *The Russian Pendulum* (1919) about his experiences. Upon departure from **Siberia** with the **American Expeditionary Force (AEF)**, he was designated a special assistant to the State Department and soon, in November 1920, chief of the Russian Division, which he resigned after a few months to return to newspaper work, serving as editor of *The World* for several years.

BULLITT MISSION (1919). During the **Paris Peace Conference** of 1919, "a dark cloud [Russia] from the North hung over the proceedings," in the words of **William Allen White**. A number of delegates attending realized the import of Russia's absence. In an effort to establish contact and bring the new Soviet Russia into the proceedings and end a bloody civil war in Russia, President **Woodrow Wilson**'s chief advisor, Colonel **Edward House**, initiated an American mission to Russia in March 1919 during the president's absence in the United States, but with his apparent agreement and that of Winston Churchill. The designated head of this mission was a young State Department official, **William Bullitt**, a fellow Yale graduate and protégé of House. Associated with him was an elderly leftist eccentric and writer (muckraker), **Lincoln Steffens**, literally "riding shotgun." This rather unlikely pair traveled through Scandinavia to pass over the Soviet frontier, guided by Captain W. W. Pettit and a secretary, and with the assistance of **Maxim Litvinov**. They managed to meet with **Vladimir Lenin** and Commissar of Foreign Affairs **Georgy Chicherin** in Moscow and drafted a peace proposal, which was brought back to Paris in April. Unfortunately, the American president was now more interested in bringing the treaty negotiations to a conclusion, and House fell out of favor. So the mission came to nothing, except to indicate that Bolsheviks were open to negotiation.

BULLITT, WILLIAM C. (1891–1967). Diplomat, socialite, and first U.S. ambassador to the Soviet Union (1933–36), Bullitt was from mainline Philadelphia society and a graduate of Yale University (1913). He was visiting Moscow with his mother in 1914 when **World War I** began. After a brief stint as a reporter for the *Philadelphia Public Ledger*, he joined the State Department in 1917. As a protégé of another Yale alumnus, Colonel **Edward House**, Bullitt attended the **Paris Peace Conference** in 1919 as a secretary to the American delegation. He was then sent by House, accompanied by socialist maverick **Lincoln Steffens**, and with the questionable approval of the president, on a special mission to Russia in 1919, where he met with **Vladimir Lenin**, **Georgy Chicherin**, and other members of the new Soviet government. Though at least indicating to Soviet leaders the willingness of the United States to negotiate on debts, confiscations, and other matters, the **Bullitt mission**, upon its return, met with the disapproval of the peace commissioners in Paris and led to a subsequent rift between President **Woodrow Wilson** and House, his longtime advisor. Wilson was especially annoyed that this mission had been launched without his approval.

Bullitt resigned from his post in the State Department in 1919 over the failure of the Russian mission and his dissatisfaction with the treaty negotiations that left out Russia. Despite this, Bullitt maintained his interest in the course of Soviet affairs, at least partially, due to his marriage in 1923 to **Louise Bryant**, the widow of **John Reed**, a founder of the **Communist Party of the United States (CPUSA)**. He spent much of the 1920s as a playboy in Paris before returning to the political scene on another mission to Europe and Russia on behalf of an aspiring president, **Franklin D. Roosevelt**, in 1932. Upon Roosevelt's inauguration the following year, Bullitt became a special assistant in the State Department, in preparation for the negotiations for diplomatic recognition. He was thus a major advisor on the negotiations for recognition with **Maxim Litvinov** in November 1933. To no one's surprise he was then named the first American ambassador to the Soviet Union, arriving initially with a hearty welcome and reception by **Joseph Stalin** in December of that year.

Initially quite enthusiastic about his new mission, Bullitt soon became disenchanted about the Soviet Union and the obstructions that were placed in the way to settling the old issues of debt and confiscation claims. He also failed to surmount his reputation as an international playboy and win the respect of a very qualified staff that included **George F. Kennan** and **Charles Bohlen**. He drifted rapidly from sympathetic approval of the Soviet cause to complete rejection by 1936, when the purges were under way. That year he achieved a requested transfer as ambassador to his beloved France, much more to his liking. There, he warned of the growing German threat and laid the foundation of a wartime alliance. Subsequently, during **World War II**, Bullitt became a strong critic of Roosevelt, especially the extent of his alliance with the Soviet Union and seeming gullibility about that country's regime. By 1948 he had joined the Republican Party, becoming a strong advocate of the political ambitions of Robert Taft and **Richard Nixon**. Bullitt's marriage to Bryant ended in 1930, but he retained custody of their daughter, Anne Moen, to whom he was much devoted. In retirement he redeveloped an association with Sigmund Freud that had begun in the early 1930s, and together they coauthored a critical study of Woodrow Wilson in 1966. The following year he died of leukemia, fittingly, in Paris.

BUSH, GEORGE H. W. (1924–). A **World War II** veteran and graduate of Yale University (1948), Bush rose through the Republican Party to serve in a number of posts, including ambassador to the **United Nations**, director of the **Central Intelligence Agency** (1976–77), and vice president in the administrations of **Ronald Reagan** (1981–89). He then served as president (1989–93) during the disintegration of the **"evil empire."** Playing the role of interested observer and holding out an olive branch, Bush met with Russian leaders **Mikhail Gorbachev** and Boris Yeltsin for a record of seven summit meetings, culminating in the signing of the **Strategic Arms Limitation Talks (SALT II)** treaty in January 1993 that was never ratified. Defeated for reelection by **Bill Clinton**, Bush became an advisor on various matters in retirement, especially for his son, **George W. Bush**, during his presidential administrations (2001–09).

BUSH, GEORGE W. (1946–). Following in the footsteps of his father, **George H. W. Bush**, George Bush graduated from Yale (1968) with a degree in history and obtained an MBA from Harvard University. After some business endeavors in Texas as owner of the Texas Rangers and ranching, but mainly in the oil industry, Bush was elected governor of the state in 1996. He established a good record in tax reduction and government reform, which, along with his father's influence, launched him into the presidential race in 2000 as the Republican candidate. He won the election in a close and controversial vote and served through two terms, including another controversial outcome in 2004.

A novice in foreign policy, Bush relied upon his vice president, Dick Cheney, and secretaries of state Colin Powell (2001–05) and **Condoleezza Rice** (2005–09) and ventured into aggressive military actions in the Middle East, especially the invasion of Iraq (March 1993), which occupied much of his attention and budget for the remainder of his presidency. Highly criticized for his arrogance and neglect of social and environmental issues, Bush would leave the presidency in 2009 with the lowest popular rating ever, in contrast with his father's high popularity in 1993 upon losing his bid for reelection to **Bill Clinton**. Fortunately, Bush continued the friendly relationship with Russian leaders established by the administration of Clinton, while following the advice of Powell and Rice. Nevertheless, a resurgent **Russian Federation** under **Vladimir Putin** gained impressively in world affairs and economic clout, thanks especially to American failures in the Middle East. The final meeting of the two outgoing presidents in April 2008 demonstrated a willingness for cooperation but solved no outstanding issues, especially the Iraq war and **NATO** expansion.

– C –

CALDER, JOHN K. (1882–1946). As Soviet Russia began to prepare for a great industrial advance in the **First Five-Year Plan** (1928–32), Soviet authorities through the **American Trading Corporation (Amtorg)**, their business agency in New York, contacted major American companies such as **Ford Motor Company** for assistance. A high priority was on the construction of large modern factories for the mass production of major items of the modern world such as tractors, cars, and trucks. As one of the best-known American builders (Dearborn complex for Ford and the Hudson Department store in Detroit), John Calder was sought after by special Soviet delegations. The result was a contract that put him in charge of building a large tractor factory at Stalingrad that would utilize **International Harvester** equipment and produce the basic "Farmall" tractor. Against odds and overlooking a number of difficulties, Calder—with the help of a large cadre of American engineers—managed to complete the project ahead of schedule. He was then asked to move on to the Urals city of Chelyabinsk, where the construction of a heavy tractor (Caterpillar) factory was encountering problems. After success on this project, Calder was again summoned to rescue the linchpin of the whole plan, the iron and steel complex at Magnitogorsk, that was floundering badly.

Calder had been able to cut through Soviet obstacles and red tape by his constant energy, his lively swearing at subordinates (apparently kicked up a notch by his Russian interpreter), and his complete transparency. As **Eugene Lyons** observed, Calder was "as honest a man as ever drew a Soviet payroll." Though finally tiring of the task and frustrated with Soviet inability to learn the basic "how-tos," Calder remained committed to the Soviet general goals and was a strong advocate of American recognition of the Soviet Union. His lunch with the president at the White House in early June 1933 may have been influential in **Franklin D. Roosevelt**'s decision in favor of diplomatic recognition.

CALVERT, HERBERT (1889–1977). Born in California, Herbert Calvert grew up in small towns in Indiana before winning a scholarship to Illinois State Normal College. His studies were interrupted by moving with his family to New Mexico, where he tried unsuccessfully to earn a living as a hardware salesman on a Navajo reservation, learning the Native American language in the process. Subsequent efforts as a farm laborer, railroad worker, and carpenter reaped few rewards. Moving back to California, he became a sewing machine salesman in Los Angeles, an adherent to socialism, and a follower of **Eugene Debs**. There he met his wife and fellow radical, Mellie Miller. Together they founded the Young People's Socialist League of Los Angeles, which soon attained a membership of more than 1,500, and became a promoter of an experimental socialist colony nearby; they soon migrated with it to Mexico. **Vladimir Lenin**'s letter to American workers of 1918 having reached these amateur Communists, the Calverts turned their attention and effort to Soviet construction. But first they became active in the **Industrial Workers of the World (IWW)** while working at the **Ford Motor Company** in a Detroit suburb. During a December 1921 holiday shutdown, Calvert led a petition for employees to continue work producing cars for themselves. Nothing came of this, but the local union in recognition of his effort named him a delegate to an "International Congress of Red Trade Unions" to be held in Moscow that spring.

Arriving in Moscow in March 1921 directly after a major shift in Soviet economic policy (the **New Economic Policy**), Calvert was one of the first to propose international assistance to Soviet industrial projects, subsequently joining a project of communal construction initiated by Dutch Communist Sebald Rutgers and promoted by **Bill Haywood**, who arrived in Moscow in May. This was the much publicized **Kuzbas** project in western **Siberia** that involved the colonization and development of the immense resources of Kuzbas by foreign workers, mainly American. Calvert's role would be the recruitment of volunteers and soliciting of funds, chiefly from a New York office. Though never achieving the expected numbers, the project nonetheless was considered a success and gained much publicity for the Soviet international cause. Owing to disagreements with Rutgers, the Calverts left the project at the end of 1923 but remained committed to socialist causes for the rest of their long lives.

CAMP DAVID. The presidential retreat in Catoctin Mountain National Park originated as a campsite for disabled children in Frederick County, Maryland, before becoming a Civilian Conservation Corps project in the 1930s. Because of the pressure of wartime duties in the summer, President **Franklin D. Roosevelt** needed a place to escape the Washington heat, but not far from the capital, and to avoid the possible dangers of cruises on the presidential yacht *Potomac*. He named the retreat (which averaged 10 degrees cooler than the capital) "Shangri-La," and it became the site of the planning of the Normandy invasion. For that and other reasons, President **Harry S. Truman** retained it as a presidential summer retreat under the supervision of the National Park Service. Upon assuming office as president, **Dwight D. Eisenhower** renamed it after his grandson and used it more frequently for entertaining summertime international visitors in a relaxed, informal environment.

The best-known guest during the Eisenhower era was Soviet premier **Nikita Khrushchev**, during his American tour in the summer of 1959. The atmosphere of a wooded and somewhat secluded mountain camp helped put a double stamp of approval on **peaceful coexistence**. The apparent reaching of an understanding between the two **cold war** leaders gave rise to the term "The Spirit of Camp David," which, unfortunately, proved illusionary, as it was followed by the **U-2** incident, the erection of the **Berlin Wall**, and the **Cuban missile crisis**. Subsequently, it was the site of a number of summit discussions with major world leaders, especially the Camp David Accords concerning the Middle East during the presidency of **Jimmy Carter**.

CANTACUZENE, COUNTESS JULIA SPERANSKY (NEE JULIA GRANT) (1876–1975). A granddaughter of President **Ulysses S. Grant** and daughter of General Frederick Grant, Julia Grant, while traveling abroad, met a Russian diplomat of Greek Phanariot (Kantakuzen in Russian) noble background, and they married in 1899. She subsequently spent many years living the life of the Russian nobility, dividing her time between a large estate in Ukraine and St. Petersburg society. During **World War I**, she was active in relief efforts, especially through the Russian Red Cross, while also being a pillar of the sizable American colony in the Russian capital, the star guest at a gala Fourth of July party at the American embassy in 1916, the last of such occasions for a number of years. As for most of the Russian nobility, her family suffered considerably through the war and revolution, her husband seriously wounded as the commander of a regiment in the Russian army.

They and their son managed to escape through Finland and return to the United States, where she again became active in relief, this time for Russian refugees and exiles. Her particular emphasis was on obtaining funds to support Russian scholars, artists, and clergymen in the 1920s and helping them to obtain entrance to the United States—with the goal of preserving the best of old Russian culture that was being threatened by Bolshevik policies and the hardships of the Russian diaspora. She wrote two sensitive (and sad) memoirs, *Revolutionary Days: Recollections of the Romanoffs and Bolsheviki, 1914–1917* (1919) and *My Life Here and There* (1921). After her return to the United States, she resided in Washington, D.C., while remaining socially active during the 1920s and 1930s as a vestige of both Civil War America and of the **Russian Civil War**. After developing a relationship with Canadian statesman McKenzie King in the 1920s through a chance meeting in

Paris, she divorced her husband in 1932 and carried on a long liaison, mostly by correspondence—and in spiritual seances—with King until his death in 1950.

CARTER, JIMMY (1924–). The 39th president of the United States (1977–81), governor of Georgia (1971–75), and Nobel Peace Laureate (2000). From the small town of Plains, Georgia, Carter graduated from the U.S. Naval Academy (1946) with a degree in nuclear physics. From 1953 he supervised the family farm and peanut processing plant, entering state politics in the 1960s. As a liberal in a modernizing Southern state, Carter won election as governor and proved to be a successful reformer for government efficiency. In 1976 he outmaneuvered Senator George McGovern to obtain the Democratic nomination for president, as a rare candidate without federal experience. He then took advantage of campaign mistakes of **Gerald Ford** to win the election. With the support of Vice President Walter Mondale and Secretary of State **Cyrus Vance**, Carter renewed the spirit of **détente** with the Soviet Union in a series of **Camp David** accords and the signing of a **Strategic Arms Limitations Talks (SALT II)** agreement with **Leonid Brezhnev** in June 1979, though it was never ratified and was withdrawn from consideration by the Senate after the Soviet invasion of **Afghanistan** in December.

The latter event, unfortunately, set the tone of the Carter administration's relations with the Soviet Union. Carter responded by declaring an embargo on grain exports to the Soviet Union and a boycott of American participation in the Olympic Games held in Moscow during the summer of 1980. Encouraged by national security advisor **Zbigniew Brzezinski**, Carter increased the training and equipping of Afghan Islamic factions in Pakistan. Some of his other efforts on the international scene were more successful: the Camp David Accords (between Israel and Egypt) and the Panama Canal Treaty, for example. His record was also excellent in the area of human rights, but his presidency was overshadowed by the Iranian hostage crisis, which he devoted much of his final year in office to resolving.

CASABLANCA CONFERENCE (JANUARY 1943). A **World War II** Allied conference was held at a North African city immortalized by a prewar film. Attending were British prime minister **Winston**

Churchill, American president **Franklin Roosevelt**, and Free French representative General Charles de Gaulle. **Joseph Stalin** was invited but chose not to come because of the critical course of the Battle of Stalingrad at the time. The meeting was probably as significant for the war effort as the succeeding and better-known conferences at **Tehran** (1944), **Yalta** (1945), and **Potsdam** (1945). The conference concerned Allied policy in the aftermath of the successful Allied North African campaign. A key decision was made in regard to delaying the launch of a cross-channel invasion in deference to an invasion of Italy during the summer of 1943. To salve Soviet disappointment, Churchill and Roosevelt agreed to increase aid (**lend-lease**) to the Soviet Union. The American president also independently issued a statement of war aims, coining the term *unconditional surrender* in an effort to discourage the possibility of a Soviet separate peace and to avoid the unsettled "armistice" of **World War I**.

CASSINI, ARTUR (1835–c. 1925). From a Russian family of Italian origin, Cassini became a professional diplomat known for his expertise in a number of languages, including English and Chinese. After serving several years as Russian minister to China, he was transferred to Washington (1902), where he managed to inspire "dislike at first sight." Egotistical, obsequious, and abrupt, Cassini did not fit well with the guardians of a newly founded American world power and especially with the personalities of Secretary of State John Hay and President **Theodore Roosevelt**, whom he constantly pestered on major and minor issues. In fact, the president considered the first priority in his effort to arbitrate the conclusion of the **Russo–Japanese War** was the removal of Cassini, which he managed to accomplish with the help of his ambassador in St. Petersburg, **George von Lengerke Meyer**. Cassini subsequently served as Russian ambassador to Spain, retiring to Paris after the **Bolshevik Revolution**.

CATHERINE II OR CATHERINE THE GREAT (NEE SOPHIE OF ANHALT ZERBST) (1729–1796). One of the most celebrated rulers of Russia, whose reign (1762–96) was marked by considerable territorial expansion through successful wars against the Ottoman Empire and by the partitioning of Poland, Catherine was also noted as an enlightened despot who corresponded with French philosophers and absorbed and practiced some of their ideas. German born, from a small principality, she was chosen by Empress Elizabeth to be the bride of her nephew, Grand Duke Peter of Holsetein and heir to the Russian throne. Catherine managed to survive this unhappy marriage and make diplomatic and wise liaisons and to produce an heir, though probably not from her husband. Popular with the guards regiments in the capital, Catherine succeeded in usurping the crown from her unpopular spouse, Peter III. She then went on, with the help of an assortment of lovers and supportive government officials, to establish one of the grandest reigns as empress in Russian history, especially rich in military and diplomatic achievements. The record, however, was not unblemished, since it also included the suppression of a major peasant revolt, led by Pugachev, who claimed to be her dead husband. This violent insurrection would be an inspiration to Russian dissident populists 100 years later.

Her reign corresponded with the American Revolution and the French Revolution. Though her diplomacy basically courted British friendship, Catherine was also quite aware of the British supremacy at sea that conflicted with her own naval aspirations. For that reason she obliquely supported the American colonial efforts at independence through her declaration of an **Armed Neutrality** (1780) that helped defend the rights of neutrals during the conflict, thus inspiring, if not actively protecting, their shipments of supplies to the rebelling colonies. Though not responding to the mission of **Francis Dana** to achieve direct diplomatic recognition, she clearly admired the American achievements, which were praised by some of her most enlightened subjects, such as Nikolai Novikov and **Alexander Radishchev**. She also welcomed the service of American naval hero **John Paul Jones** in developing Russian naval power on the Black Sea during the Second Turkish War (1787–92). Though turning more conservative later in her reign because of the French Revolution's radical turn (murder of king and queen), she remained friendly toward Americans and their successful achievement of independence.

CEDAR VALE, KANSAS, RUSSIAN COMMUNE (1871–1879).

This utopian socialist commune, formally known as the "Progressive Communist Society," was founded by **William Frey**, also known as Wilhelm Frei or by his original Russian name of Vladimir Geins

(Heinz), on a 160-acre homestead in January 1871. Frey and other Russian refugees from the Russian populist movement joined American Christian socialists in a unique frontier effort to realize the ideals of community socialism, inspired by François Fourier. Located near the Oklahoma border in southern Kansas, the community attracted considerable attention nationally by the publication of Frey's monthly newsletter, the *Progressive Communist*, that was typeset and printed by him on the community's press. Despite its name, the commune had very little relationship, if any, to Karl Marx or Bolshevism but was inspired by French utopian socialism and Russian agrarian populism. It was composed of a mix of Russian émigré dissidents, who included Russian *narodnik* **Nikolai Chaikovsky**, Ukrainian populist **Grigori Machtet**, and American Christian socialists, who practiced vegetarianism, self-sufficiency, and communal raising of children. At most only about a dozen formed the "society" at one time, but it survived longer than many utopian communities, especially considering the cleavage between the ideals of Russian atheists and American Christians.

CENTER FOR NORTH AMERICAN STUDIES, INSTITUTE OF GENERAL HISTORY. A Russian research center on the United States and Canada of the Russian Academy of Sciences directed for many years by **Nikolai Bolkhovitinov**, the center has fostered the study of objective research on various aspects of American history, usually confined to the period before **World War II**. The excellent scholarship of academician **Grigory Sevostianov**, **Irina Beliavskaya**, **Gennady Kuropiatnik**, and **Robert Ivanov**, among others, laid the foundation for a young research cadre, nurtured especially by Bolkhovitinov, Sevostianov, and the director of the institute, Alexander Chubarian. In contrast to the more ideological and politicized work of members of the **Institute of the U.S.A. and Canada**, dealing primarily with the postwar world, the production of these scholars has been of uniform high quality and objectivity as represented in the center's journal, ***Amerikanskii Ezhegodnik***.

CENTRAL INTELLIGENCE AGENCY (CIA). An American government organization that was founded in 1946 to collect information on the world situation. It concentrated its efforts on the Soviet Union and areas of instability. Its Soviet counterpart during most of the period was the **Committee on State Security (KGB)**. A successor to the wartime Office of Strategic Services, the CIA supplied critical analyses of Soviet actions and intentions during the **cold war** and after. Though often criticized for inaccuracies and bungling (such as estimating the strength of the Soviet military forces after **World War II** as twice the size of actual), it served its government well during cold war crises, such as the **Berlin blockade** (1948–49), the **Cuban missile crisis** (1962), and the Soviet invasion of Czechoslovakia (1968). It continues to gather intelligence and monitor activities of the states of the former USSR, especially that of the **Russian Federation**. *See also* PENKOVSKY, OLEG.

CHAIKOVSKY, NIKOLAI (1850–1926). As a Russian populist (*narodnik*) leader of a Russian crusade for a new Russia based on a peasant socialist society, Chaikovsky formed a discussion group in the 1870s known as the Chaikovsky Circle to promote the cause of a broad peasant revolution in Russia following the precedent of the Pugachev revolt of 1774 during the reign of **Catherine the Great**. After the resulting "to the people" movement (1874) and its suppression, Chaikovsky escaped to the United States, where he joined **Cedar Vale** commune in southern Kansas founded by **William Frey**. He added important support and recognition to that effort that endured for nearly 10 years. After many more years of exile, mainly in Great Britain, Chaikovsky returned to Russia in 1917 as a veteran socialist revolutionary and supporter of **Alexander Kerensky**. In 1918–19 he was chairman of the **Archangel** Soviet during the period of Allied Intervention and its campaign against the Bolshevik regime, a position enhanced by his American experience and good knowledge of English.

CHAIKOVSKY, PETR. *See* TCHAIKOVSKY, PETER.

CHALIAPIN, FEDOR (NE SHALYAPIN) (1873–1938). Widely acclaimed as one of the greatest opera performers and bass voices of all time, Chaliapin excelled in Russian classical roles, such as that of Prince Igor in Alexander Borodin's opera of that name and especially in the title role of Modest Mussourgsky's *Boris Godunov*. He toured the United States both before and after the Russian Revolution of 1917, achieving much popularity and causing a sensation with a debut at Carnegie Hall in 1907, to his dismay critically reviewed by the *New York Times*. He made a number of memorable recordings and was in New York to greet **Konstantin Stanislavsky** and the **Moscow Art Theater (MAT)** upon their arrival in 1923. Chaliapin remained in America performing with the Metropolitan Opera and other premier companies for several years, under the auspices of **Sol Hurok**, and later in Paris in the 1930s. His talent was a prime example of the recognition of Russian performing genius by Americans, despite — or because of — the **Bolshevik Revolution**. After all of his well-deserved international attention, Soviet officials persisted in claiming his remains until permission was finally given in 1984, and he was reburied in the artist's section of the Novodevichy Cemetery in Moscow, a site often visited by American admirers.

CHAMBERLIN, WILLIAM HENRY (1907–1969). As a long-term correspondent (1922–34) for the *Christian Science Monitor* in Soviet Russia, Chamberlin won the respect of visitors, fellow journalists, and Soviet officials. Overall, he was considered one of the most reliable and unbiased sources, unlike **Walter Duranty** of the *New York Times*, for example, who was considered "Stalin's apologist." Anyone researching the Soviet Union in the 1920s and 1930s should not miss the *Christian Science Monitor*. Still, Chamberlin, like **Louis Fischer**, was sometimes overly sympathetic to the Soviet official and social scene. He and his Russian wife, Sonia, were among the leading hosts to visitors, correspondents, and embassy personnel when they arrived in Russia. His early history of the Russian Revolution remains a classic.

CHERNOBYL NUCLEAR ACCIDENT. During a routine test on 26 April 1986 of the number 2 reactor at a Soviet atomic power station in northern Ukraine, procedures went wrong and resulted in a meltdown, a nuclear explosion, and a wide dispersal of radioactivity into the air mainly to the northwest over Belarus and as far as Scandinavia and southward by water down the Pripiat River into the Dnepr. In some respects it was similar to the accident at Three Mile Island, near Harrisburg, Pennsylvania, in 1978 in that it involved a shutdown of the cooling system. The Three Mile incident, however, was minimized by a backup system and had wide public exposure, including a visit to the site by President **Jimmy Carter**. The Chernobyl accident had much greater consequences, affecting a wide area of **Ukraine** and Belarus.

The Soviet government, under **Mikhail Gorbachev**, at first attempted to keep the Chernobyl disaster secret, following the precedent of an earlier accident near Chelyabinsk in the Urals. Ample evidence through international monitors, however, disclosed the reality. After two weeks, Gorbachev acknowledged what had happened, though the full extent of Chernobyl was still not revealed. Nevertheless, the admission was considered a breakthrough in the advance of "*glasnost*," openness. The event resulted in a reconsideration of the expansion of nuclear power plants and a new emphasis on safety procedures, especially in the United States.

CHICAGO WORLD'S FAIR. *See* COLUMBIAN EXPOSITION.

CHICHERIN, GEORGY (1872–1936). Chicherin joined the revolutionary movement as a Menshevik in 1907. After a stint in a British jail during **World War I**, he returned to Soviet Russia in January 1918 as a Bolshevik. One of the few leading Bolsheviks to boast of noble birth, a cultured education, and diplomatic experience, Chicherin replaced **Leon Trotsky**, who opposed the signing of the treaty of **Brest-Litovsk**, as commissar of foreign affairs, while the latter took on the more immediate task of saving the Bolshevik regime as commissar of defense. In his new post as head of People's **Commissariat of Foreign Affairs (NARKOMINDEL)** (1919–30), Chicherin attended the **Geneva Conference** (1922) and negotiated one of the major diplomatic coups of the 20th century in signing the Treaty of Rapallo with Germany, which brought both countries out of political isolation. Chicherin's foreign policy was concentrated on close relations with neighboring powers, Germany and China, though he also supported trade initiatives with Great Britain and the United States. Considered an eccentric, skillfully playing Mozart on the piano, even among a host of unique Bolshevik characters, he was known for his simple but odd attire (wearing the same threadbare suit for months). Chicherin nonetheless won admiration from Western diplomats as well as from his Soviet colleagues. Unfortunately, declining health (severe diabetes) limited his activities, and increasingly, foreign affairs came under the direction of his assistant, **Maxim Litvinov**, who formally succeeded him as commissar in 1930.

CHINESE EASTERN RAILWAY (CER). Early in the construction of the **Trans-Siberian Railroad**, the world's largest rail project, a much shorter, direct route was proposed across **Manchuria** to its eastern terminus, **Vladivostok**. This not only cut the distance and time considerably but also suited well the Russian imperial desire to penetrate northern China economically. The CER branched off from the main Trans-Siberian line near Chita, east of Lake Baikal. Building the CER was much easier and cheaper and led to the establishment of a major Russian administrative and financial center at **Harbin** and a direct communication—on a side line—with the Russian naval base at Port Arthur, acquired in 1898. The sharply increased Russian presence in Manchuria was one of the chief causes of the **Russo–Japanese War** (1904–05). Though Russia suffered major military reverses, especially at sea, at the **Treaty of Portsmouth** it retained control of the line, which was of special benefit as a supply route to European Russia during **World War I**.

Many Americans traveled this road both before and after the war as an adventurous journey across Asia and Europe. During the **Russian Civil War** and **Intervention** (1918–20), much of the area came under the control of the Japanese intervention army and of anti-Bolshevik forces under General Grigori Semenov at Chita and General Dmitri Horvat in **Harbin**. A four-way struggle thus commenced between the old Russian administration, the White, anti-Bolshevik armies, the Japanese, and the special **American Railway Service Corps**, whose mission was to maintain and improve the line's operation. The corps resisted Japanese authority through the intervention period and essentially preserved the CER as an escape route for refugees from Bolshevism and, ironically, for its eventual control by Soviet authorities, who claimed the earlier Russian rights. Harbin thus morphed into an unusual city in the 1920s: part Chinese, part Soviet, and part anti-Soviet, with both the United States and Japan as interested spectators. As the Japanese presence escalated after 1930 and tensions heightened, many of the Russians moved out, and, finally, the Soviet Union sold the CER to Japan with the hope of reducing the conflict.

CHURCHILL, WINSTON (1874–1965). Educated at Harrow and Sandhurst, Churchill served briefly in the British army before having a career as a war correspondent in Cuba (Spanish–American War) and in South Africa during the Boer War. He was first elected to the House of Commons as a member of the Conservative Party in 1900 and rose rapidly, benefitting especially from the downfall of the Liberal Party, to become home secretary (1910–11) in a new government and then first lord of the admiralty (1911–15). In that post, he championed the expansion of the Royal Navy before **World War I**, and during it he conceived the Dardanelles campaign in 1915 as a way to advance British interests in the Middle East, force the Ottoman Empire out of the war, and open up supply routes to Russia. The disastrous results of the Battle of Gallipoli, however, caused his resignation, only for him to be advanced again by Prime Minister David Lloyd George to minister of munitions in 1917 and secretary of state for war (1918–21). A strong opponent of the Russian **Bolshevik Revolution**, Churchill backed military intervention in Russia and convinced Lloyd George and **Woodrow Wilson** of the need for an American commitment to that cause.

Churchill is best known as the prime minister of Great Britain during **World War II**, for being a firm opponent of appeasement, for his eloquence ("blood, sweat, and tears") during the Battle of Britain, and for his success in obtaining American support—the Atlantic Charter and **lend-lease**. Though an inveterate anti-Communist, Churchill was quick to rally Allied support to the Soviet Union after the German invasion of June 1941, even supporting the diversion of American aid from Great Britain to Russia by the **northern convoy route**. He was also a major architect of the strategy of the war, sometimes perhaps wrongly (as in his emphasis on the Italian campaign and the Balkans), and the resulting victory of the "grand alliance." His presence at Allied summit meetings in the Atlantic, **Casablanca**, Cairo, **Tehran**, **Yalta**, and **Potsdam** shaped not only the conduct of the war but also the postwar world. During the latter, in July 1945, however, a Labor Party election victory resulted in his withdrawal from the British government and replacement at the conference by Clement Atlee. Churchill was also one of the first, along with **George F. Kennan**, to warn that Soviet aggressive designs were leading to a new confrontation, the **cold war**. Once again his eloquence defined the border of that war, an **iron curtain** descending across Europe, in a speech at Fulton, Missouri, in August 1946. He returned to power in the 1950s to help wage that war before his final retirement from public life to become an author of the world he had seen. *See also* ROOSEVELT, FRANKLIN D.; STALIN, JOSEPH; TRUMAN, HARRY S.

CIVIL WAR, AMERICAN (1861–1865). An American conflict over the issues of maintaining the institution of slavery in the South vis-à-vis preserving the Union that had international implications. Coming soon after the **Crimean War**, during which the United States had shown strong sympathy for Russia, the Russian Empire clearly sided with the Union. The main cause in both cases was mutual antagonism toward Great Britain, which threatened to intervene on the side of the Confederacy. Another factor was the Russian move toward emancipation of its serf population in 1861 and several decades of close Russian–American friendship and collaboration, as well as the Russian desire to rid itself of a costly administration of **Alaska**. Russia was especially concerned about the United States being broken up into two or more weakened and dependent entities, subject to British and French influence.

The chief manifestation of Russian support for the North was the sending of two naval squadrons to New York and San Francisco in 1863–64. Though offering little military support and possibly initiated by independent interests in keeping the fleet active at sea (rather than blockaded in the Baltic Sea), the visits received wide publicity and enhanced Northern morale that may have been crucial in important battles, such as the one at Gettysburg and the siege of Vicksburg. This demonstration of Russian military strength may also have influenced British refusal of official recognition to the Confederacy. It would also serve as the basis for years of close Russian–American relations, inspiring in particular the mission of **Gustavus Fox** to Russia in 1866. *See also* CLAY, CASSIUS MARCELLUS; STOEKL, EDUARD.

CIVIL WAR, RUSSIAN (1918–1920). Conflict between the **Bolsheviks** and their opponents over control of the Russian Empire after the revolution and the end of **World War I**. The seizure of power in October

1917 during the **Bolshevik Revolution** was conducted by a well-organized but small group with the support of opponents of **Alexander Kerensky** and many who were opposed to a continuation of the war. Much of the Russian population remained neutral or in support of socialist alternatives as shown by the election results to the Constituent Assembly in November, about two weeks after the Bolshevik seizure of power. The signing of the **Treaty of Brest-Litovsk** and Soviet withdrawal from the war in March 1918 also created a divisive issue, fomented by Allied efforts to support a Russian war effort by any factions willing to be so engaged.

Among the major factors causing the beginning of direct military conflict during the summer of 1918 were the continued existence of sizable military units committed to the war effort, mainly in the south of Russia; the weakness of the Bolshevik-led government, which inspired hopes of its easy overthrow; and national independence movements in non-Russian areas of the former empire, chiefly in Ukraine, the Caucasus, Central Asia, and **Siberia**. The latter provided bases of operation for the anti-Bolshevik forces, dubbed the "Whites." The latter opposition forces were encouraged by the Allied Intervention in the form of financial and material support and the presence of military forces on three fronts: North Russia around **Archangel** and **Murmansk** (mainly British and American), South Russia (chiefly French and British), and Siberia (predominantly Japanese and American). Initial rationale for the Allied Intervention in this internal Russian civil war was to protect supplies sent to Russia in 1917 from falling under German (or Bolshevik) control, the ideological motive of destroying or containing the Bolshevik-espoused ideals of world revolution, to support Russian independence movements, to check Japanese ambitions in Siberia, and, in the case of British and French involvement, to gain hegemony in strategically important territories.

The main fronts of the civil war were in the north around Archangel and Murmansk, in the south across the broad steppeland of Ukraine, and in Siberia and the Urals region. While the northern front was relatively inactive, consisting mostly of skirmishes between Red Army contingents and local units supported by Allied **Intervention** units, the main theaters of war were in the south, where General **Anton Denikin** made considerable gains in the summer campaign of 1919, and in Siberia, where Admiral **Alexander Kolchak** established an anti-Bolshevik base of power in Omsk and received crucial initial support in 1918 from the **Czechoslovak Legion**, which was trying to find its way out of Russia across Siberia. Two incidents occurred in this arena that would have major repercussions on the outcome of the civil war: an advance guard of Kolchak drove north in the Urals in the summer of 1918, causing a panic reaction of local Soviet authorities in Ekaterinburg to murder **Nicholas II** and his family; a year later the Czechoslovaks, more interested in getting out than in being involved in the Russian internal conflict, captured Kolchak and turned him over to the Red Army for immediate execution in return for safe passage across Siberia.

The victory of the Bolshevik/Soviet side was due to a central operational advantage, divisions and rivalries among White leaders, lack of popular support for the White cause, which basically stood for the return of the old regime, and limited Allied support, which in turn gave the Red forces a propaganda initiative—the motherland invaded by hostile foreign armies. The Civil War and **Intervention** would leave a major impact on the new Soviet state, in terms of fear of internal dissidence and of foreign invasion that would linger on through the **cold war**. It would also produce a long-term effect of thousands of Russian civil war refugees (largely remnants of the White armies) in Europe, Asia, and the United States. *See also* CHAIKOVSKY, NIKOLAI; GRAVES, WILLIAM S.; OMSK GOVERNMENT.

CLAY, CASSIUS MARCELLUS (1810–1903). A Kentucky plantation owner who was nonetheless a foremost abolitionist, Clay was one of the founders of the Republican Party and aspired to be its presidential candidate in 1860. Seeing this was not possible, he lent essential support to the nomination and election of **Abraham Lincoln** and expected to be rewarded with a prominent position in the new administration. He was by this time renowned for his eccentricity and irascibility. To avoid dealing with his presence in Washington, Lincoln named him minister to Russia, where he, not unexpectedly, created quite a record of wild dancing, bourbon drinking, and liaisons with ballerinas, while also successfully courting Russian support for the North in the **American Civil War**. Hoping to regain fame at home as an army commander, he abruptly left his diplomatic post to return to the United States in 1862 in order to have another unwanted person in Washington, Simon Cameron, replace him as minister. Failing to achieve a suitable military command, Clay demanded to resume his "fun and games" in St. Petersburg, where he reigned on his diplomatic throne to the amazement of many for several more years, while the Russian court warmed to his eccentric lifestyle. In this post he survived several talented secretaries, especially **Jeremiah Curtin**, who upstaged Clay during the visit of **Gustavas Fox** (1866). He eventually returned to Kentucky with a Russian-born son. Clay is seldom confused with a namesake and descendant of an African American family from his plantation, an American heavyweight boxing champion better known as Muhammad Ali.

CLIBURN, VAN (1934–). Born in Shreveport, Louisiana, as Harvey Lavan Cliburn Jr., Cliburn grew up in Kilgore and Fort Worth, Texas, where he won a statewide piano competition at age 12. In 1948 he was awarded first place at the National Music Festival in New York. He then entered the Juilliard School in 1951, where he studied in the tradition of Russian romanticists, making his debut at Carnegie Hall at age 20. Four years later, in 1958, he entered the First International **Tchaikovsky** Piano Competition in Moscow, delighting the Russian audiences with his performances of Tchaikovsky's *Piano Concerto No. 1* and Rachmaninoff's *Piano Concerto No. 3*. He was awarded first prize over a strong Chinese competitor, sometimes thought to have been through the intervention of **Nikita Khrushchev**, who personally congratulated him in the interests of **peaceful coexistence**. Cliburn was welcomed home with a New York City ticker-tape parade, unique for a classical pianist, and became a symbol of Soviet–American friendship and cultural exchanges that began more formally later the same year. His subsequent recording of the Tchaikovsky concerto was the first classical piece to sell over one million copies. After a number of years of silence, he returned to the limelight with a special performance at the White House for President **Ronald Reagan** and Soviet leader **Mikhail Gorbachev** in 1987 and with an opening performance of Tchaikovsky for the centennial celebration of the opening of Carnegie Hall (which had featured Tchaikovsky himself). In 2003 he was awarded the Presidential Medal of Freedom by President **George W. Bush** and in the following year was conferred the Russian Friendship Medal by Russian president **Vladimir Putin**.

CLINTON, BILL (NE WILLIAM JEFFERSON BLYTHE CLINTON III) (1946–). Born in Hope, Arkansas, Clinton graduated from the **Edmund A. Walsh** School of Foreign Service at Georgetown University and was awarded a Rhodes Scholarship to Oxford University, where he studied world politics, played rugby, and cheered for the Chelsea Club. He subsequently graduated from Yale Law School (1973), where he met Hillary Rodham; they married two years later. Influenced by **John F. Kennedy**, Clinton soon entered public service in Arkansas, serving 12 years as governor, then won the Democratic nomination for president in 1992, and defeated the incumbent **George H. W. Bush** in the national election.

In regard to Russia, Clinton and his secretaries of state, Warren Christopher (first term—1993–97) and **Madeleine Albright** (second term—1997–2001), faced a rather different situation from other American administrations after 1945 with the collapse of the Union of Soviet Socialist Republics (USSR) and Communism as a threat. Instead of a world military power with an aggressive foreign policy, the new **Russian Federation** was in rapid decline and in danger of internal disintegration under the presidency of **Boris Yeltsin**. With the guidance of the shrewd and adroit Christopher and Albright—and especially that of **Strobe Talbot**, his Oxford roommate—Clinton "managed" the unsteady and often inebriated Yeltsin through the transition into the steady and sober but more aggressive leadership of **Vladimir Putin** in 2001.

COLBY, BAINBRIDGE (1869–1950). A New York attorney (Columbia University Law School) and active Democratic politician in the early 20th century, Colby was appointed to the cabinet of **Woodrow Wilson**, replacing **Robert Lansing** in March 1920 to serve a year as secretary of state. During that brief tenure, however, he left his mark on the American policy of nonrecognition of Soviet Russia by issuing what became known as the **Colby Note**. Retiring from public service in 1921 and out of the political limelight during the following Republican administrations, Colby would return to render valuable service in the tenures of **Franklin D. Roosevelt** during **World War II**.

COLBY NOTE (AUGUST 1920). Responding to complaints of vagueness and indecision in regard to the American policy toward the new

Soviet government, the State Department constructed a response to a contrived query by the Italian ambassador. The catalyst of the Italian letter to the State Department was probably not Secretary of State **Bainbridge Colby** but his assistant, Norman Davis. And the formal "American Note on the Polish Situation" that it inspired was drafted mainly by John Spargo, a Wilsonian liberal turned avid anti-Communist. The "note" expressed a firm refusal to recognize formally the Soviet government, citing its effort to conquer Poland for Communism. It set more or less in concrete, ironically still in the era of **Woodrow Wilson**, the American policy toward Russia for the following three Republican administrations, until 1933. It also divided political elements in both parties more firmly between recognition, favored by Republicans such as **Raymond Robins, James Goodrich**, and Senator **William Borah** and Democrats **Norman Hapgood**, James Cox (presidential candidate in 1924), and **Edward House**. In opposition to recognition and upholding the Colby Note were the powerful voices of Secretary of State **Charles Evans Hughes, Herbert Hoover**, and **Elihu Root**.

COLD WAR (1946–1991). A period of international tension and instability between Communist-dominated countries, led by the USSR, and the freer, more democratic Western world, symbolized by the United States. The beginnings of the cold war are still much debated but stemmed mainly from unsolved problems and ideological and political power confrontations at the end of **World War II**. Controversy continues regarding the "war guilt" with "new left" historians espousing the supreme role of the United States in its long-term quest for world economic dominance, projected by **William Appleman Williams** and supported by a number of his students, including **Walter LaFeber**. The main American view (**John Lewis Gaddis**), however, is that the Soviet leadership, namely **Joseph Stalin**, distrusted democratic processes to assure the friendship of Eastern Europe and imposed by force his own regime, which caused the cold war. A major initial result was the division of Europe between the two sides, marked by the **iron curtain**, and a rivalry for military dominance and control of third-world areas, especially as conducted by **John Foster Dulles** in his **"brinkmanship"** in the 1950s. Above all, the cold war created a wasteful and very dangerous arms race involving nuclear and missile weapons systems.

The initial focus of the struggle was on Central Europe and the Soviet military control of a large part of Eastern Europe. A central point became Berlin, under four-power occupation. The Western powers were able to reconstruct their zones, while the Soviet Union was forced to concentrate on its own country. The disparity and imbalance led to the Soviet effort to force the West out by way of the **Berlin blockade** of land access routes (1948–49), while also consolidating control over Czechoslovakia and Hungary. A series of crises followed that helped fuel animosity and resentment: the Communist control of China and other parts of Asia, the **Korean War** (1950–53), the **Hungarian Revolution** (1956), the **U-2 incident** (1960), the **Berlin Wall** (1961), the **Cuban missile crisis** (1962), the Soviet armed intervention in Czechoslovakia (1968), the Soviet invasion of **Afghanistan** (1979), and the shooting down of a South Korean airliner (1983). Fortunately, interludes of relaxation—**peaceful coexistence** and **détente**—relaxed tensions, and saner minds prevailed during periods of crises. The cold war ended with the collapse of the Soviet Union and Communism in 1990–91. Dangerous remains are left: residual hostility, nuclear weapons, and psychological war. *See also* ATOMIC DIPLOMACY.

COLE, FELIX (1887–1969). Born in St. Louis, Cole graduated from Harvard University (Phi Beta Kappa, 1910) and first entered the Russian scene as an American automobile agent in St. Petersburg (1913–14). Having married a Russian and learned the language, he entered the American foreign service in 1915 and was assigned to the consulate at **Archangel** during the **Russian Revolution** in 1917 and **Russian Civil War**. He was one of the few foreign service officers to oppose military **intervention** in 1918; from his perspective, Russians simply did not want to fight anymore, so why try to force them? Back in Washington, after the American military and diplomatic withdrawal from Russia, Cole served in the newly formed "Russian Bureau" of the State Department.

Cole then directed the Russian division ("**listening post**") of the American legation in Riga during the 1920s and 1930s with the support of **Robert F. Kelley**, director of the East European Division of the State Department. The main tasks involved the sorting and translation of various communications coming out of Soviet Russia through the regular mail or through agents. In the process he accumulated enormous numbers of files and a library that was the envy of anyone interested in Soviet Russia, perhaps the largest of its kind at the time, though often in a state of disorganization, according to the memory of some of those privileged to work in it. He was admired and respected by **George F. Kennan**, **Loy Henderson**, **Charles ("Chip") Bohlen**, and other leading experts on Russia of the period. Felix Cole is certainly a neglected and unsung hero of Russian–American relations of the period. He concluded his diplomatic career as consul-general in Algiers (1939–45), minister to Ethiopia (1945–47), and ambassador to Ceylon (1947–49). In retirement he served as chair of American Friends of Russian Freedom in the 1960s.

COLLECTIVE SECURITY (1932–1938). The Soviet foreign policy designed to create common resistance to the aggressive designs of Germany and Japan. Sensing a definite threat to the Soviet Union from the rise of Adolf Hitler and German and Japanese power, Soviet Commissar of Foreign Affairs **Maxim Litvinov** sought friendly arrangements and alliances with Western liberal democracies in order to contain and restrict those totalitarian dictatorships, despite the fact that **Joseph Stalin**'s Russia was also one. Initial successes, such as recognition by the United States (1933), membership in the **League of Nations** (1934), and the Franco–Soviet alliance (1935), were defeated by the British and French policy of appeasement at the **Munich Conference** (1938) and by reversals in the **Spanish Civil War**. Abandonment of collective security was signaled by the dismissal of Litvinov from direction of foreign policy in April 1939, followed a few months later by the **Nazi–Soviet Pact**.

COLLINS' OVERLAND–WESTERN UNION EXTENSION. The triumph of telegraph technology in the mid-19th century led to projects for connecting Europe and the United States, but the possibility of a submarine cable across the Atlantic was initially discounted as impracticable. An alternative offered by Western Union after the **American Civil War** was a much longer route through **Alaska**, across the **Bering Strait**, and by way of **Siberia**. With the cooperation of the Russian government, the company organized a subsidiary with deployment of crews in Alaska and northeast Siberia to connect the main European centers to the United States. **Perry Collins**, who had traveled across Siberia in 1856, inspired the idea, though he had little to do with the actual project. He promoted the employment of veteran telegraphers and surveyors such as **George Kennan**, who became devoted to learning more about Russian life and politics. After a considerable effort in surveying and actually erecting a number of telegraph poles across Siberia, the project of Cyrus Field to lay a submarine cable across the Atlantic proved successful in 1866, and the Collins route was abandoned.

COLLINS, PERRY MCDONOUGH (1813–1900). California attorney and business promoter. Collins was attracted to the potential of Russian–American business ventures in the North Pacific by the **Crimean War** and the presence of the **Russian America Company** in the northwest of North America. Certified by a vague official designation as American "agent" for the Amur region, Collins, accompanied by Bernard Peyton, journeyed overland from St. Petersburg across **Siberia** to the Pacific in 1856–57, and then by way of Japan back to California, around the world the hard way in about 80 days. His trip received wide publicity from his descriptive account of it in *A Voyage Down the Amoor: with a Land Journey through Siberia, and Incidental Notices of Manchooria, Kamschatka, and Japan* (1860), which also received wide circulation in Russia. This book, along with the rapid development of the American West Coast, spurred American interest in the Pacific region in general and led to the project of the **Collins' Overland–Western Union Extension**.

COLTON, ETHAN (1872–c. 1960). A long-term **Young Men's Christian Association (YMCA)** secretary in Russia, he supervised a major increase in American volunteers to serve Russian soldiers behind the lines, beginning in 1916. A graduate of Wesleyan University (1898), Colton completed postgraduate work at Chicago and Columbia Universities before joining the YMCA as a secretary in 1900, with service mainly in the foreign department (1904–15). As commitments to the Russian YMCA organization rose in 1917 and 1918 with the **Russian Revolution** and **Civil War**, Colton guided its expanding operations from the "Y's" New York headquarters. Surprised by the degree of tolerance of its work by the Soviet regime in 1918, he was caught in a dilemma, ultimately siding with aid to the anti-**Bolshevik** and **Intervention** forces in North Russia and **Siberia**. He was annoyed, however, by the refusal of the **Omsk government** of **Alexander Kolchak** to allow the American volunteers into their area. Colton continued to direct from New York the relief activities to Russian refugees in Western Europe, especially Germany, in the 1920s. He described his career in *Fifty Years with Russians* (1940).

COLUMBIAN EXPOSITION (CHICAGO WORLD'S FAIR) (1893). The largest world's fair at that time, the exposition at the Great White City (now mostly occupied by the University of Chicago) celebrated the 400th anniversary of Christopher Columbus's discovery of America. Coming at a high point of Russian *Amerikanism*, it attracted much attention from Russians. A grand Russian pavilion in turn drew many American spectators, stimulated especially by the "**Tolstoy** craze" and the concurrent widely publicized American relief for famine victims in Russia. Finance Minister **Sergei Witte** sent a number of Russian "inspectors" for detailed information of fair displays as well as American innovations, many of which were published in Russian, the most important by Ivan Yanzhul. In addition, a Russian choir and orchestra performed to large audiences. The exposition represented a major vehicle for the transfer of technological innovation and for cultural appreciation.

The Russian display included Orlov horses, furs, plans and models for the **Trans-Siberian Railroad**, leather, linen, china, silver, crystal, folk arts, ore samples, and paintings (especially Ivan Aizovskii, Konstantin Makovskii, **Vasily Vereshchagin**, and Ilya Repin)—1,200 total exhibits. Official visitors attending were Russian Minister Grigory Kantakuzen, Secretary of Legation Peter Botkin, specially designated Chicago consul Peter Thal, Sergei Volkonsky (education), Liudmila Shakovskaia (women's arts), and Evgeniia Lineva (choral folk music). Wide coverage of the event appeared in the Russian press, written by **Barbara MacGahan** (*Severnyi Vestnik*), Vladimir Sviatlovskii (*Novaia Vremia* and *Russkoe Obozrenie*), **Peter Dement'ev** (*Vestnik Evropy* and *Nedelia*), and Arnold Gillin (*Dvigatel'*). Never before had the United States been so well covered in the Russian press. Similarly, all Russian happenings at the fair drew much publicity in the American press.

COMINFORM (COMMUNIST INFORMATION BUREAU) (1947–1963). Intended as a unification screen for the Soviet Union's dominance over its East European satellites and as a replacement of the **Comintern** (abolished in 1943) during the **cold war**, the strategy of the Communist Information Bureau was undermined early by the defection in 1948 of Yugoslavia from the group, especially since Belgrade was proposed initially as its center. The Cominform was essentially a lost initiative, cast aside by **Nikita Khrushchev** for more practical efforts, such as the militarily oriented **Warsaw Pact** and in new policies toward the West promoted by **Khrushchev** in **peaceful coexistence**.

COMINTERN (COMMUNIST INTERNATIONAL) (1919–1943). The Communist (or Third) International was a Soviet-sponsored organization for breakaway left-wing socialists in various countries who supported the **Bolshevik** idea of revolution and were harnessed to support it in the 1920s and 1930s. As such, it was conceived as the third socialist international, the second having collapsed at the beginning of **World War I**. The members included the **Communist Party of the United States of America (CPUSA)**, founded in 1919 as a left-wing split from the socialist movement and headed by **John Reed, Bill Haywood**, and others. The various Comintern congresses brought a number of American party members to the Moscow sessions, including, at the directorate's insistence, a number of **African Americans**. From a policy of supporting world revolution in all respects—through propaganda, funding, and so on—the organization conformed in the 1930s to the support of **Maxim Litvinov**'s moderate Soviet foreign policy. No Americans were in the high administration of the organization, though the CPUSA maintained close ties and forwarded its reports and other materials to its Moscow archives, microfilmed and available in the **Library of Congress**. The affiliation of an American party with an international organization that advocated world revolution created much public and politically hostile feeling, both toward the genuine American supporters of socialist idealism and toward the Soviet Union, as leader of the effort, for interference in the American political process, not to mention using Comintern agents as spies. In 1943, in the interests of the **World War II** Grand Alliance, the Comintern was abolished, only to be revived in a new guise in 1947 as the **Communist Information Bureau (COMINFORM)**, specifically limited, however, to Eastern Europe.

COMMERCIAL TREATY OF 1832. The "Treaty of Navigation and Commerce between the United States of America and His Majesty the Emperor of All the Russias" was signed in December 1832 by American Minister **James Buchanan** in St. Petersburg and was ratified the following year by the U.S. Senate. The treaty responded to the needs of American consuls, especially **Levett Harris**, merchants, such as **Ropes and Company**, and the rapid rise of American commerce with Russia during the first half of the 19th century. By the 1830s the main item of export to Russia was cotton, so the Southern aristocracy that dominated the State Department was naturally interested in protecting this profitable trade with Russia.

Most of the 13 articles dealt with the appointment and rights of consuls and commercial agents and the reception of ships in harbors. Articles I and X, however, covered equal rights of citizens to conduct business affairs. This was interpreted as giving the same rights to Americans in Russia as were held by Russian subjects. Because many of the "Americans" were Jewish and most of them originally from Russia and returning as naturalized U.S. citizens, the Russian government interpreted their rights as the same as those of Russian Jews whose activities were restricted in various ways. By the end of the century this led to the **passport question**, the practice of Russian consuls of denying visas on religious grounds. Considered a violation of the principle of freedom of religion, the U.S. Senate in 1911 decided to apply the right in Article XII to abrogate the treaty after a year's notice. The treaty thus became null and void in 1912. Economic relations continued as before while attempts were made to negotiate a new treaty. These were interrupted, however, by **World War I** and the **Bolshevik Revolution**.

COMMISSARIAT OF FOREIGN AFFAIRS (NARKOMINDEL). As a result of the **Bolshevik Revolution**, the former Russian Ministry of Foreign Affairs was given a new Soviet "revolutionary" title and acronym. Its first commissar, **Leon Trotsky**, proverbially entered the building of the former Imperial Ministry of Foreign Affairs and announced, "We will issue a few decrees and close up shop," indicating that the immediate approach of world revolution would eliminate the need for diplomatic relations between states. He left that post within a few months, however, to take charge of the creation of the Red Army and was replaced by **Georgy Chicherin**, who had some experience in the Russian diplomatic service before the revolution.

During the **New Economic Policy** (1921–28), a further confusion resulted from the conflicting interests of Narkomindel, dedicated to more or less diplomatic practice and courting good relations with other countries, and the Communist International (**Comintern**) that was committed to world revolution. As Chicherin's health deteriorated, his assistant, **Maxim Litvinov**, took charge and became commissar in 1930 and pursued the moderate policy of **collective security** that was aimed against the aggressions of Germany, Italy, and Japan. Not long after the failure of that policy, dramatized by the **Munich Pact**, he would be replaced by **Vyacheslav Molotov**. In 1946 the awkward title of Narkomindel would be changed to Ministry of Foreign Affairs. It continues to function in the **Russian Federation** as the implement of its foreign relations.

COMMITTEE ON PUBLIC INFORMATION (CPI). Also known as the "Creel Committee," an agency founded soon after the entry of the United States in **World War I** to develop and to supervise the American propaganda effort on behalf of the mission of **Woodrow Wilson** "to make the world safe for democracy." It inspired controversy from the beginning, especially because of its aggressive direction by George Creel. One immediate task of the Russian contingent, in charge of Edgar Sisson, was to develop a program to support the Russian **Provisional Government** and keep it in the war, which was an obvious failure, due, at least in part, to lack of sufficient American funding. During the revolutionary period in Russia, the committee was quite prominent in promoting **Alexander Kerensky** to no avail, and then faced criticism for its strongly hostile reaction to Bolshevism. It also bore the burden of certifying documents implicating the Soviet leadership with German monetary support that were later proved to be forgeries. In conclusion, the "Creel Committee" in Russia, through its mismanagement, probably contributed to **Bolshevik** success in maintaining power in 1918. *See also* SISSON DOCUMENTS.

COMMITTEE ON STATE SECURITY (KGB). The successor of the **People's Commissariat of Internal Affairs (NKVD)** and Ministry of Internal Affairs (MVD), it served the Soviet state from the 1950s to the collapse of the USSR as the equivalent of a combination of the American **Central Intelligence Agency (CIA)** and Federal Bureau of Investigation (FBI). It inherited the power of the previous organizations in regard to surveillance of population, managing arrests and sentencing of political dissidents, supervising the *gulag* empire of labor camps, maintaining a widespread network of foreign intelligence operations, and safeguarding the Soviet regime. As such, it was a major cause and participant in the **cold war**.

Nevertheless, during the years of **peaceful coexistence** and **détente** from the 1950s through the 1980s, it cultivated and assisted expertise on the outside world, with special focus on the United States. **Yury Andropov,** as director from 1967 to 1981, was especially influential in obtaining and cultivating the best talent, providing access to information, and emphasizing objective (nonideological) analyses. Much of what the *shestidesiatniki* ("men of the sixties") produced in the era of **Leonid Brezhnev**, unfortunately, was ignored by the leadership. They ascended to prominence during the reforms of **Mikhail Gorbachev** and included his important allies in **glasnost** and perestroika such as **Alexander Yakovlev** and Anatoly Chernayev. Among some of the Soviet Union's "best and brightest" who were recruited into the KGB during this period were **Vladimir Putin** and a number of others who would serve as close supporters in his administrations as president (2000–08).

COMMITTEE TO DEFEND AMERICA BY AIDING THE ALLIES (1940–1941). Created by **Franklin D. Roosevelt** to prepare the United States for a larger role in resisting fascism that began in August 1939, the president asked **William Allen White**, a leading journalist and Republican from Kansas, to chair this nonpartisan and state-oriented organization to build public support for aid to Great Britain during the 1940–41 Battle of Britain. It served its purpose as a propaganda agency for an American war effort and as a prelude to the **lend-lease** programs that would be extended to the Soviet Union immediately after the German invasion of the Soviet Union in June 1941.

COMMONWEALTH OF INDEPENDENT STATES (CIS). As independence movements grew rapidly in strength within the constituent republics of the Soviet Union in the 1980s, especially in the Baltic states and Ukraine, President **Mikhail Gorbachev** attempted to save the Soviet Union and his own position of power in 1991 by a new arrangement, outlined in a "Union Treaty." This created a crisis in the government, as the vice president and most of the council of ministers considered this move a drastic concession that would bring to an end the centralized power of the Soviet Union and the Communist Party of the Soviet Union (CPSU). The 1991 **August Coup**, an attempt to force Gorbachev to resign or back down, was the result. Its failure in the face of the opposition of Boris Yeltsin and the government of the Russian republic caused the rapid collapse of the Soviet Union in the aftermath. CIS was to keep at least some semblance of unity, similar to the British Commonwealth, and received limited support from the three Slavic republics—Russia, Ukraine, and especially Belarus—but essentially remains only on paper as nationalist divisions prevailed with the demise of the central authority of the Soviet Union and the CPSU. The idea of a confederation remains in formal existence, however, in the common *lingua franca* and in the economic interests and political ties of the states of the former Soviet Union.

COMMUNIST PARTY OF THE UNITED STATES OF AMERICA (CPUSA). The left wing of the American Socialist Party split off in 1919 to form the American Communist Party, which took its inspiration from the successful **Bolshevik Revolution** and the formation of the **Communist International (Comintern)**. Though founded by distinguished intellectuals and labor leaders, such as **John Reed** and **Bill Haywood**, and seemingly representing a real threat during the **"Red Scare"** (1919), the new party remained a small, inconsequential American presence during the 1920s. Under the unimaginative leadership of **William Foster** and **Earl Browder** and the more controversial involvement of **Jay Lovestone**, the party remained divided and weak, partly owing to its reluctance to recruit membership from dissident **African Americans**. Though posting candidates in all presidential elections, it registered an embarrassingly small percentage of the vote, even during the Depression.

Nevertheless, it unsurprisingly gained in membership, especially among young workers and intellectuals in the 1930s. Though the CPUSA received some funding from Moscow and harbored and supported intelligence activities, most of the money from abroad was devoted to propaganda publications, such as the works of **Vladimir Lenin**, and expenses for delegates to Comintern congresses. Besides internal divisions, the party was handicapped by its affiliation with the Comintern and external direction, the renewed strength of the American Socialist Party under Norman Thomas, the development of a successful National Association for the Advancement of Colored People (NAACP), and the impact of the New Deal in the administrations of **Franklin D. Roosevelt**.

CONCESSIONS (1921–1927). After the abandonment of the extreme policies of War Communism at the 10th **Bolshevik** party congress in March 1921 and the inauguration of the **New Economic Policy**, a major relaxation and retreat from the previous do-it-alone policies, the Soviet government sought accommodations with Western businesses, many of whom had suffered by way of confiscations of property as a result of the **Bolshevik Revolution**. The new Soviet regime lacked resources to purchase assistance and expertise, so it turned to concessions, which were contract arrangements with foreign companies to restore or develop specific industries (mines or factories) on concession terms. For example, a company might agree to invest a certain amount of capital and personnel to repairing and expanding a production with a guaranteed share of it that could be sold at market price abroad or in the Soviet Union. Neither the Soviet regime nor the foreign companies were happy with the results, which, nevertheless, were considerable in terms of reviving the Soviet economy. This policy would be replaced in the **First Five-Year Plan** by direct, negotiated payments for major construction projects, based on sales of art, mineral resources, and shipments of gold.

CONSTANTINE, GRAND DUKE (NE KONSTANTIN NIKOLAE-VICH) (1827–1892). The grand duke, second son of Tsar Nicholas I, emerged in the wake of the **Crimean War** to lead a reform movement for the emancipation of the serf peasant population and for the establishment of independent local governments (*zemstva*). He won the support of a number of the Russian aristocracy and bureaucratic leaders (who became known as the *konstantinovtsy*). Though he never visited the United States, he met a number of American visitors to Russia, including **Gustavus Fox** in 1866. As minister of navy and "grand admiral," he was a strong advocate of the sale of **Alaska** to the United States and of the annexation of the "Amur Provinces" (on both sides of the Amur River) by treaty with China. He was probably the most active proponent and influence on **Alexander II** in regard to the sale of the Russian territories in North America. His motivation was to concentrate Russian resources, especially naval power, in the Far East—China, Manchuria, Korea, and Japan. The foundation of **Vladivostok** as a major port and naval base in 1867 was largely owing to his initiative. Constantine was also a major factor in the building of a modern Russian navy, symbolized especially by the construction of the *Grand Admiral* in New York.

CONTAINMENT. American policy toward the USSR during the early years of the **cold war** and later, the purpose of which, as outlined in the **Long Telegram** (1946) sent from Moscow by **George F. Kennan** (and expanded upon in his 1947 "X" article in *Foreign Affairs*), was to steer American foreign policy away from the isolationism of post–**World War I** into an active and multifaceted resistance to the "Soviet threat." Among the immediate results were the **Truman Doctrine**, the **Marshall Plan**, successful resistance to the **Berlin blockade**, and the formation of the **North Atlantic Treaty Organization (NATO)**. In later years Kennan complained that what he had in mind was not an emphasis on the resulting military confrontation but an economic and political strategy of containment. He also opposed **NATO expansion** into Eastern Europe after the breakup of the Soviet Union, but the policy continues in American efforts to establish antimissile installations in Eastern Europe and to support NATO membership for states of the former Soviet Union, such as Ukraine and Georgia.

CONVENTION OF 1824. After sharp American and British reaction to the Russian Ukaz of 1821, the Russian government retreated quickly and signed with American Minister **Henry Middleton** in April 1824 a convention that nullified the ukaz and opened Russian ports on the Pacific to American ships. The boundary of Russian possessions on the Pacific coast was limited to 54°40' latitude south (later to become an American battle cry against the British regarding the northern border of the Oregon Territory). The extended territorial limits at sea were forgotten and, as if to make up for any insult, Russian ports were freely opened for 10 years (but not extended). Russia did gain, however, formal recognition by the United States of its rights in the northwest of North America.

COOLIDGE, ARCHIBALD CARY (1866–1928). As professor of history at Harvard University, Coolidge is credited with offering in the 1890s the first course in an American university that concentrated on Russian history, though it was titled, "A History of Northern Europe." He is best known as an activist for the pursuit of a knowledge of Russia in America, inspiring the creation of other programs, and for the development of the Slavic collection of the university's Widener Library. Coolidge visited Russia several times and was one of the few American experts on the country before **World War I**. In 1921 he served briefly as a consultant and advisor to the **American Relief Administration (ARA)** operations in Russia. Coolidge also served as director of the Widener Library and of its collection expansion in world areas, but perhaps his most important legacy is as a founding editor of *Foreign Affairs Quarterly*. He was instrumental in the initial programs of the **Council on Foreign Relations** in the 1920s and its emphasis on Eastern Europe.

COOLIDGE, CALVIN (1872–1933). Thirtieth president of the United States, 1923–29. A villager from Vermont, Coolidge became president by virtue of a surprise election as governor of his state in 1919, his unheralded nomination for vice president on the Republican ticket of 1920, and, of course, the sudden death of President Warren Harding during a speaking tour of the western United States. Reelected as a status quo president in 1924, Coolidge generally left foreign policy in the hands of Secretary of State **Charles Evans Hughes** and a State Department that was dominated by conservative, anti-Soviet officials. On the advice of Hughes, Coolidge refused to respond to an overture of Soviet Commissar for Foreign Affairs **Georgy Chicherin** to initiate diplomatic recognition. Despite the prorecognition stance of a number of Republican leaders, such as **James P. Goodrich**, Senator **William E. Borah**, and **Raymond Robins**, Hughes and Coolidge maintained an opposite course.

COOPER, HUGH (1865–1937). Cooper established a reputation as a builder for constructing port facilities in France in 1917–18 for large-scale unloading of American troops and supplies and internationally as a consultant on the building of the first Aswan Dam in Egypt. Subsequently, he became one of the great dam builders of American history, responsible for the Keokuk, Iowa, dam across the Mississippi and the Muscle Shoals project in Alabama. Soviet–American facilitator **Alexander Gumberg** and Soviet professor of engineering Ivan Aleksandrov (on a tour of the United States) made arrangements for him to visit the proposed site of a very large dam on the Dnepr River in Ukraine in 1926. His support transformed an idea into a giant construction project, in the vanguard of the **First Five-Year Plan**. The Dneprostroi dam not only had an output of over 500,000 kilowatts when completed in 1932, but also made the river navigable up to Kiev by essentially eliminating the famous Zaporozheny rapids. Cooper was showered with honors by Soviet authorities and by **Joseph Stalin** personally, which he repaid by support for diplomatic recognition.

COOPER, JAMES FENIMORE (1789–1851). Cooper's rise to literary popularity in Russia lagged only a few months behind his fame in America, beginning with the publication of *The Spy* in Russian in 1825. The Russian reception of German romantic philosophers prepared the way for a love of American romantic fiction. Cooper was favored over his British contemporary Sir Walter Scott because of Russia's prevailing Anglophobia and pro-American spirit. Cooper's most popular novels, *The Last of the Mohicans*, *The Deerslayer*, and *The Pathfinder*, were published in many Russian editions. One of Russia's foremost critics, Vissarion Belinsky, praised Cooper's works, and Alexander Pushkin kept a 14-volume collected works in his library and acknowledged his debt to the American writer. Though Cooper never visited Russia, he had a number of conversations with Russians in Paris salons and apparently enjoyed their company. His popularity would continue through generations of Russians, with **Mikhail Gorbachev** acknowledging that Cooper was one of his favorite writers.

CORSE, FREDERICK (1872–1928). As director of **New York Life Insurance Company** in Russia during the first two decades of the 20th century, Corse supervised the remarkable expansion of New York Life into the premier insurance company in Russia, employing several thousand employees and, by agreement for its operations in Russia, investing much of its capital in Russian stocks, making it the largest nongovernment holder of Russian securities. The company was based in prominent headquarters on Nevsky Prospect in St. Petersburg and contracted policies from many additional storefront agencies and through traveling salesmen, mostly Russian, throughout the empire. Corse naturally had many connections in Russian society and a unique knowledge of Russian affairs, political as well as economic. His collection of ragtime recordings was renowned in St. Petersburg/Petrograd, promoting another aspect of American culture in Russia. Due to his business and social prominence, he also served as a major advisor to ambassador **David Francis** and host to **Samuel Harper** during **World War I** and during the 1917 revolutionary turmoil. Because many clients in German-occupied Poland were still under his supervision, his efforts to maintain contacts there resulted in Russian suspicion of his being a German agent. In 1918 he was forced to abandon his business in Russia, leaving many life insurance policies behind for later litigation. Considering these circumstances, it is not surprising that he was an ardent opponent of the **Bolsheviks** and an influential advocate of nonrecognition in the 1920s.

COTTMAN, THOMAS (1800–1876). Physician, southern planter, **Alaska** purchase advocate. Originally from Maryland, Cottman received a medical education in Baltimore before moving to Louisiana in 1830 to supervise his wife's plantation in Ascension Parish (near New Orleans). In 1853 he left for Europe to place his daughter in school in Paris and for reasons unknown went on to St. Petersburg, where he stayed through the first half of 1854. The Russian court at the beginning of the **Crimean War** was quite happy to welcome an American who was polished, sympathetic, and fluent in French. Out of his conversations with Nicholas I and other officials came a proposal that Russia sell the Alaska territory to the United States to avoid the possibility of a British occupation and to obtain funds to finance the war. Cottman returned to the United States in mid-1854 to publicize the idea for the first time that the United States might acquire that Russian territory; the project was also supported by expansionist William McKendree Gwin, senator from California (but also formerly of Louisiana). Secretary of State William L. Marcy met with Russian Minister **Eduard Stoekl** to discuss the possibility. The project reached its zenith in public discussion in August, not a good time for any important development in Washington, when Stoekl was in Newport, Rhode Island, Gwin in California, and Cottman at home in Louisiana. By September the **Russian America Company (RAC)**, opposed to the sale, had reached a neutrality agreement with the Hudson's Bay Company that seemed to safeguard the territory for the duration of the war. Cottman would still be involved on the periphery of the actual purchase in 1867 and again in defense of the reputation of Russian Minister **Konstantin Katakazi** in 1871.

COTTON. The major item of import from the United States by Russia during the first half of the 19th century was carried by large Yankee clippers from ports such as New Orleans, Mobile, and Savannah to Russia. Cotton accounted for the largest single item of export in the 1830s and 1840s and was responsible for a very favorable American balance of trade with the Russian empire. This changed dramatically during the embargo of the **American Civil War** and the development of cotton production in Central Asia. Because of disruptions in that area during the **Russian Civil War** (1918–20), cotton would again became a major item of import from the United States in the 1920s— but only briefly—until the construction of massive irrigation projects in Central Asia along the Amu Darya and Syr Darya Rivers expanded Soviet cotton cultivation during the **First Five-Year Plan**.

COUNCIL ON FOREIGN RELATIONS. American organization devoted to promotion of the study and understanding of international relations, initiated by **Hamilton Fish Armstrong** and **Archibald Cary Coolidge** to combat the general withdrawal of the United States from world affairs after **World War I**. Officially formed in July 1921 on the eve of the beginning of a massive relief effort to Eastern Europe, the council inaugurated a high-quality journal, *Foreign Affairs Quarterly*, a year later. Under the editorship of Armstrong and Coolidge, it sought articles especially about Soviet policies and by Soviet leaders. The council was devoted to developing an American awareness of the larger world in an era of isolationism. An important step forward occurred in 1930 with the establishment of a permanent and highly visible headquarters at Park Avenue and 65th Street in New York City, where it continues to maintain a substantial library and holds regular seminars highlighted by prominent speakers. These activities flourish into the 21st century with appearances by various Soviet and Russian leaders, such as **Mikhail Gorbachev** and **Vladimir Putin**. Following this successful example, several other major American cities have similar organizations to promote awareness of international relations.

COUNTS, GEORGE S. (1889–1974). Counts received his graduate training at the University of Chicago, where he acquired a knowledge of Russian language and society under the tutelage of **Samuel Harper**. He visited Soviet Russia several times, recording his experiences in *Across Russia by Ford* and *Country of the Blind* (1930), remarkable portrayals of Russia in transformation during the **First Five-Year Plan**. Counts's main interest was the study of the new directions in Soviet education, in which he was a pioneer in regard to scholarly examination. His pro-Soviet proclivity, however, led to criticism and exclusion by the larger American Russian community, much to his and others' regret. He, however, held a long-term professorship at the Teachers' College of Columbia University.

CRANE, CHARLES R. (1858–1939). Successor—with his brother—to the management of a major plumbing fixture company of Chicago, still in existence, Crane became infatuated with Russia during the first of more than 20 trips to the country in 1891. He then spent several months in St. Petersburg in the late 1890s managing the partnership of his company with **Westinghouse** for the manufacture of air brakes for Russian railroads, especially the **Trans-Siberian**. His interest in Russian culture and especially in the Orthodox Church expanded, and Crane subsequently devoted much of his own energy and resources to the advancement of Russian studies in America. This crusade began with his shepherding William Rainey Harper, founding president of the University of Chicago, to Russia in 1900 for conversations with **Leo Tolstoy**, **Nicholas II**, and government leaders **Konstantin Pobedonostsev** and **Sergei Witte**.

In 1903, Crane sponsored the lectures in the United States of liberal Russian historian and politician **Paul Miliukov** at the Lowell Institute in Boston and at the University of Chicago. They formed a lifelong friendship, and together they toured the Balkans, which were in ferment in the years before World War I. In 1910 Crane's interest in the Russian church led to a spectacular tour of the United States by an Orthodox choir from Moscow. Crane was also active in American politics behind the scenes, becoming the largest single contributor to the campaigns for the presidency of **Woodrow Wilson** in 1912 and 1916 and his campaign manager in 1912. He was Wilson's choice for ambassador to Russia in 1913 but declined because of business affairs there. Nor were his international interests confined to Russia, as he traveled widely through the Middle East and the Far East.

Crane welcomed the **February Revolution** of 1917 and immediately pressed the president to send a delegation to that country, whose new foreign minister was his friend Miliukov. He was then included in the mission headed by **Elihu Root** and preceded it by way of the North Atlantic to Petrograd. Crane was shaken, however, by the resignation of Miliukov and was never enthused about the rise of socialist revolutionary **Alexander Kerensky**; he devoted most of his time that summer to the affairs of the Orthodox Church that was becoming separate from the state for the first time. During World War I and the **Russian Revolution**, Crane increased his financing of Russian studies by paying the salary of Harper at the University of Chicago and providing an annual allocation for library acquisitions as well as travel funds for Harper's regular trips to Russia.

Crane also sponsored the studies of **Elizabeth Reynolds (Hapgood)** at the Sorbonne and her appointment as the first instructor of Russian language at Columbia University in 1915 and financed the publication of what would become a classic history of Russia by Bernard Pares. By 1914 Crane had established "The Friendship Fund," essentially an endowment for Russian and Middle Eastern studies, and immediately after the war, because of his realization of the importance of America's being aware of international affairs, he founded the **Institute of Current World Affairs**, which sponsored a series of summer "round tables" at Williamstown, Massachusetts, and also sponsored reports of scholars on the scene in Russia in the 1930s that included, among others, future Columbia University

Soviet law scholar, **John Hazard**. The institute continues to pursue this agenda.

CRIMEAN WAR (1854–1856). This conflict resulted from diplomatic failures to resolve misunderstandings and imperial rivalry over the decline of the Ottoman Empire. Russia had a vested interest in the control of the outlet from the Black Sea through the straits to the Mediterranean but was unprepared for military engagement with Western powers, principally Great Britain and France. Because of mutual Anglophobia and commercial ties, the United States supported Russia through benevolent neutrality, causing Britain especially to exercise restraint. American arms such as Colt revolvers were smuggled into Russia in bales of cotton. More significantly, more than 30 American medical men volunteered for service with the Russian army in the Crimea. Several sacrificed their lives to cholera and typhus during their contracts. This received wide publicity in the United States and helped secure close relations between the American democracy and the Russian autocracy.

CUBAN MISSILE CRISIS (OCTOBER 1962). A major gain for the Soviet Union in the international competition with the United States was the Cuban revolution that brought to power a Marxist-oriented and anti-American charismatic leader, Fidel Castro. A number of Cubans who opposed his ascendancy fled to the United States. With the support of the American government, they staged an attempt at counterrevolution in an abortive invasion, the **Bay of Pigs**, in 1961. To shore up the Cuban defenses against any further such moves, the Soviet Union promised increased military aid, which included intermediate-range missiles. In October 1962 **U-2** high-altitude surveillance detected preparations for missile deployment, triggering a strong American reaction, even though the United States had long deployed missiles aimed at Soviet targets in neighboring countries such as Turkey.

This information and the news that the missiles were still in transit to Cuba was presented to President **John F. Kennedy** on 16 October 1962, initiating the "13 days," when the world seemed to be on the brink of nuclear war. The United States demanded that the missiles be withdrawn, and the Soviet Union resisted, claiming the right to protect a friendly country. The debate in Washington over the action to take wavered between a direct air strike on the Cuban bases and an embargo of the Soviet supply ships, some carrying the missiles, to Cuba. Military leaders preferred the direct attack, but others, such as Undersecretary of State George Ball, counseled an embargo to avoid inflicting casualties on Soviet personnel, at least in order to buy time. The more cautious approach was chosen, though it also held risks, especially with the deployment of a nuclear-armed Soviet submarine squadron.

The result was still a diplomatic and military crisis, which could have developed into a destructive nuclear war. Fortunately, saner heads prevailed, chiefly those of President Kennedy, his brother Robert, Secretary of Defense Robert McNamara, and especially Soviet leader **Nikita Khrushchev** and his new ambassador in Washington, **Anatoly Dobrynin**. For 13 days, much of the world was in suspense awaiting the outcome. There was finally a negotiated arrangement that resulted in the Soviets relenting to the American demand for withdrawal in return for a somewhat token withdrawal of outmoded American missiles from Turkey. *See also* COLD WAR.

CURTIN, JEREMIAH (1840–1906). Curtin served as secretary of the American legation in Russia (1865–68), during a very active period in Russian–American exchanges of missions following the **American Civil War**. During the visit of **Gustavas Fox** to Russia in 1866, he impressed everyone with his toasts and speeches in Russian at a formal dinner and reception, much to the annoyance of American Minister **Cassius Clay**, who demanded his recall. Curtin would retain his interest in Russian culture, publishing several pathbreaking books on Slavic folk songs and customs. Curtin is best known for his translation of the classic religious novel, *Quo Vadis*, from the Polish of Henryk Sienkiewisz, as well as a variety of Russian prose and poetry in later years.

CZECHOSLOVAK LEGION (1916–1920). Formed in Russia, beginning in 1916, from Czech and Slovak prisoners of war from the Austro-Hungarian army on the eastern front. The plan was to use them as units against the Central Powers either in Russia or on the western front. The **February Revolution** and collapse of the Russian army in 1917–18 and the successful **Bolshevik** negotiation of a peace at **Brest-Litovsk** left the only alternative of deploying these men, numbering up to 50,000, on the western front. The legion managed to become well armed through abandoned Russian army weapons. The new Soviet government refused passage through Moscow to the north of Russia, the easiest way out. The legion then decided to exit by way of the **Trans-Siberian Railroad** through **Vladivostok**. Because of the chaos in the region during the spring of 1918, the legion, well armed and organized, found it necessary to seize control of vital stretches of the rail line, with resulting clashes with early units of the Red Army and liberated groups of Hungarian and German prisoners of war, heralding the beginning of the **Russian Civil War** in **Siberia**. Fully armed and combat ready, the legion became a backbone of the White Army of **Alexander Kolchak** that was centered in Omsk, while also eliciting the support of American interventionist forces under General **William S. Graves** centered farther east around Vladivostok. Eventually, the legion, unenthusiastic about fighting in Russia in 1919 after the war was over in the west, abandoned Kolchak and turned him over to the Bolshevik forces for execution in return for unhindered passage eastward on the railroad. Returning to a newly independent Czechoslovakia in 1919, the legion formed the nucleus of its military forces.

– D –

DALL, WILLIAM (1847–1927). A naturalist for the **Smithsonian Institution**, Dall explored **Alaska** for a telegraph line to connect America with Europe through Alaska and Siberia. He explored much of the territory and became a convert to its natural beauty and resource potential while serving as chief of the mission's "scientific corps." Dall was strongly critical of the neglect of the region by the **Russian America Company**, argued for its purchase by the United States, and later defended the 1867 acquisition in a classic survey, *Alaska and Its Resources* (1870), which justified the purchase against critics, who had labeled the acquisition as "Seward's Ice Box." In his subsequent career as a prominent naturalist for the Smithsonian, Dall continued to emphasize the live and mineral resources of this new American territory in numerous publications and to lament the ignoring of its potential by the U.S. government.

DALLAS, GEORGE MIFFLIN (1792–1864). A prominent Philadelphian senator and diplomat, Dallas's first contact with Russia was as a secretary to **Albert Gallatin**'s peace commission to Russia in 1813–14. He returned to serve as minister to Russia in 1837–39. He brought his family to St. Petersburg, elevating the position of the United States at the Russian court after a series of mediocre, short-term appointments. His mission was highlighted by his arrival on the frigate USS *Independence* during a Russian naval review at the Kronstadt port. Nicholas I visited the vessel incognito, making a significant impression on the Americans in regard to imperial favor and for closer Russian–American relations. Although the Dallas mission to Russia was brief, it promoted the cause of a Russian–American rapprochement that was supported by a boom in trade between the two countries. Dallas was an ardent American expansionist (manifest destiny), well-deserving of the naming of a small Texas town (now a major city) in his honor.

DALLIN, ALEXANDER (1924–2000). The son of a prominent Menshevik activist and historian of Russian Jewish background, Dallin came to the United States from Berlin with his family in 1940. He served in the U.S. army during **World War II** in military intelligence and began his graduate studies at Columbia University, where he wrote a magisterial dissertation on the German occupation of Soviet territory during the war, published in 1957. As professor of history (1956–71) and director of the Russian Institute (later **Harriman Institute**) (1962–67) at Columbia, Dallin continued and solidified the foundations of Russian studies laid by **Geroid T. Robinson**, Philip Moseley, and Henry L. Roberts. He moved to Stanford University in 1971, where he continued to nurture students and publish important works on various aspects of past and current Soviet affairs, often in collaboration with his wife, Gail Lapidus. During his long career, he was especially active in the promotion of Slavic studies in the United States and supervised many graduate students.

DANA, FRANCIS (1743–1811). Dana served the new American republic on several missions, including one to Russia in 1781–82. Inspired by **Catherine the Great**'s perceived favors toward the United States during the Revolutionary War, especially the **Declaration of Armed Neutrality** (1780), promoted by his patron, **John Adams**, and encouraged by the Russian ambassador to the Netherlands, Dmitri Golitsyn, the Continental Congress approved sending Dana to St. Petersburg. His goal was to obtain Russian recognition of the colonies' efforts to gain independence. Dana was warned by **Benjamin Franklin** in Paris that success was unlikely, owing to French opposition. The mission, which included a 16-year-old **John Quincy Adams** as secretary, was derailed by the caution of the Russian government, for the sake of preserving at least a pretense of friendly relations with Great Britain and by French efforts to dominate any European diplomatic negotiations involving American independence; the French embassy in St. Petersburg obstructed Dana's attempts to gain access to the Russian court.

DASHKOV, ANDREI (1775–1831). Dashkov was the first Russian diplomatic representative in the United States as chargé d'affaires (1808–10) until the arrival of the first formal minister, Fedor Pahlen (Palen), in 1810. Dashkov then succeeded him as minister from 1811 to 1817. He also served initially as Russian consul-general in Philadelphia, where he established residence in July 1809, and as a representative of the **Russian America Company**. He also made an impression on President **Thomas Jefferson** by delivering a personal letter from **Alexander I** to Monticello. The major event during his tenure was the lifting of Jefferson's embargo on American trade with Europe and the consequent deluge of American ships into the Baltic to trade especially with St. Petersburg. In 1810–11 Dashkov also encouraged American assistance through **John Jacob Astor** and others for the supply of Russian America during the difficult period of continental European commercial shipping during the Napoleonic Wars. His term as minister, however, was marred by the **Kozlov affair** and by charges against the Russian consul in Boston, Aleksei Evstafyev, of being pro-British during the **War of 1812**, resulting in his recall.

DASHKOVA, EKATERINA (1743–1810). President of the Russian **Academy of Sciences** during the reign of **Catherine the Great** and of a leading noble family of Vorontsov, the princess was an early supporter of Grand Duchess Catherine and an important participant in the coup that overthrew Peter III, even though his mistress was her sister Elizabeth and others in her family were his strong supporters. Ekaterina Vorontsova had married Mikhail Dashkov in 1759; he died in 1764, leaving her with two young children. Catherine II showered favors upon her that ultimately left her in charge of Russia's cultural arena. As much as the empress herself, Dashkova was a woman of the Enlightenment. While resident in Paris in the 1770s, she became an active supporter of the American cause for independence and a friend of **Benjamin Franklin**. Impressed by her knowledge of modern sciences, Franklin proposed her membership in the American Philosophical Society. Elected unanimously in the revolutionary year of 1789, Dashkova became its first woman member. Owing to this connection, the first regular exchange of books, specimens, and other materials was inaugurated between the United States and the Russian Empire, and American scientist John Churchman was designated reciprocally as an honorary member of the Russian Academy of Sciences in 1794. Paul I expelled Dashkova from the Russian capital in 1796 for her part in the murder of his father, but she was allowed to return by his son, **Alexander I.**

DAVIES, JOSEPH (1876–1958). A successful New York attorney, Davies married wealthy socialite, businesswoman, and art collector **Marjorie Meriwether Post** in 1936, shortly before he was chosen by **Franklin D. Roosevelt** to be the second American ambassador to the Soviet Union. Davies arrived in Moscow just in time to witness the first major purge trial, which made quite an impression. Considered naive, inexperienced, and overly sympathetic to the Soviet regime by the professional diplomats in Moscow, such as **George F. Kennan, Charles Bohlen**, and **Loy Henderson**, he nevertheless seemed to perceive the reality of the Stalinist terror while maintaining good relations with Soviet leaders, abetted by his and his wife's purchases of a considerable number of art works, much of the latter on display at Post's Hillwood estate, a museum open to the public in

Washington, D.C. Davies's art collection, in contrast to his wife's, centered on contemporary Soviet artists and was presented to his alma mater, the University of Wisconsin in Madison, where it is still preserved.

During his tenure as ambassador, he traveled widely throughout the country, cultivated close relations with Soviet leaders, and is perhaps best known for a positive memoir of his Russian experience, *Mission to Moscow* (1941), subsequently made into a popular **World War II** film. His tenure also helped usher in the cooperative arrangements of the United States and the Soviet Union, such as **lend-lease**, before and during the war.

DAVIS, JEROME (1891–1979). Born in Japan of American missionary parents, Davis graduated from Oberlin College and obtained graduate degrees from Columbia University and taught evening courses in civics in Minneapolis before becoming a **Young Men's Christian Association (YMCA)** secretary in charge of activities in Russia among German prisoners of war (1916–18). After the withdrawal of the YMCA from Russia, Davis conducted research on Russian immigrants in the United States that resulted in *The Russian Immigrant* (1922). Davis began his long academic career as a professor of sociology at Dartmouth (1921–24) and then accepted the Gilbert L. Stark professorship at the Yale Divinity School in 1924. During **World War I**, Davis was associated with pro-Russian, liberal-minded Americans such as **George Kennan** and **Alice Stone Blackwell** in supporting the **Provisional Government** as an alternative to Bolshevism, but in later years Davis was a strong advocate in the United States of organized labor and for diplomatic recognition of the Soviet Union.

Davis toured Soviet Russia in 1926 and in 1927 with Boston department store scion Edward Filene, and wrote widely and favorably on what he saw and heard, especially about his six-hour interview with **Joseph Stalin**. He visited the country again in 1932 to write *The New Russia*, which contained a very positive depiction of the **First Five-Year Plan**. When negotiations began for recognition in 1933, Davis made clear his availability for the post of ambassador, which many thought foolish because of his having alienated many scholars in the field. Historian **Geroid T. Robinson** at Columbia University thought the idea had at least one merit—getting him out of the country. Davis would continue his interests in Russia and in causes related to organized labor in his contributions to the *Christian Science Monitor* in the 1930s. He was a strong advocate of peace and moderation in lectures and publications during the **cold war** and served as a special advisor to President **Harry S. Truman** at the **Potsdam Conference** (1945).

DEANE, JOHN R. (1896–?). American general, chief of the American military mission in Moscow (1943–46). Much of his responsibility in Moscow involved the coordination of **lend-lease**, which he found frustrating. Deane changed the thrust of the approach to the Soviet Union of his predecessor, **Phillip Faymonville**, from accommodation to distrust. Thus, he could claim to be "in" at the beginning of the **cold war**, following what would later become known as the **containment** policy of **George F. Kennan** and served as an advisor at the **Yalta** and **Potsdam** conferences. Deane also served as confidential assistant to U.S. Chief of Staff and later Secretary of State **George C. Marshall**. He made his case for a strong stand against Soviet policies in *The Strange Alliance: The Story of Our Efforts at Wartime Cooperation with Russia* (1946).

DEBS, EUGENE (1855–1926). Emerging by 1875 as a leader of rail workers in his native Terre Haute, Indiana, Debs would quickly rise by 1880 to national secretary and treasurer of the Brotherhood of Locomotive Firemen. Debs led a successful strike against the Great Northern Railroad and was involved in the more violent Pullman strike of 1894. Arrested and jailed, Debs read widely in prison and became converted to the cause of socialism. After release he helped found the Social Democratic Party, renamed the Socialist Party in 1901, and became its presidential candidate in 1900 and 1904 and the editor of the party's *Appeal to Reason*. Debs moved farther to the left in the activities of the **Industrial Workers of the World (IWW)** in 1905 but soon withdrew from it.

During **World War I**, Debs and his party refused to support the war effort. Arrested and sentenced to 10 years in prison for his opposition, he nevertheless gathered nearly a million votes in the presidential election of 1920, contributing to the defeat of **Woodrow Wilson**.

Though Debs led the Socialist Party into more radical positions, he was basically a pacifist and opposed the idea of revolution through violent activism promoted by Karl Marx and his Russian disciples, **Vladimir Lenin** and **Leon Trotsky**. Debs's "soft" radical leadership would lead to a split in the Socialist Party by 1919, with the left wing forming the **Communist Party of the United States of America (CPUSA)**. In poor health, Debs spent his last years as a relic and martyr of the old cause, of a world of social justice that might have been, certainly not of Lenin's Russian variety. Debs's ideals, as well as those of other prominent world socialists, would help keep the world safe from Lenin-Trotsky extremism. *See also* REED, JOHN.

DEBT ISSUE. American claims against the Soviet government. The debt that the American government and businesses claimed against the new Soviet government was a major reason for the refusal of the United States to recognize the Soviet Union after the revolution until it was acknowledged and paid. The debt was primarily of two kinds: payback of loans granted to the **Provisional Government** in 1917 and seizures of American businesses and assets mostly during 1918. It remained an obstacle to recognition and trade between the two countries during the 1920s and 1930s. During the negotiations for recognition in 1933, desirable for other reasons, the debt issue, as well as American complaints about Soviet interference in domestic affairs through the **Comintern**, was postponed for later settlement. The Soviet Union agreed to pay back a certain amount of debt but wanted it to be part of an extension of new loans and by means of a higher interest rate on those loans. The issue continued into **World War II**, which resulted in a new indebtedness from wartime **lend-lease**.

DECEMBRISTS (1825). After the Napoleonic Wars and the sharply increased Russian contacts with Western Europe and the United States, many officers and educated nobility were strongly influenced by the ideas of the French and American revolutions and by German romanticism. Two general movements looked toward the remodeling of Russia through reform or revolution after 1815. Many well-known writers and thinkers, such as Alexander Pushkin, were either involved or sympathetic to their causes. A "Southern Society," concentrated in army encampments in South Russia, was led by Paul Pestel, its program influenced mainly by the French Revolution and advocating regicide and a centralized government but with a socialist organization of the economy.

The "Northern Society," centered in St. Petersburg, took its inspiration from the American Revolution. Its program, promoted especially by Nikita Murav'ev, called for a more decentralized, federal state divided into 13 states and an executive (which might be an amenable tsar) restricted by a liberal constitution. Adherents of both became known historically as Decembrists, since a premature climax occurred in December 1825 upon the death of **Alexander I** and the confusion about who would succeed him. The Northern Society attempted to force the issue and restrict or limit the powers of a new emperor. The rebellion crushed, five of the leaders were executed, but many more were arrested and sent into exile in **Siberia**. They were important in becoming long-remembered martyrs to the cause of a liberal/socialist Russia, for the attempt at an introduction of an American model of government and society to Russia, and for the development role they played as exiles in Siberia.

DEMENT'EV, IGOR (1925–1998). Born in Kharkov and a gentleman-scholar of the old tradition, Dement'ev, a professor of American history at **Moscow State University (MGU)**, was very supportive of American students and senior scholars in the U.S.–USSR exchange program in Moscow during the 1970s and 1980s and a rare Soviet promoter of an objective study of American history during the **cold war**, along with **Nikolai Sivachev**. This orientation has been carried forth by their students, such as **Nikolai Bolkhovitinov** and **Gennady Kuropiatnik** in the **Academy of Sciences**. Dement'ev's historical contributions were mainly in the area of late 19th century American intellectual history and social thought, for example, *Ideinaia bor'ba v SShA po voprosam ekspansii (na rubezhe XIX-XX v.)* (*The Ideological Struggle in the USA on the Expansion Question, Late 19th, Early 20th Centuries*), published in 1973.

DEMENT'EV, PETER (AKA PETER DEMENS, P. A. TVER-SKOI) (1849–1919). Emigrating from the Russian Empire in 1881 for reasons that are not clear, Dement'ev, usually under the name of Demens or writing as Tverskoi, had a remarkable career in the United

States as a publicist, promoter, and businessman. After several years in the New York area, he moved south to north central Florida to exploit the timber resources in the area. This project led him to build a railroad to a Gulf coast harbor, which he named St. Petersburg after the capital of Russia. He was also a pioneer in the early development of the citrus industry in Florida before he moved on in 1893 to do the same in California. All through his life in America he wrote articles describing the country in Russian journals such as *Vestnik Evropy* (*Herald of Europe*). He also wrote for the American press, especially a series of articles in 1904 defending the Russian position in the **Russo–Japanese War**. In another venture, he corresponded with **Leo Tolstoy** about the suppression of the Molokan religious sect by the Russian government and assisted in their immigration to America, where they settled mainly in Canada and the Hawaiian Islands in the early 20th century. One of the most successful Russian immigrants, Dement'ev has a park and monument named in his honor in St. Petersburg, Florida.

DENIKIN, ANTON (1872–1947). Russian general, commander of the Volunteer ("White") Army during the **Russian Civil War**. Denikin completed the course of the Kiev Military Academy in 1892 and served with distinction in the **Russo–Japanese War**. In **World War I**, he commanded a division of the Southern army that performed better than most and rose to general rank. After the **Bolshevik Revolution**, he was one of the organizers of the White Army in the Don region of South Russia, advancing in position because of the death of the more experienced Lavr Kornilov. During the height of the campaigns in the south of Russia in 1919, Denikin was widely criticized by American observers for his lack of initiative and planning and for his unwillingness to seek compromises, for example, with the more democratic views of leaders of the former Provisional Government and with Ukrainian nationalists. As his army disintegrated in the face of Red Army offensives in 1920 and his own incompetence, he escaped across the Black Sea to Constantinople, leaving one last "hurrah" in the anti-Bolshevik cause in South Russia to General Peter Wrangel. Denikin attempted to defend his record in a long and tedious memoir in five volumes (1921–25). At least he redeemed himself to some extent by having nothing to do with Adolf Hitler and

Nazi Germany during his European exile, in contrast to a Cossack rival, Ivan Krasnov.

DETENTE. A more sophisticated version of **Nikita Khrushchev**'s **peaceful coexistence** that was mainly associated with the regime of **Leonid Brezhnev** (1964–82). Détente represented a saner, safer, and more mature rivalry between the two superpowers, symbolized by regular summit meetings of the leaders, expanded cultural exchanges, the initiation of arms limitation discussions (**Strategic Arms Limitation Talks I** and **II**), and relaxation in Soviet policy toward emigration (especially of Jews and Volga Germans). A high point of détente was the visit of President **Richard Nixon** to Moscow in the summer of 1974 for a grand reception. Growing Soviet affluence, based especially upon oil and gold sales, produced a more confident, as well as a more conservative, approach in Soviet world affairs. While some issues were resolved or put on hold (Berlin), others remained items of contention that kept the **cold war** going: the Vietnam War, the Soviet invasion of Czechoslovakia in 1968, its invasion of **Afghanistan** in 1979, and the boycott of the **Olympic Games** in Moscow (1980).

DIVISION OF EAST EUROPEAN AFFAIRS, DEPARTMENT OF STATE (1922–1937). Successor to the short-lived Russian Bureau, the division, despite its name, mainly supervised information about, and relations with, the Soviet Union under the direction of **Robert F. Kelley**. Though conservative and strongly opposed to diplomatic recognition, Kelley amassed a wealth of information about Russia that was preserved in his division's library and through the Riga "listening post" that was under his direction. Despite Kelley's strong political and religious animosity toward Communist Russia, the division attracted superior talent, including **George F. Kennan**, **Charles ("Chip") Bohlen**, and **Loy Henderson**, who would serve the United States well through the period of recognition, **World War II**, and the **cold war**. In 1937 the separate Division of East European Affairs was abolished and merged with the European Division, reducing considerably the "Russian presence" in the State Department with the attendant loss of a considerable library and intelligence data on Russia, much regretted by current and later Russian specialists.

DIXON, WALTER F. Originally from Great Britain, Dixon was employed in the building of a locomotive plant in New Jersey in the 1890s, when he was contracted to supervise the construction of the Baldwin Locomotive Works at Sormovo, a suburb of **Nizhni Novgorod**, that would produce rolling stock for the **Trans-Siberian Railroad**. He was the resident manager of that factory from 1895 until Baldwin sold it to a Russian firm in 1900. Because of his considerable Russian experience, Dixon was then hired by **Singer Sewing Machine Company** to oversee the building of its first plant in Russia at Podolsk, near Moscow, which upon completion employed 6,000 workers. He continued as director of the Singer factory, which made the name ("Zinger" in Russian) a Russian household name before **World War I** and through the harrowing years of revolution and civil war, when the Singer plant turned to the production of munitions.

DMYTRYSHYN, BASIL (1925–). An American historian of Polish-Ukrainian origin, Dmytryshyn wrote a large number and wide range of books dealing with Russian and Ukrainian history and on Russian–American relations. He came to the United States in 1947, and, after receiving his Ph.D. from the University of California, Berkeley, taught for many years at Portland State University in Oregon. He also contributed to scholarly relations by hosting a number of Soviet and Russian researchers, such as **Nikolai Bolkhovitinov**, in the United States. His works include *Moscow and the Ukraine, 1918–1953: A Study of Bolshevik Nationality Policy* (1956), *Medieval Russia* (1973), *The End of Russian America* (1979), *Russian Conquest of Siberia, 1558–1700* (1985), *The Soviet Union and the Middle East, 1917–1985* (1987), and *Russian Colonies in North America, 1799–1867* (1988).

DOBELL, PETER (1775–1852). An Irish-American adventurer from Boston and Philadelphia, Dobell was employed by the **Russian America Company (RAC)** for assistance (English speaking) in its ambitious expansion projects in the Pacific region in the early 19th century. He helped establish a temporary base for RAC in Hawaii in 1814–15, served as Russian consul in the Philippines, and also served as one of the company's agents in China. He traveled extensively along the northeastern coast of **Siberia** and inland, publishing a valuable description of his adventures in 1830, *Travels in Kamchatka and Siberia with a Narrative of a Residence in China* and of his favorable impressions of Russia, *Russia as It Is, and Not as It Has Been Represented* (1833). Dobell married a Russian and spent most of the remainder of his life as the Russian consul in Elsinor, Denmark, and was buried in St. Petersburg.

DOBRYNIN, ANATOLY (1919–). Born near Moscow, Dobrynin entered the foreign service in 1946 and was assigned to the embassy in Washington in 1952 at the height of the **cold war**. He returned to Moscow in 1955 to the ministry and then joined the Soviet mission at the **United Nations** in 1957, revolving back once more to head the American bureau in the Foreign Ministry. This led, somewhat naturally, to his formal appointment as Soviet ambassador to the United States in 1962, shortly before the unfolding of the **Cuban missile crisis**. As a genial and relaxed diplomat, he helped convert a possible nuclear catastrophe into a diplomatic issue that could be alleviated if not solved. Dobrynin remained in Washington for many years as a respected personage on the social and political scene, enhancing the American end of **Leonid Brezhnev**'s **détente**. Above all, he was a base of continuity through a frequent succession of secretary of states and American ambassadors to the USSR. Dobrynin was recalled by **Mikhail Gorbachev** in 1986 to serve as his special advisor on relations with the United States. His memoir, *In Confidence: Moscow's Ambassador to America's Six Cold War Presidents* (1995), is a candid account of the cold war times. *See also* PEACEFUL COEXISTENCE.

***DOCTOR ZHIVAGO* (1958, 1965).** A romantic and nonideological novel of Russia in war and revolution by Boris Pasternak (1890–1960). Pasternak's manuscript, for a long time "in the drawer," was transmitted to the West during the period of **peaceful coexistence**, where it was published in 1958, demonstrating that great Russian literature had survived the restrictions of Stalinist socialist realism. Its publication created a sensation in the West, as well as did the epic film version of 1965. Pasternak was chosen for the Nobel Prize for Literature but was forced to retract his initial acceptance by Soviet authorities. He spent the rest of his life isolated in the artist's colony of Peredelkino, not far from Moscow. The foreign publication of *Doctor Zhivago* and Pasternak's subsequent treatment by Soviet authorities constituted major victories for the West in the propaganda of the **cold war**. The book was published in Russian by **Young Men's Christian Association (YMCA)** Press in Paris, and many copies were smuggled into the USSR in the 1960s and 1970s. Finally, in the late 1980s, *Doctor Zhivago* was published in its homeland. The Pasternak dacha-museum and grave site at the Russian writers' colony of Peredelkino welcomes visitors from all over the world.

DOLE, NATHAN HASKELL (1852–1935). In the 1880s, Dole published superficial and popular histories of Russia. He was better known and respected as a translator of Russian fiction, especially the works of Ivan Turgenev and **Leo Tolstoy**, into American English; in this he was a rival and competitor to **Isabel Hapgood** and **George Kennan**. He recognized the difficulty of undertaking these translations, with *War and Peace* being a prime example. Though criticized for his simplifications and omissions, his efforts helped popularize Russian literature in America and fueled the American "Tolstoy craze" during the late 19th century. He is also noted for his public plea for the pursuit of academic Slavic studies in the United States.

DREISER, THEODORE (1871–1945). American novelist and social activist. Because of his fictional depictions of the darker side of American life in the 1920s, Dreiser's works were very popular in Soviet Russia, especially his *American Tragedy* (1925). For that reason, he received a special invitation to visit Russia on the occasion of the 10th anniversary of the revolution in 1927. Hosted by **Olga Kameneva** and assisted by **Ruth Kennell** as guide and secretary, Dreiser spent several months in the Soviet Union, first in witnessing the grand ceremony on Red Square in November and then by touring the south of Russia under harsh, wintry conditions. He described his experiences, as recorded by Kennell, in *Dreiser Looks at Russia* (1928). Dreiser continued to support the socialist dream of Russian progress and lent his voice to the cause of diplomatic recognition in the 1930s.

DUBININ, YURY (1930–). Russian diplomat, Soviet ambassador to the United States (1986–90). As a career foreign service officer, Dubinin served in the Soviet foreign service in France and Spain and in the Ministry of Foreign Affairs before his assignment to Washington. He completed his Russian diplomatic service as Russian ambassador to **Ukraine** (1996–99) before his retirement. A congenial and eloquent representative of both the Soviet and post-Soviet governments and as a proponent of **Mikhail Gorbachev**'s **"new thinking,"** Dubinin was a facilitator of close Russian–American relations in Washington during the administration of **Bill Clinton**. In retirement he became an important member of the "consortium of ambassadors," participating actively in sessions at the ambassadors' Conference on the 200th Anniversary of Russian–American Relations in Moscow in November 2007.

DULLES, JOHN FOSTER (1888–1959). As a nephew of **Robert Lansing**, secretary of state (1953–59) under **Woodrow Wilson**, and graduate of Princeton University (1908), Dulles represented a conservative, old-style, moralistic diplomacy associated with the Wilson era that was ill suited to the modern, more complex problems of the post–**World War II** world. A strongly committed anti-Communist as secretary of state, Dulles opposed many possible overtures to the Soviet Union and advocated increased armaments and a strong diplomatic stance to counter "the menace" of Communism and even to roll it back. He supported American commitments in Asia and the Middle East on the frontiers of the **cold war**. To his credit, however, he supported, in deference to President **Dwight D. Eisenhower**, the **containment** program of **George F. Kennan**, relented to the more peaceful approaches of **Nikita Khrushchev**, and was a patient observer of the **Camp David** proceedings. Dulles also supported Eisenhower's initiation of an innovative series of cultural exchanges with the Soviet Union. He also approved and defended—against McCarthyite opposition—the appointment of **Charles Bohlen** as ambassador in Moscow. He remained the epitome of a "cold warrior," promoting the firm policy of **"brinkmanship"** and escalated the arms race, while rejecting any idea of nuclear weapons reductions that would eventually prevail in the years of **détente**.

DUNCAN, ISADORA (1878–1927). A pioneer of modern, interpretive dance in the early 20th century in America and Europe, Duncan was attracted to Russia and its rich heritage in music and dance before **World War I** and performed before appreciative audiences in Moscow and St. Petersburg before the **Bolshevik Revolution**. Her rebellious demeanor and the liberation effect of the revolution brought her back to Russia in 1921 to even greater acclaim as she performed her risqué dances for the populous—and the artistically conservative Bolshevik leadership—as well as achieving renown for establishing a dance school for war and revolution orphans. While in Russia, Duncan became enamored of a rising, eccentric poet, **Sergei Esenin**. They formed a liaison (whether they were legally married is in dispute) in 1922, and he accompanied her on a widely publicized tour of the United States in 1923 that created sensational incidents, owing to his alcoholism and being an obvious Russian peasant misfit in America and also because of her own physical decline. Duncan returned to Russia after the tour and separated from her Russian paramour, who committed suicide the next year, 1924. She retired to her beloved France, where she soon died tragically, when her long scarf became wrapped around a rear wheel of an open car in which she was riding.

DURANTY, WALTER (1884–1957). As the chief correspondent (1922–34) of the *New York Times* in Moscow, Duranty established an unrivaled record of the most columns written and published on Soviet Russia during that period. His Moscow datelines were a regular feature of the *Times* through an important time of foreign involvement in the **First Five-Year Plan**, collectivization, and the purges. His large apartment in central Moscow, where he held court, was a center for journalists and other Americans, as well as Soviet officials, who were fond of American company and his abundance of whiskey and delicacies. He won sympathy from many for the loss of his left leg in a train accident in France (1924), but Duranty and his wife also were quite socially adept in cultivating both Soviet officials, as high as **Joseph Stalin**, and a "who's who" of American visitors.

Duranty's reporting was generally positive in regard to Soviet progress and its leadership and tended to ignore or play down the negative aspects, probably in order to maintain his position, contact sources, and luxurious way of life in Moscow. For the interwar period, however, he provided an amazing number and variety of informational articles about the events and personages of that "mystery inside an enigma." In 1932 he received the Pulitzer Prize for his comprehensive reporting on the Soviet scene. This was challenged much later by those who felt that his failures to report especially on the severity of the disastrous Ukrainian famine and other ill effects of the First Five-Year Plan were a major fault and that his Pulitzer Prize for journalism should be withdrawn. Nevertheless, information to visiting journalists, such as **William Allen White**, demonstrated that he was well aware of the severity of the conditions in the countryside and wanted others to tell the truth. Duranty was probably protecting his position as the dean of foreign journalists in the Soviet capital, either for personal gain—or perhaps for being able to provide more inside scoops on the Soviet world than anyone else was able to do.

D'WOLFE, JOHN "NORTHWEST JOHN" (1784–1862). Descendant of a prominent merchant-shipping family of Bristol, Rhode Island, in the 18th and early 19th century. As a young man, D'Wolfe captained the *Juno* around South America and up the west coast of North America to Alaska in 1805 to deliver a cargo of supplies to the new **Russian America Company**'s headquarters in **Sitka**. Desperately in need of an oceangoing ship, **Alexander Baranov** purchased for the Russian America Company (RAC) the *Juno* from D'Wolfe, who had to journey to St. Petersburg to collect the payment from the company directorate. Returning to New England in 1810, he earned an epithet for his Russian exploits as "Northwest John." D'Wolfe described his adventures in a privately printed autobiography, *A Voyage to the North Pacific and a Journey through Siberia* (1861).

– E –

EASTERN FRONT. *See* WORLD WAR I and WORLD WAR II.

EASTMAN, MAX (1883–1969). Born in upstate New York of religious minister parents, Eastman graduated from Williams College and studied under John Dewey at Columbia University, where he became immersed in Greenwich Village society before **World War I**. Developing a reputation as a bright young journalist, he became editor of a leading left-wing magazine, *The Masses*, in 1912. Eastman thus became a friend and supporter of many left-leaning American writers and artists: William English Walling, Sherwood Anderson, Upton Sinclair, **John Reed**, Boardman Robinson, **Claude McKay**, and Carl Sandburg. Under Eastman's leadership, *The Masses* argued for American neutrality during the war and was forced to spend much money and effort in court cases for violations of the Espionage Act for that cause. Eastman was removed from editorship in 1922 by Robert Minor and the **Communist Party of the United States (CPUSA)**.

In 1923 Eastman toured the Soviet Union and observed the power struggle that was then in process. Spending a few years in France, Eastman returned in 1927 as one of the earliest firm opponents of **Joseph Stalin** and an adherent to **Leon Trotsky**, a rather hopeless alternative. Eastman's disillusionment in Russia led to a renewed commitment to the American style of democracy. Nevertheless, he edited and popularized Trotsky's work and activity in the 1930s and after his assassination. After **World War II**, however, Eastman abandoned his socialist idealism and became an avid conservative, both as an active supporter of Senator Joseph McCarthy and in his writings for the *National Review* and his *Reflections on the Failure of Socialism* (1955).

EATON, CYRUS (1883–1979). Born on a farm near Pugwash Junction, Nova Scotia, Eaton was a precocious child raised in a conservative Baptist home. After attending McMaster University in Toronto, Eaton moved south, befriended by an uncle in Cleveland and then by the Rockefeller family, who had a summer home in the area. With their help he rose through the American business world to establish a stock investment company and to found and direct the Republic Steel Corporation. Expanding to other industries—shipping, railroads, rubber—by **World War II** he was a major business presence in the United States. He had also become dedicated to the quest for peaceful international relations and a strong capitalist voice for Soviet–American friendship in the era of **peaceful coexistence** in the 1950s, counting among his friends **Harry S. Truman**, **Dwight D. Eisenhower**, and **Nikita Khrushchev**. His initiatives toward better understanding are best exemplified by his financial support and promotion of the "Pugwash Conferences" at a lavish facility in his Nova

Scotia hometown. His was an important voice of moderation through difficult periods of the **cold war**.

EDDY, (GEORGE) SHERWOOD (1871–1963). Young Men's Christian Association (YMCA) secretary, executive, and international educator. Born and raised in Leavenworth, Kansas, Eddy was a brilliant student at Yale University (B.A., 1891) before committing his life to the YMCA and to international understanding. For the YMCA's new international mission he charted new ground in India and other parts of Asia before **World War I**. During that war he helped provide relief to the British army behind the lines on the western front in Europe from 1915 to 1917 for the "Y" and wrote books about his experiences. As a liberal progressive, he promoted a better understanding of the new Soviet Union and was a strong advocate of diplomatic recognition; he was one of the first to enter Russia on behalf of famine relief in early 1920 and visited that country again a few years later, recording his sympathetic descriptions of Soviet economic and social achievements in widely circulated reports.

During the 1920s and 1930s Eddy organized and led a number of summer "seminar" tours of Soviet Russia that included many academic scholars, journalists, and politicians. His pro-Soviet stance earned cooperation from Soviet authorities, allowing him to keep pledges to his tour groups on meeting high-level Soviet officials; but he also faced opposition from conservative circles at home. His summary recaps of the tours were widely distributed, thus encouraging more to join his people-to-people contacts. This exposure helped win the support of a number of leading Americans, such as **William Allen White**, in favor of diplomatic recognition by 1933. He spent the last several years of his long life teaching in liberal arts colleges, especially in a small town (Jacksonville) in Illinois. His extensive papers on his Russian experiences are in the archives of the Yale University Divinity School. *See also* MOTT, JOHN R.

EDGAR, WILLIAM C. (1856–1932). Born in Wisconsin, Edgar lived most of his life in Minneapolis, where he edited *The Northwestern Miller* (1886–1924). In this capacity he led an effort to organize the Midwestern milling industry to assist in a major **famine**

relief to Russia in 1892–93. The first shipload of Minnesota flour arrived at the Russian port of Libau in late 1892 on the USS *Missouri*. In the process he encountered a rival effort relief campaign initiated by Benjamin Tillinghast (1849–1937), a fellow journalist from Iowa, who touted the shipment and use of corn meal instead of wheat flour and enlisted the support of **Clara Barton** and the **American Red Cross** in this effort. Edgar, meanwhile, went to Russia to celebrate and help organize the distribution of the first major American relief to Russia, where he became a friend and associate of Andrei Bobrinskoi (great-grandson of **Catherine the Great**), who was in charge of the Russian side of the relief effort. Edgar would later be an advisor to **Herbert Hoover** for American relief operations in Belgium during **World War I** and in the foundation of the **American Relief Administration** and its famine relief to Russia after the war. His account of his early Russian famine experience is detailed, with many photographs, in *The Russian Famine of 1891 and 1892* (1893) and in papers at the Minnesota Historical Society.

EISENHOWER, DWIGHT DAVID (1890–1969). American general and commander in chief during **World War II**; 34th president of the United States, 1953–61. Born in Texas and raised in Abilene, Kansas, Eisenhower represented the heartland of America in honest and straightforward ideals, as did **Harry S. Truman**, and also, like his predecessor, he rose to the challenge of a series of complex international conflicts. During his presidency he took a strong stand in regard to the Suez Crisis (1956) and made a decision to commit military forces to the Middle East (the Eisenhower Doctrine, 1957). Despite the continuation of the **cold war** during his tenure as president through such incidents as the **U-2** overflights (1960) and the **Berlin Wall** (1961), he was open to, and made, overtures that would lead to a considerable reduction of tensions between the two superpowers. He met with Soviet leader **Nikita Khrushchev** at Geneva in the first postwar summit meeting in July 1955 and encouraged the new direction of Soviet foreign policy orchestrated by the Soviet leader described as **peaceful coexistence**. He subsequently welcomed Khrushchev for a celebrated tour of the United States in 1959, especially known for the Soviet leader's homespun observations and the visual effects, such as scaling a pile of corn in Iowa, and for the

Camp David personal meeting and the spirit of closer friendship it inspired.

More importantly, Eisenhower reduced tensions and launched a drive for understanding that produced the **Lacy-Zarubin Agreement** in January 1958 for mutual sponsorship of cultural exchanges for advanced students, academic professionals, performing groups, films, and so on. The exchanges would endure through subsequent difficulties, such as the **Cuban missile crisis**, and have a major cumulative effect in regard to mutual understanding and respect that eventually brought an end to the cold war. In the later years of his presidency, Eisenhower issued warnings of the dangers of an unbridled military-industrial complex in fostering the cold war.

EISENSTEIN, SERGEI (1898–1948). Eisenstein was an innovative Soviet film director with an engineering and architectural background who employed a new collage technique of filming in *Battleship Potemkin* (1925) and in *October* (1927), the latter based upon **John Reed**'s *Ten Days That Shook the World*, an account of the **Bolshevik Revolution** produced to celebrate the 10th anniversary of the revolution. These films were very popular in the United States, *Potemkin* showing in New York to standing room only audiences at the large Wurlitzer Hall on 42nd Street. They helped develop a new appreciation for Soviet revolutionary creativeness. Eisenstein met **Theodore Dreiser** during his visit to Moscow in 1927. Dreiser and especially Upton Sinclair were responsible for an invitation for Eisenstein to come to Hollywood in 1930 to film Dreiser's *American Tragedy*. Trouble with the Paramount Studio, however, led Eisenstein instead to escape to the south to make a film on the Mexican Revolution. Disenchanted by his American experiences, Eisenstein returned to Soviet Russia, where he was ostracized until commissioned to direct *Alexander Nevsky* (1938), which became another Soviet film classic. His final project, a trilogy on the life of Ivan the Terrible, had mixed results with the first part acclaimed, the second withheld for many years for political reasons, and the third never completed.

EMERY, ENOCH (c. 1850–1912). Arriving from Boston as a cabin boy on a ship in Nikolaevsk in the Russian Far East around 1868, Emory managed a spectacular rise to become one of the wealthiest men in Russia by 1900 as the "king of the Amur." He had large stores and warehouses in **Vladivostok**, Nikolaevsk, Khabarovsk, and Blagoveshchensk and maintained a lavish residence in Moscow. His assistance in providing ships and supplies in Blagoveshchensk during the Boxer Rebellion (1900) and the **Russo–Japanese War** was vital in saving the city. Though details are vague, he was probably the largest private investor in Russian securities, mainly in railroads and banks, as well as having similar holdings in American banks and railroads. Around 1905 he succumbed to mental illness, at least partly as a result of his Boxer experience, that soon left him confined to a mental hospital in Moscow, where he died, leaving the sorting out of his vast estate, complicated by an estranged Russian widow, to the American consul general and New York City Bank.

EQUITABLE LIFE ASSURANCE SOCIETY. Following the pioneering ventures of **New York Life Insurance Company**, Equitable developed a considerable business in Russia, entering the arena in 1891, and by 1900 had close to $4,000,000 in policies, ranking fifth among the several companies in Russia, but this figure expanded rapidly in subsequent years. As in the case of New York Life, Equitable would suffer as a result of the **Bolshevik Revolution** with court cases regarding lapsed policies extending beyond **World War II** and total claims on the Soviet government reaching $10,000,000 by the mid-1930s.

ESENIN, SERGEI (1895–1925). Though born into a peasant family in Riazin province, Esenin received a high-school education in a church boarding school before moving to Moscow in 1912 to work as a clerk and butcher. His first poetry was published in a children's magazine in 1914. Moving to Petrograd in 1915, he won the favor of the established poet Aleksandr Blok and soon obtained a cult following for his rural, lyrical poetry. He joined the imagist group of writers and welcomed the **Bolshevik Revolution** in 1917, though his efforts at revolutionary poetry were less successful. In 1921 he met the visiting 44-year-old American dancer **Isadora Duncan**, who became infatuated with the young, handsome, blond Esenin. They formed an unlikely bond, especially since he spoke no foreign languages and she knew very little Russian; he accompanied her in 1922 on a fund-raising tour of the United States, where he made a spectacle of himself with bad behavior and drunkenness, which seemed to become increasingly worse. He nevertheless composed some revealing descriptions of the American scene—as he saw it. They returned to Soviet Russia in 1923, but Duncan soon tired of his mental and physical illnesses and left Russia in 1924. The following year, Esenin married a granddaughter of **Leo Tolstoy** but continued to decline until his suicide, by hanging, in late December 1925, after writing his last poem with his own blood—at age 30.

EVERETT, ALEXANDER HILL (1790–1846). American diplomat, author, and statesman. Everett began a distinguished career in American public service as an unpaid secretary in St. Petersburg to **John Quincy Adams** during his term as minister to Russia (1809–14). Later, as American minister to Spain in the 1820s, Everett was instrumental in introducing **Washington Irving** to the Russian minister and to a Russian audience for his literary work. As a frequent essayist for the popular *North American Review*, he promoted the American pro-Russian stance, and as the chief editor for the journal for a number of years, he stressed the selection of articles on world affairs, including Russia.

"EVIL EMPIRE" (1983). President **Ronald Reagan**'s apt (or inept?) description of the Soviet Union. The phrase was first used by the president in a speech before an assembly of Christian conservatives in Orlando, Florida, in March 1983 as a response to the continued aggressive Soviet military activity in **Afghanistan**, subsequently supported by the **Korean airliner incident** in the fall of that year. Authorship was later credited to speechwriter Tony Dolan. It quickly became a slogan of international views of the conservative right, although Reagan formally withdrew the epithet after a meeting with **Mikhail Gorbachev** in 1989.

EXPORT-IMPORT BANK. An independent U.S. agency proposed by the administration of **Franklin D. Roosevelt** and created in February 1934 by act of Congress, this "bank" was financed to offer credits to foreign entities for the purchases of goods in the United States. The purpose in mind was to provide help to American manufacturers, still afflicted by the Depression, and to stimulate exports abroad generally but especially to the Soviet Union. These had been quite large during the **First Five-Year Plan** but had slowed considerably owing to exhaustion of Soviet gold reserves. The assistance or loans were conditioned upon the settlement of the long-standing **debt issue** that then appeared likely as part of the diplomatic **Recognition Agreement** two months earlier. The bank, moreover, was assured of a conservative, anti-Soviet orientation with R. Walton Moore and **Robert F. Kelley** of the State Department on its board of directors.

Both Foreign Commissar **Maxim Litvinov** and Ambassador **Alexander Troyanovsky** viewed the bank negatively as a political instrument of American imperialism. Partly for that reason, the debt issue remained unresolved, and a bill sponsored by Senator Hiram Johnson (the Johnson Act) firmly disallowed credits to countries owing debts to the United States. The agency, therefore, remained in being but largely moribund for many years. It finally played a role in extending credits to a new Russian government, the **Russian Federation**, in the 1990s. And in 2001 it assisted Aeroflot in the purchase of 20 Boeing Corporation passenger planes.

– F –

FAMINES, IN RUSSIA (1892–1893, 1921–1923, 1931, 1946). Russia, in both its imperial and Soviet incarnations, was subject to some of the worst famines in world history. In modern times, the one of 1892–93 was especially disastrous in suffering and loss of human life. The cause was a combination of government policy (the program of Minister of Finance **Sergei Witte** to speed the export of cheap grain to pay for industrial and transport projects) and drought. The United States—inspired by missionary and philanthropic zeal in the 1890s—responded with a major relief effort, mainly organized in Midwestern states such as Iowa and Minnesota, to send shiploads of food, especially corn and cornmeal, with special instructions on how to prepare it for the peoples of Russia, who were unfamiliar with corn.

Another serious famine, also the combined result of government policy, namely War Communism, and natural disaster resulted in an even worse condition in 1921–23, when more than five million died from starvation and disease. As in the earlier famine, the United States again responded to Russian appeals to provide major assistance through the **American Relief Administration (ARA)**, headed by **Herbert Hoover**. More than $60 million of American food and medical aid was distributed by the ARA during that period, supervised by more than 300 American administrators and 6,000 Russian employees. This was a remarkable American contribution to the saving of millions of Soviet subjects, despite having intervened in favor of opponents of that regime just two years earlier.

Another famine, even more attributable to government policy (collectivization) in the early 1930s, was especially devastating in **Ukraine** and South Russia. This time American aid was not solicited, nor offered, and many millions died. **Walter Duranty** and other American reporters were criticized then, and later, for not revealing the true extent of this disaster, which bordered on genocide in its effects in Ukraine. The aftermath of the destruction and dislocation caused by **World War II** also caused much suffering and loss of life, largely concealed from the West by the **iron curtain** of restricting access and information. Later food shortages, as in the early 1960s, were relieved, at least partially, by the Soviet ability to import food supplies from the West and China.

FAR EASTERN REPUBLIC (FER). At the conclusion of the **Russian Civil War**, **Siberia** was in political and economic shambles due to the actions of the "White" government of **Alexander Kolchak** at Omsk, the ravages of Cossack general Grigori Semenov, a large Japanese army of occupation, and other contesting authorities. In this chaos, FER was formed in 1919 with its capital at Chita and territory that extended to the Pacific coast (**Vladivostok**). Despite the FER's pro-Bolshevik tendencies, the United States recognized the republic in an effort to pressure the Japanese to withdraw. The FER was subsequently invited to the **Washington Naval Conference** in 1921, where it was represented by **Boris Skvirsky**, who later became the unofficial representative of the Soviet government in the United States for a number of years, in charge of the **Russian Information Bureau**. By 1923, however, the FER had been absorbed into the Union of Soviet Socialist Republics (USSR).

FAYMONVILLE, PHILLIP (1889–1962). A graduate of West Point (1912) and veteran of **World War I**, Faymonville's first contact with Russia was as an intelligence officer with the **American Expeditionary Force (AEF)** in **Siberia** (1918–19). During that assignment, he learned Russian and became an intelligence advisor to General **William S. Graves**, commander of the AEF. Faymonville remained as military attaché to the Russian **Far Eastern Republic (FER)** in Chita until 1923. He then performed various assignments in the United States, especially in weapons trials.

As one of a few army officers with a knowledge of Russian and experience in the country, Faymonville was chosen by Ambassador **William C. Bullitt** as military attaché for the first U.S. embassy in Soviet Russia in 1934. Very quickly he established a number of useful contacts within the Soviet military forces, operated separately from the embassy, and traveled widely through the country to visit bases, airfields, and military schools. Faymonville arranged the airplane tours of Soviet Russia by Charles Lindbergh and Howard Hughes in the 1930s, but he was also criticized by other members of the diplomatic mission for his frequent parties and close relations with the Soviet military hierarchy and for his alleged homosexual inclinations. He retained his post in Moscow until 1939 and then reemerged in 1941 as a special advisor to the mission of **W. Averell Harriman** to Moscow in October 1941 with the rank of brigadier general, remaining behind to supervise the arrival of **lend-lease** shipments to America's new ally, and he also served as guide for **Wendell Willkie**'s 1942 tour of the Soviet Union. In this role, Faymonville was again rebuked by the diplomatic corps, especially by Ambassador **William Standley**, for his independent stance. He nevertheless had a reputation as a problem solver who eased tensions associated with wartime cooperation and was considered for the post of ambassador upon Standley's resignation in May 1943. Instead, he was withdrawn in October of that year and replaced by Major General **John R. Deane**. Unfortunately, it is reported that he destroyed all personal papers connected with his Russian assignments.

FEBRUARY REVOLUTION (MARCH 1917 BY THE WESTERN CALENDAR). The terrible economic conditions inflicted upon Russia by a prolonged war and a long and diversified opposition to the old regime brought about mass demonstrations in the streets of Petrograd (St. Petersburg) and the abdication of **Nicholas II** in February/March 1917. Taking control, as the **Provisional Government**, were a mixture of liberal members of the progressive bloc (opposition) of the Fourth Duma and representatives of more radical socialist parties, such as the **Russian Social Democratic Labor Party** (both Menshevik and **Bolshevik** factions) and the Socialist Revolutionary Party, which established a rival base of power in the Petrograd Soviet of Workers' and Soldiers' Deputies. The nominal head of the new government was Georgy Lvov, while the main leaders were Alexander Guchkov (minister of war) and especially **Paul Miliukov** (foreign minister).

The revolution was welcomed in the United States because of sympathy with progressive and radical groups and because a "democratic" Russia made it much easier to enter **World War I** (in April) to "make the world safe for democracy" (in the terms of President **Woodrow Wilson**). The United States was quick to recognize the new government and send a special mission, the **Root Commission**, to Russia in May, as well as to welcome a similar Russian delegation to the United States. During the May crisis in the Provisional Government over continuing the basic foreign policy of the imperial regime, however, Miliukov resigned as foreign minister and marked the ascendancy of **Alexander Kerensky**. This change in the Allied composition, moreover, shifted the burden of providing major aid and assistance to the United States, one that could not be delivered in time to save Russia from further revolutionary upheavals, withdrawal from the war, and a desperate and costly **Civil War**. *See also* BOLSHEVIK REVOLUTION.

FEDERAL SECURITY SERVICE (FSB). Following the collapse of the Soviet Union, the **Committee on State Security (KGB)** of that entity was replaced in the **Russian Federation** under **Boris Yeltsin** by the Federal Counterintelligence Service (FSK). It essentially performed the same duties as the KGB, a combination of the **Central Intelligence Agency (CIA)** and Federal Bureau of Investigation (FBI) in the United States. In 1995 President Yeltsin, upon the recommendation of its director, Sergei Stepashin, and with the approval of the Duma, enlarged its powers and renamed it the FSB. When Stepashin moved up to the post of prime minister, **Vladimir Putin** was named director in 1998, and, after a little more than a year, Putin replaced Stepashin as prime minister and then would become acting president upon Yeltsin's resignation at the end of 1999. Stepashin would later, in 2004, resign from a subordinate government position and join the political opposition to Putin. Replacing the latter as director of FSB was Nikolai Patrushev (1951–), who was also from St. Petersburg, a former KGB official, and a loyal Putin supporter.

FEDOTOFF WHITE, DMITRI. *See* WHITE, DMITRI FEDOTOFF.

FINLAND. Governed mainly by a Swedo-Finnish aristocracy, under both Swedish rule and after it was acquired by Russia in a war against Sweden (1809), Finland retained a quasi-independence both economically and politically in the Russian Empire. As a grand duchy after 1905, Finland had a separate currency (Finnmark) and freedom from conscription into the Russian army. Thus, during **World War I** Finland was basically a neutral territory, though the main base of the Russian Baltic fleet was in Helsingfors (Helsinki). More Finns probably fought for Germany in that war than for Russia, in the cause of complete Finnish independence. During the interwar years, Finland attracted the admiration of the United States for paying its debt obligations, little though they were. After the **Nazi–Soviet Pact** (1939), Finland was again a center of American attention because of a Soviet attack on the small country that valiantly resisted in the **Winter War** of 1939–40. This invasion of a country friendly to the United States and the harsh treatment of civilians alienated many Americans from the Soviet Union and caused delays and difficulties in regard to support for Soviet resistance to the German invasion in 1941. Though Finland participated as a German ally in **World War II**, it did not take undue advantage of the siege of Leningrad, once again winning American sympathy. The Russian collection at the University of Helsinki Library is of major importance for American scholars, especially when archives and materials in Russia are not available.

FIRST FIVE-YEAR PLAN (1928–1932). A crash Soviet industrialization program, the "plan" was used by **Joseph Stalin** to claim a theoretical ascendancy from **Vladimir Lenin**, but more practically it meant the rapid industrialization of the Soviet Union and its recognition as a major industrial and military power. It also represented a resumption of the "system" of **Sergei Witte** of the 1890s, though with the force of police power and political organization behind it. The problem was how to quickly build Russia's industrial base while not interfering with its international relations. The plan would depend considerably upon American engineering expertise in the construction of large dams, new steel complexes, several tractor factories, and the largest automobile works at Nizhny Novgorod.

Many American individuals as well as large companies such as **Ford**, **International Harvester**, and the **Austin Company** were able to survive the Depression thanks to Soviet contracts. Approximately 3,000 American workers and engineers were involved in the Soviet "great offensive," a term coined by **Maurice Hindus**, most of them contracted by the **American Trading Corporation (Amtorg)**, the Soviet trade mission in New York. The plan was a demonstration of Soviet emphasis on *amerikanizm*—on building a socialist planned "new society" with American technology.

FISCHER, LOUIS (1896–1970). Born and raised in Philadelphia, Fischer was a leading member of an active and long-term American press corps that included **Walter Duranty**, **Eugene Lyons**, and **William Henry Chamberlin**. He was a popular correspondent for the *New York Evening Post*, *The Nation*, and other newspapers and journals. Fischer and his wife Sonya (a Russian) were also in the center of the American political life in Moscow. More than other journalists, however, Fischer contributed to scholarship: *The Soviets in World Affairs* (1930), *Life of Lenin* (1940), *Men and Politics* (1949), and *The God that Failed* (1949). He also wrote a memorable *Life of Mahatma Gandhi* (1950), on which a popular movie of the 1990s was based. Fischer left Russia in 1938 to settle in New York and, like **Max Eastman**, became an ardent anti-Communist after **World War II**.

FISH, HAMILTON (1808–1893). Born in New York City of a prominent political family (and named after Alexander Hamilton), Fish served as congressman, New York state governor, and senator before his appointment to the cabinet of President **Ulysses S. Grant** as secretary of state. He then became a mainstay of that administration. Regarding Russian–American relations, his tenure (1869–76) was marred by the **Katakazi affair** that involved his support of the **Perkins Claim** (1870–71), dating back to an order for rifles by the Russian government during the **Crimean War**. This caused a minor but embarrassing diplomatic rift during the visit of **Grand Duke Alexis** (1871–72). His papers in the **Library of Congress** are a rich source of information on the diplomacy of the period. Fish, as a number of other prominent Americans in foreign affairs, used the inscription "personal and confidential" on many dispatches, to which the recipient was obliged to answer the same way. This correspondence thus did not go into the official records of the State Department but was retained in the personal papers. This ruse was especially the case in the diplomatic records regarding Russia.

FLIGHT 007. *See* KOREAN AIRLINER INCIDENT.

FLORINSKY, MICHAEL T. (1895–1981). Born and raised in an educated Russian family in Kiev, after studying law at the University of Kiev, Florinsky served as an artillery lieutenant in the Russian army in **World War I**, receiving several decorations. While his elder brother would become an official in the Soviet **Commissariat of Foreign Affairs (Narkomindel)** and was later a victim of the purges, Florinsky immigrated to England after the **Bolshevik Revolution**, where he was a research assistant for Bernadotte Schmidt's *Treaty of Brest Litovsk* and then became associated with the *Economic and Social History of the World War*, a major project of the Carnegie Endowment for International Peace, which brought him in 1926 to the United States. There he received his M.A. and Ph.D. from Columbia University. His volume in the Carnegie series, *The End of the Russian Empire*, was one of its best. Joining the Columbia faculty in the department of economics (since **Geroid T. Robinson** held the position in Russian history), he became renowned for his lively, personalized lectures and elegant writing in such works as *Russia: A History and an Interpretation* (1961). Along with George Vernadsky and **Michael Karpovich**, he helped preserve objectivity in Russian history and a balanced and honest understanding of Russian culture through the difficult period of Communist rule and the **cold war**.

FLOROVSKY, FATHER GEORGES (1893–1979). The son of a priest in Odessa, adept in languages and scholarly studies, Florovsky taught at the University of Odessa beginning in 1919 but was forced to leave with his family after the **Bolsheviks** gained control of the region in 1920, first settling in Bulgaria. Associated with many of the émigré Russian intelligentsia that included Nikolai Berdyaev, Sergei Bulgakov, and John Meyendorff, he developed a close friendship with Berdyaev in the 1920s, when he was professor of patristics at the St. Sergius Orthodox Theological Institute in Paris. Ordained into the priesthood in 1932, Florovsky researched in European libraries for his classic *Ways of Russian Theology* that opposed Western influences of scholasticism, pietism, and idealism upon Orthodox theology and ignited controversy in the Russian émigré community. He immigrated to the United States in 1949 to be dean of St. Vladimir's Seminary in New York (to 1955) and then was on the faculty of the Harvard Divinity School (1956–64) and Princeton University (1964–72). A biblical scholar and ecumenical religious leader, Florovsky was also one of the founders of the World Council of Churches in the 1950s.

FORD FOUNDATION. A philanthropic fund established by **Henry Ford** and his son Edsel in 1936, following the lead of earlier American philanthropies such as those founded by John D. Rockefeller and Andrew Carnegie. Much expanded by 1950, its focus became international relations and education, which, in the climate of the **cold war**, was centered on the training of expertise in vital world areas. Many American students entered graduate study at centers such as the Russian Institute (later **Harriman Institute**) at Columbia University and the Russian Research Center at Harvard University supported by Ford Foundation fellowships. The foundation was also instrumental in urging expanded and unrestricted government funding and the establishment of student exchange programs with the Soviet Union and many other countries. It continues to provide vital funding for area studies to individuals and for major institutions.

FORD, GERALD R. (1913–2006). As a congressman from Michigan (1949–73), Ford supported the Republican Party agenda throughout his career; this involved increased defense expenditures and a hard line toward the Soviet Union. As vice president and then as successor to **Richard Nixon** after his resignation, however, Ford was an advocate of closer understanding with America's **cold war** adversary, responding to **Leonid Brezhnev**'s policy of **détente**; the new agenda included the **Strategic Arms Limitation Talks (SALT I)** negotiations and a continuation of summit meetings, such as the one at **Vladivostok** in 1974 that set the stage for the SALT II agreement, which ultimately failed to be ratified by the U.S. Senate. His steady and open hand provided stability after the abrupt political breaks caused by the assassination of **John F. Kennedy** and the Watergate scandal that forced the resignation of Nixon.

FORD, HENRY (1863–1947). A famous automobile inventor and manufacturer who pioneered assembly-line technology, Ford responded quite willingly to Soviet adoration that began with **Vladimir Lenin**. Though a promoter of capitalism and well known for anti-Semitic views, Ford welcomed overtures from the Soviet Union and its mainly Jewish agents, such as **Armand Hammer**, to supply tractors and cars to the Soviet Union in the 1920s. This led to lucrative contracts to install Ford machinery in the large State Automotive Works (GAZ) factory near Nizhny Novgorod in the 1930s. Ford stood in the forefront of *amerikanizm*, which dominated much of the Soviet thinking about industrialization during the **First Five-Year Plan**.

FORDISM. A term that defined the Soviet interest in assembly-line mass production of various products, patterned after the practice of American manufacturers, notably that engineered by **Henry Ford**. The practice was a model employed in the Soviet Union, especially in the drive for industrialization in the **First Five-Year Plan**. Fordism was a branch of *amerikanizm* that focused on production technology, borrowed mainly from the United States and applied to a number of new industrial projects.

FORD MOTOR COMPANY. Founded by **Henry Ford** in Detroit, the company quickly moved into the world arena with sales of cars, trucks, and tractors. It especially courted Russian business, and by the **Bolshevik Revolution**, most of the cars and tractors in Russia were Fords. Ford was renowned for assembly-line mass production that lowered costs and ensured a basic durability and reliability of the vehicles. The Ford system, or **Fordism**, was much admired by **Vladimir Lenin** and other **Bolshevik** leaders. A large number of Fords were purchased by the Soviet Union in the 1920s, beginning its entry into the automobile age, since practically no cars were produced there.

At the beginning of the **First Five-Year Plan**, one goal was to change that, so Soviet planners looked to Ford, or rather first to the **Austin Company** that built the factory near Nizhny Novgorod that would be furnished with Ford assembly-line equipment to produce a Soviet clone of the Model A car (GAZ 1) and Model AA truck, for years the basic Soviet vehicles. In the process a number of Ford engineers would be assigned to Russia, while over 100 select Soviet workers would work/study at Ford's premier plant in Dearborn, Michigan (1930–32). After the collapse of the Soviet Union, Ford would again become a producer of automobiles for a reviving Russian economy by building a factory near St. Petersburg.

FORT ROSS (KREPOST ROSSIYA). Following the Russian expeditions of **Nikolai Rezanov** and **Ivan Kuskov** in 1806 and 1807 to San Francisco to negotiate cooperative arrangements with the Spanish governors at Monterey, Kuskov returned to establish a base north of the main Spanish mission line (north of Bodega Bay) in early 1812, granted by Mexican authorities. The purpose of "Fort Russia" was to serve as a base for the hunting of sea otters along the California and Oregon coasts but, more importantly, to provide food for the **Russian America Company (RAC)** settlements farther north in Alaska by grain cultivation and cattle ranching. The Russian wooden fort, the Orthodox chapel, and the outlying buildings represented a new development and presence in the history of California. The population of the colony was quite small, probably no more than 25–30 Russians and around 100 resettled Aleuts. The California base was never very successful, as the sea otter soon neared extinction in the area and the production of food, mainly wheat and cattle, on the rocky terrain was always precarious. The territory was finally sold privately by the RAC to Captain John Sutter, in 1841. After many years of neglect the site was acquired by the state, but the quaint Orthodox Church burned completely in the 1960s. Today the restored and rebuilt fort and church are a tourist attraction as a California State Historic Park.

FOSTER, JOHN W. (1836–1917). A graduate of Indiana University (1855), Foster practiced law in Evansville before joining the Union forces as an officer in the 25th Indiana Volunteers, serving with distinction at Shiloh. He returned to Evansville after the war to edit a newspaper (1865–69) and then served at a number of diplomatic posts, including Russia. Though Foster's tenure (1880–81) as American minister in St. Petersburg was brief, he was among the first to be embroiled in the **passport question**, regarding conflicting interpretations of the **Commercial Treaty of 1832**, and the turmoil surrounding the assassination of **Alexander II**.

Foster was later secretary of state (1892–93), after which he headed the American delegation to the **Bering Sea** arbitration court in Paris in 1893. His careful legal work, however, was unsuccessful in obtaining a satisfactory resolution of the problem of the rapidly diminishing population of **fur seals** on the **Pribylov Islands**. Foster also took part in several other special diplomatic missions, such as the Alaska Boundary Tribunal in London in 1903. His nephew, **Robert Lansing**, another secretary of state, began his career on Foster's Paris staff, while a grandson and namesake, **John Foster Dulles**, would also leave his mark on American foreign policy during the administration of **Dwight D. Eisenhower**.

FOSTER, WILLIAM Z. (1881–1961). Beginning as an itinerant worker, Foster was first affiliated with the American Socialist Party and then with the **Industrial Workers of the World (IWW)**, for which he was a primary instigator of the 1919 steel strike. After the **Bolshevik Revolution** and the formation of the **Communist Party of the United States of America (CPUSA)**, Foster soon emerged as one of its leaders and its candidate for president in the elections of 1924, 1928, and 1932. During this period he attended several **Comintern** conferences in Moscow to present trite speeches on CPUSA achievements. Though Foster lost his leadership position in the party to **Earl Browder** in the 1930s, he regained it in 1945 and held it until 1957 to the chagrin of Moscow. Though colorless and lacking in dynamic appeal, he followed a steady course, managed to avoid arrest during the **McCarthy** era, and wrote several personal accounts of his work for "the cause": *Toward Soviet America* (1932), *From Bryan to Stalin* (1937), and *Pages from a Worker's Life* (1939).

FOX MISSION (1866). Following the end of the **American Civil War**, Assistant Secretary of the Navy Gustavus Fox led a mission to Russia, ostensibly to thank Russia for its support to the Union by the sending of naval squadrons to New York and San Francisco, but specifically to congratulate **Alexander II** on his escape from an assassination attempt. Fox sailed on a new American ironclad monitor, the USS *Miantonomoh*. It was the first and last time that a ship of this type would navigate the high seas, crossing the ocean in midwinter practically like a submarine, with the deck underwater most of the time. Arriving at the Kronstadt port near St. Petersburg in August 1866, the Fox entourage created a sensation and met with grand receptions and much celebration in St. Petersburg and Moscow, marking a high point in Russian–American friendship. Fox was inundated with a large number of valuable gifts, which he dutifully turned over to the **Smithsonian Institution** upon his return. Though the mission was successful, the Americans failed to sell the *Miantonomoh* to the Russians (a minor goal) and suffered the embarrassment of an awkward public rift between American Minister **Cassius Clay** and his secretary, **Jeremiah Curtin**. The particulars of the mission, ignoring the Curtin–Clay affair, were dutifully recorded by Fox's secretary, Joseph Loubat, in *Narrative of the Mission to Russia, in 1866, of the Hon. Gustavus Vasa Fox* (1873).

FRANCIS, DAVID R. (1850–1927). Before his appointment as ambassador to Russia (1916–18), Francis was mayor of St. Louis, governor of Missouri (1889–93), secretary of the interior in the second administration of Grover Cleveland, and director of the St. Louis World's Fair (Panamanian Exposition) in 1904. Though the latter involved some contact with foreign national exhibitors, Francis was essentially without diplomatic experience and owed his appointment to his prominence as a Democratic Party Midwestern newspaper publisher who gave crucial initial support to **Woodrow Wilson**'s first presidential campaign. In Petrograd (St. Petersburg) Francis quickly gained a reputation for drinking whiskey, playing poker, golfing in a pasture field, tooting around the Russian capital in a Model T Ford, a romantic affair with a reputed German agent, and being able to "ring" a brass spittoon at a distance. But he also gained respect from Russian officials and fellow diplomats for hard work, dedication, and a savvy intuition, which he put to good use during the difficult times of war and revolution.

In 1917, after the overthrow of the tsar and American entry into **World War I**, Francis was an able host to various visiting delegations, sought advice from experts such as **Frederick Corse**, director of the **New York Life Insurance Company** operations, his first councillor **J. Butler Wright**, and special advisor **Samuel Harper**. Also vital to his personal survival was the support of **Philip Jordan**, his faithful African American chauffeur, valet, cook, and personal advisor. His pleas in 1917 for a large influx of funding for a giant publicity effort for the war fell on deaf ears in Washington, but his equally strong insistence on American military **intervention** in 1918 did not.

As dean of the diplomatic corps after the **Bolshevik Revolution**, he won a memorable face-down meeting with **Vladimir Lenin** in February 1918 in obtaining the release of arrested diplomats. Insisting on "going down with the ship" by staying in Russia after the **Brest-Litovsk Treaty** and Russia's leaving the war, he relocated the embassy to **Vologda**, 400 miles north of Moscow, for the summer of 1918. Though a number of historians, such as **George F. Kennan**, felt he was not equal to the tasks, he has been rehabilitated by others. In later years, Francis felt betrayed by Russia, by events, and by his own country, while still pretending to be the official ambassador. His papers are preserved at the Missouri Historical Society in St. Louis. *See also* CRANE, CHARLES R.

FRANKLIN, BENJAMIN (1706–1790). As representative of the Continental Congress in Paris during the Revolutionary War, Franklin was an avid supporter of France and the diplomatic agenda of Foreign Minister Charles Comte de Vergennes in order to win vital French support for the rebelling colonies of Great Britain. He and Vergennes warned against the initiative of Franklin's fellow emissary in Europe, **John Adams** in Amsterdam, for sending **Francis Dana** on a mission to Russia in 1781 to gain Russian support for the American cause. Despite this, Franklin was celebrated in Russian writings, especially those of Alexander Radishchev and Nikolai Karamzin, as an advocate of intellectual honesty and the liberal cause of freedom. During his stay in Paris, Franklin met and conversed with **Ekaterina Dashkova**, Russia's "minister of the arts," and, significantly impressed, nominated her for membership in the American Philosophical Society in Philadelphia, and she thus became its first Russian and female member.

FREY, WILLIAM (WILHELM FREI, VLADIMIR GEINS) (1839–1888). Russian American populist/socialist. Of Baltic German origin and a graduate of a military engineering school, Geins (Heinz) became converted to the Russian populist cause in the 1860s and chose to immigrate to the United States with his wife (née Maria Slavinskaya) to find the freedom he needed. There he chose the German name for freedom, Wilhelm Frei (Americanized to William Frey). After brief residences in Jersey City and the Williamsburg section of Brooklyn, the Freys joined an American commune in Missouri. They then established a socialist commune in southern Kansas near **Cedar Vale** in January 1871 and named it the Progressive Communist Community. Its members were both Russian and American utopians and numbered fewer than 12 families, an unsuccessful mix of atheist Russians and Christian Americans. Other peculiarities of the "society" were a vegetarian regime and a communal division of work. The commune, nevertheless, attracted a number of prominent Russian exiles, such as **Nicholai Chaikovsky** and **Grigory Machtet**, who would be prominent socialist writers and revolutionaries. After nine years in Kansas and a brief venture in Oregon (New Odessa Commune), the Freys left America for London, from where Frey carried on an arcane philosophical dispute with **Leo Tolstoy**. His diaries and notes were acquired by the **New York Public Library** and formed the basis of **Avrahm Yarmolinsky**'s biography, *A Russian's American Dream* (1965).

FUR SEALS. Along with the purchase of **Alaska** in 1867, the United States gained proprietary rights to the large herd of fur seals on the **Pribylov Islands** in the **Bering Sea**. These large seals, sought after for their fine skins, numbered as many as five million at that time.

Supervision of this resource rested with the Treasury Department, which granted a 20-year contract to a California firm for the "harvesting" of this resource. The company paid an annual lease fee and around one dollar per skin (about $200,000 per year) to the American government. Over the period of the contract the revenue to the American government more than paid for the initial purchase of Alaska, $7,000,000. The seals were on the Pribylovs only for summer birthing and breeding, spending around nine months at sea, migrating from there through the Aleutians to northern California and back along the coast; the constant immersion in cold water during that period enhancing the fineness of their furs. In the mid-1880s, however, interlopers discovered the seal migration route while fishing for the cod that sustained the seals. They began to hunt for the lucrative furs of the seals, killing them indiscriminately, with a resulting sharp decline in their numbers. Concern by the American government resulted in Treasury Department revenue cutters seizing the ships of these poachers, mostly Canadian, creating an international legal controversy over maritime rights.

In 1893 the International Court of Arbitration, one of the first, met in Paris to settle the controversy, the opposing sides being the United States and Great Britain (on behalf of Canada). The former at first claimed that the Bering Sea had been purchased along with Alaska, that anything in it belonged to Alaska, and that interlopers were outlaws, citing as evidence a treaty purchase map that had a line drawn on it. The British position of the long-held doctrine of freedom of the seas prevailed. During the nine-month deliberation, the American representatives pressed a doctrine of medieval law that when a cow strays from its pasture, it still belongs to its owner. Thus, a seal born on American land carried an "invisible passport"; it was American property wherever it went. That argument was also ruled out, partly because Russia, which had a smaller but similar fur seal herd on the Kommandorsky Islands, refused to support it. With no pelagic hunting restriction resulting, the number of seals declined drastically until 1911, when another arbitration agreement resulted in the complete cessation of hunting at sea. Descendants of the original herd survive in small numbers on the Pribylovs with all commercial hunting forbidden.

FURUHJELM, JOHANN (1821–1909). Of Finnish-Swedish background, with a record of distinguished service in the Russian navy, Furuhjelm was appointed "governor" (or chief administrator) of the **Russian America Company (RAC)** in Northwest America in 1859. His administration was troubled by the increasing American presence, restless natives, and new economic endeavors. Furuhjelm, however, was one of the most creative and innovative governors in terms of establishing a close relationship with the rapidly growing American presence in Pacific waters, in exploiting new natural resources of **Alaska** in ice and timber, and in lending clear support to the Union during the **American Civil War**. His efforts to improve RAC's position, nevertheless, were ultimately doomed by the negative report of the inspection team of Pavel Golovin and Sergei Kostlivtsev (1859–60), which reinforced the Russian government's decision to sell the area to the United States in 1867. Though he gave up his authority after the traditional five-year term to the last Russian administrator, Prince Dmitri Maksutov, Furuhjelm would return to the region as governor of Eastern Siberia in 1870.

– G –

GADDIS, JOHN LEWIS (1949–). A leading American historian of **cold war** history and Soviet–American relations, Gaddis received his Ph.D. from the University of Texas and taught for several years at Ohio University, where he founded the Contemporary History Institute. He moved to Yale University in 1980, where he occupies a distinguished professorship. An associate of Russian scholars such as **Nikolai Bolkhovitinov**, Gaddis has also taught at Oxford University. His published work ranges from an excellent survey of Russian–American relations, *Russia, the Soviet Union and the United States: An Interpretive History* (1978, 1990) to a number of works on the cold war: *The United States and the Origins of the Cold War, 1941–1947* (1972); *The Long Peace: Inquiries into the History of the Cold War* (1987); *We Now Know: Rethinking Cold War History* (1997); and *The Cold War: A New History* (2005). In contrast to **William Appleman Williams** and **Walter LaFeber**, Gaddis placed primary blame for the conflict on the Soviet Union, on **Joseph Stalin** and his successors.

GAGARIN, YURY (1934–1968). The space race began in earnest in 1957 with the successful Soviet launch of an orbital module, **Sputnik**. The Soviet Union continued to lead for several years, culminating with the launching of the first man in space, Gagarin, in April 1961. The son of a collective farmer in Smolensk province, Gagarin joined the Soviet air force in 1955, was later groomed as an astronaut, and then was highly celebrated for his successful flight of 108 minutes. Unfortunately, a few years later he died during an accidental crash of a test flight and is memorialized by a striking monument in the middle of Leninsky Prospect in Moscow. *See also* KRIKALOV, SERGEI.

GALLATIN, ALBERT (1761–1849). From obscure origins as an orphan in his native Switzerland, Gallatin rose rapidly in the early American republic as a financier. He served in the House of Representatives (1795–1801) from Pennsylvania and was a strong supporter of **Thomas Jefferson**, who appointed him secretary of the treasury, a post he continued to hold in the administration of President James Madison. During the **War of 1812**, Madison assigned him to head a commission to seek Russian arbitration for a peace with Great Britain. In May 1813 he arrived in St. Petersburg with James Bayard for this cause with the assistance of Minister **John Quincy Adams**. London, however, refused to participate in this American overture, and the delegation would withdraw to join Henry Clay and Jonathan Russell in Ghent for direct negotiations on ending the war. Gallatin is credited as the chief framer of the treaty that resulted. He later performed valuable service as U.S. minister to France and Great Britain.

GARF. *See* STATE ARCHIVES OF THE RUSSIAN FEDERATION.

GARST, ROSWELL (1898–1977). Iowa farmer and activist for closer Soviet–American relations, Garst pursued an international agenda in the cause of improving the disastrous state of Soviet agriculture in the 1950s through opportunities offered by the new Soviet policy of **peaceful coexistence**. He visited the Soviet Union twice, in 1955 and 1959, and was hosted by **Nikita Khrushchev** at his Crimean dacha. Garst's mission was to assist Soviet agricultural development, especially in the cultivation of corn as a feed grain. When Khrushchev toured the United States in 1959, he visited the Garst farm in Iowa, where he admired the piles of recently harvested corn. Khrushchev subsequently ordered, somewhat recklessly considering the Russian climate, a major increase of corn production in the Soviet Union.

GARTHOFF, RAYMOND L. (1929–). A graduate of Princeton University (B.A. 1948) and Yale University (Ph.D. 1951), Garthoff was a leading American political and military advisor on the Soviet Union and Eastern Europe during the **cold war**. He served as special advisor to the Department of Defense (1957–61) and to the State Department (1961–68) on arms limitation negotiations. As an associate at the Brookings Institution, Garthoff was the author of many books on Soviet–American relations, including *Soviet Military Doctrine* (1953), *The Soviet Image of Future War* (1959), *Soviet Strategy in Nuclear War* (1962), *American-Soviet Relations from Nixon to Reagan* (1985), *Reflections on the Cuban Missile Crisis* (1987), and *The Great Transition: American-Soviet Relations and the End of the Cold War* (1994).

GAYLORD, FRANKLIN (1856–1943). Arriving in Russia in 1899, Gaylord devoted many years to the establishment of the **Young Men's Christian Association (YMCA)** in Russia. He achieved major success in St. Petersburg, where a central headquarters sponsored a variety of educational, social, religious, and athletic programs under his direction. With American—and a surprising amount of Russian—support, the YMCA expanded rapidly from its St. Petersburg base, *Mayak* (Lighthouse). This promotion of the American YMCA in Russia was strongly supported by its executive secretary, **John R. Mott**, and with the financial support of **Charles R. Crane**. Gaylord and his American assistants remained in charge until 1918, when *Mayak* was forcibly closed by the circumstances of revolution and intervention. He concluded his Russian YMCA career as director of its operations in Odessa during the **Russian Civil War**.

GENERAL-ADMIRAL. Because of the close relations of the United States and Russia during the **Crimean War** and the tendency of Russia to look to the United States for transportation development, the Russian navy contracted in 1857 with the William H. Webb shipyards of New York for the construction of a new naval ship. The result was the largest vessel (7,000 tons) ever built in America up to that time, and it attracted much public attention at a Lower East Side Manhattan dock when it was launched in October 1858. It was named in honor of Minister of Navy **Grand Duke Constantine**. Webb sailed onboard for its delivery to Kronstadt, where it served for many years as the flagship of the Baltic fleet.

GENEVA CONFERENCE (1955). The first post–**World War II** summit was noted especially for the appearance on the international scene of Soviet leader **Nikita Khrushchev**. His meeting with American president **Dwight D. Eisenhower**, as well as with British prime minister Anthony Eden and French president Edgar Faure, was the first encounter of American and Soviet leaders since the **Potsdam Conference** in the summer of 1945. The Geneva meeting heralded the initiation of the Soviet leader's policy of **peaceful coexistence** and Khrushchev's emergence as a world leader. Discussions centered on German reunification and arms limitations, but among the 17 points of recommendation was scholarly exchanges, which materialized after lengthy negotiation in January 1958 as the **Lacy-Zarubin Agreement**.

GENOA CONFERENCE (1922). First major international conference after **World War I** and the Versailles peace treaty. On 10 April, representatives of 34 nations, which did not include the United States (except as observers), met to discuss the financial and commercial repercussions of the war. It was the first time that Germany and Soviet Russia reappeared in the international arena. Those two isolated powers, however, upstaged the event by meeting separately beforehand at Rapallo to come to an agreement over mutual claims and to make a mutually beneficial alliance that would prevail until the rise of Adolf Hitler. A major issue at the conference concerned Russian debts owed to its allies of World War I, which the **Bolshevik** government refused to recognize. **Georgy Chicherin**, representing the Soviet government, offered to recognize prewar debt if the Allied representatives would agree to cancel all war debts in recognition of damages inflicted upon Russia. With a settlement impossible, the conference adjourned in mid-May.

GIBSON, ABRAHAM (c. 1780–1860). New York businessman and American consul general in St. Petersburg (1819–51), Gibson oversaw a booming American trade with Russia during the first half of the 19th century with a calm and honest demeanor for a record number of years. He was criticized, however, for taking long "vacations" in England during the winter "off seasons" of shipping. Gibson nevertheless was a mainstay of the expanding **St. Petersburg American colony** that included the Hooper, **Whistler**, **Prince**, **Ropes**, and **Winans** families.

GLASNOST. A Russian word for openness, or, in the context of **Mikhail Gorbachev**'s reforms, freedom of expression and investigation. This brought much greater access to information and the filling of "blank pages" in Soviet history, culture, and social life. Included were topics, such as crime and AIDS, previously banned from official discussion, but it also involved a wider exposure to world, and especially Russian, history, leading to the questioning of official Soviet views of all kinds. The new direction was dramatically revealed to American scholars at a Soviet–American symposium on **World War II** held at the **Franklin D. Roosevelt** presidential library in August 1986, when academician **Grigory Sevostianov** opened the meeting with an hour-long presentation of the mistakes of the past and admission of faulty, biased, and inaccurate historical works and appealed to Americans to help remedy the Soviet historical interpretations created by the **cold war**.

GLASSBORO SUMMIT. This meeting between President Lyndon Johnson and Soviet Prime Minister Aleksei Kosygin at Glassboro State College in New Jersey in June 1967 marked a return to summitry after several years of lapse. Kosygin proved to be an able exponent of **Leonid Brezhnev**'s new approach to the West known as **détente**. Though no agreements were reached, discussions included limitations on armaments that would lead to the beginning of the **Strategic Arms Limitation Talks (SALT I)** and promote the détente initiative to move beyond the Soviet armed suppression of Czechoslovakia's moves toward a moderate socialism the following year.

GOLDEN, JOHN (1892–1940). An **African American** Communist, Golden grew up picking cotton on a Mississippi plantation but learned about radical alternatives from friends. He joined the **Communist Party of the United States of America (CPUSA)** in the early 1920s. Designated a representative of the party to Moscow in 1925, he joined a number of his background in lauding the freedom and lack of discrimination in Soviet Russia. Golden returned to the United States in 1927 to organize a group for establishing a cotton plantation (collective farm) in Central Asia on behalf of the CPUSA and under the auspices of the Soviet Commissariat of Agriculture in 1931. He became a Soviet citizen in 1935. His granddaughter, Elena Hang, became a well-known journalist and television personality in the **Mikhail Gorbachev** era and author of an interesting memoir, *The Story of a Black Russian-American Family, 1865–1992*.

GOLDER, FRANK (1877–1929). As a young Jewish immigrant with his family in 1880 from Russia, Golder became a major pioneer of Russian studies in the United States, promoted especially by an early teaching assignment at a federal school in Alaska. Graduating from Harvard University in 1903, a student of **Archibald Cary Coolidge**, he subsequently studied in Paris and Berlin before resuming his teaching career at the University of Missouri in 1908. He was one of the first Americans to conduct extensive research in Russian archives, mainly on **John Paul Jones** and **Vitus Bering**, during **World War I**. Golder also served in the **American Relief Administration (ARA)** in 1921–23 as its chief historian, collecting valuable materials for the ARA archives. **Herbert Hoover**, recognizing his contributions, asked him to head the **Hoover Institution** (initially the Hoover War Library), which he directed for several years, before his premature death from cancer in 1929. Perhaps his most valuable contribution was a memoir of 1920–22 in Russia: *On the Trail of the Russian Famine* (1927). He differed from his patron (Hoover), however, in supporting the recognition of Soviet Russia by the United States in the 1920s.

GOLDMAN, EMMA (1869–1937). One of a number of Jewish immigrants from the Russian Empire who became active revolutionaries, Goldman took as her idol Vera Pavlovna, heroine of Nikolai Chernyshevsky's *What Is to Be Done?* and became identified with the anarchist **Alexander Berkman** in a crusade for social justice. In 1920 she was arrested during the **"Red Scare"** and deported with Berkman to Soviet Russia. Both were unhappy with the lack of freedom in the land of the **Bolsheviks**, which she eloquently described in *My Disillusionment in Russia* (1923), and left that country to spend the rest of her life protesting injustices in a number of other locations, though she was not allowed back into the United States until after her death in Canada, when her remains were brought to Chicago for burial.

GOLD RUSH, CALIFORNIA (1849–1850). Though the Russian **Fort Ross** outpost north of San Francisco had already been sold and abandoned by the **Russian America Company (RAC)** in 1841, some of its former territory became the site of a major gold rush that attracted many new American settlers to northern California in the middle of the 19th century. The prospect of new riches also inspired the sending of a mining expedition by RAC, which did well in California, not only in mining gold, but also in selling Russian surplus gear (clothing, axes, shovels, picks, etc.) to the "forty-niners." The San Francisco boomtown also brought new business for the Russian company in sales of ice and lumber through contracts with the **American Russian Commercial Company**.

GOLIKOV, FILIP (1900–1980). Soviet general in **World War II**, chief of Soviet army intelligence (GRU) in 1940–41. A graduate of the Frunze Military Academy (1933), Golikov rose rapidly in the Soviet military hierarchy during the purges. Golikov has often been criticized for failing to detect and warn Soviet leaders about the impending German invasion of June 1941. Nevertheless, he was entrusted with an important mission to Great Britain and the United States after the decision to send **lend-lease** aid to the Soviet Union. He headed a hastily assembled Soviet military mission that arrived in Great Britain on 8 July 1941, just over two weeks after the German invasion of the Soviet Union. Discovering that Britain had few munitions to spare, the mission moved on to the United States, which promised much greater possibilities. Golikov had a list of priorities, headed by aviation fuel, for immediate delivery. After the conclusion of this foray into the West, he was promoted to deputy commissar of defense in Moscow and subsequently had little to do with relations with the Allies. Golikov was a controversial figure during the war but was trusted by **Joseph Stalin**—and later by **Nikita Khrushchev**—with important posts.

GOLITSYN, DMITRI. *See* AUGUSTINE, FATHER.

GOODRICH, JAMES P. (1874–1940). As a banker and Republican governor of Indiana (1917–21), Goodrich became concerned about the fate of Russians during the serious **famine** of 1921–23 and volunteered to provide information for **Herbert Hoover**, who had gained an international reputation for superintending relief during **World War I**. He made two inspection trips to Russia on behalf of the **American Relief Administration (ARA)** in 1921 and 1922. In his reports to Hoover he dramatized the hardships in the Russian countryside, abetting the American support for relief. Though a loyal supporter of Hoover, he differed from him sharply on the question of recognition of the Soviet Union, which Goodrich strongly supported, but to little effect during the 1920s. He witnessed the fruition of his cause by attending the New York banquet celebrating the **Recognition Agreement** in November 1933.

GORBACHEV, MIKHAIL (1931–). As a student in the **Moscow State University** law faculty in 1957, Gorbachev became a leader of the Komsomol (Young Communist League) and then was party director in the Kuban region of South Russia, where he won recognition and support from higher party officials such as **Yury Andropov**, director of the **KGB**, who introduced him into the top leadership (Central Committee) in Moscow by 1980. Intelligent, lively, and well spoken, he stood out in comparison to other associates of **Leonid Brezhnev**, such as Konstantin Chernenko, who had dominated Soviet politics for many years. As several of the latter died in the early 1980s (notably Mikhail Suslov, Aleksei Kosygin, and Dmitri Ustinov), Gorbachev's position advanced, and in 1985, upon the death of Chernenko, he became general secretary of the party with an agenda for change.

The early years of the Gorbachev era featured the "retirements" of a number of the old guard of the Communist Party of the Soviet Union (CPSU)—**Andrei Gromyko** (foreign minister, demoted to figurehead president), Viktor Grishin (Moscow party chief), and Nikolai Tikhonov (chairman of the council of ministers)—to be replaced by younger, more liberal officials, such as **Alexander Yakovlev, Eduard Shevardnadze**, Viktor Chernyaev, Yegor Ligachev, and **Boris Yeltsin**. Supported by this younger generation that was annoyed and embarrassed by the prevailing "gerontocracy" of the Brezhnev era and by a growing scientific and professional elite who were aware of the technological gap with the West, Gorbachev pushed for greater access to information, while historians and journalists urged a greater openness (**glasnost**). The resulting influx of Western media in turn promoted another major thrust of the Gorbachev initiatives—perestroika—or reconstruction, which was especially directed at economic reform. This meant also a push toward a competitive market economy and **"new thinking"** in foreign policy.

Gorbachev responded to the new media opportunities and his ability to force the old-guard members of the upper echelon of the party into retreat. The new policies, however, unleashed a number of forces previously held in check by central authorities: a nascent market economy, strong nationalist movements in the non-Russian constituent republics, and a desire to know more about the real history of the Soviet past. Gorbachev found himself by 1988 in the position of referee between left and right tendencies represented by Yeltsin and Ligachev, respectively. A new Congress of People's Deputies met, elected by a free franchise that resulted in a much smaller influence of the Communist Party and emergence of new political forces that included longtime dissident **Andrei Sakharov**.

The rise of independence movements in the Baltic republics, Ukraine, and other areas resulted in a compromise drive for a confederation in an agreement that would transform the Soviet Union into a **Commonwealth of Independent States (CIS)**. A conservative clique placed in office by Gorbachev attempted to stem the tide of disintegration by removing him from power. The **August Coup** backfired with the disbanding of the opponents' base of power and the dissolution of the Soviet Union, at least partly engineered by Yeltsin, into 15 independent states in December 1991. Gorbachev and his initiatives were welcomed by the United States for their impact on the ending of the tensions of the **cold war**, a momentous event in Russian–American relations.

GORCHAKOV, ALEXANDER (1798–1883). One of Russia's foremost statesmen during the reign of **Alexander II**, Gorchakov was a leading diplomat and chancellor of the Russian Empire through much of the last half of the 19th century, until his resignation in 1882. Sometimes described as the Otto von Bismarck of Russia, he nevertheless acquiesced to German dominance of European affairs in the 1870s

and 1880s. He suffered a setback at the Congress of Berlin in 1878 regarding the terms of settlement of the Russo–Turkish War (1877–78) that was engineered by Bismarck. This would steer Russia toward an alliance with France in the 1890s, which would have major consequences in regard to **World War I** and the **Bolshevik Revolution**. American diplomats found Gorchakov always attentive and openly friendly in regard to special missions to the United States and in receptions of private Americans in Russia. This paved the way for the introduction of many American businesses under **Sergei Witte**.

GORKY, MAXIM (NE ALEKSEI PESHKOV) (1868–1936). As a wanderer through the Volga region in the late 19th century, Gorky won an international readership for his eloquent portrayal of the folk life of the region. His sympathies soon gravitated toward the downtrodden of Russian society and to revolutionary causes, to which he contributed most of the income from his successful books, *The Lower Depths* (1902) and *Mother* (1907). He joined the émigré Russian revolutionaries abroad, especially on the Isle of Capri. Though **Vladimir Lenin** greatly admired him and solicited his support, Gorky remained vaguely neutral among the various Russian socialist directions. He visited the United States in 1906 by invitation from American sympathizers to raise funds for revolutionary causes through a series of lectures. At a famous welcoming dinner in New York, he sat between **Mark Twain** and **Jane Addams**, much to their mutual chagrin. His American sojourn was marred by a "sensational" report that he was living with an unmarried woman at his hotel, to which Gorky responded with typically insulting comments. Twain, unimpressed, noted, "He hits the public in the face with his hat and then holds it out for contributions." Gorky sought the last word with an essay—a diatribe on New York, *City of the Yellow Devil* (1907).

Despite his condemnations of capitalist societies, especially that of the United States, Gorky was still a humanitarian who courageously sought American aid with an appeal for help in July 1921 for the millions of his countrymen who were dying of starvation, to which **Herbert Hoover** magnanimously responded with an enormous program of relief directed by the **American Relief Administration**. Though apparently not happy with the course of Soviet affairs, he returned from a prolonged stay abroad to continue his masterful and penetrating depictions of society in upheaval and, often erroneously, is considered the father of socialist realism. He nevertheless was proclaimed a hero of Soviet literature and was honored upon his death, rumored by poison, by having a major Russian city, **Nizhni Novgorod**, named for him. His memorial, the Gorky Museum in Moscow, is well worth a visit.

GRANT, JULIA. *See* CANTACUZENE, COUNTESS JULIA SPERANSKY.

GRANT, ULYSSES S. (1822–1885). Grant's first contact with Russia came during the **American Civil War**, when he entertained Russian officers, including Admiral **Stepan Lesovsky**, at the siege of Vicksburg. The prevailing good relations between Russia and the United States following that conflict were disturbed early in the Grant administration by the **Katakazi affair**, which basically involved alleged insults to Grant's imperious Secretary of State **Hamilton Fish**, who supported the **Perkins Claim**. One result was a very short interview, taken as an insult, with **Grand Duke Alexis**, son of **Alexander II**, during his extended visit to America in late 1871. After the end of his second term, Grant and his wife went on an extensive world tour that included a visit to Russia, where he was cordially received by the tsar and was given the use of an imperial rail carriage for a trip to Moscow, and Admiral Lesovsky held an official reception in his honor. Another, more lasting connection of Grant with Russia was the marriage of his granddaughter to a Russian diplomat of Russian-Greek Phanariot background. *See also* CANTACUZENE, COUNTESS JULIA SPERANSKY.

GRAVES, WILLIAM S. (1865–1940). A graduate of West Point (1889) from Texas, Graves gained his first battlefield experience in the Spanish-American War in the Philippines. In 1918 he was designated by Secretary of War **Newton Baker** as commander of the **American Expeditionary Force (AEF)** to **Siberia**. Though some controversy still exists about the contents of his "secret orders," presented to him by Baker in Union Station in Kansas City, following these directions Graves avoided as much as possible any direct engagement with either Red or White contingents in the **Russian Civil War**, confining most of the AEF to **Vladivostok** and its vicinity. With the help of Admiral **Austin Knight**, commander of the U.S. Pacific Squadron, he successfully maneuvered the AEF between local authorities in Siberia, brutal White Army commanders such as

Grigori Semenov, the forces of **Alexander Kolchak** far inland at Omsk, and especially the much larger Japanese expansionist army. Several years later he recounted his role as the American **Intervention** commander in *America's Siberian Adventure* (1931). By that time Graves was a firm supporter of recognition of the Soviet regime.

GREENE, FRANCIS V. (1850–1921). Greene was specifically assigned as a young lieutenant by General **William T. Sherman** to report in detail on the Russo–Turkish War (1877–78). He did so as he followed the Russian army through the Balkans, in detailed letters, in an official report published as *Report on the Russian Army and Its Campaigns in Turkey in 1877–1878* (1879), and in a more informal *Sketches of Army Life in Russia* (1880). In these works Greene emphasized the changing nature of warfare: infantry skirmishes from defensive trenches with artillery deployed in the rear to provide distant cover and bombardment, as in **World War I**.

GROMYKO, ANDREI (1909–1989). A veteran Soviet diplomat with expertise on the United States, having served a few years in the Soviet embassy in Washington in the 1930s and as ambassador in the 1940s, Gromyko rose to the pinnacle of the Soviet Foreign Ministry establishment in the 1950s as a moderate but serious and severe cold warrior, occasionally open to new overtures and, fortunately, committed to calm, collected approaches to crises, during his long tenure as Soviet minister of foreign affairs (1957–85). He was labeled as "Mr. Nyet" (Mr. No) and personified the **cold war** for his hostile performances before the **United Nations**. Gromyko was a stolid survivor of the Soviet regime through all of the years of **peaceful coexistence** and **détente** and contributed to discussions and resulting agreements at summit meetings with American presidents in the 1970s. He deserves credit as a stabilizing figure during the cold war and for appointing an even more moderate and flexible **Anatoly Dobrynin** as envoy to Washington in 1962 at the time of the **Cuban missile crisis**. Gromyko was forced to retire in 1985 by **Mikhail Gorbachev** to the honorary post of "president" for his few remaining years of service. His published memoirs revealed little, but Gromyko may be due for reappraisal for the preservation of what amounted to peace during the cold war.

GUMBERG, ALEXANDER (1887–1939). The son of a large family of a rabbi in Ukraine, Gumberg immigrated alone at age 15 to the United States, where he perfected his knowledge of English and quickly adjusted to the American business scene. As an early assistant (1923) of **Boris Skvirsky** at the **Russian Information Bureau** in Washington, he met a number of Americans interested in Russia, such as Senator **William E. Borah**, and served as interpreter in Russia for several of them, including members of the **Root Commission** of 1917, and for Governor **James Goodrich** during the **American Relief Administration** operations in Soviet Russia. As a friend of **Raymond Robins** and **Samuel Harper**, Gumberg made his own mark in advancing American appreciation of Soviet achievements during the 1920s and 1930s and in encouraging a number of American scholars and businessmen who were interested in Russian business. Gumberg helped organize, and was appropriately recognized at, the banquet honoring **Maxim Litvinov** at the conclusion of the **Recognition Agreement** in 1933. Owing to his many business and diplomatic connections, he thrived during the Depression years in financial dealings—with fancy cars, New York mansions, and country houses—but, unfortunately, he died prematurely of a heart attack.

GUROWSKI, ADAM (1805–1866). A descendant of Polish-Russian nobility, Gurowski followed his father's precedent in opposing the Russification of Eastern (Russian) Poland. This forced him to abandon the family estates and pursue an education in Western Europe. Though he regained some prestige in Russia by the publication of *La Civilization et la Russie* (1840), which glorified a Russian mission in Europe, he once more fled into exile, to Heidelberg and Bern, where he lectured on political economy and published works on Poland and Pan-Slavism. In 1849 he left Europe for the United States, where he became interested in national politics and an ardent advocate of various liberal and Slavic causes. While supporting himself as a translator for the State Department, Gurowski became a critic of the administration of **Abraham Lincoln** for its leniency toward slavery and its mishandling of the **Civil War** campaigns, earning him the epithet of "Lincoln's Gadfly." Upon his death in 1866, however, he was buried in the Congressional Cemetery in eastern Washington, D.C., his grave site frequently visited by Polish Americans.

– H –

HAMMER, ARMAND (1898–1990). Son of Russian-Jewish immigrant Julius Hammer (1874–1948), Armand Hammer studied medicine at Columbia University, following his father's profession and also his socialist political inclinations. His first name was derived from the symbol, arm and hammer, of the American Socialist Labor Party. Hammer would be a study in contrasts throughout his life: active socialist and successful capitalist, Soviet agent and flag-waving American, art dealer and chemical engineer. Working from a mutual admiration between his father and **Vladimir Lenin**, Hammer obtained an early concession for a monopoly for the manufacture of pencils in Russia, which turned out to be quite profitable and long lasting (until 1929). He also obtained another concession on asbestos mining in the Urals through his company, Alamerica, an affiliate of the mostly fictitious Allied Drug and Chemical Corporation of New Jersey. Though the asbestos venture was unsuccessful, Hammer found reward in acting as an intermediary between Soviet officials and **Henry Ford**, despite Ford's anti-Semitism.

The Hammer family's greatest service and most profitable venture during the interwar years was in acting as Soviet agents for the sale of Russian art, largely Western art acquired by the Romanovs and wealthy nobility before the revolution, confiscated by the **Bolsheviks**, and then sold to help pay for the industrialization projects of the **First Five-Year Plan**. From their galleries in New York in the Waldorf Astoria Hotel, at Gimbel's department store, and in Miami, Florida, the Hammers reaped lucrative commissions, especially on impressionist paintings, many of which would end up, through the largess of Andrew Mellon, in the National Gallery in Washington. In the process, Hammer also acted allegedly as a conduit for the sale of Soviet gold in the United States to finance **Comintern** activities in the United States and elsewhere.

During and after **World War II**, Hammer profited from a distillery business that had no connection with Soviet enterprises. In 1956, he founded Occidental Petroleum, which soon became a major enterprise in the world oil and chemistry industries. He reentered Soviet affairs in the 1970s by negotiating contracts for Occidental in chemical enterprises in Togliattigrad on the Volga and along the Black Sea to produce ammonia for fertilizer. Soviet business, however, was only part of what had become a Hammer multinational industrial–chemical empire.

HAPGOOD, ELIZABETH REYNOLDS (1888–1974). As a bright, ambitious New York debutante in the late 1890s and graduate of Bryn Mawr, Elizabeth Reynolds also was the goddaughter of Russian immigrant **Zenaida Ragozin,** her mother's close friend who nurtured her affinity for foreign languages and encouraged her studies of Russia. Ragozin returned to Russia in 1900 and would host her American protégé during summers at the country estates of relatives and friends before 1914. She maintained these contacts until her death in 1924, while stimulating Reynold's postgraduate study of Russian at the Sorbonne under **Paul Boyer.** Reynolds subsequently became the chair of the Russian Department at Columbia University in 1915 and the first teacher of the language at Dartmouth in 1918, where she founded its Slavic department. Her surprise marriage in 1916 to **Norman Hapgood,** a journal editor and New York theater critic, inspired her interest in Russian drama and especially in **Konstantin Stanislavsky** and the **Moscow Art Theater (MAT).**

The Hapgoods visited Russia in 1923 to renew contacts with Ragozin and to arrange the tours of Stanislavisky and MAT to the United States in 1923 and 1924. The Hapgoods obtained copyrights to all of the works of Stanislavsky in English, which she translated and which resided in the Hapgood estate for many years, much to the dismay of those who preferred new translations of his works. These publications were an essential part of the popularity of the "Stanislavsky acting method" in the United States. Her studies, publications, and travels abroad were financed and encouraged by **Charles R. Crane.** She also befriended and protected Soviet defector Victor Kravchenko and assisted him in the publication of his memoir, *I Chose Freedom* (1946).

HAPGOOD, ISABEL (1850–1928). Privately educated in New England, Isabel Hapgood proved to be quite adept in mastering foreign languages, including Russian, perfected by extended residence in Russia in the 1880s. In the late 19th century she was the leading American translator of the novels, short stories, and plays of well-known Russian writers—Nikolai Gogol, Ivan Turgenev, **Leo Tolstoy**, Fedor Dostoevsky, and Anton Chekhov. Hapgood was especially known as the American agent of Tolstoy and the first American translator of his *War and Peace* and *Anna Karenina*; she thus became a major promoter of the "Tolstoy craze" in the United States. Cantankerous and difficult in personal relations, she earned the wrath of competitors such as **Nathan Dole** and **George Kennan** for taking liberties with the originals and for excising certain "immoral" sections from them. This resulted in a celebrated rift with Tolstoy. Hapgood also wrote articles for *Nation*, *Atlantic Monthly*, and other periodicals on her Russian experiences, some collected in her *Russian Rambles* (1894), and on her observations of the **Bolshevik Revolution**. Her writings and translations were a major contribution to American awareness of Russia at the turn of the century and through the revolution.

HAPGOOD, NORMAN (1868–1937). A prominent editor of weekly journals such as *Collier's* and *Harper's Weekly* before and during **World War I**, Hapgood independently became fascinated with Russian theater, especially the "modern method" of **Konstantin Stanislavsky**. In 1914, he planned to sponsor a visit of his **Moscow Art Theater** to New York, but it was negated by the beginning of World War I. During the early years of the war, he edited **Charles R. Crane**'s *Harper's Weekly* and lectured at Columbia University, where he met **Elizabeth Reynolds (Hapgood)**, a protégé of Crane. Their marriage in December 1916 was nevertheless a surprise, as he was twice her age. As a strong supporter of **Woodrow Wilson**'s war and peace agenda, Hapgood was appointed minister to Denmark in 1919 through the initiative of **Edward House** at the **Paris Peace Conference**, specifically with **Bolshevik** representatives in mind. In the interwar years, he was a staunch opponent of isolationism and supporter of recognition of the Soviet Union, which he visited with his wife in 1923. Hapgood was the author of numerous articles and books chronicling the international scene of his times and especially an evocative memoir, appropriately entitled *The Changing Years* (1930).

HARBIN. A city in the middle of Chinese Manchuria, Harbin became a major Russian transportation center with the construction of the

Chinese Eastern Railway (CER) as a convenient shortcut for the **Trans-Siberian Railroad** in the early 20th century. It was also the junction point for a rail line that extended south to Port Arthur. As a result, a sizable Russian community of over 50,000 was established there that alarmed the Japanese. This rapid rise of Russian presence in Manchuria was thus one of the causes of the Japanese attack on Port Arthur and **Vladivostok** in 1904 that began the **Russo–Japanese War**. Thanks to American intervention at the **Portsmouth Peace Conference** (1905), the CER remained in Russian hands and the Russian community prevailed beyond the **Bolshevik Revolution**, now divided between pro-Soviet and anti-Soviet tendencies. During the **Russian Civil War** and **Intervention**, Harbin was a center of American communications with various anti-Bolshevik forces, partly in order to keep the city and CER out of the hands of the Japanese. The Russian community remained in the city through the interwar period and into and after **World War II**, when many Russian refugees would resettle in Shanghai and eventually immigrate to the United States.

HARPER, SAMUEL N. (1882–1943). Harper was a professor of Russian studies at the University of Chicago (1915–43) and son of University of Chicago president **William Rainey Harper**. Upon the urging of **Charles R. Crane**, he signed a contract with his father committing him to the study of Russian language and culture by intensive immersion during summers spent in Russia (paid for by Crane) and formal study with **Paul Boyer** at L'Ecole des Langues Orientales Vivantes in Paris (1905). After a few years as an instructor in Russian at the University of Chicago (1905–09), he became a lecturer on Russian institutional history at the University of Liverpool in England under **Bernard Pares**. He subsequently began what would be a lifelong career as a professor of Russian studies at the University of Chicago in 1915, his salary paid by Crane in regular bequests to the university. On Crane's recommendation, President **Woodrow Wilson** assigned Harper to accompany Ambassador **David Francis** to his diplomatic post in Petrograd in 1916. After the **February Revolution** of 1917, Harper accompanied Crane to Russia as special advisor to the **Root Commission** in May and again stayed for several months, witnessing the radical course of the revolution.

He also met newspaper publisher and journalist **William Allen White**, who had just toured the western front as a Red Cross representative, and that resulted in an extended lecture tour by Harper through the Midwest in early 1918.

Besides his academic and lecturing careers, Harper also served as consultant and translator for the State Department during the years of **Civil War** and **Intervention** (1918–21), mainly from his office at the university and with frequent trips to Washington. Though at first a vocal opponent of recognition of the Soviet regime, Harper converted to support of it by 1926. He also gained academic respect in the early 1930s with *Civic Training in Soviet Russia* and *Making Bolsheviks*, as well as for his many articles and conference papers. Harper supported actively the expansion of Slavic studies in the United States, for which he served as an organizational leader and communications center. His meticulously maintained papers (in the Regenstein Library's Special Collections) attest to his role as an inspirer of scholarship on Russia in general.

HARPER, WILLIAM RAINEY (1856–1906). A graduate of Muskigum College (1870) and Yale University (Ph.D. 1875), Harper taught Hebrew language and literature at Baptist Theological Seminary in Chicago and then returned to Yale as a professor of Semitic languages. Despite a lack of administrative experience, Harper was chosen in 1892 for the presidency of the University of Chicago and to oversee building (on the site of the **Columbian Exposition**) a modern campus, raising money, and hiring top-level faculty. Funds came especially from John D. Rockefeller and a number of Chicago businessmen, including **Cyrus McCormick Jr.**, Martin Ryerson, and **Charles R. Crane**. The latter also influenced Harper in the direction of Russian studies at the university by guiding him through Russia on a tour in 1900 that included visits with **Leo Tolstoy**, **Sergei Witte**, and **Nicholas II**. Crane convinced Harper to commit his son **Samuel Harper** to learning the language and culture of Russia and paid for his trips to Russia and formal study in Paris, London, and New York. Prompted by Crane, Harper hired the first teacher of Russian, **Xenephon Kalamatiano**, at the university in 1902. After his premature death, Harper's large residence on Woodlawn near the campus remained the home of his widow and son and a center of social and cultural activity through the 1930s, much of it concerning Russia and Slavic studies.

HARRIMAN (RUSSIAN) INSTITUTE. Founded in 1946 and promoted initially by **Geroid T. Robinson, John Hazard**, Philip Mosely, and others, this center of area studies at Columbia University trained many specialists on Russia, the Soviet Union, and the Communist bloc in the early years of the **cold war** and beyond. It began as the Russian Institute under the leadership of Robinson, Mosely, Henry Roberts, Ernest Simmons, and **Alexander Dallin**. After a substantial endowment from the estate of **W. Averell Harriman** in 1980 it was renamed the Harriman Institute. Many of its students entered government service or went on to Ph.D. studies in disciplines such as Russian language and literature, history, or economics and political science. The institute benefits from a distinguished faculty and the enormous resources in the area, such as the **New York Public Library**, the Butler Library at Columbia and its **Bakhmeteff Archive**, and various other manuscript collections in the New York area.

HARRIMAN, W. (WILLIAM) AVERELL (1891–1986). Born in New York City, Harriman studied at Groton and Yale University (class of 1913) and was groomed as a leading member of the eastern liberal establishment. As the son of railroad (Union Pacific) magnate E. H. Harriman, he inherited an industrial and transportation empire in the 1920s and soon expanded it into banking and shipbuilding. He ventured in 1925 into a concession in the Soviet Union for the resurrection of the manganese mines in Georgia from wartime and civil war damage. This first Russian experience was not especially fruitful, nor was it a financial loss, and it came about probably at least partly due to family connections with **George Kennan**, who wrote a biography of his father.

As a political progressive, Harriman contributed in various capacities to the New Deal during the administrations of **Franklin D. Roosevelt**. He entered the diplomatic scene as a special envoy to Europe in 1939 and especially as advisor to the president at his meeting with **Winston Churchill** at Placentia Bay in August 1941, which resulted in the Atlantic Charter. Soon after, he headed an Anglo-American mission to the Soviet Union in September 1941 that was crucial in signaling American support for the Soviet war effort and in extending **lend-lease** shipments to that country at a crucial time (Battle of Moscow). Harriman subsequently was appointed ambassador to the Soviet Union for much of the war period and into the beginning of the **cold war**, with George F. Kennan as his chief assistant; he supported Kennan's **Long Telegram** that severely warned of Soviet aggressive moves, written during the ambassador's absence in early 1946. He served several administrations in various capacities: secretary of commerce, roving ambassador, special advisor on withdrawal from Vietnam, and one-term governor of New York (1954–58), defeated for reelection by Republican Nelson Rockefeller. Harriman represented a cautious, polished, level-headed approach to Russian–American relations through the crises of the cold war. His estate left a sizable endowment to Columbia University's Russian Institute, renamed the **Harriman Institute** in recognition.

HARRIS, LEVETT (c. 1770–1839). As the first American consul in St. Petersburg (1803), Harris guided American relations with Russia through the difficult and complicated commercial period of the Continental System during the Napoleonic Wars. This involved a considerable increase in trade due to embargoes that favored American neutrality. Until the arrival in 1809 of **John Quincy Adams**, he was in charge of the relations between the two countries. Perhaps because of loss of fee income during the **War of 1812** and hoping to be named as Adams's replacement, he departed for home in 1813, leaving consular affairs in the hands of his nephew, John Levett Harris. The latter was involved in 1817 in a controversy with **William David Lewis**, brother of an American merchant in St. Petersburg; the affair did little credit to the American presence in Russia and provoked a lengthy court case in Philadelphia. Harris was replaced by **Abraham Gibson**, but he retained business interests that brought him back in later years to St. Petersburg, where he died.

HARRISON, EASTWICK AND WINANS. This 19th-century American industrial enterprise was a manufacturer of railroad engines and cars for Russian railroads. The company was founded by Thomas Winans of Baltimore, who built locomotives and cars for an early American railroad, the Baltimore and Ohio. In collaboration with

George Washington Whistler, the Winans company built the first "camel" engines that could climb steep grades for the Springfield–Albany line through the Berkshires in the 1830s. This attracted the attention of a Russian delegation inspecting American facilities in 1839. A new company, inspired by Joseph Harrison of Philadelphia, was formed and subsequently offered a 20-year contract and lease of a major government foundry, Aleksandrovsky, near St. Petersburg, for the production of the locomotives and rolling stock for the first long-distance Russian railroad from St. Petersburg to Moscow. Whistler served as its chief surveyor and supervisor. This enterprise, directed by William L. Winans in the 1840s, would be among the largest manufacturing establishments in Russia into the 1860s, netting considerable income symbolized by lavish Winans estates in Baltimore. This arrangement for the introduction of American expertise in a major Russian enterprise was one of the first of many that would later be termed *amerikanizm*, the Russian infatuation with all things technical and American.

HARVARD RUSSIAN RESEARCH (DAVIS) CENTER. Along with the **Harriman Institute** at Columbia University, the Harvard University center was a major promoter of training for expertise on Russia and the Soviet Union. Founded in 1947, it was backed by a distinguished faculty in a number of areas, headed by historians and political scientists **Michael Karpovich**, Merle Fainsod, Richard Pipes, **Zbigniew Brzezinski**, and **Adam Ulam**. It was noted as a major producer of Russian experts during the **cold war** and for its more conservative approach to Russian and Soviet history and politics, in contrast to the approach of the Harriman Institute. Renamed the William Cullom Davis Center, it continues to be a major center for scholarly research in the field.

HASKELL, WILLIAM N. (1878–1952). Hailing from Albany, New York, Haskell was a graduate of the U.S. Military Academy and a veteran of the Spanish–American War and the Mexican intervention of 1916–17. He directed the **American Relief Administration (ARA)** in Russia in 1921–23. In response to the Soviet appeal for aid to the severe Russian **famine** during the summer of 1921, **Herbert Hoover** designated Haskell, a veteran of aid to refugees of the former

Ottoman Empire, to head a large U.S. initiative to save millions of children in Russia. Hoover believed that military experience and presence was important for the success of the mission. Though a number of the approximately 300 Americans who were recruited for service in Russia were critical of his military-style administration, Haskell proved to be up to the task in providing cohesive leadership for the ARA and in negotiations with Soviet authorities. Certainly much of the success of the American mission to Russia was due to his sensible, level-headed approach that weathered most of the storms and resulted in meetings with **Lev Kamenev**, **Georgy Chicherin**, and other Soviet leaders.

Haskell subsequently obtained a law degree from Georgetown University and served for many years as commander of the New York State National Guard. To the consternation of Hoover, he became sympathetic to the Soviet Union through his service in Moscow and was a major supporter of U.S. diplomatic recognition in the 1920s that Hoover and many other government leaders opposed. He revisited the country again in 1931 to see the changes being effected by the **First Five-Year Plan** and would be an honored guest at the celebrations of the conclusion of the **Recognition Agreement** in November 1933.

HAYWOOD, WILLIAM D., "BIG BILL" (1869–1928). An American radical labor leader and a founder of the **Industrial Workers of the World (IWW)**, Haywood was born in Utah, where he became a coal miner, rising to lead some of the most memorable and violent workers' strikes, for which he achieved fame, especially for the arrests and court trials that followed. As probably the best-known American radical and antiwar socialist before and during **World War I**, Haywood was arrested for sedition and sentenced to 20 years in prison in 1917, but, while out on bail awaiting retrial for his IWW activities in 1921, he left the country and sought refuge in Soviet Russia, where he was welcomed as another example of capitalist suppression of the causes of labor. As a nominal official of the **Comintern**, Haywood's Moscow apartment became a social center for international socialists attending various Comintern and Profintern (labor international) conferences with his Russian wife serving as hostess. "Big Bill," however, was often ill—overweight, alcoholic, diabetic, and suffering from kidney failure—and he passed from the scene early in 1928, perhaps fortunate to miss the denouement of his brand of socialism in the "Stalin Revolution" and the purges (which surely would have included him).

HAZARD, JOHN N. (1909–1995). A graduate of Yale University (1930), Hazard studied law at Harvard University (LL.B. 1934), after which he went to the Soviet Union to study at the Moscow Juridical Institute under the auspices of the **Institute of Current World Affairs**. He spent several years in the country perfecting his knowledge of the language, the society, and its government. An associate of **Samuel Harper**, he became a fellow at the University of Chicago, where he received the J.S.D. (Doctor of Juristic Science) in 1939. During **World War II** he served as an assistant to **Phillip Faymonville** in the Division of Defense Aid Support (**lend-lease** to the Soviet Union) and accompanied him with the **Averell Harriman** mission to Russia in September 1941. Subsequently, Hazard joined the faculty of Columbia University and was one of the founders of the Russian Institute (later **Harriman Institute**) at Columbia University as professor of law and government (Nash Distinguished Professor). His scholarly publications were numerous: *Soviet Housing Law* (1939), *Law and Social Change in the USSR* (1953), *The Soviet System of Government* (1957), *Settling Disputes in Soviet Society* (1960), and many others, culminating in *Recollections of a Pioneer Sovietologist* (1983). Officially retired in 1977, he continued to teach as Professor Emeritus of Law at Columbia University, to which he contributed his large library on the Soviet legal system. *See also* CRANE, CHARLES R.

HEARD, AUGUSTINE, MERCHANT HOUSE (c. 1830–1890). The Heard company of Boston for three generations in the 19th century was the leading American mercantile establishment in the Far East, with its main bases in Canton and Shanghai. As such, it naturally sought the business of the **Russian America Company** of Northwest America in handling the import of **Alaska** furs, chiefly sea otter skins, for the Chinese market and in converting the receipts into Chinese goods, mainly tea, for transport overland or by sea to Russia. The Heards, acting as middlemen in the trade, also served as Russian consuls for a number of years in Chinese ports, involving periodic visits to St. Petersburg by members or agents of the Heard family. An enormous collection of business records of the company are maintained by the Baker Library of the Harvard University Business School.

HELSINKI ACCORDS AND FINAL ACT (1975). The Conference on Security and Co-operation in Europe, representing 35 countries including the Soviet Union, agreed to a comprehensive declaration that resembled **Woodrow Wilson**'s Fourteen Points. The 10-point program specified general rights of nations regarding sovereignty, frontiers, refraining from force, nonintervention, self-determination, and subordination to international law. Both the United States and the Soviet Union would be major violators of the axioms in following years. Item VII, however, required "respect for human rights and fundamental freedoms, including the freedom of thought, conscience, religion or belief." This was subject to regular neglect by the Soviet Union and by the subsequent **Russian Federation** and much condemnation by the West and the creation of a Helsinki Rights Watch, inside and outside of Russia. Though the "final act" was initially hailed by **Leonid Brezhnev**, it would become a manifesto of the Soviet and Russian dissident and liberal movements, such as Human Rights Watch.

HENDERSON, LOY W. (1892–1986). Henderson's introduction to Eastern Europe occurred as a member of an **American Red Cross** commission in Germany, supervising the repatriation of Russian prisoners of war in 1919. He entered the American foreign service in 1923 and was trained as a Soviet Russian expert. In 1934 Henderson was designated first secretary of the new embassy in Moscow and primary advisor to Ambassador **William C. Bullitt**. He coordinated the work of the embassy through difficult times that included the purge era and with a number of eccentric embassy personnel: **George F. Kennan**, **Charles Bohlen**, Elbridge Dubrow, and Charles Thayer. As a dedicated apprentice to conservative **Robert F. Kelley**, he was disliked by Soviet officials such as **Maxim Litvinov**. His tour in Moscow ended in 1938, followed by four years in the State Department dealing with Soviet affairs. In 1942 he led a special mission to the Union of Soviet Socialist Republics (USSR) to inspect the embassy, then divided between Moscow and Kuibyshev, the latter a safe retreat from the German advance. Because of his anti-Soviet stance, Henderson spent the remainder of his diplomatic career on other assignments: to Iraq during **World War II** (1943–45), as ambassador to India (1948–51), and to Iran (1951–55). He wrote *A Question of Trust, The Origins of U.S.-Soviet Diplomatic Relations: The Memoirs of Loy W. Henderson* (1986).

HERTER, CHRISTIAN A. (1895–1966). After serving in minor posts in the State Department during **World War l**, Herter became **Herbert Hoover**'s personal secretary in the Department of Commerce (1921–24). In this position he was responsible for much of the liaison correspondence with the **American Relief Administration (ARA)** office in New York and with special agents of Hoover, such as **James Goodrich** and **Frank Golder**. Herter left Washington to edit a newspaper in Boston, where he reentered politics as a Massachusetts assemblyman and as a Republican congressman (1943–52). He gained a reputation as an expert on foreign relations and was a strong supporter of the **Marshall Plan**. During the administration of **Dwight D. Eisenhower**, he served as assistant secretary of state, especially active in the American response to **Nikita Khrushchev**'s **peaceful coexistence** initiatives. He then succeeded **John Foster Dulles** as secretary of state in 1959, passing through the **U-2 incident** and the **Berlin Wall** crisis with an air of calm and caution.

HILLER, HENRY WINANS (1850–c. 1920). Hiller first became acquainted with Russia as a cabin boy stranded with an ill captain in **Siberia** (Petropavlovsk) in the 1860s, spending over a year on shore and learning Russian. He was later hired by C. S. Tiffany as a buyer of precious stones, enamelware and glassware, porcelain, and fine linens in Russia and went on annual trips during the summers from the 1870s through 1914, about 40 years. Consignments of raw material were refined, polished, and set by Russian craftsmen, mainly in Moscow, much to the economic benefit of Tiffany's. In the management of this process, Hiller was among the most knowledgeable Americans about the Russian business climate. During that period, he contributed to the considerable marketing of Russian fine arts, such as the well-known Fabergé designs, in the United States. His papers at the Mystic (Connecticut) Seaport Library and Museum provide interesting details about this unique Russian–American experience.

HINDUS, MAURICE (1891–1969). Born in a Jewish family in White Russia (Belarus), Hindus immigrated in 1905 with his family to the United States, settling, as did many other Russian Jews, in the Lower East Side of New York City. He graduated from Colgate University concentrating on the study of the Russian peasantry. After graduate study at Harvard University, he published his first scholarly work, *The Russian Peasant and the Revolution* (1920). He returned to Russia in 1923 on assignment to *Century Magazine* and stayed for several years as a freelance journalist and writer, who would provide one of the best coverages of the Soviet transformation, especially in the countryside: *Broken Earth* (1926), *Humanity Uprooted* (1929), and *The Great Offensive* (1933), as well as an epic (and little read) novel, *Moscow Skies* (1936). Hindus was admired by many of his contemporaries for his apt descriptions, honesty, and devotion to the subject. He was also a savvy prognosticator, observing publicly soon after the signing of the **Nazi–Soviet Pact** that the two countries would soon be at war.

HISS, ALGER (1904–1996). From Baltimore, Maryland, in a lower-middle class family (his father, who committed suicide when he was two years old, was a grocer), he graduated Phi Alpha Theta from Johns Hopkins University and subsequently received a law degree from Harvard University (1929), a protégé of Felix Frankfurter. He began public service in the administration of **Franklin D. Roosevelt** in 1933 as an attorney in the Agricultural Adjustment Administation, transferring to the State Department in 1936. During **World War II**, he was an important American delegate to the Dumbarton Oaks Conference on the **United Nations** and at the **Yalta Conference** (January 1945), where he was instrumental in reducing the Soviet demand for 16 members in the General Assembly to three. He was later executive secretary of the **San Francisco Conference**.

Already by 1942 Hiss was under suspicion by the Federal Bureau of Investigation (FBI) regarding his membership in the 1930s in the **Communist Party of the United States of America (CPUSA)**. During widely publicized hearings by the House of Representatives Committee on Un-American Activities in 1948, part of the **Mc-Carthyism** crusade, Hiss was declared by Whittaker Chambers to be an underground agent of the CPUSA and consequently of the Soviet Union. Under pressure from congressman **Richard Nixon**, the committee pressed the investigation, which led to both Chambers and Hiss being convicted of perjury, for which Hiss served a couple of years in prison. Hiss continually denied his guilt and fought for restitution after his release, citing misleading evidence from the FBI. Subsequent investigation in the 1990s, when Soviet archives opened, indicates circumstantial evidence (**Venona**) that Hiss was involved in transmitting vital information to the Soviet Union. The Hiss case remains debated, though historian Allen Weinstein, later director of the **National Archives**, concluded that Hiss was probably guilty of some of the allegations in his *Perjury: The Hiss-Chambers Case* (1978, revised 1997).

HOOVER, HERBERT CLARK (1874–1964). From a modest Quaker background in Iowa, Hoover rose through a Stanford University engineering degree to a major role in international business in the period before **World War I**. This included supervisory and investment roles for an international consortium based in London that managed the large Kyshtim copper mines near Chelyabinsk in the Urals region of Russia, which he visited on two occasions. By the beginning of the war, Hoover was a multimillionaire and respected manager of mineral investments worldwide. With the devastation of modern war becoming quickly apparent, Hoover disclosed his humanitarian side as the director of American relief for Belgium.

Hoover subsequently brought the cause of the destitution of many postwar refugees to the attention of the peace conference, the international relief community, and the American public. In responding to the appeal for relief from the Russian **famine** of 1921, he disposed of opposition in Congress, which actually doubled the amount of the requested grant to $20,000,000, which would be a substantial part of more than $60,000,000 in relief administered by the **American Relief Administration (ARA)**, a private agency that he directed from his office in the Commerce Department. At the same time he was instrumental in preserving records of the war and revolution—and relief—at the **Hoover Institution on War, Revolution and Peace** at Stanford University. Though his influence easily overcame objections that American relief would only bolster the **Bolshevik** regime in Russia, he remained opposed to diplomatic recognition of the Soviet Union during his presidency (1929–33) and beyond.

HOOVER INSTITUTION ON WAR, REVOLUTION AND PEACE (1919–). **Herbert Hoover**, engineer, international businessman, and organizer of relief efforts during **World War I** and administrator of the **American Relief Administration (ARA)**, believed in documentation and the preservation of records. He thus emphasized in his organizations the careful recording and filing of information and the collecting of other materials that might be of use to future historians. During the operations of the ARA in Russia, for example, carloads of records of its own operations and also those of the Soviet government were transported by pre-agreed arrangement, to the United States, where they were deposited in this special facility on the Stanford University campus. Under the leadership of **Frank Golder** and Harold Fisher, the institution continued to acquire materials, even commissioning memoirs, of the war and revolution. Supplemented by Hoover's personal and official papers at the Hoover presidential library in West Branch, Iowa, the Hoover Institution is the foremost repository (along with the **Bakhmeteff Archive** at Columbia University) on Russia in revolution and on Russian émigrés in the United States.

HOOVER, J. (JOHN) EDGAR (1895–1972). Starting as an assistant to Attorney General A. Mitchell Palmer—and earning laurels as an energetic implementer of the "Palmer raids" against suspected, mainly foreign, radical socialists, Hoover soon took over as the inaugural head of the Federal Bureau of Investigation (FBI), which soon became noted for its war against criminal organizations as well as anyone suspected of disloyalty, broadly defined. In the process the bureau (and he) acquired a large number of files on many Americans, especially those of foreign origin. His tactics included allowing the **Communist Party of the United States (CPUSA)** to operate in the open (so that it could be watched more easily). He survived several presidential administrations, bending to new policies, such as recognition of the Soviet Union and support of the **World War II** alliance. During the **cold war**, FBI operations would overlap with those of the **Central Intelligence Agency (CIA)**, creating confusion regarding jurisdiction. Hoover, nonetheless, reacted to the new **"Red Scare"** in 1950 by drawing up a list of 10,000 Americans suspected of being threats to national security to be arrested and incarcerated upon presidential order. Fortunately, that order was never issued.

HOPKINS, HARRY (1890–1946). Born in Sioux City, Iowa, and a graduate of Grinnell College in 1912, Hopkins began his career in social welfare with a settlement house on the Lower East Side of New York and was soon appointed executive secretary of the city's Bureau of Child Welfare. After a period with the **American Red Cross** in New Orleans, he helped draft the charter for the American Association of Social Workers and served as its president in 1923. He returned to New York to head several agencies. When the Depression hit New York, Governor **Franklin D. Roosevelt** asked him to direct the state's Temporary Emergency Relief Administration and won his trust and admiration.

Upon election as president, Roosevelt brought Hopkins to Washington to direct and advise on New Deal relief programs—and to live in the White House. He was instrumental in the creation of the Works Progress Administration (WPA), and his role in Washington increased dramatically with war on the horizon in 1940. He helped organize **lend-lease** for Great Britain, Soviet Russia, and China. Despite persistent ill health, Hopkins accompanied the president to various wartime conferences—Cairo, **Casablanca**, **Tehran**, and **Yalta**—and headed special missions to Moscow in July 1941 and in 1945, the latter on behalf of President **Harry S. Truman**. Some observers believe that he and another presidential advisor, Sumner Welles, had a larger role in determining American policy toward the Soviet Union than did the State Department. Historical assessments of Hopkins's role in Soviet–American relations thus vary widely, from Robert Sherwood's classic, *Roosevelt and Hopkins* (1948) to Herbert Romerstein and Eric Breinel's *The Venona Secrets* (2000).

HOUSE, "COLONEL" EDWARD (1858–1938). A "Texas colonel," House helped **Woodrow Wilson** obtain the Democratic nomination in 1912 and, upon his election, became his closest advisor on many matters, but especially on foreign policy. He served as the president's special emissary on a number of foreign missions during **World War I** and the peace conference that followed. House, along with **Breckinridge Long** in the State Department, was especially concerned about the situation of Russia and the absence of any representation at the **Paris Peace Conference**. Largely independent of the quite preoccupied president, House espoused the **Bullitt mission** directly to Soviet Russia in 1919 and the appointment (later rejected by the Senate) of **Norman Hapgood** as American minister to Denmark in view of establishing more regular contact with Bolsheviks in Scandinavia. These overextensions of authority led to a falling out with the president and the lack of his services when they were most needed during the campaign for American ratification of membership in the **League of Nations**.

HUGHES, CHARLES EVANS (1862–1948). A distinguished international attorney, Hughes was designated secretary of state (1923–25) by President Warren Harding, despite his lack of government service or diplomatic experience. He quickly became known for his conservative administration of American foreign policy, which included the continued staunch nonrecognition of the Soviet Union along the lines of the **Colby Note**, which he formally reaffirmed in 1923. Nevertheless, he supported, along with Secretary of Commerce **Herbert Hoover**, freedom of trade of American businesses with Soviet Russia and expanded cultural contacts. Faced with the formidable opposition of Republican senator **William E. Borah**, Hughes withdrew from any action against the quasi-Soviet embassy operated a stone's throw from the State Department by **Boris Skvirsky**.

HUGHES, LANGSTON (1902–1967). Born in Joplin, Missouri, Hughes grew up in Lawrence, Kansas, but soon moved on and into the Harlem Renaissance in New York as a successful writer. In 1932 he joined about 20 other **African Americans** who had been invited to Moscow to participate in a Soviet film on racial discrimination in America. Though the film, tentatively labeled "Black and White," never materialized, Hughes spent almost a year traveling around the Soviet Union to witness the "miracle" of the **First Five-Year Plan**, recorded in his autobiography, *I Wonder as I Wander*, and in a number of contemporary articles, some in Russian. While traveling in Central Asia, he met Arthur Koestler, a German journalist (Koestler would later become well known for his exposé of the brutal nature of the Stalin repressions in *Darkness at Noon*) and enjoyed playing jazz records. Hughes was the most visible of a number of African Americans attracted to what they initially perceived to be a country of nondiscrimination and opportunity.

HULL, CORDELL (1871–1955). A Tennessee democrat, Hull served several terms in the House of Representatives and then was elected to the Senate. He resigned from the latter to accept an important position in the administration of **Franklin D. Roosevelt** as secretary of state (1933–44). His main concern and expertise involved Latin American relations, and he was generally bypassed in regard to diplomatic recognition of the Soviet Union in 1933 and subsequent relations in regard to that country. Others such as his assistant, Sumner Welles, would fill that role as "acting secretary of state for European affairs." Hull's virtual exclusion from Soviet–American affairs would continue through **World War II**, though he did lead a mission to Moscow in 1943. These were left to experts such as **George F. Kennan, W. Averell Harriman, Charles Bohlen,** and, especially, Welles and **Harry Hopkins.**

HUNGARIAN REVOLUTION (1956). Inspired by the de-Stalinization programs of **Nikita Khrushchev**, especially in his February 1956 speech at the 20th Party Congress, the Hungarians, following a spring Polish precedent and led by Imre Nagy, initiated a program of reforms that would have relaxed economic controls and allowed a partial market economy and that hinted of a move away from the **Warsaw Pact** and toward an independent foreign policy. The result was a Soviet military invasion in October 1956, the replacement of Nagy by Janos Kadar, and the suppression of this "separate road to socialism." This provoked a strong response in the West, which, however, was restricted in action by contemporary problems in the Middle East (the Suez Crisis). Though Hungary succumbed to Soviet military and political pressure, it would continue to pursue an economic reform agenda under Kadar. Meanwhile, the Western alliance won a **cold war** propaganda victory through the Soviet heavy hand and the mass exodus of Hungarian political refugees. By contrast, the Soviet suppression of the Czechoslovak reforms in 1968 was much less bloody and more confined.

HUROK, SOL (1888–1974). Born and raised in a Ukrainian Jewish village, Hurok came to the United States in 1906. Wandering through the Jewish sectarian life of the Lower East Side as an aspiring actor with little success, he emerged as a strong personality and agent of a long list of performers and groups, many of them from Russia, but they also included outstanding talents such as Marian Anderson, **Fedor Chaliapin**, Anna Pavlova, Jerome Hines, Isaac Stern, Arthur Rubinstein, and **Van Cliburn**, a virtual "who's who" of American and world talent. He was especially interested in those from his native Russia and was a major force in breaking down the cultural barriers of the **cold war** in taking advantage of the cultural exchange opportunities of the 1950s and 1960s. In this period Hurok managed the American tours of the Kirov and Bolshoi Ballets, the Moiseyev folk dancers, Isaac Stern, and many others.

– I –

IMMIGRATION, "RUSSIAN" TO THE UNITED STATES. The United States was the recipient of a large number of immigrants from the Russian Empire, mainly during the last quarter of the 19th century and the first decade of the 20th. The great majority, however, were not Russian but from minority populations who felt discrimination owing to Russification policies. The largest group was Jewish, followed by Poles, Ukrainians, Volga Germans, Lithuanians, Armenians, and **Mennonites**. The Jews settled mainly in eastern urban areas, such as the Lower East Side of New York City, while Poles, Ukrainians, and Lithuanians congregated in new industrial areas such as Chicago, Cleveland, Detroit, and Pittsburgh. The Volga Germans and Mennonites settled mainly on farms on the Great Plains or in mill towns in that region. Their contributions to the cultural and ethnic variety and economic progress of the United States were enormous.

Three more waves of immigration to the United States would occur in the 20th century: an exodus of Russian refugees from the **Bolshevik Revolution** and **Civil War**; a number of expatriates fleeing Soviet rule from Eastern Europe, including territory of the USSR that had been under German occupation, immediately after **World War II**; and a smaller number seeking political asylum beginning in the 1970s. The latter would include mainly Soviet Jews allowed to emigrate, but also Soviet dissidents such as **Alexander Solzhenitsyn** and **Joseph Brodsky**.

INDUSTRIAL WORKERS OF THE WORLD (IWW, "WOBBLIES"). Beginning with a convention in Chicago in 1905 and continuing into the 1920s, the IWW, under the leadership of **Eugene Debs**, Daniel de Leon, and **William Haywood**, grew into a large organization in radical opposition to the more moderate American Federation of Labor, headed by Samuel Gompers. Perhaps the height of its success came with the Seattle General Strike of 1919. By that time, however, it was beginning to decline, owing to arrest of leaders for opposition to **World War I** conscription and its largely mixed ethnic and, consequently, disorganized membership, a number of whom were of East European immigrant background who sympathized with the **Bolshevik Revolution**. Many of them were arrested and deported to Soviet Russia during the **"Red Scare"** witch hunt of 1919–21, providing a boost of support to that Communist regime at a vital time. A few others, such as Haywood, would escape to Russia to evade prison sentences in the United States and give the Communist movement a quasi-genuine international credibility. By 1924, the IWW, weakened by arrests, deportations, and defections, but especially by the labor complacency of the interwar years and a split among leadership, ceased to have any real influence. A residue would join the nascent but perennially weak **Communist Party of the United States of America (CPUSA)**.

INNOCENT OF ALASKA. *See* VENIAMINOV, IVAN.

INSTITUTE OF CURRENT WORLD AFFAIRS. Founded by **Charles R. Crane** with a transfer of stock from his Friendship Fund in 1932, the institute sponsored research on the Soviet Union of scholars such as **Samuel Harper**, **John Hazard**, **Thomas Whittemore**, **Elizabeth** and **Norman Hapgood**, and Bruce Hopper. Recipients were expected to submit regular extensive reports on their experiences in the Soviet Union. It was a major source for scholarly exchanges before the existence of the **International Research and Exchanges Board (IREX)**, the **Ford Foundation**, the Fulbright Program, or the **Kennan Institute for Advanced Russian Studies**. The institute continues to be supported by the Crane family as a memorial to Charles Crane in the 21st century, though on a much-reduced level.

INSTITUTE OF GENERAL (WORLD) HISTORY, RUSSIAN ACADEMY OF SCIENCES. During the **cold war** and after, the institute preserved a scholarly and generally objective perspective on the world around the Soviet Union, with special focus on the United States in its **Center for North American Studies** under the direction of **Grigory Sevostianov** and **Nikolai Bolkhovitinov**. Under the longtime and steady directorship of Alexander Chubarian, the institute sponsored a number of joint Russian–American colloquia and conferences and individual scholars on exchange arrangements, as well as nurturing younger scholars, though suffering budget problems in the 1990s. For example, the institute sponsored a major academic conference in November 2007 in Moscow on the 200th anniversary of the beginning of Russian–American relations.

INSTITUTE OF THE U.S.A. AND CANADA OF THE RUSSIAN ACADEMY OF SCIENCES (ISKRAN), RUSSIAN ACADEMY OF SCIENCES. The major Soviet/Russian think tank on contemporary policies and modern history of the United States was established in 1967. Mainly devoted to the post–**World War II** period, ISKRAN (ISKAN before 1991) was a major forum and information source for contemporary American studies under the longtime directorship (1967–95) of **Georgy Arbatov** and his successor, Eduard Ivanian. It and its partner, the **Center for North American Studies** of the **Institute of General History** of the **Academy of Sciences**, which focused on the pre-1945 period, were generally objective in their studies of American history and politics. Nevertheless, ISKRAN was the source of many inaccurate and deliberately distorted publications during the **cold war**. In fact, it was a major propaganda machine of the Soviet Union, but under Arbatov's leadership, it quickly adjusted to a more friendly mode in the era of **Mikhail Gorbachev**. Most of its large quantity of publications during the cold war have been cast into Leon Trotsky's proverbial "dustbin of history."

INTERMEDIATE-RANGE NUCLEAR FORCES (INF) TREATY. Responding to major changes in international relations as a result of the reforms, especially **"new thinking"** of **Mikhail Gorbachev**, the United States and the Soviet Union agreed to the elimination of a broad category of nuclear weapons, mainly intermediate-range weapons, to be destroyed under mutual supervision. This was achieved as a significant sign of the waning of the **cold war**, despite strong opposition in both countries and disputes over the range of specific weapons, generally conceded to the American definition by Gorbachev. President **Ronald Reagan** persuaded opponents in the West to go along with these definitions and restrictions. After long negotiations the treaty was formally signed in Geneva in November 1987 between Secretary of State George Shultz and Soviet Foreign Minister **Eduard Shevardnadze**.

INTERNATIONAL HARVESTER COMPANY (IH). Built upon the invention of the famous reaper by Cyrus McCormick, the company, based in Chicago, flourished in the late 19th century and throughout much of the 20th, with expanding international sales, personified by its adopted name, derived mainly from the merger of McCormick with the Dearing Company into the International Harvesting Machine Company. The new company attracted the attention, by way of *amerikanizm*, of Russians who were seeking improvement of Russia's backward agriculture. After initial successes in the marketing of implements in that country, the company, headed by **Cyrus McCormick Jr.**, established a factory at Lubertsy in the vicinity of Moscow in 1900. IH maintained a monopoly on the production in Russia of its binder-reapers and competed with Russian companies in the production of the more primitive mowers (*lobogrieka*). Including factory workers and sales and service agencies throughout the country and especially in Ukraine and the newly developed areas of **Siberia**, the American company employed nearly 30,000 in Russia by 1914.

During **World War I** the Lubertsy factory turned to military production, while maintaining service and parts for existing equipment in Russia. At the time of the revolution, it was one of the largest private companies in Russia. The fate of the concern after the **Bolshevik** seizure of power was also unique. Respecting the continued need for American expertise in agriculture, the new government was reluctant to nationalize that enterprise during the wholesale confiscations of 1918. The factory continued to produce equipment on a temporary basis of an allowed 10 percent income over costs, until 1924, when the factory was finally brought under complete Soviet control, in part because the Chicago headquarters had decided that its further operation was not cost effective.

This was not the end of the "Harvester" story in Russia. Minor contracts continued to afford service to existing equipment and for what the Soviet machinists managed to continue to produce during the 1920s. The **First Five-Year Plan**, beginning in 1928, emphasized the increased production of all kinds of modern equipment to accompany the massive drive of collectivization of agriculture. IH, in new contracts, provided much of the design and equipment of the large new tractor factories in Kharkov and Stalingrad, where the basic Farmall 12, 14, and 20 models and accompanying equipment would be manufactured in their Soviet equivalents for many years. *See also* LEGGE, ALEXANDER.

INTERNATIONAL RESEARCH AND EXCHANGES BOARD (IREX) (1968–). A nongovernment American agency supervising exchanges of students and scholars with the Soviet Union and Eastern Europe and, after 1991, with the newly independent countries. In 1968, IREX replaced the Inter-University Committee on Travel Grants in the direction of academic exchanges with the Union of Soviet Socialist Republics (USSR). During its administration, headquartered first in Princeton, New Jersey, and later in Washington, D.C., considerable expansion occurred. A number of other organizations and direct exchanges followed as opportunities increased. Funding was provided by both government grants (such as those under the **American Council of Teachers of Russian**) and from private sources.

The basic exchanges for most of the period, beginning in 1958, involved advanced graduate-student specialists on Russia and Eastern

Europe and both junior and senior faculty from both sides. The arrangement provided for a waiving or providing substantial reduction of tuition, housing supplements, and stipends, with travel costs borne by the other partner. The fellowships also usually included a book and research expense allowance, attendance at cultural events, and travel to other major locations. A large number of the academic scholars of each country participated over the years in the exchange, which, because of the range and depth of the participants, had a major role in breaking down barriers and ending the **cold war**. Subsequently, IREX programs have included the American cultural dimensions in a much wider variety of emphases and regions, and short-term grants are available for scholars to use resources in the Washington area, such as the **Library of Congress** and the **National Archives**.

INTERVENTION, AMERICAN. After the **Bolshevik Revolution** in November 1917, the new Soviet government negotiated a separate peace with Germany at **Brest-Litovsk** in March 1918 and subsequently withdrew from **World War I**. The motivations for the Allied Intervention in Russia were several: concern about the ability of Germany to shift forces from the eastern front to the west, which led to a search for means to reestablish that front, either through a non-Soviet force from the old Russian army or by convincing the Bolsheviks to continue the war; fear that the large amounts of supplies sent to Russian ports, such as **Murmansk** and **Archangel**, would fall into German hands in the summer of 1918; and an opportunity to stop the threat of a world socialist revolution by lending assistance to anti-Bolshevik forces.

President **Woodrow Wilson** agreed during the summer of 1918, per the British plan for a military presence in Russia, to send American units under British command to Murmansk and Archangel. Landing in September and numbering about 3,000, mostly from Wisconsin and Michigan, they engaged in a protective mission of the ports, both to control the supplies and to ensure evacuation of Americans in Russia, especially the embassy relocated to Vologda from Petrograd. The latter extended their activities along railroads and rivers southward into Russia and met with limited resistance and few casualties. More Americans died of disease (mainly the Spanish influenza) than in combat. This **American Expeditionary Force (AEF)** was disturbed about its continuing deployment in the Russian Arctic in 1919—after the war was over—and about being under British command. It was withdrawn that summer, later to be memorialized as the "polar bears."

A much larger AEF was deployed in the Russian Far East in and around **Vladivostok**, constituting two regiments of about 13,000 troops under the command of General **William S. Graves**. Their mission was not only to protect supplies in the port, but also to aid the evacuation of the **Czechoslovak Legion** and to guard against the control and possible acquisition of the area by a much larger Japanese army. This operation also avoided combat as much as possible and, while lending moral support to the White Army of **Alexander Kolchak** far to the west in Omsk, refrained from direct assistance. These limited involvements of American military units in Russia became a propaganda instrument for Soviet leaders during the **cold war**. *See also* CIVIL WAR, RUSSIAN.

INTOURIST. Initially and for most of its existence as an official government travel agency, Intourist was largely staffed by the **People's Commissariat for Internal Affairs (NKVD)** and **Committee on State Security (KGB)** personnel. The agency supervised visa applications, tourist groups, and hotel arrangements in the Soviet Union, often to the consternation of any Westerners who wanted more independence in their travels. It recruited attractive young people and was sometimes notorious for its monopoly over foreign visitors (such as a plaque on the classic old Europe Hotel in Leningrad that initially read "Founded by Intourist in 1839"). Established in 1929, the agency nevertheless facilitated Western access to Russia during the **cold war**, probably to the long-term detriment of the regime. Intourist mastered the transition to privatization in the 1990s and continues as an international travel agency for visitors to the former Soviet Union and for Russians going abroad, but, of course, it no longer holds a monopoly. And its signature "Intourist Hotel" in Moscow has been razed.

IRON CURTAIN. In a speech delivered in Fulton, Missouri, in March 1946, **Winston Churchill** referred to the increasing cessation of contact between East and West after **World War II**: "From Stettin in the Baltic to Trieste in the Adriatic an iron curtain has descended across the Continent." The Soviet Union after the war was in very bad economic condition owing to the destruction caused by the war, dislocation of population, and the absorbing of a huge new territory as a result of the Red Army occupation of much of Eastern Europe, which also had suffered wartime devastation. The result was a considerable degree of insecurity but also an effort to preserve its gains of control over the region while trying to rebuild Russia. The American—and Western—response was at first muted and confused. Thanks to **George F. Kennan**'s famous **Long Telegram** from Moscow in February 1946 and Churchill's eloquent phrasing a month later, the United States responded with the **Truman Doctrine** (1947), the **Marshall Plan** (1948), and the reorganization of Western Europe under the **North Atlantic Treaty Organization (NATO)**, beginning in 1949, accompanied by the unification of the Western occupation zones of Germany.

The "curtain" was never really "iron" but rather porous, especially in the divided Berlin that remained a serious gap in the early years of the **cold war** (**Berlin Blockade** and **Berlin Wall**). Outsiders, Westerners, as well as the courted "peoples of the East" could always find means, with the help of subject supporters of the bloc, to evade restrictions. Radio transmissions (**Voice of America**, BBC, and **Radio Liberty**) were ineffectively jammed, and by the late 1950s, cultural exchanges of students, performing groups, and tourists had transformed the iron curtain into lace. Nevertheless, until 1989, a symbol of its past remained in the stone and concrete wall dividing Berlin, after which remnants of it could be purchased at souvenir shops.

IRVING, WASHINGTON (1783–1859). Irving's works, especially the best-known "Legend of Sleepy Hollow," and many other writings and essays were well known in Europe, including Russia, where he attracted a special audience in the first half of the 19th century, published in a number of Russian translations in the 1820s. "Rip Van Winkle" thus became a stock term in Russian literary circles. Irving was the first American author to receive wide circulation in Russia, partly because of an erroneous identification of his name with America's revolutionary hero and first president. As a diplomat in Spain in the 1820s he knew and associated with Dmitri Dolgorukov, who was from a prominent Russian noble family and a friend of famous Russian poet Alexander Pushkin. While traveling with Dolgorukov in Spain, Irving penned *Alhambra*, one of his most ambitious works. His writings, along with those of **James Fenimore Cooper**, established a base for a long course of American literary recognition and popularity in Russia.

IVANOV, IGOR (1945–). Russian minister of foreign affairs (1998–2004). Born in Moscow of Russian-Georgian parents, Ivanov presided over Russian diplomacy during a critical period of transition from the Soviet Union to the **Russian Federation**, from Communism to capitalism. He was an expert on Western countries, especially Spain, where he had served for many years in the embassy and as ambassador (1991–94). He returned to Moscow to be deputy minister of foreign affairs under Boris Yelstin in 1994 and to become minister in 1998. An outspoken opponent of Western actions in Kosovo and of the American invasion of Iraq, Ivanov also played a key role in the difficult Russian adjustments to the independent policies of former Soviet republics, such as Georgia. He was advanced by **Vladimir Putin** in 2004 to be secretary of the security council, from which he resigned in 2007.

IVANOV, ROBERT (1925–2003). The son of a Russian immigrant to the United States, who became involved in radical activities and was deported to Russia in 1920, Ivanov was named in memory of an American friend of his father's who was beaten to death in a Detroit jail. Remembering his American "heritage" after his **World War II** service on Russia's eastern front in Manchuria in 1945, Ivanov studied American history at **Moscow State University** and joined the staff of the **Institute of General History** of the Russian **Academy of Sciences**. His early work concentrated on the **American Civil War** and especially on **Abraham Lincoln**'s foreign policy, such as *Diplomatiia Avraama Linkol'na* (*The Diplomacy of Abraham Lincoln*). During the height of the **cold war,** Ivanov contributed a number of deservedly critical accounts of the situation of African Americans and the role of the Mafia in the United States in the interwar years.

A major accomplishment of Ivanov was his biography of **Dwight D. Eisenhower** (1983), the basic Russian work on the subject. He remained a committed Communist to the end—usually with a droll joke or shrug of the shoulders to his friends. He and his wife Nina (Petrova), a labor historian, promoted Soviet/Russian–American friendship through such organizations as the Elbe Alliance and the Lawrence, Kansas–based "People to People" exchange of 1990–91. His final (2002) and perhaps best contribution to the cause of improved historical understanding of Soviet–American relations was *Stalin i soiuzniki, 1941–1945 gg.* (*Stalin and the Allies, 1941–1945*).

IVANOV, SERGEI (1953–). Foreign intelligence advisor as director of the **Federal Security Service (FSB)** and minister of defense (2001–07) of the **Russian Federation**, Ivanov was closely associated with **Vladimir Putin** previously in the **Committee on State Security (KGB)**. From Leningrad, he rose in the last years of the presidency of Boris Yeltsin as a key advisor on national security. He was then appointed by Putin as minister of defense in 2001, a rare civilian to hold that post, while he also served in the FSB. Ivanov resigned in 2007 to accept the position as first deputy prime minister, which apparently placed him in a position to succeed Putin as president, until the surprise elevation of **Dmitri Medvedev** to prime minister later that year. In the new Putin-Medvedev government in 2008, he has been a loyal implementer of a more aggressive foreign policy in regard to the conflict with Georgia.

– J –

JACKSON-VANIK AMENDMENT (1974). As an amendment to the U.S. 1974 Trade Act, sponsored by Democratic senator Henry ("Scoop") Jackson (from Washington) and Democratic representative Charles Vanik (from Ohio), it excluded countries limiting free opportunity of departure of citizens from "favored nation" status in American exports and imports. It was a response specifically to the Soviet Union's restriction on attempts by Jews to leave for Israel or other countries. It represented a setback to the **Leonid Brezhnev** program of **détente**. Considered by Soviet leaders as interference in their domestic affairs, the amendment did little at the time to help the cause of Soviet Jewry and probably hindered advances in arms negotiations and expanded trade. Relaxation of emigration restrictions would finally occur in the 1980s in the **Mikhail Gorbachev** era, but various restrictions still applied on admission into the United States.

JACOBSON, ROMAN (1896–1982). From a prominent Jewish family in Russia, Jacobson had an early fascination with languages and was already a leading figure in the subject before the revolution. After the upheaval of war and revolution, he immigrated to Prague in 1920, joining the émigré **Russia Abroad**. His concerns with the structure and functioning of language led to his innovative solution of a plane of linguistic analysis. He fled Prague at the beginning of **World War II** for Scandinavia, and then to the United States. He became a distinguished professor at Harvard University, where he was renowned for his innovative theories in linguistics and in his later career for his comprehensive analyses of communications as a whole.

JACQUES, AGNES (1920s AND 1930s). As secretary of the **American Russian Institute** in Chicago, Jacques was one of the first serious and persistent students of Russian under **Samuel Harper** at the University of Chicago and subsequently supported herself tutoring business and other clients who wanted some knowledge of the language. In the 1920s she pioneered the establishment of a cultural group in Chicago on Russia, an American Russian Institute modeled on the first one in New York. With the assistance of the **All Russian Society for Cultural Relations with Foreign Countries (VOKS)** and its director, **Olga Kameneva**, in Moscow, and Jacques's leadership, the Chicago "institute" was very active in sponsoring lectures, exhibits, and other events aimed at promoting an American understanding of the Russian and Soviet cultural developments throughout the 1930s and into **World War II**.

JAZZ IN RUSSIA. One thing that especially brought Russia and the United States together in the 20th century was a mutual appreciation of the new music of the era—jazz—from ragtime to swing. More than any other country besides the United States, Russia was absorbed with jazz. One possible explanation was the early melding of **African American** motifs with East European Jewish folk traditions. Two of the most popular American composers of the era, **Irving Berlin** and George Gershwin, were of Russian-Jewish background. But there was also an element of *amerikanizm*. The first jazz (or ragtime) was performed in Russia at popular venues such as the circus, dance halls, cabarets, and "drinking gardens" at the turn of the century. Americans in Russia contributed to this foundation. **Frederick Corse**, director of **New York Life Insurance** in Russia, possessed a large collection of ragtime records; Frederic Thomas, the African American owner-manager of the Aquarium, ran the largest and most popular restaurant in Moscow; and the "Allied" cultural invasion of Russia during **World War I** led to regimental bands, such as the Sumskoi Hussar Regiment performing "Alexander's Ragtime Band." Various individual American artists who discovered enthusiastic audiences in Russia both before and during the war performed all over the empire.

It may come as some surprise to Americans, conditioned to the idea of Bolshevik hostility, that jazz was even more popular in Soviet Russia. This can be explained in part by a continuing fascination with all things American, but also ideologically in viewing jazz as the cultural expression of an oppressed American minority. Also, many of the writers, poets, and musicians of the Russian "silver age," roughly 1900–30, were attracted to what was new in world culture—and jazz certainly was. Among the many Russians attracted to American jazz were Sergei Diaghelev, Igor Stravinsky, **Valentin Parnakh**, and **Dmitri Shostakovich**. For Diaghelev and Stravinsky it meant exploring a new medium; for Stravinsky, composition without boundaries—"Piano-Rag-Music," "Ragtime for Eleven Instruments," and finally a jazz masterpiece, "Three Pieces for Clarinet." Shostakovich in the 1920s earned his fees for a conservatory education by playing the piano for silent films, mostly American and appropriately accompanied with modern music straight from Tin Pan Alley. This resulted in some of his early—and most interesting—compositions, especially the ballet *Golden Age* (1930), in which the influence of Cole Porter ("No, No, Nanette") is quite apparent in his unique jazz interpretation of "Tea for Two."

The initial driving force of Soviet jazz was Valentin Parnakh, stimulated especially by his exposure to African American Louis Mitchell's *Jazz Kings* in Paris in 1921. He returned to Russia to form the first Russian jazz band, to teach film director **Sergei Eisenstein** to dance the foxtrot, and to introduce jazz into several of the stage productions of Vsevolod Meyerhold. Soviet jazz also received a definite boost from resident African American artists such as **Coretta Arle-Tietz** and in early 1926 by the six-week tours of Benny Peyton and his orchestra, performing New Orleans style (Preservation Hall) improvisation and the more polished presentations of Sam Wooding and the "Chocolate Kiddies" (20 musicians and 30 dancers) that toured Russia at about the same time. The cultural impresario of the relatively open **New Economic Policy (NEP)**, Anatole Lunacharsky, financed the visit of Leopold Teplitsky to the United States in 1926 to study under Paul Whiteman in Philadelphia. Teplitsky returned to form in 1927 a premier jazz ensemble, the "First Concert Jazz Band," also known as the "jazz professors," recruited from the faculty of the Leningrad (St. Petersburg) Conservatory. The best binational jazz great, however, was **Joseph Schillinger**, who immigrated to the United States in 1927 and was a major influence on Gershwin (*Porgy and Bess*) and Glenn Miller ("Moonlight Serenade").

Jazz in the Soviet Union would suffer in the 1930s from the attacks of socialist realist propagandists and from major writers such as **Maxim Gorky** and even Shostakovich, who recanted his jazz beginnings. Still, under Georgy Landsberg and Leonid Utyosev, Soviet jazz survived and blossomed during **World War II**, when the popular music of the American ally dominated the charts. The "Russian Glen Miller," Eddie Rosner, led the most popular big band of the war era and into his fate in the gulag afterward. Though jazz during the **cold war** was ostracized as American and contaminating, it survived underground to emerge again in full force in the 1970s and 1980s with Rosner, **Dean Reed**, and countless combos across the country, invigorated and inspired by the popular tours of Duke Ellington and Benny Goodman and their orchestras through the cultural exchange agreement.

JEANNETTE **EXPEDITION (1879–1882).** In the 1870s a race was on for the first to reach the North Pole. Most contenders subscribed to the view of German geographer August Petermann that the Arctic Ocean was largely open water kept clear by warm currents and that the main problem was to find a passage through the ice ring that surrounded it. Early efforts focused on a "Northeast" passage that would skirt Greenland and Baffin Island to reach the pole. A veteran of a failed 1870 attempt, George Washington De Long (1844–81) thought that a "Northwest" passage through the **Bering Strait** held greater possibilities and convinced *New York Herald* publisher James Gordon Bennett to support a new expedition. Bennett used his influence in Washington to gain the cooperation of the Department of the Navy to refit a ship, rechristened the *Jeannette*, and to supply it with an experienced crew, headed by chief engineer George Melville and under the command of De Long. Another expedition, under explorer Nils Nordenskjold, would sail northeast over Scandinavia with a plan to meet somewhere above central Siberia.

The *Jeannette* set forth from San Francisco in July 1879 and steamed slowly through the strait and northwestward along the Siberian coast into the Arctic Ocean, soon to become frozen fast in ice. Well supplied for such an eventuality, the *Jeannette* drifted eastward for almost two years out of sight of land. Finally, with supplies exhausted and the ship in danger of being crushed by the ice, the crew set off in three parties by sledges and boats to reach the Siberian mainland. Meanwhile, the fate of the expedition had attracted considerable world attention, thanks especially to Bennett and the *Herald*. Of the three parties, those led by Melville and De Long managed to reach the Lena River delta, while the third totally disappeared. Most of the Melville group, with the assistance of Tungus natives, managed to survive to tell their story. But despite several Russian and American rescue attempts, De Long and his party succumbed to the severe winter weather in their coastal encampment in 1882. Their bodies were found during a subsequent Russian–American rescue attempt and, after an initial burial on "American Hill" on the Lena delta, were brought home in 1884. In the meantime, much acrimonious debate occurred in Congress and the press about Melville's failed rescue attempt and the insufficient efforts of the Navy Department to cooperate with it. Russian cooperation, however, was applauded.

JEFFERSON, THOMAS (1743–1826). As one of the "founding fathers" and author of the American Declaration of Independence, Jefferson gained a worldwide reputation as a Renaissance man and leading exponent of the Enlightenment. As such, he had a following in Russia among reformers and supporters of democratic ideals, even Tsar **Alexander I**, who corresponded with Jefferson during his presidency. This connection was inspired by Swiss *philosophe* Frederic Cesar de La Harpe during a visit to Russia in 1801–02 at the beginning of Alexander's reign. The tsar's interest in Jefferson, disclosed in conversation with La Harpe, was relayed through intermediaries to Jefferson, who responded, again indirectly, with a list of works on the American constitution for the tsar. In 1803 La Harpe again alerted Alexander to useful guidance in Jefferson's message to Congress. Soon a more direct communication was arranged by **Levett Harris**, first American diplomatic representative in Russia (as consul), in 1804. This set the stage for diplomatic recognition between the two countries. Despite a major step forward diplomatically, Jefferson's declaration of an embargo on trade with Europe in 1808 severely damaged the growing Russian–American direct commerce.

JEWISH JOINT DISTRIBUTION COMMITTEE (JJDC). Formed in New York specifically to aid the destitute Jewish population of Russia in the early 20th century, the JJDC became especially active in providing assistance to Jewish refugees fleeing the advance of the German armies in Poland during **World War I**. From its headquarters in New York, the committee kept track of conditions in Jewish settlements in Russia, raised alarms about **famine** in Ukraine in 1920, and provided assistance, mainly through the **American Relief Administration (ARA)**. Most of this relief was directed by means of food packages purchased from the ARA in New York and distributed by it to designated recipients. The JJDC thus acted as coordinator for American Jews who wished to aid relatives, communities, and synagogues (for their distribution) in Russia and Eastern Europe, which was facilitated by the ARA program.

JOHNSON ACT (1934). The act denied any country with indebtedness to the U.S. government from obtaining loans from American banks. This pertained to many countries but most specifically to the Soviet

Union, which had just negotiated a **Recognition Agreement** with the expectation of obtaining substantial loans. The **debt issue** remaining unresolved after the agreement, the financial and trade relations between the two countries declined substantially during the 1930s. Failure to resolve the issue was a major defeat for Foreign Affairs Commissar **Maxim Litvinov** and his program of **collective security**. The restriction was essentially suspended by the **lend-lease** arrangements during **World War II**, only to be reinstated after the war.

JONES, JOHN PAUL (1747–1792). Of Scottish origin, Jones proved his skill and gallantry at an early age and in battles at great odds in defense of the American cause of independence. The near total elimination of the American navy after the war forced Jones to seek other venues in which to continue his naval career. **Catherine the Great** welcomed the opportunity of his inclusion in her rapidly expanding navy and, in particular, to serve as commander of a nascent Black Sea fleet during her Second Russo–Turkish War (1787–91), which established Russian supremacy on the Black Sea. Jones achieved a successful record of accomplishment in the war, despite the jealousy and antagonism of a number of British officers in Russian service. His Russian sojourn, however, was marred by charges of the rape of a teenage servant girl in St. Petersburg in 1791. Dismissed from Russian employment, Jones died under a cloud and in poverty in Paris the following year. His remains were later transferred to a more fitting and heroic setting in the chapel of the United States Naval Academy in Annapolis, Maryland.

JORDAN, PHILIP. An **African American** valet, chauffeur, cook, and assistant to Ambassador **David Francis** (1916–18). Jordan, a former Pullman car attendant with some means and education, was devoted to Francis and his family and wrote a number of transparent and descriptive letters to Mrs. Francis about the Petrograd scene during the revolutionary upheavals. Jordan was largely responsible for maintaining the security and stability of the embassy during the **Bolshevik Revolution**, as well as for nursing the precarious health of the ambassador, who suffered from prostate trouble and tobacco and whiskey addictions. During those years of turmoil, he won respect for his uncanny success in finding scarce provisions for the embassy that were shared with the **St. Petersburg American colony**. He was often seen motoring around Petrograd (St. Petersburg) in Francis's Model T Ford in search of supplies for the embassy but was still on hand to greet anyone who entered the embassy. His observances of the times in letters, mainly to Mrs. Francis, are in the care of the Missouri Historical Society in St. Louis.

JUDSON, WILLIAM V. (1865–1923). A graduate of West Point (1888) and career army officer, Judson's first encounter with Russia was as an American observer with the Russian army in Manchuria during the **Russo–Japanese War** (1904–05). Because of this experience, he was assigned to accompany the **Root Commission** to Russia in 1917 as an advisor and remained as military attaché. After the **Bolshevik Revolution** in November, he was one of the most active American officials in having direct contacts with the new Soviet regime. He met frequently with **Leon Trotsky**, who was the new commissar for foreign affairs, in regard especially to safeguarding American personnel and property. He remained in Moscow well into 1918, replacing **Maddin Summers** as consul general, and until the withdrawal of the embassy from Vologda in August. As a crucial liaison at a difficult time, Judson won the respect of both American and Soviet officials. In his "final report" of 1919, suppressed by the State Department, he opposed military intervention and supported diplomatic recognition of the Soviet regime.

– K –

KAHN, ALBERT (1869–1942). Construction engineer, director of a major American construction company in Soviet Russia. Based in Detroit and closely linked to **Ford Motor Company**, Kahn Industries built a number of factories in the 1920s and 1930s. With the beginning of the **First Five-Year Plan**, Kahn was contracted by the Soviet government, through the **American Trading Corporation (Amtorg)** in New York, to provide major assistance for the construction of large projects, especially the tractor plants at Stalingrad and Chelyabinsk. Kahn was a paid consultant to more than 25 Soviet projects with an income for his company of more than two billion dollars, a lot of money for Depression years.

KALAMATIANO, XENOPHON (1883–1923). A descendant of a prominent Russian-Greek family from Odessa, Kalamatiano immigrated in the 1890s to the United States with his parents, who settled near Chicago. He attended Culver Military Academy in Indiana and then the University of Chicago, where he excelled in academic subjects as well as athletics, especially long-distance running. He also taught the first course in Russian language at the university in 1902 as a senior undergraduate assistant instructor. Making use of his knowledge of Russian, Kalamatiano subsequently served as a Russian sales agent for American agricultural implement companies such as J. I. Case, operating mainly out of sales offices in Odessa and Moscow.

During 1917, with normal business with Russia at a standstill, he was employed as a consultant and agent by the American consul general's office in Moscow. After the **Bolshevik Revolution**, Kalamatiano acted as a communications link and conduit of funds to the anti-Bolshevik forces in the south of Russia. In this role, he is sometimes referred to as the "American Sidney Reilly" (the British "ace of spies"). Arrested by the Cheka for this activity, he was incarcerated under desperate conditions in the infamous Lubianka prison for two years. Along with a few other Americans, his release was a condition of the introduction of substantial American **famine** aid under the **American Relief Administration (ARA)** and the **Riga Agreement** of August 1921. Returning to the United States, with the help of **Samuel Harper** he became an instructor of history at Culver Military Academy. Unfortunately, he was soon frostbitten during a winter hunting expedition and died of gangrene, leaving his own very intriguing story largely untold.

KALININ, MIKHAIL (1875–1946). Born in a peasant village in Tver province, though well educated, Kalinin joined the **Russian Social Democratic Labor Party** as early as 1898, the founding date, and emerged as one of the few notable **Bolsheviks** of peasant background after the **Bolshevik Revolution**. In 1919 he was thus thrust into the inconsequential post of Chairman of the Executive Committee of the

Congress of Soviets; in this position he became nominal "head of state" of the USSR. As such, he adjusted to his ceremonial role, becoming adept socially and demonstrating special interests in American contacts, such as welcoming various American visitors and presiding over the diplomatic reception of U.S. Ambassador **William Bullitt** in 1933. He has probably been underrated and overly dismissed as a docile **Stalin** henchman, but that is what he really was. Americans respected him as a genuine friend and supporter in the 1920s and 1930s, though recognizing he had little authority. Still some progress on American initiatives did get done through Kalinin. A survivor of the purge era, Kalinin is also unique in being one of the few prominent officials of the Stalin era to retain his name on the map of the present **Russian Federation** in the city of Kaliningrad, formerly the East Prussian capital of Koenigsburg.

KALUGIN, OLEG (1934–). From Leningrad, Kalugin graduated from the university there and participated in the student exchange program at Columbia University (1958–59) before (or after?) entering the service of the **Committee on State Security (KGB)**, serving as chief of its intelligence operations in the United States as deputy press officer (KGB residency) in the Soviet embassy (1965–70). He quickly rose to the rank of major general by 1980 under its KGB director, **Yury Andropov**. During the reform period of **Mikhail Gorbachev**, he promoted a more open intelligence service but was forced to retire from the KGB in 1987 and was stripped of his rank and medals by Gorbachev in 1990. He had pushed **glasnost** too far. The following year he supported **Russian Federation** president Boris Yeltsin during the **August Coup** and was elected to the Russian Congress of People's Deputies. Though an initial key advisor to KGB chairman Vadim Bakatin in 1992, his opposition to the revived role of the agency made his presence unwelcome. Kalugin defected to the United States in 1994, where he taught at Catholic University of America and cooperated in disclosing operations of the KGB during the **cold war**, especially in his exposé, *The First Directorate: My 32 Years in Intelligence and Espionage Against the West* (1994). In 2002 he was tried in absentia in Moscow and sentenced to 14 years in jail for spying for the West.

KAMCHATKA. Impressed by his tour of the USS *Independence* during its 1837 visit to St. Petersburg, **Nicholas I** dispatched a naval mission to America, headed by Captain Johann Von Schantz (né Ivan fon Shants) in 1838. After inspecting shipyards and ports on the East Coast, he contracted with George L. Schuyler and the John H. Brown Shipyards in New York for the construction of a large vessel, the largest yet constructed in the United States. The project attracted considerable public attention to the shipyards and to an ironworks in Jersey City that cast the 10-ton engine cylinders. Fully equipped, the ship weighed nearly 2,500 tons, probably the largest military vessel of the time, and cost the Russian government more than $450,000. The launch on 24 November 1840 attracted a crowd of 10,000 people. The *Kamchatka* was subsequently delivered to the Baltic by an American crew accompanied by Schuyler and his father-in-law, James A. Hamilton (a son of Alexander Hamilton). The project also was significant in breaking the British monopoly of international ship construction and in proving American capability, which attracted a number of other orders. It also heralded the advent of ***amerikanizm***, Russia looking to the United States for technology that would dominate Russian progress for the next century.

KAMENEVA, OLGA (NEE BRONSTEIN) (1883–1941). As a sister of **Leon Trotsky** and wife of **Lev Kamenev**, Olga Kameneva was naturally well positioned for a role in the early Bolshevik governmental and cultural affairs—and for her later downfall in the 1930s. She had followed her brother into revolutionary activity abroad, where she met her future husband in 1903. After the **Bolshevik Revolution**, Kameneva served as an innovative and adept administrator of a Soviet agency, the **All-Russian Society for Cultural Relations with Foreign Countries (VOKS)**, in the 1920s. She was especially interested in cultural contacts with the United States and encouraged visits of Soviet poets and writers, such as **Vladimir Mayakovsky** and **Konstantin Stanislavsky**, to the United States, while welcoming Americans, such as **Theodore Dreiser** and **Sinclair Lewis**. In 1925, she attempted to visit the United States in order to expand these contacts but was denied a visa.

Before the establishment of **Intourist** in 1929, her agency offices—in what is now the Gorky Museum in Moscow—could be counted on to assist with housing, travel arrangements, and official contacts for visiting scholars and artists. Kameneva also inspired and assisted with the establishment of **American Russian Institutes** in the United States that promoted cultural exchanges and made available various exhibits and other Soviet propaganda materials for their use. Though the Kamenevs separated by 1930, her family connections obviously made her vulnerable in the age of the Stalin purge repressions in the 1930s, directed especially against anyone associated with Trotsky. She was arrested soon after her husband in 1936, incarcerated in a Siberian prison, and executed in September 1941, in a Stalinist "cleansing" of the prisons after the German invasion, along with her two sons, one of whom, Alexander, had worked for **Ford Motor Company** in Detroit in the 1920s.

KAMENEV, LEV (NE ROSENFELD) (1883–1936). From a prominent Moscow Jewish family, Kamenev became an active social democrat and attended the crucial 1903 party congress; soon after, he married **Leon Trotsky**'s sister **Olga Kameneva** and became a member of the Bolshevik center abroad in 1907. He returned to St. Petersburg in the summer of 1914 to direct the faction's newspaper, *Pravda*, but soon after the beginning of the war was arrested. Released by the **February Revolution** in 1917, Kamenev became a leader of the moderate wing of the Bolsheviks, urging cooperation with the **Provisional Government** and, somewhat notoriously, opposing **Vladimir Lenin** and Trotsky on the decision to seize power in October. He nevertheless remained an important figure in the new Soviet government, serving as the close assistant to Lenin during the period of War Communism, the early years of the **New Economic Policy**, and the leader's illness as acting chairman of SOVNARKOM.

After Lenin's death, he at first sided with **Joseph Stalin**, along with Grigory Zinoviev, to form a triumvirate against Trotsky, though later (1925) he switched to support Trotsky against Stalin, to no avail. His main contact with Americans during this period was during the severe **famine** of 1920–22, when he directed Soviet famine relief in cooperation with the **American Relief Administration (ARA)**. He arranged for, and spoke eloquently at, a farewell banquet in Moscow for ARA officials in July 1923. Though in one sense the successor of Lenin, as acting chairman of SOVNARKOM during Lenin's illness, Kamenev was, as were Zinoviev, Nikolai Bukharin, and Trotsky, outmaneuvered by Stalin in the Soviet succession battle of the 1920s. He was ousted from the Politburo in 1925, served briefly as Soviet ambassador to Italy, but was increasingly under attack from Stalin until his arrest in 1936. At the first major purge trial, he admitted to involvement in the Kirov assassination and in the support of Trotsky. Many Americans in interwar Russia had kind feelings toward Kamenev, and his arrest and execution reduced considerably what faith and respect they may have had for the Soviet regime.

KARPOVICH, MICHAEL (1888–1959). A Russian political liberal and supporter of **Paul Miliukov** and a keen student of Russian history, in 1917 Karpovich accompanied the new ambassador of the **Provisional Government, Boris Bakhmeteff**, to the United States, and he served as his secretary during the upheavals of revolution until 1922, when Bakhmeteff formally resigned. After a short term as a trade consultant and lecturer, Karpovich obtained a position at Harvard University and became its long-term expert and lecturer on Russian history (1926–59), especially emphasizing the liberal tendencies of the Russian intellectual elite in the 19th century. Though he published relatively little in comparison with his contemporary émigré colleagues George Vernadsky and **Michael Florinsky**, Karpovich made his mark as a vocal defender of the old Russian culture and as the teacher of two generations of American students of Russian history, including major historians of Russia Richard Pipes, Nicholas Riasanovsky, and **Marc Raeff**.

KARTVELLI, ALEXANDER (NE KARTVELISHVILI) (1896–1974). Georgian born in Tiflis (Tbilisi), Kartvelli served as an artillery officer in the Russian army during **World War I**, when he became interested in warplanes. He was sent to Paris by the new Soviet government to study aeronautics and came to the attention of Americans for his design of an early transatlantic passenger plane. He immigrated to New York in 1927. Kartvelli soon joined a fledgling company founded by another Russian émigré, **Alexander de Seversky**, that was purchased by Republic Aircraft in 1939. He is best known as the designer of the Seversky Super Clipper (1938) that could carry more than 100 passengers (and remained on the drawing boards), the P-47 Thunderbolt fighter plane, of which more than 15,000 were produced during **World War II**, and its successors, the F-84 and the supersonic F-105.

KARZHAVIN, FEDOR (1735–1812). The son of a St. Petersburg merchant, Karzhavin became a protégé of Russian architect Vasily Barzhenov in Paris. He subsequently enlisted in the French support of the rebellious American colonies, more specifically in assisting the smuggling of supplies from the French West Indies (Martinique) into the Carolinas and Virginia. Karzhavin resided for a while in Williamsburg and made contact with a number of notable American supporters of independence. His offer to the Continental Congress to act as an intermediary with the court of **Catherine the Great**, however, came to nothing, in part because of his lack of noble standing. Meanwhile, he traveled extensively through the colonies and the newly independent United States in the 1780s, eventually returning to Russia, where he was employed in the Admiralty College in 1797 as a translator. During Karzhavin's stay in North America, he symbolized the Russian and French sympathy for the cause of American independence and helped lift the morale of the American cause of independence by his presence.

KASPAROV, GARRY (NE GARRI WEINSTEIN) (1963–). A noted chess grand master, Kasparov was born in Baku in Soviet Azerbaijan of an Armenian mother and Jewish father. Upon his father's death at age seven, Kasparov adopted the name of his mother, Kasparyan, later Russianized. Demonstrating early brilliance in chess, he qualified for the all-Soviet chess championship at age 15, the youngest to do so. Rising rapidly in world chess rankings during the next few years, Kasparov was rated number 2 to world champion Anatoly Karpov by 1982. A classic and seemingly never-ending match between the two was halted by the president of the International Chess Federation despite the willingness of the opponents to continue. A second match in 1984 resulted in a controversial Kasparov victory and his gaining the world title, which he held until 2000, when he was defeated by Vladimir Kramnik. In 1997, he was defeated, however, in a much publicized contest with a computer, "Deep Blue." During the last seven years, his title was disputed because of his championing of a rival chess organization.

After his formal retirement from world chess competition in 2005, Kasparov devoted much of his time to writing, promoting chess education for young schoolchildren, especially in the United States, and to Russian politics. Not a stranger to the latter, having been active in Komsomol and Communist Party activities, Kasparov left the party in 1990 and was a founder of the "Russia's Choice" coalition that backed Boris Yeltsin in 1996. By 2005, however, he had joined the vocal dissent against the leadership of **Vladimir Putin** with the creation of his own United Civil Front, which became part of an opposition coalition, "The Other Russia." His organization of marches and demonstrations brought him into conflict with Putin's **Federal Security Service**, and he was detained briefly by the police on several occasions. In October 2007 he declared his intention to run for the presidency against Putin's chosen successor, but in mid-December he withdrew, citing the inability to assemble supporters in large-scale meetings. His publications include many tributes to former chess champions and commentaries on chess itself, an interesting autobiography, *Child of Change* (1987), and *How Life Imitates Chess* (2007).

KATAKAZI, KONSTANTIN (1830–1890). Of Greek-Russian origin, Katakazi was unfortunate to be faced with a complicated diplomatic situation in Washington, the **Perkins Claim**, during his tenure as minister (1869–71). Benjamin Perkins, a New England sea captain, had ventured into arms contracts with the Russian government during the **Crimean War**, which, because of the sudden end of the war, were abruptly cancelled, leaving Perkins with many rifles on hand and facing bankruptcy. Katakazi arrived in Washington to face what had become a lengthy claim by Perkins and his heirs against the Russian government, taken up by a number of attorneys who hoped to reap an award from commissions in obtaining a share of the **Alaska Purchase** funds. Secretary of State **Hamilton Fish** supported the claim, resulting in diplomatic accusations that made Katakazi's presence unwelcome in Washington at a critical time, the royal visit of **Grand Duke Alexis** (1871–72). Katakazi retired into Russian official oblivion but had dimmed Fish's political prospects and the reputation of President **Ulysses Grant** because of this incident.

KATYN FOREST. In 1943 Germany announced the discovery of mass graves of more than 14,000 Polish soldiers, mostly officers, in a wooded area near Smolensk in the German area of occupation. Their deaths were blamed on Soviet forces after their invasion of eastern

Poland in 1939 and committed in April and May of 1940. The USSR denied any involvement and accused Germany of the crime, and the United States and the other Allies accepted the Soviet version of events at the time, in the interests of preserving the alliance against Germany. Subsequent postwar evidence clearly indicated that the Soviet **People's Commissariat of Internal Affairs (NKVD)** units were responsible. Through the **cold war** each side remained unmoved as to guilt. Finally, in 1990, with Russian archives for the period open, **Mikhail Gorbachev** admitted officially that the Soviet Union had committed this atrocity. It is believed that many more missing Poles were also victims of Soviet action.

KELLEY, ROBERT F. (1894–1976). Born in Massachusetts, Kelley received a B.A. (1915) and M.A. (1917) from Harvard University and also studied at the Sorbonne in Paris. He enlisted in the U.S. army and served as a military attaché in Russia and the Baltic states in 1918. Subsequently he was an early American expert on Soviet Russia at the **listening post** in Riga, Latvia, during the 1920s. As the foremost authority on Soviet Russia in the State Department, he was instrumental in setting American policy on the nonrecognition of Russia for 15 years. Staunchly Catholic and conservative, and influenced by Father **Edmund Walsh** of Georgetown University, Kelley amassed a substantial library on the new Soviet Russia in his office and nurtured a generation of American expertise on the Communist world.

During the administrations of **Franklin D. Roosevelt** (1934–41), Kelley became resigned to recognition—and even visited the Soviet Union as a professional duty—but was clearly out of place in the new administration's foreign relations. In 1937 the division he headed was merged with the European Division and he was reassigned (demoted) to the embassy staff in Ankara, Turkey. The United States thus lost one of its foremost experts on the USSR on the eve of **World War II**. Kelley left the State Department in 1945 but would be a founder of **Radio Liberty** and serve as its consultant, especially in sorting out differences among the various ethnic and religious groups that formed its staff, as well as softening its confrontational tone toward the Soviet Union.

KELLOGG-BRIAND PACT (1928). In June 1927 French foreign minister Aristide Briand approached the United States about a mutual agreement that neither country would ever attack the other. Since this was a somewhat meaningless overture, owing to the long-standing friendship between the two countries, Secretary of State **Frank Kellogg** transformed it into a general pact outlawing war, which was signed initially by 15 nations, led by the Soviet Union. Eventually, 62 states would adhere to the principle of "outlawing war," but the agreement lacked enforcement. It was first applied, with some success, to a rift between the Soviet Union and China over the **Chinese Eastern Railway (CER)**, but after that it descended into **Leon Trotsky**'s proverbial "dustbin of history."

KELLOGG, FRANK (1856–1937). As secretary of state (1925–29), Kellogg is best known as one of the authors of the **Kellogg-Briand Pact** (August 1928), whose signers pledged to reject war as an instrument of national policy. Somewhat to the embarrassment of the United States, the Soviet Union was the first nation to join it (September 1928). During his term of office, Kellogg continued the Republican policy of **Charles Evans Hughes** of refusing diplomatic recognition to the Soviet state, though in later years he expressed regrets and supported recognition in 1933. He was the recipient of the Nobel Prize for Peace in 1929.

KENDALL, DONALD M. (1921–). As chairman (1971–86) of a popular American soft drink company, Pepsi-Cola, Kendall broke new ground during **Nikita Khrushchev**'s policy of **peaceful coexistence** with an agreement with the Soviet authorities to produce and bottle Pepsi-Cola in the Soviet Union in the early 1970s. As a friend and supporter of **Richard Nixon**, he accompanied the vice president during his visit to the Soviet Union in 1959, witnessing the **"kitchen debate."**

KENNAN, GEORGE (1845–1924). A native of New York state and a skilled telegrapher for Western Union during the **American Civil War**, Kennan volunteered for the company's project of a telegraph connection between North America and Europe by way of **Alaska**

and **Siberia**—the **Collins' Overland–Western Union Extension**. As a surveyor in Kamchatka and Siberia, he learned the Russian language and studied local customs, which he parlayed into a successful memoir, *Tent Life in Siberia* (1870), and exhausting lecture tours through the United States. He also became a defender and supporter of liberal/radical Russian opponents of tsarism such as **Catherine Breshko-Breskovskaya**. Having obtained recognition as an authority on Russia, Kennan was sponsored by *Century Magazine* for a tour of Siberian prisons in the 1880s, which he exposed in a series of articles in *Century* and in a book, *Siberia and the Exile System* (1889).

Kennan continued his journalist career with a number of eyewitness reports on the Spanish–American War and on the **Russo–Japanese War**, in which he was clearly sympathetic to the Japanese. Many other articles on Russia, especially for *Outlook*, and collections in book form maintained his reputation as one of America's leading experts on Russia through war and revolution in that country. In later years he and his wife enjoyed gardening at his family home in Medina, New York, and at his beloved retreat in Baddeck, Cape Breton, Nova Scotia, Canada. He shared a birthday (16 February) with a distant cousin, **George F. Kennan**. The elder Kennan's extensive notes, files, and correspondence are divided between collections in the **Library of Congress** and the **New York Public Library**.

KENNAN, GEORGE F. (1904–2005). One of the foremost American experts on the Soviet Union through much of the 20th century and into the 21st, Kennan followed his namesake, **George Kennan**, a first cousin twice removed, into Russian studies but with a more formal, intellectual bent. From Wisconsin, Kennan graduated from Princeton University (1925) and entered the foreign service as a protégé of **Robert F. Kelley**, director of the East European Division of the State Department. Fluent in the Russian language from study in Germany, and with experience at the Riga **listening post**, Kennan was groomed for a key role in the new Moscow embassy after the agreement on diplomatic recognition (1933) that he helped negotiate. He accompanied the new ambassador, **William Bullitt**, on his initial visit to the Soviet Union, acting as interpreter. Kennan was instrumental in the difficult arrangements to establish the American diplomatic presence in Moscow, especially in the acquisition of the ambassador's residence, **Spaso House**.

After several years of intensive service in Moscow, Kennan was transferred to Berlin, where he was interned following the declaration of war in 1941 and subsequently exchanged. He served as an important advisor on Soviet affairs during **World War II** and was assigned to the embassy in Moscow again. One of his major contributions to American foreign policy came in March 1946, when, as first political officer in Moscow, he sent the famous **Long Telegram**, emphatically labeling the regime of **Joseph Stalin** as menacing to American interests and advocating that it should be militantly combated, the origin of the **containment** policy that shaped the American approach to the **cold war** for many years. Recalled to Washington, Kennan became an important contributor to the development of the **Marshall Plan**, the **Truman Doctrine**, and the formulation of American cold war policies in general. He achieved special recognition as "X," the author of an article in *Foreign Affairs Quarterly* in 1951 that helped define the policy of the United States during the cold war.

In the 1950s, Kennan served as ambassador to the USSR (1952) but was recalled because of negative comments about the Soviet regime; he was later ambassador to Yugoslavia (1961–63). Kennan retired from the foreign service upon completion of this assignment and joined the faculty of the Institute for Advanced Study in Princeton, where he resided as a productive scholar and an active emeritus faculty member until his death. During his long tenure at the institute, he produced a number of important historical works, beginning with his two volumes on early Soviet–American relations, 1917–20, *Russia and the West under Lenin and Stalin* (1962), historical research and publication on the background to the Franco-Russian alliance of the 1890s, and his evocative two-volume *Memoirs* (1967) of his life, with subsequent additions in *Around the Cragged Corner: A Personal and Political Philosophy* (1993) and *At a Century's End: Reflections, 1982–1995* (1996).

In the summer of 1984 Kennan led a delegation of American scholars to commemorate and reassess in Kiev the 50th anniversary of the **Recognition Agreement** of 1933, providing some intimate revelations of that historic event at its concluding banquet, which also featured many Soviet tributes to his work. This and other select public lectures and appearances added to his reputation as an aloof but serious statesman and as the voice of an America that should have been counted as credible, perhaps more than it was, in the 20th century.

Among his legacies is the **Kennan Institute for Advanced Russian Studies** of the Woodrow Wilson Center in Washington that is dedicated to the elder George Kennan.

KENNAN INSTITUTE FOR ADVANCED RUSSIAN STUDIES. Washington research center on Russia and the former Soviet Union. It was founded in 1980 by **George F. Kennan** and **James Billington** and named in honor of **George Kennan**, a pioneer of Russian studies in the United States. The institute is affiliated with the Woodrow Wilson Center for International Studies, which is part of the **Smithsonian Institution** in Washington, D.C. It sponsors academic programs relating to the region through fellowships of several months to a year, short-term (one-month) research grants, and regular programs of symposia, seminars, and guest lectures. The goals are to support research activities in the field, facilitate the use of archival and library materials in the Washington area, and host visiting scholars from the former Soviet Union. For example, in November 2007, the institute, under the direction of Blair Ruble, cosponsored with the **Institute of General History** of the **Russian Academy of Sciences** a conference on the 200th anniversary of the beginning of Russian–American relations.

KENNEDY, JOHN F. (1917–1963). Kennedy served with distinction in the U.S. navy during **World War II**. From a prominent and politically active family of Irish descent, he soon entered politics and was elected to the House of Representatives (1947) and was a consistent supporter of the administration of **Harry S. Truman**'s domestic agenda. Despite a Republican landslide in 1952, Kennedy was elected to the Senate, defeating longtime Republican leader Henry Cabot Lodge. From a distinguished record in the opposition in that body, Kennedy won the Democratic nomination as presidential candidate and was elected to the highest office in 1961. He thus became the youngest (at 43) and the first Roman Catholic president.

Though his predecessor had responded eagerly to **Nikita Khrushchev**'s **peaceful coexistence** initiatives, troubles ensued over the **U-2 incident** (1960) and the **Berlin Wall** (1961). The new president met the new Soviet threat in Europe with strong statements and a personal appearance in Berlin ("Ich bin ein Berliner"). He also viewed the Cuban revolution and rise of Fidel Castro as a Communist threat to American security and approved the **Central Intelligence Agency**–backed **Bay of Pigs** (1961) abortive attempt to overthrow that regime. His greatest challenge from the Soviet Union came the following year, when it initiated the placement of intermediate-range missiles in Cuba directed at the United States. President Kennedy and his advisors, especially his brother Robert (attorney general), took a strong stand that within two weeks forced Khrushchev to call back the missiles rather than proceed into a perilous confrontation. Level heads prevailed, especially by the two ambassadors involved, the new arrival in Washington **Anatoly Dobrynin** and the veteran **Charles Bohlen** in Moscow. Unfortunately, a former American defector to the USSR, Lee Harvey Oswald, apparently acting alone, assassinated the president in November 1963 during a motorcade in Dallas, Texas. *See also* CUBAN MISSILE CRISIS.

KENNELL, RUTH EPPERSON (1893–1977). As a young idealist, Kennell volunteered for work in the **Kuzbas American colony** in 1922, while also serving as a correspondent for *The Nation*. Though leaving Kuzbas in 1924, she remained in Russia for the journal. In 1927 she served as guide and secretary for **Theodore Dreiser** during his tour of the Soviet Union. In fact, his *Dreiser Looks at Russia* (1928) is largely her work, which reflected both his and her criticism of the Soviet scene as well as their favorable impressions of Soviet progress. Kennell returned to the United States in the 1930s but remained active as a journalist, activist for liberal causes, and author of children's books. Her papers, including an unpublished memoir of her experiences at Kuzbas, are at the University of Oregon.

KERENSKY, ALEXANDER (1879–1970). Kerensky gained a reputation as a legal defender of political dissidents in the early 20th century and joined the *trudovik* (worker) faction of the Socialist Revolutionary Party and represented it in the Duma. Immediately after the **February Revolution** of 1917, he served as minister of justice and as a link with the Petrograd Soviet of Workers' and Soldiers' Deputies. Because of the difficulties of the immediate leaders, especially **Paul Miliukov** as foreign minister, Kerensky emerged in May as minister of war and effective head of the **Provisional Government**, which he continued to consolidate as "minister-president," essentially a dictatorship. Before that he orchestrated a foolhardy Russian military offensive in June that ended badly. This was at least partly staged for the arrival of the American **Root Commission**. **Charles R. Crane**, an important member of the commission, felt betrayed by the fate of his friend, Miliukov, and thus had little faith in Kerensky's socialist military theatrics in 1917. Kerensky managed to escape Bolshevik arrest but found little support subsequently for efforts to reestablish his control, retiring to Europe along with many of his political supporters and anti-Bolshevik opponents. After a number of contentious interwar years in Prague and Paris, Kerensky would find his final refuge in the United States, where, during the **cold war**, he was celebrated exaggeratedly as the last defender of a true Russian democracy.

KERNER, ROBERT J. (1887–1956). A student of European history at Harvard University before **World War I**, Kerner concentrated on the Hapsburg Empire under the guidance of **Archibald Cary Coolidge** with an emphasis on Bohemia/Czechoslovakia. He began his teaching career at the University of Missouri in 1914 but also followed his Harvard mentor into public service as a consultant to **Edward House** in 1917 and subsequently as a member of the American Peace Commission in Paris (1918–19). He then joined the faculty of Stanford University as an assistant to **Frank Golder** in launching the **Hoover Institution**. Moving to Berkeley in 1928, Kerner founded its Slavic studies program, though he was disappointed in not being able to succeed Coolidge at Harvard; this developed into a rivalry and enmity between him and William Langer and others.

Kerner's contributions to American Slavic studies were immense. He pioneered the integration of an ecumenical Slavic idea in his expertise and publications on Czech history, as well as Russian, and in his classic interpretation of Russian expansion in *The Urge to the Sea* (1927). Kerner's scholarly contributions included studies on Siberian development and expansion, diplomatic and military affairs in the 20th century Far East, and a considerable effort devoted to compiling a bibliography of Slavic civilization. During the formative period of American Slavic studies, Kerner resented the dominance of the eastern "establishment," headed by **Michael Karpovich**, George Vernadsky, **Geroid Robinson**, **Samuel Harper**, and others.

KGB (1946–1991). The Soviet Committee on State Security was the equivalent of the **Central Intelligence Agency** and Federal Bureau of Investigation combined. With much additional jurisdiction as needed by the Soviet leadership, the KGB was the agency of political control and supervisor of the guidelines of what was permitted in the semiclosed Soviet world during the **cold war**. It was the successor to similar intelligence and police organizations, the Cheka (1917), OGPU (1924), and NKVD (People's Commissariat for Internal Affairs, 1934). The KGB would be succeeded in 1991 by the **Federal Security Service (FSB)** of the **Russian Federation**. Several leading Soviet and Russian officials made these organizations the base of considerable power: Felix Dzherzhinsky, Lavrenty Beria, **Yury Andropov**, and **Vladimir Putin**. All of these organizations were in the forefront of a continuing contest with internal dissidents and the outside world from the **Bolshevik Revolution** of 1917 until the present. They conducted extensive covert intelligence operations in the United States and in other countries, as have been documented from recently opened files and by Vladimir Pozniakov in *Sovetskaia razvedka v Amerike, 1919–1941* (*Soviet Intelligence in America, 1919–1941*) (2005).

KHILKOV, MIKHAIL (1843–1909). From the upper Russian aristocracy, of princely origin, Khilkov first visited the United States in 1860. He returned in 1864 to spend several years studying American railroads and actually operated steam locomotives on western U.S. railroads and met a number of leading Americans, including **Charles Crane** and Joseph Pangborn. Upon returning to Russia, Khilkov was a strong advocate of the building of the **Trans-Siberian Railroad**, and upon the advice of **Sergei Witte**, **Nicholas II** appointed him minister of transportation in 1895. He set off across **Siberia** for a site inspection in company with Pangborn and became convinced of the desirability of a short-cut for the railroad through **Manchuria**; thus the **Chinese Eastern Railway** was born. Khilkov was also responsible for the contract with the **Westinghouse Company** for a factory to manufacture air brakes for the Trans-Siberian. During his 10 years as minister (1895–1905), Khilkov was always open and friendly to visiting Americans.

KHODORKOVSKY, MIKHAIL (1963–). During the massive privatization of state properties in the 1990s, Khodorkovsky emerged as one of the richest businessmen in Russia. From a modest Moscow background, he became an oil tycoon and founder of Yukos Oil Company and Bank Menatep. He and his companies soared in value during the chaotic era of **Boris Yeltsin** and along the way to business success naturally attracted envy and opposition. Khodorkovsky also became known for his political activism and philanthropy.

In April 2003 he announced the approaching merger of Yukos with Sibneft, another major oil company, and began negotiations for investments from the West. The new company would be second in oil and gas reserves to ExxonMobil. Ignoring warnings in government moves against other Russian oligarches, such as Roman Abramovich and Boris Beresovsky, Khodorkovsky became even more outspoken in political affairs, advocating closer ties with the United States and supporting the latter's invasion of Iraq. On 23 October 2003, he was arrested after his private plane landed at Novosibirsk airport and charged with tax evasion. During the lengthy trial, his business empire, faced with enormous penalties, gradually collapsed with most of Yukos absorbed into state enterprises, and on 31 May 2005 he was sentenced to 10 years of imprisonment in Siberia. All of this attracted much attention in the United States, where the affair was deemed a major power move by **Vladimir Putin** and his associates, such as **Dmitri Medvedev**, who was then director of GAZPROM, the state-owned natural gas monopoly.

KHRUSHCHEV, NIKITA (1898–1971). Khrushchev served as first secretary of the Communist Party of the Soviet Union (1953–64) and chairman of the council of ministers (premier) (1958–64). The Khrushchev ascendancy was noted especially for new initiatives, such as the inauguration of the Virgin Lands program in 1954 (expansion of agriculture in Kazakhstan), delivery of the **"secret speech"** to the 20th Party Congress (February 1956), rehabilitation of victims of the Stalin era, survival of the antiparty effort to remove him (June 1957), the launching of **Sputnik** (October 1957), and a new, open approach to diplomatic relations with the West, dubbed **peaceful coexistence**, heralded by the **Austrian State Treaty** (1955). In keeping with the latter course, Khrushchev approved a new initiative of cultural exchanges (1958) and toured the United States in 1959, the first (and last) Soviet leader to do so, during which he held conversations with President **Dwight D. Eisenhower** at **Camp David** that resulted in much friendlier—or at least more realistic—relations ("The Spirit of Camp David"). In informal engagements, such as on the film set of "Can-Can" in Hollywood and in the famous **"kitchen debate"** in Moscow, Khrushchev proved himself a feisty and somewhat unpredictable competitor.

A major result of peaceful coexistence, however, was the **Lacy-Zarubin Agreement** on cultural exchanges (1958) that opened up the Soviet Union to a significant number of graduate students, scholars, performing groups, and cinema presentations, as well as to an American appreciation of Soviet/Russian culture. Nevertheless, relations between the two countries involved extremely tense episodes over the Soviet invasion of **Hungary** (1956), the **U-2 incident** (1960), and the construction of the **Berlin Wall** (1961). More important was his willingness to back down in the **Cuban missile crisis** (1962) and avert a more serious confrontation. Because of these unsettling international events, his on-and-off reforms, and the remnants of entrenched Stalinism, Khrushchev was deposed in October 1964 by a coterie of his own followers. He was allowed a comfortable "dacha" retirement, where he wrote his important memoirs, *Khrushchev Remembers*. He remains, like **Stalin**, a complicated figure to analyze and assess.

KHRUSHCHEV, SERGEI (1933–). The son of **Nikita Khrushchev** first visited the United States in company with his father in 1959, a major event in the new Soviet policy of **peaceful coexistence**. Trained as a computer engineer, Sergei and his family suffered through the eclipse of his father in the 1970s, but he was able to reemerge on the international scene in 1990 as a leading delegate of a "people for peace" initiative of more than 200 Soviet citizens hosted by Lawrence, Kansas. Subsequently, he and his wife immigrated to the United States and obtained citizenship. Sergei Khrushchev has devoted much of his time and energy to the reestablishment of his father's place in history through publication and participation in such events as the reappraisal of the **Cuban missile crisis**, during which he established close contacts with Kansas State University and the Eisenhower presidential library in Abilene and through visits to other American universities. In recent years he has become a major authority on his father and the **cold war** in general in several books devoted to the memoirs and rehabilitation of the record of his father.

KISSINGER, HENRY (1923–). Born in Germany, Kissinger immigrated to the United States with his family in 1938. He studied at Harvard University and served in the U.S. army during **World War II**. Completing his postgraduate work at Harvard after the war, he became a professor of political science there (1962–69). He was summoned to Washington by **Richard Nixon** as his national security advisor, advancing to secretary of state (1973–77) and providing continuity in foreign policy for the administration of **Gerald Ford**. During his long tenure in the highest level of government service, he was known for his steady (but unimaginative) approach to foreign affairs. He tended to look at the big picture and to concentrate on crises in the Middle East and improvement of relations with China, while taking a hard line toward the USSR. He supported his sometimes controversial approaches in tedious memoirs, such as *The White House Years* (1979) and *Years of Upheaval* (1982). He summarized these in an eloquent keynote address at **Spaso House** in Moscow for a conference on the 200th anniversary of the beginning of Russian–American relations in November 2007.

"KITCHEN DEBATE." An argumentative discussion between Soviet leader **Nikita Khrushchev** and Vice President **Richard Nixon** in Moscow over mutual Soviet and American achievements. The setting was an exhibition of American family life in Solkolniki Park in Moscow, a result of the cultural exchange agreement concluded the previous year. A purpose of Nixon's visit was to prepare the way for Khrushchev's trip to the United States a few months later. Nixon arrived in Moscow on 23 July 1959 on a direct flight from New York and proceeded to display charm and energy, beginning in Khrushchev's office in the Kremlin on the morning of 24 July. The surprising repartee that ensued continued during a walk through

Sokolniki Park and intensified at a stop at the kitchen display at the exhibition that emphasized American luxury, especially General Electric appliances, at which Khrushchev emphasized the waste of such luxury in a discussion of the relative merits of capitalist and Communist systems. The sharp but good-humored exchange continued through a festive and lavish dinner at the Kremlin that night. After a day of touring Moscow (25 July), Nixon met informally at the premier's dacha on 26 July. The trip concluded with a breakthrough television address to the Soviet people on 1 August. The "kitchen debate" and the visit in general were a boost to both Khrushchev, who showed a surprising degree of flexibility and an "on-his-feet" capability of dialogue, and Nixon's candidacy for president the following year.

KNIGHT, AUSTIN (1854–1927). As commander of the American Pacific Fleet during **World War I**, Admiral Knight established his base on the cruiser SS *Brooklyn* in the harbor of **Vladivostok** in 1918, during the **Russian Civil War**. He added his expertise and superior experience to the **American Expeditionary Force** and General **William S. Graves**. Knight was adept in negotiations with Japanese commanders and to some degree overshadowed Graves, though he supported his agenda of avoiding direct military combat with any Bolshevik or anti-Bolshevik forces in **Siberia**.

KODIAK. As Russian explorers, entrepreneurs (fur hunters), and missionaries advanced eastward across the North Pacific, they found a convenient harbor and native Aleut support for a summer hunting base that was established in 1784 by **Grigory Shelikhov**. Kodiak, the largest of the Aleutian chain of islands, would then become the first permanent outpost of the Russian Empire in North America by 1795. Though the administrative center of the **Russian America Company** would soon be moved to **Sitka**, much farther to the east and adjacent to the mainland, Kodiak would remain an important base for hunting, ice cutting (for a lucrative trade with San Francisco after 1854), and gaining Aleut conversions to Russian Orthodoxy, until the sale of **Alaska** in 1867. Kodiak and the Aleutian Islands served as the southern boundary of the large body of water, the **Bering Sea**. *See also* RUSSIAN AMERICA.

KOLCHAK, ALEXANDER (1873–1920). A respected naval officer and aspiring democratic leader, Kolchak was in many respects the last hope for a non-Bolshevik or non-Soviet alternative in Russia after the failures of **Alexander Kerensky** and General **Anton Denikin**. He was able to collect a number of White **World War I** Russian army units and the crucial support of the **Czechoslovak Legion** to establish a political and military base of power in Omsk, Siberia, in 1918. Taking advantage of the weakness of the Bolshevik Red Army, Kolchak's forces were able to occupy much of the Volga region and the Urals up to Ekaterinburg in 1918–19 before being defeated. Unfortunately, he was unable to coordinate with the larger opposition force in the south of Russia under Denikin. The Czech Legion ultimately withdrew its support of the Omsk government, in part because the **American Expeditionary Force** was not to become involved in the Siberian conflict and because its desire was to return home after the end of the war. As the Czechs withdrew along the **Trans-Siberian** in 1919, they captured and turned over Kolchak to the Red Army in return for safe passage. Kolchak was subsequently executed, a man of talent and courage who deserved a better fate for his honest effort to restore a real Russia. *See also* CIVIL WAR, RUSSIAN.

KOMPLEKTOV, VICTOR (1932–). Komplektov served in various capacities in the realm of foreign service after his graduation from the Institute of International Relations in 1955; many of these involved the United States, beginning with his apprenticeship in Washington in the 1950s that included the negotiation of the **Lacy-Zarubin** cultural exchange agreement. He continued to serve in various subordinate roles in the Soviet embassy in Washington and as an advisor on American affairs in the Ministry of Foreign Affairs in Moscow in the 1960s and 1970s. He accompanied **Leonid Breznev** to conferences in Helsinki, Vienna, Geneva, and Vladivostok in the 1970s. Komplektov was known especially for his calm, collected demeanor at these meetings and during crises, such as that of the **Korean airliner incident**. After his brief but active tenure as ambassador to the United States, he concluded his diplomatic career as ambassador to Spain (1994–99). In retirement, Komplektov has been a leader in the "conference of ambassadors," eloquently participating in their forums, such as in Moscow on the occasion of the 200th anniversary of the beginning of Russian–American relations in November 2007.

KOREAN AIRLINER INCIDENT (SEPTEMBER 1983). In one of the last serious episodes of the **cold war**, a routine South Korean Air Line Flight 007 from Anchorage to Seoul strayed, due to navigation error, into Soviet airspace over Sakhalin Island. Followed on radar and intercepted by Soviet surveillance, the plane was summarily shot down after a short and failed effort to turn the plane away. Though the situation was complicated by the existence of American air intelligence missions in the area, the episode demonstrated the dangers of overreactive responses and helped moderate tensions in later years.

KOREAN WAR (1950–1953). At the end of **World War II** in the Pacific arena, the Korean peninsula was divided artificially at the 38th parallel between American and Soviet zones of occupation and responsibility. This left an unresolved issue, since a treaty on any more logical division was never signed. While the Communists dominated north of the line, the south moved unsteadily toward democracy, successfully enough that substantial American occupation forces were withdrawn, and it seemed to be ignored as an area of vital American interest. In July 1950, North Korean forces, aided and abetted by the Soviet Union, attacked across the border and quickly occupied most of the south. The United States, under President **Harry S. Truman**, responded with direct military involvement and won **United Nations** support, owing to a Soviet boycott of the proceedings. After their impressive advance through South Korea, the invading forces were thrown back by a successful flanking amphibious operation at Inchon, engineered by General Douglas McArthur; this resulted in a rapid retreat by the North Koreans all the way to the Yalu River, the border between North Korea and China. The Chinese Red Army then intervened to force an Allied retreat, with a resulting stalemate approximately along the original border.

Though the regime of **Joseph Stalin** continued to support North Korea with military equipment and advisors, the Soviet Union refrained from direct intervention or widening the conflict and became uneasy about the growth of Chinese involvement in the conflict. A new Soviet leadership, after Stalin's death in 1953, was influential in securing an armistice, followed by protracted peace negotiations. The division of Korea into opposing north and south countries with sharply differing political and economic institutions persists into the 21st century as a remnant of the **cold war**, though in 2007 some relaxation has allowed limited direct communication (rail service) across the border. The Korean War is significant in demonstrating an American and Western resolve to stop Communist aggression in the Far East as well as in Europe, and also for the Soviet restraint in limiting military commitment. The arbitrated border, however, remains a flashpoint as it is unsanctioned by any international agreement.

KOSCIUSZKO, TADEUSZ (1746–1817). Born in Russian Poland of Polish gentry, Kosciuszko entered the Corps of Cadets in Warsaw in 1765 and became an officer the next year as an instructor in engineering. In 1774–75 he toured Europe, settling briefly in France before leaving for America to offer his services to **George Washington** in 1776. He was best known for his skill at fortification, especially at Philadelphia, Saratoga, and West Point in 1777–80. After the war, in 1784, he returned to Russian Poland to administer the family estate. He soon became involved in an attempt to secure Polish independence, suffering defeat and capture by Russian forces in 1794. After a year of friendly imprisonment in St. Petersburg, he was reprieved by Emperor Paul I and traveled through Europe and back to the United States in 1798, before settling finally in France, refusing, however, entreaties to serve Napoleon. He is widely and justly celebrated as an American hero with many place names dedicated to him.

KOSTROMITINOV, PETER. As an agent of the **Russian America Company (RAC)**, Kostromitinov brought new energy and initiatives to a fading enterprise. He first served as director (1830–38) of the **Fort Ross** colony in northern California. Taking advantage of a rapid development of the American presence on the Pacific coast in the 1840s and 1850s, he forged a cooperative relationship on business endeavors. Kostromitinov inspired and supported the San Francisco–based **American Russian Commercial Company** and encouraged its investment in the importation of ice, lumber, fish, and other products from Russian **Alaska**. Subsequently, as Russian vice consul in San Francisco he stirred up American support for Russia during the **Crimean War** and was probably the initiator of the idea of a fictitious sale of the RAC territory to avoid a possible seizure by the British.

KOUSSEVITZKY, SERGE (1874–1951). Raised in a Jewish family in Tver province, Koussevitzky began formal music studies in Moscow in 1886, specializing in the bass string instrument. He joined the Bolshoi Theater orchestra at age 20 and became its principal bassist in 1903. After marriage in 1905, he and his wife moved to Berlin, where he established a reputation as a brilliant conductor of the Berlin Philharmonic. After a brief return to Soviet Russia in 1920, Koussevitzky introduced a number of new works by **Sergei Prokofiev**, Igor Stravinsky, and Maurice Ravel in Paris before moving permanently to the United States in 1924. Koussevitzky is best known as director of the Boston Symphony Orchestra (1924–49), building it into a world-class ensemble and founding its summer concert series at Tanglewood, while commissioning a number of new works and orchestrations. The latter included Ravel's transcription of Modest Mussorgsky's *Pictures at an Exhibition* (1922) as well as his inaugural presentations of two Prokofiev symphonies, George Gershwin's *Second Rhapsody*, Aaron Copland's *Symphony No. 3*, and Benjamin Britten's *Peter Grimes*. Leonard Bernstein was among his many students and disciples. He looms large in the Russian contributions to the American musical world that included a number of other major conductors, such as Leopold Stokowski and **Mstislav Rostropovich**.

KOZLOV AFFAIR (1815–1816). Nikolai Kozlov succeeded **Andrei Dashkov** as Russian consul-general in Philadelphia in 1814. The following year, he was charged with the rape of a 12-year-old servant girl, and the case was brought before a Pennsylvania court. Dashkov, now minister, defended his colleague, publicly denouncing the case as lacking substance. Nevertheless, the affair was settled only by the withdrawal of Kozlov from the United States with much discredit to Dashkov, who was also recalled.

KRASIN, LEONID (1870–1926). One of the few truly technical experts in the upper echelon of the Bolshevik leadership, Krasin won the respect of **Vladimir Lenin** at the 1903 congress of the **Russian Social Democratic Labor Party** and was elected to its central committee. Though siding with Lenin's "left" orientation at that time, he also resumed his engineering career with the German firm of Siemens, becoming its agent first in Moscow and then in St. Petersburg until 1914; Krasin, though a "secret" Bolshevik, managed the company's plant during **World War I** under Russian government auspices. As a bearded sophisticate, a pattern of other Bolshevik leaders, he was a pronounced moderate in many ways, leading the way in charting the retreat from War Communism and in extending overtures to Western countries. As People's Commissar for Foreign Trade in 1918, he pursued normal trade relations, especially by heading a Soviet mission to London and in the negotiation of the Anglo–Soviet Trade Agreement (March 1921), a significant seal on Lenin's **New Economic Policy (NEP)**. Krasin was instrumental in the establishment of Arcos in London and the **American Trading Corporation (Amtorg)** in New York in the early 1920s. As an advocate of "Soviet laissez faire," he opposed party interference in economic matters and continued to head the trade mission in Great Britain—until his untimely natural death in London.

KRESTINSKY, NIKOLAI (1883–1938). Born in Mogilev of Ukrainian parentage, Krestinsky received an excellent secondary education. His father, a high-school (gymnasia) teacher, and his mother were both involved in populist activities in the 1870s. Krestinsky attended the law faculty of St. Petersburg University, receiving his degree in 1907, and then worked for a law firm in the capital. He had already become an active Social Democrat and revolutionary in Vilnius (Lithuania). During 1917 he was a Bolshevik leader in Ekaterinburg in the Urals while also becoming a member of the central committee of the party. After the **Bolshevik Revolution**, his international legal expertise led to his supervision of the operation of the country's banking system, and he subsequently became commissar of finance in 1918 and, in 1919, one of the five original members of the Politburo that included **Vladimir Lenin**, **Leon Trotsky**, and **Joseph Stalin**.

In 1921, with the initiation of the **New Economic Policy** (NEP), Krestinsky led an economic opening of trade with Europe and the United States. In October he was appointed Soviet ambassador to Germany, where he laid the foundation for the Treaty of Rapallo the following year and was the architect of Soviet trade missions in other countries, including the United States. As the Soviet representative in Berlin (1921–30), Krestinsky reinforced the successful alliance with Weimar Germany, and, as a supporter of **Maxim Litvinov**'s "outreach" to the West, he came back to Moscow to be the assistant commissar for foreign affairs to Litvinov until 1935. As a right-wing Communist, he was arrested and tried in the third Moscow purge trial in 1938. He created a sensation by denying his guilt of any of the charges (such as being a supporter of Trotsky) in a dramatic scene, only to recant and plead guilty the next day and to be shot soon after. Throughout his Soviet career, he represented a more traditional Russian intellectual approach that included closer ties with Europe and the United States.

KRIKALOV, SERGEI (1958–). One of the first and leading Russian participants in joint Russian–American space cooperation, Krikalov joined the missions of *Discovery* (1994) and *Endeavor* (1998) that set the stage for the establishment of the international space station. The beginning of its operation was celebrated in 2000 with his joint leadership (with American astronaut Bill Shepherd) of a cooperative mission. *See also* GAGARIN, YURY.

KRIVITSKY, WALTER (1899–1941). By the mid-1920s, Krivitsky was a leading Soviet intelligence agent in Western Europe, and especially for the German-speaking parts of it, emerging as the chief **People's Commissariat of Internal Affairs (NKVD)** agent for Western Europe by the 1930s. He felt, however, with the beginning of the purges, that his days were numbered and defected to Canada, where he delivered valuable information on Soviet operations abroad to British intelligence. Subsequently, in the United States he wrote a memoir on his activities, *I Was Stalin's Agent* (1937) but died mysteriously in a Washington hotel in February 1941, presumably murdered by the NKVD, just after testifying before the House Un-American Activities Committee, headed by Martin Dies. His death seemed to be part of a special operation by Soviet agents abroad that involved the elimination of **Leon Trotsky** in Mexico, Fedor Raskolnikov in France, and others.

KROPOTKIN, (PRINCE) PETER (1842–1921). From a family of Russian aristocracy and intellectuals, Kropotkin served as an officer in the Russian army before becoming a leading theorist of an antibureaucratic and populist orientation that promoted radical change in Russia and the world. He spent a number of years in scientific and exploration work in Manchuria and Siberia before his arrest in 1874 in a suppression of "narodniks" ("to the people" movement). Subsequently, Kropotkin served several years in prison before escaping abroad, where he spent most of his life in exile, mainly in France and England. He attracted considerable sympathy in the West, and especially in the United States, for his idealistic and utopian program. Genial and unthreatening as a personality, Kropotkin was the "gentleman's revolutionary," who might be compared with Bertrand Russell, **Eugene Debs**, and Aldous Huxley. Never a **Bolshevik** supporter, he was, nonetheless, adopted to their cause as a precursor and welcomed back to Russia in 1918. He is buried in the Novodevichy cemetery in Moscow. A prolific writer, his works are still studied for their promotion of an alternative society from those, Western and Eastern, that would dominate the 20th century.

KUROPIATNIK, GENNADY (1924–). One of Russia's leading historians of 19th-century American history, Kuropiatnik was born and raised in the Poltava region of Ukraine. As a research scholar of the Institute of General History of the **Academy of Sciences** in Moscow and an associate of **Nikolai Bolkhovitinov**, he became a productive and objective Soviet scholar on American history in the **cold war** period. Serving in the Soviet mission to the **United Nations** (1962–67), he became fluent in English and knowledgeable about American society. His scholarly work includes *Frmerskoe dvizhenie v SShA* (*The Farmers' Movement in the USA*) (1971), *Rossia i SShA: ekonomicheskie, kul'turnye i diplomaticheskie sviazi* (*Russia and the USA: Economic, Cultural and Diplomatic Connections*) (1981), and *Istoriia vneshnei politiki i diplomatii SShA, 1867–1918* (*History of the Foreign Policy and Diplomacy of the USA, 1867–1918*) (1997). Kuropiatnik has been especially supportive and encouraging of American students and faculty about their research in Russia and continues to be active in scholarly work, despite physical disabilities.

KUSKOV, IVAN (1765–1823). As a trusted and valued assistant of **Alexander Baranov** in the early years of the Russian presence in North America, Kuskov is especially noted for his survey of the northern California coast and for the establishment of a permanent base of the **Russian America Company** at **Fort Ross** in 1812, of which he served as the first commandant (1812–21). He, along with Baranov, was largely responsible for the duration of the Russian control of a vast region of Northwest America. He later retired to a monastery near his home city of Totma in North Russia. *See also* RUSSIAN AMERICA COMPANY (RAC).

KUZBAS AMERICAN COLONY (1922–1926). American utopian volunteers in 1920s Russia. The Kuznetsk basin in Siberia (generally east of Novosibirsk and south of Tomsk) had been developed as an industrial region in the early 20th century, based on its rich coal and mineral deposits. American labor radical **Bill Haywood** is credited in singling the area out for a project by American friends of the Soviet Union. This was taken up by Sebald Rutgers of Rotterdam and **Herbert Calvert** of Vincennes, Indiana. The Society for Technical Aid to Russia, headquartered in New York, signed a contract in 1922 with the Soviet government for a broad initiative of developing mining and agriculture around Kemerovo and for steel mills at Nadezhdinsk in the Urals. The American leaders promised to recruit 6,000 American volunteers, counting on the **Industrial Workers of the World (IWW)** to supply most of them. Only about 400 Americans actually participated in the project but, with the help of contributions from various sources of over a million dollars for equipment and other expenses, they accomplished more than could be expected in reviving the region. Additional information is available in the memoirs of participants, among whom were Floyd Ramp and **Ruth Kennell**.

– L –

LACY-ZARUBIN AGREEMENT (1958). The interests of Soviet party leader **Nikita Khrushchev** in **peaceful coexistence** and American president **Dwight D. Eisenhower** in people-to-people exchanges converged into negotiations in Washington beginning in late October 1957 for a Soviet–American student exchange. This was at least partly inspired by a successful tour of a Harlem company of *Porgy and Bess* in December 1955, but the main catalyst on the American side was the establishment of graduate study centers, such as the Russian Institute (later **Harriman Institute**) at Columbia University, the **Harvard Russian Research Center**, and later similar interdisciplinary centers at a number of other universities, as well as the consequent desire for access to Soviet libraries and archives. The agreement, providing for an exchange of about 20 students on each side, was signed at the end of January 1958 between special ambassadors for the negotiations, William Lacy and outgoing Soviet ambassador Georgy Zarubin, and went into effect that fall.

The exchange program endured through the ups and downs of the **cold war**, gradually expanding to include films, performing groups, and exhibits. Among the notable Americans involved were Benny Goodman, Duke Ellington, and the American Ballet Theatre, while Soviet groups included the Bolshoi Ballet, the Moiseyev Dancers, and celloist **Mstislav Rostropovich**. The impact of the exchanges was cumulative in effect, involving a large part of the American and Soviet academic communities. Mutual exposure to each other's culture certainly played a role in the collapse of the Soviet Union. Especially to be noted is that the exchanges were not limited to Soviet–American but set the example for similar exchanges between Western and third-world countries with the Soviet Union. The United States also developed smaller similar exchanges with all other nations of Eastern Europe. Direct scholarly programs of Fulbright, universities, and other organizations added to the total impact. Basically, Soviet politics and society could not effectively resist, nor survive, the Western cultural assault. Thus, the exchange program can be credited with providing a major assist to the dismantling of the "Communist world."

LAFEBER, WALTER F. (1933–). American historian of the **cold war**. A student of **William Appleman Williams** at the University of Wisconsin, LaFeber quickly emerged as a leading revisionist historian of Soviet–American relations after **World War II**, promoting especially the imperialist interpretation of American foreign relations, sometimes challenged by traditionalists such as Robert H. Ferrell and **John Lewis Gaddis**. As a professor at Cornell University he trained a number of graduate students and published widely in historical journals and scholarly standards such as *America, Russia, and the Cold War*. Throughout his career, he was a champion of closer relations between American and Russian historians, befriending and supporting such scholars as **Nikolai Bolkhovitinov** and other Russians and Americans.

LAKIER, ALEXANDER (1825–1870). Born in the South Russian port of Taganrog, Lakier studied law at the University of Moscow and served for a number of years in the Russian bureaucracy before undertaking a journey to Western Europe and the United States in 1857. He traveled around America, visiting Boston, New York, Philadelphia, Cincinnati, Chicago, St. Louis, Memphis, New Orleans, and Washington, D.C., with extensions to Canada and Cuba, and described his experiences in a number of articles in popular Russian journals, collected in *Puteshestvia po severo-amerikanskim shtatam, Kanade i ostrovu Kube* (*A Journey Through the North American States, Canada, and Cuba*) (1859). An edited English translation is *A Russian Looks at America* (1979). Lakier might be considered the Russian Alexis de Tocqueville for his shrewd and detailed observations of the United States on the eve of the **American Civil War**.

LANDFIELD, JEROME (1871–1935). A graduate of Cornell University (1894), Landfield joined with his Cornell instructor of Russian to study the Russian language in St. Petersburg (1894–97), one of the first Americans to complete a course of study there, where he met and married a daughter of prominent Russian nobility (Lobanov-Rostovsky). He subsequently developed minor business interests in Russia (such as mining in the Urals) and served as an instructor at the University of California (1902–06). After the **Bolshevik Revolution**, Landfield remained devoted to the prerevolutionary regime, based on his wife's family's Russian nobility origin, while serving on special assignment in Russia and as an advisor to the State Department in 1918–19. In this capacity he helped chart a strongly anti-Bolshevik and nonrecognition American policy. Landfield served briefly as director of the **American Russian Chamber of Commerce** in 1920 before it moved toward accommodation with Soviet Russia for business reasons.

LANSING, ROBERT (1864–1928). Replacing pacifist William Jennings Bryan, Lansing served as secretary of state (1915–20) during the difficult period of American entry into **World War I**, the **Bolshevik Revolution**, the **Paris Peace Conference**, and the **Russian Civil War**. An expert in international law, graduate of Amherst College, Lansing served as counsel for the American case at the **Bering**

Sea Arbitration (1892–93) in Paris. The son-in-law of a previous secretary of state, **John W. Foster**, and the uncle of another, **John Foster Dulles**, Lansing remained very much in the background during the **Woodrow Wilson** administration, owing to the president's own conduct of foreign relations—with the assistance of his close advisor, **Edward House**. Lansing, nonetheless, played a key role in supervising State Department operations and the regular business of the peace conference in Paris. In regard to U.S. policy toward the Soviet Union, Lansing was a hard-liner, in contrast to House, who worked to achieve an understanding, promoting and sponsoring the **Bullitt mission** and the **Prinkipo Conference**. Continually frustrated by Wilsonian liberals, Lansing resigned early in 1920 to be replaced by **Bainbridge Colby**, on the eve of the president's defeat in the Senate on U.S. membership in the **League of Nations** and his crippling stroke.

LAVROV, SERGEI (1950–). Of Armenian-Russian descent, Lavrov graduated from the Moscow State Institute of International Affairs in 1972 and joined the Soviet diplomatic service. His initial diplomatic assignment was to Sri Lanka, returning to a post in the Foreign Ministry in Moscow in 1976. Lavrov became a senior advisor to the Soviet mission to the **United Nations** (1981–88) and permanent representative of the **Russian Federation** to the UN (1994–2004). **Vladimir Putin** appointed him foreign minister in March 2004, succeeding **Igor Ivanov**. Considered an adept diplomat, he also reflects a model of stability in the **Putin** and **Medvedev** administrations while following the accepted line of being a stern critic of American involvement in the Middle East and Caucasus regions.

LEAGUE OF NATIONS (1919–1939). Promoted especially by **Woodrow Wilson** at the end of **World War I**, the league was conceived as an institution to arbitrate issues and disputes between nations before they could result in war. Unfortunately, American disillusionment in Wilson's leadership and the outcome of the war resulted in a Senate vote against membership in the organization, and the United States never joined. Another major power, the Soviet Union, was also a nonmember—until **Maxim Litvinov**'s initiation of **collective security**—after which it became a member in 1934. The league proved to be weak and ineffective in dealing with the aggressive moves of Italy, Japan, and Germany in the 1930s. It would eventually be replaced by a more workable but also often ineffective **United Nations** after **World War II**.

LEBED, ALEXANDER (1950–2002). A distinguished officer in the Soviet army from Novocherkask, Lebed took part in the invasion of **Afghanistan** and quickly rose to command an airborne division stationed in the Moscow area by 1990. During the **August Coup** of 1991, he refused to obey orders to move the tanks under his command against the Russian government of **Boris Yeltsin** and thereby helped to defeat the coup leaders, who included Minister of Defense Dmitri Yazkov. Although promoted to higher military positions in the **Russian Federation**, Lebed resigned in 1995 to enter politics and was elected to the state Duma in December. He then ran as a candidate in the presidential contest of 1996, achieving 15 percent of the vote in the first round. Lebed then threw his support to Yeltsin and was awarded with the post of secretary of the security council and in 1998 became governor of the large Krasnoyarsk region of Siberia. An adroit politician, he appeared on a possible collision course with **Vladimir Putin** when he was killed in a helicopter accident on 28 April 2002.

LEDYARD, JOHN (1751–1789). Becoming intrigued with the North Pacific while serving in the second expedition of Captain James Cook (1776–80), Ledyard, originally from Connecticut, sought funding for his own voyage in the 1780s in America and Great Britain without success. He had achieved some fame, however, by the publication of his own account of the Cook expedition, *Journal of Captain Cook's Last Voyage* (1783), which brought him to the attention of **Benjamin Franklin** and **Thomas Jefferson**. Though failing to secure adequate backing, in 1787, he decided to go to Russia to seek that government's support. After encountering bureaucratic hurdles in St. Petersburg, Ledyard decided to accompany British explorer Joseph Billings to **Siberia** without official approval. They reached Irkutsk in the fall in time to discuss North Pacific affairs with a leading fur trader (*promyshlennik*), **Grigory Shelikov**, and then journeyed as far as Yakutsk before encountering severe weather. Ledyard is credited, nevertheless, with being the first American to venture deep into Siberia. Returning to Irkutsk, Ledyard was arrested under suspicion of being a British spy and escorted back across the European Russian frontier. He died in early 1789 in Egypt on another foolhardy venture. For the documents and journal of his Russian venture, see *John Ledyard's Journey Through Russia and Siberia, 1787–1788* (1966).

LEGGE, ALEXANDER (1866–1933). Rising through the ranks of **International Harvester**, the largest agricultural implement company in the United States, to be its president (1922–29) and general manager under **Cyrus McCormick Jr.**, Legge stressed its "international" involvements and especially its commitment to the large Russian market both before and after the revolution. Recognized for his business leadership, Legge also served as vice chairman of the War Industries Board during **World War I** and as chairman of the Federal Farm Board (1929–31). In modern parlance, he was a true pioneer of early American globalization.

LEND-LEASE. The "Lend-Lease Act" was passed by Congress in March 1941, specifically to aid the defense of Great Britain during its German aerial bombardment (Battle of Britain). After the German invasion of the Soviet Union the following June, the question arose of whether to extend the program to that country. With British support, and because the Battle of Britain had been won and the Luftwaffe had shifted its commitment to the east in preparation for the invasion of the Soviet Union, a new lend-lease organization materialized in the summer of 1941, headed temporarily by Colonel **Phillip Faymonville** in Washington, to negotiate with a special Soviet mission headed by General **Filip Golikov**. The American government, prompted especially by President **Franklin D. Roosevelt** and his chief advisors on Soviet affairs, **Sumner Welles** and **Harry Hopkins**, committed to a major military assistance program for the beleaguered USSR.

Initial supplies via the Arctic **northern convoy route** to **Murmansk** and **Arkhangelsk** were quickly dispatched in July 1941, some of which, mainly fighter planes, were diverted from those already shipped to Great Britain. Additional direct shipments from the

United States were soon on the way, despite fears in some quarters that the United States should not support a Communist state or risk losing valuable equipment to a rapidly advancing German army. Hopkins led an early mission to guarantee American support in July, followed by a more official Anglo-American delegation to Moscow in September 1941, led by **W. Averell Harriman** and Lord Beaverbrook that led to the signing of the "First Protocol" on lend-lease to Russia. The United States generally adhered to the list of Soviet priorities that concentrated on fighter aircraft, high-octane aviation fuel, trucks, airplanes, and other military supplies.

As **World War II** progressed, the most important route to Russia was through the Persian Gulf and across Iran into Soviet territory. In the process Iran was brought under Allied control with Soviet forces occupying the northern third of the country. The route was especially vital for the shipment of trucks and other equipment into the front area around Stalingrad. The North Pacific route was "safe," owing to the Soviet–Japanese neutrality agreement. Typically, American "liberty" ships were turned over to Soviet crews in Seattle and made many trans-Pacific supply runs during the war. The main problems were the American priority on meeting needs of the Pacific War and the long **Trans-Siberian** journey. The route remained active, however, until the Soviet declaration of war on Japan in August 1945.

LENIN (RUSSIAN NATIONAL) LIBRARY. Founded on the large book and manuscript collection of the Rumiantsev noble family of the 18th century, similar to the library of **Thomas Jefferson** becoming the cornerstone of the **Library of Congress**, the Lenin Library served the Moscow scholarly community, but after the revolution it became *the* national library, the largest repository of books and journals in the Soviet Union, challenged only by the Saltykov-Shchedren Public Library in St. Petersburg. Though the Russian National Library has been handicapped through most of its existence by crowds of advanced students and scholars and budgetary constraints, the library still holds an immense quantity of records for all periods of Russian history, and it is also the leading collector of international materials, including those pertaining to the United States. Its manuscript collections, however, are somewhat limited compared with those of the Library of Congress. The more important materials are generally found in various state archives, especially the **State Archives of the Russian Federation (GARF)**.

LENIN, VLADIMIR ILICH (NE ULYANOV) (1870–1924). As leader and architect of the left wing of the **Russian Social Democratic Labor Party (RSDLP)**, to be known after an organizational split in 1903 as the **Bolsheviks**, Lenin emphasized, along the lines of an influential Russian populist, Nikolai Chernyshevsky, that a Russian revolutionary must be fully and absolutely committed to the cause. On the issue of party membership at the Second Congress of the party in 1903, Lenin insisted on a full-time involvement as a prerequisite to membership, in contrast to the more moderate Menshevik position. Lenin also explained the failure of a proletarian revolution in the West to the ability of imperialist countries to exploit the labor and resources of colonial areas and "throw some of the dregs" to workers at home (in *Imperialism, the Highest Stage of Capitalism*). His views on imperialism especially included analyses of the Spanish–American War. It was also clear in his many writings that Lenin paid special attention to the impressive economic progress of the United States and to the development of such practices as Ford-style assembly-line production.

Born and raised in Simbirsk, a provincial city on the Volga River, Lenin studied briefly at the University of Kazan and then law in St. Petersburg and soon became an adherent of Marxism, which was quite the fashion in late 19th-century Europe. For his support of revolution, he was sentenced to exile in **Siberia**, near the Lena River, from which he acquired a pseudonym. Released for exile, he spent several years abroad, mainly in Switzerland, where he quickly became known as a leading radical and founder of the Bolshevik wing of RSDLP at its Second Congress in Brussels/London in 1903. This faction ("party") gained additional strength during the **Revolution of 1905** and during **World War I**, taking advantage of general popular dissatisfaction with the situation of losses and economic collapse that it caused.

Gaining wide support during the summer of 1917, Lenin's party achieved power through a coup d'état in October 1917. During this crucial period, Lenin and the Bolsheviks received vital encouragement from a number of Americans, namely **John Reed, Louise Bryant**, Albert Rhys Williams, and **Raymond Robins** in Russia—and by the **Industrial Workers of the World (IWW)** and various other left-wing groups in the United States. In fact, Lenin's revolution caused a split in the American socialist movement with the left wing becoming the **Communist Party of the United States (CPUSA)**. Though the U.S. government under **Woodrow Wilson** and his Republican successors would oppose the Bolshevik regime and refuse to recognize it, business concerns won **concessions** and more or less conducted business as usual. Lenin was especially interested in friendly arrangements with the United States for economic and political reasons and actively sought diplomatic recognition without success. Nevertheless, he was encouraged by the support of a substantial number of "Americans" such as Reed, **Armand Hammer**, **Bill Haywood**, and Robins. Indeed, Lenin remained a hero of internationalism and idealism to a number of Americans for several decades.

LESOVSKY, STEPAN (1817–1884). A graduate of the Russian naval college in 1839, Lesovsky served in both the Baltic and Black Sea fleets before 1860. In 1862 he was sent to the United States to study deployment of monitor-class ironclads and returned the following year in command of a Russian squadron that created quite a sensation upon its arrival in New York, since it was interpreted as a symbol of Russian support for the Union cause. This Russian naval presence for over a year in northern ports is credited with discouraging more active British and French support of the Confederacy, which might have led to diplomatic recognition of the southern cause. While in America, Lesovsky participated in many welcoming and social occasions in New York and surrounding cities and visited battlefields as far away as observing the siege of Vicksburg, in company of General **Ulysses S. Grant**. The visit of the Russian fleet boosted Union morale at a crucial time (after the Battle of Gettysburg) and raised Russian–American friendly relations to their highest point. Small in stature, Lesovsky was, nevertheless, renowned for his discipline. He also had a reputation as a sincere, honest, and straightforward officer, much of this captured in K. M. Staniukovich's maritime stories of the late 19th century. *See also* CIVIL WAR, AMERICAN.

LEWIS, SINCLAIR (1885–1951). Born and raised in Minnesota, Lewis graduated from Yale University (1908) and pursued a journalistic career in the Midwest. From these experiences came many of his best works. His series of critical and satirical novels on the Mid-American middle class won him quick fame, especially *Main Street* (1920), *Babbitt* (1922), *Arrowsmith* (1925), and *Elmer Gantry* (1927), for which he received the Nobel Prize for Literature in 1930. Lewis achieved simultaneous popularity in Soviet Russia, partly because of a Russian tradition of interest in American writers (from **James Fenimore Cooper** to **Jack London**), but also because of his biting portrayals of the follies of "capitalist" society. In 1927 Lewis visited Moscow by invitation to help celebrate the 10th anniversary of the revolution. Unlike his rival, **Theodore Dreiser**, he and his future wife, Dorothy Thompson, stayed only for a few days. His works, as well as those of Dreiser, William Faulkner, and Ernest Hemingway, caught the imagination of the Soviet public and would remain requisite reading for at least three more generations.

LEWIS, WILLIAM DAVID (1784–c. 1850). From his native Philadelphia, Lewis went to Russia in 1813 to assist his elder brother, John Delaware Lewis, in his successful and rapidly expanding mercantile business. In pursuit of this activity, he had an encounter with the rather arrogant and supercilious American consul, **John Levett Harris**, also from Philadelphia, that led to a lawsuit that was long drawn out in Pennsylvania courts. In the meantime Lewis had been sent off by his brother to Moscow and Tver to learn Russian, St. Petersburg being considered ill advised for the purpose. As a result, William David Lewis became the first student of Russian and the first American fluent in the language, which he proved by rendering "Yankee Doodle" into Russian for his friends. Because of the feud with Harris, however, Lewis withdrew from Russia, but he retained an interest in Russian literature and years later published a volume of Russian poetry, mainly by Alexander Pushkin, in Philadelphia, the first in the English language.

LIBRARY OF CONGRESS (LC). Established by the government purchase of the library of **Thomas Jefferson**, the facility has grown enormously to include every book copyrighted in the United States, as well as maintaining the largest collection of international materials. Its manuscript collection (in the Madison Building) preserves much that is relevant to the study of Russian–American relations: presidential papers of **Theodore Roosevelt, William Howard Taft**, and **Calvin Coolidge**; the private collections of **Breckinridge Long, William Allen White, George Kennan, Norman/Elizabeth Reynolds Hapgood, Newton Baker, Alice Stone Blackwell, Charles Bohlen, Joseph Davies, W. Averell Harriman, Robert Lansing**, Laurence Steinhardt, **George von Lengerke Meyer, Elihu Root, Hamilton Fish**, Peter Demens, and many others. A long-term Librarian of Congress has been James Billington, a historian of Russia.

LIKHACHEV, DMITRI (1906–1999). Actively involved in the new, revolutionary arts of the 1920s and a friend of **Sergei Esenin** and **Vladimir Mayakovsky**, Likhachev was arrested and sent to the Solovki prison in 1928, where he spent a couple of years in forced labor on the White Sea canal system. After release, he served as editor for the **Comintern** publishing house and then as a literary editor for the **Academy of Sciences**. By 1937 he had entered the Institute of Foreign Languages in Leningrad, better known as *Pushkinskii Dom* (Pushkin House) and remained in Leningrad during the first part of the **World War II** siege (1941–43). Considered a progressive and liberal, his election as academician was blocked several times, until 1970. Politically active during the period of **détente**, Likhachev welcomed Americans on student exchange, served as their advisor, and helped pry open archives on their behalf, winning the gratitude of many American scholars. Closely associated with Raisa and **Mikhail Gorbachev** and the Gorbachev reforms, he continued to be much admired abroad and in 1995 was elected an honorary member of the American Philosophical Society. He served as an advisor to Gorbachev, Boris Yeltsin, and St. Petersburg Mayor Anatoly Sobchak on cultural and literary preservation until his death. He was also the recipient of the restored Order of St. Andrew awarded by the **Russian Federation**. Likhachev was foremost within the academic community in promoting closer Russian–American relations.

LINCOLN, ABRAHAM (1809–1865). Probably the most written about and discussed president in American history, Lincoln led the

Union through a war to preserve the United States and to abolish slavery in the "slave states." He rose from a modest frontier childhood in Indiana to the Illinois legislature during the intensive battle over slave and free states in the 1850s and achieved national distinction as an opponent of slavery during a series of debates with Stephen Douglas and by narrowly winning the nomination as the Republican candidate for president in 1860. Lincoln guided the Union government through difficult times and provided needed inspiration, such as in the Gettysburg address, delivered soon after one of the most costly battles of the **American Civil War**. Just after the surrender of the Confederacy, the president was assassinated in Ford's Theatre in Washington. He is credited with inspiring leadership through eloquent words as well as brave deeds, in putting together a "team of rivals" who could rise above intercabinet and military disputes, and, though criticized for some command decisions, ultimately could find generals—such as **Ulysses S. Grant** and **William T. Sherman**—who could win crucial battles and campaigns and who would visit Russia in later years.

Lincoln was also fortunate in having a secretary of state, **William H. Seward**, who also rose to the occasion and helped keep Great Britain and France from siding with the Confederacy. Part of that success was due to the Russian Empire, which had common cause with the United States in hostility toward the British and in the abolition of slave/serflike systems. The Russian support for the Union was manifested by the sending of naval squadrons to New York and San Francisco. Lincoln's government and cabinet also had the clear support of the Russian minister, **Eduard Stoekl**. The Russian presence in America certainly helped ward off the intervention of other European powers, but it also reinforced the existing friendship into a virtual alliance. *See also* LESOVSKY, STEPAN.

LIPPMANN, WALTER (1889–1974). Lippmann began a long and distinguished career in journalism and politics as associate editor of the *New Republic* during **World War I**. After the American declaration of war, he joined the government as assistant secretary of war and played a vital role in accumulating information for the **Paris Peace Conference**. Lippmann is credited as being one of the chief architects of the peace and as a chief advisor of **Woodrow Wilson** and of American refugee aid (**Herbert Hoover** and the **American Relief Administration**). Subsequently, he was editor and columnist for the *New York World* (1921–31), *New York Herald Tribune* (1932–62), and *Washington Post* (1962–67). Lippmann was concerned chiefly with international affairs and was a severe critic of policies that ignored rational diplomacy and decision making, such as Russia's exclusion from the peace conference in 1919, American nonrecognition of Russia in the 1920s, and the neglect of exploring avenues of negotiation during the **cold war**.

LISIANSKY, YURY (1773–1837). One of the first Russian officials to visit the United States (1793–96) after its independence, Lisiansky toured Boston, New York, and Philadelphia. At the latter he met with President George Washington (October 1795) and became acquainted with **Benjamin Franklin**. Lisiansky subsequently joined the around-the-world cruise of Ivan Kruzhenshtern, which concentrated on the North Pacific, visiting **Sitka**, **Kodiak**, and the Hawaiian Islands. He published an interesting account of it in *Voyage Around the World in 1803, 1804, 1805 and 1806* (1812).

LISTENING POST. During the period of nonrecognition of the Soviet Union by the United States (1917–33), the need for expert knowledge about the Soviet Union resulted in the establishment of a center in the U.S. legation in Riga, Latvia, to gather materials, interview travelers into and out of the USSR, and process the information for delivery to Washington, D.C. It occupied the top floor of the legation and served as a training center for expertise on that country. Under the general direction of **Robert F. Kelley**, director of the East European Division of the State Department, the listening post was manned by **Felix Cole**, **George F. Kennan**, and others. Even after recognition in 1933, it remained in existence because of the relative freedom of operation that could not be found in Moscow.

LITTLE GOLDEN AMERICA **(1936).** Ilya Ilf and Evgeny Petrov were popular in the Soviet Union in the 1920s and 1930s for their parodies of postrevolutionary Soviet society, especially in *Twelve Chairs*, a satirical commentary on Soviet bureaucracy. They took advantage of the new possibility of access to the United States after diplomatic recognition to tour the country extensively. *Little Golden America* demonstrates their mastery of satire in describing their "Soviet" impressions of an economically developing and culturally diminishing American society. It is well worth reading in the early 21st century.

LITVINENKO, ALEXANDER (1962–2006). A former officer in the Russian **Federal Security Service (FSB)**, Litvinenko received political asylum in Great Britain, where he wrote books critical of the government actions of **Vladimir Putin**. On 1 November 2006 Litvinenko became suddenly ill and died three weeks later as a result of poisoning by polonium-210 and an acute radiation syndrome. The chief suspect, FSB agent Andrei Lugovoy, remained under protection in Russia. Whether the death was ordered by Putin or was accomplished independently by the FSB remains to be known.

LITVINOV, MAXIM (NE WALLACH) (1876–1951). Born in a Jewish ghetto in Belarus (White Russia), Litvinov was a minor revolutionary figure before 1917, serving much of his time in Great Britain, where he remained as a Bolshevik agent during the revolution. There he married an Englishwoman, Ivy Low. Back in Soviet Russia in 1918, he entered the Commissariat of Foreign Affairs as a specialist on European affairs, soon becoming the deputy commissar to **Georgy Chicherin**. By the late 1920s, with Chicherin's health in decline, Litvinov was the effective head of the commissariat and was designated commissar in 1930 upon Chicherin's retirement.

In contrast to his predecessor, Litvinov courted the Western liberal democracies as support against the rising threats from Japan, Italy, and, with the rise to power of Adolf Hitler, Germany. His efforts to stem the rise of fascist militarism through the policy of **collective security** led to formal diplomatic recognition by the United States (1933), for which he visited the United States for direct negotiations with President **Franklin D. Roosevelt**, as well as Soviet membership in the **League of Nations** (1934), an alliance with France (1935), and Soviet support of the liberal side in the **Spanish Civil War** (1936). Litvinov's success, however, was limited by the setback of the Anglo-French appeasement of Germany by signing the **Munich Pact** (September 1938), which led to his dismissal in April 1939, as **Stalin** turned toward a rapprochement with Nazi Germany

(**Nazi–Soviet Pact**). After the German invasion in 1941, and in the interests of forming an alliance and enlarging the **lend-lease** program, Litvinov was appointed ambassador to the United States in late 1941. Traveling across Siberia and the Pacific to his new assignment, Litvinov visited Pearl Harbor on 6 December, arriving in Washington the next day to learn of the Japanese attack and conferring with Roosevelt at length on the drastically changing situation on 8 December. As a friendly emissary, Litvinov helped consolidate the wartime alliance.

LOMONOSOV, GEORGI (YURY) (1876–c. 1937). As a professor of economics and engineering, Lomonosov was assigned to head a mission to the United States by the Provisional Government in 1917 to obtain American aid for the deteriorating state of the country's transportation system. The effort came too late in respect to saving Russia from the Bolsheviks. Lomonosov, much to the regret of Ambassador **Boris Bakhmeteff**, sided with the new Soviet administration, resulting in the cancellation of his status in the United States and his return to Soviet Russia, where he served in various economic capacities, especially under **Leonid Krasin**, in the purchase of locomotives from the West in the 1920s.

LOMONOSOV, MIKHAIL (1711–1765). Russian scientist, poet, geographer, historian, and editor. One of the first genuinely Russian intellectuals and distinguished academicians of the Russian Academy of Sciences, founded by Peter the Great, who he honored with one of his poems. As a Renaissance man, Lomonosov has often been compared with an American contemporary, **Benjamin Franklin** (1706–90), with whom he communicated indirectly toward the end of his life. Had he not died prematurely, a more active contact with Franklin and other Americans would probably have taken place. Lomonosov had inspired a program of voyages of discovery into the Pacific and Arctic oceans. One of Russia's leading centers of higher education, Moscow State University (MGU), is quite appropriately named in his honor.

LONDON, JACK (1876–1916). A native of San Francisco and largely self-educated, London, in his early work as a newspaper reporter, covered the **Russo–Japanese War** (1904–05). A true son of the West,

London ran for mayor of Oakland in 1905 on the Socialist ticket. London's themes of sea voyages, downtrodden workers, and animal adventure (dogs, wolves, and seals) appealed especially to Russians in the early 20th century. His best-known novel, *The Call of the Wild* (1903), was published in a number of Russian editions. London's popularity in Russia probably exceeded that of **Mark Twain** but still fell behind that of **James Fenimore Cooper** among American writers. Because he was an active socialist, was from an impoverished background, and died by his own hand, in the Soviet era he was proclaimed a leading author of realism and capitalist oppression and a hero of "socialist art," although he (or his heirs) earned millions from the sustained popularity of his works.

LONG, BRECKINRIDGE (1881–1950). In his role in the State Department as third assistant secretary of state (1916–19), Long was in charge of affairs relating to Russia, which he clearly supported through the **February Revolution** but was limited by other priorities of the **Woodrow Wilson** administration. His busy schedule included the reception of the ambassadorial delegation of **Boris Bakhmeteff** in 1917 and dealing with the diplomatic implications of military intervention in Russia during the **Russian Civil War**. A sense one receives from examining Long's extensive papers in the Library of Congress is that Russia and its revolution often "fell between the cracks" because of a greatly overburdened and exhausted State Department. Excluded from a political role during subsequent Republican administrations, Long returned to the diplomatic scene as **Franklin D. Roosevelt**'s ambassador to Italy in 1933 and then held responsible posts in the Roosevelt administration during **World War II**.

LONG TELEGRAM (1946). Document signaling the beginning of the **cold war**. As chargé d'affaires at the American embassy in Moscow, **George F. Kennan**, reacting to his perception of a threat from the Soviet regime that had not yet been recognized in Washington, sent a communiqué that described a new menace to world peace. Supported by a more detailed revelation in *Foreign Affairs Quarterly* (the "X article"), the Kennan reports became the foundation of the U.S. policy of **containment** that heralded aggressive American responses: the **Truman Doctrine**, the **Marshall Plan**, and the formation of the

North Atlantic Treaty Organization. Later Kennan would decry the military aspects of this response, which he claimed had only political goals.

LOVESTONE, JAY (NE JACOB LIEBSTEIN) (1897–1990). Born in Russian Lithuania, Lovestone immigrated in 1907 with his parents to the United States, settling in the Lower East Side of New York City. While a student at City College he became a radical socialist and a leader of the **Communist Party of the United States (CPUSA)**, becoming its national secretary in 1927. Unfortunately for him, the party was beset with divisions over its own internal agenda and the shifts from **Leon Trotsky** and Nikolai Bukharin to **Joseph Stalin**. Pressed by a Stalinist faction headed by **William Z. Foster**, Lovestone appealed personally at a **Comintern** congress in Moscow in 1929 but suffered a setback with the demotion of Bukharin. Forced to resign his position in the CPUSA, essentially a victim of the purges, Lovestone nonetheless remained active in the American labor movement for many years.

LUNACHARSKY, ANATOLY (1875–1933). As one of the most Western of the Bolshevik leadership, Lunacharsky added a note of flexibility to the period of the **New Economic Policy (NEP)**. As "head" of cultural relations (commissar of enlightenment), he supported cultural contacts with the West under the auspices of the **All Russian Society for Cultural Relations with Foreign Countries (VOKS)** and **Olga Kameneva**, the tour of the **Moscow Art Theater** to the United States, and other direct exchanges that kept the Soviet Union abreast of an extremely vital and productive cultural period—the **Jazz** Age—and was responsible for the sending of jazz musician Joseph Teplitsky to study in the United States in the 1920s.

LYONS, EUGENE (1898–1985). Along with **Walter Duranty, Maurice Hindus**, and **William Henry Chamberlin,** Lyons was a leading member of the American Moscow press corps during the 1920s and 1930s. As a reporter for the United Press (UP), beginning in 1928, his dispatches were widely printed throughout the United States and focused in particular upon the great offensive of industrialization and collectivization during the **First Five-Year Plan**. He, as did some other correspondents, scored a coup with a 1930 extensive interview with **Josef Stalin**, which focused on the general secretary's family life. Lyons and his wife, Billy, similar to other correspondent families, faced the problem of finding accommodations, not easy in overcrowded Moscow. First located in a revamped stable, which also served as the UP headquarters, the Lyons moved into the often vacant and grandiose apartment of **Armand Hammer**. Thanks to Lyons, the UP had greater direct access to individuals for another 40 years. Lyons retired from United Press soon after leaving Russia in 1934 to concentrate on writing of his experiences (*Assignment in Utopia*), editing *American Mercury*, and lecturing.

– M –

MACGAHAN, BARBARA (NEE VARVARA ELAGINA) (1850–1904). As the widow of **Januarius MacGahan**, MacGahan and her infant son Paul settled around 1880 in New York City, where she became one of the most widely read correspondents on the United States for the Russian press in the 1880s and 1890s. MacGahan set a high standard for journalism. Most significant were her "25 letters" describing the **Columbian Exposition** in Chicago in 1893 in a major Russian journal, *Severnyi vestnik* (*Northern Herald*). MacGahan also wrote extensively on Russia for American newspapers and journals. She was also a stalwart of the Russian community in New York and a promoter and backer of the building of the St. Nicholas Orthodox cathedral in the city in the 1890s.

MACGAHAN, JANUARIUS (1844–1878). From a small Ohio town, MacGahan is credited as being the first American professional war correspondent. As a disciple of British journalist William Howard Russell (who covered the **Crimean War** and **American Civil War** for *The Times* of London), MacGahan first reported on the Franco-Prussian War (1870–71) and siege of Paris for the *New York Herald*. During convalescence from a fall from a horse in Odessa, he met Varvara Elagina, who soon became his wife. He then traveled with **Eugene Schuyler** through Central Asia and fully established his reputation for unbiased reporting in a series of articles, later collected into a book, *Campaigning on the Oxus and the Fall of Khiva* (1874). MacGahan remained to cover the Turkish suppression of the Bulgarian revolt of 1875 in *The Turkish Atrocities in Bulgaria* (1876), which did much to turn Western opinion in favor of Russia in the Russo–Turkish War (1877–78) that followed. Unfortunately, he succumbed at age 33 to typhus, contracted while covering that war. His remains were brought back to the United States in 1884 and interred in his hometown with much publicity. He is also celebrated as a Bulgarian national hero with a prominent statue in Sofia. *See also* MACGAHAN, BARBARA.

MACHTET, GRIGORI (1852–1901). Born in Lutsk in West Ukraine of schoolteacher parents, Machtet imbibed the ideas of Russian populism, especially those of Alexander Herzen and Nicholas Chernyshevsky, in high school and at the University of Kiev. By 1870 he was part of a small circle in Kiev that especially admired the United States, called themselves "Amerikantsy" (Americans), and saved money to go there. Arriving in New York in 1872, they headed west, reaching St. Joseph, Missouri, by midsummer. Out of money, they were befriended by a recent Russian immigrant, Ivan Moshisky, in Donophan County, Kansas. Moshisky owned a tree nursery. Machtet proceeded to record their adventures on the American prairie in planting trees with character sketches, complete with humor and the oddities of colloquialisms. Machtet then joined the Russian commune (**Cedar Vale**) of **William Frey** before returning to Russia to settle in St. Petersburg, where he was arrested in 1875 in a roundup of "narodniks" following the "to-the-people movement," but not before he had published several journal articles describing his adventures in the United States. These were collected in a separate volume and reprinted in his 12-volume collected works after his death. Machtet was well regarded by other Russian writers, such as Anton Chekhov, who attended his funeral. His vivid descriptions of frontier America and of the Frey commune were quite popular in Russia as portrayals of a "real" America.

MACMURRAY, JOHN VAN ANTWERP (1881–1960). MacMurray graduated from Princeton University in 1902 and received a law degree from Columbia University before entering the foreign service, where he became an expert on the Far East, but he also served as American vice consul in St. Petersburg (1908–11). Most of his subsequent assignments were in the Far East, where he served as ambassador to China (1925–29) before taking leave to direct the Walter Hines Page School of International Relations at Johns Hopkins University (1930–33). MacMurray was once again summoned to duty in Eastern Europe in 1933 as minister to the Baltic states, where he had a close relationship with the new U.S. embassy in Moscow. Under his supervision was the **listening post**, which, contrary to expectation, was not removed to Moscow but remained in full operation in Riga in the 1930s. MacMurray completed his career as ambassador to Turkey (1936–44). He continued to be interested in Russia and, in fact, had been seriously considered for the Moscow post in 1933, but it went to the more politically active **William Bullitt**. His papers in the Seeley Mudd Library at Princeton are an important source on Russian–American relations.

MAISKY, IVAN (NE LIAKHOVETSKY) (1884–1975). From Novgorod province, Maisky entered the University of St. Petersburg but was expelled in 1902 and sent into Siberian exile. He managed to escape abroad in 1908 and resume his studies in Munich. Later, as a long-term Soviet ambassador to Great Britain, he fully supported **Maxim Litvinov**'s **collective security** policy. Remaining in his post during the years of the **Nazi–Soviet Pact**, he was strategically important in helping to construct the Grand Alliance. Recalled to Moscow in 1943, he served as assistant commissar of foreign relations and as **Vyacheslav Molotov**'s chief advisor on relations with the Western Allies. He was one of the most important of the Soviet delegates at the **Yalta** and **Potsdam Conferences**, but his efforts to construct a friendly postwar division of power were doomed to failure. In 1953 Maisky was arrested and sent to prison as a British spy, although he was soon released at the beginning of the policy of **peaceful coexistence** in 1955, a lucky survivor.

MALKOV, VICTOR (1930–). A native Muscovite and a major scholar of America of the 20th century in the **Russian Academy of Sciences**, especially on the administration of **Franklin D. Roosevelt**,

Malkov's works include studies of the workers' movement in the United States, the New Deal, and the Manhattan Project. As a frequent contributor to journals and academic conferences and a friend and collaborator with American Russianists, Malkov demonstrated an open reception to **glasnost** and the new opportunities for scholarship with the end of the **cold war**.

MANCHURIA. The region was separated from Russia by the Amur River border for most of its history, but this did not prevent Russian interest and penetration into the area, especially in the late 19th century with the building of the **Trans-Siberian Railroad**. The original plan for the railroad was to follow a long and difficult route from Irkutsk along the north side of the Amur and then along the Ussuri to **Vladivostok**, but by looking at a map anyone could see that a much easier and shorter route could be made across central Manchuria. Thus by arrangement with the Chinese government, the Russian **Chinese Eastern Railway (CER)** was built from Chita through **Harbin** (which became an important Russian administrative center) to Vladivostok with a subsequent extension to the Liaotang peninsula and a seaport (Port Arthur). This major Russian economic expansion and presence in the area, as well as the lease of Port Arthur from China in 1898, naturally annoyed the Japanese expansionists and set the stage for the **Russo–Japanese War**. In fact, the obvious Japanese designs on Manchuria led to mediation by **Theodore Roosevelt** to limit Japanese expansion.

As an important route into Russia during **World War I**, the Trans-Siberian and its region again attracted both American and Japanese attention for control and repair of the route and to stabilize the region. This led to their military forces intervening in Vladivostok and the surrounding area, which included Manchuria. In fact, by 1918, a major reason for the dispatch of more than 12,000 Americans was to contain and restrict the Japanese army of around 70,000, most of them deployed in Manchuria. The Russian Railway Service Corps was also important in maintaining control of the route through Harbin and controlling telegraphic communications during a complicated contest for power among various Russian factions. The result was the resumption of jurisdiction of the railroad under the **Far Eastern Republic** and then the **Soviet Union**. Harbin became a major Russian refugee center, as well as a Soviet strategic foothold in China.

Beginning in 1931 Manchuria again became a zone of conflict between Soviet interests and a revived and more militant Japan, which demonstrated its military dominance in occupying the territory and renaming it "Manchukuo." To reduce tensions the Soviet government ceded the CER to Japan. Meanwhile the "Eastern crisis" was a major factor in bringing the United States and the Soviet Union into diplomatic recognition, while the border areas became a pre–**World War II** battleground between the USSR and Japan. The **Nazi–Soviet Pact** of 1939, however, led to a neutrality pact between the two countries that, surprisingly, held until near the end of the war (August 1945), which was vital to maintaining the Pacific **lend-lease** supply route. At that time, by an arrangement made at the **Yalta Conference**, the Soviet Union entered the war and occupied Manchuria as well as the northern half of Korea. As the Red Army withdrew, by agreement with China, it turned over much military equipment to the Chinese Communist forces under Mao Tse Tung that were important for his success in the ensuing civil war. *See also* KOREAN WAR.

MARSHALL, GEORGE C. (1880–1959). Marshall was chief of general staff during **World War II**, though somewhat overshadowed by European Theater commander **Dwight D. Eisenhower**. He was accused by Senator Joseph McCarthy of being overly sympathetic to the Soviet Union, supporting **lend-lease** during the war, though this was hardly the case. He is credited as secretary of state (1947–49) in the administration of **Harry S. Truman** for his establishment of the **Marshall Plan** to rebuild Western Europe and endorsing the policy of **containment** of the aggressive actions and threat of the USSR to postwar Europe.

MARSHALL PLAN (1948). Facing an apparent threat of Soviet domination of Western Europe as well as its military occupation of most of Eastern Europe, including the eastern zone of Germany, the United States reacted with large appropriations of funds for the stabilization of the political and economic foundations of Western Europe, especially Great Britain, West Germany, France, and Italy. The program, an outcome of **George F. Kennan**'s **containment** strategy, was amazingly successful in stopping Soviet penetration and led to the "German miracle" of industrial advance. The American initiative had the advantage of the support of respected European leaders, such as Winston Churchill, Konrad Adenaur, and Charles DeGaulle, and the foundation of economic advance in such enterprises as Krupp and Volkswagen in Germany. The Soviet Union, on the other hand, lacked the economic resources to effectively compete, and that resulted in such badly conceived responses as the **Berlin Blockade** (1948–49). The Soviet Union could maintain control of its side of the **iron curtain** only by military and authoritarian Communist controls, thus setting the stage for popular resentments such as East German riots (1953) and the **Hungarian Revolution** (1956). *See also* LONG TELEGRAM.

MARTENS, LUDWIG (1874–1948). Active in the early Russian revolutionary movement, Martens studied economics in Germany in the early 20th century and then immigrated to Great Britain and to the United States in 1916. His credentials as the Soviet official representative to the United States were presented in March 1919 to Secretary of State **Robert Lansing** but were refused on the grounds that a Russian ambassador, **Boris Bakhmeteff**, was still recognized. Nevertheless, owing to his old-style gentlemanly conduct, Martens was able to initiate a trade bureau in Washington and maintain a Soviet presence until he was finally expelled in 1921. If the United States had decided to recognize the Soviet government at that time, a close issue, Martens would no doubt have been the first Soviet ambassador. He returned to Moscow to serve in various economic posts, such as in the Supreme Council of the National Economy (1926–36), and as chief editor of the *Technical Encyclopedia* (1937–41). Martens managed to avoid the purges, retiring on pension in 1941, when many others of his vintage and background were being shot.

MASSIVE RETALIATION DOCTRINE. As outlined by Secretary of State **John Foster Dulles** before the **Council on Foreign Relations** in January 1954, the policy was essentially to maintain military superiority over the Communist world, no matter what the cost, the object being to deter Soviet aggression with military might. Though criticized by **George F. Kennan** as a distortion of his **containment** program and even by President **Dwight D. Eisenhower** as leading to the development of an uncontrolled "military-industrial complex," the doctrine, stemming from **cold war** hysteria, magnified the arms race and required enormous costs and waste to the detriment of social and environmental concerns. It also heightened the possibility of accidents by the employment of missile bases circling the Soviet Union as well as high-altitude overflight surveillance that would lead to the **U-2 incident**.

MATLOCK, JACK, JR. (1929–). After distinguished service in a number of diplomatic assignments, including ambassador to Czechoslovakia, Matlock was designated by the administration of **Ronald Reagan** as its envoy to Moscow. Matlock served as ambassador during a critical time of the **Mikhail Gorbachev** era that included the unclear fate of reforms and the weathering of the **August Coup** of 1991. Matlock recorded his experiences graphically in *Autopsy on an Empire* (2001) and *Reagan and Gorbachev: How the Cold War Ended* (2004). He became an active member of the "conference of ambassadors" in an attempt to moderate Russian–American relations in the 21st century. His wife, Rebecca, contributed a historical portrait of their residence in Moscow in Russian: *"Spaso-Khaus": Liudi i vstrechi: zapiski zheny amerikanskogo posla* (*Spaso House: People and Meeting: Notes of the Wife of the American Ambassador*) (2004).

MAYAK **(LIGHTHOUSE) (1900–1920).** As part of a growing international mission and presence of the **Young Men's Christian Association (YMCA)** in the early 20th century, its Russian development was most remarkable. Under the direction of Gaylord Franklin, the center in the central part of the city won many Russian adherents to its educational and athletic programs in the period before and during **World War I** (1900–18). A number of Americans, such as **Sherwood Eddy**, were involved with it, especially in translation and publication of educational literature. They also added substantially to the American presence in the city. During the war, as elsewhere, the *Mayak* and its American YMCA supporting staff were active in support roles behind the front and in general were well received by both official and nonofficial Russia. Even the Bolsheviks after the **October Revolution** were tolerant of its nonpolitical and ecumenical service—but only temporarily. Some of its programs, however, were adopted by the Communist Party–sponsored Young Pioneers and Komsomol.

MAYAKOVSKY, VLADIMIR (1893–1930). Russian poet Mayakovsky committed early, by 1915, to the **Bolshevik** revolutionary cause. During the **Bolshevik Revolution**, he promoted it in art propaganda and subsequently became one of the most prolific geniuses of the Bolshevik regime in the arts, associated with a number of others such as **Sergei Esenin** and **Vsevolod Meyerhold** and his Theatre of the Revolution. Attracted to the American material success and literary creativity of the period (**Theodore Dreiser, Sinclair Lewis,** Ernest Hemingway, and Upton Sinclair), he came to the United States in the summer of 1925 through Mexico, attracting considerable attention with his poetry readings and new interpretations of America in such poems as "Brooklyn Bridge," which symbolized Soviet praise for the idea of construction over art, that is, *amerikanizm*. By the late 1920s he had achieved stature not only as the Soviet "poet laureate" but also as the creator of futuristic plays, such as *Bath House* and *Bedbug*, during the period of the **New Economic Policy**. Interested in contemporary literary developments in the United States, Mayakovsky welcomed American writers such as Dreiser and Lewis to Soviet Russia. Discouraged by Soviet restrictions on literature in the early years of **Joseph Stalin**'s reign and by a failed love affair, Mayakovsky committed suicide by losing a game of Russian roulette in April 1930. His work would be revived in the 1950s to influence a generation of both Soviet writers and Americans such as Allen Ginsburg ("Howl").

MCCARTHYISM (1950–1955). A radical conservative movement led by Senator Joseph McCarthy (1908–57) of Wisconsin. Elected to the Senate in 1946, McCarthy really did not emerge as a force until the Republican Party won a majority in Congress in 1951 and he gained a crucial committee chairmanship. From this position he led a vicious attack on Communist infiltration of government agencies, especially the Department of State. The following "witch hunt" resembled a Soviet-style purge of anyone who ever had anything to do with a leftist organization or with the Soviet Union; it included some genuine spies and Communist supporters but also many completely innocent and loyal citizens. Fortunately, McCarthy and his crusade had little effect on the main course of the **Dwight D. Eisenhower** administration, such as that of Secretary of State **John Foster Dulles**. McCarthy's exaggerations and extremism were soon discredited and earned him a public censure by the Senate. It nevertheless gave a tone of fear and incrimination, enhanced the rhetoric of the **cold war**, left a legacy in the John Birch Society, and promoted the career of congressman **Richard Nixon**.

MCCLOY, JOHN JAY (1895–1989). Lawyer, banker, political official, and advisor. A graduate of Amherst (1919) and Harvard Law School (1921), McCloy became a rare American familiar with Europe in the 1930s by serving as legal counselor to the German chemical company I. G. Farben and was sympathetic to the goals of Hitler's Germany, at least until 1939. Appointed assistant secretary of war by **Franklin D. Roosevelt** during **World War II**, McCloy was largely responsible for setting military priorities that included the **lend-lease** program to the Soviet Union. His views were somewhat controversial, for example, for opposing both the bombing of Nazi extermination camps in 1944 and the atomic bombing of Japan in 1945. McCloy also served after the war as president of the World Bank (1947–49) and military governor of the U.S. zone of occupation in Germany (1949–52). He headed Chase Manhattan Bank from 1953 to 1960, while retaining his interest in the international scene as chairman of the **Ford Foundation** (1958–65) and of the **Council on Foreign Relations** (1954–70). He served as advisor to presidents from **John F. Kennedy** to **Ronald Reagan**.

MCCORMICK, CYRUS HALL, JR. (1859–1936). Son of the inventor of the reaper-binder grain cutter and graduate of Princeton (1879), McCormick succeeded his father as president of McCormick Harvesting Machine Company of Chicago (1884–1902) and of **International Harvester** (1902–19). Under McCormick's leadership, the leading American manufacturer of agricultural implements established a factory near Moscow (1909) and soon obtained a virtual monopoly of the production and sale of the more sophisticated agricultural machines in Russia, many of them initially of American origin. As a leading American industrialist with long-standing interests in Russia, McCormick joined the **Root Commission** to Russia in 1917 that supported the **Provisional Government**. The company's losses mounted, however, and the Harvester enterprises (factory and sales offices) in Russia were formally and reluctantly nationalized, only in

1924, by the Soviet government, though under McCormick's successors, such as **Alexander Legge**, the company would again contribute to modern progress under the **First Five-Year Plan** in supervising the construction of tractor factories in Kharkov and Stalingrad during the plan.

MCCULLY, ADMIRAL NEWTON (1867–1951). With considerable experience as an observer in the **Russo–Japanese War** (1904–05), McCully served subsequently as American naval attaché in Petrograd (1914–18) and special liaison officer with White forces in the Black Sea area (1918–20). A graduate of the U.S. Naval Academy (1887), McCully was fluent in Russian, important for his contacts with anti-Bolshevik political and military authorities during **World War I**, the **Bolshevik Revolution**, and the **Russian Civil War** (1914–20). In 1919–20 he made several trips into civil war zones in the south of Russia, under the direction of **Admiral Mark Bristol**, and assisted in the evacuation of thousands of refugees after the collapse of the anti-Bolshevik forces. His communications (in the **Library of Congress**) with Bristol are an important source of information on that area. McCully, a bachelor, adopted seven Russian orphans and brought them back to the United States in 1921.

MCKAY, CLAUDE (NE FESTUS CLAUDIUS) (1890–1948). Born and raised in Jamaica in a farming family, McKay came to the United States in 1912 to study agriculture at Tuskegee Institute in Alabama under George Washington Carver; he then transferred to Kansas State Agricultural College in Manhattan, where he was influenced toward radical perspectives by reading W. E. B. Dubois's *The Souls of Black Folk*. During **World War I**, he worked as a dining car waiter on the Pennsylvania Railroad, while growing more militant and radical. With the assistance of an English Jamaican, Walter Jekyll, he moved to New York, where he established a restaurant and contributed poetry to journals that included the *Liberator*. He was part of the generation of writers of the "Harlem Renaissance" that included **Langston Hughes**.

Having won the friendship of **Max Eastman**, while contributing to the *Liberator*, McKay became fascinated with the new Soviet Russia. He traveled by freighter to Petrograd (Leningrad) in late 1922, creating something of a sensation on the streets of the city and at the Fourth Congress of the **Comintern** in Moscow early the next year, where McKay was received as "a black icon in the flesh," much to the annoyance of the official American delegation. Asked to speak by Comintern leaders who did not realize that he was not a Communist, McKay wowed the audience with his animated address and presence. This speech inspired the Comintern to designate a special committee on "the Negro Question," and, for it, McKay wrote *Negroes in America* (1923). He soon perceived the shallowness of the international organization's concern, after six months in Soviet Russia, and became disenchanted with the possibility of a Communist answer for racial discrimination. His experience helps explain why Communism found few adherents among **African Americans**. McKay would continue to beat the drums against discrimination in America as a writer and poet, converting, to the surprise of friends, to Catholicism. McKay stands in a tradition of African American radicals who eschewed Communism and the moderate National Association for the Advancement of Colored People and instead followed a tradition of black militancy that would contribute to the rise of Malcolm X.

MEDVEDEV, DMITRI (1965–). A young Russian politician and businessman, Medvedev was named chairman of the council of ministers (Russian prime minister) in November 2007. A surprise appointment by **Vladimir Putin** to the second-highest office in Russia, Medvedev was immediately considered to be the heir to the presidency in the election of March 2008 (since the president is limited to two terms by the constitution), which he won easily. From a professional family of St. Petersburg, Medvedev has been a loyal assistant to Putin there and later in Moscow, though he lacks the **Committee on State Security (KGB)** background of other Putin associates. In addition to his high appointment, readily approved by the Duma's **United Russia** dominance, Medvedev was also chairman of Gazprom, the state natural gas monopoly and largest corporation in the **Russian Federation**. As a close collaborator and with a similar background to that of his patron (law degree from Leningrad State University), Medvedev, after his inauguration as president in May, designated Putin as "prime minister" with enlarged powers, thus maintaining the (economically) successful course of his leadership of the country.

MEDVEDEV, ROY (1925–). A twin son (with Zhores) of a Soviet Marxist scholar, who named them after prominent world Communist leaders, Medvedev graduated from Leningrad State University but became a leading dissident in the 1960s during the regime of **Leonid Brezhnev**. A leader of party reform, he was expelled from the Communist party after the publication of *Let History Judge* (1969), a masterly attack on the oppression of the Stalin era. As a dissident colleague of **Andrei Sakharov** and with similar views, Medvedev was an important source of information about the "closed" world of the Soviet Union and provided insight into that world in conversations with Western (especially American) correspondents. Zhores, a biologist, was also persecuted for speaking out in defense of Western genetics and sought asylum in Great Britain. Though hounded by the police and virtually under house arrest in Moscow, Roy Medvedev was allowed to remain free and in contact with foreign visitors, especially Americans.

MELNIKOV, PAVEL (1804–1880). As a Russian army engineer and railroad expert, Melnikov led a mission to the United States (1839–40) that resulted in Russian government contracts with **George Washington Whistler** and the Baltimore company of **Harrison, Eastwick and Winans** to provide technical and industrial expertise for the construction of the first long-distance railroad from St. Petersburg to Moscow in the 1840s. He spent several months inspecting factories and railroads in the United States and filed very positive reports, which influenced the Russian decision in favor of Americans over Europeans for the project. This heralded the beginning of *amerikanizm*, especially for the reason that Russian officials considered the American geographical situation similar to their own. Melnikov subsequently served as Whistler's guide and assistant and later, in the 1860s, became minister of ways and communications in the Russian government.

MENDELEEV, DMITRI (1834–1907). Mendeleev is best known for his formulation of the Periodic Tables (1868), his long tenure at the University of St. Petersburg (1868–90), and his two-volume *Principles of Chemistry* (1868–71), which became a basic text book in the field for generations of students at colleges and universities around the world, especially in the United States. In 1876, he visited the United States for the centennial celebration in Philadelphia and toured the oil fields of western Pennsylvania to gather information on the drilling for oil, but especially for details on the transport and refining of the product, which were subsequently employed in the Baku oil fields of Russia. His memoirs contain interesting reflections on his encounters in America.

MENNONITES FROM RUSSIA/UKRAINE. Industrious, Anabaptist, and passivist agricultural people, most originating in West Friesland (Northern Netherlands) and Switzerland in the 17th century as followers of Reformation leader Menno Simons. They came to Russia from the Danzig area of Prussia, where they were under obligation for military service (or payment to exempt them from that service) under Frederick the Great. They also came from Switzerland and the Rhineland, beginning in the 1780s, at the invitation of **Catherine the Great**, a policy she had initiated in the 1760s for Catholic and Lutheran Germans who settled in the Volga region. Her plan was to make vacant agricultural land in South Russia (now Ukraine) productive by promising free land and exemption from military conscription for these Dutch- and Swiss-speaking settlers. The main Mennonite settlement areas were Khortitsa in the rapids region of the Dniepr River south of Kiev and the large **Molochna Mennonite colony** in "New Russia," about 50 miles north of the Sea of Azov. Thanks to excellent leadership, hard work, and relative autonomy, the colonies thrived—at least in relation to Russian and Ukrainian neighbors—well into the 19th century.

By 1870, however, they felt threatened by the liberal reforms of **Alexander II** that included removal of the exemption from military service. In consideration of this, the Russian government allowed them to emigrate and eventually inaugurated a progressive policy of alternative service in the forests. Many, however, had already considered foreign migration, especially to America, where cheap railroad land in the central plains was available, thanks to the congressional land grants of 1862. A substantial number of Mennonites from the Molochna colony, especially from the central village of Alexanderwohl and from daughter villages in Crimea, decided to leave in 1873 and 1874, and most settled in Kansas, where descendants remain. Others of the initial immigration would go to Nebraska, Minnesota, Oklahoma, and Manitoba, Canada, to be followed in later years by many kinfolk.

Mennonites, like the Jews from Eastern Europe, would represent an important economic and social contribution to American development and are usually referred to as "Rooshians" though they were ethnically Swiss or Friesian. Those in the central plains would emphasize grain culture and milling, especially a variety of hard winter wheat, "Turkey Red," which was brought from Crimea to be the main crop of the Great Plains; it produced a superior flour that supported an important industry in the region and that became a major American export to Europe from the 1880s to the 1920s and, ironically, to the Soviet Union in the 1960s.

MEYER, GEORGE VON LENGERKE (1858–1918). A graduate of Harvard University (1879), classmate of **Theodore Roosevelt**, and successful businessman, Meyer rose in the political ranks in Massachusetts at the turn of the century. He then served as ambassador to Italy (1900–05) and to Russia (1905–07) and as secretary of navy in the administration of **William Howard Taft** (1909–13). Roosevelt, in his role as peace arbiter of the **Russo–Japanese War**, transferred Meyer from Rome to St. Petersburg in the summer of 1905 to serve as his personal emissary and advisor to **Nicholas II** in regard to the peace negotiations to end the conflict. In St. Petersburg Meyer won Russian acceptance of a peace conference to be conducted in the United States. The results achieved at the Portsmouth Naval Yard (in Kittery, Maine) negotiations in August–September 1905 successfully ended the war. Some might claim that Meyer deserved the Nobel Peace Prize that Roosevelt received for his role in the settlement, but it was the president who placed him in his strategic position in St. Petersburg and superintended his activities. *See also* PORTSMOUTH PEACE CONFERENCE AND TREATY; ROOSEVELT, THEODORE.

MEYERHOLD, VSEVOLOD (1874–1940). Revolutionary drama director and founder of the "Theater of the Revolution," Meyerhold collaborated with **Konstantin Stanislavsky**, **Anatoly Lunacharsky**, **Valentin Parnakh**, and **Vladimir Mayakovsky** in producing some of the best and most creative work after the **Bolshevik Revolution**.

He was known as a "constructionist" in art but also for incorporating new Western styles, such as **jazz** with onstage orchestras, thus becoming an exponent of *amerikanizm* in the cultural arena. Meyerhold and his work subsequently succumbed to the regimentation of socialist realism of the 1930s; he suffered arrest and imprisonment that led to his death in a prison camp.

MIDDLETON, HENRY (1770–1846). American minister to Russia (1820–30). From a prominent South Carolina planter family (near Charleston), Middleton received much of his education abroad and was, therefore, well prepared for a diplomatic assignment. His mission to Russia was notable for its unusual length, the establishment with his family of a notable presence in Russian imperial society that rivaled the major European states, and encompassing major American developments. U.S. western expansion and the **Monroe Doctrine** (1823) contributed to the friendly Russian–American relations of the period. Middleton was symbolic of Southern democratic predominance in American foreign affairs in the first half of the 19th century. Though the main Middleton plantation house, near Charleston, was destroyed during the **Civil War**, the gardens and outbuildings remain as a major tourist attraction, including mementos of this Southern gentleman's involvement with Russia.

MILIUKOV, PAUL (NE PAVEL NIKOLAEVICH) (1859–1943). As head of the Constitutional Democratic Party and its leader in the Duma in 1917, Miliukov became foreign minister in the **Provisional Government**. Miliukov was a long proponent of parliamentary democracy and a respected historian (University of St. Petersburg) and lecturer on Russian history at the University of Chicago (1903). He became the leader of the liberal alternative to the radical socialist revolutionary and social democratic options during and after the **Revolution of 1905** and a proponent of the American constitutional model. He emerged as a leader of the Constitutional Democrats (or Kadets — after the Russian initials) and a leader of the "Progressive bloc" in the Duma (Russian lower house of the legislature after 1905). In 1917 he was not only foreign minister, but also effective head of the government.

As a long time friend of **Charles R. Crane**, Miliukov represented "America's hope for Russia." Crane helped launch the **Root Commission** to welcome and support Miliukov's new democratic government, but by the time it arrived in Petrograd (St. Petersburg) after several unfortunate delays, Miliukov was no longer part of it. As the revolution veered from **Alexander Kerensky** to **Vladimir Lenin**, Miliukov remained in the wings as a viable alternative, but this was essentially cancelled by Bolshevik success in the **Russian Civil War**. He would spend many years in frustration and exile as one of several leaders of **Russia Abroad**.

MISSILE GAP (1957–c. 1965). A successor to the "bomber gap" that gave the United States a clear advantage in delivery of an arsenal of aerial weapons, a perception developed in the United States after **Sputnik** (1957) that the USSR had developed a superior delivery of ICBM deployment, despite contradictory evidence from **U-2** surveillance, that gave it a clear advantage in first-strike capability. The false claims of Soviet superiority in missiles by U.S. intelligence agencies was used by both the administrations of **Dwight D. Eisenhower** and **John F. Kennedy** to escalate the arms race and mitigate responses to the **peaceful coexistence** initiatives of **Nikita Khrushchev**.

MISSILE SHIELD. As a part of the National Missile Defense program, the missile shield was proposed by the United States in 2004 to be deployed in Ukraine and Poland to counter, in forward positions, the new capabilities of hostile Middle Eastern countries in nuclear arms and missiles, especially those of Iran. The program has been strongly opposed by the **Russian Federation** for the possibility that such missiles could also be used against it for an invasion of its former domain, and for the reason that such missiles would most likely traverse Russian territory and possibly be negated by Russian interception. It became a matter of serious dispute between **Vladimir Putin** and **George W. Bush** in their last meetings.

MITROKHIN ARCHIVE. Vasily Mitrokhin (1922–2004), an archivist for the **KGB**, kept notes of the materials he handled over a 30-year period and made them public in 1992, when he left Russia for Great

Britain. Analyzed and published by Christopher Andrew, they documented the extensive infiltration of Western political parties, especially in France and Germany, wiretapping of major world leaders such as **Henry Kissinger**, successful spying on major U.S. defense contractors, disinformation efforts regarding assassinations and **Central Intelligence Agency** operations, and wide-scale plans for major sabotage of communications systems in the United States, as well as actual and planned KGB assassinations in Russia and abroad. He collaborated with Andrew in the revealing *The Mitrokhin Archive and the Secret History of the KGB* (1999) and *The World Was Going Our Way: The KGB and the Battle for the Third World* (2005).

MOLOCHNA MENNONITE COLONY (1783–1943). In order to develop new territories acquired in the First Turkish War (1768–74) and the subsequent annexation of Crimea (1783), including much of the region to the north of the peninsula, labeled "New Russia," **Catherine the Great** invited settlers of Germanic background to settle in these areas. Passivist Mennonites from the region around Danzig (Gdansk), who were being pressed for conscription in the Prussian army by Frederick the Great, accepted her offer. The Molochna colony was one of the most successful foreign settlement areas in Russia in terms of agriculture and milling progress. Despite considerable emigration, it remained a successful colony through the hardships of war, revolution, civil war, and collectivization, until its abandonment with the German evacuation of the area in 1943. *See also* MENNONITES FROM RUSSIA/UKRAINE; WARKENTIN, BERNHARD.

MOLOTOV, VYACHESLAV (NE SCRIABIN) (1890–1986). An "old Bolshevik" (since 1905) of Jewish middle-class background, Molotov (meaning "The Hammer") rose to prominence in the Soviet Communist Party through his loyal support for **Vladimir Lenin** and especially **Joseph Stalin** and became a member of its inner power group, the **Politburo**, in 1925. His support for Stalin's collectivization and industrialization projects in the **First Five-Year Plan** earned him an appointment as chairman (effectively prime minister) of SOVNARKOM (Council of People's Commissars) in 1930, a post he held until Stalin himself assumed that role in 1941. In 1939 Molotov replaced **Maxim Litvinov** as Commissar of Foreign Affairs and is best known as the signer of the Soviet–German Non-Aggression Treaty, often referred to as the Molotov–Ribbentrop Pact (**Nazi–Soviet Pact**) that began **World War II** by joint invasion and occupation of Poland. Once the German government broke the agreement by invading the Soviet Union in June 1941, Molotov continued to preside over Soviet foreign policy during the alliance years with the United States and Great Britain and into the **cold war**—until 1949.

Though not known for initiative or friendliness, Molotov steered Soviet foreign policy through difficult times and was a taciturn fixture at wartime conferences such as at **Yalta** and **Potsdam**. After Stalin's death in 1953, he returned to the Foreign Ministry, going along with **Nikita Khrushchev**'s policy of **peaceful coexistence**. Molotov, however, sided with the so-called anti-party group against the Soviet leader in June 1957. Defeated, he lost his leading positions in party and state, but rather than face execution, Molotov was relegated to head the Soviet diplomatic mission to the People's Republic of Mongolia. Living for many years in isolated retirement, Molotov revealed little about himself and his times in mundane letters and memoirs.

MOLOTOV–RIBBENTROP AGREEMENT. *See* MOLOTOV, YACHESLAV; NAZI–SOVIET PACT.

MONROE DOCTRINE (1823). American statement condemning and limiting European military and political presence in the Western Hemisphere. The doctrine, drafted largely by Secretary of State **John Quincy Adams** and included in President James Monroe's address to Congress, was aimed especially at the European presence in Latin America but also at Russian expansion on the West Coast of North America as exemplified by the Ukaz of 1821. The doctrine would have an initial effect in Russia backing down from the ukaz in the **Convention of 1824**. It would become better known as a basic and enduring tenet of American foreign policy that would justify intervention in Latin American countries, but also as a contributor to an American practice of military intervention in foreign countries in general. *See also* RUSSIAN AMERICA.

MOSCOW ART THEATER (MAT). A world-renowned repertory company, associated with the revolutionary direction of **Konstantin**

Stanislavsky, the MAT entered the Moscow drama scene in 1898 and has never left it. Its performances involved the staging of Russian and Western classics, such as those of Henryk Ibsen, and the contemporary plays of Anton Chekhov. It came to the notice of American theater critic **Norman Hapgood** before **World War I**; he first made plans to bring the Russian company and its director to New York, though this was cancelled by the beginning of World War I. Soon after the peace the plan was revived. The success of **Nikita Balieff** paved the way, apparently proving that American audiences would sit through performances entirely in Russian. Stanislavsky and his cast, which included Chekhov's widow, came to New York, subsidized by **Charles Crane**, in the fall season of 1923 for a very successful—at least critically—tour, repeated the following year and celebrated by a reception at the White House of **Calvin Coolidge**. The theater, its director, and his "method school of acting" would have a major influence on American drama and film, especially through the translation of his writings into English by **Elizabeth Reynolds Hapgood**.

MOSCOW CONFERENCES OF FOREIGN MINISTERS (1941, 1943). Important **World War II** meetings of foreign affairs leaders of the Allies were supplementary to the major Big Three conferences at **Tehran, Yalta**, and **Potsdam**. The first in October 1941 was held in Moscow and consisted of Commissar of Foreign Affairs **Vyacheslav Molotov**, Ambassador **Averell Harriman**, and Lord Beaverbrook, representing Great Britain. Their major accomplishments were in solidifying the Grand Alliance and coordinating and increasing the American and British commitments to **lend-lease**. The second meeting occurred two years later in October 1943 and consisted of Molotov, Secretary of State **Cordell Hull**, and British Foreign Secretary Anthony Eden with participation also of China. A number of issues of common interest were discussed, including the establishment of a **United Nations**, coordination of a second front in Western Europe, and Soviet participation in the war against Japan, and the conference helped set the agenda for the Tehran Conference at the end of November the same year.

MOSCOW DAILY NEWS. This English-language Moscow newspaper was launched in October 1930 to provide information about Russian events to a new and growing foreign community in the capital, mainly American, and especially to a potential readership abroad. It was often considered simply as an organ of Soviet propaganda. Under the initial editorship of American **Anna Louise Strong**, it achieved a professional appearance, though most of its contents were translations from the official Soviet press. Nevertheless, under Strong, it often presented surprisingly transparent views of the course of the **First Five-Year Plan** until her departure in 1937. Published in several other languages, the paper continued as an informative, but also a propaganda instrument of the Soviet Union until it was shut down in 1949, when anything in English was considered dangerous. It resumed under tight controls in 1956 but then really came into its own in leading **Gorbachev's glasnost** after 1985 with both Western-language and Russian editions.

MOSCOW STATE (LOMONOSOV) UNIVERSITY (MGU). Originally the University of Moscow, the first Russian university, founded by **Mikhail Lomonosov** in 1755, this foremost center of higher education in the Soviet Union was relocated in the 1950s to the Lenin (Sparrow) Hills region that overlooked central Moscow. Though perhaps still surpassed by the University of St. Petersburg in some areas, such as philology and Russian literature, it has retained a leading position in the **Russian Federation** in enrollment, faculty, and as host of foreign exchange scholars. The history *fakultet* (school) includes a department of American history, for many years headed by Evgeny Yazkov, and is known for its training of experts in the field, many of whom became prominent leaders in the **Academy of Sciences Institute of General History** and the **Institute of the USA and Canada**. A former director of the American history department, Nikolai Sivachev, was well known for his scholarly contributions to 20th-century American social and political history and assistance to American students before his premature death in 1970. Thanks to his groundwork, a breakthrough in scholarly U.S.–Soviet exchanges occurred in 1974 with the establishment of a Fulbright professorship in American history at the university, held subsequently by a number of leading American historians.

MOTT, JOHN R. (1865–1950). As secretary for international operations, Mott was instrumental in expanding the activities of the **Young**

Men's Christian Association (YMCA) worldwide with a special emphasis on Russia, where **Franklin Gaylord** established and developed a Russian affiliate (*Mayak* or Lighthouse) in the early 20th century. The American YMCA was also very active in Russia during **World War I** and the revolution with contingents in Petrograd, Moscow, and many other cities. It provided essential services to Russian army units and to German and Austrian prisoners of war. Closely associated with **Charles R. Crane**, Mott was a member of the **Root Commission** to Russia in 1917 and accompanied Crane to a special council of the Orthodox Church in Moscow. He also supported and financed the Russian missions of **Ethan Colton**, **Paul Anderson**, and Donald Lowrie. His papers in the Yale Divinity School Library reveal much about these special missions of the YMCA in Russia.

MUNICH PACT. Preliminary efforts of British Prime Minister Neville Chamberlain and German Chancellor Adolf Hitler at Berchtesgarden in September 1938 had failed to achieve an agreement on German demands for a plebiscite in the predominantly German region of "Sudetenland" in Czechoslavkia. Joint pressure by American president **Franklin D. Roosevelt** and Italian leader Benito Mussolini resulted in a broader conference at Munich in October. This meeting, however, significantly excluded the Soviet Union and the United States. Concessions of Great Britain and France to Germany, known as "appeasement," undermined the defensive ability of Czechoslovakia and effectively destroyed the **collective security** policy of the Soviet Union headed by Commissar of Foreign Affairs **Maxim Litvinov**, its linchpin of a Franco–Soviet Alliance, and the prospects for avoiding a major war. Chamberlain, meanwhile, arrived home waving a piece of paper and declaring "peace in our time." The result of the pact, however, was a carte blanche for Hitler's aggression in Czechoslovakia and beyond.

MURMANSK. This Russian port city on the Barents Sea is located about 900 miles due north of St. Petersburg. During **World War I** access to Russia from the west was limited by German control of the Baltic Sea and Turkish control of the outlet from the Black Sea. A northern route was the main alternative. The port of **Archangel** on the White Sea was restricted in use by ice during the winter and spring months. A site on the Kola peninsula at the mouth of the Murman River, open year round due to the Gulf Stream over Scandinavia, was developed as a more convenient access to Russia in 1915–16 by a rail line connecting this new port with Petrograd that would allow more convenient shipments of Allied aid. American assistance was provided in its construction as well as in the port itself, and in 1917 it became a major facility for the import of a variety of American munitions and other goods for the Russian war effort. Unfortunately, supplies were backed up at Murmansk in 1917–18. Allied concern about the possibility that they would fall into German hands as a result of the **Treaty of Brest-Litovsk** (March 1918) contributed to the decision to send troops to occupy the area as well as to Archangel that summer.

Murmansk would emerge again as an access port for **lend-lease** aid to the Soviet Union during **World War II** (1941–45) as a major terminus (along with Archangel) of the **northern convoy route**, delivering essential supplies, mainly from the United States, for the Soviet war effort. During the **cold war** Murmansk would be a major naval base for submarines and other vessels because of its direct access to the Atlantic Ocean, and the largest city (over 300,000) north of the Arctic Circle. *See also* INTERVENTION, AMERICAN; NORTHERN CONVOY ROUTE.

– N –

NABOKOV, VLADIMIR (1899–1977). An American-Russian writer, born in St. Petersburg in 1899 into a professional and politically active family (his uncle was a secretary to **Alexander Kerensky** in 1917), Nabokov immigrated to England in 1919 and then to Germany in 1922. He left for France in 1937 and went from there to the United States in 1940, where he became an American citizen in 1945. Emerging as a major writer, Nabokov is best known for his short stories and *Lolita* (1958), which became an American classic, and for being an erudite leader of the intellectual life of **Russia Abroad**. His memoir of growing up in prerevolutionary Russia, *Speak, Memory* (1966), is a classic of its genre. Nabokov was also known as an avid lepidopterist (butterfly collector).

NATIONAL ARCHIVES AND RECORDS ADMINISTRATION (NARA). As the official depository of American government documents, including State Department and military records, NARA (Archives II) is located just outside Washington, D.C., in College Park, Maryland. Materials relating to Russian–American relations are concentrated in record group (RG) 59 in the official diplomatic correspondence, but also appear in RG 84 (post records of consulates, legations, and embassies in Russia) and various military collections. Also available are the records of special expeditions such as the **American Expeditionary Force (AEF)** in Siberia and the **American Red Cross (ARC)**. A knowledgeable staff is available for consultation. Its materials are supplemented by the **Library of Congress** manuscript division for research on Russian–American relations, especially since many government officials, such as secretaries of state, retained important "private" correspondence in their personal files. The national archives contain many special collections regarding military reports, American Expeditionary Force operations, and so on.

NARKOMINDEL. *See* COMMISSARIAT OF FOREIGN AFFAIRS.

NATIONAL CITY BANK, NEW YORK. A major Western bank established in Russia from 1899 to 1918. The Russian branch bank flourished in St. Petersburg due to the large expansion of Western investment in Russia, especially by American companies such as **Singer**, **International Harvester**, **New York Life Insurance Company**, and **Westinghouse** in the late 19th and early 20th centuries. Under the directorship of Harry Fessenden Meserve, it expanded rapidly and provided convenience in currency exchanges and credits for companies, tourists, and governmental agencies. In 1918 it was the last of the foreign banks in Russia to be closed by the new Soviet government.

NAZIMOVA, ALLA (1879–1945). Born the daughter of a Jewish pharmacist in Yalta as Mariam Ediz Adelaida Leventon, she was renamed Alla by her mother and later assumed "Nazimova" from the name of the heroine of a Russian novel. She studied violin at an early age and first performed onstage at age 10 in a Christmas play in 1889, while living with a family in Switzerland. She became more seriously interested in drama as resident in a boarding school in Odessa but soon "escaped" to Moscow, where she allegedly worked as a prostitute and then was "kept" by a millionaire. She subsequently managed to continue her acting interests during an exciting period that witnessed the birth of the **Moscow Art Theater** under **Konstantin Stanislavsky**, under whom she began her serious acting career as an understudy of that institution, and she married a fellow student, Sergei Golovin.

Soon after her marriage, Nazimova left the Stanislavsky company to become a leading actress on the Moscow and St. Petersburg stages by 1903. She continued to rise in stature and popularity by appearances in Berlin, London, and finally New York, where in 1906 she became the darling of Broadway and signed lucrative contracts with producer Lee Schubert, performing serious drama, such as that of Henryk Ibsen, as well as lighter fare. In New York she also met Charles Bryant, with whom she would live for many years. By 1915, however, Nazimova had turned to a new genre, silent films, and moved to California, where she helped make Hollywood Hollywood by starring in such films as *Camille* (1921), *Salome* (1923), and *Madonna of the Streets* (1924), and by her flamboyant lifestyle. She and Bryant lived in a mansion on Sunset Boulevard, where both had numerous relationships, mainly with those of the same sex. Nazimova was renowned for her assistance to—and affairs with—young American actresses, who included June Marlowe and Tallulah Bankhead.

At the zenith of her career in the mid-1920s, Nazimova failed financially in producing and screenwriting her own films and by 1925 had returned to the Broadway stage. Late in life she played minor movie parts, such as Tyrone Power's mother in the swashbuckling *Blood and Sand* (1941). A legend in her own time, Nazimova would be featured in films centering on one of her earlier male opposites, Rudolph Valentino, in a part performed by Leslie Caron in *Valentino* (1977) and by Laura Harring in *Return to Babylon* (2004). She was also the subject of a stage retrospective by opera singer/actress Irene Castle in the 1990s, à la Nazimova.

NAZI–SOVIET PACT. The nonaggression agreement between Communist Russia and Nazi Germany in August 1939 came as a surprise to most of the world. It occurred after the signing of the **Munich Agreement** in October 1938 and the British and French policy of "appeasing" Hitler's demands in Czechoslovakia, an ally of the Soviet Union, which was not invited to participate in the deliberations. This was the final blow to **Maxim Litvinov**'s crusade for **collective security**, already damaged by the effects of the **Spanish Civil War**. Litvinov was consequently retired as commissar of foreign affairs and replaced by **Joseph Stalin**'s loyal ally, **Vyacheslav Molotov**. Though there were clear indications of initiatives on the part of both Adolf Hitler and Stalin, Allied diplomacy provided virtually no response to prevent it.

The pact and its subsequent amendments provided for the division of most of Eastern Europe between Germany and the Soviet Union, beginning with Poland. That country was invaded simultaneously by forces of both countries immediately after the pact, establishing a long common border between the two countries. Poland was thus partitioned one more time, but its futile defense by Great Britain and France led to general declarations of war and the beginning of **World War II**. The pact also provided for a division of spheres of influence in Eastern Europe, Czechoslovakia already having fallen into the Nazi orbit. The Baltic states of Lithuania, Latvia, and Estonia belonged to Russian disposition, while the Balkan area remained in contention.

The United States was dismayed by the "betrayal" of the Soviet Union and its attack on **Finland** (as part of the division of Eastern Europe specified by the pact) and the resulting **Winter War** (1939–40). Signs of strain in the Nazi–Soviet alliance were soon apparent, and German plans for a massive invasion of the Soviet Union, planned in November 1940, were known to many intelligence services and relayed to the Soviet Union. The Nazi–Soviet Pact was thus brought to a sudden conclusion by Operation Barbarossa, launched in June 1941, setting off a whole new dimension to the war.

NEW ECONOMIC POLICY (NEP) (1921–1928). The effort by the new Soviet government to introduce quickly a Communist economy and also to conduct a very destructive **civil war** had led to a virtual economic collapse. The distinguishing features of War Communism were nationalization of industry and communization of agriculture, that is, a system whereby peasants should provide everything they did not need for their own consumption to the state without payment. The result, naturally, was less production, leading to a disastrous **famine** situation. Recognizing the need for a change in policy, **Lenin** pushed for a more relaxed, semicapitalist regime at the 10th Party Congress in March 1921. The NEP abandoned the agrarian policy and returned many smaller industries to their owners or transformed them into cooperatives; a free market dominated the consumer economy. Foreign enterprises were encouraged to support Soviet economic development through **concessions**. Americans were especially welcomed and participated widely in short- and long-term plans for economic rehabilitation in the 1920s. *See also* FIRST FIVE-YEAR PLAN.

"NEW THINKING." As a vital part of the liberal reforms of **Mikhail Gorbachev** that included **glasnost** and perestroika, "new thinking" was basically a more objective, less ideological approach to foreign policy issues. Introduced in 1987, it involved a more open and friendly attitude toward Western powers, specifically the United States, and signaled the end of the **cold war**. Outcomes included an increasing number of summit meetings and open discussions by, and access to, ambassadors. More important were nuclear weapons safeguards and dismantling in the aftermath of the collapse of the Soviet Union. A key architect was **Alexander Yakovlev**, a major advisor to Gorbachev.

NEW YORK LIFE INSURANCE COMPANY (NYLIC). Establishing its Russian headquarters in St. Petersburg in the late 19th century, NYLIC quickly became the largest insurance company in the Russian empire, exceeding the size of its American rival, **Equitable Life Assurance Society**, until after the **Bolshevik Revolution**, when all foreign insurance companies were forced from the Soviet scene. Although employing only about 50 at its central offices, the company maintained a large corps of sales personnel throughout the empire. One of the conditions of its operations in Russia was that the company invest most of its capital gains from insurance sales in Russian capital stocks such as railroads, factories, and banks. As a result, NYLIC became the largest holder of Russian securities by 1917 and, consequently, suffered some of the largest financial losses from the revolution. The longtime director of its Russian operations, **Frederick Corse**, was also a leader of the American colony in the capital, as well as a close friend of **Samuel Harper** and a chief advisor to Ambassador **David Francis**. NYLIC was also a symbol of the rapid growth of American economic presence abroad at the turn of the century; other companies dominant on the Russian business scene included **Singer**, **International Harvester**, and **Westinghouse Air Brake**.

NEW YORK PUBLIC LIBRARY (NYPL). Responding to the influx of a large number of Jewish immigrants from the Russian Empire into New York City in the late 19th century, the main public library at Fifth Avenue and 42nd Street subscribed to many Russian-language periodicals and collected books and materials for them and other researchers. The resulting Slavonic Division was an important repository of regular and arcane materials relating to all aspects of Russian history and culture, surpassing the **Library of Congress (LC)** in holdings of prerevolutionary publications. Under the able direction of **Avrahm Yarmolinsky** and his successors, the division became a major study center for Russian history and culture to the benefit of many students and scholars. While LC and some university libraries, such as that of the University of Illinois, may have larger holdings on the Soviet period, NYPL remains unsurpassed in the United States on prerevolutionary Russia. The manuscript division also contains many valuable collections for researchers in Russian history and culture, for example, Anna Whistler, **William Frey**, **Isabel Hapgood**, **George Kennan**, and **Francis Greene**. NYPL also sponsors public exhibitions and study programs for teachers that pertain to Russia.

NICHOLAS II (1860–1918). The last of the Romanov dynasty to preside over Russia (1894–1917), Nicholas II possessed few of the qualities needed to manage that empire through difficult times. His reign was beset by a transition to modern times, both economically and politically, by a growing revolutionary movement, and by a rising national consciousness from the many ethnic minorities, constituting half of the population. Some challenges were met, but only partially, by granting some degree of autonomy, for example, to the Finns, and by establishing a national parliament (Duma) after the **Revolution of 1905**. But Nicholas was unable to cope with conflicting advice from different directions, chiefly from his arch-conservative former tutor **Konstantin Pobedonostsev**, his progressive Minister of Finance **Sergei Witte**, his domineering spouse, Grand Duchess Alexandra, and his mother, Maria Fedorovna, nor was he able to form a working relationship with the liberal progressive bloc of the Duma. He also faced the problem of his only son's hemophilia, temporarily alleviated by treatments of hypnosis by Valentin Rasputin. Above all and beyond his and his ministers' capabilities were alliances with France and Serbia that brought Russia into **World War I**.

The war came at the wrong time for Russia and resulted in the **February Revolution** of 1917, during which Nicholas abdicated for himself and his son, leaving Russia for the first time without a tsar figure in control. He was held with his family under house arrest, and they were moved to Ekaterinburg in the Urals by the Bolsheviks during the winter of 1917–18. The approach of units of the **Omsk government** of **Alexander Kolchak** and the **Czechoslovak Legion** in July 1918 resulted in the execution of the family to avoid their becoming a symbol of the anti-Bolshevik movement. Throughout his reign Nicholas II was especially open and friendly to Americans, devoting many hours to visiting Americans and allowing President **Theodore Roosevelt** to arbitrate an end to the **Russo–Japanese War** (1905). In post-Soviet Russia Nicholas II has been a center of attention and rehabilitation in several scholarly (and not-so-scholarly) works. Remains of him and the family have been relocated in St. Petersburg, where DNA evidence on distinguishing members of the family remains controversial.

NIKOLIUKIN, ALEXANDER (1928–). A leading Russian expert on American literature and a philologist. Born in Voronezh and graduate of **Moscow State University (MGU)** (1953), Nikoliukin quickly became a leading scholar on a wide range of American literature and its reception in Russia. He specialized in American romanticism, his extensive publications including studies on the literary connections of the United States and Russia (1981), William Faulkner (1985), Russian and Soviet writers about America (1987),

Robert Penn Warren (1988), and American romanticism (1990). Since 1976 he has been a member of the Institute of Scholarly Information on the Social Sciences of the **Academy of Sciences**. Though often cited, little of his scholarly study has been translated into English with the exception of a collection of valuable Russian descriptions of the United States that he edited as *A Russian Discovery of America* (1986).

NIXON, RICHARD M. (1913–1994). A graduate of Whittier College (1934) and Duke University Law School (1937), Nixon won election to Congress in 1946 and soon achieved national attention in the **Alger Hiss** spy case (1948), which launched him into the Senate in 1950 and as the conservative running mate of **Dwight D. Eisenhower** in 1952 and 1956. Groomed as his successor, Nixon lost narrowly to **John F. Kennedy** in the hotly fought 1960 presidential election. He gained the highest office after the withdrawal of Lyndon B. Johnson from the 1968 campaign over the Vietnam debacle. His celebrated **"kitchen debate"** as vice president, during a meeting with **Nikita Khrushchev** at an American exhibition in Moscow in 1959, advanced his credibility as a strong but flexible negotiator with Soviet leaders and contributed to his later election. As president, he responded to the **Leonid Brezhnev** initiatives of **détente**, resulting in a grand welcome to Moscow in July 1974. However, his involvement later that year in the clandestine infiltration of the Democratic Party Headquarters in Washington (Watergate) resulted in his resignation, the first by an American president.

NIZHNY NOVGOROD (GORKY). A city on the Volga known historically for its summer "fairs" that featured goods from the Orient with exotic color (camel caravans) and fanfare, "Nizhny" became a major tourist attraction in the 19th century for many American visitors. During the **First Five-Year Plan**, the city became a focus for the construction of a large automobile and truck factory, the State Automobile Works (GAZ), an American project by the **Austin Company** of Cleveland and the **Ford Motor Company** of Detroit. Over 50 American engineers worked in the city and its vicinity in the early 1930s. It remains the major producer of cars and trucks in Russia and the third-largest city in the **Russian Federation**. Upon the death of **Maxim Gorky** in 1936 the city was renamed in his honor, only to return to its original name in the 1990s. It is also known as the place of "house arrest" of **Andrei Sakharov** in the 1970s and 1980s until his summons back to Moscow by **Mikhail Gorbachev** in 1987.

NKVD. *See* PEOPLE'S COMMISSARIAT OF INTERNAL AFFAIRS.

NOOTKA SOUND CONTROVERSY (1788–1793). This conflict in the waters around Vancouver Island over territorial control along the Pacific coast of North America involved Great Britain and Spain. Though the encounter was part of a series of confrontations between the squadrons of Spanish Admiral Juan Francisco de la Bodega and British explorer George Vancouver, it brought international attention to the area, and through diplomatic reports from Madrid and London, to Russia. The resulting Russian concern was described by historian Moisei Alperovich as a major factor in drawing Russian attention and presence to Northwest America in the 1790s. While Vancouver "won" the contest with Bodega, both left their names prominently on the American coast. Under **Catherine the Great**, Russia took advantage of this confrontation to "sneak in by the back door." Soon after, Russia established its first permanent American settlement on **Kodiak Island** (1795). *See also* RUSSIAN AMERICA.

NORTH ATLANTIC TREATY ORGANIZATION (NATO). In response to the **Berlin blockade** (1948–49) and other Soviet aggressive actions in Europe, West European countries joined the United States, Canada, and others to form a military coordination effort. By this joining of forces of resistance to actual and potential Soviet threats, NATO helped stabilize the **cold war** by presenting a common front and also discouraging maverick acts by a Western power. It thus restrained both the USSR and the United States from independent moves that would involve all members. Soviet leaders responded by establishing a similar institution in the **Warsaw Pact**. These arrangements still left problems, namely the overlying competition and rivalry between the two major powers, as would be demonstrated during the **Cuban missile crisis**. NATO remains a symbol of Western, democratic solidarity with its headquarters in Brussels, Belgium, and the continued existence of American military bases in Western Europe.

More controversial has been the expansion of the membership in NATO after the collapse of Communism and the USSR in the 1990s to a number of former Soviet satellites or to the newly independent countries of the former Soviet Union. Many, such as Poland and the Baltic countries, have sought the assurance and security against any possible hostile moves by the **Russian Federation**, which, under **Vladimir Putin** especially, considers these efforts to maintain the cold war and take advantage of the military weakness of the region. A number of Western experts, such as **George F. Kennan**, consider the expansion unnecessary and harmful to friendly relations with the Russian state and its allies, especially when such membership may include the establishment of missile bases in those countries.

NORTHERN CONVOY ROUTE. From a precedent established during **World War I**, when the Baltic and Black Seas were closed by enemy control, a major alternative sea route was used over the north of Scandinavia to the Russian port of **Murmansk** that was open the year around and to **Archangel** on the White Sea that was closed by ice during the winter months. It became an essential lifeline for **lend-lease** assistance to the Soviet Union in the summer of 1941, with British and American ships delivering a large quantity of military supplies that were critical in the Battle of Moscow that fall. The most important initial items were P-40 fighter planes, airplane fuel, and trucks. Though a dangerous route to Russia owing to German U-boat activity and air attacks (an important convoy in June 1942 would lose 21 of 35 ships), the northern route would perhaps be the most important because of delivery nearer to battle zones in central Russia. It was augmented by the Persian Gulf route through Iran and by another across the North Pacific directly to **Vladivostok**. *See also* WORLD WAR II.

NOVIKOV, NIKOLAI (1744–1818). Novikov was a leading example of the penetration of the French Enlightenment into Russia during the reign of **Catherine the Great**. A widely respected editor, essayist, and satirist, Novikov was especially interested in American themes and publicized American achievements, especially in his 1780s articles on **George Washington** and **Thomas Jefferson**. Though freed from his arrest and imprisonment in 1792 for his outspoken criticism of the Russian autocracy and bureaucracy, Novikov failed to regain his former status as the thorn in the side of the Russian regime.

NOVOE RUSSKOE SLOVO. A leading Russian-language newspaper in the United States published in New York beginning in 1910 for the rapidly growing Russian immigrant population in the 20th century. The daily newspaper received wide dissemination with an average circulation of 65,000 in the 1930s and after. As such, it was an important and influential voice of **Russia Abroad**. Though stridently anti-Soviet and pro-American, it maintained an open and fairly liberal perspective that was welcomed by the new diaspora after the collapse of the Soviet Union in the 1990s.

– O –

OCTOBER REVOLUTION. *See* BOLSHEVIK REVOLUTION.

OLYMPIC GAMES BOYCOTTS (1980, 1984). In response to the Soviet invasion of **Afghanistan** in December 1979, the administration of **Jimmy Carter** decided that the United States would not participate in the Moscow Olympic Games, which was to be a star attraction and the culmination of **Leonid Brezhnev**'s policy of **détente**. Much costly Soviet preparation, such as building a grand "Olympic Village," went for little, as most Western nations followed the American lead. In return for this "insult," the Soviet Union would boycott the next Olympic Games held in Los Angeles in 1984. In reflection, this **cold war** gamesmanship seems somewhat silly and misplaced.

OMSK GOVERNMENT (1918–1920). After the **Bolshevik Revolution** of November 1917, considerable opposition remained in respect to this "coup d'état" from many political and military organizations. The largest anti-Bolshevik forces gathered in the Kuban region and in Ukraine under Generals Anton Deniken and Petr Wrangel. But an equally formidable challenge to Bolshevik rule emerged in **Siberia** under the leadership of Admiral **Alexander**

Kolchak. Though considered by many at the time the best alternative to Bolshevism—and with the greatest chance of success—with the resources of Siberia behind it, the Omsk government proved to be weak and incapable. It was initially sustained by remnants of the White Army, the weakness of the Bolshevik forces, and especially by the **Czechoslovak Legion**, which controlled much of the area. Receiving some material and financial support from American loans to the **Provisional Government** and from the **American Red Cross**, Kolchak's possibilities were undermined by lack of coordination with Deniken and other opponents to the Bolsheviks, by ambitious, independent, and brutal Cossack generals such as Grigori Semenov, by failure of Washington to recognize his legitimacy, and finally by the withdrawal of the Czech forces. The sizable **American Expeditionary Force** remained around **Vladivostok**, while the Japanese army preferred to support opposition elements in hopes of establishing their own protectorate. The Czechs captured Kolchak and turned him over to the Red Army in return for safe passage across Siberia, and he was quickly executed.

OPEN SKIES. An accord reached at the **Geneva Conference** of July 1955, upon the initiative of Soviet leaders **Nikita Khrushchev** and Nikolai Bulganin and President **Dwight D. Eisenhower**, to ban the use of outer space and of aircraft over each other's territory. A significant limitation of the arms race, it was unfortunately soon violated by the American overflights of Soviet territory by high-altitude **U-2** planes. It was to be revived, however, in the 1990s as a multinational accord and ratified by Russian president **Boris Yeltsin** and American president **Bill Clinton** in 1997.

OPEN SOCIETY FUND. *See* SOROS, GEORGE.

ORTHODOX CHURCH IN AMERICA. The Russian Orthodox Church came to Northwest America with Russian fur hunters and missionaries at the end of the 18th century and continued to win native converts during the long administration of the **Russian America Company** (1797–1867), with the result that most of the native population of **Alaska** was converted. The company established an advance hunting and supply base at **Fort Ross**, north of San Francisco, that resulted in the first Russian Orthodox Church on American territory. The Russian and native Orthodox population in that area gained considerably with the sale of Alaska (1867) and resettlement of many of them in San Francisco. By the 1870s an Orthodox diocese, headed by a metropolitan (bishop), included the community in California and the whole of Alaska.

Most of the immigration into the United States from 1880 to1910, however, was non–Russian Orthodox: Jewish predominantly, Roman Catholic (Polish, Lithuanian, and Volga German), Lutheran (Volga German and Baltic), Armenian, and **Mennonite**. A number of Orthodox Russians, however, settled in the New York area and established congregations and seminaries, notable examples being the St. Nicholas Orthodox Church at 96th Street and Fifth Avenue and the St. Vladimir Seminary on the Hudson River. These institutions would be strengthened by a large number of new arrivals in the early 20th century, especially by the Russian diaspora after the revolution.

OSINSKY, NIKOLAI (NE VALERIAN OBOLENSKY-OSSINSKY) (1887–1938). Born on a small estate in Kursk province, Osinsky grew up in a middle-class family in Moscow and participated in the **Revolution of 1905** as a student at the University of Moscow. The following year he left for Germany, where he continued his studies. Back in Russia, he joined the Russian Social Democratic Party, spent a brief period in jail in 1910, and played a minor role in the Bolshevik seizure of power but emerged quickly as an economic leader, as first chairman of the Russian Socialist Federated Soviet Republic's Supreme Council of the People's Economy and as deputy commissar of agriculture. During this period he was associated with the left Communist position of Nikolai Bukharin. Osinsky followed Bukharin into the pro-**New Economic Policy** camp in 1921. Through the 1920s and early 1930s he was a delegate to party congresses and a candidate member of the party central committee. More importantly, Osinsky was an active member of the State Planning Commission (GOSPLAN) and one of the strongest proponents of the **First Five-Year Plan** and of its American emphasis on cars, trucks, tractors, dams and electricity, and mass production.

One of the Bolshevik technical supporters and quite familiar with the foreign environment, Osinsky was briefly in 1923–24 ambassador to Sweden, considered an important post, and he spent six months in the United States in 1925 studying both agriculture and industry. He became a dedicated advocate of *amerikanizm* in the plan, and wrote a very positive survey of American agriculture. He returned for another investigative tour in 1927, making a number of initial contacts with American companies and engineers. As the First Five-Year Plan got underway in 1928, Osinsky was appointed chairman of the All-Union Automobile and Tractor Industries Corporation with specific responsibility for a new automobile plant to be built near Nizhny Novgorod. In this role he planned to return to the United States to negotiate a contract, but he was denied a visa on account of his attendance at a Comintern congress. Instead, he established offices in Windsor, Ontario, and carried on his work from there, "across the channel," much to the embarrassment of American clients. Taking a special interest in cars, he was the founding editor of *Za Rulyom* (*Behind the Wheel*), a popular Soviet journal in the field, and served as its chief editor for 10 years. Because of his major role in the industrialization drive and its American aspects, Ossinsky found himself a target of the purges. Arrested in late 1937, he was tried as a member of the "anti-Soviet Trotskyite bloc" in March 1938 and executed a few months later.

OSWALD, LEE HARVEY (1939–1963). After service in the U.S. army, Oswald defected to the USSR in October 1959, where he spent over a year and a half. He married a Russian, Marina Prusakova, and converted to the cause of international Communism. He returned to the United States through Mexico in 1963 and with a long-range rifle assassinated President **John F. Kennedy** during a motorcade in Dallas, Texas, on 22 November. Though rumors circulated about a second gunman and/or a calculated plot involving Soviet intelligence, the Warren Commission concluded that the act was that alone of a strangely motivated Oswald. Immediately after the shooting in Dallas, he was apprehended and then murdered by a deranged Jack Ruby before he could be arraigned and tried. Both Kennedy and Oswald were victims of the hysteria of the **cold war**.

OZEROV, IVAN (1869–1942). Born in a peasant family in Kostroma province, Ozerov studied law and political economy at the University of Moscow and soon became an authority on budget finances and international economics, through his dissertation on the income tax system in England. Subsequently, he taught at universities in Moscow and St. Petersburg. His early publications include *Ocherki ekonomicheskoi i finansovoi zhizni Rossii i Zapada* (*Essays on Economic and Financial Life of Russia and the West*) (1904), *Russkii budget* (1907), and *Osnovi finansovoi nauki* (*Fundamentals of Finance*), a basic textbook. He was a critic of the system of forced industrialization pioneered by Minister of Finance **Sergei Witte** because it benefitted the state at the cost of the lower classes.

Ozerov championed free trade and liberal economic policies that he found in the United States and fostered them in such publications as *Amerika idyot na Evropu* (*America Is Taking Over Europe*) (1903) and *Chemu uchit nas Amerika* (*What Can America Teach Us*) (1908). He advocated agricultural loan banks, rural electrification, and estate taxes and predicted that the economic powers in the future would be the United States and China. In 1914 Ozerov helped organize—with American consul general John Snodgrass—the Russian–American Chamber of Commerce in Moscow, served as its vice president, and continued to promote close economic cooperation between the two countries. After the **Bolshevik Revolution**, his name was on a list of "professors" to be expelled from the country but then withdrawn, his expertise in finance apparently considered still of use to the new regime. He retained his teaching position through the 1920s and 1930s at **Moscow State University**, occasionally consulted by visiting Americans. Though he would have opposed the forced industrialization of **Joseph Stalin**, he simply quietly retired and escaped being a victim of the purges.

– P –

PARES, SIR BERNARD (1867–1949). One of the first Western scholars to study seriously and appreciate Russia and its language, Pares was largely self-taught in the language and the history of the country and spent much time living in, and reporting on, the social and political course of the late Russian Empire and its crises. Realizing the importance of nurturing further studies, he established the first Western

Russian studies department at the University of Liverpool in 1910. Among his first students and disciples was **Samuel Harper** of Chicago. Among Pares's early works are *Russia and Reform* (1907), *Day by Day with the Russian Army* (1915), and *The Fall of the Russian Monarchy* (1939). Pares, meanwhile, won recognition through his articles and books, especially his *A History of Russia* (1930), which remained for decades the classic survey, published in many subsequent and expanded editions.

After **World War I** and the **Bolshevik Revolution**, Pares moved from Liverpool to found the School of Slavonic and East European Studies at the University of London and its *Slavonic and East European Review*, with the assistance of R. W. Seton Watson, a specialist in Balkan history and politics. While American involvement in Slavic studies expanded considerably during the 1920s and 1930s, Pares continued to claim premiership in the field and for his journal, but he also encouraged efforts by young American scholars of accepting their articles for his *Review*. After some reluctance, Pares succumbed to the inevitability of American dominance of his field, at least financially, by the mid-1930s. He would then be revered by nearly all scholars as the Western elder statesman and the School of Slavonic and East European Studies would continue to foster training and research on the Slavic world for American as well as British students.

PARIS PEACE CONFERENCE (1919). After the armistice of 11 November 1918, world attention centered on the peace negotiations conducted in Paris by the "Big Four," representing the victors: Great Britain, France, Italy, and the United States. The latter, headed by **Woodrow Wilson**, was the catalyst of a new, open diplomacy, the chief goal being the remapping of Europe according to national self-determination, especially in Eastern Europe, which was in turmoil due to the demise of both the Austro-Hungarian and Russian empires. The Russian side of the equation was complicated by the revolution, early withdrawal from the war (**Brest-Litovsk**), and the **Russian Civil War**. Because in the spring of 1919 nothing in Russia was yet settled, and the Great Powers' leaders, especially Wilson, still counted on a Bolshevik defeat or overthrow, Russian representatives were left out of the proceedings. Americans present, including members of a large press corps, were quite divided about the "Russian question," with **Walter Lippmann** and **William Allen White** being among those who favored olive branches to Soviet Russia, such as those extended by the abortive **Prinkipo Conference** and the **Bullitt Mission**, promoted by **Edward House**. The result, however, was disappointment, frustration, and, ultimately, the exclusion of the "Russian question" from the results of the conference, leaving half of Europe unresolved and festering for a future war.

PARNAKH, VALENTIN (1891–1951). Born in Taganrog, Parnakh traveled widely in his youth and studied romance languages at the University of St. Petersburg and music and theater under Mikhail Gnesin and **Vsevolod Meyerhold**. He returned to Europe during **World War I**, settling in Paris, where he studied at the Sorbonne, published poetry, and, most importantly, was exposed to African American **jazz** music. He returned to Russia in 1922 to form the first Russian jazz ensemble, "The First Eccentric Orchestra of the Russian Federated Socialist Republic—Valentin Parnakh's Jazz Band," which held its first performance at the Russian Academy of Theater Arts in Moscow on 1 October 1922, now widely recognized as the birthdate of Russian jazz. The following year his band performed onstage during Meyerhold's staging of Ilya Ehrenburg's *Trest D. E.*, a major event in the development of Soviet jazz. Becoming disillusioned with the Soviet cultural scene, Parnakh went back to Paris to work on his poetry and articles for the Russian immigrant press, returning to Russia finally in 1931, where, like Boris Pasternak, he survived mainly as a translator of Western literature. Though living modestly for many years, upon his death he received a prominent burial in the Novodevichy Cemetery and in later years was honored as the "founding father" of Russian jazz in the American style.

PASSPORT QUESTION (1890–1912). This major problem in Russian–American relations arose in the 1880s and 1890s as a result of continuing Russian oppression of its Jewish population and the large number of them who had immigrated to the United States and become naturalized citizens. Some wanted to return to visit family, settle estates, or enter into legitimate business (having a knowledge of Russian and the assumed protection of American passports). In the eyes of the Russian government, however, many had not left legitimately and were simply draft evaders, still subject to military service. Local authorities saw an opportunity to exact bribes from these returning visitors. Whether refusing or just on principle, a few were arrested and sentenced to jail terms, which became a major problem for the American embassy in St. Petersburg, which claimed that the **Commercial Treaty of 1832** gave them all rights equal to Russians. The Russian government, however, interpreted this as only those rights (or restrictions) applied to its Jewish subjects.

In order to minimize and reduce the growing number of legal cases involving these Jewish expatriates, the Russian Consul General in New York (where most of them resided) developed a questionnaire for visa applications that required the revealing of religious preference; those who indicated Jewish were usually denied visas (exceptions were always granted on the basis of wealth or profession). This, in American eyes, was obvious discrimination on grounds of religion, while Jews, meanwhile, evaded it by fictitious conversions to vague or nonexistent churches, such as "the World Old Testament Christian Church." American protests and offers to renegotiate the treaty were rebuffed, the Russian government citing claims of reciprocity because of its other treaty arrangements. Congress, in disgust, and charged by representatives from New York City, led an initiative in 1911 to abrogate the treaty of 1832 under a provision in its terms requiring a year of advance warning. That expiring in 1912, the Russian American Treaty of Commerce became null and void. Though the whole affair was embarrassing to both countries, the actual situation, however, was that everything continued as before, and there was virtually no effect on economic or political relations.

PEACE CORPS. Though the idea of a volunteer American mission to the world had been raised on several separate occasions after **World War II**, the main impetus came during the presidential campaign of **John F. Kennedy** in a speech at the University of Michigan on 14 October 1960, later dubbing the idea of youth volunteers as the "peace corps." Though obviously a **cold war** strategy of winning friends in vital third-world countries, while correcting the image of the "ugly American," it hit a responsive chord in the United States. The idea was to finance volunteers to provide their work and skills to construction and alleviation of illnesses and obstacles around the world. It was to show America as the opposite of what **Ronald Reagan** termed the **"evil empire."**

After Kennedy's election an executive order created the agency on 1 March 1961, later funded and authorized by Congress the following September. By that time the first group of volunteers had left for Ghana. Within two years more than 7,000 volunteers were spread over 44 countries. The high point was reached in 1966 with 15,000 involved in Peace Corps programs. Since then the program dipped (to just over 5,000 in 1982), and then rose again, with special emphasis from President **George W. Bush** in 2002 to include 15 percent or more over 50 in age. The program, numbering around 10,000 participants, has been extended to the former Soviet Union and Eastern Europe with around 100 assigned to that area by 2008. The Peace Corps has without doubt been one of the most successful American initiatives abroad.

PEACEFUL COEXISTENCE. A widely publicized initiative by **Nikita Khrushchev** to reduce conflicts with the Western powers, namely the United States, and win favorable world opinion. It was symbolized by the **Austrian State Treaty** (1955), **Van Cliburn**'s first prize at the Tchaikovsky piano competition in Moscow, the Khrushchev-Bulganin world tours, the **Lacy-Zarubin Cultural Exchange Agreement** (1958), Khrushchev's tour of the United States (1959), and a general increase in East–West contacts. Unfortunately, the program was marred by continued **cold war** incidents: suppression of the **Hungarian Revolution** (1956), the **U-2 incident** (1960), the **Berlin Wall** (1961), the **Cuban missile crisis** (1962), and, above all, the continuing arms race of potential mutual nuclear annihilation. It was replaced after 1964 by a more sophisticated but equally inadequate version, **détente**.

PENKOVSKY, OLEG (1919–1963). Penkovsky was a career Soviet army officer, who served with distinction during the **Winter War** with Finland (1939–40) and during **World War II**, rising to the rank of lieutenant-colonel. He subsequently served in the diplomat corps as military attaché in Ankara and in military scientific research. In the latter capacity he began in 1961 to pass secret papers to a British embassy contact, Greville Wynne. More than 5,000 sensitive papers, regarding Soviet missile development and about locations and missions of **KGB** officers, were passed to the **Central Intellignce Agency** in the early 1960s, alerting President **John F. Kennedy** to Soviet intentions in advance of the **Cuban missile crisis**. Recorded as one of the most successful spies of the **cold war**, Penkovsky was arrested in 1962 and executed in 1963. Much of the material that gave the West an intelligence victory was published in *The Penkovsky Papers* (1966).

PEOPLE'S COMMISSARIAT OF INTERNAL AFFAIRS (NKVD). Through the 1930s and beyond **World War II**, the NKVD sustained the USSR as a police state. Known especially for its role in the great purges of the 1936–38 period, to Americans it represented the most visible evidence that the Soviet Union was committed to physical elimination of any opposition or those who might tender such possibilities, or otherwise innocent victims of "the Terror." Under the administration of Lavrenty Beria, it became renowned, not only as the chief instrument of oppression within the country, but also for its aggressive intelligence-gathering agency (spy network), though it also provided valuable service during World War II as a backup chain of command to the Red Army. It would be succeeded in 1946 by the Ministry of Internal Affairs and in the 1950s by the **Committee on State Security (KGB)**.

PERKINS CLAIM. Benjamin Perkins was a Connecticut sea captain who became involved in what promised to be a lucrative American arms sale to Russia during the **Crimean War**. Trusting a verbal contract with the Russian consul general in New York, he purchased rifles for shipment to Russia. The war, however, came to a sudden end, and the Russians refused to honor the deal, leaving Perkins to face bankruptcy. Agents and attorneys pursued a legal adjustment on behalf of Perkins and his heirs, hoping to claim a substantial commission, especially because of the prevailing close relations between the United States and Russia. The case also involved New England politicians who hoped to gain from a successful outcome, particularly **Hamilton Fish**, secretary of state in the **Ulysses S. Grant** administration. A successful outcome of the claim was bolstered by the possibility of obtaining part of the money allocated for the purchase of **Alaska** to be held for recompense.

The claim came to a head in 1870–72, when the Russian minister in Washington, **Konstantin Katakazy**, apparently circulated a note, undiplomatically, that Fish had a personal monetary interest in the affair. Though Katakazy denied authorship, damage had been done to his and Fish's reputations as well as to a much heralded impending visit of **Grand Duke Alexis**, resulting in a White House reception that was very short and cool. The revelations by Katakazy and the popularity of the grand duke would cast Perkins's heirs and defenders, Fish, and the Grant administration all into virtual political oblivion.

PETROGRAD CHILDREN'S COLONY (1918–1920). Early in 1918 with Petrograd—and Russia in general—in the process of economic and political collapse, Soviet authorities arranged for the evacuation of around 800 children to the Urals area, accompanied by a few teacher-chaperones. As Russian control of the area shifted, the colony fell into the hands of the **Czechoslovak Legion**, which turned it over to the **American Red Cross (RAC)**. Among the RAC workers who took a special interest in these Russian children were Riley Allen and Hannah "Mother" Campbell. They managed to evacuate the children to **Vladivostok** and then in 1920 by a remodeled Japanese cargo ship back to Russia by way of San Francisco, the Panama Canal, and New York. An early **"cold war** issue" involved whether to return them to their families in Communist Russia or put them under the orphanage care of the anti-Communist Russian exile community in Western Europe. Humanity prevailed in the midst of the **"Red Scare,"** and the children passed over the Finnish frontier to be united with their parents in Petrograd in October 1920.

PIERCE, RICHARD A. (1918–2004). Canadian scholar of the Russian presence in Northwest America and historian at Queen's University in Kingston, Ontario, Pierce received his doctorate at the University of California, Berkeley, and published his first scholarly study of **Russian America Company** activities in 1965, *Russia's Hawaiian Adventure, 1815–1817*. Subsequently, he was chiefly known as a major promoter of scholarship on the Russian presence in America through the many translations of Russian publications by his own Limestone Press, based in Kingston, though in later years he had migrated to Fairbanks, Alaska. Pierce was also noted for extensive cooperation with Russian scholars such as Svetlana Federova and **Nikolai Bolkhovitinov** and for his many contributions to academic conferences in the United States, Canada, and Russia.

POBEDONOSTSEV, KONSTANTIN (1827–1907). As a major influence on the Romanov dynasty and as Procurator of the Holy Synod (minister of religion), 1880–1905, Pobedonostsev promoted an official creed of autocracy, orthodoxy, and Russification. These policies naturally alienated both radical and liberal opponents of the regime and led Russia into a police state of Siberian exiles, refugees abroad, and **Russian anti-Semitism**. Due to his considerable influence on Tsars **Alexander III** and **Nicholas II**, he may also be blamed for the demise of the dynasty and of pushing Russia toward Communism. The United States, for example, through the reporting of **George Kennan** and others of the miserable conditions in Russia, turned increasingly hostile toward Russia. Another effect on the relationship was the **immigration** of a very large number of anti-Russian Jews to the United States, many of them subscribing to left-wing political movements. On the other hand, Pobedonostsev was the author of a sophisticated critique of democracy in his *Reflections of a Russian Statesman*, which eloquently described the dangers of democracy, freedom of the press, and unenlightened leadership (with the United States as the leading example). The problem was that Russia was not exactly a model alternative.

POGROMS. A Russian term for the storming of Jewish settlement districts (ghettos) of towns and villages, almost all in the Pale of Settlement of Eastern Europe, where most of the Jewish population of the Russian Empire was confined. The raids, occurring usually during a few days after Easter, first involved chiefly vandalism of property but gradually became more violent as the Jews armed and prepared themselves for such events. These attacks, such as the one in Kishinev in 1903, received much publicity in the United States and added to strong anti-Russian public opinion, especially inspired by Jewish émigré media. Anti-Semitic violence in the Russian Empire seemed to correspond to bad times of war, revolution, and civil war; thus, the greatest loss of Jewish life occurred in Odessa in October 1905 and in Kiev in 1919 in the midst of civil war.

POINSETT, JOEL ROBERTS (1779–1851). Diplomat, congressman, horticulturist. Poinsett is best known for developing a Mexican plant into a ubiquitous American Christmas season decoration, poinsettia. Originally from South Carolina, Poinsett traveled widely on special missions for the American government, especially in Latin America. Well educated and ambitious, in his youth Poinsett journeyed in 1806 to St. Petersburg, where he gained entrance to the court and impressed **Alexander I** and his family at private dinners with his stories of America, thus inspiring the Russian emperor's interest in the United States and in writing a special message that Poinsett carried back to President **Thomas Jefferson**. This helped pave the way for diplomatic recognition. He subsequently toured Russia as far as the Caucasus and Central Asia, the first American to do so. President James Monroe wanted to appoint Poinsett minister to Russia in 1820 but deferred to the pressure for Poinsett's fellow Carolinian, **Henry Middleton**. Poinsett subsequently served as congressman (1821–25), minister to Mexico (1825–29), and secretary of war (1837–41) in the Van Buren administration.

POLETIKA, PETR (1778–1849). Poletika arrived in the United States in 1809 as Russian consul general to inaugurate diplomatic relations. He served subsequently in the legation under Minister **Andrei Dashkov** for a number of months and returned as minister in 1819 at a busy and confused time in Russian–American–Spanish relations, when many of the Spanish colonies in the Americas were becoming independent. Poletika pressed upon St. Petersburg the value of recognizing the inevitable and not to support Spain, the Russian government's first inclination (on behalf of the "Holy Alliance"). Secretary of State **John Quincy Adams**, however, was annoyed by the Russian Ukaz of 1821 that made extravagant territorial claims in the Pacific Northwest and may have acted to secure Poletika's recall. A book, published in Paris and Baltimore in 1826, *A Sketch of the Internal Condition of the United States of America and of Their Political Relations with Europe*, "by a Russian," was attributed to Poletika but more likely was the work of **Pavel Svinin**.

POLITBURO (LATER PRESIDIUM). The political bureau of the Communist Party of the Soviet Union was the highest decision-making body of the USSR from its establishment in 1919 until the presidency of **Mikhail Gorbachev**. Though composed of a small number (five at the beginning), it met regularly, normally two or three times a week, and drew on the presence of experts from commissariats and ministries. For example, when matters concerning the United States were discussed, Commissar of Foreign Affairs **Maxim Litvinov** or Minister of Foreign Affairs **Andrei Gromyko** might be present for consultation. The protocols of the meetings, consisting of agendas and actions taken, are available in the party archives.

POOLE, DEWITT CLINTON (1885–1952). A graduate of the University of Wisconsin (1906), Poole studied at George Washington University before entering the American foreign service in 1910. In July 1917 he was United States consul in Moscow, where he served through the **Bolshevik Revolution**. Returning to the United States, Poole headed the Russian Bureau of the State Department, where he took a strong stand against diplomatic recognition. Resigning his government position in 1922, Poole joined the faculty of Princeton University as head of its School of Public and International Affairs. Though maintaining his negative position toward the Soviet Union, in early 1933, in an address before the Foreign Policy Association in Boston, he responded to the question, "Should the United States Now Recognize Soviet Russia," with a definite "yes." He later served in the Office of Strategic Services (OSS) during **World War II** and was one of the founders of **Radio Free Europe**.

PORTSMOUTH PEACE CONFERENCE AND TREATY (AUGUST–SEPTEMBER 1905). President **Theodore Roosevelt** intervened to call for a peace negotiation to end the **Russo–Japanese War**. After considerable negotiations on all sides and the essential assistance of **George von Lengerke Meyer** as the new ambassador to the Russian Empire, the respective parties sent delegates, the Russian party headed by **Sergei Witte**, the Japanese by Jutaro Komura, to meet at the Portsmouth Naval Shipyards in Kittery, Maine, in August 1905. The site was selected on the basis of good communications, mild resortlike climate, a federal site under police control, and the existence of a new building that could be easily modified for the event. The war had resulted in a clear victory for Japan at sea but a standstill on land in Manchuria. The main considerations were the Japanese insistence on an indemnity to repay loans that supported the war and a considerable grant of Russian territory. Though the Japanese delegation pressed hard for an indemnity to help pay much of the cost of the war, Witte successfully opposed any compensation but settled for relinquishing the southern half of Sakhalin Island, which would remain Japanese until the end of **World War II**.

POS'ET, ADMIRAL KONSTANTIN (1819–1889). Pos'et commanded the squadron that brought **Grand Duke Alexis** to the United States in 1871. He accompanied the grand duke on his lengthy foray into the country as far as Wyoming and Colorado with the express purpose of examining the new railroad transportation facilities in the region. The Russian delegation continued its journey by way of Mississippi steamer from Memphis to New Orleans and rejoined the squadron in Pensacola. The diminutive Pos'et won laurels for his chaperoning of the grand duke and a few years later was appointed by **Alexander II** as minister of transportation (1874–88). In this office he was an important catalyst of railroad construction, especially in promoting the idea of the **Trans-Siberian Railroad**, and he was later named an honorary member of the Russian **Academy of Sciences**.

POST, MARJORIE MERIWETHER (1887–1973). Heir to the C. W. Post cereal fortune, she married as her fourth husband prominent Wisconsin attorney **Joseph Davies**, shortly before his appointment as ambassador to the Soviet Union in 1936 by President **Franklin D. Roosevelt**, and she accompanied him to his Moscow assignment. Marjorie Post was already a very wealthy businesswoman who had pioneered in the marketing not only of cereals, but also of frozen foods (Birdseye brand). She had also developed an early interest in art collecting, especially French and Russian works, and devoted much of her time in the Soviet Union to acquiring additions to her collection. These included many 18th- and 19th-century ceramic items, Faberge crafts, and so on. The Soviet government aided her efforts for the money received and in the interests of promoting good relations. She later built a home/museum that was designed to display much of it; Hillwood in Washington, D.C., overlooking Rock Creek Park, is open to the public by appointment.

POTSDAM CONFERENCE (17 JULY–2 AUGUST 1945). Conference of major Allies in **World War II**, after the victory in Europe.
The major participants were **Joseph Stalin, Harry S. Truman**, and
Winston Churchill (replaced by the new British prime minister,
Clement Attlee). They faced an old agenda from the **Yalta Conference**, six months earlier, to settle and modify agreements reached
there but also to deal with new problems in the aftermath of the war
in Europe. The major agreement provided for a military occupational
authority to be administered by the Soviet Union, the United States,
Great Britain, and France. A "Potsdam Declaration" warned Japan of
their mutual commitment to continuing the war effort. Most importantly, the conference defined the boundaries of a new Germany,
shifting a major region of the country to Poland in the east and rear-
ranging the zones of occupation. A major shadow—the successful
testing of the atomic bomb by the United States—loomed over the
proceedings.

PRIBYLOV ISLANDS. Located in the **Bering Sea** and discovered in
the 1780s by Russian explorer Gavril Pribylov, these uninhabited (until the late 19th century) islands were the breeding grounds and summer habitat for a large herd of fur seals, whose skins were in high demand in the 19th century. The United States acquired the islands as a
result of the **Alaska Purchase** in 1867. In order to take advantage of
the demand for these furs and control their production, the Treasury
Department granted a long-term lease to the Alaska Fur Company,
based in San Francisco. Following Russian custom, the company limited the summer "harvest" to young, "surplus" male ("bachelor")
seals. The United States government received an annual lease fee in
addition to a certain amount for each skin; the harvest averaged
100,000 per year, resulting in a substantial revenue for the American
treasury. The total more than paid for the purchase price of **Alaska**
($7,200,00) during the first 20-year contract, 1870–90.

Unfortunately, problems with interlopers had begun before the end
of that period. The fur seals annually migrated from the Pribylovs in
the fall through the Aleutian Islands and to the West Coast of North
America as far as northern California and back through the Bering
Sea by spring, the long immersion in cold water enhancing their furs.
In the 1880s a number of Canadian, British, and American ships in-

tersected the migration route and the food foraging of the cows off the Pribylovs, killing them indiscriminately by net, harpoon, and rifles, often killing pregnant females and thus severely diminishing the herd in short order. Treasury Department revenue cutters sought remedy through seizure of the "poaching" sealers, which resulted in counterclaims based on the old principle of "freedom of the seas." This resulted in an international court of arbitration in Paris that began in early 1893 and lasted almost a year.

This arbitration court, the first of its kind, ruled against the American propositions that the United States had purchased the Bering Sea along with the territory of Alaska and the Aleutian Islands, or that the seals were born on American territory and thus traveled (swam) with "invisible passports" that protected them in international waters, adopting the medieval principle that if a cow strays from its pasture it still belongs to its owner. The court, however, ruled in favor of freedom of the seas, and the seals were subsequently hunted at sea almost to extinction. A major factor in the proceedings for the United States was a failure to secure the support of Russia, which was engaged in a similar problem with a separate herd of seals on the Komandorsky Islands, off the Kamchatka peninsula. A subsequent international agreement in 1911 attempted to repair the damage by outlawing all hunting of seals at sea (except for traditional native use) and prescribed quotas for harvesting them on their respective islands. Further concerns of environmental impact on the seals led to a complete ban on hunting on and around the Pribylovs in the 1970s.

PRIMAKOV, EVGENY (1929–). Born in Kiev, Primakov grew up in Tbilisi, Georgia. He was educated at the Moscow State Institute of Oriental Studies (1953), where he became fluent in Chinese and Arabic. He served as deputy director of the Institute of World Economy and International Relations (1970–77), head of its Department of Oriental Studies (1978–85), and director (1985–89) and gained the respect of the Soviet academic community. He subsequently served as **Mikhail Gorbachev**'s special advisor on the Middle East and as envoy to Iraq (1990–91). His professional and astute approach to foreign policy (multilateralism vs. U.S. hegemony) led to his appointment by Boris Yeltsin, after the failed **August Coup** of 1991, as first deputy chairman of the **KGB** and later as Russian foreign minister (1996–98). In the latter role he was a firm opponent of expansion of the **North Atlantic Treaty Organization** membership into the former Eastern bloc.

Primakov's approach to foreign policy, however, was distinguished by primacy on negotiation rather than confrontation, thus heralding the end of the **cold war**. As a reward for his moderation and tact, he ascended to the post of prime minister in September 1998 and is credited with providing firm guidance to domestic reforms before his surprise dismissal in May 1999 and replacement by Sergei Stepashin, who was soon succeeded (also a surprise) by **Vladimir Putin**. After at first deciding to compete for the presidency in the election of 2000, he withdrew, gave his support to Putin, and remained a staunch ally. After 2000 he served as an advisor on Middle-Eastern affairs, during which he tried to prevent the U.S. invasion of Iraq (2003), and as president of the Russian Chamber of Commerce and Industry (2001–).

PRINCE, NANCY GARDNER (1799–c. 1856). Born in Newburyport, Massachusetts, of a seafaring African American family, she resisted following many of her ethnicity and gender into prostitution in Boston. In 1823 she met Nero Prince, a Boston seaman who had first sailed to Russia in 1810 and found lucrative employment as one of about 20 "colored" guards of the imperial palace in St. Petersburg. After their marriage she accompanied him back to the Russian capital, where she was easily accepted into the growing American community, quickly winning laurels for her courageous relief efforts during the famous Neva flood of 1824. She subsequently became a stellar member of the **American colony in St. Petersburg** by establishing a sewing shop that served especially the imperial and noble families with children's clothing; she also continued her welfare and religious activities in distributing bibles for the New England Bible Society.

In 1833 she returned to New England in advance of her husband, who was expected to bring savings from his Russian employment for investment in a business. Unfortunately, he died before he could depart Russia, leaving her to make her own mark, not in business, but as a vocal abolitionist and missionary, concentrating on Jamaica, where she established an orphanage in 1840 as well as one in Boston. Prince won legendary status for her survival of stormy voyages from New England to Jamaica and back, but little else is known about her later life. Her autobiography, *A Narrative of the Life and Travels of*

Mrs. Nancy Prince, was first published in 1850, with subsequent printings in 1853 and 1856—and a paper edition in 1995.

PRINKIPO CONFERENCE (1919). At the **Paris Peace Conference** that concluded **World War I** a question arose in regard to Russia, a major participant in the war, that was not represented in the negotiations because of the **Bolshevik Revolution** and an emerging **civil war** that produced a number of rival claimants to authority. How could a peace be effectively concluded without representation by a major participant? One solution was to invite all major contenders to be the voice of Russia to meet and come to agreement on a representative. A neutral site, the Prinkipo—or Princess Islands—in the Sea of Marmora, near Constantinople, was selected to bring the various factions together, from the beginning probably a long shot. The Bolshevik-controlled central government in Moscow quickly accepted the invitation, but various parties representing opposing views refused to participate. The designated American observers, including **William Allen White**, were frustrated by the anti-Bolshevik parties' refusals. The result was that a very consequential country was totally left out of the treaties that ended World War I, leaving many issues unsettled.

PROKOFIEV, SERGEI (1891–1953). Composer, pianist, director. Along with Igor Stravinsky, Prokofiev was a student of Nikolai Rimsky-Korsakov at the St. Petersburg Conservatory of Music before **World War I**. Discouraged about the prospects for a musical career in Russia, Prokofiev left in the spring of 1918 across Siberia to Japan and the United States. After successful concerts in Japan, he sailed to Honolulu and San Francisco, and from there to New York. Befriended by other Russian expatriate musicians, Prokofiev performed in New York and Chicago with acclaim in 1919. While funded by the management of the Chicago Opera, Prokofiev composed one of his most original and popular pieces, *The Love for Three Oranges*. Because of the sudden death of the director of the Chicago Opera and his own demands, however, it was not performed until several years later. From 1921, he was drawn more to performing in London and Paris with occasional visits to the United States; in 1923 *The Love for Three Oranges* was finally performed for the first time in Chicago by the Chicago Opera under his direction—and also in New York. Prokofiev continued to compose and perform successfully in Europe and the United States until 1933, when he returned to Soviet Russia. His music is best known for the variety of his compositions and their liveliness and innovations, regularly performed by orchestras throughout the world.

PROVISIONAL GOVERNMENT (1917). After the abdication of **Nicholas II** in early March 1917, a new government was formed from the progressive (opposition) bloc of the Fourth Duma. The members were the liberal successors to the imperial regime and included Alexander Guchkov as minister of war, Georgi Lvov as head of government, **Paul Miliukov** as foreign minister, and **Alexander Kerensky** as minster of justice. It received immediate recognition by the United States, which hoped to see Russia transformed into an American-style liberal democracy. With the tsar removed from the scene, American entry into a war "to make the world safe for democracy" in April was much easier. A special **Root Commission** was belatedly dispatched to present the new Russian government with American blessings in May, but the course of the revolution was already turning more radical, due to the rise of the power of worker and soldier soviets, led by social democrats and socialist revolutionaries, that challenged the Provisional Government on economic issues and especially the continued prosecution of the war. Kerensky, the leader of the Provisional Government, inspired little American political support, leaving him more vulnerable to a radical opposition that triumphed in the **Bolshevik Revolution**. The considerable financial (major loans) and advisory (railroads) assistance came too late to save Russia for democracy.

PUTIN, VLADIMIR (1952–). As president of the **Russian Federation** (1999–2008), Putin has been the architect of an economic resurgence and the revival of Russia as a regional and world power. He has accomplished this by winning popular support, building a constructive and loyal administration, and suppressing opposition in the media and political arenas. He nevertheless probably merited his designation by *Time Magazine* as "man of the year" in December 2007.

Born in Leningrad (St. Petersburg), Putin attended Leningrad State University (University of St. Petersburg), specializing in international law. As one of Russia's "best and brightest," he was recruited into the **Committee for State Security (KGB)** in 1975, where he first worked in the Leningrad bureau before being posted to Dresden in East Germany (1985–90), after which he returned to head the international section of the University of Leningrad. There he became acquainted with Anatoly Sobchak and would serve as a capable assistant in his reform administration as mayor of the city (1991–96). Upon Sobchak's defeat in election, Putin moved to Moscow, where he demonstrated his administrative abilities in several capacities under President Boris Yeltsin, rising to head the **Federal Security Service (FSB)**, the Russian Federation successor to the KGB, in July 1998. In the following year in August, he was named by Yeltsin as a first deputy prime minister.

Despite this phenomenal rise through the Russian administration, his appointment by Yeltsin as prime minister and approval by the Duma the same month was a surprise to Russians and foreign observers of the tumultuous Russian scene. Also a surprise was Yeltsin's resignation as president on 31 December 1999, thus, according to the Russian constitution, elevating Putin as acting president. Required to stand in a popular election, he won handily in March 2000 to the first of his two terms. Putin subsequently skillfully outmaneuvered an old guard of reformers, employing former KGB associates and carrying out a series of economic reforms that brought much of the major privatized entities under state control and supervision. A celebrated state–private contest with a major Russian oil company, Yukos, resulted in the trial of its director, **Mikhail Khodorkovsky**, for tax evasion and his sentencing for a number of years to a Siberian prison.

While courting American support and gaining the respect of American leaders, Putin used strong measures against internal opposition, such as in Chechnya and the independent states of the former Soviet Union, for example, in Ukraine and Georgia. He also strongly opposed the expansion of **North Atlantic Treaty Organization (NATO)** membership into former Soviet domination areas, especially Ukraine and Georgia, and opposed the American invasion and occupation of Iraq. He took advantage of the unpopularity of U.S. military involvements in the Middle East to advance his own agenda in promoting the development of energy resources and opposing the **missile shield** that was proposed by the administration of President **George W. Bush** to be employed in Poland. By 2008, thanks especially to Russian economic gains and successful foreign initiatives, Putin's internal popularity rating was at least three times that of the U.S. president.

Limited to two terms as president by the constitution, Putin followed the Yeltsin precedent of hand-picking a successor, **Dmitri Medvedev**, as prime minister in November 2007, who subsequently easily won the

March 2008 presidential election. And Medvedev, assuming office in May, named his patron as prime minister. Thus, the Putin era continues and presents a rising challenge to American foreign policy and in economic and military spheres. In his last months as president, his criticism of U.S. policy, as well as his internal police regime, increased, though he voiced support for negotiation, as indicated in his last meeting with the American president at Sochi in April, though no differences were resolved. In May 2008 his appointment by Medvedev as prime minister (chairman of the council of ministers) was ratified by the State Duma. Thus, Putin remains a major force in Russia and a strong opponent of **NATO** membership for Georgia and Ukraine.

– R –

RADEK, KARL (1885–1939). A Jewish native of Austrian Galicia, Radek became a Marxist revolutionary and participated in radical activity in Warsaw during the **Russian Revolution of 1905**. His main concentration, however, remained in Austria-Hungary and Germany as a left-wing social democrat. After the beginning of **World War I**, he sought refuge in Switzerland, where be became an associate of **Vladimir Lenin** in the Zimmerwald (antiwar) movement. This attachment led to his following Lenin back to Russia in 1917 and lending his assistance to the Bolshevik cause. Fluent in German, he played a leading role in the negotiations for the **Treaty of Brest-Litovsk** and subsequently filled a number of troubleshooting roles in the Soviet government. Radek became a controversial and contradictory figure in the 1920s and 1930s, earning a reputation as an extreme radical within Bolshevik circles but also as a socially comfortable pro-American who frequented the headquarters of the **American Relief Administration (ARA)** in the early 1920s and provided liaison support. A true Leninist, but never a Trotskyite nor Stalinist, Radek represented a voice of Western outreach and intellectual brilliance in the Soviet Union. He became a central figure in the January 1937 purge trial of Trotskyites, often referred to at the time as the "Radek trial." Surprisingly, he was not executed immediately as many others, but sentenced to hard labor in a Siberian camp, where he died, reportedly, at the hands of a fellow inmate.

RADIO FREE EUROPE (RFE). With headquarters in Munich and as the communications program of the National Committee for a Free Europe, RFE began broadcasting to Czechoslovakia on 4 July 1950. It received appropriations indirectly from the U.S. Congress through the **Central Intelligence Agency (CIA)** as part of a psychological warfare campaign until 1971. By that time it was broadcasting over 1,000 hours per week in 28 languages, mainly to the Soviet Union and Eastern Europe. In 1975, to avoid duplication and possible conflict in goals, RFE merged with **Radio Liberty** (as RFE/RL), which was more centered on Soviet émigrés.

RADIO LIBERTY (RL) (1953–1975). Founded by the American Committee for Liberation from Bolshevism, RL commenced broadcasting in Russian from Western Europe, mainly from Munich, into the Soviet Union on 1 March 1953. Programs in non-Russian languages began a few weeks later. Central offices located in New York City employed a large staff of Soviet émigrés and exiles. As was suspected and later confirmed, must of its funding came from the **Central Intelligence Agency (CIA)** through congressional appropriations. Funding and staff increased as its value as a **cold war** propaganda instrument was realized and as Soviet jamming became more of an obstacle. Its early and formative leaders included Soviet experts such as journalist **Eugene Lyons** (president) and **Robert F. Kelley** (retired from the State Department), who was a chief consultant/advisor (1951–64). In 1975 RL merged with **Radio Free Europe (RFE)**. RFE/RL continues to broadcast but now concentrates on sensitive world areas such as the Middle East.

RADISHCHEV, ALEXANDER (1749–1802). A Russian *philosophe*, writer, poet, and one of the first internationally recognized western-oriented Russian liberals; along with Nikolai Novikov, Radishchev thrived under the "enlightened" regime of **Catherine the Great** in the 1780s. He was especially enamored of the American revolution and its heroes. He concluded his "Ode to Liberty" (1784) with a tribute to America: "But, since my spirit is not enslaved, Let my ashes rest on your shores." In Russian history, he emerged as a stern critic of the social and economic conditions he found in *Journey from St. Petersburg to Moscow*. Thus, the American revolution was an inspiration for many Russian idealists who followed Radishchev.

RAEFF, MARC (1923–2008). Born in Moscow, Raeff immigrated to the United States in 1941 from Germany with his family. After studying at Harvard University under **Michael Karpovich**, he taught several years at Clark University before moving to Columbia University in 1961. Raeff quickly became a leading scholar in 18th- and early 19th-century social and political history. In 1973 he was named **Bakhmeteff** Professor of History at Columbia. His *Russia Abroad* (1990), a study of the Russian emigration after the **Bolshevik Revolution**, is of special importance to students of Russian–American relations and Russian emigration. Throughout his career, he fostered Russian–American scholarly communications as a sharp critic of American research on Russian history in book reviews, but also as a kind and sympathetic mentor to students and peers.

RAGOZIN, ZENAIDA (1839–1924). A remarkably bright, sophisticated, and colorful Russian woman, Ragozin came to the United States with her husband around 1870 to promote the Russian populist cause. He returned to Russia and apparently soon died, while she remained in the United States, surviving on her talents in language (fluency in English, French, and German, as well as Russian) and her expanding New York social connections. Her stay of 30 years in the United States remains to be fully researched, but her main occupation in New York was as a tutor to the debutante sector of upper-class American society and as the writer of four volumes for Putnam's "history of nations" series in the 1880s, some of which still stand as classics. She also translated the first real history of Russia into English from the French of Anatole Leroy Beaulieu. As a friend of Margaret Reynolds, she became the godmother of her daughter, **Elizabeth Reynolds Hapgood**. Deciding to return to Russia in 1900 to see remaining family and to reproduce her publications in Russian, Ragozin invited her American protégé Elizabeth Reynolds as a guest for summers on friends' estates.

"Madam" Ragozin published many articles in the Russian press on America and books on American figures such as Helen Keller and George Washington Carver in Russian. She excelled especially in children's literature, for which she won a special grant from **Nicholas II** in 1910. During **World War I**, she wrote for the liberal Petrograd newspaper, *Volos* (*Voice*), while also translating several volumes of

Russian short stories for Putnam. She survived after the revolution by translating materials for the **Comintern**, commenting to a friend, "Beggars cannot be choosers." As long as possible she recounted her life and the events of the times in remarkably well-written English letters to American friends, especially Margaret Reynolds, preserved in the Hapgood Papers in the **Library of Congress**. Ragozin finally received support from the **American Relief Administration (ARA)** in 1921–22 and from a welcome visit from Elizabeth Hapgood in 1923. She died in her small apartment in Petrograd in 1924, probably the last and most remarkable of the **St. Petersburg American colony**.

RAILWAY SERVICE CORPS, AMERICAN. A direct program of technical assistance to Russian railroads resulted from a special American mission to Russia, headed by **John F. Stevens** in May–June 1917. By this time it was obvious that the Russian railroad system was in desperate condition and must be improved in order for Russia to continue the war. A major concern was the **Trans-Siberian Railroad** that was a major artery for transporting vital war materials into Russia from the port of **Vladivostok**. The "corps" began to arrive in January 1918 and was finally withdrawn in 1922. Eventually totaling just over 300 railroad and telegraph specialists, its work was concentrated on the **Chinese Eastern Railway (CER)** and the Trans-Siberian as far as Chita. The officers, headed by Stevens, faced a number of obstacles: Japanese military control of the region, hostile Russian White guard units, and the very poor condition of the equipment, as well as the unreliable labor, mainly Chinese. The unit, however, established a clear record of progress, especially in restoring telegraphic and rail communication and in diplomatic negotiations with the **Far Eastern Republic**. Its members, who much later won the right to military pensions, were the first and the last of Americans officially assigned to Russian duty during this period.

RAKHMANINOFF, SERGEI (1873–1943). Russian romantic composer and virtuoso pianist from North Russia, Rakhmaninoff graduated from the Moscow Conservatory in 1892 and was widely praised for his first concerto that year. He first visited the United States in 1902, when he was a soloist with the Boston Symphony Orchestra. Rakhmaninoff returned to Russia, where he directed the Bolshoi

Opera in Moscow, but after the revolution he fled to Sweden and remained abroad, mainly in the United States, as a concert performer, settling there permanently in 1935. He was one of a number of the Russian intelligentsia who abandoned their homeland after the **Bolshevik Revolution** in order to preserve the best of Russian creative performing arts. He remained Russian at heart, however, and was a strong advocate of American aid (**lend-lease**) to the Soviet Union at the beginning of **World War II**.

RANDOLPH, JOHN (1773–1833). An adroit and troublesome Virginia Democrat but a sharp legal expert on parliamentary law, Randolph served several terms in Congress in the period from 1815 to 1833 and briefly as a senator (1825–27). Perhaps best known for his irascibility and for fighting a drawn duel with Henry Clay (both luckily surviving), Randolph also served in 1830 as minister to Russia, owing to President Andrew Jackson's being obliged to reward him for his support—but definitely not with an appointment in Washington. In poor health and disgusted with his St. Petersburg fate, he nevertheless created a scene at the Russian court by falling to his knees (perhaps drunk) before Nicholas I. He is also noted for some memorable observations on Russia, drunk or sober, such as: "It is Egypt in all but fertility. The extremes of human misery and human splendour here meet." He had expected to sign a treaty with Russia and return home to much acclaim, but Russian delays and his own mental and physical illnesses would leave that task to his successor, **James Buchanan**.

REAGAN, RONALD (1911–2004). After establishing a reputation as a good (if not outstanding) performer in Hollywood films, Reagan proved to be an excellent administrator as a several-term president of the Screen Actors Guild in the early post–**World War II** era. A Roosevelt Democrat, he supported **Dwight D. Eisenhower** and **Richard Nixon** in the 1950s and formally became a Republican in 1962. Reagan entered the political arena seriously in 1966, when he defeated incumbent Edmund "Pat" Brown for governor of California, running on a conservative fiscal program. He subsequently cut funding for welfare and higher education and became the idol of "Goldwater Republicans." He rode this popularity into the White House in 1981, serving two terms.

Though perhaps best known for labeling the Soviet Union as an
"evil empire," for priming the American economy (Reaganomics),
and for developing the "star wars" (Strategic Defense Initiative) policy aimed at Russia, he nevertheless responded adroitly to the reform
agenda of **Mikhail Gorbachev**, especially through the appointment
of veteran diplomats to the "new" Russia, such as **Jack Matlock Jr.,**
and his cordial summit meeting with the Soviet leader at **Reykjavik**
in October 1986 in a crucial encouragement of Gorbachev's new
policies of perestroika and **"new thinking."** Reagan's legacy was
thus one of flexibility toward the Soviet Union—speaking harshly
while waving a soft stick.

RECHT, CHARLES (1907–1976). Born in Austrian Bohemia of
Jewish parents who immigrated to America, he was a graduate of
New York University Law School. Recht served for many years on
the staff of the New York Bureau of Legal Advice, becoming especially known for his defense of immigrant radicals who were threatened with deportation during the **"Red Scare"** of 1920. Recht subsequently represented Soviet organizations, such as the **American
Trading Corporation (Amtorg)**, in the 1920s and lavishly entertained Soviet visitors, for example, the Soviet poet **Vladimir
Mayakovsky** in 1925. Respected as a Renaissance man, Recht published two novels and a book of poetry as well as numerous articles
dealing with civil rights and Jewish history. An unpublished autobiography is among his papers preserved in the Robert F. Wagner
Labor Archives of the Elmer Holms Bobst Library (New York University).

RECOGNITION AGREEMENT (1933). Diplomatic recognition between the United States and Soviet Russia was negotiated in Washington, D.C., by Soviet Commissar for Foreign Relations **Maxim
Litvinov** and President **Franklin D. Roosevelt** in November 1933.
Though a reversal of the long Republican policy of nonrecognition
was expected with the advent of the Roosevelt administration, it was
not consummated until nearly a year after the election. The president's first priority was in setting up agencies and the passage of bills
to inaugurate the New Deal to counter the lingering Depression. Finally, in early October 1933, Roosevelt sent a message to Soviet

"president" **Mikhail Kalinin**, proposing the opening of formal negotiations. Litvinov responded quickly and offered to come personally
for the event. Arriving in New York, accompanied by veteran American reporter **Walter Duranty**, Litvinov cut quite a swath, reminis-
cent of **Sergei Witte**'s appearance in 1905 to negotiate the peace of
the **Russo–Japanese War**.

Direct negotiations in Washington were prepared behind the scenes
by State Department officials, especially veterans such as William R.
Castle Jr., assistant secretary of state and long an opponent of recognition, now restrained by the return of William Phillips of the Wilson
administration, who supported recognition. The main work on details
was done by another department assistant secretary, Judge R. Walton
Moore, the career officer **George F. Kennan**, and **William F. Bullitt**,
just returned from reconnaissance tours of Europe for Roosevelt and
designated special assistant in the State Department. It was a strange
mix with Secretary of State **Cordell Hull**, meanwhile, concentrating
his energy on Latin America. More important, probably, was support
from Middle-American Republicans such as **William Allen White**
and Henry Justin Allen, who had just returned from Russia. Some of
the strongest opposition came from traditional Democratic supporters,
such as labor unions, Polish immigrants, and the Roman Catholic
Church. The latter had been somewhat muted, however, by Roosevelt's cultivating of Father **Edmund Walsh** of Georgetown University, who agreed not to oppose recognition.

The main issues were the Soviet payment of the outstanding
World War I debt, the promise of a substantial American loan, and
the cessation of **Comintern** propaganda in the United States. The situation of a high-level visit on American invitation, however, practically guaranteed that recognition would occur. In the background was
the situation in the Far East, where both the Soviet Union and the
United States were alarmed by aggressive Japanese actions in
Manchuria and the need for joint action. The result was that these
major issues would be agreed upon in principle with details to be
worked out later (which did not happen). The "treaty" was signed on
13 November, followed by a grand celebration at the Waldorf Astoria in New York with many longtime friends of Soviet recognition in
attendance, including **Hugh Cooper**, **Raymond Robins**, **William
Haskell**, and **Samuel Bertron**. Though there was much criticism and

opposition to an agreement that left unresolved issues and troublesome subsequent diplomatic relations, recognition would be a lasting legacy of the Roosevelt international agenda.

"RED SCARE" (1919–1920 AND 1948–1950). Disillusioned with the results of **World War I** and the peace arrangements that followed in Paris, many Americans in business and political circles—and in general—overreacted to the growth of labor protests, inspired by Bolshevik victories, such as the Seattle General Strike of 1919, to advocate a strong suppression of radical movements in the United States. This was officially conducted by Attorney General A. Mitchell Palmer and his assistant, J. Edgar Hoover, and took the form of Federal Bureau of Investigation (FBI) raids on editorial offices of leftist publications and those of political movements, thorough and violent suppression of strikes and demonstrations, and many arrests without benefit of legal rights. Mass involuntary deportations, especially of immigrants from Eastern Europe, followed in 1920–21. These included many who were sympathetic to socialist beliefs but also opponents of the Bolshevik variety.

A case in point is that of Fedor Ivanov, who jumped ship from a Russian vessel in New York Harbor in 1912 to become a political refugee. He moved west to Michigan, where he worked for **Ford Motor Company** in Dearborn. As did many new immigrants, he became active in the **International Workers of the World (IWW)** and joined the **Communist Party of the United States of America (CPUSA)** soon after its founding in 1919. He was arrested in 1920 and deported to what was now Soviet Russia, where he never joined the Communist Party of the Soviet Union. His first son, **Robert Ivanov**, who became a leading Soviet/Russian expert on Russian–American relations, was named in memory of an American socialist friend who was beaten to death in a Detroit jail.

A similar wave of public hysteria accompanied the **McCarthy** era, following **World War II** and another perception of a "red threat." The focus was on left-leaning "fellow travelers" in government agencies and in certain industries, such as motion pictures. In addition to Senator Joseph McCarthy, J. Edgar Hoover of the FBI again played a leading role, and by 1950 Hoover had composed a list of 10,000 (97 percent American citizens) who he recommended for arrest and incarceration on presidential orders as national security threats. Fortunately, neither President **Harry S. Truman** nor **Dwight D. Eisenhower** followed his advice.

REED, DEAN (1948–1987). Born and raised in Denver, Colorado, Reed initially sought a film career in Hollywood and earned roles in a few popular B pictures for his handsome good looks and Elvis Presley–type persona. In the 1970s, he set off on a tour of South America as a rock concert artist, where he became converted to leftist views. Moving to Europe, Reed toured the continent, winning especially receptive audiences in Eastern Europe, including the Soviet Union, in the late 1970s and 1980s with many popular recordings. Reed truly had a good voice and ability to capture the ambiance of the era, as his many extant recordings demonstrate—a more restrained, more modest, but political Presley.

Reed then married an East German actress and settled in East Berlin, where he died by drowning in a lake. His premature death remains a mystery—whether it was an accident or whether the **Central Intelligence Agency (CIA)**, the **Committee on State Security (KGB)**, the *stazi* (East German KGB equivalent), or a jealous lover was involved. Reed still has a large cult following in Eastern Europe and more recently in the United States. He was the subject of an American television documentary in 1985, "American Rebel: The Dean Reed Story," and a biography by Reggie Nadelson, *Comrade Rockstar: The Search for Dean Reed* (2004), the film rights for which Tom Hanks apparently purchased.

REED, JOHN "JACK" (1887–1920). From Oregon, Reed graduated from Harvard University (1910) and became a reporter for a number of publications, such as *The Masses* in 1913. Covering the silk workers' strike in Paterson, New Jersey, that year converted Reed permanently to radical socialist causes. He was soon busy reporting critically on the American intervention in Mexico (1916) and covering both the western and eastern fronts during **World War I**. In 1915, Reed and Boardman Robinson went to Russia on assignment for *Metropolitan Magazine*. His reports, illustrated by Robinson, were also published in *The War in Eastern Europe* (1917). He returned to revolutionary Russia in the summer of 1917 with his wife, **Louise**

Bryant, also a journalist, to capture the drama of the Bolshevik seizure of power in *Ten Days that Shook the World* (1918). He and Bryant, assisted by other American sympathizers such as Albert Rhys Williams, **Raymond Robins**, and **Bessie Beatty**, were among the American journalists and eyewitnesses who demonstrated avid, perhaps naive, support for what they saw as the social and political ideals of the **Bolshevik Revolution**.

Reed returned to America to speak on behalf of that revolution and to create a split in the American Socialist Party that resulted in the formation of the **Communist Party of the United States of America (CPUSA)** by 1919. He returned to Russia, however, to devote the remainder of his short life to the cause of world revolution. While attending the Congress of Peoples of the East in Baku in 1920, he contracted typhus and subsequently died in a Moscow hospital with his wife at his side. Reed was honored with burial along the Kremlin wall, one of the first true heroes of Russian Communism and a martyr to that cause, to be memorialized in various leftist "John Reed clubs." His story is told dramatically in an epic film, *Reds*, with Warren Beatty portraying Reed and Diane Keaton as Bryant.

REMINGTON, FREDERIC (1861–1909). An American artist and sculptor, especially of scenes of the American West, Remington graduated from Yale University and soon became known for his exploits and travels and ability to capture Western life in motion. Remington ventured into Russia in 1891 with a former Yale classmate, Poultney Bigelow. They challenged Russian authorities on an ill-conceived canoe trip down a fortified border stream, were briefly arrested, and saw some of the worst of Russia, which Remington sketched in his ubiquitous style. Their experiences naturally attracted much publicity to the credit of neither them nor Russia. His sketches of Russian soldiers and border guards, however, rank with the best of his large art portfolio.

REYKJAVIK SUMMIT (OCTOBER 1986). This historic meeting between Russian leader **Mikhail Gorbachev** and American president **Ronald Reagan** in the capital of Iceland was the first encounter of Gorbachev with an American leader. Though the session was cordial, the Soviet side was disappointed that Reagan refused to compromise on his Strategic Defense Initiative ("star wars"). It was nonetheless notable for Reagan's retreat from the branding of the Soviet Union as the **"evil empire"** in 1983.

REZANOV, NIKOLAI (1764–1807). Rezanov received a typical "guards" education during the reign of **Catherine the Great** and transferred to the civil service (Bureau of Petitions) with aspirations of becoming a writer. In 1794, he was designated to supervise a detachment of priests and serfs destined for service in **Russian America** for **Grigory Shelikhov**'s settlement at **Kodiak**. On their trip across Siberia, Rezanov fell in love with Shelikhov's daughter, Anna, and they were married. Upon the sudden death of his father-in-law in 1795, he inherited, through his wife, the privileges and rights of North Pacific hunting expeditions, for which he sought government support. This soon resulted in the issuance of a charter by Emperor Paul (1799) for the **Russian America Company (RAC)** that conferred it monopoly rights to a large part of Northwest America. Thus, Rezanov was the true founder of the company and of the initial Russian occupation of what would become known as **Alaska**.

He, with his wife Anna, promoted the Russian presence in the area with permanent bases at Kodiak and **Sitka** and by acquiring the services of **Alexander Baranov** as the first administrator of the region for the exploitation of its fur resources. Anna, however, soon died. Despite the resource and navigational difficulties created by the Napoleonic Wars, Rezanov mounted an inspection expedition in 1803 to Russian America. Suffering considerably from the long voyage around South America and across the Pacific, Rezanov made a historic Russian port call at Nagasaki, Japan. Finally arriving at Sitka in 1805, he found the Russian settlement destitute. Taking advantage of an American ship, the *Juno*, that came there under **John D'Wolfe**, Rezanov set forth for California in April 1806 to obtain supplies.

During the negotiations with Spanish officials, Rezanov became enamored of the 16-year-old daughter, Conception de Arguello, of the commandant of San Francisco and was engaged for a marriage to be celebrated upon his return. To add to this Pushkinesque story, on the trip home across the Pacific and Siberia, Rezanov fell ill with a "fever" and died in Krasnoyarsk. After a long wait for her lover's return, Conception retired to a convent for the rest of her life. More importantly, Rezanov had reaffirmed Russian governmental support for the region and paved the way for a more permanent Russian California connection that was consolidated a few years later with the founding of **Fort Ross**. A romantic opera of this tragedy was produced in St. Petersburg in the 1990s.

RIBBENTROP–MOLOTOV AGREEMENT. *See* NAZI–SOVIET PACT.

RICE, CONDOLEEZZA (1954–). Born in Birmingham, Alabama, Rice graduated from the University of Denver in 1974, received an M.A. from the University of Notre Dame (1975), and earned a Ph.D. in international studies from the University of Denver in 1981, learning Russian in the process. She moved to Stanford that year as a member of the Center for International Security and Arms Control (1981–86) and served as provost (1991–99) of the university, which had a vested interest in international affairs. As a professor of political science, she published a number of articles and received several teaching awards. Rice also participated in a number of major scholarly organizations, such as the Carnegie Endowment for International Peace and the Rand Corporation, while also serving as a member of the board of directors of Chevron Corporation and Charles Schwab.

Rice joined the administration of **George H. W. Bush** as a director of Soviet and East European affairs of the National Security Council (1989–91) and returned to Washington as special assistant to the Joint Chiefs of Staff in 1997. She became national security advisor in the administration of **George W. Bush** in 2001. She was designated secretary of state in 2005, the first scholar of Russian studies in that position. Her tenure continued through the Bush second term under the shadow of the agenda of Bush and Vice President Dick Cheney, to whom she has been criticized as being overly subservient. While strong on social graces and presence, Rice did not achieve much in her own right in political affairs, with the exception of a few orchestrated peace initiatives in the lower Middle East in 2007–08. Speaking Russian, however, enabled her to ease communications and reduce formalities with **Vladimir Putin** and his associates.

RIGA AGREEMENT (AUGUST 1921). The United States responded to a general appeal for assistance issued by **Maxim Gorky** on behalf of **Vladimir Lenin** and the Soviet government for relief supplies to alleviate desperate famine conditions in July 1921. Director of the **American Relief Administration (ARA)** and Secretary of Commerce **Herbert Hoover** agreed to a conference in August with Soviet officials in Riga, Latvia, where American conditions were proposed and accepted: that all American citizens (especially **Xenephon Kalamatiano**) detained in Russia be released, that the distribution of relief be entirely under American control, and that the transportation (mainly rail) for relief be of the highest priority for use by ARA. After the signature by Hoover's representative, Walter Lyman Brown, substantial assistance was almost immediately on its way from European stocks, the first train crossing the Soviet border within a week — along with a carload of American journalists to cover the event.

ROBESON, PAUL (1898–1976). A son of a former slave, Robeson won an academic scholarship to Rutgers University, where he overcame racial discrimination to become a two-time African American All-American in football (as well as achieving varsity letters in basketball, baseball, and track and field) and class valedictorian. After graduation (1919), he moved to Harlem, studied law at Columbia University, and became a partner in a prominent New York law firm in 1923, but he had already begun his career as a singer and actor while working his way through law school. He was acclaimed for his performance in the title role of Eugene O'Neill's *The Emperor Jones* (1924) and went on to star status as "Porgy" in the stage version of DuBose Heyward's novel and in Shakespeare's *Othello*. Robeson is probably best remembered for his bass voice rendering of Jerome Kern's "Ol' Man River" as Joe in the stage and film versions of *Show Boat*. No one since has done it better.

Though always an outspoken critic of American racial injustice, Robeson first emerged as a supporter of the Soviet Union during **World War II**, when he performed at Madison Square Garden for a Soviet benefit rally, chaired by Albert Einstein. There he met Soviet Jewish poet Itzik Feffer and actor/director Solomon Mikhoels of the Moscow Jewish Theatre, beginning a warm relationship. He subsequently and consistently opposed American **cold war** policies and actively supported the progressive candidacy for president of Henry Wallace in 1948. During a 1949 tour of the Soviet Union, Robeson paid tribute to both of his Soviet Jewish friends, who were then being persecuted in a wave of Soviet (Stalinist) anti-Semitism. Despite this, he was accorded the Stalin Peace Prize in 1952 and, in return, he praised **Joseph Stalin**, perhaps misguidedly.

By this time (the McCarthy era), Robeson had earned the enmity of **J. Edgar Hoover** and the Federal Bureau of Investigation (FBI) for his criticism of discrimination against the American black population in appearances abroad. All of his films were blacklisted, and he was denied permission to leave the country, even to Canada, for a number of years. He flaunted this restriction by giving a concert on the American border to a large Canadian audience on the other side. When his passport was finally returned to him in 1958 by a Supreme Court ruling, Robeson left for England, where he resumed performances of *Othello* at Stratford-upon-Avon and in the Soviet Union with much acclaim. Suffering from poor health, Robeson returned to the United States in 1963 to live quietly with his family in Philadelphia. He recounted his experiences in *Here I Stand* (1958).

ROBINS, RAYMOND (1873–1954). From remarkable wanderings through North America in early life—from Florida to Ohio to Colorado to Alaska—Robins achieved success in gold mining in Colorado and even greater riches from ventures into the Klondike region of **Alaska** in the 1890s. Becoming a "social worker," Robins was a partner at Hull House with **Jane Addams** and in other "settlements" in the early 20th century. An active supporter of **Theodore Roosevelt** and his Progressive (Bull Moose) Party, Robins ran for the Senate on the ticket in Illinois in 1912 without success. He subsequently joined the Republican Party's moderate wing, despite his social and political ideals that more resembled those of **Woodrow Wilson** and **Franklin D. Roosevelt**. During **World War I** Robins devoted his considerable energies to **American Red Cross (RAC)** activities, becoming a senior member of its mission to Russia in 1917 under the leadership of William Boyce Thompson and succeeding him as head in 1918. In Russia, he moved into the political arena in support of Soviet Russia after the **Bolshevik Revolution** and worked to secure American assistance to keep that country in the war during the peace negotiations at **Brest-Litovsk**. American diplomats and the Department of State strongly opposed and basically sabotaged his efforts for an American–Soviet rapprochement, and he was forced to leave Russia in May 1918. Robins subsequently continued to support reconciliation with Soviet Russia and diplomatic recognition through Republican Party channels.

During the interwar years, Robins remained a thorn in the side of all Republican officials, who felt obliged to listen to him. While presiding over a Florida estate (Chisenut), which he later bequeathed to the state as a wildlife preserve, Robins suffered a curious mental lapse (amnesia and disappearance for several months) and, later, a freak accident that left him a quadriplegic. He campaigned for recognition, touring through the Soviet Union during the summer of 1933 on its behalf, while continuing to maintain close contact with Republican moderates, such as Senator **William E. Borah**, who were also committed to that cause. Robins well deserved the place of honor at the New York banquet that celebrated the conclusion of the **Recognition Agreement** in November 1933. Robins was one of those unique American eccentrics: entrepreneur, social worker, Republican, internationalist, Russianist, environmentalist, and crusader for various causes.

ROBINSON, GEROID TANQUARY (1893–1971). Born and raised in Virginia as Rodney G. Robinson and known familiarly as "GTR" by his many students, he served in **World War I** and began a career in journalism on the staffs of *The Dial* and *The Freeman* in the early 1920s, while completing an M.A. in history at Columbia University, where he became interested in Russian agrarian history. He was among the first Americans to study extensively in Soviet archives (1925–27) after the revolution. The result was an enduring classic of American historical literature, *Rural Russia Under the Old Regime*, for which he received his doctorate in 1930. He subsequently was an avid promoter of the field of Slavic studies in the United States along with **Samuel Harper**, **Michael Karpovich**, Samuel Cross, and others. Robinson left academia temporarily to serve in the Office of Strategic Services during **World War II**.

Becoming aware of the importance of scholarly Russian studies in the United States in the postwar world, he helped establish the Russian Institute (later **Harriman Institute**) at Columbia University in 1946. In recognition of his leadership in the field, he was named the Seth Low Professor of History at Columbia in 1950. Professor Robinson was renowned as a taskmaster in his seminars for graduate students in Russian history that produced a substantial number of American Russian scholars in the 1950s and 1960s—though he was always a Virginia gentleman.

ROBINSON, ROBERT (1907–1991). As a **Ford Motor Company** lathe operator from Jamaica in Detroit, Robinson decided to seek a more secure employment and freedom from racial discrimination in 1930 during the Depression by securing employment in Russia, during the **First Five-Year Plan**. There he went from one job to another, meeting other **African American** visitors, such as **Langston Hughes**, and soon found himself ensconced in the Soviet world. He was one of a number of Americans who were attracted to the semi-egalitarian, less racially discriminating Soviet society, but most of the others soon left, disenchanted by Soviet life. After many travails, he was finally able to return to the United States in the 1970s to record his experiences in *Black on Red: My 44 Years Inside the Soviet Union* (1988).

ROOSEVELT, FRANKLIN D. (1882–1945). Born at Hyde Park, New York, Roosevelt was a graduate of Harvard University (1904) and of Columbia University Law School. He married Eleanor Roosevelt (1884–1962), a distant cousin and niece of **Theodore Roosevelt**, in 1905. She would be an active promoter of his political career, beginning with his early tenure as a fledgling attorney in New York City. Soon entering politics, Roosevelt was elected to the New York State Senate in 1910 and led fellow democratic rebels (against Tammany Hall) in support of **Woodrow Wilson** as president in 1912. For his loyal service, he was appointed assistant secretary of the navy (1913–20). Proving quite adept at administration in that role, Roosevelt became the vice presidential running mate of James Cox against the Republican ticket of Warren G. Harding and **Calvin Coolidge**, which won convincingly. A year later, while vacationing at the family's summer home on Campobello Island, Roosevelt was stricken with poliomyelitis, which left him paralyzed from the waist down. His political career seemed to be at an end, but encouraged by his wife and friends and through his own determination, he kept active in 1928 by supporting Alfred Smith for the presidency and in being elected governor of New York. Proving his ability to handle administration despite a severe disability, the next step would be his candidacy for president in 1932, conducted with skill but also with the incumbent, **Herbert Hoover**, saddled with the consequences of a severe economic depression.

As president, Roosevelt dealt with a number of crucial issues that involved the Soviet Union. First was the problem of diplomatic recognition, which was achieved despite many opponents, such as the State Department, the Roman Catholic Church, and labor unions, the latter two being traditionally Democratic. His agreement with **Maxim Litvinov** in November 1933 solved few outstanding issues, namely debt payments, an American loan, **Comintern** propaganda in the United States, and guarantees of religious freedom. Nonetheless, a channel of dialogue had been instituted that would endure through many crises of the **cold war**. One of his most significant contributions would be the early (summer 1941) extension of **lend-lease** to the Soviet Union, which grew and became a major basis of the "Grand Alliance" during **World War II**. During those years, FDR prided himself on an ability to deal with the Soviet Union and, particularly, with **"Uncle Joe" (Joseph Stalin)**. He relied on loyal assistants in his administration—Henry Morgenthau, **Harry Hopkins**, Sumner Welles, and **W. Averell Harriman**—to develop good wartime relations and was confident in guiding and understanding the Soviet leaders at conferences at **Tehran** and **Yalta**. Roosevelt was subsequently criticized by opponents for giving in too much to Soviet demands, especially because of winning Soviet accession to a new international body, the **United Nations**, and entry into the war against Japan. His sudden death in April 1945 left much unfinished international business to his successor, **Harry S. Truman**, who basically followed the Roosevelt agenda in regard to the Union of Soviet Socialist Republics (USSR).

ROOSEVELT, THEODORE (1858–1919). A graduate of Harvard University and one of the most literate and literary American presidents— with an impressive portfolio of writings and publications—Roosevelt included in his repertoire the works of **Leo Tolstoy**, which he read on his many ventures into wilderness regions of the world. As president (1901–09) during the **Russo–Japanese War** (1904–05), he saw an opportunity for arbitrating a peace and thus ending the war, while enhancing his own international standing. His mastery of the diplomacy of 1905 was truly remarkable, obtaining the recall of Russian ambassador **Artur Cassini**, who few in the American government could tolerate, and of maneuvering his friend and Harvard classmate, **Alfred von Lengerke Meyer**, into position as ambassador in St. Petersburg. Roosevelt, through Meyer, thus put pressure upon **Nicholas II** to agree to negotiations and, despite Russian objections, to hold them in the United States, which was clearly preferred by Japan. "Teddy" Roosevelt thus guided the deliberations of the **Portsmouth Peace Conference** at the U.S. Naval Shipyards in Kittery, Maine, from his Oyster Bay, Long Island, summer home in August and September 1905, which successfully ended the war. The results left both sides at first unhappy but eventually resigned to the outcome. The president clearly deserved his Nobel Peace Prize for this accomplishment (though it probably should have been shared with Meyer).

ROOT COMMISSION (1917). Sent by President **Woodrow Wilson** to support and recognize the new **Provisional Government** of Russia after the **February Revolution** of 1917 and headed by the elderly (age 72) former secretary of state **Elihu Root**, the commission was composed of a number of distinguished Americans and a military contingent. Among the leaders of the delegation that arrived in Petrograd in May 1917 were **Charles R. Crane**, who is credited with inspiring the idea, **John R. Mott**, chief secretary of the **Young Men's Christian Association (YMCA)**, **Cyrus McCormick Jr.** of **International Harvester**, New York attorney and stock broker **Samuel R. Bertron**, railroad engineer **John F. Stevens**, and labor leader Charles Russell. The military contingent was less distinguished: Vice-Admiral James Glennon and the senior army chief of staff General Hugh Scott. All, of course, had attendants, making up a considerable delegation—with **Samuel Harper** assigned as official guide and chaperone. Harper and Crane preceded the main group, traveling via the Atlantic route and through Scandinavia, while the main party suffered a stormy voyage across the North Pacific.

The results of the commission were mixed, owing partly to the transition in the Provisional Government from the Americanophile **Paul Miliukov**, minister of foreign affairs and de facto leader, to that of the more socialistic, charismatic, and generally disliked **Alexander Kerensky**, who misguidedly staged a military offensive in June for the Americans to prove Russia's military capability. This resulted in a disastrous retreat and the end of the Russian army as an effective fighting force. The commission's reports to the president in July and August would instigate, belatedly, a series of substantial loans to the Provisional Government and the delivery of many military supplies to **Murmansk**, **Archangel**, and **Vladivostok** that arrived too late to be of use before the **Bolshevik Revolution**. The control of these materials would be a factor in the decision for **intervention**.

ROOT, ELIHU (1845–1937). Root served as secretary of war (1899–1904) under two presidents, William McKinley and **Theodore Roosevelt**, a tenure that included the Spanish–American War. In this capacity he inaugurated many reforms in the U.S. military organization and established the Army War College. After the death of Secretary of State John Hay in 1905, Root assumed that position (1905–09), devoting much energy to international conciliation, for which he received the Nobel Peace Prize in 1912. Removed from Washington politics by the election of a Democrat, **Woodrow Wilson**, in 1912, Root retired to legal practice in New York City. In 1917, after the **February Revolution** in Russia and the abdication of **Nicholas II**, Root was asked by Wilson to head a committee of distinguished and representative Americans to Petrograd to welcome what was believed to be a new democratic era for that country. Root (at 72) did not provide the dynamic leadership for such an occasion and was somewhat at a loss in the tumultuous Russian scene. Nonetheless, the **Root Commission** accomplished an important objective of signaling American support for the **Provisional Government** during its relatively brief existence. The commission's recommendation for a major propaganda effort to shore up the Russian military commitment, unfortunately, fell on deaf ears in Washington.

ROPES AND COMPANY. Established in the Russian–American trade in the 1830s by William H. Ropes, the company flourished until the 1850s owing to Russian demand for American cotton and the large number of New England ships involved in this commerce. The large Ropes family and assistants, such as George Prince, settled more or less permanently in St. Petersburg after the conclusion of the **Commercial Treaty of 1832** and were very active in the **Anglo-American Church** that supported a variety of charity and missionary endeavors, backed by the New England Bible Society. A son of W. H. Ropes spent several years as a missionary among the Buriats of Eastern Siberia. Though the direct commerce of the company declined after 1850 under management of George Henry Prince and Ernest Ropes, Ropes and Company moved into oil refining and other Russian business opportunities to survive in Russia beyond the end of the century. After the **Bolshevik Revolution** and the end of the company's business in Russia, Ernest Ropes would become an expert on Russia in the U.S. Department of Commerce for a number of years.

ROSENBERG, JULIUS AND ETHEL (1918–1953). Along with Harry Gold, Elizabeth Bentley, and Klaus Fuchs, the Rosenbergs were among the most important Soviet intelligence agents in the United States during and after **World War II**. The Rosenbergs were arrested in 1950 on the basis of information gained from intercepting and decoding cable traffic (**Venona**). With additional evidence furnished by Fuchs and Gold, the Rosenbergs were tried and convicted of treason and, despite considerable public opposition, were executed in 1953 as traitors, a rare example of a precedent going back to Benedict Arnold.

ROSEN, ROMAN (1847–1921). Having served previously as minister to Japan, Rosen accompanied the Russian peace delegation led by **Sergei Witte** to the negotiations for concluding the **Russo–Japanese War**, arranged by **Theodore Roosevelt** and that resulted in the **Portsmouth Peace Conference** (August–September 1905). He had the advantage of knowing both Japanese and English and used these linguistic skills well. After the successful conclusion of peace, he remained as ambassador (1905–11). During his tenure, Rosen was personally very well liked but unable to reduce the tensions accruing from Russian anti-Semitism, the resulting **passport question**, and the abrogation of the **Commercial Treaty of 1832** by the United States. Rosen reemerged in 1918 as an anti-Bolshevik and pro-American spokesman in **Russia Abroad**.

ROSENSTRAUS, HERMAN AND THEODORE. These brothers immigrated to the United States in the 1860s from Wurttemburg (Germany) and became American citizens before going to Russia to establish a retail business in Kharkov in the 1870s. Their "*Amerikanskii magazin*" (American store) thrived selling Western goods, especially **Singer** sewing machines, but they were periodically in trouble with local authorities, despite payment of bribes, for allegedly selling "French postcards" to local university students but more for being Jewish during a period of intense Russian anti-Semitism. The Rosenstraus brothers regularly appealed their cases to the American legation in St. Petersburg on the basis of the **Commercial Treaty of 1832** that stipulated that Americans had the same rights as Russians in doing business in the country. This would raise the issue of the **passport question**, a Russian effort to restrict American Jews from entry into the Russian Empire by denying visas on the basis of religion.

ROSTROPOVICH, MSTISLAV (1927–2007). Born in Baku of musician parents, Rostropovich debuted on the cello in 1940 and was soon known as a virtuoso with that instrument on a wide range of compositions that included those of Anton Dvorak, Joseph Haydn, Sergei Prokofiev (an early mentor), and Benjamin Britten. In 1955 he and Galina Vishnevskaya, another premier Soviet performer who was lead soprano with the Bolshoi Opera, were married. Outspoken as an advocate of freedom of the arts and for democratic reform, Rostropovich soon fell under a political cloud, along with a close friend, **Alexander Solzhenitsyn**, for whom he provided shelter in Moscow in the early 1970s. Expelled from his positions and deprived of Soviet citizenship in 1974, he would follow Solzhenitsyn into exile in the West.

Rostropovich subsequently established a high reputation in the American musical world as conductor and musical director of the National Symphony Orchestra (1977–94) in Washington D.C., while also serving in guest roles with other leading groups, such as the London Symphony Orchestra. With his Soviet citizenship restored in 1990, he visited Russia and his native Azerbaijan for much-acclaimed performances and tributes from Boris Yeltsin and **Vladimir Putin**. He had the distinction of earning the highest awards from both Russia and the United States: Lenin and Stalin prizes, State Prize of Russia, and the American Medal of Freedom, as well as many other distinctions from other countries, such as the French Legion of Honor. Having retired to Paris, Rostropovich flew to Moscow in early 2007 for medical treatment of what turned out to be terminal intestinal cancer. After his death there in April, he was honored by a memorial service at the new Church of Christ the Saviour, attended by many dignitaries, including Putin, and burial in the artists' section of the famed Novodevichy Cemetery.

RUBENSTEIN, ANTON (1829–1894). Born in a Jewish family in what is now Transdnistria in Moldava, but was then part of the Russian Empire, Rubenstein made his piano concert debut at the age of nine and was soon touring Europe to great acclaim. For six months in 1872–73, on the heels of the U.S. tour of **Grand Duke Alexis**, he made an exhausting visit to America, where he was widely admired. It began in September 1872 with a "serenade" by the New York Philharmonic at Steinway Hall and proceeded through Boston, Buffalo, Montreal, Toronto, Detroit, Cleveland, Cincinnati, Memphis, Baltimore, and Philadelphia and ended with a triumphal return to New York. The American "Rube craze" was phenomenal and added to the complex love–hate relationship between the two countries, helped by Rubenstein's own efforts, such as performing all six Beethoven piano concertos at one concert and gladly enduring many encores that featured several Rubenstein variations on "Yankee Doodle." The income from the American tour helped solidify the eminence of the St. Petersburg Conservatory of Music, which he had founded 10 years earlier. His younger brother Nicholas (1835–81) was also successful in establishing the Moscow Conservatory and claiming **Peter Tchaikovsky** as a prize student but remained in the shadow of his brother.

Though also a respected composer in his time with 20 operas, six symphonies, and numerous concertos, Anton Rubenstein's works were rarely performed in later years, clearly overshadowed by Tchaikovsky,

Nikolai Rimsky-Korsakov, Igor Stravinsky, Sergei Prokofiev, Dmitri Shostakovich, and others. He summed up his life best: "Russians call me German, Germans call me Russian, Jews call me a Christian, Christians a Jew. Pianists call me a composer, composers call me a pianist. The classicists think me a futurist, and the futurists call me a reactionary. My conclusion is that I am neither fish nor fowl—a pitiful individual." He would not be alone among Russians who deserved that epithet.

RUSSIA ABROAD. This term is applied to a substantial number of refugees from the Russian Empire after the **Bolshevik Revolution** who established what they believed would be temporary residences abroad until the Bolsheviks failed. They included a variety of political exiles, White Army veterans, those of foreign origins, and intellectuals seeking to preserve traditional Russian culture. Concentrated in Europe during the interwar years in centers such as Prague, Berlin, and Paris, the Russians (many of whom were Jewish) gave Europe a new "feel." They would include **Paul Miliukov**, **Anton Denikin**, **Boris Bakhmeteff**, **Vladimir Nabokov**, and historians such as George Vernadsky, **Michael Karpovich**, and **Michael Florinsky**. Though most of these expatriate Russians were restricted by immigration rules from the United States, they generally preferred Europe because of knowledge of languages and being closer to Russia. The American **Young Men's Christian Association (YMCA)** was especially sympathetic to their situation and provided educational programs to assist in their adjustments, especially in Berlin and Paris. Many, however, especially of the second generation, would gain admission to the United States just before and after **World War II**, for example, Richard Pipes, **Marc Raeff**, **Alexander Dallin**, and Nicholas Riasanovsky.

RUSSIAN ACADEMY OF SCIENCES. *See* ACADEMY OF SCIENCES.

RUSSIAN AMERICA. Having conquered **Siberia** in the 17th century, Russia launched explorations of the North Pacific, especially those of **Vitus Bering** in the 18th century, that were inspired especially by Peter the Great and **Catherine the Great**. Especially after awakening to the international competition in the area by the **Nootka Sound controversy** and the quest for sea otter skins, Russian entrepreneurs (*promyshenniki*) established hunting camps and then permanent settlements at **Kodiak** and **Sitka**. This led to the consolidation and expansion of the Russian occupation under the aegis, after 1797, of the **Russian America Company** of what would later be the American territory and state of **Alaska**, with a temporary extension into northern California (**Fort Ross**) and briefly to the Hawaiian Islands. Russian America would officially cease with the sale of the territory to the United States in 1867 but would survive culturally in monuments left behind at Sitka and other places, as well as in the enduring presence of the **Russian Orthodox Church** and its Alaska native adherents.

RUSSIAN AMERICA COMPANY (RAC) (1799–1867). The Russian advance to the Pacific coast and into Northwest America was due mainly to the quest for furs, especially those of the sea otter, but also by government interest in exploration and by geopolitics, such as the **Nootka Sound controversy**. After fur hunters had established camps at **Kodiak** by the 1790s, the Russian government of Paul I issued an ukaz in 1799 establishing a Russian stock company that was granted a monopoly contract to exploit the resources of Northwest America (**Alaska** and the **Aleutian Islands**). An administrative center was soon established at **Sitka**, just off the mainland under the company's chief representative, "Governor" **Alexander Baranov**. Though beset by many problems with natives, climate, supplies, and threats of foreign (British) invasion, the company survived—and even flourished at times—on the exchange in China of furs harvested in Alaska for tea shipped overland or later by sea to Baltic ports. Thus, for Russians RAC was mainly a tea company.

Though subsidized by the Russian government, especially in the furnishing of naval ships for security and personnel, RAC faced increasing problems of viability due to the exhaustion of fur resources, the increasing costs of administration, international conflict (**Crimean War**), and commercial competition in Pacific waters with other countries, especially the United States. Also, in the reform period of **Alexander II**, the company was perceived as a throwback to monopoly and feudal treatment of natives. The Russian government sought a way to divest itself of a losing situation by selling the area by the

1850s. This was finally arranged with the United States after the **American Civil War** in 1867. Though RAC technically continued to exist for several more years on the basis of tea supplies, but without a base for the future, it came to an end by 1880. *See also* RUSSIAN AMERICA.

RUSSIAN AMERICAN TREATY OF 1832. *See* COMMERCIAL TREATY OF 1832.

RUSSIAN FEDERATION (RF). In the aftermath of the **August Coup** and rapidly rising independence movements in the Union of Soviet Socialist Republics (USSR), the latter disintegrated, its 15 constituent republics, representing separate major ethnic peoples, becoming independent countries. The largest, the former Russian Socialist Federated Soviet Republic (RSFSR), was reconstituted as the Russian Federation. In fact, **Boris Yeltsin**, already president of the RSFSR, helped engineer the breakup of the USSR, in his own power interests vis-à-vis **Mikhail Gorbachev**. Yeltsin continued as president of the RF, followed in 2001 by **Vladimir Putin**, his chosen successor. The new "Russia" was about 85 percent ethnic Russian, in contrast with about 50 percent in the former Soviet Union, the largest remaining minorities being Turkic or other smaller native groups, such as Chechens, who would pose a continuing problem for the new Russian government.

The United States maintained regular diplomatic relations with the RF while forming modest new representations with the other 14 countries and continued to negotiate with the RF on remaining and new issues, such as arms reduction and control of nuclear weapons. The new Russia also faced economic, social, and political instability that concerned American officials during the administration of **Bill Clinton** and led to a considerable amount of support by the American government and other organizations to assist Russia through its transition difficulties. Under Vladimir Putin, the RF has rebounded, especially with the spiraling price of oil, to forge ahead of the other states of the former USSR into a realm of comparative prosperity and, at the same time, restore some of its dominance over the other republics.

RUSSIAN INFORMATION BUREAU. Established in 1922 in Washington, D.C., and directed by **Boris Skvirsky** on behalf of the Soviet

Union, the bureau served as a pseudo-embassy during the period of nonrecognition until 1933. During this period, it facilitated contacts through direct communication with the **Commissariat of Foreign Affairs (Narkomindel)** in Moscow regarding such things as permissions for relatives of Americans to leave Russia and obtaining visas for Americans by running a courier service to Montreal or providing forms to be processed at Russian consulates in Europe. By all accounts it was a beehive of activity, patronized especially by the conservative Republican chairman of the Senate Committee on Foreign Relations, **William E. Borah**, who might be considered for this period as the American "minister to Russia" in absentia. The bureau would merge into the Soviet embassy after the **Recognition Agreement** in 1933 with Skvirsky remaining as advisor to the new Soviet ambassador.

RUSSIAN INSTITUTE. *See* HARRIMAN (RUSSIAN) INSTITUTE.

RUSSIAN RESEARCH CENTER. *See* HARVARD RUSSIAN RESEARCH (DAVIS) CENTER.

RUSSIAN REVIEW. During the 1930s there was much discussion among American scholars of Russia about launching a new scholarly journal devoted to Russia. Reservations involved a natural competition that would result with the *Slavonic and East European Review*, edited by the long-recognized dean of Western studies of Russia, **Bernard Pares**. Many American scholars, such as **Samuel Harper**, had longtime connections with Pares. Nevertheless, an independent American journal, supported by Harper, Samuel Cross, **Robert Kerner**, and others materialized with its first issue appearing on 7 December 1941. Though in the early years dominated by Russian émigré exiles, such as Dmitri Mohrenschildt, the *Russian Review* continued to provide the best of American scholarship on Russia. It gravitated more toward objective works under the editorships of Alan Wildman and Eve Levin and from moving from Ohio State University to its current home at the University of Kansas. In contrast to its only American competitor, *Slavic Review*, the *Russian Review* emphasizes Russia and history as opposed to broad interdisciplinary and wider geographic coverage. While the *Slavic Review* is the journal of the major scholarly organization devoted to the subject, the **American Association for the Advancement of Slavic Studies (AAASS)**, the *Russian Review* stands alone in its dedication to Russian studies.

RUSSIAN REVOLUTION OF 1905. A long period of Russian activism and gestation of revolutionary ideas from the 1870s into the 20th century culminated in a spontaneous protest by workers and students in January 1905 (Bloody Sunday), setting off a year-long series of conflicts. A major catalyst was an unpopular and losing war against Japan in the Far East. A number of Americans were involved as observers diplomatically and militarily, while many others expressed sympathy for the Russian liberal and radical agendas. The United States also helped extricate the imperial regime from a near disaster by arbitrating an end to the **Russo–Japanese War** (1904–05) at the **Portsmouth Peace Conference**. The upheaval included a famous naval mutiny in the Black Sea (Battleship *Potemkin*), a general strike in St. Petersburg, and the issue of the "October Manifesto" that initiated a new elected Duma for Russia. Though many of the hopes for a real democracy were thwarted in the following years—not only by the government of **Nicholas II** but also by the extremist radical movements—the 1905 revolution remained for many the "dress rehearsal" for the one of 1917. *See also* BOLSHEVIK REVOLUTION.

RUSSIAN REVOLUTION OF 1917. *See* BOLSHEVIK REVOLUTION; FEBRUARY REVOLUTION.

RUSSIAN SOCIAL DEMOCRATIC LABOR PARTY (RSDLP). A Russian Marxist party was formed from a small intellectually oriented "emancipation of labor" group led by Georgy Plekhanov and held its first congress in 1898 in Minsk (only nine delegates attended). From there it gathered momentum under the younger leadership of **Vladimir Lenin**, **Leon Trotsky**, and Peter Struve. At the Second Congress in 1903 in Brussels and London, it would split into two factions: the **Bolsheviks** under Lenin and the Mensheviks. The former would forge ahead during 1917 to take power in revolutionary Russia in the **Bolshevik Revolution**, attracting sympathy from a number of Americans, such as **John Reed** and Albert Rhys Williams.

RUSSO–JAPANESE WAR (1904–1905). Expansionist policies by Russia in the 1890s were resented by the rising power of Japan, especially as a result of the construction of the **Trans-Siberian Railroad**, the selection of a shortcut across Manchuria (the **Chinese Eastern Railway [CER]**), the establishment of a considerable Russian presence in **Harbin**, and the acquisition of timber rights in North Korea, which Japan considered to be in its sphere of influence. Failure to negotiate differences led to the surprise Japanese attacks on Port Arthur and a siege of **Vladivostok** in February 1904. The Russians were totally unprepared and initially suffered serious naval defeats. Port Arthur fell, and Vladivostok was blockaded, leading to most of the war being bogged down in central Manchuria.

The United States was clearly sympathetic to the Japanese at the beginning, and American bankers, mainly Jewish, provided essential loans to support the Japanese cause. A number of American reporters, such as **George Kennan**, and military observers also favored Japan because of animosity toward Russia's policies toward its Jewish population and its persecution of revolutionaries. Japanese success, however, led to fears of a new challenge to U.S. interests in the Far East. President **Theodore Roosevelt** won Russian acceptance of mediation in a peace conference at the Portsmouth Naval Shipyards to resolve the conflict. Thanks to the successful courting of public opinion by **Sergei Witte**, head of the Russian delegation, and the pressure of the president on the Japanese, a peace was brokered that retained Russian presence and reputation in the world arena. In the treaty (September 1905), Russia lost some territory, including Port Arthur and the southern half of Sakhalin Island, but avoided payment of an indemnity.

– S –

SAKHAROV, ANDREI (1921–1989). As a nuclear physicist and political dissident, Sakharov attracted the attention and sympathy of Americans, especially after his protests in the 1960s resulted in exile and house arrest in Gorky (**Nizhny Novgorod**) in the 1980s. Born and educated in Moscow, Sakharov became a leading physicist employed in scientific laboratory work during **World War II**. After the war, he led the Soviet Union into the nuclear age with atomic research, culminating with the country's surprising gain in the field with hydrogen bomb capability. He became disenchanted with the results in an arms race and ICBM delivery capability that raised the possibility of mutual atomic destruction. In 1968 he called for a new rationality between the United States and the Soviet Union in *Reflections on Progress, Peaceful Coexistence, and Intellectual Freedom* and became a courageous human rights activist. For this he was awarded the Nobel Peace Prize in 1975, though he was not allowed to leave the country to accept it.

Sakharov became increasingly critical of the political blindness and stagnation of the era of **Leonid Brezhnev**. His outspokenness led to his exile in Gorky in 1980 with his second wife and fellow human rights activist, Yelena Bonner, despite many American appeals on his behalf. Sakharov would reemerge into the Russian political scene in 1987 by means of a phone call from **Mikhail Gorbachev** inviting him back to Moscow. He subsequently became a major spokesman for a Russian open democracy and was elected as a delegate to the Congress of People's Deputies in March 1989. Unfortunately, he died later that year of a sudden heart attack.

SAN FRANCISCO CONFERENCE. Following the agreement by the "Big Three," **Joseph Stalin**, **Franklin D. Roosevelt**, and **Winston Churchill**, at **Yalta** to Roosevelt's proposal for a new international organization, a conference of Allied countries and others met to support this initiative. Delegations from over 50 countries, numbering around 850, met in San Francisco in June 1945 to draft and sign the charter of the **United Nations**. The total number of staff, reporters, and observers reached 6,000, making it one of the largest international conferences ever held. The heads of principal delegations took turns chairing plenary meetings: Secretary of State Edward Stettinius of the United States, Foreign Minister Anthony Eden of Great Britain, **Vyacheslav Molotov** of the Union of Soviet Socialist Republics (USSR), and T. V. Soong of China. The negotiations for the charter occurred behind the scenes, resulting in an agreement on a veto power for the "Big Five"—United States, USSR, Britain, France, and China. A ceremonial signing of the charter took place on 25 June, culminating in an address by President **Harry S. Truman**. The UN formally existed upon the ratification of the charter by the "Big Five" and a majority of the other signatories on 24 October 1945.

SANDERS, BEVERLEY C. (1815–c. 1875). Originally from Baltimore, where he managed a general store, Sanders went to California in 1850 attracted by business opportunities of the gold rush in San Francisco. He founded a bank partnership with Samuel Brenham, established a gas company, and was the first president of the San Francisco Chamber of Commerce. In 1853 he organized the **American Russian Commercial Company (ARCC)** to bring ice from the **Russian America Company (RAC)** territories in **Alaska** to serve the demand for refrigeration for a burgeoning population and for cooling mint juleps on the hot Panama steamers that connected California with the East Coast. In 1854 he journeyed to St. Petersburg to negotiate a 20-year contract with the RAC for ARCC that included all items that might be imported from the Russian territories, such as lumber, to California, or, in other words, a monopoly arrangement. Unfortunately, the investment in ice cutting and storage overextended his credit, causing his bank to fail and his departure from the American company.

SCHILLINGER, JOSEPH (1895–1943). Born in Kharkov, Schillinger was a true Russian American virtuoso in abstract design, mathematics, physics, and musical composition. Maturing in the fairly open and free artistic society of 1920s Russia, Schillinger became a friend and inspirer of **Dmitri Shostakovich** and of the "tsar" of Soviet art and literature, **Anatoly Lunacharsky**. He was sent by the latter in 1928 to the United States, where he collaborated with a number of Russian and American iconic musicians, while teaching at Columbia University on his system of music composition. With a fellow Russian-Jewish émigré, Lev Termin (Leon Theremin), he composed the first work, "Symphonic Air," for electronic music (the Theremin box), first performed in Carnegie Hall with the Cleveland Symphony Orchestra in 1930. Schillinger, however, is best known for his collaboration with George Gershwin on *Porgy and Bess* and with Glen Miller on "Moonlight Serenade" and "Pennsylvania 6500."

SCHLEY, REEVE (1881–1960). A graduate of Yale University (1903) and receiving a law degree from Columbia University (1906), Schley became a leading American banker during the first half of the 20th century. As vice president of Chase Bank in New York, he superintended the substantial accounts of the Soviet government during the 1920s and early 1930s to pay for the contract arrangements with such companies as the **Austin Company**, **Ford**, **International Harvester**, General Electric, and many others. Schley also served as president of the **American Russian Chamber of Commerce** in close association with the **American Trading Corporation (Amtorg)** during the **First Five-Year Plan**. He was, of course, a strong advocate of U.S. diplomatic recognition of Soviet Russia.

SCHUYLER, EUGENE (1840–1890). From a New York aristocratic family, Schuyler earned one of the first doctoral degrees from Yale University, learned Russian mainly from association with the Russian fleet that visited New York City during the **Civil War**, and subsequently received diplomatic appointments as consul in Moscow (1867–69) and secretary of legation in St. Petersburg (1870–76). He spent much time away from his assigned posts, however, traveling in the Caucasus and Central Asia, which he described in many articles in American newspapers and journals and collected in books, such as *Turkistan* (1877). While serving as consul in Moscow, he collected a number of original documents that were the basis of the first genuine American history of Russia that centered on the life of Peter I, *Peter the Great, Emperor of Russia: A Study of Historical Biography* (1884).

SECOND DIVISION, U.S. EMBASSY (1915–1918). In 1915, the United States, as a leading neutral country during the initial years of **World War I**, agreed to serve under the Geneva Convention as supervisor of the Russian prisoner-of-war camps for German, Austro-Hungarian, and Turkish captives and deserters who were scattered across the country, mainly in **Siberia**. The continuation of the war, the vast distances, and the internal problems of the empire required a considerable American presence, designated as the Second Division of the embassy in Petrograd. The United States also assumed jurisdiction of government properties of the enemy countries. The Austrian embassy in Petrograd thus became the headquarters of the Second Division, headed by Basil Miles. A sizable contingent was established in a more central location in Moscow. In all, the commitment more than doubled the official American personnel in Russia and made it by far the largest diplomatic colony in Russia during the war. By most accounts (contained in a large file in the **National Archives**), the American service was appreciated by all sides and contributed to internal stability during the upheavals of 1917–18, as well as assisting in the forming of the **Czechoslovak Legion**. After American entry into the war and elimination of its neutral status, the duties were transferred gradually to Sweden and Norway, both of which lacked the facilities for coping with the growing number of prisoners.

"SECRET SPEECH" (25–26 FEBRUARY 1956). A surprise late-night and somewhat extemporaneous four-hour speech by First Secretary **Nikita Khrushchev** in a secret session at the conclusion of the 20th Congress of the Communist Party of the Soviet Union in Moscow became a major turning point in Soviet policy from the rigidity of the era of **Joseph Stalin** to a more flexible approach that acknowledged the "crimes" of Stalin, especially for the extent of the great purges (1936–38) and the cult of the personality. Khrushchev's pronouncements caused reverberations throughout the Soviet-controlled sphere and led to abortive efforts by Poland and Hungary to steer independent paths. It was also followed by the liberation of many survivors of the purges from the gulag camp system, the posthumous rehabilitation of a number of those who had perished, and the advent of a new policy of **peaceful coexistence**. The speech was naturally heralded in the West as a breakthrough and loosening of the tensions of the **cold war**.

SEVERSKY, ALEXANDER (NE ALEXANDER PROKOFIEV DE SEVERSKY) (1894–1974). A highly decorated Russian naval aviator during **World War I**, Seversky is credited with downing six German planes, despite having lost a leg. He was a member of a Russian air mission to the United States in 1917 and stayed to become an assistant to General Billy Mitchell in founding the U.S. Air Corps. A pioneer advocate of air power, Seversky devised the first air-to-air refueling system in 1921, married a New Orleans socialite and pilot (Evelyn

Oliphant) in 1923, and founded Seversky Aircraft Corporation in 1931, later reorganized as the Republic Aviation Company that produced the P-47 Thunderbolt and a prototype luxury 100-passenger airship, the Seversky Super Clipper, for Pan American Airways in 1938. He was also the author of *Victory Through Air Power* (1942), the **World War II** book immortalized in the film version by Walt Disney. Seversky was an advocate of long-range bombers and the creation of the Strategic Air Command during the **cold war**.

SEVOSTIANOV, GRIGORY (1916–). Academician and historian of American history in the Russian **Academy of Sciences** and first director of its Center for North American Studies, Sevostianov is the editor of a number of valuable document collections on Soviet–American relations for the interwar years. A veteran of partisan campaigns in **World War II**, during which he was badly wounded, he studied history in Rostov before the war and diplomacy after it. In 1948 Sevostianov joined the **Institute of General History** of the Academy and has been a leading member for 60 years. In this role he was an advocate of objective history, a promoter of young scholars, a protector of those who fell under the shadow of the **Committee on State Security (KGB)**, and a proponent of collaboration with American scholars during the **cold war** and beyond. On one very memorable occasion he led a Soviet delegation to a symposium at the **Franklin D. Roosevelt** library at Hyde Park on World War II in August 1987, just as **glasnost** was beginning; by his initiative the parameters of scholarly exchange shifted dramatically from belligerence to open discussion and compromise. In the early 21st century, he edited a number of valuable documentary publications.

SEWARD, WILLIAM H. (1801–1872). From a Whig abolitionist position, Seward became a founder of the Republican Party by 1860. Though hoping to gain nomination for the presidency for himself, he supported **Abraham Lincoln** and upon Lincoln's election was named secretary of state. His activist career included an agitation for war against Britain and expansionist aims in North and South America. During the **Civil War**, Seward successfully courted Russian support for the Union that resulted in visits of Russian naval squadrons to New York and San Francisco, which helped discourage British and

French support for the Confederacy. He is perhaps best known for the negotiation of the purchase of **Alaska** in 1867, named prematurely as "Seward's Folly." The negotiation with Russian Minister **Eduard Stoekl**, following the mission of **Gustavas Fox** to Russia in 1866, was deftly accomplished secretly and confirmed an era of close Russian–American relations that followed the Civil War. Seward, by the purchase, consolidated a major territorial expansion of the north vis-à-vis the south (Cuba).

SEYMOUR, THOMAS HENRY (1807–1868). As U.S. minister to Russia (1854–58), Seymour served at the head of the American legation in Russia during the **Crimean War** (1854–56) that was growing considerably in political stature, owing mainly to mutual Russian–American Anglophobia. He was instrumental in maneuvering the United States into a position of benevolent neutrality, boosting Russian morale and resistance to the British and French invasion of the south of Russia. Seymour also adroitly supported, encouraged, and maintained communications with a number of American surgeons who volunteered to minister to the needs of Russian casualties in the theater of battle. His assignment also reflected a shift of orientation in the State Department from the South to the North before the **Civil War**.

SHATOFF, WILLIAM (BILL) (?–c. 1937). Involved in the **Russian Revolution of 1905**, Shatoff sought political refuge in 1907 in the United States, where he worked as a railroad engineer, became an activist in the **Industrial Workers of the World (IWW)**, and organized with Aleksandra Kollontai, **Emma Goldman**, and **Leon Trotsky** the return of Russian political exiles to Russia in 1917. Joining this exodus, Shatoff, a rather corpulent, colorful figure, emerged after the **Bolshevik Revolution** as an important facilitator, especially in managing the transfer of the government from Petrograd/St. Petersburg to Moscow in March 1918. He subsequently held midlevel positions in the Soviet government and was a resource person for many visiting Americans. During the **First Five-Year Plan**, he supervised the construction of the 1,000-mile Turk-Sib Railroad that connected Central Asia to the **Trans-Siberian Railroad** from Tashkent to Novosibirsk, an exploit recorded by **Anna Louise Strong** in *Moscow*

News and the *New York Times*. Later in the 1930s, an American inquiring about his whereabouts was told, "Change the *a* in his name to an *o*."

SHELIKHOV, GRIGORY (1747–1795). Russian/Irkutsk fur merchant and entrepreneur. In 1775 Shelikhov set off to exploit the fur resources of the Aleut and Kurile Islands. Concerned about British presence in the North Pacific, he organized a larger company in 1783 in partnership with Ivan Golikov with the aim of settling the islands of the North Pacific. He and his wife Natalia set off from Okhotsk to found the first Russian settlement in North America on **Kodiak** Island. Shelikhov and Golikov traveled to St. Petersburg in 1788 to obtain the support of **Catherine II** for their American objectives as well as to unite a number of fur companies, which resulted in the formation of the **Russian America Company** (1799). This visit coincided with the empress's becoming alarmed about international interest in the area. Though Shelikhov failed to see the fruition of his goal of a strong Russian presence in the North Pacific, his widow would continue in his footsteps to achieve it, with the help of **Nikolai Rezanov**. *See also* BARANOV, ALEXANDER; NOOTKA SOUND CONTROVERSY.

SHERMAN, WILLIAM TECUMSEH (1820–1891). As a hero of the **American Civil War**, Sherman was much admired and respected in Russia for his striking Cossack-like accomplishments in his march through Georgia. Afterwards, he organized from a Chicago base a Western (Nebraska and Colorado) buffalo hunt for **Grand Duke Alexis** in 1872. Later that year, Sherman, accompanied by the son of President **Ulysses S. Grant**, traveled through Russia from the Black Sea to St. Petersburg, receiving many honors along the way. In the Russian capital, Sherman met with Chancellor **Alexander Gorchakov** and dined with Emperor **Alexander II**. He also reminisced about the Civil War (over glasses of Kentucky bourbon) with Admiral **Stepan Lesovsky**, who commanded the Russian squadron that visited New York in 1863.

SHEVARDNADZE, EDUARD (1928–). Mikhail Gorbachev, in a surprise move in July 1985, replaced longtime Soviet foreign minister

Andrei Gromyko with a party liberal inexperienced in foreign affairs. At the time the event was celebrated more for the significant "changing of the guard" than for Shevardnadze's appointment. He nevertheless met the challenge and paved the way for a new dimension of Soviet foreign relations, dubbed **"new thinking,"** that is, a rational approach to international relations devoid of ideology. In 1990, however, he resigned his position in protest of the Gorbachev shift to the right that led to the **August Coup** of 1991. Shevardnadze returned to Georgia to become its first president after it became an independent country due to the collapse of the Soviet Union. His tenure, however, was marred by corruption and difficult economic conditions, which damaged his reputation and led to his solid defeat in a popular referendum in 1998. He failed to solve internal ethnic problems that involved Osetians in the north, Abkazians in the west, and other minorities, and he was forced to retire from political life in 1999.

SHEVCHENKO, ARKADY (1930–1998). Born in eastern Ukraine, Shevchenko grew up in Crimea, though the family was dispersed by the German occupation (1941–44) during **World War II**. After study at the Moscow State Institute of Foreign Relations, he joined the Soviet diplomatic service in 1956, assigned to a special department on the **United Nations (UN)**. Most of his service was subsequently in the Soviet delegation to the UN except for a brief period (1970–73) as a special advisor to Foreign Minister **Andrei Gromyko**, after which he returned with his family to New York as under-secretary-general of the UN. By 1975, however, he had decided to defect and established contact with the **Central Intelligence Agency**, which convinced him to stay in Soviet service and provide information. By 1978 he became aware of **Committee on State Security (KGB)** suspicions of his activities and formally asked for political asylum. Sadly, his wife returned to Russia to die mysteriously two months later. He recounted these experiences in *Breaking with Moscow* (1985).

SHOSTAKOVICH, DMITRI (1906–1975). One of the major musical geniuses of the 20th century, Shostakovich contributed much to maintaining the tradition of Russian musical compositions in the Soviet area, mainly in the classical genre and within the shifting guidelines of Soviet controls over the arts. Early in his career, however,

Shostakovich demonstrated a talent for **jazz** improvisations. He first became caught up in the Jazz Age by playing piano for American silent films in the 1920s in order to pay for his studies at the conservatory in Petrograd/Leningrad. Among his early compositions were "Jazz Suite," "Tahiti Trot," and the jazz ballet *Zolotoi Vek* (*The Golden Age*) (1930). He would soon conform, however, to the Stalinist restrictions on culture and denounce his early infatuation with American jazz. Shostakovich might have been the Soviet George Gershwin. Instead he became a major composer of classical symphonies and operas, whose works are part of the repertoire of all major orchestras and especially popular in the United States.

SIBERIA. Russian expansion into the large northern part of the Asian continent began in the 17th century with settlements in the southern region extending to the Pacific coast that was being explored by sponsored voyages as early as the reign of Peter the Great. By the first half of the 19th century, Siberia had gained a permanent Russian presence in cities such as Irkutsk, Tomsk, Chita, and Novosibirsk. By that time Americans and Russians discussed their mutual "manifest destinies," going west for America, east for Russia, producing in more recent years comparative studies of frontier settlement. Also in the early 19th century, the expansion of the United States and the Russian Empire met in the North Pacific and, though Russia would "retreat" by selling **Alaska**, the two countries would continue to have common borders.

Siberia also had a fascination for Americans conscious of their own conquest of a huge land mass and in the second half of the 19th century would attract American entrepreneurs such as **Perry McDonough Collins**, **George Kennan**, **Enoch Emery**, and others interested in the development of the enormous mineral resources of the area. In the early 1900s, the construction of the **Trans-Siberian Railroad** would provide an alternative route to Europe across the North Pacific and Siberia for the many adventurous Americans, including **William Howard Taft**. During both **World War I** and **World War II**, Siberia would be an important lifeline for essential supplies from America to Russia. *See also* INTERVENTION, AMERICAN; LEND-LEASE.

SINGER SEWING MACHINE COMPANY. An American pioneering company, Singer held a virtual monopoly on production and sales of its sewing machines in Russia from 1890 into the 1920s. By 1880, Singer had become well established in Europe with a central base in Hamburg and had begun to explore the possibilities of sales in Russia. The company had already developed an inexpensive model for the general market due to mass production's ability to reduce costs. Sales boomed owing especially to the technique of term payments and readily available service. After initial excursions into the Russian market, the company determined to make a major investment there in the late 19th century. A landmark office building was constructed on Nevsky Prospect in St. Petersburg, with a tower featuring a globe on top. In Soviet times it would be known as *dom knigi* (House of Books). A factory was built in Lubertsy, a suburb of Moscow, to manufacture simplified "Zinger" machines, and the headquarters would shift to that location later.

With sales and repair shops scattered throughout the empire, Singer was one of the largest private companies in Russia, employing more than 30,000 by 1914. At the beginning of **World War I**, many of these shops would be ransacked as the company was (mistakenly) popularly considered German and/or Jewish. The Singer heavy-duty machines, imported from the United States, nonetheless sewed most of the uniforms for the Russian army. In Russia the company would suffer during the war because of a forced conversion to the manufacture of munitions. Due to these losses, Singer reluctantly relinquished its operations to nationalization in 1924. The factory continued to manufacture Singer-type sewing machines through the Soviet era and more recently has been modernized by Singer of Canada. *See also* INTERNATIONAL HARVESTER COMPANY (IH).

SISSON DOCUMENTS. Papers collected by Edgar Sisson, representative of the American Committee of Public Safety in Russia, in early 1918 purported to show that the Bolshevik leaders had accepted financial aid from Germany during **World War I** and were, therefore, "German agents." Initial inspection of the papers by American experts, including **Samuel Harper**, certified them as authentic, thus contributing to the U.S. decision for **intervention** and the subsequent policy of nonrecognition. They were later dismissed as crude forgeries. The issue of

German funding of the **Bolshevik Revolution** remained, with the conclusion that some was involved but had no real effect on the outcome of events.

SITKA (NEW ARCHANGEL). Situated on an island off the southern coast of **Alaska**, Sitka became the administrative center of the **Russian America Company** from 1799 to 1867, when the territory was sold to the United States. Its advantages were a good harbor, a relatively mild climate, and closeness to both British (Hudson's Bay Company) and American settlements and military and political centers. The first "manager" of the company, **Alexander Baranov**, enhanced the small town with a large administrative building, the "Baranov Castle," and a prominently displayed Russian Orthodox church; they represent a monument to the Russian presence in North America and serve as a tourist attraction, especially for visitors from Alaskan coast cruise ships. *See also* RUSSIAN AMERICA.

SIVACHEV, NIKOLAI (1934–1983). A leading historian of modern American history at the **Moscow State University** (MGU), Sivachev headed the department of American history in the historical faculty for several years and promoted closer ties with American scholars and the nurturing of American studies in Russia and of Soviet studies of the United States. One of his achievements was the establishment of a regular Fulbright lectureship in American history at MGU in 1974. Unfortunately, Sivachev died suddenly and prematurely on the verge of major advances in Russian–American scholarly cooperation. He has been much recognized for his pioneering efforts in cultural exchange, his dedication to students, and his honest efforts at objectivity during the **cold war**.

SKVIRSKY, BORIS (1887–1941). Skvirsky first came to the United States in late 1921 as a representative of the **Far Eastern Republic (FER)** to the **Washington Conference**. He stayed in the United States as the "minister" of the FER, which was soon absorbed into the Soviet Union. Skvirsky then managed an adroit transition to a basically private status as the unofficial Soviet representative during the period of nonrecognition (1922–33). His **Russian Information Bureau**, centrally located in Washington, provided information to businessmen, the press, Congress, and others. With the initial assistance of **Alexander Gumberg**, Skvirsky facilitated the obtaining of visas to the Soviet Union with advice, forms, and, if needed, courier service to an official Soviet consulate in Montreal. He could also intervene in emergencies for relatives trapped in Russia via direct communication with **Maxim Litvinov** in the **Commissariat of Foreign Affairs** in Moscow. His "business" was much appreciated and valued by many who desired to go to, or communicate with, Soviet Russia, ranging from Senator **William E. Borah** to academics such as **Samuel Harper**. After recognition (1933), Skvirsky remained as first councilor to the embassy for a few years before returning to Moscow, where he ultimately became a victim of a "clean-up purge" during the summer of 1941.

SLAVIC REVIEW. Founded in 1961 by the **American Association for the Advancement of Slavic Studies (AAASS)**, the *Slavic Review* and its predecessors, such as the *American Slavic and East European Review* (1945–61), established a high scholarly reputation for the field and promoted current and future studies in the area. In contrast to the ***Russian Review***, which is not affiliated with an organization, *Slavic Review* includes all Slavic peoples and countries and extends into Central Asia—and includes more interdisciplinary subjects. Since 1996, its editorial office has been at the University of Illinois in Champaign-Urbana, where it was edited by Diane Koenker and Mark Steinberg, and maintains its position as the leading American journal in the field.

SMITH, CHARLES EMORY (1841–1908). Smith, publisher of the *Philadelphia Ledger*, was American minister to Russia at a crucial time (1890–92), during one of the worst **famines** in Russian history. At first reluctant to become involved in a complicated internal situation, Smith soon rallied to the cause, appealed eloquently for American assistance, and succeeded in cutting through the Russian bureaucracy to master local authorities and obtain the necessary transportation for a major American relief effort. He was an advocate of closer Russian–American relations in subsequent years.

SMITH, CHARLES HADDELL (?). An adventurer in Russia from Indiana, Smith set off to strike it rich in the goldfields of **Siberia** in the early 20th century with little success. He returned to Russia, however, in 1922 to seek Bolshevik support—and that of the American government—in ousting the Japanese from Siberia. He was also involved with the management of the **Chinese Eastern Railway (CER)** for a period, but by 1925, he had gravitated to Moscow, where he served as an advisor to various American business interests and "general secretary" of the **American Russian Chamber of Commerce**. He had the advantage of knowledge of Russian and experience in business and connections in Soviet circles. Smith continued as a freelance resident agent in Moscow through the 1930s, assisting American engineers, workers, and business executives, who were bewildered by the Soviet scene. Smith was one of those elusive Americans who served as facilitators of Russian–American business relations during the first half of the 20th century. *See also* FIRST FIVE-YEAR PLAN.

SMITHSONIAN INSTITUTION. This well-known research facility in Washington, D.C., was founded in 1846 through a bequest of British philanthropist James Smithson. From the very beginning it was involved in exchanges of books and scientific objects with major countries, including Russia. The Russian **Academy of Sciences** was its major partner in these transactions, though quite a few of them involved Russian government ministries, independent agencies (such as the Saltykov Shchedrin Imperial Library, the Pulkovo observatory, and the Hermitage gallery), as well as individual gifts directly to the institution or indirectly to government officials, such as those involved in the 1866 visit of **Gustavus Fox** to Russia and that of **Grand Duke Alexis** to the United States. Many of these became scattered through the various divisions of the Smithsonian, while most of the printed items, such as special publications of the Russian/Soviet Academy of Sciences, were transferred to the **Library of Congress**.

SOLZHENITSYN, ALEXANDER (1918–2008). A Soviet mathematics instructor and **World War II** veteran, Solzhenitsyn emerged as a surprisingly new voice in Soviet literature, following the removing of the restraints of socialist realism and the condemnation of the "crimes" of the **Joseph Stalin** era in the **"secret speech"** and subsequent **peaceful coexistence** policy of **Nikita Khrushchev**. Having suffered a series of arrests and imprisonments after the war, Solzhenitsyn dramatized his own experiences, first in *One Day in the Life of Ivan Denisovich* (1962), an exposé of the gulag system that was approved for publication personally by Khrushchev. He was influenced by Aleksandr Tvardovsky, editor of the prominent literary journal *Novyi Mir* (*New World*), where the book was first published. Solzhenitsyn's other works, including *First Circle* (1968) and *Cancer Ward* (1968) established his position as a leading Soviet and world writer. For these he received the Nobel Prize in Literature in 1970 but declined to travel to accept it. He continued to write works strongly critical to the Soviet regime, such as *Gulag Archipelago*, for which he was arrested and deported in 1974.

For the next 20 years Solzhenitsyn resided in exile in the United States, most of the time in isolation in Vermont, while publishing a fictional series on **World War I** that began with *August 1914* (1983). Fully committed to the Orthodox Christian world and critical of Western materialism, he returned to Russia in 1994, where he remained once again in somewhat aloof seclusion, emerging only occasionally, such as for the funeral of his close friend **Mstislav Rostropovich** in 2007. His legacy in Soviet–American literary relations remains enormous, with extensive evaluations beginning with obituaries after his death in August 2008.

SOROS, GEORGE (NE SCHWARTZ) (1930–). From a Jewish family in Budapest, Soros immigrated in 1947 to England, where he graduated from the London School of Economics in 1952 and worked at odd jobs, eventually securing an entry-level position in a London bank. In 1956 he moved to the United States, where he quickly rose in the investment world and established First Eagle with lucrative hedge funds. Through the Quantum Fund he reached the upper levels of high finance, though not without charges and convictions of insider trading. To his credit, much of his profit from various speculative involvements has been devoted to good causes—as well as to questionable political activism. Most notable has been the Soros contributions to the establishment of computer access at a number of Russian and East European universities. He became a strong critic of the **George H. W. Bush** administration and vocal proponent of gun control, provoking Republican Party leaders, especially Dennis Hastert, to question the sources of his funding (implying drug trafficking).

SPANISH CIVIL WAR (1936–1938). A weak and divided democratic and republican Spanish government was challenged by right-wing military leaders, led by General Francisco Franco. The resulting civil war expanded into a conflict between the fascist/Nazi world led by Germany and Italy and the "democracies" of Great Britain, France, the Soviet Union, and the United States. Because the latter were far from united, Franco's forces had the advantage in terms of military supply and advice. The Soviet Union, especially, committed substantial material and ideological support to the republican cause, alongside the volunteer, liberal aid made famous by participants such as Ernest Hemingway and George Orwell. This cause was seriously damaged by division, especially that between Soviet-sponsored armed units and the idealistic and opposing Trotskyite and anarchist elements that were still strong in Spain. The defeat of the republican forces by the summer of 1938, largely due to failure of a real commitment by "the democratic world," was a major blow to **Maxim Litvinov**'s campaign for **collective security** and a factor that supported the British policy of appeasement in the decisions of the **Munich Conference** in September 1938.

SPASO HOUSE. The residence of the American ambassadors to Soviet Russia (1934–) was built by Moscow merchant Nikolai Vtorov in 1912–13 in the neoclassical style of older buildings in the area of Spasopeskovskaya Square in Moscow. At the time of the recognition of the Soviet Union by the United States in 1933, a desperate housing crunch existed in the Russian capital. In advance of the arrival of Ambassador **William F. Bullitt**, the house, then occupied by the Peoples' **Commissariat of Foreign Affairs**, was secured by **George F. Kennan**. Subsequently, Spaso House has been the scene of many social events. Among notable occasions was the celebration of the bicentennial of the American Revolution in 1976, another Fourth of July reception in 1985 upon the advent of perestroika, and the keynote address of **Henry Kissinger** for the conference on 200 years of Russian–American relations in November 2007. Many distinguished American leaders, including several presidents attending summit meetings, have stayed there.

SPUTNIK. The successful launch on 4 October 1957 of a small module into orbit by the Soviet Union as the first earth satellite caught the United States by surprise. That **cold war** adversary had suddenly outreached the United States in space. Though Sputnik was a rather small and primitive object, it nevertheless emitted a "beep-beep" heard on radios around the world and was a major propaganda victory for **Nikita Khrushchev**, both at home and abroad. Sputnik, followed by the first man in orbit, **Yuri Gagarin**, ushered in a space race that would lead to an American concentration on landing a man on the moon. In later years these events would be regarded as a pathway for Russian–American cooperation in space explorations.

STALIN, JOSEPH (1879–1953). Though a significant contributor to the Bolshevik revolutionary organization from 1905, particularly in obtaining funds by criminal actions, Stalin ranked in the secondary echelon of the party. **Vladimir Lenin**, however, valued his dedication and administrative skill and designated him editor of *Pravda* in 1917, subsequently awarding him important **Civil War** assignments and finally appointment as party secretary in 1919. Though Lenin had reservations about his crude behavior and perhaps intended to demote him in the ranks, owing to his illness after 1922, he was unable to head off a power struggle after his death in 1924.

In the 1920s Stalin gradually consolidated his power by playing one faction against another and winning the allegiance of a large number of new members of the rapidly growing party apparatus. His innovative program of crash industrialization launched in 1928 was both daring and initially disastrous in terms of expenditure of resources, both material and human, through the **First Five-Year Plan.** One important inspiration was the rapid American industrial advance with similarly gigantic engineering projects, mass-production techniques, and large-scale, mechanized farms. The program had its earlier incarnations in the **Sergei Witte** system and the **Peter Stolypin** plan, all often referred to under the rubric of *amerikanizm*. Assisting with the construction were a number of major American companies—**International Harvester**, **Singer**, **Austin Company**, **Ford Motor Company**, and General Electric and Westinghouse. Imported engineering talents included **Hugh Cooper** and **John Calder**.

While the construction of factories, dams, and the Moscow Metro system were impressive, the human cost was terribly high, especially during a severe **famine** that resulted in the deaths of millions of peasants in Ukraine and the Volga region. Accompanying the new regime was a cleansing of the old in mass arrests and show trials and purges conducted during the period 1935–39. Many of the old Bolsheviks, who had been friends and supporters of Lenin, were eliminated. Among them were **Lev Kamenev**, **Karl Radek**, eventually **Leon Trotsky**, and many others. This caused much disillusionment among American admirers of Soviet accomplishments in the midst of a major capitalist world depression.

During this period, Stalin generally followed the lead of his Commissar of Foreign Affairs, **Maxim Litvinov**, approving his successful negotiation of diplomatic recognition with the United States. This came to a close, however, with the rise of Adolf Hitler and the shift in direction toward accommodation with Nazi Germany. Another abrupt change in international affairs occurred with the German invasion of the Soviet Union in 1941. The "Grand Alliance" of **World War II** won the Soviet leader the epithet of **"Uncle Joe"** and prominent display of his picture on the covers of American magazines as a great ally. This harmony ended rather suddenly after the war and with the power and ideological rivalries of the **cold war**, of which he was a major architect.

STANDLEY, WILLIAM H. (1872–1963). From California, Standley graduated from the U.S. Naval Academy in 1895 and began his active service in the Spanish–American War. Subsequently, he served in a number of assignments, rising to the rank of rear admiral in the 1930s. As chief of naval operations in the 1930s he won the respect of an old navy man and then president, **Franklin D. Roosevelt**. In early 1942, after **W. Averell Harriman** declined an appointment as wartime ambassador to the Soviet Union, Standley accepted. From the beginning he was disappointed in having his authority undercut by special missions headed by Harriman, **Harry Hopkins**, **Wendell Willkie**, and **Joseph Davies**, and especially by the independence of **Philip Faymonville**, who directed the **lend-lease** deliveries on the Soviet end. Though having little previous knowledge of Soviet affairs, Standley during his tenure (February 1942–October 1943) took a harder line toward the USSR than was popular at the time, especially in regard to **Joseph Stalin**. Despite this he later criticized American policy for not being forthright about the failure to launch a second front in 1943. Annoyed by the obvious efforts to bypass his authority, Standley resigned his post in October 1943. He would win more respect for his cautionary attitude during the **cold war**, especially after the publication of his memoirs, *Admiral Ambassador to Russia* (1955).

STANISLAVSKY, KONSTANTIN (1863–1938). Actor, theater director, founder of the **Moscow Art Theater (MAT)**, Stanislavsky began as a stage actor in Moscow in the late 19th century but advanced to founding of the MAT, which quickly established a reputation as a premier repertory company in Russia—and the world. The theater was renowned for its new renditions of classics and for performances of Anton Chekhov, Henryk Ibsen, and other early 20th-century contemporaries. New York theater critic **Norman Hapgood** planned to bring Stanislavsky and the MAT to New York in 1914, but this was thwarted by the beginning of **World War I**. A visit was finally staged in New York in 1923 to much acclaim, followed by a return engagement in 1924. Hapgood's wife, **Elizabeth Reynolds Hapgood**, translated Stanislavsky's works, such as *An Actor Prepares*, into English; they had a major impact on the Actor's Studio and American theater in general.

STATE ARCHIVES OF THE RUSSIAN FEDERATION (GARF). Constituting a combination of a number of previous archives, GARF is approximately equivalent to the United States **National Archives**. Housed in Moscow, it contains most of the governmental records of the Russian Empire and the Soviet Union. This includes documents of many of the ministries and commissariats, and even personal papers of the Romanov family, such as the letters from the United States of **Grand Duke Alexis** to his mother in 1871–72, and records of various Soviet agencies. The archives are generally open to scholars. An exception is the documents of the Russian and Soviet foreign ministries/commissariats—Archive of the Foreign Policy of the Russian Federation (AVPRF), which is located separately and under much stricter administration, and in general not open to foreign scholars, or only with great difficulty and many restrictions. The other major research collection in Moscow is the Russian State Archive of Social-Political History (RGASPI) that maintains the records of the Russian/ Soviet Communist Party, including the protocols of the **Politburo**, papers of party members, and papers of the **Comintern**. Much of the latter that pertains to the **Communist Party of the United States of America (CPUSA)** is available on microfilm at the **Library of Congress**.

STEFFENS, LINCOLN (1866–1936). As a leading American journalist, Steffens, along with Ida Tarbell and Ray Stannard Baker, was a practitioner of muckraking and was associated with *McClure*'s and *American Magazine*. As a social reformer he is best known for *Shame of the Cities* (1904). Sympathetic to socialist revolutions, Steffens accompanied **William C. Bullitt** in 1919 on a mission to Soviet Russia, where they met with **William Shatoff**, Commissar of Foreign Affairs **Georgy Chicherin**, and **Vladimir Lenin**, the experience related in detail in his *Autobiography* (1931). The mission, an effort of **Edward House** to bring Russia into the **Paris Peace Conference**, though reaching a preliminary agreement with Lenin, was scuttled by the British. Steffens was one of a number of Americans, including **John Reed**, Albert Rhys Williams, **Louise Bryant**, and **Bessie Beatty**, who were sympathetic to the **Bolshevik Revolution**. During a subsequent visit to Russia in 1922, Steffens is credited with the classic remark, "I've seen the future and it works."

STEVENS, JOHN F. (1853–1933). Born in Maine, Stevens served on the staffs of a number of American railroads and was the supervisor for the construction of the Canadian-Pacific Railroad before becoming the chief engineer for the construction of the Panama Canal. In 1917 he headed an American railroad inspection mission to Russia and subsequently directed the Russian Railway Service Corps (1918–23), mainly in Manchuria, through the **Russian Civil War** and during the existence of the **Far Eastern Republic (FER)**. His leadership and presence confronted and successfully avoided a permanent occupation by the Japanese intervening forces in the region by establishing technological direction and control of telegraphic communications traffic along the eastern **Trans-Siberian Railroad**.

STOEKL, EDUARD (1804–c. 1875). Succeeding long-term minister **Alexander Bodisco** after his accidental death in 1854, Stoekl already had several years of experience in the United States as secretary of the Russian legation. He would subsequently steer Russian diplomacy through the difficult years of the **American Civil War**. Sometimes styled as a "baron," Stoekl was of modest Baltic German origin and, like his predecessor, was married to an American. He is best known for engineering the sale of **Alaska** that began with contacts with Senator William McKendree Gwin and **Beverley C. Sanders** of California during the **Crimean War**. Pursuit of this goal was interrupted by the war, during which Stoekl was adept in shifting his own allegiance from the South to the North and in facilitating the reception of the Russian squadrons to New York and San Francisco.

After the war Stoekl resumed discussions with Secretary of State **William H. Seward** about Alaska. Any serious step, however, depended on St. Petersburg, where councils under the influence of Grand Duke **Constantine** prevailed in the decision to sell. The actual negotiation in Washington was done secretly and in haste, virtually overnight, at the end of March 1867. Stoekl, unfortunately, was soon charged with corruption in bribing key figures to achieve the vital approval of Congress and perhaps in payoffs to Seward himself. Under this cloud, Stoekl would retire from Russian service (though with a substantial pension in dollars) to spend his remaining years in the Russian and American societies of Paris.

STOLYPIN, PETER (1862–1911). As Russian minister of interior and chairman of the council of ministers (1906–11), Stolypin was successful in temporarily stabilizing the empire after the turmoil of the **Revolution of 1905**. He is best known for the initiation of major reforms of the countryside that would have eventually liquidated the peasant village commune, considered a target of revolutionary activism. By special decree, provisions were made to divide the traditional communal allotments to peasant families into permanent possessions and then to the removal of the dwellings to the land, essentially dissolving the villages (communes). This was quite a radical change for Russia, patterned clearly after the American independent farms. Unfortunately, Stolypin's assassination in 1911, a reversion to conservatism, and the advent of **World War I** would terminate this promising initiative. His program was an example of *amerikanizm* that pervaded Russian and Soviet policy through the **Joseph Stalin** era of collectivization.

ST. PETERSBURG AMERICAN COLONY. A distinctive American community in the Russian capital emerged in the early 19th century with the establishment of diplomatic relations and the flourishing of commerce between the two countries. The fact that the city was both the governmental center and a major port brought American merchants and diplomats together, especially fostered by the prominence of the first minister, **John Quincy Adams**, who was from Boston, and a successor, **Henry Middleton**, of Charleston. The colony was nurtured by the **Anglo-American Church** and the American legation/embassy. Merchant families, such as that of John D. Lewis and William H. Ropes, found common ground with industrialists and engineers of the **Winans**, **Whistler**, and **Berdan** families and a number of **African Americans** that would include **Nancy Prince** and **Ira Aldridge**. They would also associate with and assist many visiting Americans to the Russian Empire and include a number of Russians returning from the United States, for example, **Zenaida Ragozin**, and spouses of Russians, such as **Julia Grant Cantacuzene**.

The colony expanded considerably in the late 19th and early 20th centuries with the expansion of major American companies into Russia: **Singer**, **International Harvester**, **Westinghouse** (William E. Smith), **New York Life Insurance** (**Frederick Corse**), and so on. A symbol of the American presence was the landmark Singer building on Nevsky Prospect. During **World War I**, the American military and diplomatic personnel multiplied, due especially to the establishment of the **Second Division** of the embassy and growing political and economic connections. Major expansions of the **American Red Cross** and **Young Men's Christian Association** were also significant. These and the **Root Commission** of 1917 to Petrograd symbolized the new Russian–American connections introduced by the war and revolution. Another contingent of Americans attracted to Russia at the time were journalists who included **John Reed**, **Louise Bryant**, and others.

After the **Bolshevik Revolution**, the Soviet withdrawal from the war in the **Treaty of Brest-Litovsk**, and the move of the capital to Moscow in 1918, the American community dissipated, many fleeing through Finland, while the embassy transferred temporarily to Vologda. By 1924, when the city was renamed Leningrad, the American colony had disappeared, to be replaced by a smaller and more fragmented community in Moscow during the 1920s and 1930s.

STRATEGIC ARMS LIMITATION TALKS (SALT I AND SALT II). These were a major focus of Soviet–American relations during the **détente** era of **Leonid Brezhnev**. The idea of limiting and perhaps even decreasing the large number of nuclear arms (that represented the possibility of mutual self-destruction) was perceived as desirable on both sides of the **cold war**. Negotiating the details was not easy owing to calculating numbers of multiple warheads and complex delivery systems, for which both the United States and the USSR were reluctant to provide information. Decreasing tensions, however, spurred progress in protracted, behind-the-scenes negotiations that concluded with a "treaty" (SALT I) in 1972 with a complicated series of inspections and restrictions. This, however, was never ratified by the U.S. Senate. Progress toward another stage (SALT II) proceeded but was caught up in the instability of Russia after the collapse of the Soviet Union in the **Mikhail Gorbachev** and **Boris Yeltsin** eras. The existence of nuclear stockpiles and missile systems remained a major problem for the future.

STRATEGIC ARMS REDUCTION TREATY (START). Proposed first by President **Ronald Reagan** at Geneva in 1982, the program was designed to reduce the possibility of mutual assured destruction (MAD). Negotiation on reducing the numbers of nuclear warheads and the missiles that carry them continued over a number of years and resulted in the signing of START I on 31 July 1991 between the United States and the USSR. It was later signed by Kazakhstan, Ukraine, and Belarus, which agreed to remove their nuclear weapons. The far-ranging results helped end the **cold war** with arms reduction, such as the destruction of 365 U.S. B-52 bombers. A further advance in this program resulted in the signing of START II between President **George H. W. Bush** and Boris Yeltsin on 3 January 1993. The **Russian Federation**, however, withdrew from this agreement in 2002 after the United States abandoned the **Anti-Ballistic Missile (ABM) Treaty**.

STRATEGIC OFFENSIVE REDUCTIONS TREATY (SORT). On 24 May 2002 the United States and the **Russian Federation** agreed to decrease their nuclear arsenals to 1,700–2,200 operational warheads. It has been criticized for lack of a verification system and, though ratified in June 2003, remained largely ignored and unimplemented. It is due to expire in 2012.

STRONG, ANNA LOUISE (1885–1970). An American social worker, journalist, and international socialist who was born in a small town in Nebraska in a Congregational minister's family, Anna Strong was an unusually gifted child. She graduated from Oberlin College in 1905 and received a Ph.D. in philosophy from the University of Chicago three years later. Strong worked initially for the U.S. Office of Education as an advocate of social welfare programs and then joined her father in Seattle, where she became a labor advocate, school board member, and avid mountain climber. As a social pacifist Strong opposed American entry into **World War I**, joined the **Industrial Workers of the World**, and was an active participant in the Seattle General Strike (1919). She joined the **famine** relief in Russia of the **American Friends Service Committee** and remained to sponsor an agricultural colony for orphan victims, described in her *Children of Revolution* (1925). She became devoted to the Soviet "experiment," returning to the United States to win support among the business community. Strong also traveled to Central Asia and China, where Communist leader Zhou Enlai won her admiration, described in *China's Millions* (1928) and *Red Star Over Samarkand* (1929).

Strong returned to Russia in 1930 to found and edit *Moscow News*, the first Russian newspaper in English that was specifically geared to publicize the accomplishments of the **First Five-Year Plan** and to record her experiences and views in a number of revealing books: *The Soviets Conquer Wheat* (1931), *I Change Worlds: The Remaking of an American* (1935), and *This Soviet World* (1936). She traveled widely throughout the Soviet Union and, perhaps, knew the country better than any other American at that time. She remained there through **World War II**, interviewing many average citizens as well as the leaders, but her real sympathies remained with the Chinese revolution, for which she was, ironically, arrested in Moscow in 1949 and expelled. She settled in China in the 1950s, renewing her close relationship with Zhou Enlai until her death.

STRUVE, OTTO (1897–1963). Struve's great-grandfather, Friedrich Georg Wilhelm von Struve (1793–1864), emigrated from Germany to the Russian Empire in 1817 to direct the observatory at Dorpat in Estonia and then became the founding director of a new observatory on Pulkovo Heights near St. Petersburg in 1839. He was succeeded by his son Otto Wilhelm Struve (1819–1905). The first Otto Struve established contacts with American astronomers by hosting **Cleveland Abbe** at Pulkovo in the 1860s and touring the United States in 1879, during which he purchased a 30-inch lens from the Clark Company of Cambridgeport, Massachusetts, for a new telescope at Pulkovo. His namesake grandson, trained in Russia, came to the United States in 1921 to obtain a doctorate from the University of Chicago and to join its faculty in astronomy and physics, as well as to direct the university's Yerkes Observatory in California and the MacDonald Observatory of the University of Texas. Realizing the community of interests of Russia's transported intelligentsia, in 1924 Struve organized the Society of Russian Intellectuals of Chicago. He was later (1950–59) a professor at the University of California and director of the university's Leuschner Observatory.

SUMMERS, MADDIN (1877–1918). Born in Nashville, Tennessee, Summers graduated from Vanderbilt University and attended Columbia University before entering the foreign service. He served at various consular posts, including Barcelona, Madrid, Belgrade, and Sao Paulo, before his assignment in April 1917 as consul general in Moscow to augment the staff of beleaguered ambassador **David Francis**. There he inherited the major responsibility for the oversight of the German, Austrian, and Turkish prisoners of war in Russia. The appointment was largely due to his marriage to a Russian noblewoman (née Gorianov) in Spain and his dedication to service. Moscow, already significant because of its central location, loomed in importance, owing to the moving of the capital to that city in March 1918 and the withdrawal of the American embassy to Vologda. The pressures on the consul general naturally increased and, according to many accounts, led to Summers's premature death of "overwork" (heart attack) at age 41. Contributing to it was his facilitating contacts with the new government, despite his pronounced anti-Bolshevik views, which were at least partly due to his marriage into an aristocratic Russian family. The State Department would subsequently employ his widow in Washington, D.C., as a translator.

SURGEONS IN CRIMEAN WAR, AMERICAN (1854–1856). Because of American sympathy toward Russia during its defense against the invading forces of Great Britain, the Ottoman Empire, and France in Crimea, more than 30 American physicians volunteered for duty in the rear of the Russian army, mainly in hospitals in and around Simferopol, where they treated wounded and those who had fallen ill to typhus and cholera. Most had studied or were studying medicine in Paris and thus arrived in the early stages of the war. This demonstration of American support was much appreciated by Russian officials and helped boost morale. Their sacrifice was indeed genuine, owing not to the danger of battles some distance away, but to disease—typhus and cholera—of which 12, a substantial percentage, were victims.

SVININ, PAVEL (1787–1839). Svinin served in the Russian Ministry of Foreign Affairs as a translator and was assigned to the legation in Philadelphia in 1811 for his knowledge of English and geography. He was thus in residence in the United States during the upheavals of the Napoleonic invasion of Russia and the **War of 1812**. Svinin wrote a popular descriptive account of the leading Russian cities for the American audience, published in Philadelphia in 1813: *Sketches of Moscow and St. Petersburg Ornamented with Nine Coloured Engravings, Taken from Nature* by "Paul Svenin." In the United States, he became infatuated with river steam navigation, meeting Robert Fulton and admiring his work, and convinced Svinin of opportunities in Russia. His most interesting work, including a chapter on steamboats and his paintings and sketches, was published in Russia in 1814. A later translation is by Avrahm Yarmolinsky, *Picturesque United States of America, 1811, 1812, 1813* (1930). After his return to Russia, Svinin had a distinguished career as founder and editor (1820–30) of a leading literary journal, *Otechestvennye zapiski (Fatherland Notes)* that would feature articles on America.

– T –

TAFT, WILLIAM HOWARD (1857–1930). As secretary of war in the administration of **Theodore Roosevelt**, and in the absence of a secretary of state (owing to the death of John Hay), Taft was involved in the president's efforts to arbitrate a peace of the **Russo–Japanese War** (and the **Portsmouth Conference and**

Treaty). Subsequently, in 1908, he made an around-the-world trip, traveling on the new **Trans-Siberian Railroad** through Russia, which was widely publicized and helped gain him the election to the presidency. He and his entourage created quite a sensation as they crossed Russia to meet with **Nicholas II** in St. Petersburg. During his administration, the **passport question** came to a crisis, resulting in the abrogation in 1911 of the Russian–American **Commercial Treaty of 1832**.

TALBOTT, STROBE (1946–). After graduating from Yale University (1968), Talbott received a Rhodes scholarship to Oxford, where he met and roomed with **Bill Clinton**. After serving a number of years as a correspondent for *Time Magazine* on Russian affairs, he joined the Clinton administration as a special assistant and its chief advisor on communications with Russian president Boris Yeltsin. Talbott's experiences in "handling" the pro-American but often unsteady and unpredictable Russian leader are detailed in *The Russia Hand* (2002). He subsequently became director of the Brookings Institution.

TAUBMAN, WILLIAM (1941–). A graduate of Harvard University (1962), Taubman earned a Ph.D. at Columbia University (1969) specializing in Soviet politics, particularly of the era of **Nikita Khrushchev**. His scholarly works include *Stalin's American Policy* (1982) and *Khrushchev, the Man and His Era* (2003). He also collaborated with and translated **Sergei Khrushchev**'s *Khrushchev on Khrushchev* (1990). Taubman teaches at Amherst College and is an associate of the **Davis Center** at Harvard University.

TCHAIKOVSKY, PETER (1840–1893). A famous Russian composer whose works still occupy the repertoire of leading orchestras, Tchaikovsky was invited to preside over the dedication of Carnegie Hall in 1891 and conducted a concert that featured his works with an array of dignitaries present. He also visited Niagara Falls and Washington, D.C., and directed orchestras in Baltimore and Philadelphia. As **Leo Tolstoy** was to world literature in the American mind, so Tchaikovsky was instrumental in promoting an appreciation of Russian symphonic music. Both have enduring positions in the classrooms, libraries, and concert halls of the United States.

TEHRAN CONFERENCE (1943). Codenamed "Eureka," the "Big Three" leaders of **World War II**—**Franklin D. Roosevelt, Winston Churchill**, and **Joseph Stalin**—met for the first time in the capital of Iran from 28 November to 1 December 1943. The meeting would be followed by similar conferences at **Yalta** and **Potsdam** in 1945. The Tehran meeting was mainly a result of the desire of Roosevelt to meet with the Soviet leader. The British, in turn, insisted on a preparatory session in Cairo (Cairo conference), but Roosevelt was ill and uncooperative, so the conference in Iran resulted in a series of concessions to the Soviet Union. The main decisions, however, were open to future discussion and definition: Allied support of Yugoslav partisans; Soviet support of Turkey if that country became an Ally; improving communications between the three powers; a promise by Great Britain and the United States to begin an offensive into Western Europe in the spring of 1944 (Operation Overlord); recognition of the future boundaries of Poland along the Oder-Neisse line and the Curzon line in the east; tentative approval of mutual support for a **United Nations** organization; and an agreement by the Soviet Union to enter the war against Japan once Germany was defeated. The conference succeeded in defining many of the central issues of the war but was no doubt influenced by the superior position of Stalin, having won the major and crucial battles at Stalingrad and Kursk that year. *See also* CASABLANCA CONFERENCE; YALTA CONFERENCE.

TEN DAYS THAT SHOOK THE WORLD **(1919).** **John Reed**'s evocative, sympathetic, and stylized account of the **Bolshevik Revolution** (October/November 1917) was based on the author's firsthand observations and materials he gathered in Petrograd/St. Petersburg while covering the dramatic events with fellow journalists **Louise Bryant** (his wife) and Albert Rhys Williams. **Sergei Eisenstein**'s classic film, "October," celebrating the 10th anniversary of the revolution, was broadly based on Reed's account. The book and film are widely used in undergraduate history classes in both Russia and the United States.

THOMPSON, LLEWELLYN E., JR., "TOMMY" (1904–1972). As ambassador to the Soviet Union (1957–62 and 1967–69), Thompson was a leading American expert on Soviet Russia, along with **George**

F. Kennan and **Charles (Chip) Bohlen**. Thompson began his long diplomatic service in Russia in the 1930s and later became one of the most successful American diplomats on the front line of the **cold war**, heading the mission in Moscow through many of the most acute crises of the period: the **U-2 incident, Berlin Wall, Cuban missile crisis**, and **Soviet invasion of Czechoslovakia**.

TOLSTOY, LEO (LEV) (1828–1910). Perhaps the best-known Russian writer of the 19th century, Tolstoy attracted a wide following in the United States, reaching its height in the 1880s "Tolstoy craze." Although probably few Americans read all of his novels or even one completely, much discussion occurred in salons and journal reviews, abetted by popular translations such as those by **Isabel Hapgood**, who took liberties with the texts, notably omitting certain "salacious" passages. Some prominent Americans adhered to what was becoming a cult, notably **Theodore Roosevelt**, who read *Anna Karenina* while on a hunting expedition in the American West. The writer himself often went out of his way to host visiting Americans, such as **Jane Addams, Charles R. Crane**, Hapgood, and **William Rainey Harper** at his country estate, Yasnaya Polyana, or his Moscow dacha, preserved as a museum. Though he considered several invitations to visit America, Tolstoy, a true Russian aristocrat and patriot, never left Russia, which endeared him even more to Americans as an eccentric "peasant" pacificist.

TRANS-SIBERIAN RAILROAD (1892–1908). The idea of a trans-Asia railroad was inspired by the American examples of transcontinental enterprises and the Russian quest for economic expansion in the Far East. The main promoter, **Sergei Witte**, as minister of communications and later minister of finance, was enamored of American economic success, which certainly included railroads. The object was not only overland connections but especially consolidation of a far-flung empire. The project, when it began in the early 1890s, captured the American imagination, and many Americans would be among the first to try it out. Though incomplete during the **Russo–Japanese War**, that conflict attracted attention to it. Perhaps the most widely publicized debut of the completed line was the around-the-world journey of **William Howard Taft** as secretary of war in 1908.

The Trans-Siberian would serve as an important means of communication during both **World War I** and **World War II**, when the United States and Russia were allies. In the former, a large amount of supplies were shipped to **Vladivostok**, but the deterioration of the service on the rail line was a factor in the **American intervention** in 1918. The construction of the **Chinese Eastern Railway (CER)** across **Manchuria** also attracted the attention of Japan, which had imperial interests in that area. Again, in World War II, the Trans-Siberian served as a major conduit for **lend-lease** aid to the Soviet war effort, operational until August 1945 thanks to a Soviet–Japanese neutrality treaty. The line, with its secondary Baikal-Amur extension, continues to be an important avenue of development and exploitation of resources in the Russian Far East.

TREATY OF NAVIGATION AND COMMERCE OF 1832. *See* COMMERCIAL TREATY OF 1832.

TREATY OF PORTSMOUTH. *See* PORTSMOUTH PEACE CONFERENCE AND TREATY.

TROTSKY, LEON (1870–1940). From a Ukrainian-Jewish family (Bronstein), Trotsky became one of the most vocal and active Russian Marxists, recognized especially by his speeches, writings, and activism, the latter especially noted in 1903 at the Second Congress of the **Russian Social Democratic Labor Party** in Brussels and London. He disagreed with both the Menshivik broad-based membership policy and the **Lenin**-inspired **Bolshevik** tight-knit organization and formed his own party. As in the case of other radical leaders, he spent much time outside Russia in Switzerland, France, England, and finally the United States, where he edited a socialist newspaper on the Lower East Side of New York. He was there when the **February Revolution** of 1917 occurred and hastened to return to Russia, since all political exiles were welcomed back (with travel expenses paid) by the new **Provisional Government**.

Upon return to Petrograd in May, detained by the British in Halifax, Trotsky subscribed to Vladimir Lenin's slogan of "All Power to the Soviets," and thus became a leader of his Bolshevik party. He subsequently became an eloquent orator and organizer of the seizure of power in the **Bolshevik Revolution** as Lenin's right arm. With an excellent knowledge of Western languages—German, French, and English—he was an important leader of the revolution, with foreign contacts, and as commissar of foreign affairs in the initial Soviet government. He, however, resigned that position over disagreement on the negotiations for peace at **Brest-Litovsk** to head the Soviet effort in the **Civil War**. The question of who was most important for Soviet success and survival—Lenin or Trotsky—remains the subject of debate.

During the initial and Civil War period, Trotsky was open to Americans, such as Moscow consul **DeWitt Clinton Poole** and helped resolve problems pertaining to Americans still resident in Soviet Russia. Subsequently, Trotsky, often considered the natural successor to Lenin in the 1920s, lost out to **Joseph Stalin**, and he and his followers became targets of persecution, culminating in his assassination in Mexico in 1940. Trotsky's program and legacy as an alternative to Stalinism has been much discussed and debated.

TROYANOVSKY, ALEXANDER (1882–1955). From Tula, Troyanovsky was an early activist in the **Russian Social Democratic Labor Party (RSDLP)** but also was an officer in the Russian army during the **Russo–Japanese War** (1904–05). Arrested for revolutionary activity, Troyanovsky escaped abroad and spent several years (1910–17) in Austria and France. Returning to Soviet Russia, he served as an officer in the Red Army during the **Civil War**. Having left the Menshevik branch of the RSDLP by 1921, he became an official in the Commissariat of Foreign Trade during the **New Economic Policy**. Transferring to the foreign service, he was Soviet minister to Japan (1927–33) during a difficult period of increasing tensions.

After the U.S.–Soviet **Recognition Agreement**, and following a long tradition from the imperial period of transferring envoys from Japan to the United States, Troyanovsky was named ambassador immediately after its conclusion. His tenure began with the renovation of the old Russian embassy and the hosting of a gala reception there in April 1934. He was unsuccessful, however, in resolving the several outstanding issues in Soviet–American relations in the 1930s, such as the **debt issue**, **Comintern** interference, and a closer union against fascism. At the end of his term (1938), Troyanovsky was withdrawn from diplomatic assignments and devoted his time to publicity (the war effort) and to educational activities, fortunate to have escaped a worse fate in the purges.

TRUMAN DOCTRINE (1947). The doctrine was a hasty response to what was perceived to be a Soviet aggressive action that was taking advantage of instability in Western Europe but especially in regard to southeastern Europe—Greece and Turkey—where a civil war was in progress in the former. The doctrine essentially was a pronouncement of commitment of military and economic aid that sent a message to the Soviet Union of American intentions to stop its actions through a policy of **containment**. In retrospect, the doctrine may have been a harsher response than necessary, an overreaction to a particular situation in Greece, but it became a fundamental commitment of the United States to Western Europe in general and was followed by the successful **Marshall Plan**. For example, one factor missed at the time was that the aid to the Greek Communist revolution came primarily from Yugoslavia, not from the Soviet Union, and it ironically would soon (1948) become a Western "ally" by defecting from the Soviet bloc.

TRUMAN, HARRY S. (1884–1972). With the death of **Franklin D. Roosevelt** in April 1945, Truman became the American president in the midst of a war that was soon to end with a dramatic Allied victory. With little experience in foreign affairs, Truman relied on advisors such as secretaries of state **George C. Marshall** and **Dean Acheson** and experienced diplomat **George F. Kennan**. For even these "experts," the Soviet hostility and isolation (phrased by **Winston Churchill** in 1946 as the **iron curtain**) was perplexing. Considering the multitude of problems associated with Soviet military power, its occupation of Eastern Europe, and the economic and political instability of Western Europe, the United States responded adequately and responsibly with major economic assistance (the **Marshall Plan**) and military strategy (the **Truman Doctrine** and **North Atlantic Treaty Organization**). With a surprise victory in the 1948 election, Truman was able to refine the organizations and policies that would be in place for the waging of a long **cold war**.

TSARITSA. This 1,089 ton "Yankee clipper," built in Portsmouth, New Hampshire, in 1854, was originally registered as the *Coeur de Lion.*

It was purchased by the **Russian America Company (RAC)** in Hamburg in 1858 to transport ice from **Alaska**, mainly from St. Paul (**Kodiak Island**), to San Francisco under contract to the **American Russian Commercial Company**. It represented one of the largest capital investments of the RAC and served as the workhorse for ice exports to the United States. For such cargoes, the larger the ship, the better (less ice melt)—and steamships definitely were not suitable. On one voyage the *Tsaritsa* suffered serious damage from hitting rocks while entering San Francisco bay with a load of ice, but, since ice floats, it was easily towed to a wharf for repairs. One of the most venerable of the American "Yankee clippers," it would sail on to other waters under other proprietors for a number of years after the sale of Alaska until its final demise in 1914, a long record for a wooden sailing ship.

TSFASMAN, ALEXANDER (1906–1969). Pianist, composer, and leader of American-style **jazz** bands in Soviet Russia. Born in Ukraine, Tsfasman studied violin and piano from the age of seven and entered a conservatory in **Nizhny Novgorod** at the age of 12. He continued his classical music education at the Moscow conservatory but was soon concentrating on the jazz that invaded Russia. By 1924, he was known for his jazz renditions of "Excentrical Dance" and "Sad Mood," among others. Late in 1926, after the sensational Russian tours of the Benny Peyton and Sam Wooding **African American** ensembles, he formed one of the first genuine Soviet jazz orchestras, performing jazz music on programs of the Soviet radio in 1927. He continued to direct the premier jazz group through the 1930s, recording such popular compositions as "At the Sea-shore," "The Sounds of Jazz," "O'Key Toots," "Jolly Walk," and "I'm Blue Without You." He also composed a jazz ballet, "Rot-Front" (1931), for concert piano and jazz orchestra and achieved great popularity, despite the restrictions of socialist realism.

Tsfasman was also widely admired and respected as a concert pianist, for example, by **Dmitri Shostakovich**, who asked him, and only him, to perform some of his early jazz compositions; by the late 1930s he and his orchestra had become a fixture on the state's "Radio Moscow," which competed with the recordings of Glenn Miller, Count Basie, and **Irving Berlin**. He strangely thrived in this socialist-oriented society (Stalin liked jazz?), rivaling Eddy Rosner during

World War II with such hits as "Jolly Tankist," "My Love," "Young Sailors," and "Lyrical Foxtrot," mixing the patriotic with the romantic, as in the case of his American counterparts. Though somewhat eclipsed during the early **cold war**, Tsfasman was widely recognized as the "Soviet Duke Ellington" in symphojazz, as musical director of the Hermitage Theatre, and for his original piano accompaniments to Leonid Utyosov's "When Youth Is Passing By," and "Little House on Lesnaya Street." Tsfasman demonstrates especially the persistent legacy of musical *amerikanizm* throughout the Soviet period. His contributions were celebrated at a jubilee concert in 1956, as part of new Soviet relaxations and **peaceful coexistence**.

TWAIN, MARK (NE SAMUEL CLEMENS) (1835–1910). Best known for his Middle American classics, *The Adventures of Tom Sawyer* (1876) and *The Adventures of Huckleberry Finn* (1884), Twain gained much popular acclaim abroad, and especially in Russia, for his caustic social commentaries, pointed satire, and humorous short stories. Before achieving fame for these works, in 1867 Twain visited the south of Russia—Odessa, Crimea, and mainly Yalta—with a party of tourists sailing on *The Quaker City*; his encounter with Russia was hilariously depicted in *The Innocents Abroad* (1869). Twain subsequently became one of the most popular American authors in Russia in the late 19th century, continuing through the 20th century, becoming a Soviet and Russian icon—as well as an American one—for his social satire.

– U –

U-2 INCIDENT (1960). The United States for a few years had been conducting high-altitude surveillance of the Soviet Union in violation of an international agreement ("open skies") safeguarding airspace, in order to detect changes in Soviet nuclear missile deployment via high-altitude photography. Though these overflights were known to Soviet officials, they lacked the capability to intercept them until May 1960. The Soviet claim of a successful interception over the Urals seemed at first doubtful, so the United States, personally by

President **Dwight D. Eisenhower**, denied any knowledge of the flight. The display of wreckage and the surviving pilot, Gary Powers, left no doubt, and became an American embarrassment. The incident is most important for its sabotage of a Soviet–American rapprochement that had been symbolized by the cultural exchange agreement of 1958 and the visit of **Nikita Khrushchev** to the United States in 1959. The **cold war** was still flourishing.

ULAM, ADAM (1922–2000). Born in Lviv, Poland (now Ukraine), of a Polish-Jewish family, Ulam immigrated with his family to the United States at the last moment in August 1939 before the German and Soviet invasions as a result of the **Nazi–Soviet Pact**. He was rejected from American military service because of poor eyesight, studied at Brown University, and received a Ph.D. from Harvard University in 1947. Ulam was associated with that university for the remainder of his long career as a leading American Kremlinologist and major scholar in the **Davis (Harvard Russian) Research Center**. His many publications varied from solid historical scholarships to polemical (anti-Soviet) works. Among the best are *The Bolsheviks: The Intellectual and Political History of the Triumph of Communism in Russia* (1965), *Expansion and Co-Existence: The History of Soviet Foreign Policy, 1917–67* (1968), and *Rivals: America and Russia since World War II* (1971).

UMANSKY, KONSTANTIN (1902–1945). Umansky was Soviet ambassador to the United States (1939–41) at the beginning of **World War II**. In the early 1920s, Umansky served in the Soviet telegraph agency in Vienna and then for 10 years as a leading reporter for the Soviet foreign press agency in Western Europe. He transferred to the press department of the **Commissariat of Foreign Affairs** in 1932, and in 1936 he was assigned to the post of first counselor of the Soviet embassy in Washington while **Alexander Troyanovsky** was ambassador. Succeeding the latter, he became notorious in Washington for pestering anyone he could contact in the State Department or the White House about a variety of important and unimportant issues and for his hostile attitude in general. His removal from the office and replacement by **Maxim Litvinov** in late 1941 was especially welcomed by the American government.

"UNCLE JOE." An American popular term for **Joseph Stalin** during **World War II**. Despite ample evidence that Stalin was a tyrant and mass murderer during the 1930s, an image of a kinder, gentler, heroic leader emerged after 1940 in the interests of supporting the "Grand Alliance" against Nazi Germany. This view of the Soviet leader was especially cultivated by the mass media (*Time* and *Life*), press services, Hollywood films, and Western journalists who were reporting from Moscow. His quaint image contrasted with that of the bearded "Uncle Sam."

UNITED NATIONS (UN). The UN is an international organization that replaced the defunct **League of Nations** after **World War II**. Its initial architect was **Franklin D. Roosevelt**, who conceived the idea of fulfilling **Woodrow Wilson**'s mission of a regular association of all nations for the preservation of peace. At World War II conferences at **Tehran**, **Yalta**, and especially at a foundation meeting at the **San Francisco Conference** in June 1945, the groundwork was laid and concessions made, the main ones being a veto right of the major powers in the Security Council and the location of the headquarters in New York City. Despite many problems and the use of the UN as a propaganda forum, the organization maintained and enlarged its role during the **cold war**. It continued to have its proponents and critics and often lacked essential authority to deal with issues such as the **Korean War**, **Cuban missile crisis**, and Middle Eastern conflicts. As membership grew and military encounters continued, the UN has become more cumbersome and bureaucratic and less effective in its operations. The UN was often ignored by the Soviet Union and the United States during the cold war, but it still represents an important forum for the exchange of views and for international mediating.

UNITED RUSSIA (2001–). A phenomenon, surprising to many Americans, in post-Communist Russia was the absence of truly effective political parties. The Communist Party still loomed large, but as something of a well-worn and discredited shadow of its past. The emergence of another conservative opposition during the 1990s headed by **Vladimir Zhirinovsky**, the Liberal-Democratic Party, became something of a joke to both Russians and Americans. President Boris Yeltsin, glaringly, lacked an effective political organization, relying instead on his own personality—such as it was—to carry him through. This problem was clearly perceived by his successor, **Vladimir Putin**. The subsequent quest for a "Putin party" was aided by the existence of organizations loyal to particular politicians such as Yury Luzhkov, mayor of Moscow. A resulting consolidation began in April 2001 and culminated in United Russia, which holds a monopoly position of political authority, not unlike that of the Communist Party in the Soviet era. Still, a semblance of democracy is preserved since United Russia polled only 37 percent of the vote in 2003 though still controlling 305 seats of the Duma out of 450, a "constitutional majority." In the December 2007 Duma election, as the party of Putin, United Russia won 64 percent of the vote, increasing its majority and obtaining the power to amend the constitution and basically control the presidential election in March 2008 of **Dmitri Medvedev** and his selection of Putin as prime minister.

UNIVERSITY OF MOSCOW. *See* MOSCOW STATE UNIVERSITY.

– V –

VANCE, CYRUS (1917–2002). From Clarksburg, West Virginia, Vance graduated from Yale University in 1939, where he excelled in hockey and also obtained a law degree in 1942. He served with distinction as a naval gunnery officer in **World War II**. After practicing as an attorney for a prominent law firm in New York City, Vance was appointed secretary of the army in the administration of **John F. Kennedy** and was involved in the policing of desegregation efforts in Mississippi. Subsequently as deputy secretary of defense in the **Lyndon Johnson** administration, he was one of the first to advocate withdrawal from Vietnam. Vance is best known as secretary of state in the administration of **Jimmy Carter**, during which he supervised and advanced negotiations on the **Strategic Arms Limitation Talks (SALT II)** and dealt with the Iranian hostage crisis. He lost influence to the more hawkish national security advisor **Zbigniew Bzrezinski** but is given much credit for the **Camp David** Accords (Israeli–Egyptian agreement). He later served on diplomatic missions in Bosnia, Croatia, and

South Africa but unfortunately succumbed to a long battle with Alzheimer's disease and was buried at Arlington National Cemetery.

VENIAMINOV, IVAN (AKA INNOCENT OF ALASKA) (1797–1879). Veniaminov, born and raised in the Irkutsk district of **Siberia**, is known for his zeal and dedication to the Russian Orthodox Church and his ability as a scholar, linguist, and administrator. In early 1823 he departed for Northwest America (**Alaska**) with his wife, mother, infant son, and brother to be the parish priest for a portion of the Aleutian Islands. In 1834 he moved to **Sitka**, from where he expanded his studies of native culture and languages, publishing major works on the ethnography and linguistics of native peoples. In 1838, Veniaminov went to Moscow and St. Petersburg to report on his activities and to appeal for additional funding; there he learned that his wife had died. He took vows as a monk, choosing the name Innocent, and was consecrated as metropolitan (bishop) with an expanded territory that included all of Northwest America and Kamchatka. Noted for his physical size and athletic endurance, Veniaminov established many legends in the area for his religious devotion, courageous explorations, and innovations. After 1853, however, he spent most of his time in Yakutsk in Siberia and then was designated metropolitan of Moscow (1867–79). Upon his death, he was buried at the Sergeevsky Monastery in Zagorsk. By formal initiation of the Russian Orthodox Church in America in 1977, he was proclaimed a saint. *See also* RUSSIAN AMERICA.

VENONA PROJECT. A highly secret intelligence operation of the United States and Great Britain, Venona revealed much information by interception of communications traffic, especially between Germany and Japan, and decoding of messages during **World War II**. Though initiated in 1943 in regard to fears of a possible Soviet separate peace with Germany, the decoding of message traffic resulted instead in uncovering a substantial Soviet spy operation in Great Britain and the United States. Venona was also applied to the interception and analysis of Soviet communications that reached 50 percent in 1944. Most significant was the revelation about Soviet acquisition of atomic weapon technology through the activities of Kim Philby, Donald MacLean, Harry Dexter White, **Julius** and **Ethel**

Rosenberg, **Alger Hiss**, and others. This resulted in arrests and a general infiltration of a wide range of Soviet secret intelligence operations in the West, a clear **cold war** victory.

VERESHCHAGIN, VASILI (1842–1904). Achieving fame as a battlefield artist and for his realistic paintings of the Russian conquest of Central Asia, Vereshchagin was probably the most popular Russian artist in the late 19th century and early 20th century United States. Born into the landed nobility, he entered the Tsarskoe Selo cadet corps at an early age and was commissioned an officer in the navy. Vereshchagin soon left military service, however, to study art in St. Petersburg and then in Paris in 1864, making his first exhibition there in 1868. He joined a Russian military expedition to Turkestan in 1969 and traveled as far as Tibet in 1873 and India in 1884. Meanwhile, the artist accompanied the Russian army into the Balkans during the Second Russo–Turkish War (1877–78). Much of his work aroused controversy for its antiwar and antireligious interpretations. An exhibition of his works on the Russo–Turkish War had mixed reactions in St. Petersburg but more success on tour in Europe and in the United States. One American patron and collector of his works was **Charles R. Crane**.

A major exhibition of Vereshchagin's works was held in New York in 1888, and the artist himself came to New York and Washington, D.C., in 1891 but left discouraged and unhappy. He would return by invitation of the Chicago Art Institute in 1901: a number of his paintings were part of an impressive exhibit of Russian art at the St. Louis Pan-American Exhibition in 1904. Unfortunately, that year the artist, in an effort to depict the events of yet another war, perished in an explosion onboard the Russian battleship *Petropavlovsk* during a Japanese attack on **Vladivostok** during the **Russo–Japanese War**.

VERSAILLES, TREATY OF (1919). *See* PARIS PEACE CONFERENCE.

VLADIVOSTOK. Founded in 1867 as a Russian naval base on the extreme tip of the "maritime provinces" to assert Russian power in the Pacific region, Vladivostok quickly became an important port for Russia's Far Eastern trade. This was according to the design of **Grand**

Duke Constantine (brother of **Alexander II**) to shift Russian attention away from North America (sale of **Alaska**) to Asia and especially China. Its importance was magnified by becoming the terminus of the **Trans-Siberian Railroad** in the 1890s, enhanced even more by the construction of the **Chinese Eastern Railway** as a shortcut across Manchuria to Vladivostok. Americans were fascinated by this new entry point to European Russia, and many used it and wrote about it, most notably Secretary of War **William Howard Taft** in 1908.

Vladivostok became a major port of access to European Russia during both **World War I** and **World War II**, when normal Baltic and Black Sea routes were cut off. During the **Russian Civil War**, the city became the main base of the **American Expeditionary Force** in **Siberia** under command of General **William S. Graves** and the cruiser USS *Brooklyn*, flagship of the American Pacific squadron. During World War II, Vladivostok was also a major entry port for American **lend-lease** supplies to the Soviet ally until the Soviet declaration of war against Japan in August 1945.

VOICE OF AMERICA (VOA). The Voice of America was initiated by the Office of War Information in February 1942 with programs aimed at areas of Europe and northern Africa under German occupation, borrowing short-wave transmitters from the NBC and CBS networks. Considered a successful media for providing information to stimulate resistance movements during **World War II**, the service in February 1947 became a major propaganda instrument of the **cold war** with programs in Russian. The Soviet Union and the East European satellite bloc became the major target of its broadcasts during the cold war. Its broadcasts were patterned after—and often in competition with—BBC World Service, Radio Moscow, and the "sister" services of **Radio Free Europe** and **Radio Liberty** that also received their primary funding from the U.S. government. The impact of VOA was considerable, though it is not easily measured. It was heard especially in urban areas, where short-wave radios were commonplace but sustained interference until the 1970s by Soviet jamming efforts. VOA maintained many field stations and transmitters, serving up to 50 languages and international regions. Its English broadcasts, however, remained popular because of the opportunity they provided for learning American colloquial English. Since the apparent end of the cold war, VOA has followed American spheres of interest and military activity in the Balkans, the Middle East, Africa, and South Asia, where it has occasionally encountered charges of infringing on territorial sovereignty.

VOLOGDA. As a provincial and railroad center about 400 miles north of Moscow, Vologda also became an important diplomatic base of operations in 1918, after the **Bolshevik Revolution** and the withdrawal of Russia from **World War I** at the **Treaty of Brest-Litovsk** (March 1918). U.S. Ambassador **David Francis** decided to move the American embassy there from Petrograd/St. Petersburg after the Soviet transfer of the capital to Moscow. Some of the other foreign posts followed, though Great Britain and France abandoned Russia completely. Vologda had the advantage of a direct rail route to **Archangel** to the north, Moscow to the south, and Petrograd to the west, and being on the main line of the **Trans-Siberian Railroad** to the east. Francis set up headquarters in a merchant's house as a temporary embassy from March through July 1918, from where he maintained contacts with Petrograd and Moscow, but was finally forced to abandon Vologda due to **Allied intervention** and Bolshevik opposition to his presence without a formal recognition of the Soviet government. In 1998 the house was restored by a local businessman/historian, Alexander Bitov, and opened as a museum on the occasion of the 80th anniversary and in conjunction with an international conference sponsored by the American embassy.

– W –

WALSH, EDMUND (1885–1956). A Jesuit Catholic priest, Walsh was the founder of the School of Foreign Service at Georgetown University in 1919. This was the first formal training center for future American diplomats and did much to attract young scholars into careers in the foreign service, though clearly conservative and Catholic. Father Walsh's interest in Russia began with his service on the Papal Famine Relief Mission (1922–23) to Ukraine. He subsequently became strongly opposed to the Soviet refusal to uphold agreements to allow

Roman Catholic churches to remain open in Ukraine and especially for the persecution and even execution of priests by Soviet authorities.

Throughout the remainder of his life, Walsh was a professor of politics and international relations at Georgetown as well as dean of the school that he founded. An inveterate anti-Communist and vocal opponent of diplomatic recognition, he was nonetheless dedicated to developing expertise on the Communist world. One of his students, **Robert F. Kelley**, headed the East European division of the State Department for many years and helped shape official policy toward the Soviet Union during the interwar years. When the formal **Recognition Agreement** was approaching in the early administration of **Franklin D. Roosevelt**, Walsh met with the president and agreed to refrain from opposition in exchange for a proviso in the agreement guaranteeing freedom of religion and that the United States be allowed two chaplaincies in Moscow, Protestant and Roman Catholic. It is also claimed that Walsh provided vital encouragement to Joseph McCarthy's campaign against Communists after **World War II**.

WARKENTIN, BERNHARD (1847–1908). The son of a wealthy landowner and mill owner in Altona, a village in the **Molochna Mennonite colony** in southern Russia (now Ukraine), Warkentin was of West Friesian (Northern Netherlands) roots and a follower of Menno Simon's Anabaptist belief in salvation through passivism and opposition to military service. Knowing of ethnic and religious compatriot settlements in the United States, he came there in 1872 as a young "tourist" and quickly became a convert to the religious freedom of that country. He visited Mennonite settlements in Pennsylvania, Indiana, and Illinois and conducted a fact-finding mission through the American Great Plains, including Canada, with the goal of finding suitable settlement areas for those threatened by conscription into the Russian army by the reforms of **Alexander II**.

Warkentin was especially attracted to the fellowship of a Mennonite elder, Christian Krebhiel, in Summerfield, Illinois, and joined that congregation's move to a new location on railroad land near Halstead, Kansas, where in 1873 Warkentin built a flour mill patterned on ones he had known in Russia. Throughout his journey in America, he maintained contact with friends and family in Russia and encouraged kindred Mennonites to consider immigration to the United

States. This contributed to a flood of new settlers from "Rooshia," as they pronounced their origin upon arrival, thus earning their designation as "Rooshian," whether German Volga Lutheran and Roman Catholic or Dutch-speaking Mennonites.

Warkentin, as an important flour miller, became an advocate of a variety of hard-grained wheat, "Turkey Red," *krasnaya turetskaya* in Russian (because it was red in color and believed to have originated in the Ottoman Empire). It was grown by Mennonites in Crimea, where Tatars were the first to cultivate it. His adaptation of cylindrical steel rollers for milling in the late 1880s made the production of flour from this hard wheat commercially feasible and a source of the best flour for the European market. Warkentin subsequently became the founder of a number of additional mills in the area, a long-term president of the Kansas Flour Millers Association, and the creator of the wheat phenomenon of the American Great Plains. Unfortunately, he died as a result of an errant revolver discharge on a train near Beirut, Lebanon. His house in Newton, Kansas, is open to the public as a monument to his important contributions to American agriculture.

WAR OF 1812 (1812–1815). The conflict between the United States and Great Britain was an outgrowth of the Napoleonic Wars and the commercial contest that resulted between France and Britain (continental system vs. blockade). Neutral American shippers took advantage of the situation in 1809–12 to seize a virtual monopoly of trade with European countries, especially with Russia through the Baltic. As many as 200 "American" flag vessels entered Russian ports, mainly St. Petersburg, in 1810 and 1811. Suspecting that some of these ships and their crews were not really from the United States, the British navy began stopping and searching them, a major cause of the war. The result was that when military action began, Russia and the United States were on opposite sides due especially to Napoleon's invasion of Russia. Russia attempted to mediate the trans-Atlantic war in 1814 to no avail. The rise of American commercial and political interests in Europe in the background of the conflict inspired the beginning of diplomatic relations between the United States and Russia in 1809. The United States sought Russian mediation to end the war and sent **Albert Gallatin** to aid Minister **John Quincy Adams** in what was a fruitless effort.

WARSAW PACT. A treaty signed by Soviet-controlled East European nations in 1955 in response to the admission of the Federal Republic of Germany to the **North Atlantic Treaty Organization (NATO)** was designated formally as the "Warsaw Treaty of Friendship, Cooperation and Mutual Assistance," and it included Albania, Bulgaria, Czechoslovakia, the German Democratic Republic (East Germany), Hungary, Poland, Romania, and the Soviet Union, often referred to as the "Soviet bloc." The pact allowed for the Soviet army to be based in member states and, subsequently, for a multinational Czechoslovakia invasion in 1968. The pact was thus strengthened by the **Brezhnev Doctrine** that stipulated, formally, that all members were permanently committed to its unity, that is, could not withdraw from it. This arrangement of the bipolar world of the **cold war** would, of course, vanish with the growing separatist movement in Poland, the fall of the **Berlin Wall**, and the collapse of the Soviet Union in 1991.

WASHINGTON, GEORGE (1732–1799). Thanks to military experience during the French and Indian War (Seven Years' War in Europe), "Colonel" Washington, a Virginia plantation owner, emerged as the commander of the Continental Army by 1777, despite considerable difficulties and hardships, such as at Valley Forge, and facing defections (Benedict Arnold). One of the keys to his success was the willing acceptance of outside assistance, beginning with the substantial French naval and military support under the Marquis de Lafayette; another was his use of a number of other European volunteers, who included **John Paul Jones** from Scotland, **Thaddeusz Kosciuszko** and Casimir Pulaski from Russian Poland, and John Rose (Rosenthal) from the Russian Baltic provinces. Washington's leadership of the successful war of American independence was much admired in Russia by **Catherine the Great** and by enlightened spokesmen of reform such as **Alexander Radishchev.**

WASHINGTON NAVAL CONFERENCE (1921–1922). Despite American rejection of **Woodrow Wilson**'s pleas for membership in the **League of Nations**, the United States initiated a conference of major powers to place limits on numbers and types of military vessels. The conference succeeded in developing a formula for the naval powers, though it was subsequently amended by other conferences and then cast aside in the 1930s arms race. Though Soviet Russia was not invited, the **Far Eastern Republic (FER)** participated as a ploy against Japan, especially to force evacuation of remaining Japanese forces in **Siberia**. Since the FER joined (or was assimilated by) the USSR during the conference, its representative, **Boris Skvirsky**, remained in the United States as an "unofficial ambassador" (1923–33) and director of the **Russian Information Bureau** in Washington.

WESTINGHOUSE COMPANY. In the 1890s, through an arrangement with Crane Plumbing Company, Westinghouse established a factory near the Russian capital to manufacture air brakes, especially for the **Trans-Siberian Railroad**, then under construction. The factory's initial operation was supervised by **Charles R. Crane** and directed for several years by his brother-in-law, William E. Smith. During **World War I**, the factory was removed to Yaroslavl, where it was still functioning in the summer of 1921 when Crane passed through on his way from China. Westinghouse also had plants in St. Petersburg and Moscow for the production of electricity and was responsible for the first street lights in many Russian urban centers.

WHISTLER, GEORGE WASHINGTON (1800–1848). As a graduate of West Point and an army officer trained as a surveyor and engineer, Whistler was especially known in the United States for surveying and constructing the railroad through the Berkshires—the Springfield–Albany line—around 1840 (the New York Central line). A Russian mission to secure American assistance for the development of its first long-distance railroad from St. Petersburg to Moscow, contracted with Whistler to supervise its construction in 1842. He brought his family to St. Petersburg while engaged in this long-term enterprise. His son, James McNeil Whistler, a precocious art student, advanced his career by study at the St. Petersburg Academy of Art in the 1840s. Unfortunately, Whistler succumbed to cholera while working on the project, and his widow, Anna, was left to raise and promote the careers of their children, especially that of artist James McNeil Whistler, who painted his mother as well as his sister Deborah (often depicted in a white dress). Deborah was celebrated in the **American colony in St. Petersburg** for her musical talents and beauty.

WHITE, ANDREW DICKSON (1832–1918). Early in his career, White went to Russia during the **Crimean War** as an attaché to the legation, assisting many of the American **surgeons** who had come to lend their assistance to the Russian cause. Subsequently, he was a distinguished educator and the first and long-term president of Cornell University (1867–85). White was afterward appointed minister to Russia during the American relief to the severe **famine** of 1892–93, when he also stimulated and encouraged Russian participation in the **Columbian Exposition** in Chicago (1893). He subsequently served as American ambassador to Germany (1897–1902) and as head of the American delegation to the first Hague Peace Conference (1899).

WHITE, DMITRI FEDOTOFF (1889–1950). During **World War I**, under his Russian name of Dmitri Fedotoff, White served as Russian assistant naval attaché in London and then commanded a destroyer in the Baltic fleet during the 1917 upheavals. He was one of a number of liberal naval officers who supported the **February Revolution** but opposed the **Bolsheviks**. During the **Russian Civil War**, he enlisted in the army of **Alexander Kolchak** in **Siberia** and briefly commanded a flotilla on the Volga River. He was captured by the Red Army but rescued by friends who had sided with the Bolsheviks. Fedotoff White edited the official naval journal, *Morskoi Sbornik*, for several months before fleeing from Soviet Russia in 1921. He came to the United States, where he was employed as an agent of the British Cunard Line in Philadelphia in the 1920s and 1930s. Interested in naval history, White wrote a number of articles on Russian naval exploits in the Napoleonic Wars. He also published one of the best memoirs of the revolution, *Survival Through War and Revolution* (1939), while completing his doctorate in history at Columbia University. White was recognized as one of the leading experts on Soviet military affairs, especially with *The Growth of the Red Army* (1940). His papers, including a more complete draft of his memoirs, are preserved in the **Bakhmeteff Archive** at Columbia University.

WHITE, WILLIAM ALLEN (1868–1944). From the small Midwestern town of Emporia, Kansas, White traveled extensively but never left his roots. After studying English at the University of Kansas (1886–90), he acquired the *Emporia Gazette* and made it into the voice of middle America for half a century, having a circulation well beyond Kansas. He achieved early fame for his editorials, such as the anti-Populist "What's the Matter with Kansas?" (1896) and a poignant eulogy for his daughter, "Mary White." Among his best-known books are *A Certain Rich Man* (1909), *The Martial Adventures of Henry and Me* (1918) about **World War I**, biographies of **Woodrow Wilson** (1924) and **Calvin Coolidge** (1925), and his *Autobiography* (1946), which received the Pulitzer Prize.

White's interest in Russia began during the revolutions of 1917, when he met **Samuel Harper** on his return from Europe. They were both lively talkers, and Harper had just spent several months witnessing the Russian turmoil. White then arranged for Harper's lecture tour of Colorado and Kansas in early 1918 on the meaning of the Russian Revolution. In the vanguard of American reporters on the scene of the **Paris Peace Conference** in 1919, White consulted with Colonel **Edward House** and **Walter Lippmann** on world affairs, especially about the glaring absence of Russia in the negotiations. Through them he was designated by Wilson as one of two American observers for the **Prinkipo Conference**, an attempt at sorting out various Russian political entities that had resulted in **civil war**. Though the meeting in Constantinople never took place because of anti-Bolshevik opposition, White retained his interest in the Russian situation and was one of the first to see a silver lining in the **Bolshevik Revolution**: "Today in Russia, all uninformed, all blind, all mad and tremendously stupid, stands a new man in the world—the worker" (*Emporia Gazette* editorial, January 1919).

Several years later, White joined a **Sherwood Eddy** "academic" tour of Soviet Russia in September and October 1933, when diplomatic **recognition** was being seriously considered. He spent most of his time in Moscow and its vicinity consulting with journalist friends such as **Eugene Lyons** and **Walter Duranty**. He returned to write a series of columns for the *New York Times*, syndicated to a number of other newspapers, expressing his views of the Soviet Union and strongly advocating recognition, mainly on the commonsense position that it is an important country that clearly exists. His views virtually neutralized most Republican opposition to **Franklin D. Roosevelt**'s recognition plans in November 1933. His final contribution to international history was to head, after a telephone plea from the president in December 1940, the Committee to Defend America by Aiding the Allies at the height of the Battle of Britain. With chapters in every state, the "committee," though White was outspoken in trying to keep the United States out of **World War II**, was crucial in paving the way for **lend-lease**, not only to Great Britain but also to the Soviet Union.

WHITTEMORE, THOMAS (1874–1950). A graduate of Tufts College (1894), Whittemore studied medieval history at Harvard University on his road to becoming one of the world's leading Byzantine scholars and archeologists. Before, during, and after **World War I**, he led relief efforts in southern Russia and the Middle East on behalf of the American Near East Relief fund, directed by **Charles R. Crane**. He subsequently became a protégé of Crane, who funded much of his activities in the region of the former Ottoman Empire. He is known mainly for his pioneering work in restoring the early Greek-Christian mosaics of St. Sophia in Istanbul, beginning in 1932 and continuing through the 1940s as director of the Byzantine Institute of Harvard and Istanbul. He also led important excavations on early Christian sites in the Holy Land and of Egyptian burial tombs. Whittemore served as Crane's agent in the purchase and shipping of the bells of the Danilevsky Monastery in Moscow to Harvard in 1929–30 (returned in 2008). Just after receiving an honorary degree from Brown University, he fell dead of a heart attack at the door of the office of **John Foster Dulles** in the State Department.

WILEY, JOHN COOPER (1893–1967). Born in an American diplomatic family in Bordeaux, France, Wiley was a graduate of Union College in Schenectady and of Columbia University Law School. He entered the foreign service in 1915 and served in a variety of posts in Europe and South America before his appointment as first counselor at the American embassy in Moscow under Ambassador **William C. Bullitt** in 1934. He performed many of the duties of the ambassador during this early difficult period, especially during Bullitt's frequent absences. Described as a tall and heavyset man with a keen sense of humor and with a grave, booming voice, Wiley passed through a number of assignments after his tenure in Moscow: minister to the Baltic states (1938–40) and ambassador to Colombia (1944), Portugal (1947), Iran (1948), and Panama (1951). In the latter post, he negotiated an important agreement on joint administration of the Panama Canal before his retirement from the foreign service in 1953. During the administration of **Dwight D. Eisenhower**, Wiley was a vocal opponent of summit meetings, arguing for emphasizing normal channels in diplomatic negotiations. He and his wife subsequently presided over many diplomatic/international gatherings at their stately Georgetown home.

WILLIAMS, WILLIAM APPLEMAN (1921–1990). American revisionist historian and leader of the "old left" perspective on American history, Williams argued that the United States bore a major responsibility for the **cold war** as the promoter of a global empire after **World War II**, illustrated by his classic study, *The Tragedy of American Diplomacy* (1962), and the disciples he attracted to the University of Wisconsin, who included **Walter LaFeber** and Lloyd Gardner, both authors of major works on Soviet–American relations. Williams also acquired related manuscript collections—such as **Singer** and **International Harvester** and those of **Alexander Gumberg** and **Raymond Robins**—for the State Historical Society of Wisconsin on the university campus. He also wrote the pioneering *American–Russian Relations, 1781–1947* (1952).

WILLKIE, WENDELL (NE LEWIS WENDELL WILLKIE) (1892–1944). Known primarily as the losing Republican candidate in the presidential election of 1940, Willkie was a respected attorney from Indiana who managed to win a large popular vote but was overwhelmed in the electoral college. Graduating from Indiana University Law School, Willkie became politically active in campaigning for **Franklin D. Roosevelt** in 1932. He became disenchanted with the Roosevelt program, however, especially with the roughshod promotion of the Tennessee Valley Authority. An underdog all the way, Willkie faced formidable opposition from the main Republican contenders, Robert Taft, Arthur Vandenberg, and Thomas Dewey, but a swell of popular support won him nomination as a dark-horse candidate at the 1940 Republican convention. After his defeat, Willkie supported the Roosevelt agenda in foreign affairs, including especially the **United Nations**, in *One World* (1943), inspired in part by his tour through the Soviet Union that year. A voice of moderation from "both sides of the aisle," his premature death would leave a void no one would fill on the threshold of the **cold war**.

WILSONIAN INTERNATIONALISM. A term for the foreign policy direction of the administration of **Woodrow Wilson**, it involved advancing the global role of the United States through expansionism, in intervention in the affairs of countries of American vital interests, and in forwarding an agenda of international cooperation and justice, symbolized especially by support of the **League of Nations** and the peace proposals embodied in the Fourteen Points. Though this program had precedents in previous administrations, it was given a new thrust due to the global conflict of **World War I** and American involvement in it. Proponents included Colonel **Edward House**, a chief advisor to the president, Newton Baker (secretary of war), **Breckinridge Long** (assistant secretary of state), and Josephus Daniels (secretary of the navy) in the administration and influential journalists such as **Walter Lippmann** and **Norman Hapgood**, as well as **Charles R. Crane**. A number of leading Republicans also supported a greater world presence: **Herbert Hoover**, **Raymond Robins**, **William Allen White**, and **James Goodrich**. Some important results were American intervention in Mexico, entry into World War I, promotion of the League of Nations, and intervention in the **Russian Civil War**.

WILSON, WOODROW (1856–1924). Wilson served as president and commander in chief during a critical period in American history that witnessed growing global economic and political influence. A university professor and president, and governor of New Jersey, Wilson won election mainly due to a split of the opposition vote between incumbent **William Howard Taft** and elder statesman **Theodore Roosevelt**. An important aspect was the defection of **Charles R. Crane** from Taft because of an awkward and embarrassing withdrawal of his appointment as minister to China. Crane was thus a major contributor to the Wilson campaign and served as its chairman.

The new president promoted an active role for the United States in world affairs with intervention in areas of vital interest to the country, such as Mexico in 1916. He also faced major challenges with the beginning of **World War I**. Though steering a policy of neutrality,

Wilson clearly supported the Western allies in their war effort, including special assistance in the sending of supplies to Russia through **Vladivostok**, **Archangel**, and the new port of **Murmansk**. The Wilson administration welcomed the **February Revolution**, which, by removing the Romanov autocracy, made possible the American entry into the war "to make the world safe for democracy." The subsequent effort was shackled by the Allied commitment to primacy for the western front. With Russia in a desperate situation militarily and economically by the summer of 1917, however, major loans were granted to the **Provisional Government** for the purchase of badly needed supplies, which piled up at the Russian ports during the summer of 1917 owing to deterioration of the rail transport.

Wilson, spurred especially by Crane, sent a special commission to welcome the new Russian government under the nominal leadership of **Elihu Root** in May 1917. Other initiatives included a propaganda effort to keep Russia in the war led by Ambassador **David Francis**, the Committee on Public Safety representative **Edward Sisson**, and **American Red Cross** director **Raymond Robins**. Their efforts proved too little and too late to avoid the overthrow of the Provisional Government in the **Bolshevik Revolution**. After these events, the administration and its representatives in Russia were torn between hostility toward the revolutionary socialism of the Soviet regime and the need to keep Russia in the war. Wilson's famous Fourteen Points, issued in January 1918, in point six declared support for the integrity of Russia, opposing a possible division of the former empire into independent and dependent client states, such as Ukraine. Though refusing to recognize the new Soviet government in Russia, Wilson at first sought some informal contacts but then gave in to Allied pressure in the summer of 1918 to follow a policy of **intervention** in North Russia and Siberia, which became a controversial issue in the Wilson administration and subsequently. The resulting absence of Soviet Russia at the **Paris Peace Conference** left, as **William Allen White** commented, a "dark cloud" hanging over Europe. The subsequent failure of the United States to approve Wilson's advocacy of a **League of Nations** undermined an American presence in Europe in the interwar years.

WINANS, HARRISON, AND WINANS (1843–1866). The Baltimore locomotive manufacturing company of Thomas Winans produced the most powerful early engines for the Baltimore and Ohio Railroad and later for the Springfield–Albany line through the Berkshires in 1840. Along with surveyor and construction engineer **George Washington Whistler**, the Russian government contracted with a partnership of William R. Winans, William L. Winans, and Joseph Harrison (the latter of Philadelphia) to produce the locomotives and cars for the first long-distance railroad in Russia from St. Petersburg to Moscow. A large iron foundry near the capital, in the suburb of Aleksandrovsk, was leased to the Baltimore company for 20 years. The Winans families and engineers contributed substantially to the growth of the **American colony in St. Petersburg** that would also include the **William H. Ropes** and Whistler families. The arrangement proved quite profitable, at least for the Americans, as they built substantial estates in the Baltimore area from the profits.

WINTER WAR (1939–40). As a result of the **Nazi–Soviet Pact**, the Soviet Union occupied the eastern half of Poland and was given carte blanche on adding additional territories on its western border. **Finland**, long a grand duchy of the Russian Empire, gained its independence during the upheavals that followed the **Russian Revolution**, extending its territory to within a few miles of Petrograd, then Russia's largest city. The Soviet government claimed that much of this territory was not Finnish because it was inhabited largely by a related Karelian ethnic people and a large Russian minority. It declared war in November 1939 and advanced into that area. A superior defense, organized by Marshall Carl Gustav Mannerheim, plus Red Army inadequacy in operations in wooded, winter conditions made the campaign costly and embarrassing to the Soviet government. The conflict also elicited sympathy from Western countries, especially the United States, winning their respect for the underdog Finland. By the Treaty of Moscow, the Soviet Union acquired an important buffer zone to the north of Leningrad around Lake Ladoga and much of Finnish Karelia, including the port city of Vyborg. Separately, it also occupied with little opposition the Baltic states of Estonia, Latvia, and Lithuania. *See also* WORLD WAR II.

WITTE, SERGEI (1845–1915). A descendant of a Dutch family living in Russia for several generations, Witte emerged from the obscure middle-class intelligentsia to rise to the pinnacle of the Russian state bureaucracy. His speciality was railroads in the last half of the 19th century, beginning from the ground level. Cognizant that European and American economic progress was based on efficient and extensively developed transportation networks, Witte argued the case for major government intervention to promote railroad construction as a mainspring for rapid economic progress. Much of the theoretical background was borrowed from Prussian Franz List and from American applications in the Homestead Act and congressional land grants to railroads. The American model predominated, and Witte would follow it as Russia's resources and defense priorities would allow. A keynote to the "Witte system" was borrowing from abroad (and improving internal taxation) to finance construction and technological advance. His *amerikanizm* was especially demonstrated in the sending of a number of experts in 1893 to the **Columbian Exposition** to study American progress and report back in detail.

By that time the construction of the **Trans-Siberian Railroad** was under way. Though conceived as a state enterprise to promote Russian industrialization as well as land settlement, Witte also sought others' expertise, such as a contract with **Westinghouse** to erect a factory to produce air brakes for the Siberian trains. His program also had adverse implications: increased peasant poverty and strains on the society, heavy reliance on foreign loans and investment; the former resulting in an alliance with France (in return for favorable interest rates on loans), and imperialist adventures in the Far East resulting from the Trans-Siberian project and its **Chinese Eastern Railway** shortcut across **Manchuria** that led to the **Russo–Japanese War** (1904–05). Ironically, it was left to Witte to construct a peace under American supervision to end that war, and in August 1905 he became quite popular in America. Though not in favor with **Nicholas II** for his giveaway in the **Portsmouth Treaty**, Witte was summoned once more to bail out the regime with the October Manifesto, which ushered in a quasi-constitutional government, and he served as its first "premier," chairman of the council of ministers. Inability to work with the tsar forced his retirement to write an important memoir of the period.

WORLD WAR I (1914–1918). The first and perhaps the only truly "great war" in all respects, it tore Europe apart politically and culturally. Russia is often blamed for the conflict's escalation from a minor

Balkan issue into a conflict of horrendous human loss by supporting Serbia against Austria-Hungary after the assassination of an Austrian grand duke by a Serb nationalist. Clearly, Europe was already a tinderbox owing to hostile alliances, the arms escalation, leadership arrogance, and a general willingness to solve matters by military means.

On the resulting Russian eastern front, as on the western front, military superiority was not gained by either side, despite major offensives. Russia's main allies, Britain and France, dominated the strategy of the war, which was to concentrate all efforts—men and supplies—on the western front, leaving Russia to "just hold on" in the east. The increasing need for orders for equipment from the United States thus placed Russia's needs in lower priority. On another level, the U.S. presence in Russia dramatically increased in its role as the chief neutral observer (under the Geneva Convention) of prisoner-of-war installations through the American embassy's **Second Division**.

As the war developed into a war of attrition, Russia was unable to carry on economically, cut off in the Baltic and Black Seas from support from outside. The resulting shortages, rampant inflation, and poor leadership were major causes of the **February Revolution** in 1917. But the abdication of **Nicholas II** and the promise of a new democratic leadership in Russia in the **Provisional Government** eased the way for U.S. entry into the war in April. The other main allies in the increasingly bitter conflict with the Central Powers shifted the responsibility of saving democracy in Russia to the United States while still insisting on the priority of the western front. Despite a modest propaganda effort and major financial commitments by the United States, Russia descended rapidly into radical revolution. The **Bolsheviks** took power in October largely on a commitment to achieve peace, which was accomplished in March 1918 in the **Brest-Litovsk Treaty**. Though Russia had formally left the war, many questions of the future of Eastern Europe remained unresolved and neglected by the **Paris Peace Conference**, a major cause of international conflict in the rest of the century.

WORLD WAR II (1939–1945). Although the Union of Soviet Socialist Republics (USSR), because of the **Nazi–Soviet Pact**, did not formally enter the war until invaded by Germany in June 1941, it had contributed to its beginning by cooperating with Germany in the invasion and occupation of Poland in August 1939. The United States and Russia would again be allies, as in **World War I**, as a result of the Japanese attack on Pearl Harbor in December 1941 and general American sympathy for Great Britain, under attack by Germany during the winter of 1940–41 (Battle of Britain). America responded first with a massive supply effort under the **lend-lease** program to both Britain and the USSR. But while the United States gathered its forces to defeat German armies in North Africa and plan for an invasion of the continent, the Red Army struggled to halt and defeat the Nazi invasion at Moscow, Stalingrad, and Kursk, three of the largest battles of the war.

In the meantime, Allied councils prepared for achieving victory and agreeing on peace terms at the **Casablanca**, **Tehran**, **Yalta**, and **Potsdam Conferences** in meetings of the wartime leaders, namely, **Franklin D. Roosevelt**, **Winston Churchill**, and **Joseph Stalin**. Each had a particular agenda, for example, Roosevelt to secure agreement to a **United Nations** and Stalin to push boundaries of the state and influence as far as possible to the west in the interests of defense of the Russian state, and also to advance the Communist agenda of world revolution. The result would be a bipolarized, divided Europe and the beginning of the **cold war**. The memory of the alliance would resurface, however, in such movements as the "Elbe Alliance" in the 1990s, celebrating the victory meeting of Soviet and American armies in eastern Germany in 1945.

WRIGHT, J. (JOSHUA) BUTLER (1877–1939). From New York state, Wright graduated from Princeton University (1899) and, after a stint at stock raising in Wyoming, entered the American foreign service. He served primarily in Latin America—Honduras and Brazil—until his appointment as counselor of the embassy in Petrograd in 1916. Wright was a stabilizing presence for Ambassador **David Francis** during the revolutionary upheaval and oversaw the large **Second Division** of the embassy that supervised prisoner-of-war camps throughout Russia. As a career diplomat, Wright subsequently held posts as minister to Hungary (1927–30), Uruguay (1930–34), and Czechoslovakia (1934–37). His diary of the events through the **Bolshevik Revolution** in Petrograd is a valuable source on the period.

– Y –

YAKOBSON, ROMAN. *See* JACOBSON, ROMAN.

YAKOVLEV, ALEXANDER (1923–2005). From a small village on the Volga River, through extensive service in the Red Army during **World War II**, Yakovlev was an early cultural exchange journalism student in 1958 at Columbia University, where he met a number of young American specialists on Russian affairs, academically and socially. Returning to the Soviet Union, Yakovlev edited party publications, emerging as head of the Department of Ideology and Propaganda (1969–73), taking critical stands in regard to Soviet policies. He was "demoted" from that position to Soviet ambassador to Canada (1973–83). Somewhat by happenstance, in 1983, **Mikhail Gorbachev** came to Canada on an agricultural inspection and was naturally guided by the ambassador. They formed a mutual understanding on the need for major reforms, and Yakovlev was summoned back to Moscow, where in 1985 he would become a major advisor to Gorbachev on **glasnost** and perestroika. He would later be critical of the Soviet president for failing to perceive the **August Coup**. In retirement he wrote memoirs, delved into revelations from archival materials, and founded the International Democracy Foundation.

YALTA CONFERENCE. A crucial meeting of the big three — **Franklin D. Roosevelt**, **Winston Churchill**, and **Joseph Stalin** — took place at the recently liberated resort of Yalta in the Russian Crimea in January 1945 to settle outstanding issues of **World War II**. Important decisions were reached: the Soviet Union agreed to enter the war against Japan within three months after the war in Europe ended; it also promised to cooperate in the establishment of the **United Nations**, and Great Britain and the United States agreed to support a Soviet plan for the organization of postwar Poland (the Lublin Committee). The conference, held in wintry January Crimea, was uncomfortable and perhaps added to the illnesses and strain of all those attending, especially Roosevelt.

YARMOLINSKY, AVRAHM (1890–1975). Yarmolinsky emigrated from Russia in 1913, graduated from the City College of New York

(1916), and obtained a doctorate from Columbia University (1921). Meanwhile he joined the staff of the **New York Public Library (NYPL)** and served as long-term director of its Slavonic division (1918–55). Yarmolinsky was instrumental in developing it as one of the leading centers of Slavic studies in the United States at the Fifth Avenue research library, following in the footsteps of, and assisted by, **Alexis Babine**. Yarmolinsky was also an accomplished and widely recognized scholar with many publications. Chief among them were studies of Ivan Turgenev (1926), Fedor Dostoyevsky (1934), and Anton Chekhov (1973). He was married to Babette Deutsch, with whom he collaborated on a number of literary studies and anthologies. Yarmolinsky also contributed a much-heralded history of the Russian revolution, *Road to Revolution* (1957), and a lesser-known *An American's Russian Dream* (1967), about a Russian commune in Kansas, based on manuscripts in the NYPL.

YELTSIN, BORIS (1930–2007). First president of the **Russian Federation** (1991–1999) after the collapse of the Soviet Union. Yeltsin was born in the Sverdlovsk (Ekaterinburg) region of the Urals and grew up in the Perm area, the son of a peasant/construction worker. He then attended Ural Polytechnic Institute in Sverdlovsk, where he excelled in athletics (volleyball) and academics and was employed as a construction engineer on various projects in the area, rising rapidly in that profession. In 1961 he joined the Communist Party of the Soviet Union (CPSU), in which he also distinguished himself, becoming first secretary of the Sverdlovsk Region Committee by 1976.

Recognized as a talented administrator by **Michail Gorbachev**, Yeltsin was promoted to head the Moscow party organization early in 1985. He soon, however, criticized the slow pace of Gorbachev reforms and was demoted in 1987. In the ensuing process of democratization, he concentrated on the political institutions of the Russian republic and was elected president in June 1991. During the August coup against Gorbachev that year, he emerged as a vocal and colorful defender of the reform efforts. And with the resulting collapse of the Soviet Union and resignation of Gorbachev in December, he was in a position to head an "independent" Russian Federation.

His tenure as president was beset with political and economic upheavals, which he barely survived, especially a revolt of his own parliament (duma) in October 1993. Americans generally supported his jovial personal and sometimes reckless behavior, and under the administration of President **Bill Clinton** he received vital American economic and political support, especially through Clinton's former Oxford Rhodes classmate and Russian expert **Strobe Talbot**, who helped "manage" the Russian leader through periods of inebriation, ill health, and internal opposition. The reign of "Tsar Boris" came to a surprising end with his appointment of **Vladimir Putin** as prime minister and his resignation of 31 December 1999, which made Putin acting president and heir apparent to Yeltsin's reform agenda and move toward a more authoritarian regime.

YOUNG MEN'S CHRISTIAN ASSOCIATION (YMCA). Though initially established in London in 1844, the association expanded considerably in North America with centers in Montreal and Boston. It became a major factor in American social and educational life by the end of the 19th century, receiving large contributions from philanthropists such as John D. Rockefeller, Andrew Carnegie, James Stokes, **Charles R. Crane**, and many others. With this American backing, the YMCA expanded rapidly at the turn of the century throughout the world, as part of the new American global outreach and extended philanthropy.

A special target of this activity was Russia. By 1900 a major center was established in St. Petersburg under **Franklin Gaylord** and Clarence Hicks as the "Society for Cooperating with St. Petersburg Young Men in the Attainment of Moral and Physical Development." It was better known by the name of its journal, *Mayak* (*Lighthouse*). Supported by American secretary **John Mott** and by others groomed for Russian leadership by study in universities there, such as **Sherwood Eddy**, the YMCA prospered in several Russian cities in the early 1900s. The organization was part of a rise of Western religious-based assistance to Russia that included the Society of Friends, the Methodists under George Simon, the **Jewish Joint Distribution Committee**, and various Baptist and Mennonite organizations. Somewhat surprisingly, the **Bolsheviks** respected the YMCA presence for its nonpolitical stance and the aid it could provide in desperate circumstances. Its activities in Russia were eventually concluded by 1920, but many of its ideas were adopted by the Young Communist League (Komsomol).

The YMCA, along with its sister Young Women's Christian Association, was poised to deliver major spiritual and material comfort to the many Allied forces in **World War I**, in cooperation with another rapidly rising and American-supported organization, the **American Red Cross**. Both of these organizations would expand considerably in Russia during the war. The YMCA, after considerable effort, won the right to serve directly behind the Russian lines just before the **February Revolution**. It continued to play a role, though somewhat restricted by the military and economic collapse in Russia and demands on the western front. Backed by its Cleveland-based training center, stalwart volunteers such as **Paul Anderson**, Donald Lowrie, and Helen Ogden remained at their posts in Russia through 1918. They would provide an important reservoir of expertise on Russia, and many would join the relief effort of the **American Relief Administration** in 1921.

YUDIN COLLECTION. A large private library of a Siberian merchant and distiller, Gennady Yudin (1840–1912) of Krasnoyarsk, was purchased for the **Library of Congress** in 1906 by **Alexis Babine**. It became the cornerstone of the Russian collection of the library as a unique assemblage of more than 80,000 volumes and a number of rare sketches, drawings, and maps. Weighing five tons, it was crated and shipped to the United States in 1907 and incorporated into the library's holdings of rare books, manuscripts, and photographs. It also represented an official commitment by the United States to the development of resources on Russian historical and cultural studies.

– Z –

ZARUBIN-LACY AGREEMENT (1958). *See* LACY-ZARUBIN AGREEMENT.

ZAVALISHIN, DMITRI (1804–1892). As a naval officer and participant in a Pacific exploring expedition (1822–24) on behalf of the **Russian America Company (RAC)**, Zavalishin became an early advocate of Russian expansion into northern California and of the founding of **Fort Ross**. Unfortunately for his career, he was also associated with a number of liberal reformers, known as **Decembrists**.

Arrested and sentenced to 20 years of exile in **Siberia**, Zavalishin remained a strong proponent of a Russian Pacific empire, publishing a number of articles for Russian newspapers such as *Moskovskie vedomosti* (*Moscow Herald*) in the 1860s. As a journalist, he came once again to the United States in 1866 and wrote enthusiastically about the economic and political growth of the country, with special emphasis on Chicago, but also warned about the rising American presence on the Pacific shores as a threat to Russian interests. *See also* RUSSIAN AMERICA.

ZHIRINOVSKY, VLADIMIR (1946–). From Alma-Ata (Almaty) in Kazakhstan, Zhirinovsky was a student at **Moscow State University (MGU)** in African and Turkish studies before entering military service in the 1970s. A son of a Polish Jew (Wolf Eidelshtein), Zhirinovsky first became politically active on behalf of Jewish dissidents in the politically wide-open situation during the perestroika era of **Mikhail Gorbachev**. He emerged, to the surprise of many, as the leader of an ultranationalist, anti-Semitic fringe party, the Liberal Democratic Party of Russia (LDPR), which, as became common to say, was neither liberal nor democratic. Though laughed at by both domestic and foreign observers, the party nonetheless scored impressively in the 1993 Duma elections, gathering 23 percent of the popular vote in a popular reaction to the economic chaos during the administration of **Boris Yeltsin**. This rang an alarm in the West of a neo-Nazi takeover of Russia, though this prospect was soon weakened by Zhirinovsky's extravagant claims, such as that the sale of **Alaska** was fraudulent and the territory should be returned to Russia. Though declining subsequently, owing to the popularity of **Vladimir Putin**, Zhirinovsky and his party retain a voice and presence in the **Russian Federation** State Duma, welcomed by some as a critic of the Putin regime.

Appendix 1

Ministers/Ambassadors from the
United States to Russia/Soviet Union

Note: Those who were appointed but never reached their post are not
included.

TO RUSSIA

Representatives and States	Years at Post	Presidents and Secretaries of State
Francis Dana, Massachusetts (1743–1811)	1780–83	(Not received)
John Quincy Adams, Massachusetts (1767–1848)	1809–15	Thomas Jefferson James Madison
William Pinkney, Maryland (1764–1822)	1816–18	Madison James Monroe
George Washington Campbell, Tennessee (1768–1848)	1818–20	Monroe J. Q. Adams
Henry Middleton, South Carolina (1770–1846)	1820–30	Monroe/J. Q. Adams/ Andrew Jackson Henry Clay/Martin Van Buren
John Randolph, Virginia (1773–1833)	1830–31	Jackson Van Buren
James Buchanan, Pennsylvania (1791–1868)	1831–33	Jackson Edward Livingston

William Wilkins, Pennsylvania (1779–1865)	1834–36	Jackson John Forsyth
George M. Dallas, Pennsylvania (1792–1864)	1837–39	Martin Van Buren Forsyth
Churchill Cambrelling, New York (1786–1862)	1840–41	Van Buren Daniel Webster
Charles S. Todd, Kentucky (1791–1871)	1841–46	James Polk Webster/John Calhoun
Ralph Ingersoll, Connecticut (1789–1872)	1847–48	Polk Buchanan
Arthur Bagby, Alabama (1796–1858)	1848–49	Polk/Andrew Taylor Buchanan
Neill Brown, Tennessee (1810–86)	1850–51	Millard Fillmore Daniel Webster
Thomas H. Seymour, Connecticut (1807–68)	1854–58	Franklin Pierce/ James Buchanan William L. Marcy
Francis Pickens, South Carolina (1805–69)	1858–60	Buchanan Lewis Cass
John Appleton, Maine (1815–64)	1860–61	Buchanan Jeremiah Black
Cassius Marcellus Clay, Kentucky (1810–1903)	1861–69	Abraham Lincoln/Andrew Johnson William H. Seward
Simon Cameron, Pennsylvania (1799–1889)	1862–63	Lincoln Seward
Andrew Curtin, Pennsylvania (1817–94)	1869–72	Ulysses Grant Hamilton Fish
James Orr, South Carolina (1822–73)	1872–73	Grant Fish

Marshall Jewell, Connecticut (1825–83)	1873–74	Grant Fish
George Henry Boker, Pennsylvania (1823–90)	1875–78	Grant/Rutherford Hayes Fish
Edwin W. Stoughton, New York (1818–82)	1880–81	Hayes William Evarts
John W. Foster, Indiana (1836–1917)	1881–82	Chester A. Arthur James Blaine
William H. Hunt, Louisiana (1823–84)	1882–84	Arthur Frederick Frelinghuysen
Alphonso Taft, Ohio (1810–91)	1884–85	Arthur Frelinghuysen
George Van Ness Lothrop, Michigan (1817–97)	1885–87	Grover Cleveland Thomas Bayard
Lambert Tree, Illinois (1832–1910)	1888–89	Benjamin Harrison Bayard
Charles Emory Smith, Pennsylvania (1842–1908)	1889–92	Harrison James Blaine
Andrew Dickson White, New York (1832–1918)	1892–94	Harrison/Cleveland John W. Foster
Clifton Breckinridge, Arkansas (1846–1932)	1894–97	Cleveland Walter Gresham
Ethan Allen Hitchcock, Missouri (1854–1914)	1897–98	McKinley John Sherman (ambassador rank)
Charlemagne Tower, Pennsylvania (1848–1923)	1899– 1902	McKinley/Roosevelt John Hay
Robert McCormick, Illinois (1849–1919)	1903–05	Theodore Roosevelt Hay

George von Lengerke Meyer, Massachusetts (1858–1918)	1905–07	Roosevelt Elihu Root
John Wallace Riddle, Minnesota (1864–1941)	1907–09	William H. Taft Root
William Rockhill, Washington, D.C. (1854–1914)	1909–11	Taft Philander Knox
Curtis Guild, Massachusetts (1860–1915)	1911–12	Taft Knox
George Marye, California (1857–1933)	1914–16	Woodrow Wilson William Jennings Bryan
David Rowland Francis, Missouri (1850–1927)	1916–18	Wilson Robert Lansing

TO THE SOVIET UNION

Representatives and States	Years at Post	Presidents and Secretaries of State
William C. Bullitt, Pennsylvania (1891–1967)	1933–36	F. D. Roosevelt Cordell Hull
Joseph Davies, Wisconsin (1876–1958)	1936–38	Roosevelt Hull
Laurence Steinhardt, New York (1892–1950)	1939–41	Roosevelt Hull
William H. Standley, California (1872–1963)	1942–43	Roosevelt Hull
W. Averell Harriman, New York (1891–1986)	1943–45	Roosevelt Hull
Walter Bedell Smith, Indiana (1895–1961)	1946–49	Harry Truman James Brynes

Alan Kirk, Pennsylvania (1888–1963)	1949–51	Truman George Marshall
George F. Kennan, Wisconsin (1904–2005)	1952	Truman Dean Acheson
Charles Bohlen, Washington, D.C. (1904–74)	1953–57	Dwight Eisenhower John Foster Dulles
Llewellyn Thompson, Colorado (1904–72)	1957–62	Eisenhower Dulles/Christian Herter
Foy Kohler, Ohio	1962–66	J. F. Kennedy/ Lyndon Johnson Dean Rusk
Llewellyn Thompson, Colorado	1966–69	Johnson
Jacob Beam, New Jersey (1908–74)	1969–72	Richard Nixon William Rogers
Walter Stoessel Jr., California (1920–86)	1973–76	Nixon/Gerald Ford Henry Kissinger
Malcolm Toon, New York (1916–96)	1976–79	Ford Kissinger
Thomas J. Watson Jr., Connecticut (1914–93)	1979–81	Jimmy Carter Cyrus Vance
Arthur Hartman, Maryland (1926–)	1981–87	Ronald Reagan George Shultz
Jack Matlock, New Jersey (1928–)	1987–91	Reagan Shultz/James Baker
Robert Strauss, Texas (1918–)	1991–92	George H. W. Bush Lawrence Eagleburger
Thomas Pickering, New Jersey (1931–)	1992–96	Bill Clinton Warren Christopher
James Collins, Illinois (1939–)	1997–2001	Bill Clinton Madeleine Albright
Alexander Vershbow, Massachusetts	2001–05	George W. Bush Colin Powell
William J. Burns, Washington, D.C.	2005–	Bush Condoleezza Rice

Appendix 2

Ministers/Ambassadors from Russia/ Soviet Union to the United States

Representatives *Russian Empire*	Term	Tsar and Foreign Minister
Andrei Dashkov (1775–1831)	Charge d'affaires 1808–10 Minister 1811–17	Alexander I Adam Cartoryski and Ionnes Capodistrias
Fedor Palen (1780–1863)	1810–11	Alexander I Karl Nesselrode
Petr Poletika (1778–1849)	1817–22	Alexander I Nesselrode
Fedor Tuyll van Serooskerken (1772–1826)	1823–25	Alexander I Nesselrode
Paul Krudener (1784–1858)	1828–37	Nicholas I Nesselrode
Alexander Bodisko (1786–1854)	1837–54	Nicholas I Nesselrode
Edward Stoeckl (1814–69)	1854–68	Alexander II Alexander Gorchakov
Konstantin Katakazi (1830–90)	1869–72	Alexander II Gorchakov
Henrickh Offenberg (1821–88)	1872–75	Alexander II Gorchakov
Nikolai Shishkin (1830–1912)	1875–80	Alexander II Gorchakov
Nikhail Bartolomei (1836–95)	1881–82	Alexander III Nikolai Giers

Karl Struve 1882–92 Alexander III
(1835–1907) Giers
Grigori Kantakuzin 1892–95 Alexander III/Nicholas II
(1843–1902) Giers
Ernst Kotzebue 1895–97 Nicholas II
(1838–1914) Aleksei Lobanov-Rostovsky
Arthur Cassini 1897– Nicholas II
(1835–?) 1905 Vladimir Lamzdorf
Roman Rosen 1905–11 Nicholas II
(1847–1921) Alexander Izvolsky
Georgi Bakhmetev 1911–17 Nicholas II
(1848–1928) Sergei Sazonov

Provisional Government

Boris Bakhmeteff 1917–23 Alexander Kerensky
(1880–1951) Mikhail Tereshchenko

Soviet Union

Boris Skvirsky 1922–33 Lenin/Stalin
(1887–1941) Georgi Chicherin/Maxim
Litvinov
Alexander Troyanovsky 1933–38 Stalin
(1882–1955) Litvinov
Konstantin Umansky 1939–41 Stalin
(1902–45) Vyacheslav Molotov
Maxim Litvinov 1941–43 Stalin
(1876–1951) Molotov
Andrei Gromyko 1943–46 Stalin
(1909–89) Molotov
Nikolai Novikov 1946–47 Stalin
(1903–89) Molotov
Aleksandr Paniushkin 1947–52 Stalin
(1905–74) Andrei Vyshinsky
Georgi Zarubin 1952–58 Stalin/Nikita Khrushchev
(1900–58) Molotov
Mikhail Menshikov 1958–61 Khrushchev
(1902–76) Andrei Gromyko

Anatoly Dobrynin (1919–)	1962–86	Khrushchev/Leonid Brezhnev/ Yuri Andropov/Konstantin Chernenko/Mikhail Gorbachev Gromyko
Yuri Dubinin (1930–)	1986–90	Gorbachev Edoard Shevardnadze
Aleksandr Bessmertnykh (1933–)	1990–91	Gorbachev Shevardnadze

Russian Federation

Victor Komplektov (1932–)	1991–92	Boris Yeltsyn Andrei Kosyrev
Vladimir Lukin (1937–)	1992–93	Yeltsyn Kosyrev
Iulii Vorontsov (1929–)	1994–98	Yeltsyn Kosyrev/Yevgeny Primakov
Yuri Ushakov (1947–)	1999–	Yeltsyn/Vladimir Putin Igor Ivanov/Sergei Lavrov

Selected Bibliography

CONTENTS

Introduction   385
Reference and General Works   389
The United States and the Russian Empire, 1763–1867   391
The United States and Russia, 1867–1914   398
War, Revolution, and Civil War, 1914–1921   402
The United States and Soviet Russia, 1921–1941   408
The United States, the Soviet Union, and World War II,   418
    1941–1945
The Cold War, 1945–1990   422
The United States, Russia, and the Post-Soviet World,   432
    1990–2008

INTRODUCTION

In the following bibliography the emphasis is on scholarly studies and travel accounts that concentrate on Russia and the United States. While the large majority are by Americans and in English, a select number by Russian scholars are included. In fact, they have probably contributed more to the overall study and understanding of Russian–American relations in the 20th century than Americans, perhaps because of the long-term fascination by Russians with the United States. Obviously, many of the sources, especially for the period after World War II, have a cold war bias on both sides. Yet there remains a surprising amount of excellent scholarship, probably because of the importance of the subject and the attraction of excellent scholars to it.

Credit for the productivity on Russian–American research and publication is also due to the funding of study centers by government agencies, private entities such as the Ford Foundation, and university and academic support. For the latter, the establishment of the Russian Institute at Columbia University and the Russian Research Center at Harvard produced many specialists, as did the "American" institutes of the Soviet Academy of the Sciences. Of special note is the promotion of research by the Kennan Institute for Advanced Russian Studies at the Woodrow Wilson Center in Washington. It has provided research support not only for American scholars, but also for a large number of Russians and those of the former Soviet Union who needed access to National Archives and the Library of Congress.

Much can also be credited to a number of Russian scholars who have devoted much of their careers to the scholarly pursuit of objective Russian–American relations. Foremost are Nikolai Bolkhovitinov, Grigory Sevostianov, Aleksandr Fursenko, Aleksandr Nikoliukin, Igor Dement'ev, Gennady Kuropatnik, Irina Beliavskaya, Eduard Ivanian, and Robert Ivanov, whose contributions are listed in the bibliography and in the dictionary. Special mention for their promotion of their studies when it was not exactly politically correct on the Soviet side of the cold war are Bolkhovitinov and Sevostianov and the director of the Institute of World History of the Russian Academy of Sciences, Aleksandr Chubarian.

That important and very productive generation of Russian/Soviet scholars who aided and assisted the research of American students and senior scholars in Russia has been succeeded by a new group of productive scholars on Russian–American relations. To mention only a few: Viktoria Zhuravleva of the Russian State Humanities University, Vladimir Pozniakov of the Institute of General History of the Academy of Sciences, Vladimir Sogrin of the Institute of International Relations in Moscow, Alexander Petrov of the Institute of General History, and Ivan Kurilla of Volgograd University.

Comprehensive studies on Russian–American relations are restricted to some older surveys, for example those by Robert Allen, Thomas Bailey, Rhea Foster Dulles, and William Appleman Williams. They are of limited value because of their early publication and ideological bias. The best overall survey is that by John Lewis Gaddis, *Russia, the Soviet*

Union and the United States, though it concentrates on the Soviet period and has not been updated to include the post-Soviet period. A general survey of Russian–American relations from the beginning to the present is certainly needed.

For that endeavor a number of valuable reference sources exist. They include the *Modern Encyclopedia of Russian and Soviet History*, published by Academic International Press under the guidance of Peter von Walhde and Eduard Ivanian's superb encyclopedia of Russian–American relations, published in 2001. The latter, about three times in extent of this volume, was a major resource for the author. Also of note is the little-known work of Eric Amburger, which has a detailed list of Russian ministers, ambassadors, and consuls to the United States with previous and subsequent appointments. The more recent interpretive works by David Engerman and David Foglesong are especially recommended, as is the Russian periodical *Amerikanskii Ezhegodnik* (American Yearbook), which is devoted to American history and Russian–American relations.

The early period of Russian–American relations has been the most fruitful in terms of scholarship, the standard set especially by Nikolai Bolkhovitinov and his associates, such as Nikoliukin, Gennady Kuropiatnik, and Vladimir Ponomarev. Major contributions have also been made by a number of North American scholars: James Gibson, Frank Golder, David Griffiths, Richard Haywood, Anatole Mazour, Richard Pierce, and Avrahm Yarmolinsky. A focus in this period has been on Russian establishment and experience in Alaska, featured in the works of Bolkhovitinov, but also in the publications of Pierce, Gibson, Svetlana Fedorova, Howard Kushner, and Lydia Black.

The emergence of American industrial relations with Russia in the 19th century is examined in the publications of Joseph Bradley, Fred Carstensen, Vladimir Lebedev, John McKay, and Hans Rogger, but much more remains to be done. The best other scholarly contributions in the realm of cultural relations during the late 19th and early 20th centuries are by Frederick Travis, Patricia Herlihy, Norman Saul, Albert Parry, and Robert C. Williams.

The period of war, revolution, and intervention has naturally produced a concentration of publications, including a number of firsthand accounts, such as those of Carl Ackerman, William Allison, Bessie

Beatty, David Francis, John Reed, Dmitri Fedotov White, Albert Rhys Williams, Louise Bryant, and many others. While some of the best scholarly analyses come from Americans—George F. Kennan, David Foglesong, David McFadden, Albert Weeks, John White, and Betty Unterberger to mention a few—anyone who studies the period of the first half of the 20th century owes a great debt to Grigory Sevostianov, who has collected and published volumes of documents from Russian archives. They remain to be fully appreciated and analyzed. An exellent overall survey of the Russian Revolution background is *A People's Tragedy* by Orlando Figes.

The interwar period (1918–41) still needs more attention. Diplomatic relations have been surveyed thoroughly in the studies of Edward Bennett, Donald Bishop, Michael Cassella-Blackburn, Thomas Maddux, Joan Hoff Wilson, Robert Ferrell, Hugh Ragsdale, George Lensen, Hugh DeSantis, and Jonathan Haslam. Cultural relations are investigated by Jeffrey Brooks, James Libbey, Robert Williams, Fred Starr, and Marc Raeff, while intelligence operations have been the focus of the recent works of Raymond Leonard, Bradley Smith, Vladimir Pozniakov, and Katherine Sibley.

Of the many studies of the World War II relationship, some that stand out are by John R. Deane, Mary Glantz, George Herring, Robert Ivanov, Warren Kimball, Steven Minor, Richard Overy, Bradley Smith, Mark Stoler, and Albert Weeks. A large number of memoirs and firsthand accounts, such as those of Margaret Bourke-White, remain to be fully analyzed, while some materials, such as the papers of the American embassy and other officials, seem to be lost. The period also remains a difficult one in terms of access to Russian archives.

The publications on the cold war are, of course, enormous and wide ranging in focus and quality. Among the best are those of Michael Beschloss, Robert Ferrell, Raymond Garthoff, George F. Kennan, Walter La Feber, Ernest May, Jack Matlock, Thomas Paterson, Ilya Gaiduk, and William Taubman. Probably the leading expert, at least from the American side, is John Gaddis. Anyone studying this period will need to consult the revealing memoirs of Dean Acheson, Georgy Arbatov, Jimmy Carter, Anatoly Chernyaev, Anatoly Dobrynin, Mikhail Gorbachev, George F. Kennan, George Shultz, Strobe Talbott, and Alexander Yakovlev. The several works of the pioneer of Russian archives, Dmitri Volkogonov, are also important for revealing the sense of the times.

REFERENCE AND GENERAL WORKS

Adams, Bruce F., ed. *The Supplement to the Modern Encyclopedia of Russian, Soviet & Eurasian History.* 7 vols. Gulf Breeze, Fla.: Academic International Press, 2000–07.

Allen, Robert V. *Russia Looks at America: The View to 1917.* Washington, D.C.: Library of Congress, 1988.

Amburger, Erik. *Geschichte der Behordenorganisation Russlands von Peter dem Grossen bis 1917.* Leiden: E. J. Brill, 1966.

Anschel, Eugene, ed. *The American Image of Russia, 1775–1917.* New York: Ungar, 1974.

Babey, Anna. *Americans in Russia, 1776–1917: A Study of the American Travelers in Russia from the American Revolution to the Russian Revolution.* New York: Comet Press, 1938.

Bailey, Thomas A. *America Faces Russia: Russian–American Relations from Early Times to Our Day.* Ithaca, N.Y.: Cornell University Press, 1950.

Billington, James H. *Russia in Search of Itself.* Baltimore, Md.: Johns Hopkins University Press, 2004.

Bolkhovitinov, N. N., et al., eds. *Amerikanskii Ezhegodnik* (American Yearbook). Moscow: Nauka, 1974–.

—— et al., eds. *Istoriia Russkoi Ameriki, 1732–1867* (A History of Russian America, 1732–1867). 3 vols. Moscow: Nauka, 1998–2000.

——, ed. *Russia and the United States: An Analytical Survey of Archival Documents and Historical Studies.* Translated by J. Dane Hartgrove. Armonk, N.Y.: M. E. Sharpe, 1986.

Chubarian, A. O., and Blair Ruble, eds. *200 let Rossiisko–Amerikanskikh otnoshenii: nauka i obrazovanie: sbornik statei* (Two Hundred Years of Russian–American Relations: Scholarship and Education: Collection of Articles [includes those in English by Peter Kolchin, Robert Levgold, David Engerman, Steven Minor, Martin Malia, George F. Kennan, David Nordlander, and Susan Smith-Peter]). Moscow: OLMA, 2007.

Chubarian, A. O., et al. *Russkoe otkrytie Ameriki: Sbornik statei, posviashchennyi 70-letiiu akademika Nikolaia Nikolaevicha Bolkhovitinova* (The Russian Discovery of America: A Collection of Articles Honoring the 70th Anniversary of Academician Nikolai Nikolaevich Bolkhovitinov [including articles in English by Marcus Rediker, Michael Zuckherman, Philip Morgan, David Griffiths, Norman Saul, Walter La Feber, Basil Dmytryshyn, and James Gibson]). Moscow: Rosspen, 2002.

Dean, Vera Micheles. *The United States and Russia.* Cambridge, Mass.: Harvard University Press, 1948.

Dulles, Foster Rhea. *The Road to Teheran: The Story of Russia and America, 1781–1943.* Princeton, N.J.: Princeton University Press, 1944.

Engerman, David C. *Modernization from the Other Shore: American Intellectuals and the Romance of Russian Development.* Cambridge, Mass.: Harvard University Press, 2003.

Florinsky, Michael T. *McGraw-Hill Encyclopedia of Russia and the Soviet Union.* New York: McGraw-Hill, 1961.

Foglesong, David S. *The American Mission and the "Evil Empire."* Cambridge: Cambridge University Press, 2007.

Gaddis, John Lewis. *Russia, the Soviet Union and the United States: An Interpretive History.* 2nd ed. New York: McGraw Hill, 1990.

Geisinger, Adam. *The Story of Russia's Germans from Catherine to Khrushchev.* Battleford, Sask.: Marian Press, 1974.

Goldberg, Harold, and James Libbey, eds. *Documents of Soviet–American Relations. 1917–1945.* 4 vols. Gulf Breeze, Fla.: Academic International Press, 1999–2005.

Grant, Steven A., and John H. Brown, comps. *Russian Empire and Soviet Union: A Guide to Manuscripts and Archival Materials in the United States.* Washington, D.C.: Kennan Institute for Advanced Russian Studies [G. K. Hall], 1981.

Haupt, Georges, and Jean-Jacques Marie. *Makers of the Russian Revolution: Biographies of Bolshevik Leaders.* Ithaca, N.Y.: Cornell University Press, 1974.

Hunt, William R. *Arctic Passage: The Turbulent History of the Land and People of the Bering Sea, 1697–1975.* New York: Charles Scribner's Sons, 1975.

Ivanian, Eduard A. *Kogda govoriat Muzy: istoriia rossiisko–amerikanskikh kul'turnykh sviazei* (When the Muses Speak: A History of Russian–American Cultural Connections). Moscow: Mezhdu. otnosh., 2007.

———. comp. *Entsiklopediia rossiisko–amerikanskikh otnoshenii, XVIII–XX veka* (Encyclopedia of Russian–American Relations, 18–20th Centuries). Moscow: Mezhdu. otnosh., 2001.

Jados, Stanley S. *Documents on Russian–American Relations: Washington to Eisenhower.* Washington, D.C.: Catholic University of America Press, 1965.

McCauley, Martin. *Who's Who in Russia Since 1900.* London: Routledge, 1997.

Nerhood, Harry W. *To Russia and Return: An Annotated Bibliography of Travelers' English-Language Accounts of Russia from the Ninth Century to the Present.* Columbus: Ohio State University Press, 1968.

Papers Relating to the Foreign Relations of the United States. Various series. Washington, D.C.: Government Printing Office, 1867–.

Russkii biograficheskii slovar (Russian Biographical Dictionary). 25 vols. St. Petersburg: Lissner and Sovko, 1896–1914.

Saul, Norman E., and Richard McKenzie, eds. *Russian–American Dialogue on Cultural Relations, 1776–1914.* Columbia: University of Missouri Press, 1997.

Sevost'ianov, G. N., et al., eds. *Istoriia SShA* (History of the USA). 4 vols. Moscow: Nauka, 1983–87.

Smelev, Anatol, ed. *Tracking a Diaspora: Emigres from Russia and Eastern Europe in the Repositories.* New York: Haworth Press, 2006.

Startsev, Abel. *Russko–Amerikanskie etiudy* (Russian–American Studies). Moscow: Russian Academy of Sciences, 1995.

Stephan, John J. *The Russian Far East: A History.* Stanford, Calif.: Stanford University Press, 1994.

Toews, John B. *Czars, Soviets & Mennonites.* Newton, Kans.: Faith and Life Press, 1981.

Vneshnaia politika Rossii XIX i nachala XX veka: Dokumenty Rossiskogo ministersva inostrannykh del (The Foreign Policy of Russia in the 19th and Beginning of the 20th Centuries: Documents of the Russian Ministry of Foreign Affairs). Ser. 1, 8 vols. Moscow: Nauka, 1960–72; Ser. 2, 9 vols. Moscow: Nauka, 1974–.

Volkov, Solomon. *The Magical Chorus: A History of Russian Culture from Tolstoy to Solzhenitsyn.* Translated by Antonina W. Bouis. New York: Alfred A. Knopf, 2008.

Wieczynski, Joseph L., ed. *Modern Encyclopedia of Russian and Soviet History.* 46 vols. (plus supplements). Gulf Breeze, Fla.: Academic International Press, 1976–2005.

Williams, William Appleman. *American–Russian Relations, 1781–1947.* New York: Rinehart, 1952.

Zhuravleva, Viktoria, et al., eds. *Rossiisko–Amerikanskie otnosheniia v proshlom i nastoiashchem: obrazy, mify, real'nost': materialy mezhdunarodnyi konferentsii, posviashchennoi 200 letiiu ustanovleniia diplomaticheskikh otnoshenii mezhdu Rossiei i SShA* (Russian–American Relations in Past and Present: Images, Myths, and Reality: The Materials of the International Conference Dedicated to the Bicentenary of Russian–American Relations in Past and Present: Images, Myths, and Reality [including articles in English by Norman Saul, Frank Costigliola, David Foglesong, William Shade, Dina Fainberg, and Elizabeth Elliott]). Moscow: Russian State Humanities University, 2007.

THE UNITED STATES AND THE RUSSIAN EMPIRE, 1763–1867

Abrahams, Robert D. *The Uncommon Soldier: Major Alfred Mordecai.* New York: Farrar, Straus & Cudahy, 1958.

Alden, John R. *Stephen Sayre, American Revolutionary Adventurer.* Baton Rouge: Louisiana State University Press, 1983.

Alexander, John T. *Catherine the Great: Life and Legend.* Folio ed. New York: Oxford University Press, 1999.

Arnaud, Colonel Charles A. De. *The Union, and Its Ally, Russia: An Historical Narrative of the Most Critical and Exciting Period of Our Late War.* Washington, D.C.: Gibson Bros., 1890.

Barratt, Glynn. *Russia in Pacific Waters, 1715–1825: A Survey of Russian Naval Presence in the North and South Pacific.* Vancouver: University of British Columbia Press, 1981.

Bartley, Russell H. *Imperial Russia and the Struggle for Latin American Independence, 1808–1828.* Latin American Monographs, no. 43. Austin: University of Texas Press, 1978.

Batueva, T. M. *Ekspansiia SShA na Severe tikhogo okeana v seredene XIX v. i pokupka Aliaski v 1867 gg.* (The Expansion of the USA in the North Pacific Ocean in the Middle of the 19th Century and the Purchase of Alaska in 1867). Tomsk: TGU, 1976.

Belohlavek, John M. *Let the Eagle Soar! The Foreign Policy of Andrew Jackson.* Lincoln: University of Nebraska Press, 1985.

——. *George Mifflin Dallas: Jacksonian Politician.* University Park: Pennsylvania State University Press, 1977.

Bemis, Samuel Flagg. *John Quincy Adams and the Foundations of American Foreign Policy.* New York: Knopf, 1949.

Berquist, Harold E., Jr. *Russian–American Relations, 1820–1830: The Diplomacy of Henry Middleton, American Minister at St. Petersburg.* Ph.D. diss., Boston University, 1970.

Black, Lydia. *Russians in Alaska, 1732–1867.* Fairbanks: University of Alaska Press, 2004.

Bolkhovitinov, Nikolai. *The Beginnings of Russian–American Relations, 1775–1815.* Translated by Elena Levin. Cambridge, Mass.: Harvard University Press, 1975.

——. *Doktrina Monro: Proiskhozhdenie i kharakter* (The Monroe Doctrine: Origins and Character). Moscow: Nauka, 1959.

——, ed. *Istoriia russkoi Ameriki: 1732–1867* (The History of Russian America, 1732–1867). 3 vols. Moscow: Mezhdu. otnosh., 1997–99.

——. *Rossiia i voina SShA za nezavisimost', 1775–1783* (Russia and the War of the USA for Independence, 1775–1783). Moscow: Mysl', 1976.

——. "Russian–American Rapprochement and the Commercial Treaty of 1832." Translated and edited by J. Dane Hartgrove. *Soviet Studies in History* 19 (3) (Winter 1980–81): 3–92.

——. *Russko–Amerikanskie otnosheniia i prodazha Aliaski, 1834–1867* (Russian–American Relations and the Sale of Alaska). Moscow: Nauka, 1990.

———. *Russko–Amerikanskie otnosheniia, 1815–1832* (Russian–American Relations, 1815–1832). Moscow: Nauka, 1975.

Brayard, Frank O. *S.S. Savannah: The Elegant Steam Ship.* New York: Dover, 1963.

Buchanan, James. *James Buchanan's Mission to Russia, 1831–1833: His Speeches, State Papers and Private Correspondence.* New York: Arno Press, 1970.

Burrows, Silas E. *America and Russia: Correspondence, 1818 to 1848.* N.p.: 1848.

Chevigny, Hector. *Russian America: The Great Alaskan Venture, 1741–1867.* New York: Viking Press, 1965.

Collins, Perry McDonough. *A Voyage Down the Amoor: With a Land Journey through Siberia, and Incidental Notices of Manchooria, Kamschatka, and Japan.* New York: D. Appleton, 1860.

Cresson, William Penn. *Francis Dana: A Puritan Diplomat at the Court of Catherine the Great.* New York: Dial Press, 1930.

Crosby, Alfred W., Jr. *America, Russia, Hemp, and Napoleon: American Trade with Russia and the Baltic, 1783–1812.* Columbus: Ohio State University Press, 1965.

Curti, Merle Eugene. *The American Peace Crusade, 1815–1860.* Durham, N.C.: Duke University Press, 1929.

Dallas, George Mifflin. *Diary of George Mifflin Dallas.* Edited by Susan Dallas. Philadelphia: J. B. Lippincott, 1892.

Darby, William. *The Northern Nations of Europe, Russia and Poland.* Chillicothe, Ohio: author, 1841.

Davis, Curtis Carroll. *The King Chevalier: A Biography of Lewis Littlepage.* Indianapolis, Ind.: Bobbs-Merrill, 1961.

Dolgova, S. R. *Tvorchestva put E. V. Karzhavina.* Leningrad: Nauka, 1984.

Dowty, Alan. *The Limits of American Isolation: The United States and the Crimean War.* New York: New York University Press, 1971.

Dvoichenko-Markov, Eufrosina. "Americans in the Crimean War." *Russian Review* 13, no. 2 (April 1954): 137–45.

———. "Benjamin Franklin, the American Philosophical Society, and the Russian Academy of Science." *Proceedings of the American Philosophical Society* 96, no. 3 (August 1947): 250–58.

D'Wolf, Captain John. *A Voyage to the North Pacific and a Journey through Siberia.* Cambridge, Mass.: author, 1861.

Fedorova, Svetlana G. *The Russian Population of Alaska.* Kingston, Ontario: Limestone Press, 1995.

Fischer, LeRoy H. *Lincoln's Gadfly, Adam Gurowski.* Norman: University of Oklahoma Press, 1964.

Fisher, Raymond H. *Bering's Voyages: Whither and Why.* Seattle: University of Washington Press, 1977.

Gibson, James R. *Feeding the Russian Fur Trade: Provisionment of the Okhotsk Seaboard and the Kamchatka Peninsula, 1639–1856.* Madison: University of Wisconsin Press, 1969.

——. *Imperial Russia in Frontier America: The Changing Geography of Supply of Russian America, 1784–1867.* New York: Oxford University Press, 1976.

——. *Otter Skins, Boston Ships, and China Goods: The Maritime Fur Trade of the Northwest Coast, 1785–1941.* Montreal: McGill-Queen's University Press, 1992.

Golder, Frank A. *John Paul Jones in Russia.* Garden City, N.Y.: Doubleday, 1927.

——. "The Purchase of Alaska." *American Historical Review* 25, no. 3 (April 1920): 411–25.

——. "Russian American Relations During the Crimean War." *American Historical Review* 31, no. 3 (April 1926): 462–65.

——. *Russian Expansion on the Pacific, 1641–1850.* New York: Paragon Book Reprint Corp., 1971.

Golovin, Ivan. *Stars and Stripes, or American Impressions.* New York: Appleton, 1856.

Golovin, P. N. *Civil and Savage Encounters: The Worldly Travel Letters of an Imperial Russian Navy Officer, 1860–1861.* Edited and translated by Basil Dmytryshyn and E. A. P. Crownhart-Vaughan. Portland: Oregon Historical Society, 1983.

Griffiths, David M. "American Commercial Diplomacy in Russia, 1780–1783." *William and Mary Quarterly,* 3rd Ser. 27, no. 3 (July 1970): 379–410.

——. "An American Contribution to the Armed Neutrality of 1780." *Russian Review* 30, no. 2 (April 1971): 164–72.

——. "Nikita Panin, Russian Diplomacy, and the American Revolution." *Slavic Review* 28, no. 1 (March 1969): 1–24.

Grimsted, Patricia Kennedy. *The Foreign Ministers of Alexander I: Political Attitudes and the Conduct of Russian Diplomacy, 1801–1825.* Berkeley: University of California Press, 1969.

Grossman, Joan Delaney. *Edgar Allan Poe in Russia: A Study in Legend and Literary Influence.* Wurzburg: Jal-Verlag, 1973.

Grzelonski, Bogdan. *Poles in the United States of America, 1776–1865.* Warsaw: Interpress, 1976.

Gurowski, Adam. *America and Europe.* New York: Appleton, 1856.

Haiman, Miecislaus. *Kosciuszko: Leader and Exile.* New York: Kosciuszko Foundation, 1977.

Harrison, Joseph, Jr. *The Iron Worker and King Solomon.* 2nd ed. Philadelphia: Lippincott, 1869.

Haywood, Richard Mowbray. *The Beginnings of Railway Development in Russia in the Reign of Nicholas I, 1835–1842.* Durham, N.C.: Duke University Press, 1969.

Hildt, John C. *Early Diplomatic Negotiations of the United States with Russia.* Johns Hopkins University Studies in Historical and Political Science: 25, 5–6. Baltimore, Md.: Johns Hopkins University Press, 1906.

Ivanov, Robert F. *Diplomatiia Avraama Linkona* (The Diplomacy of Abraham Lincoln). Moscow: Mezhdu. otnosh., 1987.

Jensen, Ronald J. *The Alaska Purchase and Russian–American Relations.* Seattle: University of Washington Press, 1975.

Kirchner, Walther. *Studies in Russian–American Commerce, 1820–1860.* Leiden: E. J. Brill, 1975.

Kolchin, Peter. *Unfree Labor: American Slavery and Russian Serfdom.* Cambridge, Mass.: Harvard University Press, 1987.

Kroll, C. Douglas. *"Friends in Peace and War": The Russian Navy's Landmark Visit to Civil War San Francisco.* Dulles, Va.: Potomac Books, 2007.

Kurilla, Ivan. *Zaokeanskie partnery: Amerika i Rossiia v 1830–1850-e gody* (Trans-Ocean Partners: America and Russia, 1830s–1850s). Volgograd: VGU, 2005.

Kushner, Howard I. *Conflict on the Northwest Coast: American–Russian Rivalry in the Pacific Northwest, 1790–1867.* Westport, Conn.: Greenwood Press, 1975.

Ledyard, John. *Journey through Russia and Siberia, 1787–1788: The Journals and Selected Letters.* Edited by George D. Watrous. Madison: University of Wisconsin Press, 1966.

Lensen, George Alexander. *The Russian Push Toward Japan: Russo–Japanese Relations, 1607–1875.* Princeton, N.J.: Princeton University Press, 1959.

Lerski, Jerzy Jan. *A Polish Chapter in Jacksonian America: The United States and the Polish Exiles of 1831.* Madison: University of Wisconsin Press, 1958.

Lewis, William David. *The Bakchesarian Fountain, by Alexander Pooshkeen, and Other Poems, by Various Authors.* Translated by William David Lewis. Philadelphia: author, 1849.

Lobanov-Rostovsky, Andrei A. *Russia and Europe, 1789–1825.* New York: Greenwood Press, 1968.

Madariaga, Isabel de. *Britain, Russia and the Armed Neutrality of 1780.* New Haven, Conn.: Yale University Press, 1963.

———. *Russia in the Age of Catherine the Great.* New Haven, Conn.: Yale University Press, 1981.

Maggs, Barbara. "Fedor Karzhavin and Vasilii Baranshchikov: Russian Travellers in the Caribbean and Colonial America." In *Russia and the World of the Eighteenth Century.* Edited by R. P. Bartlett. Columbus, Ohio: Slavica, 1988.

Malkin, M. M. *Grazhdanskaia voina v SShA I Tsarskaia Rossiia.* Moscow–Leningrad: OGIZ, 1939.

May, Ernest R. *The Making of the Monroe Doctrine.* Cambridge, Mass.: Harvard University Press, 1975.

Mazour, Anatole G. "The Russian–American and Anglo–Russian Conventions, 1824–1825: An Interpretation." *Pacific Historical Review* 14, no. 3 (September 1945): 303–10.

McPherson, Hallie M. "The Interest of William McKendree Gwin in the Purchase of Alaska, 1854–1861." *Pacific Historical Review* 3, no. 1 (March 1934): 28–38.

Miller, Martin A. *The Russian Revolutionary Emigres, 1825–1870.* Baltimore, Md.: Johns Hopkins University Press, 1986.

Mohrenschildt, Dmitri von. *Toward a United States of Russia: Plans and Projects of Federal Reconstruction in the Nineteenth Century.* Rutherford, N.J.: Fairleigh Dickinson University Press, 1981.

Morison, Samuel Eliot. *John Paul Jones: A Sailor's Biography.* Boston: Little, Brown, 1959.

Mumford, Elizabeth. *Whistler's Mother.* Boston: Little, Brown, 1939.

Nakajima, Hiroo. "The Monroe Doctrine and Russia: American Views of Czar Alexander I and Their Influence upon Early Russian–American Relations," *Diplomatic History* 31, no. 3 (June 2007): 439–63.

Narochnitskii, A. L. "Ekspansiia SShA na Dalnem Vostoke v 50–70-e gody XIX veka" (The Expansion of the USA in the Far East in the 50s–70s of the 19th Century). *Istoricheskie Zapiski* (Historical Notes) 44 (1953): 130–76.

Neatby, L. H. *Discovery in Russian and Siberian Waters.* Athens: Ohio University Press, 1973.

Nichols, Irby C., Jr. "The Russian Ukase and the Monroe Doctrine: A Reevaluation." *Pacific Historical Review* 36, no. 1 (February 1967): 13–26.

Nikoliukin, Alexander. *Literaturnye sviazi Rossii SShA: Stanovlenie literaturnykh kontaktov* (Literary Relations of Russia and the USA: The Foundations of Literary Contacts). Moscow: Nauka, 1981.

———. *A Russian Discovery of America.* Moscow: Progress Publishers, 1986.

———. *Vzaimosviazi litertur Rossii i SShA: Turgenev, Tolstoi, Dostoevskii i Amerika* (Interconnections of the Literature of Russia and the USA: Turgenev, Tolstoy, Dostoevsky and America). Moscow: Nauka, 1987.

Okun, S. B. *The Russian–America Company.* Translated by Carl Ginsberg. Cambridge, Mass.: Harvard University Press, 1951.

Parry, Albert. "American Doctors in the Crimean War." *South Atlantic Quarterly* 54, no. 4 (October 1955): 478–90.

———. *Whistler's Father.* Indianapolis, Ind.: Bobbs-Merrill, 1939.

Petrov, Alexander. *Obrazovanie Rossiisko–Amerikanskoi kompanii* (The Formation of the Russian–American Company). Moscow: Nauka, 2001.

Petrov, Viktor. *Russie v istorii Ameriki* (Russians in the History of America). Moscow: Nauka, 1991.

Pierce, Richard A. *Builders of Alaska: The Russian Governors, 1818–1867.* Kingston, Ont.: Limestone Press, 1986.

———. *Russia's Hawaiian Adventure, 1815–1817.* Kingston, Ont.: Limestone Press, 1976.

Ponomarev, V. N. *Krimskaia voina i russko–amerikanskie otnosheniia* (The Crimean War and Russian–American Relations). Moscow: Nauka, 1993.

Richardson, H. Edward. *Cassius Marcellus Clay: Firebrand of Freedom.* Lexington: University of Kentucky Press, 1976.

Rippy, J. Fred. *Joel R. Poinsett: Versatile American.* Durham, N.C.: Duke University Press, 1935.

Robertson, James Root. *A Kentuckian at the Court of the Tsars: The Ministry of Cassius Marcellus Clay to Russia, 1861–1869.* Berea, Ky.: Berea College Press, 1935.

Robertson, William Spence. "Russia and the Emancipation of Spanish America, 1816–1826." *Hispanic American Historical Review* 21, no. 2 (May 1941): 196–221.

Saul, Norman E. "America's First Student of Russia: William David Lewis of Philadelphia." *Pennsylvania Magazine of History and Biography* 96, no. 4 (October 1972): 469–79.

———. "The Beginnings of American–Russian Trade, 1763–1766." *William and Mary Quarterly, 3rd Series* 26, no. 4 (October 1969): 596–601.

———. *Distant Friends: The United States and Russia, 1763–1867.* Lawrence: University Press of Kansas, 1991.

Schrier, Arnold, and Joyce Story, eds. *A Russian Looks at America: The Journey of Aleksandr Borisovich Lakier in 1857.* Chicago: University of Chicago Press, 1979.

Smiley, David L. *Lion of Whitehall: The Life of Cassius M. Clay.* Madison: University of Wisconsin Press, 1962.

Startsev, Abel. *Russko–Amerikanskie etiudy* (Russian–American Studies). Moscow: RAN, 1995.

Suchukova, Nataliia. *Diplomaticheskaia missiia Dzhona Kuinsi Adamsa v 1809–1814 godakh* (The Diplomatic Mission of John Quincy Adams, 1809–1814). Moscow: Rosspen, 2007.

Starr, S. Frederick, ed. *Russia's American Colony.* Durham, N.C.: Duke University Press, 1987.

Swoboda, Marina, and William Benton Whisenhunt. *A Russian Paints America: The Travels of Pavel P. Svin'in, 1811–1813.* Montreal: McGill-Queen's University Press, 2008.

The United States and Russia: The Beginning of Relations, 1765–1815. Washington, D.C.: State Department and Government Printing Office, 1980. Also available in Russian translation.

Thomas, Benjamin Platt. *Russo–American Relations, 1815–1867.* Johns Hopkins University Studies in Historical and Political Science, 48, no. 2. Baltimore, Md.: Johns Hopkins University Press, 1930.

Tumarkin, D. D. *Gavaiskii narod i amerikanskie kolonizatory, 1820–1865 gg.* (The Hawaian People and American Colonialism, 1820–1865). Moscow: Nauka, 1971.

Watrous, Stephen D. *Fort Ross: The Russian Settlement in California.* Jenner, Calif.: Fort Ross Interpretive Association, 1975.

——, ed. *John Ledyard's Journey Through Russia and Siberia, 1787–1788: The Journal and Selected Letters.* Madison: University of Wisconsin Press, 1966.

Wheeler, Mary E. "Empires in Conflict and Cooperation: The Bostonians and the Russian–American Company." *Pacific Historical Review* 40 (1971): 419–41.

Woldman, Albert A. *Lincoln and the Russians.* Cleveland, Ohio: World Company, 1952.

Yarmolinsky, Avrahm. *Picturesque United States of America, 1811, 1812, 1813.* New York: Rudge, 1930.

THE UNITED STATES AND RUSSIA, 1867–1914

Abbot, Lawrence F. *The Story of NYLIC: A History of the Origin and Development of the New York Life Insurance Company from 1845 to 1929.* New York: The Company, 1930.

Barratt, Glynn. *Russian Shadows on the British Northwest Coast of North America, 1810–1890: A Study of Rejection of Defence Responsibilities.* Vancouver: University of British Columbia, 1983.

Barton, Clara. *The Red Cross: A History of This Remarkable International Movement in the Interest of Humanity.* Washington, D.C.: American National Red Cross, 1898.

Bates, Lindon, Jr. *The Russian Road to China.* Boston, Mass.: Houghton Mifflin, 1910.

Beveridge, Albert. *The Russian Advance.* New York: Harper, 1904.

Bouton, John Bell. *Roundabout to Moscow: An Epicurean Journey.* New York: Appleton, 1887.

Bradley, Joseph. *Guns for the Tsar: Technology Transfer and the Small Arms Industry in Nineteenth-Century Russia.* DeKalb, Ill.: Northern Illinois University Press, 1990.

Buckley, James Monroe. *The Midnight Sun, the Tsar and the Nihilist: Adventures and Observations in Norway, Sweden and Russia.* Boston, Mass.: D. Lothrop, 1886.

Buel, James W. *Russian Nihilism and Exile Life in Siberia.* St. Louis, Mo.: Historical Publishing Company, 1883.

Buley, R. Carlyle. *The Equitable Life Assurance Society of the United States, 1859–1961.* Vol. 2. New York: Equitable reprint, 1983.

Carstensen, Fred V. *American Enterprise in Foreign Markets: Studies of Singer and International Harvester in Imperial Russia.* Chapel Hill: University of North Carolina Press, 1984.

Cary, Clarence. *The Trans-Siberian Route, or Notes of a Journey from Peking to New York in 1902.* New York: Evening Post, 1902.

Catacazy, M. de [Konstantin Katakazi]. *An incident diplomatique: lettre au Chief Justice S. Chase.* Paris: Arnyot, 1872.

Child, Theodore. *The Tsar and His People, or Social Life in Russia.* New York: Harper and Bros., 1891.

Clay, Cassius Marcellus. *The Life of Cassius Marcellus Clay: Memoirs, Writings, Speeches.* Cincinnati, Ohio: J. Fletcher Brennan, 1886.

Curtin, Jeremiah. *A Journey in Southern Siberia.* Boston, Mass.: Little, Brown, 1909.

Dall, William H. *Alaska and Its Resources.* Boston, Mass: Lee and Shepard, 1870.

De Long, George Washington. *The Voyage of the Jeannette: The Ship and Ice Journals.* Boston, Mass.: Houghton Mifflin, 1883.

Dole, Nathan Haskell. "A Plea for the Study of Russian." *Harvard's Graduate Magazine* 3, no. 10 (December 1894): 180–85.

Edgar, William C. *The Russian Famine of 1891 and 1892.* Minneapolis, Minn.: Millers and Manufacturers Insurance, 1893.

Emmons, Terence. *Alleged Sex & Threatened Violence: Doctor Russel, Bishop Vladimir, and the Russians in San Francisco, 1887–1892.* Stanford, Calif.: Stanford University Press, 1997.

Engel', V. V. *"Evreiskii vopros" v russko–amerikanskikh otnosheniizkh: (na premere "pasportnogo voprosa", 1864–1913)* (The "Jewish Question" in Russian–American Relations: the "Passport Question," 1864–1913). Moscow: RAN, 1998.

Foglesong, David S. "Redeeming Russia? American Missionaries and Tsarist Russia, 1886–1917." *Religion, State & Society* 25, no. 4: 353–68.

Ford, Alexander Hume. "Russia as a Market for Machinery and Machine Tools." *Engineering Magazine* 21, no. 4 (July 1901): 493–507.

Gatrell, Peter. *The Tsarist Economy, 1850–1917.* New York: St. Martin's Press, 1986.

Gorky, Maxim. *The City of the Yellow Devil: Pamphlets, Articles and Letters about America.* Moscow: Progress Publishers, 1972.

Greene, Francis V. *Report on the Russian Army and Its Campaigns in Turkey in 1877–1878.* 2 vols. New York: D. Appleton, 1879.

Guild, Curtis. *Britons and Muscovites, or Traits of Two Empires.* Boston, Mass.: Lee and Shepard, 1888.

Hapgood, Isabel. *Russian Rambles.* Boston, Mass.: Houghton Mifflin, 1895.

Hecht, David. *Russian Radicals Look to America, 1825–1894.* Cambridge, Mass.: Harvard University Press, 1947.

Herlihy, Patricia. *Odessa: A History, 1794–1914.* Harvard Ukrainian Research Institute Monograph Series. Cambridge, Mass.: Harvard University Press, 1986.

Hoffman, Wickham. *Leisure Hours in Russia.* London: George Bell and Sons, 1883.

Holbo, Paul S. *Tarnished Expansion: The Alaska Scandal, the Press, and Congress, 1867–1871.* Knoxville: University of Tennessee Press, 1983.

Hughes, Michael. *Diplomacy before the Russian Revolution: Britain, Russia and the Old Diplomacy, 1894–1917.* London: Macmillan, 2000.

Hundley, Helen. "George Kennan and the Russian Empire: How America's Conscience Became an Enemy of Tsarism." Kennan Institute Occasional Paper, no. 277. Washington, D.C.: Woodrow Wilson Center, 2000.

Jackson, Sheldon. *Alaska and Missions on the North Pacific Coast.* New York: Dodd, Mead, 1880.

Kennan, George F. *The Fateful Alliance: France, Russia, and the Coming of the First World War.* New York: Pantheon, 1984.

Kuropiatnik, Gennady, ed. *Istoriia vneshnei politiki i diplomatii SShA, 1867–1918* (The History of the Foreign Policy and Diplomacy of the USA, 1867–1918). Moscow: Nauka, 1997.

Laserson, Max M. *The American Impact on Russia, 1784–1917: Diplomatic and Ideological.* New York: Macmillan, 1950.

Lebedev, V. V. *Russko–Amerikanskie ekonomicheskie otnosheniia (1900–1917 gg.)* (Russian–American Economic Relations, 1900–1917). Moscow: Mezhdu. otnosh., 1964.

Lied, Jonas. *Siberian Arctic: The Story of the Siberian Company.* London: Methuen, 1960.

MacDonald, David M. "Lever without a Fulcrum: Domestic Factors and Russian Foreign Policy, 1905–1914." In *Imperial Russian Foreign Policy,* edited by Hugh Ragsdale, 268–311. New York: Woodrow Wilson Center, 1993.

March, G. Patrick. *Eastern Destiny: Russia in Asia and the North Pacific.* Westport, Conn.: Praeger, 1996.

Marshall, Herbert, and Mildred Stock. *Ira Aldridge, the Negro Tragedian.* Carbondale and Edwardsville, Ill.: Southern Illinois University Press, 1968.

McDaniel, Tim. *Autocracy, Capitalism, and Revolution in Russia.* Berkeley: University of California Press, 1988.

McKay, John P. *Pioneers for Profit: Foreign Entrepreneurship and Russian Industrialization, 1885–1913.* Chicago: University of Chicago Press, 1977.

Miller, David Hunter. *The Alaska Treaty.* Kingston, Ont.: Limestone Press, 1981.

Parry, Albert. *America Learns Russian: A History of the Teaching of the Russian Language in the United States.* Syracuse, N.Y.: Syracuse University Press, 1967.

Reznikoff, Charles. *Family Chronicle: An Odyssey from Russia to America.* New York: Marcus Weiner, 1988.

Rieber, Alfred J. *Merchants and Entrepreneurs in Imperial Russia.* Chapel Hill: University of North Carolina Press, 1982.

Rogger, Hans. "America in the Russian Mind or Russian Discoveries of America." *Pacific Historical Review* 47, no. 1 (February 1978): 27–51.

———. "*Amerikanizm* and the Economic Development of Russia." *Comparative Studies in Society and History* 23, no. 1 (July 1981): 382–420.

Saul, Norman E. *Concord and Conflict: The United States and Russia, 1967–1914.* Lawrence: University Press of Kansas, 1996.

———. "A Diplomatic Failure and an Ecological Disaster: The United States, Russia, and the North Pacific Fur Seals." In *Russkoe otkrytie Ameriki* (The Russian Discovery of America), 255–66. Moscow: Rosspen, 2002.

Schuyler, Eugene. *Turkistan: Notes of a Journey in Russian Turkistan, Khokand, Bukhara, and Kuldja.* 2 vols. New York: Scribner, Armstrong, 1877.

Smith, C. Henry. *The Coming of the Russian Mennonites: An Episode in the Settling of the Last Frontier, 1874–1994.* Berne, Ind.: Mennonite Book Concern, 1927.

Travis, Frederick F. *George Kennan and the American–Russian Relationship, 1865–1924.* Athens: Ohio University Press, 1990.

Williams, Robert C. *Russian Art and American Money, 1900–1940.* Cambridge, Mass.: Harvard University Press, 1983.

Yarmolinsky, Avraham. *A Russian's American Dream: A Memoir on William Frey.* Lawrence: University of Kansas Press, 1965.

Yoffe, Elkhonon. *Tchaikovsky in America: The Composer's Visit to Celebrate the Opening of Carnegie Hall in New York City, 1891.* New York: Oxford University Press, 1986.

Zabriskie, Edward H. *American–Russian Relations in the Far East: A Study in Diplomacy and Power Politics, 1895–1914.* Philadelphia: University of Pennsylvania Press, 1946.

WAR, REVOLUTION, AND CIVIL WAR, 1914–1921

Abbott, Lawrence F. *The Story of NYLIC: A History of the Origin and Development of the New York Life Insurance Company from 1845 to 1929.* New York: The Company, 1930.

Abraham, Richard. *Alexander Kerensky: The First Love of the Revolution.* New York: Columbia University Press, 1987.

Ackerman, Carl W. *Trailing the Bolsheviki: Twelve Thousand Miles with the Allies in Siberia.* New York: Charles Scribner's Sons, 1919.

Albertson, Ralph. *Fighting Without a War: An Account of Military Intervention in North Russia.* New York: Harcourt, Brace and Howe, 1920.

Allison, William. *American Diplomats in Russia: Case Studies in Orphan Diplomacy, 1916–1919.* Westport, Conn.: Praeger, 1997.

Ambrosius, Lloyd E. *Wilsonian Statecraft: Theory and Practice of Liberal Internationalism during World War I.* Wilmington, N.C.: Scholarly Resources, 1991.

Anderson, Paul B. *No East or West.* Edited by Donald E. Davis. Paris: YMCA Press, 1985.

Barnes, Harper. *Standing on a Volcano: The Life and Times of David Rowland Francis.* St. Louis: Missouri Historical Society, 2001.

Beatty, Bessie. *The Red Heart of Russia.* New York: Century, 1919.

Beaver, Daniel R. *Newton D. Baker and the American War Effort, 1917–1919.* Lincoln: University of Nebraska Press, 1966.

Berezkin, Aleksandr. *Oktiabrskaia revolutsiia i SShA, 1917–1922 gg.* (The October Revolution and the USA). Moscow: Nauka, 1967.

Boylan, James. *Revolutionary Lives: Anna Strunsky and William English Walling.* Amherst: University of Massachusetts Press, 1998.

Bryant, Louise. *Six Red Months in Russia: An Observer's Account of Russia Before and During the Proletarian Dictatorship.* New York: George H. Doran, 1918.

Bykov, Aleksandr, and Leonid Panov. *Diplomaticheskaia stolitsaia Rossii* (Diplomatic Capital of Russia). Vologda: Ardvisura, 1998.

Byrnes, Robert F. *Awakening American Education to the World: The Role of Archibald Cary Coolidge, 1866–1928.* South Bend, Ind.: University of Notre Dame Press, 1982.

Cantacuzene-Speransky [Kantakuzen], Julia (née Grant). *My Life Here and There.* New York: Charles Scribner's Sons, 1921.

Capelotti, P. J. *Our Man in the Crimea: Commander Hugo Koehler and the Russian Civil War.* Columbia: University of South Carolina Press, 1991.

Carey, Neil G., ed. *Fighting the Bolsheviks: The Russian War Memoirs of Private First Class Donald E. Carey, U.S. Army, 1918–19.* Novato, Calif.: Presidio Press, 1997.

Carley, Michael. *Revolution and Intervention: The French Intervention and the Russian Civil War.* Montreal: McGill-Queen's University Press, 1983.

Cockfield, Jamie H. *With Snow on Their Boots: The Tragic Odyssey of the Russian Expeditionary Force in France during World War I.* New York: St. Martin's Press, 1998.

Crosley, Pauline S. *Intimate Letters from Petrograd.* New York: Dutton, 1920.

Davis, Donald E., and Eugene Trani. *The First Cold War: The Legacy of Woodrow Wilson and U.S. Soviet Relations.* Columbia: University of Missouri Press, 2002.

———. "The American YMCA and the Russian Revolution." *Slavic Review* 33, no. 3 (September 1974): 467–91.

Dearborn, Mary V. *Queen of Bohemia: The Life of Louise Bryant.* Boston, Mass.: Houghton Mifflin, 1996.

Debo, Richard K. *Revolution and Survival: The Foreign Policy of Soviet Russia, 1917–1918.* Liverpool, U.K.: Liverpool University Press, 1979.

———. *Survival and Consolidation: The Foreign Policy of Soviet Russia, 1918–1921.* Montreal: McGill-Queen's University Press, 1992.

Decker, Clinton J., ed. *An American Journal: Letters by Clinton A. Decker.* New York: author, 1994.

Dorn, Harold. "Hugh Lincoln Cooper and the First Detente." *Technology and Culture* 20 (1979): 322–47.

Dubie, Alain. *Frank A. Golder: An Adventure of a Historian in Quest of Russian History.* New York: Columbia University Press, 1989.

Dubofsky, Melvyn. *We Shall Be All: A History of the IWW, the Industrial Workers of the World.* New York: Quadrangle/New York Times, 1969.

Duncan, Isadora. *My Life.* New York: Boni and Liveright, 1927.

Evgen'ev, G., and B. Shapik. *Revoliutsioner, Diplomat, Uchenyi: L. K. Martens* (Revolutionary, Diplomat, Scholar: L. K. Martens). Moscow: Nauka, 1960.

Fedotoff White, Dmitri. *Survival through War and Revolution.* Philadelphia: University of Pennsylvania Press, 1939.

Feist, Joe Michael. "Theirs Is Not to Reason Why: The Case of the Russian Railway Service Corps." *Military Affairs* 42 (February 1978): 1–6.

Ferrell, Robert H. *Woodrow Wilson & World War I, 1917–1921.* New York: Harper & Row, 1985.

Fic, Victor M. *The Collapse of American Policy in Russia and Siberia, 1918: Wilson's Decision Not to Intervene (Jan.–March 1918).* New York: Columbia University Press, 1995.

Figes, Orlando. *A People's Tragedy: The Russian Revolution, 1891–1924.* London: Allen Lane, 1996.

Fike, Claude E. "The Influence of the Creel Committee and the American Red Cross on Russian–American Relations, 1917–1919." *Journal of Modern History* 31, no. 2 (June 1959): 93–109.

Foglesong, David S. *America's Secret War against Bolshevism: U.S. Intervention in the Russian Civil War, 1917–1920.* Chapel Hill: University of North Carolina Press, 1995.

———. "Xenophon Kalamatiano: An American Spy in Revolutionary Russia?" *Intelligence and National Security* 6 (January 1991): 154–95.

Francis, David R. *Russia from the American Embassy: April 1916–November 1918.* New York: Charles Scribner's Sons, 1921.

Ganelin, Rafail Sh. *Rossiia i SShA, 1914–1917: ocherki istorii Russko–Amerikanskikh otnoshenii.* Leningrad: Nauka, 1969.

———. *Sovetsko Amerikanskie otnosheniia v kontse 1917–nachale 1918 g.* Leningrad: Nauka, 1975.

Gardner, Lloyd. *Safe for Democracy: The Anglo–American Response to Revolution, 1913–1923.* New York: Oxford University Press, 1983.

Gardner, Virginia. *Friend and Lover: The Life of Louise Bryant.* New York: Horizon, 1982.

Gaworek, Norman H. "From Blockade to Trade: Allied Economic Warfare against Soviet Russia, June 1919 to January 1920." *Jahrbucher fur Geschichte Osteuropas* 23 (1975): 39–69.

Glenny, Michael, and Norman Stone. *The Other Russia: The Experience of Exile.* New York: Viking, 1991.

Goldhurst, Richard. *The Midnight War: The American Intervention in Russia, 1918–1920.* New York: McGraw-Hill, 1978.

Good, Jane E., and David R. Jones. *Babushka: The Life of the Russian Revolutionary E. K. Breshko-Breshkovskaia.* Newtonville, Mass.: Oriental Research Partners, 1991.

Gordon, Dennis, ed. *Quartered in Hell: The Story of the American North Russian Expeditionary Force.* Missoula, Mont.: Doughboy Historical Society, 1982.

Graves, William S. *America's Siberian Adventure, 1918–1920.* New York: Jonathan Cape & Harrison Smith, 1931.

Grayson, Benson Lee. *Russian–American Relations in World War I.* New York: Ungar, 1979.

Grow, Malcolm C. *Surgeon Grow, an American in the Russian Fighting.* New York: F. A. Stokes, 1918.

Hagedorn, Ann. *Savage Peace: Hope and Fear in America, 1919.* New York: Simon & Schuster, 2008.

Hagedorn, Hermann. *The Magnate: William Boyce Thompson and His Times, 1869–1930.* New York: Reynal and Hitchcock, 1935.

Hapgood, David. *Charles R. Crane: The Man Who Bet on People.* New York: Institute of Current World Affairs, 2000.

Harper, Samuel N. *The Russia I Believed In: The Memoirs of Samuel N. Harper, 1902–1941.* Edited by Paul V. Harper. Chicago: University of Chicago Press, 1945.

Harrison, Marguerite. *Marooned in Moscow: The Story of an American Woman Imprisoned in Russia.* New York: Doran, 1921.

Heenan, Louise E. *Russian Democracy's Fatal Blunder: The Summer Offensive of 1917.* New York: Praeger, 1987.

Hopkins, C. Howard. *John R. Mott, 1865–1955: A Biography.* Grand Rapids, Mich.: William Eerdmans, 1979.

Houghteling, James L. *A Diary of the Russian Revolution.* New York: Dodd, Mead, 1918.

Ivanian, Eduard. *Y istokov Sovetsko–Amerikanskikh otnoshenii* (Sources of Soviet–American Relations). Moscow: Mezhdu. otnosh., 2007.

Jahns, Hubertus F. *Patriotic Culture in Russia during World War I.* Ithaca, N.Y.: Cornell University Press, 1995.

Kennan, George F. *Soviet–American Relations, 1917–1920.* Vol. 1, *The Decision to Leave the War;* Vol. 2, *The Decision to Intervene.* Princeton, N.J.: Princeton University Press, 1958.

Kerensky, Alexander. *Russia and History's Turning Point.* New York: Duell, Sloan and Pearce, 1965.

Killen, Linda. *The Russian Bureau: A Case Study in Wilsonian Diplomacy.* Lexington: University of Kentucky Press, 1983.

———. "The Search for a Democratic Russia: Bakhmetev and the United States." *Diplomatic History* 2 (Summer 1978): 237–57.

Kurth, Peter. *Isadora: A Sensational Life.* Boston: Little, Brown, 2001.

Lasch, Christopher. *The American Liberals and the Russian Revolution.* New York: Columbia University Press, 1962.

Lincoln, W. Bruce. *Passage through Armageddon: The Russians in War and Revolution, 1914–1918.* New York: Oxford University Press, 1986.

———. *Red Victory: A History of the Russian Civil War.* New York: Oxford University Press, 1994.

Listikov, Sergei V. *SShA I revoliutsionnaia Russiia v 1917 godu: k voprusu ob al'terativakh amerikanskoi politiki ot Fevralia k Oktiabriu* (USA and Revolutionary Russia in 1917: Alternatives in American Policy from February to October). Moscow: Nauka, 2006.

Lohr, Eric. *Nationalizing the Russian Empire: The Campaign against Enemy Aliens during World War I*. Cambridge, Mass.: Harvard University Press, 2003.

Long, John W. "American Intervention in Russia: The North Russian Expedition, 1918–1919." *Diplomatic History* 6, no. 1 (Winter 1982): 45–67.

Lyandres, Semion. *The Bolsheviks' German Gold Revisited: An Inquiry into the 1917 Accusations*. Pittsburgh, Penn.: Center for Russian and East European Studies (The Carl Beck Papers), 1995.

MacMillan, Margaret. *Paris 1919: Six Months That Changed the World*. New York: Random House, 2002.

Maddox, Robert J. *The Unknown War with Russia: Wilson's Siberian Adventure*. San Rafael, Calif.: Presidio Press, 1997.

———. *William E. Borah and American Foreign Policy*. Baton Rouge: University of Louisiana Press, 1969.

———. "Woodrow Wilson, the Russian Embassy and Siberian Intervention." *Pacific Historical Review* 36 (November 1967): 435–48.

Marye, George Thomas. *Nearing the End in Imperial Russia*. London: Selwyn & Blount, 1929.

Mayer, Arno. *Politics and Diplomacy of Peace Making: Containment and Counterrevolution at Versailles, 1918–1919*. New York: Knopf, 1967.

———. *Wilson vs. Lenin: Political Origins of the New Diplomacy, 1917–1918*. New Haven, Conn.: Yale University Press, 1958.

McCormick, Robert. *With the Russian Army*. New York: Macmillan, 1915.

McFadden, David. *Alternative Paths: Soviets & Americans, 1917–1920*. New York: Oxford University Press, 1993.

———, and Claire Gorfinkel. *Constructive Spirit: Quakers in Revolutionary Russia*. Pasadena, Calif.: Intentional Productions, 2004.

McNeal, Shay. *The Secret Plot to Save the Tsar: The Truth behind the Romanov Mystery*. New York: William Morrow, 2001.

Morley, James W. *The Japanese Thrust into Siberia, 1918*. New York: Columbia University Press, 1957.

Neilson, Keith. *Strategy and Supply: The Anglo–Soviet Alliance, 1914–17*. London: Allen & Unwin, 1984.

O'Connor, Timothy Edward. *Diplomacy and Revolution: G. V. Chicherin and Soviet Foreign Affairs, 1918–1930*. Ames: Iowa State University Press, 1988.

———. *The Engineer of Revolution: L. B. Krasin and the Bolsheviks, 1870–1926*. Boulder, Colo.: Westview Press, 1992.

Paasiverta, J. *The Victors in World War One and Finland: Finland's Relations with the British, French, and United States Governments in 1918–1919*. Helsinki: Finnish Historical Society, 1965.

Pereira, Norman G. O. *White Siberia: The Politics of Civil War.* Montreal: McGill-Queen's University Press, 1996.

Ponafidine, Emma Cochrane. *Russia—My Home: An Intimate Record of Personal Experiences Before, During and After the Bolshevist Revolution.* Indianapolis, Ind.: Bobbs-Merrill, 1931.

Reed, John. *Ten Days That Shook the World.* New York: Boni and Liveright, 1919.

Rhodes, Benjamin D. *The Anglo-American Winter War with Russia: A Diplomatic and Military Tragedy.* New York: Greenwood Press, 1988.

Rosenberg, William G. *Liberals in the Russian Revolution: The Constitutional Democratic Party, 1917–1921.* Princeton, N.J.: Princeton University Press, 1974.

Russell, Charles Edward. *Bolshevism and the United States.* Indianapolis, Ind.: Bobbs-Merrill, 1919.

Saul, Norman E. *War and Revolution: The United States and Russia, 1914–1921.* Lawrence: University Press of Kansas, 2001.

Sevostianov, Grigorii, ed. *Rossiia i SShA: torgovo-ekonomicheskie otnosheniia, 1900–1930* (Russia and the USA: Commercial-Economic Relations, 1900–1930). Moscow: Nauka, 1996.

Sisson, Edgar. *One Hundred Red Days: A Personal Chronicle of the Bolshevik Revolution.* New Haven, Conn.: Yale University Press, 1931.

Smith, Daniel M. *Aftermath of War: Bainbridge Colby and Wilsonian Diplomacy, 1920–1921.* Philadelphia: American Philosophical Society, 1970.

Somin, Ilya. *Stillborn Crusade: The Tragic Failure of the Western Intervention in the Russian Civil War, 1918–1920.* New Brunswick, N.J.: Transaction Publishers, 1996.

Spence, Richard B. "The Tragic Fate of Kalamatiano: America's Man in Moscow." *International Journal of Intelligence and Counterintelligence* 12, no. 3 (Fall 1999), 347–74.

Stockdale, Melissa Kirschke. *Miliukov and the Quest for a Liberal Russia, 1880–1918.* Ithaca, N.Y.: Cornell University Press, 1996.

Stoff, Laurie S. *They Fought for the Motherland: Russia's Women Soldiers in World War I and the Revolution.* Lawrence: University Press of Kansas, 2006.

Strakhovsky, Leonid. *American Opinion about Russia, 1917–1920.* Toronto: University of Toronto Press, 1961.

———. *Intervention at Archangel: The Story of Allied Intervention and Russian Counter-Revolution in North Russia, 1918–1920.* Princeton, N.J.: Princeton University Press, 1944.

———. *The Origins of American Intervention in North Russia (1918).* Princeton, N.J.: Princeton University Press, 1937.

Swan, Jane. *The Lost Children: A Russian Odyssey.* Carlisle, Penn.: South Mountain Press, 1989.

Tang, Peter S. H. *Russian and Soviet Policy in Manchuria and Outer Mongolia, 1911–1931.* Durham, N.C.: Duke University Press, 1959.

Thompson, Donald. *Blood Stained Russia.* New York: Leslie-Judge, 1918.

Thompson, John M. *Russia, Bolshevism, and the Versailles Peace.* Princeton, N.J.: Princeton University Press, 1966.

Trask, David F. *The United States in the Supreme War Council: American Aims and Inter-Allied Strategy, 1917–1918.* Middletown, Conn.: Wesleyan University Press, 1961.

Uldricks, Teddy J. *Diplomacy and Ideology: The Origins of Soviet Foreign Relations, 1917–1930.* London: Sage, 1979.

Ullman, Richard H. *Anglo–Soviet Relations, 1917–1921.* 3 vols. Princeton, N.J.: Princeton University Press, 1961–1973.

Unterberger, Betty Miller. *America's Siberian Expedition, 1918–1920: A Study of National Policy.* Durham, N.C.: Duke University Press, 1956.

———. *The United States, Revolutionary Russia, and the Rise of Czechoslovakia.* Chapel Hill: University of North Carolina Press, 1989.

Warth, Robert D. *The Allies and the Russian Revolution from the Fall of the Monarchy to the Peace of Brest-Litovsk.* Durham, N.C.: Duke University Press, 1954.

Washburn, Stanley. *On the Russian Front in World War I: Memoirs of an American War Correspondent.* New York: Robert Speller, 1982.

Weeks, Albert J., Jr., and Joseph O. Baylen. "Admiral Kolchak's Mission to the United States, 10 September–9 November 1917." *Military Affairs* 40, no. 2 (April 1976): 64–75.

———. *An American Naval Diplomat in Revolutionary Russia: The Life and Times of Vice Admiral Newton A. McCully.* Annapolis, Md.: Naval Institute Press, 1992.

White, Christine A. *British & American Commercial Relations with Soviet Russia, 1918–1924.* Chapel Hill: University of North Carolina Press, 1992.

White, John Albert. *The Siberian Intervention.* Princeton, N.J.: Princeton University Press, 1950.

Wightman, Orrin Sage. *The Diary of an American Physician in the Russian Revolution, 1917.* Brooklyn, N.Y.: Brooklyn Daily Eagle, 1928.

Williams, Albert Rhys. *Journey into Revolution: Petrograd, 1917–1918.* Chicago: Quadrangle Books, 1969.

Willis, Edward F. *Herbert Hoover and the Russian Prisoners of War: A Study in Diplomacy and Relief, 1918–1919.* Stanford, Calif.: Stanford University Press, 1951.

UNITED STATES AND SOVIET RUSSIA, 1921–1941

Abramson, Rudy. *Spanning the Century: The Life of W. Averell Harriman, 1891–1996.* New York: Morrow, 1992.

Adams, Frederick C. *Economic Diplomacy: The Export–Import Bank and American Foreign Policy, 1933–1939*. Columbia: University of Missouri Press, 1976.

Alexander, Robert Jackson. *The Right Opposition: The Lovestoneites and the International Communist Opposition of the 1930s*. Westport, Conn.: Greenwood Press, 1981.

Anderson, Paul B. *Nor East or West*. Paris: YMCA Press, 1985.

Armstrong, Hamilton Fish. *Peace, and Counterpeace from Wilson to Hitler: Memoirs of Hamilton Fish Armstrong*. New York: Harper & Row, 1971.

Ashby, LeRoy. *Spearless Leader: Senator Borah and the Progressive Movement in the 1920s*. Urbana: University of Illinois Press, 1972.

Asquith, Michael. *Famine: Quaker Work in Russia, 1921–1923*. New York: Oxford University Press, 1943.

Austin, Richard Cartwright. *Building Utopia: Erecting Russia's First Modern City, 1930*. Kent, Ohio: Kent State University Press, 2004.

Bailes, Kendall E. "The American Connection: Ideology and the Transfer of American Technology to the Soviet Union, 1917–1941." *Comparative Studies in Society and History* 23, no. 2 (April 1981): 426–39.

Baker, Nicholson. *Human Smoke: The Beginnings of World War II, the End of Civilization*. New York: Simon & Schuster, 2008.

Ball, Alan M. *Imagining America: Influence and Images in Twentieth-Century Russia*. Lanham, Md.: Rowman & Littlefield, 2003.

Bassow, Whitman. *The Moscow Correspondents: Reporting from the Revolution to Glasnost*. New York: Paragon House, 1989.

Beal, Fred E. *Proletarian Journey: New York, Gastonia, Moscow*. New York: Hillman-Carl, 1937.

Bennett, Edward M. *Franklin D. Roosevelt and the Search for Security: American–Soviet Relations, 1933–1939*. Wilmington, Del.: Scholarly Resources, 1985.

——. *Franklin D. Roosevelt and the Search for Victory: American–Soviet Relations, 1939–1945*. Wilmington, Del.: Scholarly Resources, 1990.

——. *Recognition of Russia: An American Foreign Policy Dilemma*. Waltham, Mass.: Blaisdell, 1970.

Bishop, Donald G. *The Roosevelt–Litvinov Agreements: The American View*. Syracuse, N.Y.: Syracuse University Press, 1965.

Boe, Jonathan E. *American Business: The Response to the Soviet Union, 1933–1947*. New York: Garland, 1987.

Bolkhovitinov, Nikolai N. "Zhizn'i deiatel'nost G. V. Vernadskogo (1887–1973) i ego arkhiv" (The Life and Activity of G. V. Vernadsky). Sapporo, Japan: Slavic Research Center, Hokkaido University, 2002.

Bourke-White, Margaret. *Eyes on Russia*. New York: Simon & Schuster, 1931.

Bowers, Robert E. "Hull, Russian Subversion in Cuba, and Recognition of the USSR." *Journal of American History* 52, no. 3 (December 1966): 542–55.

Braun, Leopold L. S. *In Lubianka's Shadow: The Memoirs of an American Priest in Stalin's Moscow, 1934–1945*. Edited by G. M. Hamburg. South Bend, Ind.: University of Notre Dame Press, 2007.

Brooks, Jeffrey. "The Press and Its Message: Images of America in the 1920s and 1930s." In *Russia in the Era of the NEP: Explorations in Soviet Society and Culture*. Bloomington: Indiana University Press, 1991.

Bryant, Louise. *Mirrors of Moscow*. New York: Liveright, 1923.

Burrell, George A. *An American Engineer Looks at Russia*. Boston, Mass.: Stratford, 1932.

Carr, E. H. *Twilight of the Comintern, 1930–1934*. New York: Pantheon, 1982.

Cassella-Blackburn, Michael. *The Donkey, the Carrot, and the Club: William C. Bullitt and Soviet–American Relations, 1917–1948*. Westport, Conn.: Praeger, 2004.

Castle, Alfred L. *Diplomatic Realism: William R. Castle, Jr. and American Foreign Policy, 1919–1933*. Honolulu: University of Hawaii Press, 1999.

Chamberlin, William Henry. *Russia's Iron Age*. Boston, Mass.: Little, Brown, 1934.

Cohen, Stephen F. *Bukharin and the Bolshevik Revolution: A Political Biography, 1888–1938*. New York: Norton, 1973.

Cohen, Warren I. *Empire without Tears: America's Foreign Relations, 1921–1933*. Philadelphia, Penn.: Temple University Press, 1987.

Colton, Ethan. *Forty Years with Russians*. New York: Association Press, 1940.

Coopersmith, Jonathan. *The Electrification of Russia, 1880–1926*. Ithaca, N.Y.: Cornell University Press, 1992.

Costigliola, Frank. *Awkward Dominion: American Political, Economic, and Cultural Relations with Europe, 1919–1933*. Ithaca, N.Y.: Cornell University Press, 1987.

Counts, George S. *A Ford Crosses Soviet Russia*. Boston: Stratford, 1930.

Dallek, Robert. *Franklin D. Roosevelt and American Foreign Policy, 1932–1945*. New York: Knopf, 1979.

Dalrymple, Dana. "American Technology and Soviet Agricultural Development, 1924–1933." *Agricultural History* 40, no. 3 (July 1955): 187–206.

Danforth, William H. *Russia under the Hammer and Sickle: Impressions Written to the Purina Family*. St. Louis, Mo.: Ralston Purina, 1927.

Davies, Jessie. *Isadora Duncan's Russian Husband or Child of the Terrible Years*. Liverpool, U.K.: Lincoln Davies, 1990.

Davies, Joseph. *Mission to Moscow*. New York: Simon & Schuster, 1940.

Davis, Kenneth S. *FDR: The New Deal Years, 1933–1937*. New York: Random House, 1986.

DeSantis, Hugh. *The Diplomacy of Silence: The American Foreign Service, the Soviet Union and the Cold War, 1933–1947*. Chicago: University of Chicago Press, 1980.

Desmond, Robert W. *Crisis and Conflict: World News Reporting between Two Wars, 1920–1940.* Iowa City: University of Iowa Press, 1982.

Dewey, John. *Impressions of Soviet Russia and the Revolutionary World.* New York: New Republic, 1929.

Dorn, Harold. "Hugh Lincoln Cooper and the First Detente." *Technology and Culture* 20 (1979), 322–47.

Draper, Theodore. *American Communism and Soviet Russia: The Formative Period.* New York: Viking, 1960.

Dreiser, Theodore. *Dreiser Looks at Russia.* New York: Liveright, 1928.

Dubie, Alain. *Frank A. Golder: An Adventure of a Historian in Quest of Russian History.* Boulder, Colo.: East European Monographs, 1989.

Dukes, Paul. *The USA in the Making of the USSR: The Washington Conference, 1921–1922, and "Uninvited Russia."* London: Routledge/Curzon, 2004.

Duncan, Isadora. *My Life.* New York: Boni and Liveright, 1927.

Dunn, Dennis J. *Caught between Roosevelt and Stalin: America's Ambassadors to Moscow.* Lexington: University Press of Kentucky, 1998.

Duranty, Walter. *I Write as I Please.* New York: Simon & Schuster, 1935.

Eagles, Keith David. *Ambassador Joseph E. Davies and American–Soviet Relations, 1937–1941.* New York: Garland, 1984.

Eddy, Sherwood George. *The Challenge of Russia.* New York: Farrar & Rinehart, 1931.

Ehrenburg, Ilya. *Memoirs: 1921–1941.* Translated by Tatania Shebunina. Cleveland, Ohio: World, 1964.

Epstein, Edward Jay. *Dossier: The Secret History of Armand Hammer.* New York: Random House, 1996.

Farnsworth, Beatrice. *William C. Bullitt and the Soviet Union.* Bloomington: Indiana University Press, 1967.

Ferrell, Robert. *American Diplomacy in the Great Depression: Hoover-Stimson Foreign Policy, 1929–1933.* New Haven, Conn.: Yale University Press, 1957.

———. *Peace in Their Time: The Origins of the Kellogg-Briand Pact.* New Haven, Conn.: Yale University Press, 1952.

Figes, Orlando. *Whisperers: Private Life in Stalin's Russia.* London: Allen Lane, 2007.

Filene, Peter G. *Americans and the Soviet Experiment, 1917–1933.* Cambridge, Mass.: Harvard University Press, 1967.

Fischer, Louis. *Machines and Men in Russia.* New York: Harrison Smith, 1932.

———. *Soviet Journey.* New York: Harrison Smith and Robert Haas, 1935.

Fisher, Harold H. *The Famine in Soviet Russia, 1919–1923: The Operations of the American Relief Administration.* New York: Macmillan, 1927.

Fitzpatrick, Sheila, et al., eds. *Russia in the Era of NEP: Explorations in Soviet Society and Culture.* Bloomington: Indiana University Press, 1991.

Furaev, V. K. *Sovetsko–amerikanskie otnosheniia, 1917–1939*. Moscow: Nauka, 1964.

Gardner, Lloyd. *Safe for Democracy: The Anglo–American Response to Revolution, 1913–1923*. New York: Oxford University Press, 1983.

Gardner, Virginia. *"Friend and Lover": The Life of Louise Bryant*. New York: Horizon, 1982.

Getty, J. Arch, and Oleg V. Naumov. *The Road to Terror: Stalin and the Self-Destruction of the Bolsheviks, 1932–1939*. New Haven, Conn.: Yale University Press, 1999.

Glad, Betty. *Charles Evans Hughes and the Illusions of Innocence: A Study in American Diplomacy*. Urbana: University of Illinois Press, 1966.

Glenny, Michael, and Norman Stone, eds. *The Other Russia: The Experience of Exile*. New York: Viking, 1991.

Golder, Frank, and Lincoln Hutchinson. *On the Trail of the Russian Famine*. Stanford, Calif.: Stanford University Press, 1927.

Goldman, Emma. *My Disillusionment in Russia*. New York: Thomas Y. Crowell, 1950.

Grew, Joseph. *Turbulent Years: A Diplomatic Record of Forty Years, 1904–1945*. 2 vols. London: Hammond, 1953.

Hammer, Armand. *The Quest of the Romanoff Treasure*. New York: Paisley Press, 1932.

Hapgood, David. *Charles R. Crane: The Man Who Bet on People*. New York: Institute of Current World Affairs, 2000.

Harper, Samuel N. *The Russia I Believed In: The Memoirs of Samuel N. Harper, 1902–1941*. Chicago: University of Chicago Press, 1945.

Harriman, W. Averell. *America and Russia in a Changing World: A Half-Century of Personal Observation*. Garden City, N.Y.: Doubleday & Company, 1971.

Haslam, Jonathan. *Soviet Foreign Policy, 1930–1933: The Impact of the Depression*. New York: St. Martin's Press, 1983.

———. *The Soviet Union and the Struggle for Collective Security in Europe, 1933–1939*. New York: St. Martin's Press, 1984.

———. *The Soviet Union and the Threat from the East, 1933–1941: Moscow, Tokyo, and the Prelude to the Pacific War*. Basingstoke, U.K.: Macmillan, 1992.

Haywood, Harry. *Black Bolshevik: Autobiography of an Afro-American Communist*. Chicago: Liberator Press, 1978.

Henderson, Loy. *A Question of Trust: The Origins of U.S.–Soviet Relations—The Memoirs of Loy W. Henderson*. Edited by George W. Baer. Stanford, Calif.: Hoover Institution Press, 1986.

Herndon, James S., and Joseph O. Baylen. "Col. Philip R. Faymonville and the Red Army, 1934–1943." *Slavic Review* 34, no. 3 (September 1975): 483–505.

Heywood, Anthony. *Modernizing Lenin's Russia: Economic Reconstruction, Foreign Trade and the Railways.* Cambridge: Cambridge University Press, 1999.

Hiebert, Peter Cornelius, and Orie O. Miller. *Feeding the Hungry: Russian Famine, 1919–1925.* Scottsdale, Penn.: Mennonite Central Committee, 1929.

Hindus, Maurice. *The Great Offensive.* New York: Harrison Smith and Robert Haas, 1933.

Hochman, Jonathon. *The Soviet Union and the Failure of Collective Security, 1933–1938.* Ithaca, N.Y.: Cornell University Press, 1984.

Hogan, Michael J. *The Ambiguous Legacy: U.S. Foreign Relations in the "American Century."* Cambridge: Cambridge University Press, 1999.

Hopper, Bruce. *Pan-Sovietism: The Issue before America.* Boston: Houghton Mifflin, 1931.

Hughes, Langston. *I Wonder as I Wander: An Autobiographical Journey.* New York: Thunder's Mouth Press, 1986.

——. *Moscow and Me: A Noted American Writer Relates His Experiences.* Moscow: International Union of Revolutionary Writers, 1933.

Hull, Cordell. *The Memoirs of Cordell Hull.* 2 vols. New York: Macmillan, 1948.

Huntington, W. Chapin. *The Homesick Million: Russia-out-of-Russia.* Boston, Mass.: Stratford, 1933.

Huppert, Hugo. *Men of Siberia: Sketchbook from the Kuzbas.* New York: International Publishers, 1934.

Ickes, Harold L. *The Secret Diary of Harold L. Ickes.* 3 vols. New York: Macmillan, 1948.

Ilf, Ilya, and Eugene Petrov. *Little Golden America: Two Famous Soviet Humourists Survey the United States.* London: George Routledge & Sons, 1946.

Iriye, Akira. *After Imperialism: The Search for a New Order in the Far East, 1921–1931.* Chicago: Imprint Publications, 1990.

Jacobson, Jon. *When the Soviet Union Entered World Politics.* Berkeley: University of California Press, 1994.

Kaltenborn, H. V. *Fifty Fabulous Years, 1900–1950: A Personal Review.* New York: Putnam's, 1950.

Kennan, George F. *Memoirs, 1925–1950.* Boston: Houghton Mifflin, 1970.

Kennell, Ruth Eppeerson. *Theodore Dreiser and the Soviet Union, 1927–1945: A First-Hand Chronicle.* New York: International Publishers, 1969.

Kern, Gary. *Death in Washington: Walter G. Krivitsky and the Stalin Terror.* New York: Enigma Books, 2003.

Klehr, Harvey. *The Heyday of American Communism: The Depression Decade.* New York: Basic Books, 1984.

——, John Earl Haynes, and Fridrikh Igorevich Firsov. *The Secret World of American Communism.* Russian documents translated by Timothy D. Sergay. New Haven, Conn.: Yale University Press, 1995.

Krivitsky, Walter G. *In Stalin's Secret Service: An Expose of Russia's Secret Policies by the Former Chief of the Soviet Intelligence in Western Europe.* New York: Harper and Brothers, 1939. Reprinted edition, New York: Enigma Books, 2001.

Kutulus, Judy. *The Long War: The Intellectual People's Front and Anti-Stalinism, 1930–1940.* Durham, N.C.: Duke University Press, 1995.

Leder, Mary M. *My Life in Stalinist Russia: An American Woman Looks Back.* Edited by Laurie Berstein. Bloomington: Indiana University Press, 2001.

Lee, Ivy. *Present-Day Russia.* New York: Macmillan, 1928.

Lensen, George Alexander. *The Damned Inheritance: The Soviet Union and the Manchurian Crises, 1924–1935.* Tallahassee, Fla.: Diplomatic Press, 1974.

Leonard, Raymond W. *Secret Soldiers of the Revolution: Soviet Military Intelligence, 1918–1933.* Westport, Conn.: Greenwood Press, 1999.

Levine, Isaac Don. *Eyewitness to History: Memoirs and Reflections of a Foreign Correspondent of Half a Century.* New York: Hawthorne Books, 1973.

Libbey, James K. *Alexander Gumberg and Soviet American Relations, 1917–1933.* Lexington: University of Kentucky Press, 1977.

Liberman, Simon. *Building Lenin's Russia.* Chicago: University of Chicago Press, 1945.

Lindbergh, Anne Morrow. *North to the Orient.* New York: Harcourt, Brace, 1935.

Littlepage, John, with Demaree Bess. *In Search of Soviet Gold.* New York: Harcourt, Brace, 1938.

Litvinov, Maxim. *Notes for a Journal.* Introduction by E. H. Carr. New York: Macmillan, 1955.

Long, Ray. *An Editor Looks at Russia: One Unprejudiced View of the Land of the Soviets.* New York: Ray Long and Richard Smith, 1931.

Lotz, Rainer. *Black People: Entertainers of African Descent in Europe and Germany.* Bonn: Birgit Lotz Verlag, 1997.

Lyons, Eugene. *Assignment in Utopia.* New York: Harcourt, Brace, 1937.

MacLean, Elizabeth Kimball. *Joseph E. Davies: Envoy to the Soviets.* Westport, Conn.: Praeger, 1992.

Maddox, Robert James. *William E. Borah and American Foreign Policy.* Baton Rouge: Louisiana State University Press, 1969.

Maddux, Thomas. *Years of Estrangement: American Relations with the Soviet Union, 1933–1941.* Tallahassee, Fla.: University Presses of Florida, 1980.

Mahoney, Barbara. *Dispatches and Dictators: Ralph Barnes for the Herald Tribune.* Corvallis: Oregon State University Press, 2002.

Margolies, Sylvia R. *The Pilgrimage to Russia: The Soviet Union and the Treatment of Foreigners, 1924–1937.* Madison: University of Wisconsin Press, 1968.

Marshall, Mildred Widmer. *Two Oregon Schoolma'ams, Around the World, 1937, via Trans-Siberian Railroad.* Woodburn, Ore.: Widdy Publishing, 1985.

Marx, Harpo, with Rowland Barber. *Harpo Speaks!* New York: Limelight Editions, 2000.

McKay, Claude. *A Long Way from Home.* New York: Lee, Furman, 1937.

Meiburger, Anne Vincent. *Efforts of Raymond Robins toward Recognition of Soviet Russia and the Outlawry of War, 1917–1933.* Washington, D.C.: Catholic University of America Press, 1958.

Metlok, Rebekka [Rebecca Matlock]. *"Spaso-Khaus": Liudi i vstrechi: zapiski zheni amerikanskogo posla* ("Spaso House": People and Meetings: Notes of the Wife of an American Ambassador). Moscow: Eksmo, 2004.

Morray, J. P. *Project Kuzbas: American Workers in Siberia (1921–1926).* New York: International Publishers, 1983.

Nabokov, Nicolas. *Bagazh: Memoirs of a Russian Cosmopolitan.* New York: Atheneum, 1975.

Nadzharov, D. G. *Neitralitet SshA (1935–1941).* Moscow: Nauka, 1990.

Nemrad, Semen. *Maiakovskii v Amerike: Stranitsy biografii.* Moscow: Sovetskii pisatel', 1970.

O'Connor, Timothy Edward. *Diplomacy and Revolution: G. V. Chicherin and Soviet Foreign Affairs, 1918–1930.* Ames: Iowa State University Press, 1988.

———. *The Engineer of Revolution: L. B. Krasin and the Bolsheviks, 1870–1926.* Boulder, Colo.: Westview, 1992.

Page, Dorothy Myra. *Soviet Main Street.* Moscow: International Press, 1933.

Patenaude, Bertrand M. *The Big Show in Bololand: The American Relief Expedition to Soviet Russia in the Famine of 1921.* Stanford, Calif.: Stanford University Press, 2002.

Phillips, Hugh D. *Between the Revolution and the West: A Political Biography of Maxim M. Litvinov.* Boulder, Colo.: Westview, 1992.

Phillips, William. *Ventures in Diplomacy.* Portland, Maine: Anthoensen Press, 1952.

Pozniakov, Vladimir V. *Sovetskaia razvedka v Amerike, 1919–1941* (Soviet Intelligence in America, 1919–1941). Moscow: Mezhdu. otnosh., 2005.

Prokofiev, Sergey. *Diaries 1915–1922: Behind the Mask.* Translated and edited by Anthony Phillips. Ithaca, N.Y.: Cornell University Press, 2007.

Raeff, Marc. *Russia Abroad: A Cultural History of the Russian Emigration, 1919–1939.* New York: Oxford University Press, 1990.

Ragsdale, Hugh. *The Soviets, the Munich Crisis, and the Coming of World War II.* Cambridge: Cambridge University Press, 2004.

Rassweiler, Anne. *The Generation of Power: The History of Dneprostroi.* New York: Oxford University Press, 1988.

Remple, Henry. *From Bolshevik Russia to America: A Mennonite Family History.* 2nd ed. Sioux Falls, S.D.: Pine Hill Press, 2007.

Reuther, Victor G. *The Brothers Reuther and the Story of the UAW: A Memoir.* Boston: Houghton Mifflin, 1976.

Rhodes, Benjamin D. *James P. Goodrich, Indiana's "Governor Strangelove": A Republican's Infatuation with Soviet Russia.* Selinsgrove, Penn.: Susquehanna University Press, 1996.

Robinson, Robert, with Jonathan Slavin. *Black on Red: My 44 Years Inside the Soviet Union.* Washington, D.C.: Acropolis, 1988.

Rogger, Hans. "*Amerikanizm* and the Economic Development of Russia." *Comparative Studies in Society and History* 23, no. 1 (July 1881): 382–420.

Ruddy, T. Michael. *The Cautious Diplomat: Charles E. Bohlen and the Soviet Union, 1929–1969.* Kent, Ohio: Kent State University Press, 1986.

Rukeyser, Walter Arnold. *Working for the Soviets: An American Engineer in Russia.* New York: Covici-Friede, 1932.

Salzman, Neil V. *Reform and Revolution: The Life and Times of Raymond Robins.* Kent, Ohio: Kent State University Press, 1991.

Saul, Norman E. *Friends or Foes? The United States and Soviet Russia, 1921–1941.* Lawrence: University Press of Kansas, 2006.

Schmidt, Regin. *Red Scare: FBI and the Origins of Anticommunism in the United States, 1919–1943.* Copenhagen: Museum Tusculanum Press, University of Copenhagen, 2000.

Schultz, Kurt S. "Building the 'Soviet Detroit': The Construction of the Nizhnii-Novgorod Automobile Factory, 1927–1932." *Slavic Review* 49, no. 2 (Summer 1990), 200–212.

Scott, John. *Behind the Urals: An American Worker in Russia's City of Steel.* Bloomington: Indiana University Press, 1989.

Sevost'ianov, G. N., et al., eds. *Sovetsko–Amerikanskie otnosheniia: gody nepriznaniia, 1927–1933, dokumenty* (Soviet–American Relations: Years of Non-Recognition, 1927–1933: Documents). Moscow: Fond "demokratiia" (Aleksandr Iakovlev), 2002.

Sevost'ianov, Grigorii. *Moskva-Vashington: Dipomaticheskie otnosheniia, 1933–1936.* Moscow: Nauka, 2002.

Sheinis, Zinovy. *Maxim Litvinov.* Translated by Vic Schneierson. Moscow: Progress, 1990.

Shirer, William L. *20th Century Journey: The Nightmare Years: A Memoir of the Life and the Times.* Boston: Little, Brown, 1984.

Siegel, Katherine A. S. *Loans and Legitimacy: The Evolution of Soviet–American Relations, 1919–1933.* Lexington: University of Kentucky Press, 1996.

Skariatina, Irma (Mrs. Victor Blakeslee). *First to Go Back: An Aristocrat in Soviet Russia.* Indianapolis, Ind.: Bobbs-Merrill, 1933.

Smith, Canfield F. *Vladivostok under Red and White Rule: Revolution and Counterrevolution in the Russian Far East, 1920–1922.* Seattle: University of Washington Press, 1974.

Sorokin, Pitirim A. *Russia and the United States.* New York: E. P. Dutton, 1944.

Sovetsko–Amerikanskie otnosheniia, 1934–1939: dokumenty (Soviet–American Relations, 1934–1939: Documents). Moscow: fond "demokratiia" (Aleksanr Iakovlev), 2003.

Starr, S. Frederick. *Red and Hot: The Fate of Jazz in the Soviet Union, 1917–1980.* New York: Oxford University Press, 1983.

Steffens, Lincoln. *The Autobiography of Lincoln Steffens.* New York: Harcourt, Brace, 1931.

Strong, Anna Louise. *Children of Revolution: Story of the John Reed Children's Colony on the Volga.* Seattle, Wash.: Pigott, 1926.

———. *I Change Worlds: The Remaking of an American.* New York: Garden City Publishing Co., 1937.

Sutton, Antony. *Western Technology and Soviet Economic Development, 1917–1930.* Palo Alto, Calif.: Stanford University Press, 1968.

———. *Western Technology and Soviet Economic Development, 1930–1945.* Palo Alto, Calif.: Stanford University Press, 1971.

Taylor, Sally J. *Stalin's Apologist, Walter Duranty: The New York Times's Man in Moscow.* New York: Oxford University Press, 1990.

Thayer, Charles W. *Bears in the Caviar.* Philadelphia, Penn.: Lippincott, 1950.

Trotsky, Leon. *My Life.* New York: Grosset and Dunlap, 1960.

Tzouliadis, Tim. *The Forsaken: An American Tragedy in Russia.* New York: Penguin, 2008.

Uldricks, Teddy. *Diplomacy and Ideology: The Origins of Soviet Foreign Relations, 1917–1930.* London: Sage, 1979.

Weinberg, Steve. *Armand Hammer: The Untold Story, an Unauthorized Biography.* Boston, Mass.: Little Brown, 1989.

Weinstein, Allen, and Alexander Vassiliev. *The Haunted Wood: Soviet Espionage in America—The Stalin Era.* New York: Random House, 1999.

Weissman, Benjamin B. *Herbert Hoover and Famine Relief to Soviet Russia, 1921–1923.* Palo Alto, Calif.: Hoover Institution Press, 1974.

Wettlin, Margaret. *Fifty Russian Winters: An American Woman's Life in the Soviet Union.* New York: Pharos, 1992.

White, Christine. *British and American Commercial Relations with Soviet Russia, 1918–1924.* Chapel Hill: University of North Carolina Press, 1992.

White, William Allen. *The Autobiography of William Allen White.* New York: Macmillan, 1946.

Williams, Robert C. *Russian Art and American Money, 1900–1940.* Cambridge, Mass.: Harvard University Press, 1983.

Wilson, Joan Hoff, *American Business and Foreign Policy, 1920–1933*. Lexington: University of Kentucky Press, 1971.

———. *Ideology and Economics: U.S. Relations with the Soviet Union, 1918–1933*. Columbia: University of Missouri Press, 1974.

Witkin, Zara. *An American Engineer in Stalin's Russia: The Memoirs of Zara Witkin, 1932–1934*. Edited by Michael Gleb. Berkeley: University of California Press, 1991.

Yakobson, Helen. *Crossing Borders: From Revolutionary Russia to China to America*. Tenafly, N.J.: Hermitage, 1994.

Youngblood, Denise J. *Movies for the Masses: Popular Cinema and Soviet Society in the 1920s*. Cambridge: Cambridge University Press, 1992.

THE UNITED STATES, THE SOVIET UNION, AND WORLD WAR II, 1941–1945

Allen, Paul. *Katyn: The Untold Story of Stalin's Polish Massacres*. New York: Macmillan, 1991.

Alperovitz, Gar. *Atomic Diplomacy: Hiroshima and Potsdam*. New York: Elizabeth Sifton, 1985.

Andrew, Christopher, and Vasili Mitrokhin. *The Sword and the Shield: The Mitrokhin Archive and the Secret History of the KGB*. New York: Basic Books, 1999.

Beitzell, Robert. *The Uneasy Alliance: America, Britain, and Russia, 1941–1943*. New York: Knopf, 1972.

Bennett, Edward M. *Franklin D. Roosevelt and the Search for Victory: American–Soviet Relations, 1929–1945*. Wilmington, Del.: Scholarly Resources, 1990.

Bentley, Elizabeth. *Out of Bondage: The Story of Elizabeth Bentley*. New York: Ivy, 1988.

Beschloss, Michael. *The Conquerors: Roosevelt, Truman and the Destruction of Hitler's Germany, 1941–1945*. New York: Simon & Schuster, 2002.

Bohlen, Charles E. *Witness to History, 1929–1969*. New York: Norton, 1972.

Bourke-White, Margaret. *Shooting the Russian War*. New York: Simon & Schuster, 1942.

Carley, Michael Jabara. *The Alliance That Never Was and the Coming of World War II*. Chicago: Ivan R. Dee, 1999.

Cienciala, Anna M., Natalia Lebedeva, Wojciech Materski, eds. *Katyn: A Crime Without Punishment*. New Haven, Conn.: Yale University Press, 2008.

Dallek, Robert. *Franklin D. Roosevelt and American Foreign Policy, 1932–1945*. Oxford: Oxford University Press, 1979.

Dawson, Raymond H. *The Decision to Aid Russia, 1941*. Chapel Hill: University of North Carolina Press, 1959.

Deane, John R. *The Strange Alliance: The Story of Our Efforts at Wartime Co-operation with Russia.* Bloomington: Indiana University Press, 1973. First published 1946.

DeSantis, Hugh. *The Diplomacy of Silence: The American Foreign Service, the Soviet Union, and the Cold War, 1933–1947.* Chicago: University of Chicago Press, 1980.

Eisenhower, David. *Eisenhower at War, 1943–1945.* New York: Random House, 1986.

Erikson, John. *The Road to Berlin.* London: Grafton, 1985.

Eubank, Keith. *Summit at Teheran.* New York: Morrow, 1985.

Gardner, Lloyd. *Architects of Illusion: Men and Ideas in American Foreign Policy, 1941–1949.* Chicago: Quadrangle Books, 1970.

Garrett, Garet. *Defend America First: The Antiwar Editorials of the Saturday Evening Post, 1939–1942.* Caldwell, Idaho: Caxton Press, 2003.

Gellman, Irwin F. *Secret Affairs: Franklin Roosevelt, Cordell Hull, and Sumner Welles.* Baltimore, Md.: Johns Hopkins University Press, 1995.

Glantz, Mary E. *FDR and the Soviet Union: The President's Battles over Foreign Policy.* Lawrence: University Press of Kansas, 2005.

Goldberg, Harold J., ed. *Documents of Soviet-American Relations.* Vol. 4: *Economic Relations, Military Alliance, Second Front, Plans for Peace, 1941–1945.* Gulf Breeze, Fla.: Academic International Press, 2001.

Golikov, F. I. *On a Military Mission to Great Britain and the USA.* Moscow: Progress, 1987.

Harriman, W. Averell, and Elie Abel. *Special Envoy to Churchill and Stalin, 1941–1946.* New York: Random House, 1975.

Hasegawa, Tsuyoshi. *Racing the Enemy: Stalin, Truman, and the Surrender of Japan.* Cambridge, Mass.: Harvard University Press, 2006.

Herring, George C., Jr. *Aid to Russia, 1941–1946.* New York: Columbia University Press, 1973.

Herzstein, Robert E. *Roosevelt & Hitler: Prelude to War.* New York: Paragon House, 1989.

Hull, Cordell. *The Memoirs of Cordell Hull.* 2 vols. New York: Macmillan, 1948.

Ivanov, Robert F. *Duait Eizenkhauer: Chelovek, politik, polkovodets* (Dwight Eisenhower: Man, Politician, Commander). Moscow: Poligran, 1998.

———. *Stalin i soiuzniki, 1941–1945 gg.* (Stalin and the Allies, 1941–45). Smolensk: Rusich, 2000.

———, and Nina K. Petrova. *Obshchestvenno-politicheskie sily SSSR i SShA v gody voiny, 1941–1945* (The Social-Political Forces of the USSR and USA in the Years of War, 1941–1945). Voronezh: Voronezh State University, 1995.

Jones, Robert Huhn. *The Roads to Russia: United States Lend-Lease to the Soviet Union.* Norman: University of Oklahoma Press, 1969.

Ketchum, Richard M. *The Borrowed Years, 1938–1941: America on the Way to War.* New York: Random House, 1989.

Kimball, Warren F. *The Juggler: Franklin Roosevelt as Wartime Statesman.* Princeton, N.J.: Princeton University Press, 1991.

———. *The Most Unsordid Act: Lend-Lease, 1939–1941.* Baltimore, Md.: Johns Hopkins University Press, 1969.

Klingaman, William K. *1941: Our Lives in a World on the Edge.* New York: Harper & Row, 1989.

Kolko, Gabriel. *The Politics of War: The World and United States Foreign Policy, 1943–1945.* New York: Pantheon, 1990.

Langer, William L., and S. Everett Gleason. *The Challenge to Isolation, 1937–1940.* New York: Harper and Brothers, 1952.

———. *The Undeclared War, 1940–1945.* New York: Harper and Brothers, 1953.

Leahy, William D. *I Was There: The Personal Story of the Chief of Staff as Presidents Roosevelt and Truman Based on His Notes and Diaries Made at the Time.* New York: Whittlesey House, 1950.

Levering, Ralph B. *American Opinion and the Russian Alliance, 1939–1945.* Chapel Hill: University of North Carolina Press, 1976.

Lundestad, Geir. *The American Non-Policy towards Eastern Europe, 1943–1947.* Tromso, Norway: Universitetsforlaget, 1978.

Maddox, Robert James. *Weapons for Victory: the Hiroshima Decsion.* Columbia: University of Missouri Press, 2004.

Maisky, Ivan. *Memoirs of a Soviet Ambassador: The War, 1939–1943.* Translated by Andrew Rothstein. London: Hutchinson, 1967.

Martel, Leon. *Lend-Lease, Loans, and the Coming of the Cold War: A Study of the Implementation of Foreign Policy.* Boulder, Colo.: Westview, 1979.

Mastny, Vojtech. *Russia's Road to the Cold War: Diplomacy, Warfare, and the Politics of Communism, 1941–1945.* New York: Columbia University Press, 1979.

Mayle, Paul D. *Eureka Summit: Agreement in Principle and the Big Three at Tehran, 1943.* Newark: University of Delaware Press, 1987.

McNeill, William Hardy. *America, Britain, and Russia: Their Cooperation and Conflict, 1941–1946.* London: Oxford University Press, 1953.

Mee, Charles L., Jr. *Meeting at Potsdam.* New York: Dell, 1976.

Miner, Steven Merritt. *Between Churchill and Stalin: The Soviet Union, Great Britain, and the Origins of the Grand Alliance.* Chapel Hill: University of North Carolina Press, 1988.

Motter, T. H. Vail. *The Persian Corridor and Aid to Russia.* Washington, D.C.: Center of Military History, 1989.

Murphy, David E. *What Stalin Knew: The Enigma of Barbarossa.* New Haven, Conn.: Yale University Press, 2005.

Overy, Richard. *The Dictators: Hitler's Germany, Stalin's Russia.* New York: Norton, 2004.

Persico, Joseph E. *Roosevelt's Secret War: FDR and World War II Espionage.* New York: Random House, 2001.

Pleshakov, Constantine. *Stalin's Folly: The Secret History of the German Invasion of Russia, June 1941.* Boston: Houghton Mifflin, 2005.

Raack, R. C. *Stalin's Drive to the West. 1938–1945.* Stanford, Calif.: Stanford University Press, 1995.

Roberts, Geoffrey. *The Soviet Union and the Origins of the Second World War: Russo–German Relations and the Road to War, 1933–1941.* New York: St. Martin's Press, 1995.

———. *The Unholy Alliance: Stalin's Pact with Hitler.* Bloomington: Indiana University Press, 1989.

Rzheshevskii, Oleg. *Stalin i Cherchill': vstrechi, besedy, diskussii* (Stalin and Churchill: Meetings, Conversations, Discussions). Moscow: Nauka, 2004.

Sainsbury, Keith. *The Turning Point: Roosevelt, Stalin, Churchill and Chiang-Kai-Shek, 1943: The Moscow, Cairo, and Teheran Conferences.* Oxford: Oxford University Press, 1985.

Scott, Mark, ed. *Eyewitness Accounts of the World War II Murmansk Run, 1941–1945.* Lewiston, N.Y.: Mellen Press, 2006.

———, and Semyon Krasilshchik, eds. *Yanks Meet Reds: Recollections of U.S. and Soviet Vets from the Linkup in World War II.* Santa Barbara, Calif.: Capra Press, 1988.

Sherwood, Robert E. *Roosevelt and Hopkins: An Intimate History.* Rev. ed. New York: Enigma Books, 2001.

Smith, Bradley F. *Sharing Secrets with Stalin: How the Allies Traded Intelligence, 1941–1945.* Lawrence: University Press of Kansas, 1996.

Smith, Gaddis. *American Diplomacy during the Second World War, 1941–1945.* 2nd ed. New York: Knopf, 1985.

Snell, John L. *Illusion and Necessity: The Diplomacy of Global War, 1939–1945.* Boston: Houghton Mifflin, 1965.

Stafford, David. *Roosevelt and Churchill: Men of Secrets.* Woodstock and New York: Overlook Press, 1999.

Standley, William H., and Arthur A. Ageton. *Admiral Ambassador to Russia.* Chicago: Henry Regnery, 1955.

Stettinius, Edward R., Jr. *Lend-Lease, Weapon for Victory.* New York: Macmillan, 1944.

———. *Roosevelt and the Russians: The Yalta Conference.* Garden City, N.Y.: Doubleday, 1949.

Stimson, Henry L., and McGeorge Bundy. *On Active Service in Peace and War.* New York: Harper & Brothers, 1947.

Stoler, Mark. *Allies and Adversaries: The Joint Chiefs of Staff, the Grand Alliance, and U.S. Strategy in World War II*. Chapel Hill: University of North Carolina Press, 2000.

Tuttle, Dwight William. *Harry L. Hopkins and Anglo–American Relations, 1941–1945*. New York: Garland, 1983.

Wanke, Paul. *Russian/Soviet Military Psychiatry, 1904–1945*. London: Frank Cass, 2005.

Weeks, Albert L. *Russia's Life-Saver: Lend-Lease Aid to the U.S.S.R. in World War II*. Lanham, Md.: Lexington Books, 2004.

———. *Stalin's Other War: Soviet Grand Strategy, 1939–1941*. Lanham, Md.: Rowman & Littlefield, 2002.

Weinberg, Gerhard L. *Germany and the Soviet Union, 1939–1941*. Leiden: E. J. Brill, 1954.

Welles, Benjamin. *Sumner Welles: FDR's Global Strategist*. New York: St. Martin's Press, 1997.

Werth, Alexander. *Moscow War Diary*. New York: Knopf, 1942.

———. *Russia at War, 1941–1945*. New York: Carroll & Graf, 1964.

West, Nigel. *Mortal Crimes: The Greatest Theft in History—Soviet Penetration of the Manhattan Project*. New York: Enigma Books, 2004.

———. *A Thread of Deceit: Espionage Myths of World War II*. New York: Random House, 1985.

THE COLD WAR, 1945–1990

Abramson, Rudy. *Spanning the Century: The Life of W. Averell Harriman, 1891–1986*. New York: Morrow, 1992.

Acheson, Dean. *Present at the Creation: My Years in the State Department*. New York: Norton, 1969.

Adelman, Kenneth L. *The Great Universal Embrace: Arms Summitry—A Skeptic's Account*. New York: Simon & Schuster, 1989.

Allison, Graham T. *Essence of Decision: Explaining the Cuban Missile Crisis*. Boston, Mass.: Little, Brown, 1971.

Alperovitz, Gar. *Atomic Diplomacy: Hiroshima and Potsdam*. Rev. ed. New York: Penguin, 1985.

———. *The Decision to Use the Atomic Bomb and the Architecture of an American Myth*. New York: Knopf, 1995.

Andrew, Christopher, and Oleg Gordievsky. *KGB: The Inside Story of Its Foreign Operations from Lenin to Gorbachev*. New York: HarperCollins, 1990.

———, and Vasili Mitrokhin. *The Sword and the Shield: The Mitrokhin Archive and the Secret History of the KGB*. New York: Basic Books, 1999.

———, and Vasili Mitrokhin. *The World Was Going Our Way: The KGB and the Battle for the Third World.* New York: Basic Books, 2006.

Arbatov, Georgi. *The System: An Insider's Life in Soviet Politics.* New York: Random House, 1992.

Bailey, Thomas A. *The Marshall Plan Summer.* Stanford, Calif.: Hoover Institution Press, 1977.

Barron, John. *Operation Solo: The FBI's Man in the Kremlin.* Washington, D.C.: Regnery, 1996.

Beisner, Robert L. *Dean Acheson: A Life in the Cold War.* New York: Oxford University Press, 2006.

Beschloss, Michael R. *The Crisis Years: Kennedy and Khrushchev, 1960–1963.* New York: HarperCollins, 1991.

———. *Mayday: Eisenhower, Khrushchev, and the U-2 Affair.* New York: Harper & Row, 1986.

———, ed. *Reaching for Glory: Lyndon Johnson's Secret White House Tapes, 1963–1964.* New York: Simon & Schuster, 1997.

Blight, James G. *On the Brink: Americans and Soviets Examine the Cuban Missile Crisis.* New York: Noonday Press, 1989.

Bohlen, Charles E. *Witness to History, 1929–1969.* New York: Norton, 1973.

Borawski, John. *From the Atlantic to the Urals: Negotiating Arms Control at the Stockholm Conference.* Washington, D.C.: Pergamon-Brassey, 1988.

Borowski, Harry R. *A Hollow Threat: Strategic Air Power and Containment before Korea.* Westport, Conn.: Greenwood, 1982.

Brands, H. W. *Inside the Cold War: Loy Henderson and the Rise of the American Empire, 1918–1961.* New York: Oxford University Press, 1991.

Brinkley, Douglas. *Dean Acheson: The Cold War Years, 1953–71.* New Haven, Conn.: Yale University Press, 1992.

Brugioni, Dino A. *Eyeball to Eyeball: The Inside Story of the Cuban Missile Crisis.* Rev. ed. New York: Random House, 1991.

Buhite, Russell D. *Decisions at Yalta: An Appraisal of Summit Diplomacy.* Wilmington, Del.: Scholarly Resources, 1986.

Bundy, McGeorge. *Danger and Survival: Choices about the Bomb in the First Fifty Years.* New York: Random House, 1988.

Byrnes, James F. *Speaking Frankly.* New York: Harper, 1947.

Byrnes, Robert F. *Soviet-American Academic Exchanges, 1958–1975.* Bloomington: Indiana University Press, 1976.

Carter, Jimmy. *Keeping Faith: Memoirs of a President.* New York: Bantam, 1982.

Caute, David. *The Great Fear: The Anti-Communist Purge under Truman and Eisenhower.* New York: Simon & Schuster, 1978.

Chace, James. *Acheson: The Secretary of State Who Created the American World.* New York: Simon & Schuster, 1998.

Chernyaev, Anatoly. *My Six Years with Gorbachev.* University Park: Pennsylvania State University Press, 2000.

Clemens, Diane S. *Yalta.* New York: Oxford University Press, 1970.

Cold War International History Project. *Bulletin.* Washington, D.C.: Woodrow Wilson International Center for Scholars, 1992–.

Craig, Campbell. *Destroying the Village: Eisenhower and Thermonuclear War.* New York: Columbia University Press, 1998.

Cronin, James E. *The World the Cold War Made: Order, Chaos, and the Return of History.* New York: Routledge, 1996.

Dallin, Alexander. *Black Box: KAL 007 and the Superpowers.* Berkeley: University of California Press, 1985.

DeSantis, Hugh. *The Diplomacy of Silence: The American Foreign Service, the Soviet Union and the Cold War, 1933–1947.* Chicago: University of Chicago Press, 1979.

Divine, Robert A. *Blowing on the Wind: The Nuclear Test Ban Debate, 1954–1960.* New York: Oxford University Press, 1978.

———. *The Sputnik Challenge.* New York: Oxford University Press, 1993.

Djilas, Milovan. *Conversations with Stalin.* Translated by Michael Petrovich. New York: Harcourt, Brace & World, 1962.

Dobrynin, Anatoly. *In Confidence: Moscow's Ambassador to America's Six Cold War Presidents.* New York: Random House, 1995.

Dulles, John Foster. *War or Peace.* New York: Macmillan, 1950.

Earley, Pete. *Family of Spies: Inside the John Walker Spy Ring.* New York: Bantam, 1988.

Fawcett, Louise. *Iran and the Cold War: The Azerbaijan Crisis of 1946.* New York: Cambridge University Press, 1992.

Feis, Herbert. *From Trust to Terror: The Onset of the Cold War, 1945–1950.* New York: Norton, 1970.

Ferrell, Robert H. *Harry S. Truman and the Cold War Revisionists.* Columbia: University of Missouri Press, 2006.

Fischer, Beth A. *The Reagan Reversal: Foreign Policy and the End of the Cold War.* Columbia: University of Missouri Press, 1997.

FitzGerald, Frances. *Way Out There in the Blue: Reagan, Star Wars and the End of the Cold War.* New York: Simon & Schuster, 2000.

Foot, Rosemary. *The Wrong War: American Policy and the Dimensions of the Korean Conflict, 1950–1953.* Ithaca, N.Y.: Cornell University Press, 1985.

Ford, Gerald R. *A Time to Heal: The Autobiography of Gerald R. Ford.* New York: Harper & Row, 1979.

Freedman, Lawrence. *Kennedy's Wars: Berlin, Cuba, Laos and Vietnam.* New York: Oxford University Press, 2000.

Freeland, Richard M. *The Truman Doctrine and the Origins of McCarthyism: Foreign Policy, Domestic Politics, and Internal Security, 1946–1948.* New York: New York University Press, 1971.

Fried, Richard M. *Nightmare in Red: The McCarthy Era in Perspective.* New York: Oxford University Press, 1990.

Friedberg, Aaron L. *In the Shadow of the Garrison State: America's Anti-Statism and Its Cold War Grand Strategy.* Princeton: Princeton University Press, 2000.

Fursenko, Aleksandr, and Timothy Naftali. *"One Hell of a Gamble": Khrushchev, Castro, and Kennedy, 1958–1964.* New York: Norton, 1997.

Gaddis, John Lewis. *The Cold War: A New History.* New York: Penguin Press, 2005.

——. *The Long Peace: Inquiries into the History of the Cold War.* New York: Oxford University Press, 1987.

——. *Strategies of Containment: A Critical Appraisal of American National Security Policy during the Cold War.* Rev. ed. New York: Oxford University Press, 2005.

——. *The United States and the Origins of the Cold War, 1941–1947.* 2nd ed. New York: Columbia University Press, 2000.

——. *We Now Know: Rethinking Cold War History.* New York: Oxford University Press, 1997.

Gaiduk, Ilya. *Confronting Vietnam: Soviet Policy toward the Indochina Conflict, 1954–1963.* Stanford, Calif.: Stanford University Press, 2003.

——. *The Soviet Union and the Vietnam War.* Chicago: I. R. Dee, 1996.

——, and N. I. Egorova, eds. *Stalin i kholodnaia voina* (Stalin and the Cold War). Moscow: RAN, 1998.

Gardner, Lloyd C. *Architects of Illusion: Men and Ideas in American Foreign Policy, 1941–1949.* Chicago: Quadrangle Books, 1970.

——. *Spheres of Influence: The Great Powers Partition Europe, from Munich to Yalta.* Chicago: I. R. Dee, 1993.

Garrison, Mark, and Abbott Gleason, eds. *Shared Destiny: Fifty Years of Soviet–American Relations.* Boston: Beacon Press, 1985.

Garthoff, Raymond L. *Detente and Confrontation: American–Soviet Relations from Nixon to Reagan.* Washington, D.C.: Brookings Institution Press, 1985.

——. *The Great Transition: American–Soviet Relations and the End of the Cold War.* Washington, D.C.: Brookings Institution Press, 1994.

——. *A Journey through the Cold War: A Memoir of Containment and Coexistence.* Washington, D.C.: Brookings Institution Press, 2001.

——. *Reflections on the Cuban Missile Crisis.* Rev. ed. Washington, D.C.: Brookings Institution Press, 1989.

Garton Ash, Timothy. *In Europe's Name: Germany and the Divided Continent.* New York: Random House, 1991.

Gates, Robert M. *From the Shadows: The Ultimate Insider's Story of Five Presidents and How They Won the Cold War.* New York: Simon & Schuster, 1996.

Goldgeier, James M. *Leadership Style and Soviet Foreign Policy: Stalin, Khrushchev, Brezhnev, Gorbachev.* Baltimore, Md.: Johns Hopkins University Press, 1994.

Goldman, Marshall I. *Detente and Dollars: Doing Business with the Soviets.* New York: Basic Books, 1975.

Gorbachev, Mikhail. *Memoirs.* New York: Doubleday, 1996.

Graham, Loren R. *Moscow Stories.* Bloomington: Indiana University Press, 2006.

Haig, Alexander M., Jr. *Caveat: Realism, Reagan, and Foreign Policy.* New York: Macmillan, 1984.

Haines, Gerald K., and Robert E. Heggett, eds. *CIA's Analysis of the Soviet Union, 1947–1991.* Washington, D.C.: Cold War Studies Center, 2001.

Hanhimaki, Jussi. *The Flawed Architect: Henry Kissinger and American Foreign Policy.* New York: Oxford University Press, 2004.

———, and Odd Arne Westad, eds. *The Cold War: A History in Documents and Eyewitness Accounts.* New York: Oxford University Press, 2003.

Hardesty, Von, and Gene Eisman. *Epic Rivalry: The Inside Story of the Soviet and American Space Race.* Washington, D.C.: National Geographic, 2008.

Harriman, W. Averell. *America and Russia in a Changing World: A Half Century of Personal Observation.* Garden City, N.Y.: Doubleday, 1971.

———, and Elie Abel. *Special Envoy to Churchill and Stalin, 1941–1946.* New York: Random House, 1975.

Harrison, Hope M. *Driving the Soviets Up the Wall: Soviet–East German Relations, 1953–1961.* Princeton, N.J.: Princeton University Press, 2003.

Haynes, John Earl, and Harvey Klehr. *Venona: Decoding Soviet Espionage in America.* New Haven, Conn.: Yale University Press, 1999.

Heinrichs, Waldo. *Threshold of War: Franklin D. Roosevelt & American Entry into World War II.* New York: Oxford University Press, 1988.

Hersh, Seymour M. *"The Target Is Destroyed": What Really Happened to Flight 007 and What America Knew about It.* New York: Random House, 1986.

Herz, Martin F. *The Beginnings of the Cold War.* Bloomington: Indiana University Press, 1966.

Hitchcock, William I. *The Struggle for Europe: The Turbulent History of a Divided Continent, 1945–2002.* New York: Doubleday, 2002.

Hixson, Walter L. *George F. Kennan: Cold War Iconoclast.* New York: Columbia University Press, 1989.

Holloway, David. *Stalin and the Bomb: The Soviet Union and Atomic Energy, 1939–1954.* New Haven, Conn.: Yale University Press, 1994.

———. *The Soviet Union and the Arms Race.* New Haven, Conn.: Yale University Press, 1983.

Huchthausen, Peter A. *October Fury.* New York: John Wiley & Sons, 2002.

Hunter, Robert W. *Spy Hunter: Inside the FBI Investigation of the Walker Espionage Case.* Annapolis, Md.: Naval Institute Press, 1999.

Hutchings, Robert L. *American Diplomacy and the End of the Cold War: An Insider's Account of U.S. Policy in Europe, 1989–1992.* Washington, D.C.: Woodrow Wilson Center Press, 1997.

Hyland, William G. *Mortal Rivals: Superpower Relations from Nixon to Reagan.* New York: Random House, 1987.

Immerman, Ruchard H., ed. *John Foster Dulles and the Diplomacy of the Cold War.* Princeton, N.J.: Princeton University Press, 1990.

Isaacson, Walter, and Evan Thomas. *The Wise Men: Six Friends and the World They Made: Acheson, Bohlen, Harriman, Kennan, Lovett, McCloy.* New York: Simon & Schuster, 1986.

Israelyan, Victor. *On the Battlefields of the Cold War: A Soviet Ambassador's Confession.* University Park: University of Pennsylvania Press, 2003.

Johnson, Loch K. *America's Secret Power: The CIA in a Democratic Society.* New York: Oxford University Press, 1989.

Judt, Tony. *Postwar: A History of Europe Since 1945.* New York: Penguin, 2005.

Kalugin, Oleg, with Fen Montaigne. *The First Directorate: My 32 Years in Intelligence and Espionage against the West.* New York: St. Martin's Press, 1994.

Kaplan, Lawrence S. *The United States and NATO: The Formative Years.* Lexington: University Press of Kentucky, 1984.

Kennan, George F. *Around the Cragged Hill: A Personal and Political Philosophy.* New York: Norton, 1993.

———. *Memoirs, 1925–1950.* Boston, Mass.: Little, Brown, 1967.

———. *Memoirs, 1950–1963.* Boston, Mass.: Little, Brown, 1972.

———. *The Nuclear Delusion: Soviet–American Relations in the Atomic Age.* New York: Pantheon, 1982.

———. *Russia, the Atom and the West.* New York: Harper, 1957.

———. *Sketches from a Life.* New York: Pantheon, 1989.

Kennedy, Paul. *The Rise and Fall of the Great Powers: Economic Change and Military Conflict from 1500 to 2000.* New York: Random House, 1987.

Kennedy, Robert F. *Thirteen Days: A Memoir of the Cuban Missile Crisis.* New York: Norton, 1969.

Khrushchev, Nikita. *Khrushchev Remembers.* Translated and edited by Strobe Talbot. New York: Bantam Books, 1971.

———. *Khrushchev Remembers: The Last Testament.* Translated and edited by Strobe Talbot. Boston: Little, Brown, 1974.

——. *Memoirs of Nikita Khrushchev.* Edited by Sergei Khrushchev. New translation by George Shriver. University Park: Pennsylvania State University Press, 2004.

Khrushchev, Sergei. *Khrushchev on Khrushchev: An Inside Account of the Man and His Era.* Edited and translated by William Taubman. Boston, Mass.: Little, Brown, 1990.

——. *Nikita Khrushchev: Creation of a Superpower.* University Park: Pennsylvania State University Press, 2000.

Killen, Linda R. *The Soviet Union and the United States: A New Look at the Cold War.* Boston, Mass.: Twayne Publishers, 1989.

Killian, James R. *Sputnik, Scientists, and Eisenhower: A Memoir of the First Special Assistant to the President on Science and Technology.* Cambridge, Mass.: MIT Press, 1977.

Kissinger, Henry A. *A World Restored.* New York: Houghton Mifflin, 1957.

Klehr, Harvey, John Earl Haynes, and Fridrickh Igorevich Firsov. *The Secret World of American Communism.* New Haven, Conn.: Yale University Press, 1995.

Kohler, Foy D., and Mose L. Harvey. *The Soviet Union: Yesterday, Today, Tomorrow: A Colloquy of American Long Timers in Moscow.* Miami, Fla.: University of Miami Press, 1975.

Korchilov, Igor. *Translating History: Thirty Years on the Front Lines of Diplomacy with Top Russian Interpreter.* New York: Scribner's, 1997.

Korey, William. *The Promises We Keep: Human Rights, the Helsinki Process, and American Foreign Policy.* New York: St. Martin's Press, 1994.

LaFeber, Walter. *America, Russia, and the Cold War, 1945–1996.* 10th ed. New York: McGraw-Hill, 2006.

Larson, Deborah Welch. *Origins of Containment: A Psychological Explanation.* Princeton, N.J.: Princeton University Press, 1985.

Leffley, Melvyn P. *A Preponderance of Power: National Security, the Truman Administration, and the Cold War.* Stanford, Calif.: Stanford University Press, 1992.

Levering, Ralph B. *American Opinion and the Russian Alliance, 1939–1945.* Chapel Hill: University of North Carolina Press, 1976.

——. *The Cold War: A Post–Cold War History.* Arlington Heights, Ill.: Harlan Davidson, 1994.

Libby, James K., ed. *Documents of Soviet–American Relations.* Vol. 5: *The Cold War Begins, 1946–1949.* Gulf Breeze, Fla.: Academic International Press, 2006.

Lukacs, John. *A New History of the Cold War.* Garden City, N.Y.: Doubleday, 1966.

Lundestad, Geir. *The American Non-Policy towards Eastern Europe, 1943–1947.* New York. Columbia University Press, 1978.

Maddox, Robert James. *The New Left and the Origins of the Cold War.* Princeton, N.J.: Princeton University Press, 1973.

Mastny, Vojtech. *The Cold War and Soviet Insecurity: The Stalin Years.* New York: Oxford University Press, 1996.

May, Ernest R. *American Cold War Strategy: Interpreting NSC-68.* Boston, Mass.: St. Martin's Press, 1993.

——, and Philip D. Zelikow, eds. *The Kennedy Tapes: Inside the White House during the Cuban Missile Crisis.* Cambridge, Mass.: Harvard University Press, 1997.

Mayers, David. *George Kennan and the Dilemmas of US Foreign Policy.* New York: Oxford University Press, 1995.

McNeill, William H. *America, Britain, and Russia: Their Cooperation and Conflict, 1941–1946.* London: Oxford University Press, 1953.

McPhee, John. *The Ransom of Russian Art.* New York: Farrar Straus Giroux, 1994.

Medvedev, Grigori. *The Truth about Chernobyl.* New York: Basic Books, 1989.

Mee, Charles L., Jr. *The Marshall Plan: The Launching of the Pax Americana.* New York: Simon & Schuster, 1984.

Mendelson, Sarah E. *Changing Course: Ideas, Politics, and the Soviet Withdrawal from Afghanistan.* Princeton, N.J.: Princeton University Press, 1998.

Messer, Robert. *The End of an Alliance: James F. Byrnes, Roosevelt, Truman, and the Origins of the Cold War.* Chapel Hill: University of North Carolina Press, 1982.

Miner, Steven Merritt. *Between Churchill and Stalin: The Soviet Union, Great Britain, and the Origins of the Grand Alliance.* Chapel Hill: University of North Carolina Press, 1988.

Miscamble, Wilson D. *George F. Kennan and the Making of American Foreign Policy, 1945–1950.* Princeton, N.J.: Princeton University Press, 1992.

Mueller, John. *Retreat from Doomsday: The Obsolescence of Major War.* New York: Basic Books, 1989.

Murphy, David E., Sergei A. Kondrashev, and George Bailey. *Battleground Berlin: CIA vs KGB in the Cold War.* New Haven, Conn.: Yale University Press, 1997.

Naimark, Norman N. *The Russians in Germany: A History of the Soviet Zone of Occupation, 1945–1949.* Cambridge, Mass.: Harvard University Press, 1995.

Nash, Philip. *The Other Missiles of October: Eisenhower, Kennedy and the Jupiters, 1957–1963.* Chapel Hill: University of North Carolina Press, 1997.

Nitze, Paul H., with Ann M. Smith and Steven Rearden. *From Hiroshima to Glasnost: At the Center of Decision—A Memoir.* New York: Grove Weidenfeld, 1989.

Oberdorfer, Don. *From the Cold War to a New Era: The United States and the Soviet Union, 1983–1991.* Baltimore, Md.: Johns Hopkins University Press, 1998.

Offener, Arnold A. *Another Such Victory.* Stanford, Calif.: Stanford University Press, 2002.

Olmsted, Kathryn S. *Red Spy Queen: A Biography of Elizabeth Bentley.* Chapel Hill: University of North Carolina Press, 2002.

Osgood, Kenneth. *Total Cold War: Eisenhower's Secret Propaganda Battle at Home and Abroad.* Lawrence: University Press of Kansas, 2006.

Oshinsky, David M. *A Conspiracy So Immense: The World of Joe McCarthy.* New York: Free Press, 1983.

Ouimet, Matthew J. *The Rise and Fall of the Brezhnev Doctrine in Soviet Foreign Policy.* Chapel Hill: University of North Carolina Press, 2003.

Overy, Richard. *The Dictators: Hitler's Germany, Stalin's Russia.* New York: Norton, 2004.

Palazchenko, Pavel. *My Years with Gorbachev and Shevardnadze: The Memoir of a Soviet Interpreter.* University Park: Pennsylvania State University Press, 1997.

Paterson, Thomas G., ed. *Cold War Crisis: Alternatives to American Foreign Policy in the Truman Years.* Chicago: Quadrangle, 1971.

———, ed. *Kennedy's Quest for Victory: American Foreign Policy, 1961–1963.* New York: Oxford University Press, 1989.

———. *Meeting the Communist Threat: Truman to Reagan.* New York: Oxford University Press, 1988.

———. *On Every Front: The Making and Unmaking of the Cold War.* Rev. ed. New York: Norton, 1992.

———. *Soviet–American Confrontation: Postwar Reconstruction and the Origins of the Cold War.* Baltimore, Md.: Johns Hopkins University Press, 1973.

Pisani, Sallie. *The CIA and the Marshall Plan.* Lawrence: University Press of Kansas, 1991.

Quandt, William B. *Camp David: Peacemaking and Politics.* Washington, D.C.: Brookings Institution, 1986.

Raach, R. C. *Stalin's Drive to the West, 1938–1945: The Origins of the Cold War.* Stanford, Calif.: Stanford University Press, 1995.

Reagan, Ronald. *An American Life: The Autobiography.* New York: Simon & Schuster, 1990.

Reid, Escott. *Time of Fear and Hope: The Making of the North Atlantic Treaty, 1947–1949.* Toronto: McClelland & Stewart, 1977.

Resis, Albert, ed. *Molotov Remembers: Inside Kremlin Politics: Conversations with Felix Chuev.* Chicago: I. R. Dee, 1993.

Reynolds, David. *One World Divisible: A Global History since 1945.* New York: Norton, 2000.

———. *Summits: Six Meetings That Shaped the Twentieth Century.* London: Allen Lane, 2008.

Richmond, Yale. *Cultural Exchange and the Cold War: Raising the Iron Curtain.* University Park: Pennsylvania State University Press, 2003.

Romerstein, Herbert, and Breindel, Eric. *The Venona Secrets: Exposing Soviet Espionage and America's Traitors.* New York: Regnery, 2000.

Rothchild, Sylvia. *A Special Legacy: An Oral History of Soviet Jewish Emigres in the United States.* New York: Simon & Schuster, 1985.

Rusk, Dean, as told to Richard Rusk. *As I Saw It.* New York: Norton, 1990.

Sarotte, M. E. *Dealing with the Devil: East Germany, Detente, and Ostpolitik, 1969–1973.* Chapel Hill: University of North Carolina Press, 2001.

Schecter, Jerold, and Leona Schecter. *Sacred Secrets: How Soviet Intelligence Operations Changed American History.* Washington, D.C.: Brassey's, 2002.

Sherwin, Martin J. *A World Destroyed: The Atomic Bomb and the Grand Alliance.* New York: Knopf, 1975.

Shevardnadze, Eduard. *The Future Belongs to Freedom.* New York: Free Press, 1991.

Shevchenko, Arkady N. *Breaking with Moscow.* New York: Knopf, 1985.

Shirer, William L. *20th Century Journey: A Memoir of a Life and the Times.* Vol. 3: *A Native's Return, 1945–1988.* Boston, Mass.: Little, Brown, 1990.

Shlaim, Avi. *The United States and the Berlin Blockade, 1948–1949.* Berkeley: University of California Press, 1983.

Shultz, George P. *Turmoil and Triumph: My Years as Secretary of State.* New York: Scribner's, 1993.

Sibley, Katherine A. S. *Red Spies in America: Stolen Secrets and the Dawn of the Cold War.* Lawrence: University Press of Kansas, 2004.

Sivachev, Nikolai, and Nikolai N. Yakovlev. *Russia and the United States: U.S.–Soviet Relations from the Soviet Point of View.* Chicago: University of Chicago Press, 1979.

Smith, Bradley F. *Sharing Secrets with Stalin: How the Allies Traded Intelligence, 1941–1945.* Lawrence: University Press of Kansas, 1996.

Smith, Gaddis. *The Last Years of the Monroe Doctrine, 1945–1993.* New York: Hill & Wang, 1994.

Steinbeck, John. *A Russian Journal.* New York: Viking Press, 1948.

Stern, Sheldon M. *Averting "The Final Failure": John F. Kennedy and the Secret Cuban Missile Crisis Meetings.* Stanford, Calif.: Stanford University Press, 2003.

——. *The Week the World Stood Still: Inside the Secret Cuban Missile Crisis.* Stanford, Calif.: Stanford University Press, 2005.

Stoler, Mark A. *Allies and Adversaries: The Joint Chiefs of Staff, the Grand Alliance, and U.S. Strategy in World War II.* Chapel Hill: University of North Carolina Press, 2000.

——. *The Politics of the Second Front: American Military Planning and Diplomacy in Coalition Warfare, 1941–1943.* Westport, Conn.: Greenwood Press, 1977.

Stueck, William. *Rethinking the Korean War: A New Diplomatic and Military History.* Princeton, N.J.: Princeton University Press, 1995.

Talbott, Strobe. *The Russians and Reagan.* New York: Vintage, 1984.

Taubman, William. *Khrushchev: The Man and His Era.* New York: Norton, 2003.

——. *Stalin's American Policy: From Entente to Detente in Cold War.* New York: Norton, 1982.

Theoharis, Athan G. *The Yalta Myths: An Issue in U.S. Politics, 1945–1955.* Columbia: University of Missouri Press, 1970.

Thomas, Daniel C. *The Helsinki Effect: International Norms, Human Rights, and the Demise of Communism.* Princeton, N.J.: Princeton University Press, 2001.

Thomas, Hugh. *Armed Truce: The Beginnings of the Cold War, 1945–46.* London: Hamish Hamilton, 1986.

Ulam, Adam B. *The Rivals: America and Russia since World War II.* New York: Viking, 1971.

Volkogonov, Dmitri. *Autopsy for an Empire: Seven Leaders Who Built the Soviet Regime.* New York: Free Press, 1998.

——. *Stalin: Triumph and Tragedy.* Translated by Harold Shukman. New York: Free Press, 1996.

West, Nigel. *The Third Secret: The CIA, Solidarity, and the KGB's Plot to Kill the Pope.* London: HarperCollins, 2000.

Westad, Odd Arne. *Cold War and Revolution: Soviet–American Rivalry and the Origins of the Cold War, 1944–1946.* New York: Columbia University Press, 1993.

Wise, David. *The Inside Story of How the FBI's Robert Hanssen Betrayed America.* New York: Random House, 2002.

Wohlfort, William C. *Witnesses to the End of the Cold War.* Baltimore, Md.: Johns Hopkins University Press, 1996.

Woods, Randall B., and Howard Jones. *Dawning of the Cold War: The United States' Quest for Order.* Athens: University of Georgia Press, 1991.

Yakovlev, Alexander. *The Fate of Marxism in Russia.* New Haven, Conn.: Yale University Press, 1993.

Zubok, Vladislav M. *A Failed Empire: The Soviet Union in the Cold War from Stalin to Gorbachev.* Chapel Hill: University of North Carolina Press, 2007.

——, and Constantine Pleshkov. *Inside the Kremlin's Cold War: From Stalin to Khrushchev.* Cambridge, Mass.: Harvard University Press, 1996.

THE UNITED STATES, RUSSIA, AND THE POST-SOVIET WORLD, 1990–2008

Arbel, Daniel, and Ran Edelist. *Western Intelligence and the Collapse of the Soviet Union: The Ten Years That Did Not Shake the World.* London: Frank Cass, 2003.

Aron, Leon. *Yeltsin: A Revolutionary Life.* New York: St. Martin's Press, 2000.

Baker, Peter, and Susan Gasser. *Kremlin Rising: Vladimir Putin's Russia and the End of Revolution.* New York: Scribner, 2005.

Billington, James H. *Russia in Search of Itself.* Washington, D.C.: Woodrow Wilson Center, 2005.

Breslauer, George W. *Gorbachev and Yeltsin as Leaders.* New York: Cambridge University Press, 2002.

Bumiller, Elisabeth. *Condoleezza Rice: An American Life.* New York: Random House, 2007.

Christopher, Warren. *In the Stream of History.* Stanford, Calif.: Stanford University Press, 1998.

Draper, Robert. *Dead Certain: The Presidency of George W. Bush.* New York: Free Press, 2008.

English, Robert D. *Russia and the Idea of the West: Gorbachev, Intellectuals and the End of the Cold War.* New York: Columbia University Press, 2000.

FitzGerald, Frances. *Way Out There in the Blue: Reagan, Star Wars and the End of the Cold War.* New York: Simon & Schuster, 2000.

Freeland, Chrystia. *Sale of the Century.* New York: Crown, 2000.

Goldgeier, James M. *Not Whether but When: The U.S. Decision to Enlarge NATO.* Washington, D.C.: Brookings Institution, 1999.

———, and Michael McFaul. *Power and Purpose: U.S. Policy toward Russia after the Cold War.* Washington, D.C.: Brookings Institution, 2003.

Gorbachev, Mikhail. *On My Country and the World.* New York: Columbia University Press, 2000.

———. *Perestroika: New Thinking for Our Country and the World.* New York: Harper & Row, 1987.

Gorbacheva, Raisa. *I Hope: Reminiscences and Reflections.* New York: Harper-Collins, 1991.

Herspring, Dale, ed. *Putin's Russia: Past Imperfect, Future Uncertain.* Latham, Md.: Rowman & Littlefield, 2007.

Hutchings, Robert L. *American Diplomacy and the End of the Cold War: An Insider's Account of U.S. Policy in Europe, 1989–1992.* Washington, D.C.: Woodrow Wilson Center Press, 1997.

Jack, Andrew. *Inside Putin's Russia: Can There Be Reform without Democracy?* New York: Oxford University Press, 2005.

Kessler, Glenn. *The Confidante: Condoleezza Rice and the Creation of the Bush Legacy.* New York: St. Martin's Press, 2007.

Kreutz, Andre J. *Russia in the Middle East: Friend or Foe?* Westport, Conn.: Praeger Security International, 2006.

Ledeneva, Alena V. *How Russia Really Works: The Informal Practices That Shaped Post-Soviet Politics and Business.* Ithaca, N.Y.: Cornell University Press, 2006.

Lieven, Anatole. *Chechnya: Tombstone of Russian Power.* New Haven, Conn.: Yale University Press, 1998.

Lucas, Edward. *The New Cold War: How the Kremlin Menaces Both Russia and the West.* London: Bloomsbury, 2008.

Matlock, Jack F., Jr. *Autopsy on an Empire: The American Ambassador's Account of the Collapse of the Soviet Union.* New York: Random House, 1995.

———. *Reagan and Gorbachev: How the Cold War Ended.* New York: Random House, 2004.

Oberdorfer, Don. *From the Cold War to a New Era: The United States and the Soviet Union, 1783–1991.* Baltimore, Md.: Johns Hopkins University Press, 1998.

Odom, William E. *The Collapse of the Soviet Military.* New Haven, Conn.: Yale University Press, 1998.

Putin, Vladimir. *First Person.* New York: PublicAffairs, 2000.

Shevardnadze, Eduard. *The Future Belongs to Freedom.* New York: Free Press, 1991.

Shiraev, Eric, and Vladislav Zubok. *Anti-Americanism in Russia: From Stalin to Putin.* New York: Palgrave, 2000.

Steele, Jonathan. *Eternal Russia: Yeltsin, Gorbachev, and the Mirage of Democracy.* Cambridge, Mass.: Harvard University Press, 1994.

Stokes, Gale. *The Walls Came Tumbling Down: The Collapse of Communism in Eastern Europe.* New York: Oxford University Press, 1993.

Talbot, Strobe. *The Russia Hand: A Memoir of Presidential Diplomacy.* New York: Random House, 2002.

Trenin, Dmitri. *Getting Russia Right.* Washington, D.C.: Carnegie Endowment, 2007.

Wise, David. *Spy: The Inside Story of How the FBI's Robert Hanssen Betrayed America.* New York: Random House, 2002.

Yakovlev, Alexander. *The Fate of Marxism in Russia.* New Haven, Conn.: Yale University Press, 1993.

Yeltsin, Boris. *Midnight Diaries.* New York: PublicAffairs, 2000.

———. *The Struggle for Russia.* New York: Time Books, 1994.

Zelikow, Philip, and Condoleezza Rice. *Germany Unified and Europe Transformed: A Study in Statecraft.* Cambridge, Mass.: Harvard University Press, 1995.

About the Author

Norman E. Saul is professor of history and of Russian and East European studies at the Center for Russian, East European, and Eurasian Studies at the University of Kansas, where he also served for nine years as chair of the Department of History.

Dr. Saul was born and raised on a small farm in the American Midwest and graduated with a degree in Slavic studies from Indiana University. He began his postgraduate studies at the School of Slavonic and East European Studies of the University of London on a Fulbright Scholarship. After two years of service in the U.S. army, he resumed his graduate work at Columbia University with concentrations in Russian and East European history and international relations and was awarded an M.A. degree, certificate of the Russian Institute, and his doctorate in 1965. He taught Russian history at Purdue and Brown Universities before beginning his tenure at the University of Kansas and also has been a visiting professor at Northwestern and at University College Dublin.

Dr. Saul's first book, *Russia and the Mediterranean, 1797–1807* (University of Chicago Press, 1970), was based on his dissertation and on research in Russia, Corfu, Dubrovnik, Rome, Paris, Naples, London, and Vienna. His master's thesis, *Sailors in Revolt: The Russian Baltic Fleet in 1917*, was also published after additional work in Finnish and Russian archives. Since the 1970s, however, Saul's major focus has been on Russian–American relations, and he has completed four books in a chronological series: *Distant Friends: The United States and Russia, 1763–1867* (1991); *Concord & Conflict: The United States and Russia, 1867–1914* (1996); *War and Revolution: The United States and Russia, 1914–1921* (2001); and *Friends or Foes? The United States and Soviet Russia* (2006), all published by the University Press of Kansas, two of them receiving prestigious book awards. He was also the coeditor, with Richard McKenzie, of

Russian–American Dialogue on Cultural Relations, 1776–1914 (1997). These publications stress all aspects of the Russian–American relationship, especially cultural contacts and personal experiences. A large number of published articles focus on Russian–American relations, but also on Russian settlements in the Great Plains region, the Russian Revolution, and cold war studies. During 2007 he presented retrospective papers at two international conferences in Moscow and one in New Orleans on the bicentennial of the beginning of Russian–American relations. His future projects involve a biographical study of American philanthropist and Russophile Charles R. Crane and a fifth volume in the Russian–American series, tentatively entitled *From Allies to Enemies: The United States and the Soviet Union, 1941–1951.*